The Business Writer's Handbook

The Business Writer's Handbook

Charles T. Brusaw
NCR Corporation

Gerald J. Alred
University of Wisconsin—Milwaukee

Walter E. Oliu
U.S. Nuclear Regulatory Commission

St. Martin's Press
New York

Preface

The Business Writer's Handbook is designed to be a comprehensive, thoroughly practical reference guide for courses in business writing or business communication. We assume that most instructors will use it along with a standard textbook, but an instructor wishing to avoid the constraints imposed by a textbook could easily use the *Handbook* as the basic resource, supplementing it as necessary in the classroom.

The Business Writer's Handbook goes far beyond the scope of conventional English handbooks. It not only provides comprehensive coverage of grammar, usage, style, format, and writing procedure—planning, research, outlining, methods of development, etc.—but includes information on letters, memorandums, proposals, reports of various kinds (including oral reports), minutes of meetings, job descriptions, and other types of business communication. The abundant examples —even those illustrating grammatical points—reflect real business situations to provide the greatest possible relevance for career-oriented students.

The three authors have brought different and complementary perspectives to the preparation of this book: one of us is a professional writer for a large corporation, one is a writer for a government agency, and one is a teacher of business and technical writing in a university. We hope this diversity of experience has made *The Business Writer's Handbook* a book that students will find valuable not only now, in the classroom, but later, on the job. We are encouraged in this hope by the fact that preliminary forms of the book have been used successfully at the University of Wisconsin; at NCR Corporation and Price Waterhouse & Company; and at the Department of Housing and Urban Development. The valuable lessons learned from these various uses, as well as from detailed prepublication critiques by teachers of business writing, have been incorporated in this final version.

We have tried to make *The Business Writer's Handbook* more flexible and convenient than other writing handbooks we have seen. Its unique four-way access system is explained in "How to Use This Book" on page xi, which every student should read in order to gain the greatest possible advantage from the book. The Alphabetical Entries on pages 1–515 constitute the principal section of the *Handbook*. The Index, page 523, provides an exhaustive listing of the topics covered; it lists these topics not only under the terms used in the entries but also under other terms that students might think of instead. The Topical Key, page xxii, classifies the entries into subject categories; it serves as a topical table of contents to assist students in reviewing a broad subject covered by several entries and facilitates the correlation of the *Handbook* with a standard textbook. The introduction, "Five Steps to Successful Writing," page xiii, sets forth a practical, step-by-step approach to the writing process, which is summarized in a convenient checklist form (with page references to the pertinent entries) by the Checklist of the Writing Process, page xx.

The entries themselves are complete without being exhaustive; that is, they focus on solutions to specific writing problems. Therefore, the general tone is prescriptive. For example, questions about the history of a term such as *data* and the controversy surrounding its use may be interesting, but they are secondary to the advice the user seeks. So, although debate over divided usage is acknowledged, a guideline is offered to get the writer on with the business of writing. This principle holds true for the grammatical entries as well; they do not attempt to settle the debate between traditional and linguistically oriented grammarians, although current linguistic thinking about grammatical problems is presented where it contributes to the explanation of a concept. The guidance offered in the entries will solve most of the problems users of this book will encounter, but students should, of course, understand that some companies and government agencies have their own special standards governing some of the subjects dealt with in this book and that persons employed by those companies and agencies must conform to those standards.

For instructors adopting *The Business Writer's Handbook* who like to use a system of marginal symbols in correcting student writing, a Correction Chart listing the most commonly used correction symbols, with page references to the *Handbook,* is available upon request in class quantities, at no charge, from the publisher: St. Martin's Press, Inc., College Department, 175 Fifth Avenue, New York, New York 10010.

We are deeply indebted to a number of people for assistance with this book, though its faults are ours alone. Acknowledgments must begin with Conrad R. Winterhalter of both the University of Dayton and NCR Corporation, who reviewed and criticized the entire manuscript on four separate occasions during the book's development and wrote the entries on the Résumé, Letter of Application, Letter of Acceptance, and Letter of Technical Information. Keith Palmer of the Harnischfeger Corporation reviewed the final draft and wrote the entry on Specifications. Others to whom we are grateful for reviewing the manuscript and contributing valuable suggestions and examples are Lee Newcomer and John Taylor of the University of Wisconsin—Milwaukee, Brian Murphy of NCR Corporation, Clare Bedillion of the University of Akron, James H. Chaffee of Normandale Community College, Merrily A. Enquist of Portland Community College, Bertrand Heflin of Daytona Beach Community College, Julie Whitmore of the United States League of Savings Associations, and Bobby Wooten of Louisiana State University, Baton Rouge. We must also express our appreciation to NCR Corporation, Harnischfeger Corporation, and Johnson Service Company for their permission to use many different examples of their business writing.

Instructors who also teach technical writing courses may wish to examine our *Handbook of Technical Writing*, also published by St. Martin's Press. Its organization is identical to that of *The Business Writer's Handbook*, with which it has a great deal of material in common, but its examples are drawn primarily from technical and industrial contexts. In a course combining business and technical writing, either book might be used, depending on the desired emphasis.

Charles T. Brusaw
Gerald J. Alred
Walter E. Oliu

Contents

Preface
v

How to Use This Book
xi

Five Steps to Successful Writing
xiii

Checklist of the Writing Process
xx

Topical Key to the Alphabetical Entries
xxii

THE BUSINESS WRITER'S HANDBOOK:
ALPHABETICAL ENTRIES
1-515

Bibliography
517

Index
523

How to Use This Book

The purpose of this book is to help you solve specific writing problems as quickly and efficiently as possible. To get the greatest benefit from the book, you should be familiar with the four different ways you can find the advice and examples you need.

1. The Alphabetical Text Entries (pages 1–515)

To solve many problems, you will find it most convenient to go directly to the handbook entries on pages 1–515. These entries are in alphabetical order, just as in a dictionary or encyclopedia. For example, if you wish to know the difference between *activate* and *actuate*, or want to review the uses of adverbs, or need information about writing an annual report, you can go directly to the "A" section of the handbook and find the entries: **activate/actuate**, **adverbs**, **annual report**. Key words at the top of each page will help you locate any alphabetical entry quickly. Within each entry, cross-references to other entries are printed in **bold type**, so that you can easily investigate any problem to whatever depth may be necessary to solve it. For example, if you go to the entry on **conjunctions**, you will find not only brief explanations of the various kinds of conjunctions but also bold-type cross-references to more detailed entries about each kind: **coordinating conjunctions**, **correlative conjunctions**, **subordinating conjunctions**, and **conjunctive adverbs**. Within each of these entries, you will find still further cross-references, in case you wish to explore a particular problem in even more detail. This reference system enables you to get out of the book and on with the job as soon as you have enough information to solve a specific problem.

2. The Index (page 523)

If you are uncertain about what entry to look for, the Index will help you. There you will find the item you need, with its page reference, listed not only under the term used in the handbook but under various other terms that you might think of instead. For example, if you wish to know how to handle the omission of words in quoted material, you can look under "omitted words" in the Index and be directed to the page with the entry for **ellipses** (the spaced dots indicating that words have been left out). You can also find the discussion of ellipses by looking up "dots, spaced," "periods, spaced," or "quotations."

The index is especially valuable for locating information about the usage of individual words or phrases. For example, if you want to know the difference between *diagnosis* and *prognosis,* you can look up either word in the Index and be directed to the page for the entry **diagnosis/prognosis** in the "D" section of the handbook.

3. Checklist of the Writing Process (page xx)

The Checklist of the Writing Process is a tool not only to help you locate information but to help you detect your specific writing problems. It presents a disciplined step-by-step approach to successful writing, with page references to the entries that discuss each step in detail. The Checklist is a guide to planning, organizing, and writing your draft, and it is equally valuable as a guide to revision, to help you pinpoint and eliminate specific problems in a systematic way. The Checklist is preceded, on page xiii, by a brief, thoroughly practical discussion of the writing process entitled "Five Steps to Successful Writing."

4. Topical Key to the Alphabetical Entries (page xxii)

Should you wish to review a broad subject that is dealt with in a number of entries—for instance, the parts of speech, the various methods of development, the elements of style, or the types of illustrations—you will find the alphabetical entries conveniently grouped by subject in the Topical Key, which is, in effect, a topical table of contents. Further, if you are using *The Business Writer's Handbook* along with a standard textbook, the Topical Key provides an easy way to correlate the contents of the handbook with those of your textbook. Thus, if a particular discussion within the textbook is inadequate, unclear, or lacking in examples, you can readily turn to the related entries in the handbook for additional help.

Five Steps
to Successful Writing

The main reason that many business people have difficulty writing, no matter how proficient they may be in their business specialties, is that they do not know how to begin. They sit down at a typewriter or with a pen in hand and hope to fill a blank page; they do not realize that skill in writing, like any other business skill, requires a systematic approach.

Successful writing is not the product of inspiration, nor is it merely the spoken word transferred to paper—it is primarily the result of knowing how to *structure ideas* on paper. The best way to ensure that a writing project will be successful—whether it is a letter, a proposal, or a formal report—is to divide the writing process into five major steps: preparation, research, organization, writing the draft, and revision. At first, these five steps must be consciously—even self-consciously—followed. But so, at first, must the steps involved in operating a typewriter or computer, preparing a balance sheet, closing a sale, interviewing a candidate for a job, or chairing a meeting of the board of directors. With practice, the steps involved in each of these business processes become nearly automatic. This is not to suggest that writing becomes easy; it does not. But the easiest way to do it—and the only way to ensure that your writing will accomplish its objective—is to do it *systematically*.

The following pages describe the five major steps of the writing process, and the Checklist that follows provides a summary that can guide you as you write. The Checklist can also help you detect any problem you may have and refer you to the specific entry that explains the cause of the problem and shows you how to solve it. In the following discussion, as elsewhere throughout this book, words and phrases printed in **bold type** refer you to specific alphabetical entries on pages 1–515.

Step 1. Preparation

Writing, like most business tasks, requires solid **preparation**—in fact, adequate preparation is as important as writing the draft. Preparation for writing consists of (1) establishing your objective, (2) identifying your reader, and (3) determining the scope of your coverage.

Establishing your **objective** is simply determining what you want your reader to know or be able to do when he has finished reading your report or paper. But you must be precise; it is all too common for a writer to state his objective in terms so broad that it is almost useless. An objective such as "To report on possible locations for a new manufacturing facility" is too general to be of real help. But "To present the relative advantages of Chicago, Minneapolis, and Salt Lake City as possible locations for a new manufacturing facility in such a way that top management can choose the best location" gives you an objective that can guide you throughout the writing process.

The next problem is to identify your **reader**—again, precisely. What are your reader's needs in relation to your subject? What does your reader already know about your subject? You need to know, for example, whether you must define basic terminology or whether such definitions will merely bore, or even insult, your reader. Is your reader actually several readers with differing interests and levels of technical knowledge? For the objective stated in the previous paragraph the reader was described as "top management." But *who* is included in this category? Will one of the people evaluating the report on three cities as possible plant locations be the personnel manager? If so, he is likely to have a special interest in such things as the availability of qualified personnel in each city, the presence of colleges where special training would be available for employees, housing conditions, perhaps even recreational facilities. The purchasing manager will be concerned about available sources for the materials needed by the plant. The marketing manager will give priority to such things as the plant's closeness to its primary markets and the available transport facilities for distribution of the plant's products. The financial vice-president will want to know about land and building costs and the local tax structure. The president may be interested in all of these things, and more; for example, he might be concerned about the convenience of personal travel between corporate headquarters and the new plant.

In addition to knowing the needs and interests of these readers, you should know as much as you can about their backgrounds. For example, have they visited all three cities? Have they already seen other studies of the three cities? Is this the first new plant, or have they been through the process of choosing locations for new plants before? Finally, if you have multiple readers, then the best course, once you have learned as much as possible about their needs and backgrounds, is to combine all of your readers in your mind into one composite reader and write to *that reader*. By writing as if to a single reader, you are less likely either to adopt a lecturing tone (as if you were addressing a group rather than individuals) or to be intimidated by your audience.

Determining your objective and identifying your reader will help you decide what to include and what not to include in your writing. When you have distinguished the important from the unimportant on the basis of your objective and your reader, you have established the **scope** of your writing project. If you do not clearly define the scope before beginning your research (the next step), you will inevitably spend needless extra hours on research because you will not be sure what kind of information you need, or even how much. For example, given the objective and reader established in the preceding two paragraphs, the scope of your report on plant locations would include such things as land and building costs, the available labor force, transportation facilities, proximity to sources of supply, and so forth; but it probably would not include information on the history of the cities being considered or on the altitude and geological features (unless these were directly pertinent to your particular business).

Step 2. Research

The purpose of most business writing is to explain something— usually something that is complex. This kind of writing cannot be done by someone who does not understand the subject he is writing about. The only way to be sure that you can deal adequately with a complex subject is to compile a complete set of notes during your **research** and then to create a working outline from the notes. Three sources of information are available to you: the library (see **library research**), personal **interviews** (or written **questionnaires**), and your own knowledge. Consider them all when you begin your research, and use those that fit your needs. Of course, the amount of research you need to do depends on your project; for a simple memo or letter your "research" may amount to nothing more than jotting down all your ideas before you begin to organize them.

Step 3. Organization

Without **organization**, the material gathered during your research would be incomprehensible to your reader. To provide effective organization, you must determine the sequence in which your ideas should be presented—that is, you must choose a **method of development**.

An appropriate method of development is the writer's tool for keeping things under control and the reader's means of following the writer's presentation. Your subject may obviously lend itself to a particular method of development. For example, if you were giving instructions for starting an engine, you would naturally present the steps of the process in the order of their occurrence. This is the sequential method of development. If you were writing about the history of your company, your account would go from the beginning to the present. This is the chronological method of development. If your subject naturally lends itself to a certain method of development, use that method—don't attempt to impose another method on it. Many different methods of development are available to you; this book includes all of those that are likely to be used by business people: chronological, sequential, spatial, increasing or decreasing order of importance, comparison, analysis, general-to-specific, specific-to-general, and cause-and-effect. As the writer, you must choose the method of development that best suits your subject, your reader, and your objective. You are then ready to prepare your outline.

Outlining makes large or complex subjects easier to handle by breaking them into manageable parts, and it ensures that your writing will move logically from idea to idea without omitting anything important. It also enables you to emphasize your key points by placing them in the positions of greatest importance. Finally, by forcing you to structure your thinking at an early stage, creating a good outline releases you to concentrate exclusively on writing when you begin the rough draft. Even if the task is only a letter or short memo, successful writing needs the logic and structure that a method of development and an outline provide, although for such simple projects the method of development and outline may be in your head rather than on paper.

If you intend to include **illustrations** with your writing, a good time to think about these is when you have completed your outline—especially if the illustrations need to be prepared by someone else while you are writing and revising the draft. If your outline is reasonably detailed, you should be able to determine which ideas will require graphic support in order to be clear.

Step 4.   Writing the Draft

When you have established your objective, reader, and scope, when you have done adequate research, and when you have chosen a method of development and created a good outline, **writing the draft** is relatively easy. Writing the draft is simply the process of transcribing and expanding the notes from your outline into **topic sentences** and then into **paragraphs**. Write the draft quickly, concentrating entirely on converting your outline to sentences and paragraphs. Don't worry about a good **opening** or **introduction** unless it comes easily. Concentrate on ideas. Don't attempt to polish or revise. Don't let concern about grammatical rules or spelling get in your way, for these are of little importance in the rough draft. Do, above all, keep your reader's needs and knowledge in mind.

Step 5.   Revision

Chances are that the clearer a piece of writing seems to the reader, the more effort the writer has put into **revision**. If you have followed the steps of the writing process to this point, you have a very rough draft that could hardly be considered a finished product. Revision is the obvious final step. A different frame of mind is required for revising than for writing the draft. Read and evaluate the draft from the point of view of the reader. Be anxious to find and correct faults, and be honest. Be hard on yourself for the reader's convenience; never be easy on yourself at the reader's expense.

Do not try to do all your revision at once. Read through your rough draft several times, each time looking for and correcting a different set of problems or errors.

Check your draft for accuracy and completeness. Your draft should give the reader exactly what he needs, but it should not burden him with unnecessary information or get sidetracked into loosely related subjects. If you have not yet written an **opening** or **introduction**, this is the time to do it. Your introduction should serve as a frame into which your reader can fit the information that follows in the body of your draft; check your introduction to see that it does, in fact, provide the reader with such assistance. Your opening should both suggest the subject and capture the reader's attention.

Check your draft for unity, coherence, and transition. If it has **unity**, all of the sentences in each paragraph contribute to the development of that paragraph's central idea (expressed in the topic sentence), and all of the paragraphs contribute to the development of the main topic. If the draft has **coherence**, the sentences, and also the paragraphs, flow smoothly from one to the next; the relationship of each sentence or paragraph to the one before is clear. Coherence is accomplished in many ways, but especially by the careful use of **transition** devices and by the maintenance of a consistent **point of view**. Also check your draft for proper **emphasis** and **subordination** of your ideas. This is also a good time to adjust the **pace**: if you find places where too many ideas are jammed together, space the ideas out and slow the pace; conversely, if you find a series of simple ideas expressed in a series of short, choppy sentences, combine them into fewer sentences and speed the pace.

Check your draft for **clarity**. Much of the revision you have done has already contributed to greater clarity. But check now for any terms that need to be defined or explained for your reader (see **defining terms**), and also check for **ambiguity**. Is your writing free of **affectation**? Is it free of **jargon** that your reader (or some of your readers) may not understand? Are there **abstract words** that could be replaced by concrete words? Check your entire draft for appropriate **word choice**.

Check your draft for **style**. By now you have already done much to improve the style, but there is more you can do. Check for **conciseness**: can you eliminate useless words or phrases—what some writers call deadwood? It is almost always possible to do so, and your writing (and your reader) will benefit greatly. Get rid of **clichés** and other **trite language**. Is your writing active? Especially in business writing there is a great temptation to use the passive **voice** when the active would be far stronger (and also more concise). Replace negative writing with **positive writing**. Check, too, for **parallel structure**. Examine your **sentence construction** and look for ways to achieve more interesting **sentence variety**.

Check your draft for **awkwardness** and for departures from the appropriate **tone**. Awkwardness and tone are hard to define because they are the result of a great many different things, most of which you have already dealt with in your revision. But try reading your draft aloud (better still, have someone read it to you) while you listen as if you were the reader. You will recognize awkwardness because it sounds forced or clumsy—like something you would never say if you were *talking* to your reader because it would sound unnatural to both of you. You will recognize departures from the proper tone because they are words, phrases, or statements which are inappropriate to the relationship that exists between you and your reader. For example, in a memo to a superior in your organization you would want to avoid phrases or statements that sounded like lecturing. If your reader is serious about your subject (and it is best to assume that he is), don't try to be witty. Correcting the tone is frequently a matter of replacing a word with another that has more appropriate **connotations**. For example, consider the difference in tone between "I'm puzzled by your *stubbornness* in opposing the plan" and "I'm puzzled by the *firmness* of your opposition to the plan."

Finally, check slowly and carefully for problems of **grammar**, **punctuation**, mechanics (**spelling**, **abbreviations**, **capital letters**, etc.), and **format**.

The following Checklist of the Writing Process is designed to guide you as you follow the five steps to successful writing. It can help you to diagnose any problem you may have, and it also refers you to the specific entry that explains the causes of the problem and shows you how to correct it.

Checklist of the Writing Process

Note: This checklist arranges key entries from pages 1–515 of the handbook into a recommended sequence of steps for any writing project. The exact titles of the entries are in **bold type** for quick reference, and the page numbers are given. When you turn to the entries themselves, you will find bold-type cross-references to further entries that may be helpful. (You may also wish to refer to the Topical Key to the Alphabetical Entries on page xxii and to the Index on page 523.)

1. **Preparation** 376

Establishing your **objective (purpose)** 318
Identifying the **reader** 400
Determining the **scope** 432

2. **Research** 411

Taking notes (**note-taking**) 306
Conducting **library research** 281
Interviewing 253
Creating and using a **questionnaire** 391

3. **Organization** 336

Choosing the best **method of development** 292
Outlining 338
Creating and using **illustrations** 236

4. **Writing the Draft** 512

Choosing a **point of view** 368
Developing **topic sentences** 487
Writing **paragraphs** 343
Using **quotations** and **paraphrase** 396, 352
Writing an **introduction** 256
Writing an **opening** 323
Writing a **conclusion** 112
Choosing a **title** 486

5. **Revision** 421

Checking for completeness (**revision**) 421
Checking for accuracy (**revision**) 421

Checking for **unity** and **coherence**   496, 87

Achieving effective **transition**   489

Checking for consistent **point of view**   368

Emphasizing main ideas (**emphasis**)   155

Subordinating less important ideas (**subordination**)   468

Adjusting the **pace**   342

Checking for **clarity**   81

Defining terms   131

Eliminating **ambiguity**   35

Checking for appropriate **word choice**   511

Eliminating **affectation** and **jargon**   24, 262

Replacing **abstract words** with concrete words   12

Achieving **conciseness**   108

Eliminating **clichés** and **trite language**   85, 496

Making writing active (**voice**)   507

Changing negative writing to **positive writing**   373

Checking for **parallel structure**   349

Checking **sentence construction** and achieving **sentence variety**   437, 445

Eliminating **awkwardness**   53

Checking for appropriate **tone**   486

Eliminating problems of **grammar**   209

Eliminating **sentence faults**   441

Checking for **agreement**   27

Checking for proper **case**   74

Checking for clear reference of **pronouns**   381

Eliminating **dangling modifiers** and **misplaced modifiers**   126, 297

Checking for correct **punctuation**   389

Checking for mechanics: **spelling** (463), **abbreviations** (2), **capital letters** (70), **contractions** (119), **dates** (129), **indentation** (242), **italics** (259), **numbers** (314), **symbols** (472), **syllabication** (471), **footnotes** (175), and **bibliography** (60)

Checking for correctness of **format** and **illustrations**   196, 236

Topical Key to the Alphabetical Entries

Note: This tabulation arranges the alphabetical entries on pages 1–515 into subject categories. Within each category the entries are listed mainly, but not strictly, in alphabetical order. Excluded from this tabulation are the numerous entries concerned with the usage of particular words or phrases (*imply/infer, already/all ready,* etc.); to locate any such usage entry, look up the specific word or phrase in the Index, page 523. (For a listing of key entries in a recommended sequence of steps for any writing project, see the Checklist of the Writing Process, page xx.)

Types of Business Writing

Abstract   10
Articles:
   House Organ Article   228
   Journal Article   265
Brief   65
Correspondence   121
   Acceptance, Letter of   14
   Application, Letter of (*see also* Résumé)   46
   Inquiry, Letter of   247
   Technical Information, Letter of   478
   Memorandum   291
Essay Questions, Answering   160
Instructions   250
Job Description   263
Letters (*see* Correspondence)   121

Memorandum   291
Minutes of Meeting   296
Proposal   388
    Government Proposal   202
    Sales Proposal   424
Questionnaire   391
Reports   410
    Annual Report   39
    Formal Report   180
    Laboratory Report   274
    Oral Report   327
    Police Report   370
    Progress Report   380
    Trip Report   494
Résumé   413
Specifications   455
Technical Manual   479

Planning and Research

Preparation   376
    Objective (Purpose)   318
    Reader   400
    Scope   432
Research   411
    Interviewing   253
    Library Research   281
        Bibliography   60
        Copyright   120
        Footnotes   175
        Library Classification System   279
        Note-Taking   306
        Paraphrase   352
        Plagiarism   368
        Reference Books   401
    Questionnaire   391
    Quotations   396

Organization, Writing, and Revision

Forms of Discourse   197
    Description   137

Explaining a Process 163
Exposition 167
Instructions 250
Narration 302
Persuasion 364

Methods of Development 292
Analysis 37
Cause-and-Effect 79
Chronological 81
Comparison 103
Decreasing Order of Importance 130
Definition 132
General-to-Specific 199
Increasing Order of Importance 240
Sequential 449
Spatial 455
Specific-to-General 455

Outlining 338
Writing the Draft 512
Point of View 368
Introduction 256
Openings 323
Conclusion 112
Title 486

Revision 421
Clarity 81
Coherence 87
Conciseness 108
Defining Terms 131
Transition 489
Unity 496

Format and Illustrations

Format 196
Appendix 46
Bibliography 60
Footnotes 175
Foreword/Preface 180
Glossary 199
Header/Footer 222

Heads   222
Indentation   242
Index   243
Quotations   396
Tables   475
Tables of Contents   474
Illustrations   236
Drawings   147
Flowchart   174
Graphs   210
Maps   289
Organizational Chart   337
Schematic Diagrams   430
Tables   475

Language and Style

Language:
Absolute Words   10
Abstract/Concrete Words   12
Affectation   24
Antonyms   44
Blend Words   64
Cliché   85
Clipped Form of Words   86
Compound Words   108
Connotation/Denotation   117
Contractions   119
Diction (*see also* Word Choice)   141, 511
Dictionary   141
Double Negative   145
Elegant Variation   152
Epithet   159
Euphemism   161
Foreign Words in English   179
Gobbledygook   200
Idiom   234
Intensifiers   251
Jargon   262
Long Variants   287
Malapropism   288

New Words   304
Prefixes   375
Suffixes   470
Synonyms   474
Thesaurus   485
Trite Language   496
Usage (see the Index for particular words and phrases)   497
Vague Words   498
Varieties of English:
    Nonstandard English   305
    Standard English   464
Vogue Words   506
Word Choice   511

Style   464
Allusion   34
Ambiguity   35
Analogy   37
Anecdote   38
Awkwardness   53
Balance   57
Business Writing Style   66
Clarity   81
Coherence   87
Comparison   102
Conciseness/Wordiness   108
Emphasis   155
Figures of Speech   170
    Hyperbole   231
    Metaphor   292
    Simile   450
Formal Writing Style   195
Informal Writing Style   246
Pace   342
Parallel Structure   349
Paraphrase   352
Positive Writing   373
Repetition   409
Rhetorical Question   424
Subordination   468
Sweeping Generalization   470
Technical Writing Style   479

Tone   486
Unity 496

Paragraphs, Sentences, Clauses, and Phrases

Paragraphs   343
    Coherence   87
    Topic Sentence   487
    Transition   489
    Unity 496
Sentences   434
    Simple Sentence   451
    Compound Sentence   106
    Complex Sentence   105
    Compound-Complex Sentence   107
    Inverted Sentence Order   258
    Modifiers   299
        Dangling Modifiers   126
        Misplaced Modifiers   297
    Sentence Construction   437
        Subject   466
        Predicate   374
        Object   317
            Direct Object   144
            Indirect Object   243
        Complement   103
            Subjective Complement   467
            Objective Complement   318
        Expletive   166
        Connective   115
        Mixed Construction   298
        Sentence Faults   441
        Sentence Variety   445
        Subordination   468
        Voice   507
Clauses   83
    Adjective Clause   19
    Adverb Clause   23
    Dependent Clause   135
    Noun Clause   313
    Restrictive and Nonrestrictive Elements   412
    Subordination   468

Phrases   366
    Absolute Phrase   9
    Infinitive Phrase   244
    Participial Phrase   354
    Prepositional Phrase   378
    Restrictive and Nonrestrictive Elements   412
    Verb Phrase   505

Parts of Speech, Inflection, and Agreement

Parts of Speech   357
    Adjective   16
        Article   49
        Comparative Degree   101
        Demonstrative Adjective   134
        Indefinite Adjective   241
        Infinitive (as adjective)   243
        Numeral Adjective   317
        Participle   355
        Possessive Adjective   373
        Predicate Adjective   374
        Relative Adjective   408
    Adverb   20
        Conjunctive Adverb   115
        Infinitive (as adverb)   243
        Interrogative Adverb   253
    Conjunction   113
        Coordinating Conjunction   119
        Correlative Conjunction   120
        Subordinating Conjunction   467
    Interjection   252
    Noun   310
        Abstract Noun   12
        Appositive   48
        Collective Noun   89
        Common Noun   100
        Concrete Noun   113
        Count Noun   125
        Gerund   199
        Infinitive (as noun)   243
        Mass Noun   290

　　Predicate Nominative   375
　　Proper Noun   388
　　Substantive   470
Preposition   377
Pronoun   381
　　Agreement   27
　　Case   75
　　Demonstrative Pronoun   135
　　Gender   198
　　Indefinite Pronoun   241
　　Interrogative Pronoun   253
　　Number   314
　　Person   362
　　Personal Pronoun   363
　　Reciprocal Pronoun   401
　　Reflexive Pronoun   408
　　Relative Pronoun   408
Verb   499
　　Agreement   27
　　Finite Verb   173
　　Helping Verb   227
　　Intransitive Verb   255
　　Linking Verb   286
　　Mood   300
　　Number   314
　　Person   362
　　Tense   481
　　Transitive Verb   492
　　Verbals   505
　　　　Gerund   199
　　　　Infinitive   243
　　　　Participle   355
　　Verb Phrase   505
　　Voice   507
Inflection:
　　Case   74
　　Gender   198
　　Mood   300
　　Number   314
　　Person   362

Tense   481
Voice   507
Agreement   27

Punctuation and Mechanics

Punctuation   389
Apostrophe   44
Brackets   65
Colon   89
Comma   91
Dash   127
Ellipses   152
Exclamation Mark   162
Hyphen   231
Parentheses   353
Period   359
Question Mark   390
Quotation Marks   394
Semicolon   432
Slash   453
Mechanics (*see also* Format)   196
Abbreviations   2
Bibliography   60
Capital Letters   70
Contractions   119
Dates   129
Diacritical Marks   140
Footnotes   175
Indentation   242
Italics   259
Numbers   314
Proofreaders' Marks   386
Spelling   463
Syllabication   471
Symbols   472

The Business Writer's Handbook

Alphabetical Entries

A

a, an

A and *an* are indefinite **articles**; "indefinite" implies that the **noun** designated by the article is not a specific person, place, or thing but is one of a group.

> *Example:* *A* program was run by the computer. (Not a specific program, but an unnamed program.)

Use *a* before words beginning with a consonant or consonant sound (including "y" or "w" sounds).

> *Examples:* The year's activities are summarized in *a* one-page report. (Although the "o" in *one* is a vowel, the first *sound* is "w," a consonant sound. Hence the article *a* precedes the word.)
> *A* manual has been written on that subject.
> It was *a* historic event for the company.
> The office manager felt that it was *a* unique situation.

Use *an* before words beginning with a vowel or vowel sound.

> *Examples:* The report is *an* overview of the year's activities.
> He seems *an* unlikely candidate for the job.
> The interviewer arrived *an* hour early. (Although the "h" in *hour* is a consonant, the word begins on a vowel *sound;* hence it is preceded by *an.*)

Be careful not to use unnecessary indefinite articles in a sentence.

> *Change:* There is no more complex *a* subject than accounting.
> *To:* There is no more complex subject than accounting.

> *Change:* I will meet you in *a* half *an* hour.
> *To:* I will meet you in *a* half hour.
> *Or:* I will meet you in half *an* hour.

a la

The literal meaning of *a la* in French is "in the style of" or "in the manner of." In business and technical writing, it is better to avoid the term.

> *Change:* The consumer representative presented a penetrating report *a la* Ralph Nader.

> *To:*   The consumer representative presented a penetrating report in the manner of Ralph Nader.

The accent mark (*à la*) need not be used in English. (See also **foreign words in English**.)

a lot/alot

A lot is often incorrectly written as one word *(alot)*. Write the phrase as two words: *a lot*. The phrase *a lot* is very informal, however, and should not normally be used in business and technical writing.

> *Change:*   There are *a lot* of objections.
> *To:*   There are many objections.

abbreviations

Abbreviations, like **symbols**, can be important space savers in business and technical writing, where it is often necessary to provide the maximum amount of information in limited space. Use abbreviations, however, only if you are certain that your **reader** will understand them as readily as he would the terms for which they stand. Remember also that a **memorandum** or **report** addressed to a specific person may be read by others, and you must not confuse those readers. Use common sense to decide when abbreviations are appropriate. Do not use them if they might become an inconvenience to the reader. A good rule of thumb: When in doubt, spell it out.

FORMING ABBREVIATIONS

Some abbreviations are formed by omitting letters from a word or words.

> *Examples:*   Mister   Mr.
> square feet   sq. ft.
> Chapter   Ch.
> January   Jan.

Other abbreviations are made by combining the first letters of several words in a term.

> *Examples:*   U.S.A.   United States of America
> c.o.d.   collect on delivery
> M.B.A.   Master of Business Administration
> a.m.   *ante meridiem*

Abbreviations that are pronounced as if they were single words are called acronyms. They are never punctuated and are written in all **capital letters** unless they have become accepted as **common nouns**.

Examples: CORE   Congress of Racial Equality
WAC   Women's Army Corps
NATO   North Atlantic Treaty Organization
NASA   National Aeronautics and Space Administration
radar   radio detecting and ranging

The plural of acronyms is formed by adding lower-case "s" (WACs).

HOW TO USE ABBREVIATIONS

Except for commonly used abbreviations (U.S.A., p.m.), a term to be abbreviated should be spelled out the first time it is used, with the abbreviation enclosed in **parentheses** following the term. Thereafter, the abbreviation can be used with confidence that the **reader** will understand its meaning.

Example: The annual report of the National Retail Dry Goods Association (NRDGA) will be issued next month. In it, the NRDGA will detail shortages in several widely used textiles.

Normally, you should not attempt to make up your own abbreviations; you will almost surely confuse your reader.

PUNCTUATING ABBREVIATIONS

Although punctuation of abbreviations varies considerably, the following guidelines will help you.

Names of companies, government agencies, and social organizations are not normally punctuated. A few are, however, and you should follow the practice of the company, agency, or organization itself.

Examples: FHA   Federal Housing Authority
FBI   Federal Bureau of Investigation
IBM   International Business Machines
YMCA   Young Men's Christian Association
CIA   Central Intelligence Agency
RCA   Radio Corporation of America
USIA   United States Information Agency

Lower-case abbreviations made up of single letters usually require a period after each initial.

Examples: a.m.   f.o.b.
p.m.   c.o.d.

Other lower-case abbreviations are followed by a period when confusion could otherwise result.

Example: in. for "inch"

Upper-case abbreviations require no periods, with the exception of geographical names (U.S.A., U.S.S.R.), academic degrees (B.A., M.B.A.), and a few miscellaneous expressions (R.S.V.P.).

Examples:	TV	UN
	ESP	NAACP
	FM	GI

Acronyms are always in capital letters (unless they have become accepted as common nouns) and are never punctuated.

Examples: NATO, UNESCO, CORE, radar

Use of the period with other abbreviations, such as measurements (ft., gal.) and months and days (Sept., Mon.), varies widely. This book recommends use of the period with such abbreviations.

ABBREVIATIONS IN SPECIALIZED FIELDS

All technologies have specialized abbreviations. The following are typical examples:

Examples:	EDP	Electronic Data Processing
	COBOL	Common Business Oriented Language
	Spec	Specification

Abbreviations common to various technologies can most easily be found in specialized dictionaries or in style manuals designed for publications in a specific subject. See **reference books**.

The business terms that are most often abbreviated can be found in reference works such as the *University Dictionary of Business and Finance,* edited by Donald T. Clark and Bert A. Gottfried (New York: Thomas Y. Crowell, 1967). The following are typical examples of abbreviations used in business.

Examples:	CIF (or c.i.f.)	Cost, Insurance, and Freight
	FOB (or f.o.b.)	Free On Board
	EOM (or e.o.m.)	End Of Month
	GNP	Gross National Product
	NRDGA	The National Retail Dry Goods Association

A type of organization (company, corporation, etc.) is usually spelled out unless it appears as an abbreviation in the official name of the organization; when this occurs, the following abbreviations should be used.

Examples:	Assn.	Association	Corp.	Corporation
	Bros.	Brothers	Inc.	Incorporated
	Co.	Company	Ltd.	Limited

Television and radio networks and stations. Names of television and radio networks and stations should appear in all capital letters, and they should not be punctuated.

Examples: NBC, CBS, ABC, KBZ, WHIO, WLW

Measurements. When you abbreviate terms that refer to measurement, be sure your reader is familiar with the abbreviated form. The following list contains some typical abbreviations used with units of measurement:

ac., alternating current
AM or am, amplitude modulation
amp., ampere
bbl., barrel
b.h.p., brake horsepower
Btu., British thermal unit
bu., bushel
C., Centigrade or Celsius
cal., calorie
cc., cubic centimeter
cm., centimeter
cos, cosine
ctn., cotangent
dc., direct current
doz. or dz., dozen
emf or EMF, electromotive force
F., Fahrenheit
fig., figure (illustration)
FM or fm, frequency modulation
ft., foot (or feet)

g., gram
gal., gallon
h.p., horsepower
hr., hour
ID, inside diameter
in., inch
kc., kilocycle
km., kilometer
OD, outside diameter
psi, pounds per square inch
qt., quart
rpm, revolutions per minute
sec., second or secant
tan., tangent
v., volt
vac, volts of alternating current
vdc, volts of direct current
w., watt
yd., yard
yr., year

Personal Names and Titles. Personal names should generally not be abbreviated in business and technical writing.

Change:	Chas., Thos., Wm., Geo.
To:	Charles, Thomas, William, George

An academic, civil, religious, or military title should be spelled out when it does not precede a name.

Example: The *doctor* asked that the report be finished.

When it precedes a name, the title may be abbreviated.

Examples: Dr. Smith, Mr. Mills, Capt. Hughes

Reverend and *Honorable* are abbreviated only if the surname is preceded by a first name.

Examples: The Reverend Smith, Rev. John Smith (but not Rev. Smith)
The Honorable Commissioner Curran, Hon. Charles J. Curran

An abbreviation of a title may follow the name; however, be certain that it does not duplicate a title before the name.

Change: Dr. William Smith, Ph.D.
To: Dr. William Smith
Or: William Smith, Ph.D.

Following is a list of common abbreviations for personal and professional titles.

Atty.	Attorney
B.A. or A.B.	Bachelor of Arts
B.S.	Bachelor of Science
B.S.E.E.	Bachelor of Science in Electrical Engineering
D.D.	Doctor of Divinity
D.D.S.	Doctor of Dental Science (or Surgery)
Dr.	Doctor (used with any doctor's degree)
Ed.D.	Doctor of Education
Esq.	Esquire (*Esquire* is a nearly obsolete title following a name. It never precedes the name. Equivalent to *mister*, it is used primarily in legal notices.)
Hon.	Honorable
Jr.	Junior (used when a father with the same name is living)
LL.B.	Bachelor of Law
LL.D.	Doctor of Law
M.A. or A.M.	Master of Arts
M.B.A.	Master of Business Administration
M.D.	Doctor of Medicine
Messrs.	Plural of Mr.

Mr.	Mister (spelled out only in the most formal contexts)
Mrs.	Married woman
Ms.	Woman of unspecified marital status
M.S.	Master of Science
Ph.D.	Doctor of Philosophy
Rev.	Reverend
Sr.	Senior (used when a son with the same name is living)

Abbreviations in Reports and Papers. Abbreviations are used extensively in **footnotes**, **bibliographies**, and manuscripts. The following are typical abbreviations for such uses.

app., appendix

ca., circa, about (with reference to an approximate time, in years)

cf., compare

ch., chapter

col., column

diss., dissertation

ed. or eds., edited by, editor, editors

e.g., for example

et al., and others

f. or ff., and the following page or pages

ibid., in the place of the citation above

i.e., that is

il., illustrated

loc. cit., in the place cited

MS or ms, manuscript; MSS or mss, manuscripts

n., note

N.B., note well

n.d., no date

n.n., no name

n.s., new series

no., number; nos., numbers

op. cit., in the work cited

o.s., old series

p., page; pp., pages

pass., cited here and there

q.v., which see

rev., revised

sec., section

supp., supplement

tr. or trans., translated by

viz., namely

vol., volume; vols., volumes

Use Latin abbreviations only if you are certain your readers will understand them.

Geographical Abbreviations. It is generally better to spell out geographical locations, including the names of streets, cities, states, regions, and countries (except for long multiword official titles, such as United States of America, Union of Soviet Socialist Republics, and

United Kingdom). Spelling out such names avoids possible misunderstanding and makes reading much easier. The following is a list of a few common geographical abbreviations.

N.E.	Northeast	Ave.	Avenue
N.H.	New Hampshire	Blvd.	Boulevard
N.Y.	New York	Ct.	Court
U.K.	United Kingdom	Dr.	Drive
U.S.A.	United States of America	Ln.	Lane
		St.	Street

The Post Office recommends the following abbreviations for states and protectorates.

Alabama	AL	Montana	MT
Alaska	AK	Nebraska	NE
Arizona	AZ	Nevada	NV
Arkansas	AR	New Hampshire	NH
California	CA	New Jersey	NJ
Colorado	CO	New Mexico	NM
Connecticut	CT	New York	NY
Delaware	DE	North Carolina	NC
District of Columbia	DC	North Dakota	ND
Florida	FL	Ohio	OH
Georgia	GA	Oklahoma	OK
Guam	GU	Oregon	OR
Hawaii	HI	Pennsylvania	PA
Idaho	ID	Puerto Rico	PR
Illinois	IL	Rhode Island	RI
Indiana	IN	South Carolina	SC
Iowa	IA	South Dakota	SD
Kansas	KS	Tennessee	TN
Kentucky	KY	Texas	TX
Louisiana	LA	Utah	UT
Maine	ME	Vermont	VT
Maryland	MD	Virgin Islands	VI
Massachusetts	MA	Virginia	VA
Michigan	MI	Washington	WA
Minnesota	MN	West Virginia	WV
Mississippi	MS	Wisconsin	WI
Missouri	MO	Wyoming	WY

Chronological Abbreviations. The following are typical chronological abbreviations.

A.D. *anno Domini* (beginning of calendar time—A.D. 1790)

B.C. Before Christ (before the beginning of calendar time —647 B.C.)

Jan. January (always spell out when only the month and year are given)

Feb. February

Mar. March

Apr. April

Aug. August

Sept. September

Oct. October

Nov. November

Dec. December

The proper forms for standard abbreviations are in your **dictionary**, either in regular alphabetical order (by the letters of the abbreviation) or in a separate **index**.

above

Be careful in using *above* to refer to a preceding passage in your writing. Its reference is often vague, and, if the passage being referred to is far from the current one, the use of *above* is distracting because your **reader** must go back to the earlier passage to understand your reference. The same is true of *aforesaid, aforementioned, above mentioned, the former,* and *the latter.* In addition to distracting the reader, these words also contribute to a heavy, wooden **style**. If you must refer to something previously mentioned, either repeat the **noun** or **pronoun** or construct your **paragraph** so that your reference is obvious. (See also **former/latter**.)

absolute phrase

An absolute phrase is a **verbal** phrase—either a **participial phrase** or an **infinitive phrase**—that modifies a statement *as a whole* and is not linked to it by a **subordinating conjunction** or a **preposition**.

> *Examples:* *Considering the cost of materials today,* the building was a bargain. (participial phrase)
> *To speak bluntly,* the proposal is unacceptable. (infinitive phrase)

An absolute phrase may have its own subject (in which case it is sometimes called a nominative absolute).

Example: *His experience* (subject) *being exactly right for the job,* he was hired at once.

Sometimes the subject of an absolute phrase is stated but the verbal is implied rather than stated.

Example: *His accounts in order,* the bookkeeper left for the day. (The participle *being* is implied.)

Because an absolute phrase modifies an entire statement rather than a specific part of it (such as the subject), it does not create a **dangling modifier**.

An absolute phrase is often useful because it contributes to **conciseness**.

Change: His accounts were in order, and so he left for the day. (less concise)
To: His accounts in order, he left for the day. (more concise)

absolute words

Absolute words (such as *round, unique, perfect*) are not logically subject to comparison (*rounder, roundest*); however, language is not always logical, and these words are sometimes used comparatively.

Example: We modified our contract to make it *more exactly* reflect our current needs.

Absolute words should be used comparatively only with the greatest caution in business and technical writing, where accuracy and precision are critical.

absolutely

Absolutely means "definitely," "entirely," "completely," or "unquestionably." It is not an **intensifier** and should not be used to mean "very" or "much." Where it is used as an intensifier, it can be deleted.

Change: A new analysis is *absolutely* impossible.
To: A new analysis is impossible.

abstract

An abstract is a condensed version of a longer piece of writing, summarizing or highlighting the major points covered in the longer work. Abstracts, which are generally one paragraph long and seldom exceed two hundred words, help the **reader** by allowing him to review the content of the **report** in an abbreviated form. If the subject matter is pertinent, the reader can then read the complete report. Scientific and technical reports, as well as business and industrial manuals, are often accompanied by abstracts.

Abstracts are usually classified as either descriptive or informative. A descriptive abstract tells what the report investigated but does not reveal its conclusions. Descriptive abstracts are intended for readers who will decide whether to read a full report exclusively on the basis of its subject matter. The following abstract is descriptive:

Example: The thesis describes the development of a computer surveillance program that identifies potential cases of abuse in the Medicaid reimbursement of claims submitted by physicians. The basic logic of the program is to establish claiming patterns for all physicians, select out certain physicians who have patterns "deviant" from normal patterns, and print out individual claims from these physicians for further examination. At least 75% of Tennessee's 3800 licensed physicians are members of the program.

—Vanderbilt Univ., Nashville, Tenn. "Computer Surveillance of Medicaid Provider Claims in Tennessee." Master's thesis. John David Lander, 1973.

An informative abstract tells what the report investigated and how the subject was investigated. It also gives the report's conclusions. Informative abstracts allow other researchers to grasp the essentials of a report without having to read it. The following abstract is informative:

Example: A 1970 Plymouth Duster, equipped with a 225 cu. in. six-cylinder engine and automatic transmission was modified, with changes to the intake manifold, lean main jets in the carburetor and revised camshaft. The intake modification consisted of truncated cone inserts placed in each inlet port. The following standard emission tests were run: (1) standard 1970 Federal test procedure for exhaust emissions (FTP); (2) closed, constant volume sampling technique using 9 repeats on the 7-mode Federal emissions test cycle (CVS); (3) closed constant volume sampling technique using the LA4-S3 driving schedule as specified for 1972 and later. Performance tests were also conducted consisting of wide open accelerations from 0–60 mph, 20–50 mph, and 40–80 mph. The results indicate that the Roberts' device: (1) caused no significant change in unburned hydrocarbons or carbon monoxide; (2)

caused some (27%) reduction in oxides of nitrogen, and (3) had a small detrimental effect on performance at high loads.

—"Exhaust Emissions from a Vehicle Equipped with the Roberts' Induction Modification Supplied Under CPA 70–51," John C. Thompson. Environmental Protection Agency, Ann Arbor, Michigan Division of Motor Vehicle Research and Development (December 1970), 8 pp.

Tips on Creating an Abstract. The major and minor **heads** of your **outline** can be useful in creating an abstract from a report you have written. If you are condensing someone else's work, use the **introduction** and **conclusion** as starting points for determining what should be included in the abstract. Begin the abstract with a **topic sentence**.

When writing an abstract, condense information. This is best accomplished by eliminating words and ideas that are repetitious or simply unnecessary. Also eliminate any references to the report that the abstract condenses, since the reader knows that the information came from the longer work.

| *Change:* | This report describes a test sequence on a General Motors prototype using a catalytic exhaust manifold system concept. |
| *To:* | A test sequence was conducted on a General Motors prototype using a catalytic exhaust manifold system. |

Even though the material must be condensed, articles (*a, an, the*) and transitional words (*and, however, but*) should not be dropped. When they are omitted, the language of the abstract is too brusque and choppy.

Certain journals—*Chemical Abstracts, Journal of Economic Abstracts, Highway Research Abstracts*—are devoted exclusively to abstracts of articles or reports in specific fields of study. These journals allow the researcher to scan large portions of the literature in a specialized field in a short time. (See also **reference books**.)

abstract noun

An abstract noun, as opposed to a **concrete noun**, refers to something that is intangible, something that cannot be discerned by the five senses. Abstract nouns are those that are used to name qualities, concepts, and actions, such as *kindness, fantasy, love, idealism, sportsmanship, hate.* (See also **abstract words/concrete words**.)

abstract words/concrete words

Abstract words refer to general ideas, qualities, conditions, acts, or relationships.

Examples: work, courage, crime

Abstract words must frequently be qualified with other words.

Change: What the Research and Development Department needs is *freedom.*

To: What the Research and Development Department needs is *freedom to explore the problem further.*

Concrete words refer to specific objects, persons, places, and acts that can be perceived by the senses.

Examples: sawing, soldier, auto theft
Bookkeeping (concrete) is hard *work* (abstract).

Concrete words create a specific sensory image.

Example: His feelings about his business rival are so bitter that in recent conversations with his staff he has returned to the subject compulsively, like *a man scratching an itch.*

Since the human mind can absorb sensory information easily and quickly, we generally prefer concrete words. Concrete words can be absorbed and assimilated more easily than abstract words, and the **reader** can create his own mental image, which is more meaningful to him.

Example: The file room is *conveniently arranged* (abstract) *with files at the center and the desks and work tables placed around them* (concrete).

Abstract words are appropriate to many subjects, even in business and technical writing. When using abstract words, however, remember that to be effective they must often be qualified with concrete words.

accept/except

Accept is a **verb** meaning "to consent to," "to agree to take," or "to admit willingly." *To receive*

Example: I *accept* the appointment and the responsibility that goes with it.

Except is normally a **preposition** meaning "other than" or "excluding."

Example: We agreed on everything *except* the schedule.

acceptance, letter of

When you have received an offer of a job that you want to accept, reply as soon as possible—certainly within a week. The format for such a letter is simple: begin by accepting, with pleasure, the job you have been offered. Identify the job you are accepting and state the salary so there is no confusion on these two important points.

The second **paragraph** might go into detail about moving dates and reporting for work. The details will vary depending on what occurred during your interview. Complete the letter with a statement that you are looking forward to working for your new employer. The following is a typical letter of acceptance.

2647 Patterson Road
Beechwood, Ohio 45432

March 6, 1976

Mr. F. E. Cummins
Personnel Manager
Calcutex Industries, Inc.
3275 Commercial Park Drive
Bintonville, Michigan 49474

Dear Mr. Cummins:

State the job and salary you are accepting. →

I am pleased to accept your offer of $865 per month as a junior design engineer in the Calcutex Servocontrol Group.

Specify the date on which you will report to work. →

Since graduation is August 30, I plan to leave Dayton on Tuesday, September 2. I should be able to locate suitable living accommodations within a few days and be ready to report for work on the following Monday, September 8. Please let me know if this date is satisfactory to you.

State your pleasure at joining the firm. →

I look forward to what I am sure will be a rewarding future with Calcutex.

Very truly yours,

Craig Adderly

accumulative/cumulative

Accumulative and *cumulative* are synonyms that mean "amassed" or "added up over a period of time." *Accumulative* is rarely used except with reference to accumulated property or wealth.

> *Examples:*   Last month's expenses were acceptable, but the *cumulative* expenses since the project was begun are excessive.
> The corporation's *accumulative* holdings include nineteen real-estate properties.

activate/actuate

Even linguists disagree on the distinction between these two words, although both mean "to make active." *Actuate* is usually applied only to mechanical processes.

> *Examples:*   The governor *activated* the National Guard.
> The relay *actuates* the trip hammer. (mechanical process)
> The electrolyte *activates* the battery. (chemical process)

actually

Actually is an **adverb** meaning "really" or "in fact." Although it is often used for **emphasis** in speech, such use of the word should be avoided in writing.

> *Change:*   Did he *actually* finish the report on time?
> *To:*   Did he finish the report on time?

(See also **intensifiers**.)

A.D.

A.D. is an **abbreviation** for the Latin *anno Domini*, meaning "in the year of the Lord" (dating from the year Christ was born). In formal usage, *A.D.* precedes the year indicated (A.D. 43) although it follows a designated century (in the first century A.D.). In informal usage, it is used like B.C., which always follows the date indicated (1543 A.D.; the third century A.D.).

A.D. does not mean "after (Christ's) death," a confusion that arises from the false analogy that because B.C. means "before Christ," *A.D.* must mean "after death."

ad hoc

Ad hoc is Latin for "for this" or "for this particular occasion." An *ad hoc* committee is one set up to consider a particular issue, as opposed to a permanent committee. (See also **foreign words in English**.)

adapt/adept/adopt

Adapt is a **verb** meaning "to adjust to a new situation." *Adept* is an **adjective** meaning "highly skilled." *Adopt* is a verb meaning "to take or use as one's own."

> *Example:*   The company will *adopt* a policy of finding executives who are *adept* administrators and who can *adapt* to new situations.

adherence/adhesion

Adherence refers to psychological or moral commitment.

> *Example:*   His *adherence* to the company's quality-control standards was never questioned.

Adhesion refers to physical attachment.

> *Example:*   The *adhesion* of barnacles to the ship's hull made cleaning difficult.

adjectives

An adjective modifies a **noun** or **pronoun**; that is, it makes the meaning of a noun or pronoun more exact by pointing out one of its qualities (descriptive adjective) or by imposing boundaries upon it (limiting adjective).

> *Examples:*   a *hot* iron (descriptive)
> He is *cold.* (descriptive)
> *ten* automobiles (limiting)
> *his* desk (limiting)

Limiting adjectives include some common and important categories:

Articles (a, an, the)
Demonstrative Adjectives (this, that, these, those)
Possessive Adjectives (my, his, her, your, our, their)
Interrogative and Relative Adjectives (whose, which, what)

Numeral Adjectives (two, first)
Indefinite Adjectives (all, none, some, any)

Of these, the demonstrative adjectives, the possessive adjectives, and the interrogative and relative adjectives are forms from pronouns and are sometimes called pronominal adjectives.

COMPARISON OF ADJECTIVES

Most adjectives add the **suffix** "-er" to show comparison with one other item and the suffix "-est" to show comparison with two or more other items. The three degrees of comparison are called the positive, comparative, and superlative.

The second ingot is *brighter*. (comparative form)
The third ingot is *brightest*. (superlative form)

> *Examples:* Interest rates at bank A are *high*. (positive form)
> Interest rates at bank B are *higher*. (comparative form)
> Interest rates at bank C are *highest*. (superlative form)

However, many two-syllable adjectives and most three-syllable adjectives are preceded by "more" or "most" to form the comparative or the superlative.

> *Examples:* The new facility is *more impressive* than the old one.
> The new facility is the *most impressive* in the city.

A few adjectives have irregular forms of comparison *(much, more, most; little, less, least).*

Absolute words (round, unique) are not logically subject to comparison (rounder, roundest); however, language is not always logical and these words are sometimes used comparatively.

> *Example:* We recently modified our standard contract to make several clauses *more exact*.

PLACEMENT OF ADJECTIVES

When limiting and descriptive adjectives appear together, the limiting adjectives precede the descriptive adjectives, with the articles usually in the first position.

> *Example:* *The ten gray* cars (article, limiting adjective, descriptive adjective)

Within a sentence, an adjective is in an attributive position when it precedes its noun and in a predicative position when it follows its noun.

Examples: The *small* jobs are given priority. (attributive position)
Priority is given when a job is *small*. (predicative position)

An adjective in an attributive position may shift to a predicative position in a larger, more complex construction.

Examples: We passed a *big* budget. (attributive position)
We negotiated a contract *bigger by far than theirs*. (predicative position for adjective phrase)

When an adjective is in a predicative position following a **linking verb**, it is called a **predicate adjective**.

Examples: The warehouse is *full*.
The lens is *convex*.
His department is *efficient*.

A predicate adjective is one kind of **subjective complement**. By completing the meaning of a linking verb, a predicate adjective describes or limits the subject of the **verb**.

Examples: The job is *easy*.
The manager was very *demanding*.

An adjective that follows a **transitive verb** and modifies its **direct object** is one kind of **objective complement**.

Example: We appointed Mr. James *chairman*.

(See **complement**.)

USAGE OF ADJECTIVES

Because of the need for precise qualification in business and technical writing, it is often necessary to use nouns as adjectives.

Example: The *test* conclusions led to a redesign of the system.

A common weakness of business and technical people is to attempt to string together a series of nouns to form a unit modifier. Therefore, exercise caution when using nouns as adjectives.

Change: The test control group meeting was held last Wednesday.
To: The meeting of the test control group was held last Wednesday.

As a rule of thumb, it is better to avoid general (*nice, fine, good*) and trite (a *fond* farewell) adjectives; in fact, it is good practice to question the need for most adjectives in your writing. Often, your writing will not only read as well without an adjective, but it may be even better without it. If an adjective is needed, try to find one that is as exact as possible for your meaning.

adjective clause

An adjective clause is a subordinate **clause** that functions as an **adjective** by modifying a **noun** or **pronoun** in another clause.

> *Example:*   The designer *we commissioned last year* (modifying "designer") has delivered the drawings, *which we have approved* (modifying "drawings").

Adjective clauses are often introduced by **relative pronouns** (*who, that,* and *which*).

> *Example:*   Our culture is beginning to produce a breed of people *who are very mobile.*

Adjective clauses are also sometimes introduced by relative **adverbs** (*when, where,* and *why*).

> *Example:*   The fourth quarter is the period *when cost control will be crucial.*

Adjective clauses may be **restrictive** or nonrestrictive. If the clause is essential to limiting the meaning of the noun, it is restrictive and not set off by **commas**.

> *Example:*   The statistics *that accompany this report* were compiled from a series of questionnaires.

If the clause is not intended to limit the meaning of the noun but merely provides further information about it, the clause is nonrestrictive and set off by commas.

> *Example:*   New statistics, *which will be submitted soon,* suggest a different conclusion.

If adjective clauses are not placed carefully, they may appear to modify the wrong noun or pronoun.

> *Change:*   The factory in the suburbs *that we bought* has increased in value. (This sentence implies that we bought the suburbs rather than the factory.)
> *To:*   The factory *that we bought* in the suburbs has increased in value.
> *Or:*   The suburban factory *that we bought* has increased in value.

adverbs

An adverb modifies the action or condition expressed by a **verb**.

> *Example:*   Three of the four applicants passed the business aptitude tests *satisfactorily.* (The adverb tells *how* the applicants passed the test.)

An adverb may also modify an **adjective**, another adverb, or a **clause**.

> *Examples:*   The graphics department used *extremely* bright colors. (modifying an adjective)
> The redesigned brake pad lasted *much* longer. (modifying another adverb)
> *Surprisingly,* the machine failed. (modifying a clause)

An adverb answers one of the following questions:

Where? (adverb of place)

> *Example:*   The office will be moved *downtown.*

When? (adverb of time)

> *Example:*   Please give me the estimate *tomorrow.*

How? (adverb of manner)

> *Example:*   Open the container *gently.*

How much? (adverb of degree)

> *Example:*   The *nearly* completed report was lost in the move.

An adverb may be a common, a conjunctive, an interrogative, or a numeric modifier. Typical common adverbs are *almost, seldom, down, also, now, ever,* and *always.*

> *Example:*   I *rarely* work on the weekend.

Typical **conjunctive adverbs** are *however, therefore, nonetheless, nevertheless, consequently, accordingly,* and *then.*

> *Example:*   I rarely work on the weekend; *however,* this weekend will be an exception.

Typical **interrogative adverbs** are *where, when, why,* and *how.*

> *Example:*   *How* many hours did you work last week?

Typical numeric adverbs are *once* and *twice.*

> *Example:*   I have worked overtime *twice* this week.

COMPARISON OF ADVERBS

Adverbs are normally compared by adding *-er* or *-est* to them or by inserting *more* or *most* in front of them. One-syllable adverbs use the comparative ending *-er* and the superlative ending *-est*.

> *Examples:* This copier works *faster* than the old one.
> This copier works *fastest* of the three tested.

Most adverbs with two or more syllables end in *-ly*, and most adverbs ending in *-ly* are compared by inserting the comparative *more* or the superlative *most* in front of them.

> *Examples:* He moved *more quickly* than the other company's salesman.
> *Most surprisingly*, the engine failed during the test phase.

Less and *least* are **antonyms** of *more* and *most*.

> *Examples:* He moved *less quickly* than the other company's salesman.
> *Least surprisingly*, the engine failed during the test phase.

There are a few irregular adverbs that require a change in form to indicate comparison.

> *Examples:* The training program functions *well*.
> Our training program functions *better* than most others in the industry.
> Many consider our training program the *best* in the industry.

ADVERBS MADE FROM ADJECTIVES

Many adverbs are simply adjectives with *-ly* added, such as *dashingly* and *richly*. Sometimes, the adverb form is identical to the adjective form: *early, cheap, fair, hard, right,* and *fast*.

Resist the temptation to drop the *-ly* ending from such adverbs as *surely, differently, seriously, considerably, badly,* and *really*.

> *Change:* The breakdown of the air conditioning equipment damaged the computer system *considerable*.
> *To:* The breakdown of the air conditioning equipment damaged the computer system *considerably*.

On the other hand, resist the temptation to coin awkward adverbs by adding *-ly* to adjectives (*firstly, muchly*).

> *Change:* He slumped *tiredly* into the chair.
> *To:* *Tired*, he slumped into the chair.

PLACEMENT OF ADVERBS

An adverb may appear almost anywhere in a **sentence**, but its position may affect the meaning of the sentence. Avoid placing an adverb between two verb forms where it can be read ambiguously as modifying either.

Change: The supplier wanted *belatedly* to thank the purchasing agent for the order.

To: The supplier *belatedly* wanted to thank the purchasing agent for the order.

The adverb is commonly placed in front of the verb it modifies.

Example: The accountant *meticulously* checked the figures.

An adverb may, however, follow the verb (or the verb and its **object**) that it modifies.

Examples: The gauge dipped *suddenly*.
They repaired the computer *quickly*.

The adverb may be placed between a **helping verb** and a main verb.

Example: He will *surely* call.

If an adverb modifies only the main verb, and not any accompanying helping verbs, place the adverb immediately before the main verb.

Example: The alternative proposal has been *effectively* presented.

An adverb phrase should not be inserted between the words of a compound verb.

Change: This suggestion has *time and time again* been rejected.
To: This suggestion has been rejected *time and time again*.

To place **emphasis** on an adverb, put it before the subject of the sentence.

Examples: *Clearly,* he was ready for the promotion when it came.
Unfortunately, fuel rationing has been unavoidable.

In writing, such adverbs as *nearly, only, almost, just,* and *hardly* are placed immediately before the words they limit. A speaker can place these words earlier and avoid **ambiguity** by stressing the word to be limited; in writing, however, only correct placement of the adverb will ensure clarity.

Change: The punch press *only* costs $47,000.
To: The punch press costs *only* $47,000.

(See also **misplaced modifiers**.)

adverb clause

An adverb clause is a subordinate **clause** used to modify a **verb**, **adjective**, or **adverb** in the main clause.

> *Example:*   The property is located *where the railroad track crosses the road.*

Like adverbs, adverb clauses normally express such ideas as those of time, place, condition, cause, manner, or comparison.

> *Examples:*   It stopped *after we installed the new bearings.* (time)
> It stopped *where the previous model stopped.* (place)
> *If we install the new bearings again,* it will stop again. (condition)
> It stopped *because we installed the new bearings.* (cause)
> It stopped *as though it had run into a wall.* (manner)
> The new bearings perform no better *than the old ones did.* (comparison)

Adverb clauses are often introduced by **subordinating conjunctions** (*because, when, where, since,* and *though*). If the adverb clause follows the main clause, a **comma** should not normally separate the two clauses.

> *Example:*   We are being especially cautious about expansion *because of the cost-price squeeze.*

If the adverb clause precedes the main clause, the adverb clause should be set off by a comma.

> *Example:*   *Because of the cost-price squeeze,* we are being especially cautious about expansion.

Placement of an adverb clause can change the **emphasis** of a sentence. Do not allow this to happen inadvertently.

> *Examples:*   Ruins and artifacts are mere objects of curiosity *unless they are used to reconstruct the daily activities of prehistoric peoples.*
>
> *Unless they are used to reconstruct the daily activities of prehistoric peoples,* ruins and artifacts are mere objects of curiosity.
>
> Ruins and artifacts, *unless they are used to reconstruct the daily activities of prehistoric peoples,* are mere objects of curiosity.

An adverb clause cannot act as the subject of a sentence.

> *Change:*   *Because medical expenses have increased* is the reason health insurance rates have gone up.
> *To:*   Health insurance rates have gone up *because medical expenses have increased.*
> *Or:*   *Because medical expenses have increased,* health insurance rates have gone up.

advice/advise

Advice is a **noun** that means "counsel" or "suggestion."

> *Example:*   His *advice* was to sign the contract immediately.

Advise is a **verb** that means "to give advice."

> *Example:*   I *advise* you to handle the situation carefully.

affect/effect

Affect is a **verb** meaning "to influence" or "to pretend."

> *Examples:*   Viewers' experiences tend to *affect* their observations.
> The researcher *affected* a fancy writing style in his report.

(See also **affectation**.)

Effect can function either as a verb meaning "to bring about" or as a **noun** meaning "result."

> *Examples:*   He *effected* many changes in the organization. (verb)
> The *effect* of the stock market's sharp plunge was felt by many. (noun)
> The ruling had a good *effect* on our business. (noun)

affectation

Affectation is the use of language that is more technical, or showy, than is necessary to communicate information to the **reader**. Writing that is unnecessarily ornate, pompous, or pretentious is affected, and the writer is usually attempting to impress the reader by showing off a repertoire of fancy or flashy words. Affected writing forces the reader to work harder to understand the writer's meaning. Affected writing typically contains abstract, highly technical, pseudo-technical, pseudo-legal, or foreign words and is often liberally sprinkled with **vogue words**. **Jargon** can become affectation if it is misused. **Euphemisms** can contribute to affected writing if their purpose is to hide the facts of a situation rather than treat them with dignity or restraint.

The easiest kind of affectation to be lured into is the use of **long variants**: words created by adding **prefixes** and **suffixes** to simpler words (*analyzation* for analysis, *telephonic communication* for telephone call). The practice of **elegant variation**—attempting to avoid repeating the same word in the same **paragraph** by substituting pretentious **synonyms**—is also a form of affectation. Another contributor to affectation is **gobbledygook,** which is wordy, roundabout writing that has many pseudo-legal and pseudo-scientific terms sprinkled throughout.

Wordiness, when it attempts to make the trivial seem important, is a cause of affectation. This is apparent in the first version of the following example, taken from a specification soliciting bids from local merchants for the operation of a television repair shop in an Air Force Post Exchange.

Change: In addition to performing interior housekeeping services, the concessionaire shall perform custodial maintenance on the exterior of the facility and grounds. Where a concessionaire shares a facility with one or more other concessionaires, exterior custodial maintenance responsibilities will be assigned by Post Exchange management on a fair and equitable basis. In those instances where the concessionaire's activity is located in a Post Exchange complex wherein predominant tenancy is by Post Exchange-operated activities, then Post Exchange management shall be responsible for exterior custodial maintenance except for those described in a, b, c, and d below. The necessary equipment and labor to perform exterior custodial maintenance, when such a responsibility has been assigned to the concessionaire, shall be furnished by the concessionaire. Exterior custodial maintenance shall include the following tasks.
a. Clean entrance door and exterior of storefront windows daily.
b. Sweep and clean the entrance and customer walks daily.
c. Empty and clean waste and smoking receptacles daily.
d. Check exterior lighting and report failures to the contracting officer's representative daily.

To: The merchant awarded this concession shall be responsible for performing, with his own equipment, the following duties daily: (1) maintaining a clean and neat appearance inside the store, (2) cleaning the entrance door window and the outsides of the store windows, (3) sweeping the entrance and sidewalk, (4) emptying and cleaning waste cans and ash trays, (5) checking the exterior lighting and reporting failures to the representative of the contracting officer.

The merchant shall also be responsible for the maintenance and appearance of any grounds surrounding his store. Where two or more merchants share the same building, Post Exchange management shall equitably assign responsibility for the grounds. Where the merchant's store is in a building that is occupied predominantly by Post Exchange operations, Post Exchange management shall be responsible for the maintenance and appearance of the grounds.

Affectation is the most serious single problem in business and technical writing because many people apparently feel that affectation lends a degree of formality, and hence authority, to their writing. Nothing could be further from the truth. Affectation simply lays down a smoke screen that the reader must penetrate to get to the writer's meaning. Revise your writing carefully if you have a weakness for affected writing. (See also **conciseness/wordiness**.)

affinity

Affinity means the attraction of two persons or things to each other.

> *Example:* The *affinity* between these two elements can be explained in terms of their valence electrons.

Affinity should never be used to mean "ability" or "aptitude."

> *Change:* She has an *affinity* for chemistry.
> *To:* She has an *aptitude* for chemistry.
> *Or:* She has a *talent* for chemistry.

afflict/inflict

Afflict is a **transitive verb** meaning "to inflict suffering upon."

> *Example:* The Havertown plant has been *afflicted* by labor-management trouble since it began production.

Inflict is a **transitive verb** meaning "to cause by aggressive action."

> *Example:* The truck hit a parked car and *inflicted* severe damages.

In summary, *afflict* is an action from the receiver's perspective that is *inflicted* from the doer's perspective.

> *Example:* The training program has been *afflicted* by delays that were *inflicted* by budget cuts.

aforesaid

Aforesaid means "stated previously," but it is legal **jargon** and should be avoided in nonlegal writing.

> *Change:* The Sturgess contract was concluded on June 16, 1976. The *aforesaid* contract expires three years from that date.
> *To:* The Sturgess contract was concluded on June 16, 1976. It expires three years from that date.
> *Or:* The Sturgess contract, concluded on June 16, 1976, expires in three years.

agree to/agree with

When you *agree to* something, you are "giving consent."

Example: I *agree to* the terms of the contract.

When you *agree with* something, you are "in accord" with it.

Example: I *agree with* the recommendations of the advisory board.

agreement

Agreement, grammatically, means the correspondence in form between different elements of a **sentence** to indicate **person, number, gender**, and **case**. A **pronoun** must agree with its antecedent, and a **verb** must agree with its **subject**.

A subject and its verb must agree in number and in person.

Examples: *I am* going to approve his promotion. (The singular, first person subject, *I*, requires the singular, first person form of the verb, *am*.)
His *colleagues are* envious. (The plural, third person subject, *colleagues*, requires the plural, third person form of the verb, *are*.)

A pronoun and its antecedent must agree in person, number, and gender.

Examples: The *employees* report that *they* become less efficient as the humidity rises. (The third person, plural subject, *employees*, requires the third person, plural pronoun, *they*.)
Mr. Joiner offered *his* services during negotiations. (The third person, singular, masculine subject, *Mr. Joiner*, requires the third person, singular, masculine form of the pronoun, *his*.)

AGREEMENT OF SUBJECT AND VERB

A verb must agree with its subject. Do not let intervening **phrases** and **clauses** mislead you.

Change: The use of insecticides, fertilizers, and weed killers, although they offer unquestionable benefits, often result in unfortunate side effects.
To: The *use* of insecticides, fertilizers, and weed killers, although they offer unquestionable benefits, often *results* in unfortunate side effects. (The verb *results* must agree with the subject of the sentence, *use*, rather than with the subject of the preceding clause, *they*.)

Be careful to avoid making the verb agree with the **noun** immediately in front of it if that noun is not its subject. This problem is especially likely to occur when a plural noun falls between a singular subject and its verb.

> *Examples:* Only *one* of the emergency lights *was* functioning when the accident occurred. (The subject of the verb is *one,* not *lights.*)
> *Each* of the switches *controls* a separate circuit. (The subject of the verb is *each,* not *switches.*)
> *Each* of the managers *supervises* a very large region. (The subject of the verb is *each,* not *managers.)*
> The proper *use* of the tools *requires* practice. (The subject of the verb is *use,* not *tools.*)

Be careful not to let modifying phrases obscure a simple subject.

> *Example:* The *advice* of two engineers, one lawyer, and three executives *was* obtained prior to making a commitment. (The subject of the verb is *advice,* not *executives.*)

Sentences with inverted word order can cause problems with agreement between subject and verb.

> *Example:* From this work *have come* several important *improvements.* (The subject of the verb is *improvements,* not *work.*)

Such words as *type, part, series,* and *portion* take singular verbs even when they precede a phrase containing a plural noun.

> *Examples:* A *series* of meetings *was* held about the best way to market the new product.
> A large *portion* of most industrial annual reports *is* devoted to promoting the corporate image.

Subjects expressing measurement, weight, mass, or total often take singular verbs even though the subject word is plural in form. Such subjects are treated as a unit.

> *Examples:* *Four years is* the normal duration of the apprenticeship program.
> *Twenty dollars is* the wholesale price of each unit.

Indefinite pronouns such as *some, none, all, more,* and *most* may be singular or plural depending upon whether they are used with a **mass noun** (*oil* in the following examples) or with a **count noun** (*driver* in the following examples).

> *Examples:* *None* of the oil *is* to be used.
> *None* of the truck drivers *are* to go.
> *Most* of the oil *has* been used.
> *Most* of the drivers *know* why they are here.
> *Some* of the oil *has* leaked.
> *Some* of the drivers *have* gone.

One and *each* are normally singular.

> *Examples:* *One* of the brake drums *is* still scored.
> *Each* of the original founders *is* scheduled to speak at the dedication ceremony.

A verb following the relative pronouns *who* and *that* agrees in number with the noun to which the pronoun refers (its antecedent).

> *Examples:* Steel is one of those *industries* that *are* hardest hit by high energy costs. (*That* refers to *industries*.)
> This is one of those engineering *problems* that *require* careful analysis. (*That* refers to *problems*.)
> She is one of those *employees* who *are* rarely absent. (*Who* refers to *employees*.)

Some **abstract nouns** are singular in meaning though plural in form: *mathematics, news, physics,* and *economics.*

> *Examples:* *News* of the merger *is* on page four of the *Chronicle.*
> *Textiles is* an industry in need of import quotas.

Some words are always plural, such as *trousers* and *scissors.*

> *Example:* His *trousers were* torn by the machine. (But: A *pair* of trousers *is* on order.)

Collective subjects take singular verbs when the group is thought of as a unit, plural verbs when the individuals are thought of separately. (See also **collective noun.**)

   Relative pronouns (*who, which, that*) may take either singular or plural verbs depending upon whether the antecedent is singular or plural.

> *Examples:* He is an *executive* who *takes* work home at night.
> He is one of those *executives* who *take* work home at night.

(See also **who/whom.**)

   A singular subject that is followed by a phrase or clause containing a plural noun still requires a singular verb.

> *Change:* One in twenty transistors we receive from our suppliers are faulty.
> *To:* *One* in twenty transistors we receive from our suppliers *is* faulty. (The subject is *one*, not *transistors*.)

The number of a **subjective complement** does not affect the number of the verb—the verb must always agree with the subject.

> *Example:* The *topic* of his report *was* rivers. (The subject of the sentence is *topic*, not *rivers*.)

A book with a plural title requires a singular verb.

> *Example:* *Monetary Theories is* a useful source.

Compound Subjects. A compound subject is one that is composed of two or more elements joined by a **conjunction** such as *and, or, nor, either . . . or,* or *neither . . . nor.* Usually, when the elements are connected by *and,* the subject is plural and requires a plural verb.

> *Example:* *Chemistry and accounting are* both prerequisites for this position.

There is one exception to the *and* rule. Sometimes the elements connected by *and* form a unit or refer to the same person. In this case, the subject is regarded as singular and takes a singular verb.

> *Examples:* *Bacon and eggs is* a high-cholesterol meal.
> The *red, white, and blue flutters* from the top of the capitol.
> His *secretary and biographer was* also his toughest critic. (His secretary was also his biographer.)

A compound subject with a singular and a plural element joined by *or* or *nor* requires that the verb agree with the element nearest to it.

> *Examples:* Neither the office manager nor the *secretaries were* there.
> Neither the secretaries nor the office *manager was* there.
> Either they or *I am* going to write the report.
> Either I or *they are* going to write the report.

If *each* or *every* modifies the elements of a compound subject, use the singular verb.

> *Examples:* *Each* manager and supervisor *has* a production goal to meet.
> *Every* manager and supervisor *has* a production goal to meet.

AGREEMENT OF PRONOUN AND ANTECEDENT

A pronoun must have a logical antecedent, or a noun to which it refers.

> *Change:* Accountants must constantly struggle to keep up with the professional literature because *it* is a dynamic science.
> *To:* Accountants must constantly struggle to keep up with the professional literature because *accounting* is a dynamic science.
> *Or:* Accountants must continue to study *accounting* because *it* is a dynamic science.

Using the relative pronoun *which* to refer to an idea instead of a specific noun can be confusing.

> *Change:* He acted independently on the advice of his consultant, *which* the others thought unjust. (Was it the fact that he acted inde-

pendently or was it the advice that the others thought unjust?)

To: The others thought it unjust for him to act independently.

Or: The others thought it unjust for him to act on the advice of his consultant.

(See also **misplaced modifiers**.)

Gender. A pronoun must agree with its antecedent in gender.

Example: Mr. Swivet in the Accounting Department acknowledges *his* share of the responsibility for the misunderstanding, just as Mrs. Barkley in the Research Division must acknowledge *hers.*

There is a long-standing tradition of using a masculine, singular pronoun to agree with such indefinite antecedents as *one, anyone,* and *person.*

Example: *Each* may stay or go as *he* chooses.

Many people are now sensitive to an implied sexual bias in such usage. When graceful alternatives are available, use them. One solution is to use the plural.

Change: Every *employee* will have *his* supervisor sign *his* slip.

To: All *employees* will have *their* supervisors sign *their* slips.

Do not, however, attempt to avoid expressing gender by resorting to a plural pronoun when the antecedent is singular.

Change: A *technician* can expect to advance on *their* merit.

To: A *technician* can expect to advance on *his* merit.

Or: *Technicians* can expect to advance on *their* merit.

Number. A pronoun must agree with its antecedent in number. Many problems of agreement are caused by expressions that are not clear in number.

Change: Although the typical *engine* runs well in moderate temperatures, *they* often stall in extreme cold.

To: Although the typical *engine* runs well in moderate temperatures, *it* often stalls in extreme cold.

Use singular pronouns with the antecedents *everybody* and *everyone* unless to do so would be illogical because the meaning is obviously plural.

Examples: *Everyone* pulled *his* share of the load.

Everyone laughed at my sales slogan, and I really couldn't blame *them.*

(See also **everybody/everyone**.)

A compound antecedent joined by *or* or *nor* is singular if both elements are singular, and plural if both elements are plural.

Examples: Neither the *engineer* nor the *draftsman* could do *his* job until *he* understood the new concept.
Neither the *executives* nor the *board of directors* were pleased at the performance of *their* company.

When one of the antecedents connected by *or* or *nor* is singular and the other plural, the pronoun agrees with the nearer antecedent.

Example: Either the *supervisor* or the *operators* will have *their* licenses suspended.

A compound antecedent with its elements joined by *and* requires a plural pronoun.

Example: Jim and Ed took *their* layout drawings with *them*.

If both elements refer to the same person, however, use the singular pronoun.

Example: The respected *economist and author* departed from *his* prepared speech.

Collective nouns may be singular or plural, depending on meaning.

Examples: The *committee* arrived at the recommended solutions only after *it* had deliberated for days.
The *committee* quit for the day and went to *their* respective homes.

albeit

Albeit is an archaic **conjunction** meaning "even though" or "although." Avoid using it in your writing.

Change: The union approved the contract, *albeit* reluctantly.
To: The union reluctantly approved the contract.

all around/all-around/all-round

All-round and *all-around* both mean "comprehensive" or "versatile."

Example: The company started an *all-round* training program.

Do not confuse these words with the two-word phrase *all around*, as in "The police were *all around* the building."

all right/alright/all-right

All right means "all correct." In formal writing it should not be used to mean "good" or "acceptable." It is always written as two words, with no **hyphen**; *all-right* and *alright* are incorrect.

> *Change:*   The decision that the committee finally reached was *all right.*
> *To:*   The decision that the committee finally reached was acceptable.

all the farther

All the farther is an unacceptable substitute for "as far as."

> *Change:*   That was *all the farther* we could go.
> *To:*   That was as far as we could go.

all together/altogether

All together means "all acting together," or "all in one place."

> *Example:*   The parties involved in the merger were *all together* at the attorney's office.

Altogether means "entirely" or "completely."

> *Example:*   The trip was *altogether* unnecessary.

allude/elude

Allude means to make an indirect reference to something not specifically mentioned.

> *Example:*   The report simply *alluded* to the problem rather than coming to grips with it.

Elude means to escape notice or detection.

> *Examples:*   The discrepancy in the account *eluded* the auditor.
> The leak *eluded* the inspectors.

allude/refer

Allude means to make an indirect reference to something not specifically mentioned.

Examples: He *alluded* to the rumors of stock failure in his speech to the trustees.
The memo *alluded* to past equipment failures.

Refer is used to indicate a direct reference to something.

Example: He *referred* to the chart three times during his speech.

allusion

The use of allusion (implied or indirect reference) promotes economical writing because it is a shorthand way of referring to a body of material in a few words, or of helping to explain a new and unfamiliar process in terms of one that is familiar. Be sure, however, that your **reader** is familiar with the material to which you allude. In the following paragraph, the writer sums up the argument he has been developing with an allusion to the Bible. The biblical story is well known, and the allusion, with its implicit reference to "right standing up to might," concisely emphasizes the writer's point.

Example: As it presently exists, the review process involves the consumer's attorney sitting alone, usually without adequate technical assistance, faced by two or three government attorneys, two or three attorneys from the XYZ Corporation, and large teams of experts who support the government and corporation's attorneys. The entire proceeding is reminiscent of David versus Goliath.

Allusion should be used with restraint. If overdone, it can become **affectation**.

allusion/illusion / DELUSION

An *allusion* is an indirect reference to something not specifically mentioned.

Example: The report made an *allusion* to the company's declining sales.

An *illusion* is a mistaken perception or a false image.

Example: The general manager is under the *illusion* that all is going well in the manufacturing department.

DELUSION: FIXED ABERRATION OF THE MIND

almost/most

Do not use *most* as a colloquial substitute for *almost* in your writing.

Change: New shipments arrive *most* every day.
To: New shipments arrive *almost* every day.

If you can substitute *almost* for *most* in a sentence, *almost* is the word you need.

along the line of

Along the line of is an overworked and inexact expression that should be eliminated from your writing.

Change: What we need is something *along the line of* a hand calculator.
To: What we need is something similar to a hand calculator.

already/all ready

Already is an **adverb** expressing time.

Example: The shipment had *already* been made when the stop order arrived.

All ready is a two-word **phrase** meaning "completely prepared."

Example: He was *all ready* to start work on the project when it was suddenly canceled.

also

Also is an **adverb** that means "additionally."

Example: He brought the reports and letters. He *also* brought the section supervisor's recommendations.

It should not be used as a **connective** in the sense of "and."

Change: He brought the reports, letters, *also* the section supervisor's recommendations.
To: He brought the reports, letters, *and* the section supervisor's recommendations.

ambiguity

A word or passage is ambiguous when it is susceptible to two or more interpretations, yet provides the **reader** with no certain basis for choosing among the alternatives.

Example: Mathematics is more valuable to an engineer than a computer. (Does this mean that an engineer is more in need of mathematics than a computer is? Or does it mean that mathematics is more valuable to an engineer than a computer is?)

Ambiguity can take many forms: ambiguous **pronoun** reference, misplaced **modifiers**, **dangling modifiers**, ambiguous coordination, ambiguous juxtaposition, incomplete comparison, incomplete **idiom**, ambiguous **word choice**, and so on.

Change: Inadequate quality-control procedures have resulted in more equipment failures. *These* are our most serious problem at present. (ambiguous pronoun reference; does *these* refer to "quality-control procedures" or "equipment failures"?)

To: Inadequate quality-control procedures have resulted in more equipment failures. These failures are our most serious problem at present.

Or: Inadequate quality-control procedures have resulted in more equipment failures. Quality control is our most serious problem at present.

Change: Ms. Jones values rigid quality control standards more than Mr. Johnson. (incomplete comparison)

To: Ms. Jones values rigid quality control standards more than Mr. Johnson *does.*

Change: His hobby was cooking. He was especially fond of cocker spaniels. (missing modifier)

To: His hobby was cooking. He was *also* especially fond of cocker spaniels.

Change: She *almost* wrote a million dollars in insurance policies last month. (misplaced modifier)

To: She wrote *almost* a million dollars in insurance policies last month.

Ambiguity is also often caused by thoughtless word choice.

Change: The general manager has denied reports that the plant's recent fuel allocation cut will be *restored.* (inappropriate word choice)

To: The general manager has denied reports that the plant's recent fuel allocation cut will be *rescinded.*

amount/number

Amount is used with things thought of in bulk (**mass nouns**).

Examples: The *amount* of electricity available for industrial use is limited. The *amount* of oxygen was insufficient for combustion.

Number is used with things that can be counted as individual items (**count nouns**).

Examples: A large *number* of stockholders attended the meeting.
The *number* of employees who are qualified for early retirement has increased in recent years.

analogy

Analogy is a **comparison** between two objects or concepts to show ways in which they are similar. In effect, analogies say, "A is to B as C is to D."

Example: Pollution is to the environment as cancer is to the body.

The resemblance between the concepts represented in an analogy must be close enough to illuminate the relationship the writer wants to establish. Analogies may be brief or extended, depending on the writer's purpose.

Analogy can be a particularly useful tool to the business or technical person writing for an intelligent and educated but nontechnical audience, such as top management, because of its effectiveness in **defining terms** and **explaining processes**. Like all figurative language, analogy can provide a shortcut means of communication if it is used with care and restraint.

Example: The search technique used in indexed sequential processing is similar to the search technique used to look up a word in a dictionary. To locate a specific word, the dictionary user scans the key words located at the top of each page (these key words identify the first and last words on the page) until he finds the key words that confine his word to a specific page. Assume that all the key words that reference the last words on each page of a dictionary were placed in a file (the index file), along with their corresponding page numbers, and that all the words in the dictionary were placed in another file (the data file). The dictionary would then be organized as an indexed sequential system. To locate any word, the user would simply scan the index file until he found a key word greater in alphabetical sequence than the desired word and go to the indicated page number.

—The NCR File Management Manual, NCR Corporation

analysis as a method of development

Analysis, as a **method of development**, separates a whole into its component parts. It is a form of examination that seeks to distinguish and separate things, situations, experiences, or concepts and thereby to establish the identities of parts or particulars. For example, if you were describing the requirements for establishing a small business you might develop your subject in terms of (1) location, (2) background of personnel, (3) training of personnel, (4) required equipment, and (5) facilities. This would be development by analysis of the component parts of the whole.

The purpose, or **objective**, of your writing must determine the parts to be analyzed and the relevant material to be included in analyzing them. The sequence of the parts should depend upon the relationship between the parts and the whole and upon the support given to the whole by the parts being analyzed.

and/or

And/or means that either both circumstances are possible or only one of two circumstances is possible; however, it is clumsy and awkward because it makes the **reader** stop to puzzle over your distinction. As Wilson Follett said, "English speakers and writers have managed to express this simple relationship without *and/or* for over six centuries."* Avoid it.

anecdote

An anecdote is an interesting or humorous incident or story indirectly related to the writer's subject. It is used to develop or clarify a point. For example, Isaac Asimov, discussing pre-scientific thinking, tells an anecdote about the tendency of men to explain the outcome of their actions on the basis of astronomical phenomena.

Example: Thus in 1066, the comet we now call Haley's Comet appeared in the sky just as William of Normandy was making ready to invade England. It predicted catastrophe and that is exactly what came, for the Saxons lost the Battle of Hastings and passed under the permanent rule of the Normans. The Saxons couldn't have asked for a better catastrophe than that.

On the other hand, if the Saxons had won and had hurled William's expeditionary force into the Channel, that would have been catastrophe enough for the Normans.

Whichever side lost, the comet was sure to win.

—*The Stars in Their Courses* (New York: Ace Books, 1971), p. 20.

* *Modern American Usage* (New York: Hill & Wang, 1966), p. 65.

annual report

The corporate annual report is a legally required document that is, in effect, a "state of the company" message. It is written primarily for stockholders, although many other audiences must be kept in mind when the report is prepared (bankers, financial press, labor unions, employees, etc.). An annual report usually covers the high points of the previous year's operations and attempts to forecast the coming year's operations. It may also explain the company's present directions and highlight its present strengths. If weaknesses have developed or failures have occurred, the annual report may analyze them and explain the efforts being made to overcome them.

A wide variety of annual reports are published every year. Some are lavish in presentation and paint the company and its operations in glowing terms; others are spartan financial recitations that merely meet the legal requirements for annual financial reporting. Most annual reports are combinations of legally required financial reporting and narrative articles presenting the company with its best foot forward.

Although they vary greatly, the annual report can be loosely divided into five major divisions: (1) financial highlights, (2) a statement to stockholders or letter from the president, (3) a narrative section containing articles on the company's operations, (4) a financial statement, and (5) a listing of the company's board of directors and officers.

Financial Highlights. The financial highlights section is a quick review of the company's sales and earnings that usually precedes the president's message to the stockholders, sometimes even appearing on the inside of the front cover. The most-read part of the annual report, this section often compares sales and earnings for three years, and it often includes the percentage of change from year to year.

Statement to Stockholders. This section of the annual report is a direct statement to stockholders from the company's president or chairman of the board of directors. This statement (which is sometimes presented in the form of a letter) is second in readership only to the financial highlights. It is the place to set the stage for the rest of the report. It should avoid repeating financial facts already cited in the financial highlights; instead, it can be used to (1) interpret the entire year's performance, (2) touch upon plans and future directions, (3) give the company's explanations for any failures.

The statement to stockholders may be an in-depth review of the company's operations during the past year, or it may be a brief summary of the entire report. A brief summary of the annual report is sometimes followed by an article in "interview" (question and answer) format that reviews the past year's operations as though an actual verbal interview were taking place between the writer and the president of the company.

Avoid stereotyped language and clichés when you write this statement. Also avoid technical terms. Use simple sentences and short paragraphs, and use a straightforward and informal style.

Narrative Feature Articles. This section of the annual report is normally used to present company operations and new products or developments in a positive light. Select the topics for these articles very carefully, making certain that they are timely and meaningful and that they contribute to the primary objective of the annual report. The following list includes topics that are often dealt with in annual reports.

Major profit factors in last year's performance
Sales trends
How well or poorly the company is doing against its competition
International operations
An analysis of what world problems may mean to the company
An analysis of the dependability of the company's overseas markets
Research and development efforts
Significant organizational changes
The company's labor relations outlook
How productivity is being increased
Acquisitions and their significance
Prospects for increasing stock dividends
Outlook for next year (for the company as a whole or by divisions)
Significant new products or services
Current market performance of existing products or services
Service and support operations
How the company is meeting its social responsibilities—on environmental protection, energy conservation, safety, hiring minorities and the handicapped, and so on. (Be certain to document the company's efforts in this area because overstated claims by a few companies in the past have generated suspicion of all such claims.)

Most readers merely scan an annual report, but they stop to look at photographs and **illustrations** and to read their captions. Therefore, use photographs and illustrations liberally in this section of the annual report, and make your captions informative and well-written.

Financial Statement. The financial statement should not be forbidding in appearance; it should be uncluttered, inviting, and consistent with the other sections of the annual report. The financial statement may appear at the beginning, middle, or end of the annual report; however, it most often appears at the end. It is frequently prepared as a separate booklet, printed on colored paper, and then stitched into the report.

Minimum normal contents of the financial statement include (1) balance sheet, (2) statement of income, (3) changes in financial position, (4) the auditor's statement, and (5) footnotes. Most annual reports also include a fairly comprehensive comparison of financial results of the past ten to fifteen years.

Footnotes in the financial section should be written in simple, direct language rather than in accounting terms. The auditor's statement should be limited to no more than one-third of a page.

Board of Directors and Company Officers. The final part of the annual report lists the company's board of directors, along with their corporate affiliations. Many annual reports also include a portrait photograph of each director. Also listed by name and title (sometimes with photographs) are the company's officers. These generally include the chairman of the board of directors, president, vice-presidents, secretary, treasurer, and legal counsel. To avoid hard feelings about some being shown in photographs and others not, establish a logical cut-off point. For example, if there are too many officers to include photographs of them all, show only the executive committee. Do not, however, underestimate the importance of these photographs; all your reading audiences are interested in seeing what your company's top men look like.

PREPARING THE REPORT

In large and medium-sized companies, annual reports are prepared by professional writers in the company's advertising or public relations department or by an outside agency. If you work for a small company, however, it is possible that you may one day find yourself faced with the task of preparing the annual report, or that you may be responsible for getting it done even if you do not do it yourself. A top executive in the company is usually given responsibility for "getting out" the annual report. This executive may be the president of the company, the secretary, the marketing manager, the advertising manager, the public relations manager, or even the sales manager—depending on the size of the company. The executive won't actually do the job but will designate someone to do it.

Assuming you are to prepare the annual report, the first thing you must do is interview the president of the company or the chairman of the board of directors to determine the general directions the report is to take. Next, you must interview the various vice-presidents, or division heads, to learn the highlights of each division's operations during the year. Determine from these executives the proper emphasis to place on their divisions' performances—but stay within the general direction established by the president or chairman of the board.

The primary objective of the annual report often depends upon which of several audiences (shareholders, bankers, business and financial analysts, the financial press, employees, labor unions, the communities in which your company operates) you are most concerned about. Since you cannot satisfy all these groups with one report, you must establish priorities among them. Having done that, you can compose a list of "must" topics, then a list of secondary topics (such as diversification, expansion of markets, product development, etc.). You can also make such decisions as (1) selection of main topics for brief coverage in the statement to stockholders, (2) whether to show sales and earnings by division, (3) the amount of space to allot to various divisions and subsidiaries, (4) contents of charts and graphs, (5) whether to include photographs of the executives of branches, divisions, and subsidiaries, (6) whether to include a frank discussion of company problems and solutions, and (7) how lavish or spartan the report should be in appearance (and costs).

Tone is a critical factor in writing and designing an annual report. Companies are as different as people; some are conservative, and some are aggressively youthful. The annual report should convey the image your company has or wants to establish. Static, formal page layout with traditional typography will suggest a conservative, dignified company, for example; and bold graphics, dynamic design, and unusual typography will suggest an aggressive company. Don't mix the two, however; photographs of executives in dark business suits would not be compatible with bold graphics.

Be selective in your choice of photographs and illustrations, choosing only those that will make the maximum contribution to the report's theme. Remember that most readers merely scan an annual report, looking carefully only at photographs and captions. So both photographs and their captions are critical to the success of your annual report. A photograph of a machine can be dull. But put an operator in it, and the caption can tell what he is doing and why it is meaningful.

Study your company's annual reports of the past several years for content, style, and format. Within reason, try to emulate these, since they presumably were successful. Review the writing process outlined in the Checklist of the Writing Process at the beginning of this book, and use all the steps listed there to the best of your ability— your company's annual report could well be the most important writing you will ever be asked to do.

The following information is normally printed on the inside front and back covers of the annual report: (1) notice of the annual meeting, (2) corporate address, (3) names of transfers agents, (4) registrar, (5) stock exchange, and so on. Some annual reports use the inside front cover for the announcement of the annual meeting alone.

Use of Charts and Graphs. **Graphs** and charts enable readers to grasp statistical material quickly and easily—provided the charts and graphs are not so complex that they defeat that purpose. Some companies scatter graphs throughout the annual report at strategic locations near the financial highlights, in the statement to stockholders, throughout the feature articles, and so forth. Others group them in the financial statement.

The subjects that most easily lend themselves to graphs and charts —usually shown in a five-year comparison arrangement—are (1) assets, (2) capital expenditures, (3) dividends, (4) earnings (by product groups or by divisions), (5) industry growth, (6) inventories, (7) liabilities, (8) net worth, (9) prices (trend of), (10) reserves, (11) sales (by product groups or by divisions), (12) source and disposition of funds (taxes, wages, working capital).

ante-/anti-

Ante- means "before" or "in front of."

>   *Examples:* *Ante*room, *ante* meridiem (abbreviated a.m., "before noon"), *ante*diluvian (before the flood)

Anti- means "against" or "opposed to."

Examples: *anti*body, *anti*clerical, *anti*neutrino

Anti- is hyphenated when joined to proper nouns or to words beginning with the letter *i*.

Examples: *anti-*intellectual, *anti-*American

When in doubt, consult a good **dictionary**. (See also **prefix**.)

antonym

An antonym is a word that is nearly the opposite, in meaning, of another word.

Examples: good/bad, well/ill, fresh/stale

Many pairs of words that look as if they were antonyms are not. Be careful not to use these words wrongly.

Examples: famous/infamous, flammable/inflammable, limit/delimit

When in doubt about the pronunciation, correct use, or exact meaning of a word, use your **dictionary**.

apostrophe

The apostrophe (') is used to show possession, to mark the omission of letters, and to indicate the plural of Arabic numbers and letters.

POSSESSION

An apostrophe is used with an "s" to form the possessive **case** of some **nouns**.

Example: A recent scientific analysis of *New York City's* atmosphere concluded that a New Yorker on the street took into his lungs the equivalent in toxic materials of 38 cigarettes a day.

With compound nouns, the last noun takes the possessive form to show joint possession.

Example: Michelson and *Morley's* famous experiment on the velocity of light was made in 1887.

To show individual possession with compound nouns, each noun should take the possessive form.

Example: *Tom's* and *Mary's* desks are at opposite ends of the office.

Singular nouns ending in "s" may form the possessive either by an apostrophe alone or by 's.

> *Examples:* a waitress' uniform, an actress' career
> a waitress's uniform, an actress's career

Use only an apostrophe with plural nouns ending in "s."

> *Examples:* a managers' meeting, the technicians' handbook, a motorists' rest stop

When a noun ends in multiple consecutive "s" sounds, form the possessive by adding only an apostrophe.

> *Examples:* Jesus' disciples, Moses' sojourn

The apostrophe is not used with possessive **pronouns**.

> *Examples:* yours, its, his, ours, whose, theirs

It's is a **contraction** of *it is,* not the possessive form of *it.*

In names of places and institutions, the apostrophe is usually omitted.

> *Examples:* Harpers Ferry, Writers Book Club

OMISSION

An apostrophe is used to mark the omission of letters in a word or date.

> *Examples:* can't, I'm, I'll
> the class of '61

PLURALS

Apostrophes are often used to indicate the plural of numbers.

> *Examples:* 5's, 30's, two 100's

An apostrophe and an "s" may be added to show the plural of a word as a word. (The word itself is italicized.)

> *Example:* There were five *and*'s in his first sentence.

If the term is in all capital letters or ends with a capital letter, however, the apostrophe is not required to form the plural.

> *Examples:* The university awarded seven *Ph.D.s* in engineering last year.
> He had included 43 *ADDs* in his computer program.

appendix/appendices

An appendix is a collection of supplementary material at the end of a **report** or book. The plural form of the word may be either *appendices* or *appendixes*.

Although not a mandatory part of a report, an appendix can be quite useful for (1) explanations that are too long for **footnotes** but could be helpful to the **reader** seeking further assistance or clarification, (2) passages from documents and laws that reinforce or illustrate the text, and (3) long lists of charts and **tables**.

Do not use the appendix as a wastebasket for miscellaneous bits and pieces of information you were unable to work into the text. If you could not fit them into the text, they very likely do not belong in the report.

application, letter of

The letter of application is, essentially, a sales letter. You are trying to sell your services, and you are competing with other applicants. Therefore, your letter of application must do three things: (1) catch the **reader's** attention favorably, (2) create a desire for your services, and (3) ask for an interview. Try to do all these things on a single page, in three to five well-organized paragraphs. Your immediate **objective** is to catch the reader's interest; your ultimate objective is to obtain an interview.

A letter of application requires careful planning. Begin by determining that you are, in fact, qualified for the job. One way to do that is to write a **résumé** (a summary of your education, work experience, personal data, and references) before writing the letter of application. Once you have determined that you are qualified for the job, you are ready to write the letter of application. In your letter, be certain to do each of the following.

1. State that you are applying for a specific job, not just any job, and state where you learned about the opening.
2. Give specific information showing that you are qualified for that specific job. Stress your special qualifications, and refer the reader to your résumé for less important details.
3. Ask for an interview. State when and where you can be reached and when you will be available for an interview.

The importance of the letter of application makes special attention to the following details unusually important.

1. Address the letter to a person rather than to a department, if possible. You can often get the correct name and title by telephoning the local representative of the company to which you are applying.
2. Check your letter and résumé for accuracy of facts, spelling, grammar, and appearance. Neatness is important.
3. Clean the keys on your typewriter if they are smudged, and put in a new ribbon if the old one is faded. If you do not type well, have someone who does type well do the letter for you. Neatness counts!
4. Use paper and envelopes of good quality. The small expense required to purchase these could prove to be an excellent investment.

The following is an example of an effective letter of application.

```
                                        2647 Patterson Road
                                        Beechwood, Ohio 45432

                                        January 23, 1976


        Mr. F. C. Cummins
        Personnel Manager
        Calcutex Industries, Inc.
        3275 Commercial Park Drive
        Bintonville, Michigan 49474

        Dear Mr. Cummins:

        Through the placement office of the University
        of Dayton, I have learned that you have an
        opening for a design engineer in your servo-
        controls section.  The four-year program in
        electrical engineering technology that I will
        complete on August 30, when I will receive
        my degree, has provided me with the basic
        qualifications for the job.

        The extensive use of microprocessors in your
        servo systems interests me greatly.  In
        addition to the courses I have taken on
        microprocessors and system design, I had the
        valuable experience of working with a team of
        three other students in designing and building
        an electro-mechanical robot.  My role in this
        project was to design the microprocessor-based
        servocontrol system; certain peculiarities in
        the drive train and sensor system made it
```

State the specific job for which you are applying. →

Give specific information that shows you are qualified for the job. →

necessary to create original designs for three
of the interfaces. There seems to be a very
strong similarity between the system I designed for our robot and the products of your
servocontrols group. Our project was successful, meeting all the design specifications.

My work on this project has increased my
interest in designing with and for micro-
processors; it has also given me valuable
experience in working on an interdisciplinary
team consisting of two mechanical engineers
and one other electrical engineer.

Details of my education and work experience
are contained in the enclosed résumé. Those
persons listed as references in the resume
will attest to my efficiency and dependability
as a worker. Should you be interested, I will
be happy to send you a copy of the final
report on the robot project.

May I have an appointment for an interview
with you to discuss my qualifications in
greater detail? Any time the week of February
25-29 would be especially convenient for me
since I have no classes that week. Please
telephone me at (513) 555-2952 or write me at
the above address.

Ask for an interview.
→

                                    Sincerely yours,

                                    Craig Adderly

Encl: Résumé

appositives

An appositive is a **noun** or noun **phrase** that follows and amplifies
another noun or noun phrase. It has the same grammatical function
as the noun it complements.

Examples: Dennis Gabor, *a British scientist,* experimented with coherent
light in the 1940s.
The British scientist *Dennis Gabor* experimented with coherent
light in the 1940s.
George Thomas, *head of the Economic and Planning Branch of
PRC,* summarized the president's speech in a confidential
memo to the advertising staff.

For detailed information on the use of commas with appositives, see
restrictive and nonrestrictive phrases.

When in doubt about the **case** of an appositive, you can check it by substituting the appositive for the noun it modifies.

Example: My boss gave the two of us, Jim and *me,* the day off. (You wouldn't say, "My boss gave *I* the day off.")

argumentation

(See **persuasion**.)

article

As a **part of speech**, articles are considered to be **adjectives** because they modify the items they designate by either limiting them or making them more exact. There are two kinds of articles, indefinite and definite.

Indefinite: *a* and *an* (denotes an unspecified item)

Example: *A* program was run on our new computer. (Not a specific program, but an unspecified program. Therefore, the article is indefinite.)

Definite: *the* (denotes a particular item)

Example: *The* program was run on the computer. (Not just any program, but *the* specific program. Therefore, the article is definite.)

The choice between *a* and *an* depnds on the sound rather than the letter following the article. Use *a* before words beginning with a consonant sound (*a* person, *a* happy person, *a* historical event). Use *an* before words beginning with a vowel sound (*an* uncle, *an* hour). With abbreviations, use *a* before initial letters having a consonant sound (*a* TWA flight); use *an* before initial letters having a vowel sound (*an* SLN report).

Do not omit all articles from your writing. This is, unfortunately, an easy habit to develop. To include the articles costs nothing; to eliminate them is a disservice to your **reader** and can make unclear reading.

Change: Remove nuts from bolts and lift plate from body. Remove gasket and clean sealing surface.

To: Remove *the* nuts from *the* bolts and lift *the* plate from *the* body. Remove *the* gasket and clean *the* sealing surface.

Change: There has been decline in domestic output of crude oil.
   To: There has been *a* decline in *the* domestic output of crude oil.

On the other hand, don't overdo it. An article can at times be superfluous.

Examples: There is no more difficult *a* subject than calculus. (Eliminate the article.)
           I'll meet you in *a* half *an* hour. (Choose one and eliminate the other.)
           Fill with *a* half *a* pint of fluid. (Choose one and eliminate the other.)

Do not capitalize articles when they appear in titles except as the first word of the title.

Example: *Time* magazine reviewed *An Analysis of Europe in the Seventies.*

(See also **capital letters**.)

as

Since *as* can mean so many things (*since, because, for, that, at that time, when, while,* etc.) and can be at least four **parts of speech** (**conjunction, preposition, adverb, pronoun**), it is often overused and misused, especially in speech. In writing, *as* is often weak or even ambiguous.

Example: *As* we were together, he revealed his plans.
                 (could mean)
           Because we were together, he revealed his plans.
                   (or)
           While we were together, he revealed his plans.

The word *as* can also contribute to **awkwardness** by appearing too many times in a sentence.

Change: *As* we realized *as* soon *as* we began the project, the problem needed to be solved.
   To: We realized the moment we began the project that the problem needed to be solved.

as . . . as/so . . . as

In positive expressions, *as . . . as* is the correct form (His letter was *as* short *as* mine.). In negative expressions, the choice between *as . . . as* and *so . . . as* is a matter of taste (His letter was not *so* good *as* mine. His letter was not *as* good *as* mine.).

as much as/more than

These two **phrases** are sometimes illogically run together, especially when intervening phrases delay the completion of the phrase.

Change: The engineers had *as much,* if not more, influence in planning the program *than* the accountants.

To: The engineers had *as much* influence in planning the program *as* the accountants, if not more.

Or: The engineers had *as much* influence *as* the accountants, if not more, in planning the program.

as regards/with regard to/in regard to/regarding

With regards to and *in regards to* are incorrect **idioms** for *with regard to* and *in regard to. As regards* and *regarding* are both acceptable variants.

Change: *With regards to* the building contract, several questions are pertinent.

To: *With regard to* the building contract, several questions are pertinent.

Or: *In regard to* the building contract, several questions are pertinent.

Or: *As regards* the building contract, several questions are pertinent.

Or: *Regarding* the building contract, several questions are pertinent.

as such

The **phrase** *as such* is usually unnecessary and should often be omitted.

Change: Throw-away cans, *as such,* contribute to pollution.
To: Throw-away cans contribute to pollution.

Use *as such* only when it helps clarify your meaning. When the phrase makes such a contribution, do not hesitate to use it.

Example: An engineer, *as such,* has no special expertise for solving theological problems. (This says, in effect, that an engineer, *as an engineer,* is not capable of solving theological problems—although as a person, he may be.)

as well as

The **phrase** *as well as* should not be used with *both*.

> *Change:*   *Both* General Motors, *as well as* Ford, are developing electric cars.
> *To:*   *Both* General Motors *and* Ford are developing electric cars.
> *Or:*   General Motors, *as well as* Ford, is developing an electric car.

Notice that, in addition to being redundant, using *both* and *as well as* together causes some confusion over whether the **verb** is singular or plural.

as to whether

The **phrase** *as to whether (as to when* or *as to where)* is clumsy and redundant. Either omit it altogether or use only *whether*.

> *Change:*   *As to whether* we will commit our firm to a long-term contract, we have decided to do so.
> *To:*   We have decided to commit our firm to a long-term contract.

Be wary of all phrases starting with *as to;* they are often redundant, vague, or indirect.

> *Change:*   *As to* his policy, I am in full agreement.
> *To:*   I am in full agreement with his policy.

at about/at around

These are redundant **phrases**. Use only one of the **prepositions**, not both.

> *Change:*   He arrived at the office *at around* nine o'clock.
> *To:*   He arrived at the office *at* nine o'clock.
> *Or:*   He arrived at the office *around* nine o'clock.

attribute/contribute

Attribute (with the accent on the "i") is a **verb** that means "to point to a cause or source."

> *Example:*   He *attributes* the plant's improved safety record to the new training program.

Attribute (with the "a" accented) is a **noun** meaning a "quality belonging to someone."

> *Example:*   His mathematical skill is his most valuable *attribute*.

Contribute means "to give."

> *Example:* His mathematical skills will *contribute* much to the project.

augment/supplement

Augment means to increase or magnify in size, degree, or effect.

> *Example:* Many of our employees *augment* their income by working over-time.

Supplement means to add something to make up for a deficiency.

> *Example:* The physician suggested that he *supplement* his diet with vitamins.

average/mean/median

Average, or arithmetical *mean,* is determined by dividing a sum of two or more quantities by the number of quantities. For example, if one report is ten pages, another is thirty pages, and a third is twenty pages, their *average* (or *mean*) length is twenty pages. It is incorrect, therefore, to say that *"each* averages twenty pages" because *each* report is a specific length.

> *Change:* Each report *averages* twenty pages.
> *To:* The three reports *average* twenty pages.

A *median* is the middle number in a sequence of numbers.

> *Example:* The *median* of the series 1, 3, 4, 7, 8 is 4.

awhile/a while

Awhile is an **adverb** meaning "for a short time." It is not preceded by *for* because the meaning of *for* is inherent in the meaning of *awhile*. *A while* is a **noun** phrase that means "a period of time."

> *Change:* Wait for *awhile* before investing more heavily.
> *To:* Wait for *a while* before investing more heavily.
> *Or:* Wait *awhile* before investing more heavily.

awkwardness

Any construction that strikes the **reader** as being unnatural is awkward. Awkwardness can sometimes be corrected by altering **sentence** structure. The more complex the idea, the more important it is to state it as simply as possible. For this reason, it is often better to use simple sentence structure to express complex ideas. The reader then absorbs the ideas at a more comfortable **pace**.

Change: The agreement, reached on January 19, 1976, between the Acme Research and Development Corporation and the Natural Resources Corporation, was for the purpose of establishing arrangements for the exchange of technical information, preliminary and final experimental data, analytical methods and results, evaluations, and other information pertinent to their respective research and development programs with special emphasis on data related to nuclear reactor and fuel cycle safety, reactor safeguards, and environmental impact.

To: The agreement was reached on January 19, 1976, for the exchange of technical information between the Acme Research and Development Corporation and the Natural Resources Corporation. The information to be exchanged will include preliminary and final experimental data, analytical methods and results, and other information pertinent to their respective research and development programs. Special emphasis will be given to data related to nuclear reactor and fuel cycle safety, reactor safety, and environmental impact.

On the other hand, a series of simple thoughts is often better stated in a complex sentence than in a string of choppy simple sentences. (See also **sentence variety**.)

Change: A computer is a calculating device. It was once referred to as a "mechanical brain." The computer has revolutionized industry.

To: The computer, once known as a "mechanical brain," is a calculating device that has revolutionized industry.

Sentence fragments cause awkwardness. Check the subject-verb-object pattern of a sentence suspected of being a fragment to determine whether the **subject** or the **verb** is missing. If either is missing, the "sentence" is really only a fragment.

Change: I saw him. Leaving the branch office with our regional sales representative.

To: I saw him leaving the branch office with our regional sales representative.

Lengthy **phrases** or **clauses** inserted between a subject and its verb can cause awkwardness.

Change: The use of insecticides, although they offer unquestionable benefits, often results in unfortunate side effects.

> *To:* Although insecticides offer unquestionable benefits, their use often results in unfortunate side effects.

Subordination is normally one of the writer's most effective tools for making sentences flow naturally; however, if it is overdone, even subordination can cause awkwardness. Using too many modifying clauses in a sentence often violates the principles of **unity** and **emphasis**. When too many ideas—even subordinate ideas—are included in one sentence, the major thought is obscured. The most effective way to solve the problem is to break the series of thoughts into two or more sentences.

> *Change:* When I was in Pittsburgh, I interviewed Bill Foss, who at that time was working for the Connors brothers, who were expanding their operations but who failed to give Bill a pay raise, let alone an anticipated promotion.
>
> *To:* When I was in Pittsburgh, I interviewed Bill Foss, who at that time was working for the Connors brothers. Although they were expanding their operations, they failed to give Bill either a pay raise or an anticipated promotion.

To avoid causing confusion or **ambiguity** in your **sentence construction**, place **modifiers** as close as possible to the words they modify.

> *Change:* The four new—slope reduction, box cutting, valley filling, and area mining of mountain tops—mining methods are more than theories conceived in a laboratory.
>
> *To:* The four new mining methods—slope reduction, box cutting, valley filling, and area mining of mountain tops—are more than theories conceived in a laboratory.

Placing a string of compound modifiers in front of a noun causes awkwardness.

> *Change:* The physically-handicapped-children fund raising meeting is scheduled for Friday.
>
> *To:* The meeting to plan the fund raising for physically handicapped children is scheduled for Friday.

The use of too many **expletives** can also be a cause of awkwardness.

> *Change:* *It is* essential that the technician understand that *it is* the lever rather than the switch that controls upward movement. *There is* danger of causing damage to the equipment if one attempts to use the switch.
>
> *To:* The technician must understand that the lever, not the switch, controls upward movement and that attempting to use the switch may damage the equipment.

Dangling modifiers are a common cause of awkwardness. Because dangling modifiers are sometimes humorous, the writer may make himself the butt of his own unintentional joke.

> *Change:* While eating lunch in the cafeteria, the computer malfunctioned. (The problem, of course, is that the sentence neglects to mention *the operator,* who just happens to be the one eating lunch in the cafeteria.)
>
> *To:* While the operator was eating lunch in the cafeteria, the computer malfunctioned.

(See also **misplaced modifiers**.)

Another common cause of awkwardness is overuse of the passive **voice**, or use of the passive voice when the active voice would make the meaning of the sentence clearer or more direct.

> *Change:* The pocket calculator costs so little that it *can be afforded* by anyone who wants it.
>
> *To:* The pocket calculator costs so little that anyone who wants it *can afford* it.

Lack of logic can cause not only awkwardness but incomprehensibility, as in the following statement from an air conditioner warranty.

> *Change:* The warranty is not valid for defects that result from accidents, abuse, or unauthorized repairs *unless such defects are not a result of this.* (The ending clause is meaningless.)
>
> *To:* The warranty is not valid for defects that result from accidents, abuse, or unauthorized repairs.

Purposeless repetition makes a sentence awkward and hides its key ideas.

> *Change:* He *said that* the invoice *said that* the shipment arrived on the 24th.
>
> *To:* He *said that* according to the invoice the shipment arrived on the 24th.

The harm caused to your writing by careless repetition is not limited to words and phrases; the needless repetition of an idea can be equally damaging.

> *Change:* In this modern world of ours today, the well-informed knowledgeable executive will be well ahead of the competition.
>
> *To:* To succeed, the contemporary executive must be well informed.

B

back of/in back of

The **phrases** *back of* and *in back of* are colloquial for "behind."

Change: The operator stands *back of* the panel.
To: The operator stands *behind* the panel.

bad/badly

Bad is the **adjective** form that follows such **linking verbs** as *feel* and *look*.

Examples: You will feel *bad* for three days with the flu.
We don't want our department to look *bad* at the meeting.

Badly is an **adverb**.

Example: The test model performed *badly* during the trial run.

To say "I feel badly" would mean, literally, that your sense of touch was impaired.

balance

When parallel constructions are similar in thought and equal in length and construction, they balance one another. Balance is particularly useful for comparing and contrasting ideas.

Example: A qualified staff without a sufficient budget is helpless; a sufficient budget without a qualified staff is useless.

(See also **parallel structure**.)

balance/remainder

One meaning of *balance* is "a state of equilibrium"; another meaning is "the amount remaining in a bank account after balancing deposits and withdrawals." *Remainder,* in all applications, is "what is left over." *Remainder* is the more accurate word, therefore, to mean "that which is left over."

Examples: The personnel department must attempt to maintain a *balance* between looking after the company's best interests and being sensitive to the needs of individuals.

The *balance* in the corporate account after the payroll has been met is a matter for concern.

Round the fraction off to its nearest whole number and drop the *remainder.*

When using these words figuratively (outside of banking and mathematical contexts), use *remainder* to mean "what is left over."

Change: Four of the cars in the auto show were from General Motors, and the *balance* were from Ford and Chrysler.

To: Four of the cars in the auto show were from General Motors, and the *remainder* were from Ford and Chrysler.

be sure and/be sure to

The **phrase** *be sure and* is colloquial and unidiomatic when used for *be sure to.*

Change: When you get to the branch office, *be sure and* phone me.

To: When you get to the branch office, *be sure to* phone me.

because

To express cause, *because* is the strongest and most specific **connective** (others are *for, since, as, inasmuch as, insofar as*). *Because* is unequivocal in stating causal relationship.

Example: We didn't complete the project *because* the raw materials became too costly. (The use of *because* emphasizes the cause/effect relationship.)

For can express causal relationships, but it is weaker than *because,* and it allows the **clause** that follows to be a separate independent clause.

Example: We didn't complete the project, *for* raw materials became too costly. (The use of *for* expresses but does not emphasize the cause/effect relationship.)

As a connective to express cause, *since* is also a weak substitute for *because.*

Example: *Since* the computer is malfunctioning, paychecks will be delayed.

However, *since* is an appropriate connective when the emphasis is on circumstances or conditions rather than on cause and effect.

> *Example:* *Since* I was in town anyway, I stopped at the branch office.

As is the least definite connective to indicate cause; its use for this purpose is better avoided.

> *Change:* I left the office early, *as* I had finished my work.
> *To:* I left the office early *because* I had finished my work.
> *Or:* *Since* I had finished my work, I left the office early.

Inasmuch as implies concession; that is, it suggests that a statement is true "in view of the circumstances."

> *Example:* You may as well complete the project, *inasmuch as* you have already begun it.

being as/being that

These **phrases** are nonstandard in writing. Use *because* or *since*.

beside/besides

Besides, meaning "in addition to" or "other than," should be carefully distinguished from *beside,* meaning "next to" or "apart from."

> *Example:* *Besides* the two of us from the Marketing Department, three people from Production were standing *beside* the president when he presented the award.

between/among

Between is normally used to relate two items or persons.

> *Examples:* The roll pin is located *between* the grommet and the knob.
> Preferred stock offers a buyer a middle ground *between* bonds and common stock.

Among is used to relate more than two.

> *Example:* The subcontracting was distributed *among* the three companies.

between you and me

People sometimes use the incorrect expression *between you and I.* Because the **pronouns** are objects of the **preposition** *between,* the objective form of the **personal pronoun** *(me)* must be used.

Change: *Between you and I,* John should be taken off the job.
   To: *Between you and me,* John should be taken off the job.

(See also **case.**)

bi/semi

When used with periods of time, *bi* means "two" or "every two." Bimonthly means "once in two months"; biweekly means "once in two weeks."

When used with periods of time, *semi* means "half of" or "occurring twice within a period of time." Semimonthly means "twice a month"; semiweekly means "twice a week."

Both *bi* and *semi* are normally joined with the following element without space or hyphen.

biannual/biennial

By conventional usage, *biannual* means "twice during the year," and *biennial* means "every other year." (See also **bi/semi.**)

bibliography

A bibliography is a list of books or articles, usually on one subject, and usually arranged alphabetically at the end of a **report** or research paper. The purpose of a bibliography is to present the sources of your information in a convenient, standardized form helpful to someone seeking additional information about your subject.

A bibliography may consist of all the material used for a research paper (a full bibliography), or it may list only the material directly referred to in the text (a selected bibliography). An annotated bibliography includes a brief description of some or all works listed.

When typing a bibliography, single-space within an entry and double-space between entries. Indent the second line of an entry three spaces so that the author's name stands out.

The details of bibliographic systems vary from one field of study to another, but all bibliographic entries, no matter how complicated the work cited, should contain (1) the author's name, (2) the full title of the work cited, and (3) the publication facts.

AUTHOR'S NAME

Give the author's last name first, then his first name. Where there is more than one author, give the last name first of the first author *(Doe, John Q.)* because of the alphabetic arrangement of bibliographies, and then list the other names in normal order *(Fred R. Roe)*. Separate the names from each other by commas, and separate the authors' names from the work's title with a period.

Alphabetize all works by the same author according to their titles. When listing multiple works by the same author, replace the author's name in all entries except the first with a line followed by a period.

> *Example:* Sperry, R. W. "The Eye and the Brain." *Scientific American* (August 1958): 48–52.
>
> ———. "The Growth of Nerve Circuits." *Scientific American* (November 1959): 68–75.

When a work lists no author, alphabetize it according to the first major word in the title.

TITLE OF WORK

Capitalize the key words in the title, italicize (underline) the complete title, and conclude the title with a period.

PUBLICATION FACTS

Include all pertinent facts about the publication of the work in the publication facts.

BOOK

For a book, the pertinent facts to be included in a bibliographic entry are as follows: (1) name of the author (or authors), editor, or institution responsible for the work cited, followed by a period; (2) title of the work, followed by a period; (3) title of the series, if applicable, followed by a comma; (4) volume number, if applicable, followed by a period; (5) edition, if it is not the first edition, followed by a period; (6) number of volumes, followed by a period; (7) city where the book was published, followed by a colon; (8) publisher's name, followed by a comma; and (9) year of publication, followed by a period to end the entry.

JOURNAL ARTICLE

For a journal article, the pertinent facts to be included in a bibliographic entry are as follows: (1) name of the author (or authors), followed by a period; (2) title of the article, in quotation marks, followed by a period; (3) name of the periodical in which the article was published (no punctuation follows); (4) volume number of the periodical and date of its publication (the date in parentheses), followed by a colon; and (5) page numbers of the article within the periodical, followed by a period.

EXAMPLES OF BIBLIOGRAPHIC ENTRIES

The following examples are typical for general works.

Book, One Author:

Bernstein, Theodore M. *Watch Your Language.* Manhasset, N.Y.: Channel Press, 1958.

Book, Two or More Authors:

Hammond, J. D., and Arthur L. Williams. *Essentials of Life Insurance.* New York: Scott, Foresman and Company, 1968.

Meadows, Donella H., Dennis L. Meadows, Jorgen Randers, and William W. Behrens III. *The Limits of Growth: A Report for the Club of Rome's Project on the Predicament of Mankind.* New York: Universe Books, 1972.

Book Edition, If Not the First Edition:

Woodson, Wesley E., and Donald Conover. *Human Engineering Guide for Equipment Designers.* 2nd ed. Berkeley, Calif.: University of California Press, 1964.

Multivolume Book:

Bartholemew, John, ed. *Times Atlas of the World.* Midcentury Edition. 5 vols. London: Times Publishing Co., Ltd., 1955–1959.

Give the full number of volumes in the set either following the book title or the book's edition.

Book in a Series:

Cooper, E. L., ed. *Invertebrate Immunology.* Contemporary Topics in Immunology, vol. 4. New York: Plenum Publishing Corporation, 1974.

Give the series title and the volume number following the title of the book.

Editor of a Collection:

Estrin, Herman A., ed. *Technical and Professional Writing.* New York: Harcourt, Brace and World, Inc., 1963.

Corporate Author:

Commission on Vocational Education. *Job Selection in the 1980's.* Washington, D.C.: American Vocational Institute, 1973.

Journal Article:

Haughness, Norman. "Clarity—The Technical Writer's Tightrope." *STC Journal* 18 (November 1971): 13–14.

Symposium or Conference Paper:

Eisenbud, Merril. "Standards of Radiation Protection and Their Implications for the Public's Health." In *Nuclear Power and the Public,* ed. Harry Foreman, M.D. Garden City, N.Y.: Doubleday & Company, Inc., 1972.

Magazine Article:

"Going Private." *Newsweek,* June 3, 1975, p. 56.

Encyclopedia Article:

"Electricity." *Encyclopaedia Britannica.* 14th ed.

If the article is signed, begin the entry with the author's last name.

Report:

Evans, Parker. *The Erosion of Buried Cables.* Dayton, Ohio: Ohio Bell Telephone Company, 1970.

Pamphlet or Booklet:

U.S. Bureau of the Census. *We, the First Americans.* Washington, D.C.: Government Printing Office, 1973.

Thesis or Dissertation:

Lander, John D. "Computer Surveillance of Medicaid Provider Claims in Tennessee," Master's thesis, Vanderbilt University, 1973.

Personal Correspondence:

Brady, Robert T. July 7, 1975. Personal Correspondence.

Interview:

Denlinger, Virgil, Assistant Chief of Police. Milwaukee, Wisconsin: March 27, 1975. Interview.

SCIENTIFIC BIBLIOGRAPHIES

In scientific works, where journal and periodical references are common, do not put the title in quotation marks, capitalize only the first word and proper names in the title, abbreviate the name of the periodical and omit any prepositions it may contain, italicize the volume number, and include the article's full number of pages. The following example is typical.

Dalldorf, G. The sparing effect of Coxsackie virus infection on experimental poliomyelitis. Jour. Exper. Med., 1951, *94:* 65–71.

Bibliography entries in scientific writing may be listed either alphabetically or in the order they are referred to in the text. In the second method, the entries are arranged in numerical sequence (1, 2, 3, etc.), according to the order in which they first appear in the text. Thus, in the text, the number 1 in parentheses after a quotation or reference to a book or article (1) refers the reader to the reference information in the first bibliographic entry. Number 5 in parentheses (5) refers the reader to the fifth entry in the bibliography, and so on. (See **footnotes** for full details of this method.)

blend words

A blend word is formed by combining part of one word with part of another.

> *Examples:*   motor + hotel = motel
> breakfast + lunch = brunch
> smoke + fog = smog
> electric + execute = electrocute

Although blend words (sometimes called "portmanteau words") may occasionally be created by a specialist to meet a specific need—such as *stagflation* (a stagnant economy coupled with inflation)—resist creating blend words in your writing unless an obvious need arises. If you must create a blend word, be sure to define it clearly for your **reader**. Otherwise, creating blend words is at best merely "cute" and could be confusing. (See also **new words**.)

both . . . and

Statements using the *both . . . and* construction should always be balanced both grammatically and logically.

Example: A successful photograph must be *both* clearly focused *and* adequately lighted.

Notice that *both* and *and* are followed logically by ideas of equal weight and grammatically by identical constructions.

Change: For success in engineering, it is necessary both *to develop* writing skills and *master* calculus.

To: For success in engineering, it is necessary both *to develop* writing skills and *to master* calculus.

Be careful to avoid the common error of substituting *as well as* for *and* in this construction.

Change: For success in engineering, it is necessary *both* to develop writing skills *as well as* to master calculus.

To: For success in engineering, it is necessary *both* to develop writing skills *and* to master calculus.

(See also **parallel structure**, **balance**, and **correlative conjunction**.)

brackets

The primary use of brackets is to enclose a word or words inserted by an editor or writer into a quotation from another source.

Example: He stated, "Wheat prices will continue to rise [no doubt because of the Russian wheat purchase] until next year."

Brackets are also used to set off a parenthetical item within **parentheses**.

Example: We should be sure to give Emanuel Foose (and his brother Emilio [1812–1882] as well) credit for his role in founding the institute.

Brackets are also used in academic writing to insert the Latin word *sic*, which indicates that the writer has quoted material exactly as it appears in the original, even though it contains an obvious error.

Example: Dr. Smith pointed out that "the earth does not revolve around the son [sic] at a constant rate."

brief

A brief is a condensed statement of a long document or series of documents. In law, a brief is a statement (which an attorney files before arguing a case in court) containing the points of law and facts relevant to a specific case. In short, a brief is a summary, much like an **abstract**.

bunch

Bunch refers to like things that grow or are fastened together. Do not use the word *bunch* to refer to people.

> *Change:* A *bunch* of trainees toured the site.
> *To:* A *group* of trainees toured the site.

business writing style

At one time, business writing style was as formal as the starched collars every businessman wore. The following example was typical.

> *Example:* My Dear Sir:
> Yours of the 12th received and in reply beg to state that herewith are forwarded the reports under consideration. Please be advised of general concurrence in desire to expedite matters. . . .

Although **style** is always difficult to define, this style was clearly extremely formal and impersonal. Business writing today (especially business **correspondence**) is generally much more personal and conversational, as the following revision of the previous example illustrates.

> *Example:* Dear Mr. Watson:
> I received your letter of the 12th, and I am enclosing the reports for your company to study. Certainly, we agree with you that time is important to the project. . . .

Even though business writing style is less formal today than in the past, it must adhere to the conventions of **standard English** by using conventional spelling and standard grammatical forms.

Business writing may legitimately vary all the way from the chatty style of a letter to a close business associate to the very formal style found in contracts. In **memorandums** and letters, however, a position between the two extremes is generally appropriate. Writing that is too formal can be irritating to the **reader**, and an obvious attempt to be casual and informal may strike the reader as insincere. In business writing, as in all writing, knowing your reader is critical.

Change: Dear Jane,
  I'm crazy about your proposal! . . .
  To: Dear Jane:
  I received your proposal today, and I think it is excel-
  lent. . . .

Your **point of view** (the way you address your readers and the attitude you display toward them) is important in letters and memos. For example, do not use *the writer* or *one* to refer to yourself; it is perfectly natural and appropriate to refer to yourself as *I* and to the reader as *you.* In a report, however, you may not be writing to a single reader and should not normally refer to collective readers as *you.* Be careful also when you use the **pronoun** *we* in a business letter that is written on company stationery, since it commits your company to what you have written. When a statement is your opinion, use *I;* when it is company policy, use *we.* Leave no doubt about whom you are speaking for.

The best writers strive to write in a style that is so clear that their message cannot be misunderstood. **Clarity** should be the ultimate goal of your business writing style. A clear style is achieved primarily through proper and conscientious use of the different steps of the writing process—**preparation**, **research**, **organization**, **writing the draft**, and **revision**. (See also the Checklist of the Writing Process.)

One way to achieve a clear style, especially during revision, is to eliminate overuse of the passive **voice**, which is prevalent in most poor business writing. The passive voice not only saps the life of your writing, it can sometimes be ambiguous or uninformative.

Change: Use the following material as required. (Who requires it? Company policy? Or the task itself?)
  To: Company policy requires that you use this material.
  Or: Use this material as you need it.

You can also achieve clarity with **conciseness**. Proceed cautiously here, however, because business writing should not be telegraphic, with an endless series of short, choppy **sentences**.

Finally, clarity is achieved through the wise use of **punctuation**. The businessman who says "I don't worry about every **comma**, I get my message across" does not realize that a misplaced comma (or other mark of punctuation) can often cause misunderstanding and confusion.

In the following example, notice that the tone is dignified, yet neither too formal nor too informal. Extensive use of the active voice keeps the **pace** of the letter moving well. Use of personal pronouns and a positive point of view keeps the writing interesting.

March 6, 1976

Ms. Harriet L. Bussman, President
Bussman Engineering, Inc.
2731 Janus Street
Plaines City, Iowa 50705

Dear Ms. Bussman:

Thank you very much for allowing us to present to you
our recommendation for a PLR Air Conditioning System.
We would like also to express our appreciation to
Mr. Lindsay and Mrs. Smoot for their time and the
courtesy they extended to us as we collected the data
necessary for this proposal.

After thoroughly analyzing your company's requirements,
and discussing in detail the intricacies of your
engineering requirements, it is our mutual agreement
that this proposed PLR system will provide the maximum
return on your investment dollar. In addition, you
are assured against obsolescence in the near future--if
your business continues to experience the normal growth
you have experienced the last few years--because the
equipment PLR proposes to install is a modular design
to which additional units may be added as the need
arises. The system we have designed for you provides
flexibility, allowing for any special conditions and
policies that your company may wish to incorporate in
the near future.

We feel that you will find this system practical,
efficient, and economical for the needs of your company
both now and in the near future. It is our sincere
hope that the information in the enclosed proposal will
make your decision to install a PLR Air Conditioning
System much easier.

Sincerely yours,

James P. Callahan

James P. Callahan
Sales Manager

(See also **formal writing style**, **informal writing style**, and **English, varieties of**.)

C

can/may

In writing, a distinction should be made between *can* and *may*. *Can* refers to capability, and *may* refers to possibility or permission.

> *Examples:*   I *can* have the project finished by the first of the year. (capability)
> I *may* be in Boston on Thursday. (possibility)
> I *can* be in Boston on Thursday. (capability)
> *May* I have an extra week to finish the project? (permission)

cancel out

In the **phrase** *cancel out,* the word *out* is redundant.

> *Change:*   We should *cancel out* the order.
> *To:*   We should *cancel* the order.

cannot/can not

Cannot is one word.

> *Change:*   We *can not* meet the deadline that your contract would impose upon us.
> *To:*   We *cannot* meet the deadline that your contract would impose upon us.

cannot help but

Avoid the **phrase** *cannot help but* in writing. (See also **double negative**.)

> *Change:*   We *cannot help but* cut our staff.
> *To:*   We cannot avoid cutting our staff.

canvas/canvass

Canvas is a **noun** meaning "heavy, coarse, closely woven cotton or hemp fabric." *Canvass* is a **verb** for the act of soliciting votes or opinions.

> *Examples:*   The maintenance crew spread the *canvas* over the equipment.
> The election committee decided to *canvass* the neighborhood.

capital/capitol

Capital may refer either to wealth or to the city that hosts the government of a state or a nation. *Capitol* refers to the building in which the state or national legislature meets. *Capitol* is often written with a small "c" when it refers to a state building, but it is always capitalized when it refers to the home of the United States Congress in Washington, D.C.

capital letters

The use of capital letters (or upper-case letters) is determined by custom and tradition. Capital letters are used to call attention to certain words, such as **proper nouns** and the first word of a **sentence**. Care must be exercised in using capital letters because they can affect the meaning of words (march/March, china/China, turkey/Turkey). For the same reason, however, capital letters can help eliminate **ambiguity**.

FIRST WORDS

The first letter of the first word in a sentence is always capitalized.

>   *Example:*   Of all the plans you mentioned, the first one seems most appropriate.

The first word after a **colon** may be capitalized if (1) the statement following is a complete sentence, (2) the thought is not closely related to the preceding **clause**, or (3) it introduces a formal resolution or question.

>   *Example:*   Today's meeting will deal with only one issue: What is the firm's role in environmental protection?

If a subordinate element follows the colon, however, or if the thought is closely related, use a lower-case letter following the colon.

>   *Example:*   We had to keep working for one reason: our deadline was upon us.

The first word of a complete sentence inside **quotation marks** is capitalized.

>   *Example:*   He said, "When I arrive, we will begin."

Complete sentences contained as numbered items within a sentence may also be capitalized.

Example: He recommended two ways to increase sales: (1) Next year we should spend more on television advertising, and (2) Our quality control should be improved immediately.

The first word in the salutation and complimentary close of a letter is capitalized. (See also **correspondence**.)

Examples: Dear Mr. Smith:
Sincerely yours,
Best regards,

SPECIFIC PEOPLE AND GROUPS

Capitalize all personal names.

Examples: Walter Bunch, Mary Stewart, Bill Krebs

Capitalize ethnic groups and nationalities.

Examples: American Indian, Italian, Jew, Chicano
Thus *Italian* immigrants contributed much to the industrialization of the United States.

Do not capitalize names of social and economic groups.

Example: The speaker attacked the *bourgeoisie* and the *nouveaux riches* but supported the *lower class* and the *intelligentsia*.

SPECIFIC PLACES

Capitalize the names of all political divisions.

Examples: Chicago, Cook County, Illinois, United States, Ontario, Iran, Ward Six

Capitalize the names of geographical divisions.

Examples: Europe, Asia, Africa, North America, the Middle East, the Orient

Do not capitalize geographical features unless they are part of a proper name.

Example: The *mountains* in this area are not comparable to the Smoky *Mountains*.

The words *north, east, south,* and *west* are capitalized when they refer to sections of the country. They are not capitalized when they refer to directions.

Examples: I may travel *south* this winter.
The *South* may decide next year's election.

The street we live on runs *east* and *west*.
Such a move might cause a nuclear confrontation between the *East* and *West*.

Capitalize the names of stars, constellations, and planets.

Examples: Saturn, Andromeda, Earth

Earth, sun, and *moon* are not capitalized, however, except in formal astronomical writing.

Example: Although the *sun* rises in the east and sets in the west, the *moon* may appear in any part of the night sky when darkness settles over the *earth*.

SPECIFIC INSTITUTIONS, EVENTS, AND CONCEPTS

Capitalize the names of institutions, organizations, and associations.

Example: The *American Society of Mechanical Engineers* and the *Office of Housing and Urban Development* are cooperating in the project.

An organization usually capitalizes its internal divisions and departments.

Examples: Faculty, Board of Directors, Engineering Department

Types of organizations are not capitalized unless they are part of an official name.

Examples: Our group decided to form a *writers' association;* we called it the *American Association of Writers*.
I attended *Patterson High School*. What *high school* did you attend?

Capitalize historical events.

Example: Dr. Jellison discussed the *Boston Tea Party* at the last class.

Capitalize words that designate specific periods of time.

Examples: Labor Day, the Renaissance, the Enlightenment, January, Monday, the Great Depression, Lent

Do not, however, capitalize seasons of the year.

Examples: fall, autumn, winter, summer

Capitalize scientific names of classes, families, and orders, but do not capitalize species or English derivatives of scientific names.

Examples: Mammalia, Carnivora
mammal, carnivorous

TITLES OF BOOKS, ARTICLES, PLAYS, AND FILMS

Capitalize the first and last words of a title of a book, article, play, or film, as well as all major words in the title. Do not capitalize articles *(a, an, the)*, conjunctions *(and, but, if)*, or short prepositions *(at, in, on, of)*. Capitalize prepositions that contain more than four letters *(between, because, until, after)*.

PERSONAL TITLES

Titles preceding proper names are capitalized.

> *Examples:* Miss March, Professor Galbraith, Senator Church

Appositives following proper names are not normally capitalized. (The word *President* is usually capitalized when it refers to the chief executive of a national government.)

> *Example:* Frank Church, *senator* from Idaho (but *Senator* Church)

The only exception is an **epithet**, which actually renames the person.

> *Examples:* Alexander the *Great,* Solomon the *Wise*.

Use capital letters to designate family relationships only when they occur before a name or substitute for a name.

> *Examples:* One of my favorite people is *Uncle Fred*.
> Jim and *Mother* went along.
> Jim and my *mother* went along.

ABBREVIATIONS

Capitalize **abbreviations** if the words they stand for would be capitalized.

> *Examples:* OSU (Ohio State University), p. (page), Ph.D. (Doctor of Philosophy)

LETTERS

Certain single letters are always capitalized. Capitalize the **pronoun** *I* and the **interjection** *O* (but do not capitalize *oh* unless it is the first word in a sentence).

> *Examples:* When *I* say writing, *O* believe me, *I* mean rewriting.
> When *I* say writing, *oh* believe me, *I* mean rewriting.

Capitalize letters that serve as names or indicate shapes.

> *Examples:* X-ray, vitamin *B*, *T*-square, *U*-turn, *I*-beam

MISCELLANEOUS CAPITALIZATIONS

The word *Bible* is capitalized when it refers to the Christian Scriptures; otherwise, it is not capitalized.

> *Example:* He quoted a verse from the *Bible,* then read from Blackstone, the lawyer's *bible.*

All references to the Deity are capitalized.

> *Example:* *God* is the *One* who sustains us.

A complete sentence enclosed in **dashes, brackets,** or **parentheses** is not capitalized when it appears as part of another sentence.

> *Examples:* Extra effort in sales (last year's sales were down 10%) should be made next year.
> Extra effort in sales should be made next year. (Last year's sales were down 10%.)

Certain units, such as parts and chapters of books, rooms in buildings, etc., when specifically identified by number, are normally capitalized. (See also **abbreviations**.)

> *Examples:* Chapter 5, Ch. 5, Room 72, Rm. 72

Minor divisions within such units are not capitalized unless they begin a sentence.

> *Examples:* page 11, verse 14, seat 12

When in doubt about whether or not to capitalize, check a **dictionary**.

case (grammatical)

Grammatically, *case* indicates the functional relationship of a **noun** or a **pronoun** to the other words in a **sentence.** Nouns change form only in the possessive case; pronouns may show change for the subjective, the objective, or the possessive case. The case of a noun or pronoun is always determined by its function in its **phrase, clause,** or sentence. If it is the subject of its phrase, clause, or sentence, it is in the subjective case; if it is an object within its phrase, clause, or sentence, it is in the objective case; if it reflects possession or ownership and modifies a noun, it is in the possessive case. The subjective case indicates the person or thing acting (*He* sued the vendor.); the objective case indicates the thing acted upon (The vendor sued *him*.);

and the possessive case indicates the person or thing owning or possessing something (It was *his* company.).

The different forms of a noun or pronoun indicate whether it is functioning as a subject (subjective case), as a **complement** (usually objective case), or as a **modifier** (possessive case).

Subjective	Objective	Possessive (Modifier)
I	me	my, mine
we	us	our, ours
he	him	his, his
she	her	her, hers
they	them	their, theirs
you	you	your, yours
who	whom	whose

SUBJECTIVE CASE

A pronoun is in the subjective case (also called nominative case) when it represents the person or thing acting.

Example: *I* wrote a letter to that company before I graduated.

A **linking verb** links a pronoun to its subject to show that they identify the same thing. Because they represent the same thing, the pronoun is in the subjective case even though it follows the **verb,** which makes it a **subjective complement**.

Examples: *He* is the president of the company. (subject)
The president of the company is *he*. (subjective complement)

Whether a pronoun is a subject or a subjective complement, it is in the subjective case. This situation causes much confusion with one sentence in particular—*It is I* versus *It is me.* The sentence consists of a subject (*it*), a linking verb (*is*), and a personal pronoun (*I* or *me*). Although "It is me" appears to fit the normal subject-verb-object pattern of English sentences, it really does not. The pronoun actually stands for the subject and is therefore a subjective complement—hence "It is I" is the grammatically correct way to express the thought. However, we are so accustomed to the subject-verb-object pattern in English sentences that we instinctively expect the objective form of the pronoun (*me*). For this reason, "It is me" is more natural-sounding in speech and is therefore also appropriate to the type of writing in which the expression is likely to appear. (See **comple-ment**.)

The subjective case is used after the words *than* and *as* because of the understood (although unstated) portion of the clauses in which these words appear.

Examples: George is as good a designer as *I* [am].
Our subsidiary can do the job better than *we* [can].

OBJECTIVE CASE

A pronoun is in the objective case when it indicates the person or thing receiving the action expressed by the verb. (Objective case is also called accusative case.)

Example: They wrote *me* a letter stating that they had received my ré-sumé.

A pronoun is in the objective case when it is the object of a verb, **gerund,** or **preposition,** and when it is the subject of an **infinitive.** Pronouns that follow prepositions must be in the objective case.

Examples: Between you and *me*, his facts are questionable.
Many of *us* attended the conference.

Pronouns that follow action verbs (which excludes all forms of the verb *be*) must be in the objective case.

Example: The company gave *me* the responsibility for the job.

Pronouns that follow gerunds must be in the objective case.

Example: Phoning *him* was the best thing I could have done.

Subjects of infinitives must be in the objective case.

Example: We asked *them* to return the deposit.

In determining the case of an object, English does not differen-tiate between **direct objects** and **indirect objects;** both require the objective form of the pronoun. (See also **complement**.)

POSSESSIVE CASE

A noun or a pronoun is in the possessive case when it represents a person or thing owning or possessing something.

Example: John's intelligence was evident in *his* work.

Nouns. Although exceptions are relatively common, it is a good rule of thumb to use the *'s* form of the possessive case with nouns referring to persons and living things, and to use an *of* phrase for the possessive case of nouns referring to inanimate objects.

Examples: The *chairman's* address was well received.
The leaves *of the tree* look healthy.

If this rule leads to **awkwardness** or **wordiness**, however, be flexible.

Examples: The *company's* branches are doing well.
The *plane's* automatic pilot failed.

Established **idiom** calls for the possessive case in many stock phrases.

Example: A day's journey, a day's work, a moment's notice, at his wit's end, the law's delay

In a few cases, idiom even calls for a double possessive employing both the *of* and *'s* forms.

Example: That friend *of* George's was at the meeting yesterday.

Plural words ending in "s" need only add an **apostrophe** to form the possessive case.

Example: the *laborers'* union

When several words compose a single term, add the *'s* to the last word only.

Examples: The Chairman of the Board's statement was brief.
The fact that his *father-in-law's* business address was the Pentagon gave rise to some suspicion.

To show individual possession with coordinate nouns, make both nouns possessive.

Example: The *Senate's and House's* chambers were packed.

To show joint possession with coordinate nouns, make only the last possessive.

Example: The *Senate and House's* joint declaration was read to the press.

Pronouns. The use of possessive pronouns does not normally cause problems except with gerunds and **indefinite pronouns.** Several indefinite pronouns (*all, any, each, few, most, none,* and *some*) require *of* phrases to form the possessive case.

Example: Both dies were stored in the warehouse, but rust had ruined the surface *of each*.

Others, however, use the apostrophe.

Example: *Anyone's* contribution is welcome.

Only the possessive form of a pronoun should be used with a gerund.

Examples: The boss objected to *my* arriving late every morning.
My working has not affected my grades.

Pronouns in compound constructions should be in the same case.

Examples: This is just between *them* and *us*.
Both *they* and *we* must agree to the arrangement.

APPOSITIVES

An **appositive** should be in the same case as the noun with which it is in apposition.

Examples: Two accountants, Merle Fosnight and *I*, were appointed to represent the department. (subjective case)
The accountants selected two members to represent the department—Merle Fosnight and *me*. (objective case)
We all came—Jim and Bill and *I*. (subjective case)
He gave us both, Rod and *me*, a week to make up our minds. (objective case)

TIPS ON DETERMINING THE CASE OF PRONOUNS

One test to determine the proper case of a pronoun is to try it with some transitive verb such as *resembled* or *hit*. If the pronoun would logically precede the verb, use the subjective case; if it would logically follow the verb, use the objective case.

Examples: *She* (he, they) resembled her father. (subjective case)
Angela resembled *him* (her, them). (objective case)

In the following type of sentence, try omitting the noun to determine the case of the pronoun.

Example: (*We/Us*) pilots fly our own airplanes.
Us [pilots] fly our own airplanes. (This incorrect usage is obviously wrong.)
We [pilots] fly our own airplanes. (This correct usage sounds right.)

To determine the case of a pronoun that follows *as* or *than*, try mentally adding the words that are normally omitted.

Examples: The other bookkeeper is not paid as well as *she* [is paid]. (You would not write, "*Her* is well paid.")
His partner was better informed than *he* [was informed]. (You would not write, "*Him* was informed.")

If compound pronouns cause problems, try using them singly to determine the proper case.

> *Example:*   (*We/Us*) and the Johnsons are going to the Grand Canyon next year.
> *We* are going to the Grand Canyon next year. (You would not write, "*Us* are going to the Grand Canyon.")

WHO/WHOM

Who and *whom* cause much trouble in determining case. *Who* is the subjective case form, *whom* is the objective case form, and *whose* is the possessive case form. When in doubt about which form to use, try substituting a personal pronoun to see which one fits. If *he* or *they* fits, use *who*.

> *Example:*   *Who* is the congressman from the 45th district?
> *He* is the congressman from the 45th district.

If *him* or *them* fits, use *whom*.

> *Example:*   It depended upon *them*.
> It depended upon *whom*?
> It was they upon *whom* it depended.

It is becoming common to use *who* for the objective case when it begins a clause or sentence, although some writers still object to such an "ungrammatical" construction.

> *Example:*   *Who* should I call to report a fire?

The best advice is to know your **reader**.

case (usage)

The word *case* is often merely filler. Be critical of the word, and eliminate it if it contributes nothing.

> *Change:*   In the *case* of those closely connected with the project, an exception was made.
> *To:*   An exception was made for those closely connected with the project.

cause-and-effect method of development

The cause-and-effect method of development, by stressing the connection between a result and a preceding event, explains why something happened or why the writer predicts that something is going to happen. For example, a report on an automobile accident would naturally follow this **method of development.** Such reports are normally developed sequentially, but the sequence is a special one based on cause and effect. The cause-and-effect relationship must be sound and plausible. Be careful not to oversimplify in establishing a cause-and-effect relationship or to attribute too broad an effect to an inadequate cause. (The abolition of cigarettes would not be likely to end lung cancer, for example.)

The cause-and-effect method of development can be developed from the cause, or causes, to the resulting effect, or it can begin with the resulting effect and from it establish the cause or causes.

censor/censure

To *censor* is "to examine in order to prohibit objectionable material." To *censure* is "to criticize severely" or "to blame."

Examples: The Committee for Decent Literature *censored* the book for its alleged pornographic content.
The director *censured* him for his unbecoming conduct.

center around

Substitute *on* or *in* for *around* in this redundant and illogical expression.

Change: The experiments *center around* the new discovery.
To: The experiments *center on* the new discovery.

Usually the idea intended by *center around* is best expressed by *revolve around*.

Example: The Senate hearings on no-fault insurance *revolved around* present insurance rates.

chairman/chairwoman/chairperson

Although *chairwoman* is quite acceptable and *chairperson* is common, in business and industry *chairman* is still the most widely used title for a presiding officer of either sex. Know your reading audience, however, because many people have become sensitive to any word that may imply sexual bias.

Examples: Mary Roberts preceded John Stevens as *chairman* of the executive committee.
Mary Roberts was *chairwoman* of the executive committee before John Stevens became *chairman*.
Mary Roberts preceded John Stevens as *chairperson* of the executive committee.

character

Character, used in the sense of "nature" or "quality," is often an unnecessary and inexact filler that should be omitted from your writing. Choose instead a word that conveys your meaning more specifically.

Change: The modifications changed the whole *character* of the engine.
To: The modifications changed the performance of the engine.

chronological method of development

The chronological **method of development** arranges the events being discussed in an orderly time sequence, starting with the first event and proceeding chronologically to the last event; it is therefore well suited to **explaining a process** in which time relationships are important. The process of biological evolution, for example, would logically be described in chronological sequence.

cite/site/sight

Cite means "to acknowledge" or "to quote an authority"; *site* is the place or plot of land where something is located; *sight* is the ability to see.

Examples: The speaker *cited* several famous economists to support his prediction about the stock market.
The *site* for the new factory is three miles from the middle of town.
After the accident, his vision was blurred and he feared that he might lose his *sight*.

clarity

Clarity in writing is difficult to achieve, and also to explain, because so many factors can contribute to it and so many other factors can defeat it. Logical development, unity, coherence, emphasis, subordination, pace, transition, an established point of view, conciseness, and word choice contribute to clarity. **Ambiguity**, **awkwardness**, vagueness, poor use of **idiom**, **clichés**, and inappropriate level of usage detract from clarity.

It is surely evident that a logical **method of development,** based on a good **outline,** is essential to clarity. Without a logical method of development and an outline, you may communicate only isolated thoughts to your **reader,** and your **objective** cannot be achieved by a jumble of isolated thoughts. You must use a method of development that puts your thoughts together in a logical, meaningful sequence. Only then will your writing achieve the **unity** and **coherence** so vital to clarity.

Proper **emphasis** and **subordination** are mandatory if you wish to achieve clarity. If you do not use these two complementary techniques wisely, your **clauses** and **sentences** may all appear to be of equal importance. Your reader will be forced to guess which are most important, which are least important, and which fall between the two extremes. At the very least, this will puzzle and annoy your reader; at worst, it will render your writing incoherent.

The **pace** at which you present your ideas is important to clarity because if the pace is not carefully adjusted to both the **topic** and the reader, your writing will appear cluttered and unclear.

Point of view establishes through whose eyes, or from what vantage point, the reader views the subject. A consistent point of view is essential to clarity; if you switch from the first person to the third person in midsentence, you are certain to confuse your reader.

Clear **transition** contributes to clarity by providing the smooth flow that enables the reader to connect your thoughts with one another without conscious effort. This enables the reader to concentrate solely on absorbing your ideas.

That **conciseness** is a requirement of clearly written communication should be evident to anyone who has ever attempted to decipher an insurance policy or legal contract. Although words are our chief means of communication, too many of them can impede communication just as effectively as too many cars on a freeway can impede traffic. For the sake of clarity, prune excess verbiage from your writing.

The selection of precise words over **vague words** is **word choice.** Thoughtful choice of the right word advances clarity by defeating **ambiguity** and **awkwardness.**

Another important contributor to clarity is a careful and methodical approach to your writing project, including proper application of all the steps of the writing process—**preparation, research, organization, writing the draft,** and **revision.**

clauses

A clause is a syntactical construction, or group of words, that contains a **subject** and a **predicate** and functions as part of a complex or compound **sentence.** A clause that could stand alone as a simple sentence is an independent clause.

> *Example:* *The scaffolding fell* when the rope broke.

A clause that could not stand alone if the rest of the sentence were deleted is a dependent clause.

> *Example:* I was at the St. Louis branch *when the decision was made.*

Every subject-predicate word group in a sentence is a clause. Unlike a **phrase,** a clause can make a complete statement because it contains a finite **verb** (as opposed to **verbals**) as well as a subject. Every sentence must contain at least one clause, with the obvious exception of minor sentences (sentence fragments that are acceptable because the missing part is clearly understood, such as "At last." or "So much for that.").

A clause may function as a **noun,** an **adjective,** or an **adverb** in a larger sentence, or it may be modified by one or more other clauses that are subordinate to it.

> *Example:* While I was in college, I studied differential equations.

While I was in college is an **adverb clause** modifying the independent clause *I studied differential equations.*

A clause may be connected with the rest of its sentence by a **coordinating conjunction,** a **subordinating conjunction,** a **relative pronoun,** or a **conjunctive adverb.**

> *Examples:* Peregrine falcons are about the size of a large crow, *and* they have a wingspread of three to four feet. (coordinating conjunction)
>
> Mission control will have to be on the alert *because* at launch the space laboratory will contain a highly flammable fuel. (subordinating conjunction)
>
> It was Robert M. Fano *who* designed and developed the earliest "Multiple Access Computer" system at M.I.T. (relative pronoun)

It was dark when we arrived; *nevertheless,* we began the tour of the factory. (conjunctive adverb)

INDEPENDENT CLAUSE

Unlike a dependent clause, which is part of a larger construction, an independent clause is complete in itself; it could stand alone as a separate sentence if taken out of its larger sentence.

Example: *We abandoned the project* because the cost was excessive.

DEPENDENT CLAUSE

A dependent, or subordinate, clause is a group of words that has a subject and a verb but must nonetheless depend upon a main clause to complete its meaning. Within the sentence as a whole, a **dependent clause** can function as a noun, an adjective, or an adverb.

A **noun clause** is a subordinate clause that functions as a noun. It can be a subject, an object, or a complement.

Examples: *That the noise level on Eighth Street in New York City on a weekday is as loud as an alarm clock ringing three feet away* is more readily perceived by a sound meter than by a native New Yorker. (subject)
Mr. Rich told me *that you are a key-punch operator.* (direct object)
That is not *what I meant.* (subjective complement)

An **adjective clause** is a subordinate clause that functions as an adjective by modifying a noun or pronoun in the main clause.

Examples: The laboratory technician *we met yesterday* showed us his equipment, *which included an electron microscope.*
The man *who called earlier* is here.

An **adverb clause** is a subordinate clause used to modify a verb, an adjective, or another adverb in another clause or phrase. As an adverb, a dependent clause may express a relationship of time, cause, result, degree, or contrast.

Examples: I go fishing *when I need to forget the pressures of my job.* (time)
I left work early *because I felt sick.* (cause)
I worked late *so I could finish the project on time.* (result)
He was hurt so badly *that he limped for a week.* (degree)
The office seemed smaller *than when I last saw it.* (contrast)

ELLIPTICAL CLAUSE

An elliptical clause is a clause that is clearly understood even though one or more words are not stated.

Example: *While* [he was] *achieving great success at his research,* Dr. Brandt was backed by an outstanding research team.

This construction works, of course, only if the subject of the clause and the sentence are the same (*he* and *Dr. Brandt*). (See **dangling modifiers.**)

clench/clinch

Clench and *clinch* both mean "to secure" or "to hold" something. When you tighten your fingers into a fist or clamp your teeth together, the word *clench* is more appropriate. *Clinch* should be used when a bargain, argument, or verdict is secured.

Example: He *clenched* his teeth as his opponent *clinched* the argument.

cliché

A cliché is an expression that has been used for so long that it is no longer fresh (although some clichés were, at one time, fresh **figures of speech**). Because they have been used continuously over a long period of time, clichés come to mind easily.

Examples: quick as a flash
straight from the shoulder
vehemently opposed
with reference to
abreast of the times

In addition to being trite, clichés are usually wordy and often vague.

Clichés	*Substitutes*
quick as a flash	quickly (or, specifically, how quickly: one minute, four seconds, etc.)
straight from the shoulder	frank
vehemently opposed	against
with reference to	about (or omit altogether)
abreast of the times	up-to-date (or current)

Clichés are often used in an attempt to make writing elegant or impressive (see also **affectation**). Because they are wordy and vague, however, they slow communication and can even irritate your **reader.** So, although clichés come to mind easily while you are

writing the draft, they normally should be eliminated during the **revision** phase of the writing process.

On rare occasions, certain clichés, because they are so much a part of the language, may provide (much like **jargon**) a time-saving and efficient means of relating an idea.* For example, "guardedly optimistic" or "inextricably interwoven" may, in appropriate contexts, best express your idea—provided you are certain that the expression is meaningful and acceptable to your reader. Be on guard, however, because clichés can too easily become the pattern of your **word choice.** The best advice is to avoid clichés if *any* other choice of words will work. Consider the following **paragraphs,** first with clichés, then rewritten without them.

> *Change:* Our new computer system will have a positive impact on the company *as a whole.* It will keep us *abreast of the times* and make our competition *green with envy.* The committee deserves a *pat on the back* for its *herculean efforts* in convincing management that it was *the thing to do.* I'm sure that their *untiring efforts* will *not go unrewarded.*
>
> *To:* Our new computer system will have a positive impact throughout the company. It will keep our operations up-to-date and make our competition envious. The committee deserves credit for their efforts in convincing management of the need for the computer. I'm sure that the value of their efforts will be recognized.

clipped form of words

When the beginning or end of a word is cut off to create a shorter word, the result is called a clipped form.

> *Examples:* dorm, lab, demo, phone

In the insurance business, for example, policies that pay dividends are called "participating" policies, and policies that do not pay dividends are called "nonparticipating" policies. In the insurance industry, they are known respectively as *par* and *nonpar* policies. As a rule, it is better to avoid clipped forms; however, where these are part of a special vocabulary, such as *par* and *nonpar* in the insurance industry, they are acceptable.

Apostrophes are not normally used with clipped forms of words

*Charles Sukor, "Clichés: A Re-assessment," *College Composition and Communication,* 26 (May 1975): 159–162.

(not *'phone,* but *phone*). Since they are not strictly **abbreviations,** clipped forms are not followed by **periods** (not *lab.,* but *lab*).

Do not use clipped forms of spelling (*thru, nite,* etc.).

coherence

Coherence, in writing, is the quality of being logically consistent throughout; in other words, all parts are naturally connected with one another. Writing that flows smoothly from one point to another, from one **sentence** to another, and from one **paragraph** to another is coherent, and the reason one sentence or paragraph follows another is clearly evident to the **reader.** Many things contribute to the smooth flow that is indicative of coherent writing; however, the major components of coherence are (1) a logical sequence of ideas, (2) a **pace** that is right for both your topic and your reader, (3) proper **subordination** and **emphasis,** and (4) thoughtful **transition**.

A logical sequence of presentation is the most important single requirement in achieving coherence, and the key to achieving the most logical sequence of presentation is the use of a good **outline.** The outline forces you to establish a beginning (**introduction**), a middle (body), and an end (**conclusion**), and this alone contributes greatly to coherence. The outline also enables you to lay out the most direct route to your **objective**—without digressing into interesting but only loosely related side issues, a habit that inevitably defeats coherence. Drawing up an outline permits you to experiment with different sequences and choose the best one.

For the most coherent communication between writer and reader, the pace of the writing (the speed with which the writer presents ideas to the reader) must be right for both the subject and the reader. If facts are piled on top of each other at a rapid-fire pace, the writing may become incoherent to the reader. Note the difference between the following two paragraphs.

Examples: The thermal unit is powered by a 150-horsepower engine and is designed to operate under normal conditions of temperature and humidity, producing 12,000 Btu., is also designed for use under emergency conditions, and may be coupled with other units of the same type.

The thermal unit, which is powered by a 150-horsepower engine, produces 12,000 Btu. under normal conditions of temperature and humidity. Designed especially for use under emergency conditions, this thermal unit may be coupled with other units of the same type to produce additional capacity when needed.

In the first paragraph, the facts are presented too fast for comfortable reading; the reader must reread and ponder to absorb the information contained in the paragraph. In the second paragraph, the same facts are spread out and presented in a more digestible manner—in other words, the second paragraph is more coherent than the first.

Proper emphasis and subordination are essential to coherence; without them, every **clause** and sentence would carry the same weight. The reader would be forced to guess which elements were the most important, which were the least important, and which should fall between the two extremes. The result would be confusion.

Thoughtful transition is also essential to coherence, for without it your writing cannot achieve the smooth flow from sentence to sentence and from paragraph to paragraph that is required for coherence. Note the difference between the following two paragraphs; the first has no transition, the second has transition added.

Examples: The moon had always been an object of interest to human beings. Until the 1960s, getting there was only a dream. Some thought that we were not meant to go to the moon. In 1969 Neil Armstrong stepped onto the lunar surface. Moon landings became routine to the general public.

The moon had always been an object of interest to human beings, *but* until the 1960s, getting there was only a dream. *In fact,* some thought that we were not meant to go to the moon. *However,* in 1969 Neil Armstrong stepped onto the lunar surface. *After that* moon landings became routine to the general public.

The transitional words and expressions of the second paragraph fit the ideas snugly together, making that paragraph read more smoothly than the first. Attention to transition in longer works is essential if your reader is to move smoothly from point to point in your writing.

Check your draft carefully for coherence during **revision;** if your writing is not coherent, you are not really communicating with your reader.

collective noun

A collective noun names a group or collection of persons, places, things, concepts, actions, or qualities.

Examples: army, committee, crowd, team, public, class, jury, humanity, data

When a collective noun refers to a group as a whole, it takes a singular **verb** and **pronoun**.

Example: The jury *was* deadlocked; *it* had to be disbanded.

When a collective noun refers to individuals within a group, it takes a plural verb and pronoun.

Example: The jury *were* allowed to go to *their* homes for the night.

Another way to emphasize the individuals in the jury would be to use the **phrase** *members of the jury*.

Example: The members of the jury *were* allowed to go to *their* homes for the night.

Some collective nouns regularly take singular verbs (*crowd*); others do not (*people*).

Examples: *The crowd was* growing impatient.
Many *people were* unable to watch Armstrong's walk on the moon.

Some collective nouns have regular plural forms (*team, teams*); others do not (*mankind*).

For additional information about the **case, number,** and function of collective nouns, see **nouns.**

colon

The colon is a mark of anticipation and introduction that halts the **reader,** then connects the first statement to the one following.

A colon may be used to connect a list or series to a clause, word, or phrase with which it is in apposition.

Example: We carry three brands of watches: Timex, Bulova, and Omega.

Do not, however, place a colon between a **verb** and its **objects.**

> *Change:*   The three fluids for cleaning pipettes are: water, alcohol, and acetone.
>
> *To:*   The three fluids for cleaning pipettes are water, alcohol, and acetone.

Do not use a colon between a **preposition** and its object.

> *Change:*   I would like to be transferred to: Tucson, Boston, or Miami.
>
> *To:*   I would like to be transferred to Tucson, Boston, or Miami.

A colon may be used to link one statement to another that develops, explains, amplifies, or illustrates the first. A colon may be used in this way to link two independent clauses.

> *Example:*   Any large organization is confronted with two separate, though related, information problems: it must maintain an effective internal communication system, and it must see that an effective overall communication system is maintained.

A colon may be used to introduce a stacked list.

> *Example:*   The following corporations manufacture computers:
>
> | | |
> |---|---|
> | Univac | Control Data Corporation |
> | NCR Corporation | IBM, Inc. |
> | Burroughs | Honeywell |

A colon may be used to link an **appositive** phrase to its related statement if greater **emphasis** is needed.

> *Example:*   There is only one thing that will satisfy Mr. Sturgess: our finished report.

Colons are used to link numbers signifying different identifying nouns.

> *Examples:*   Genesis 10:16 (chapter 10, verse 16)
>
> 9:30 a.m. (9 hours, 30 minutes)

In proportions, the colon indicates the ratio of one amount to another.

> *Example:*   The cement is mixed with the water and sand at 7:5:14. (In this case, the colon replaces *to*.)

Colons are often used in mathematical ratios.

> *Example:* $7:3 = 14:x$

In **bibliography** and **footnote** entries, colons link the place of publication with the publisher.

> *Example:*   Aaron, John. *Business Letters*. Boston: Bane Publishing Co., 1970.

A colon follows the salutation in business letters, even when the salutation refers to a person by name.

Examples: Dear Ms. Jeffers:
Dear Sir:
Dear George:

The initial capital letter of a quotation is retained following a colon if the quoted material originally began with a capital letter.

Example: The senator stated: "We are not concerned about the present, we are worried about the future."

A colon always goes outside quotation marks.

Example: This was the real meaning of his "suggestion": the division must show a profit by the end of the year.

When quoting material that ends in a colon, drop the colon and replace it with **ellipses.**

Change: "Any large corporation is confronted with two separate, though related, information problems:"
To: "Any large corporation is confronted with two separate, though related, information problems . . ."

The first word after a colon may be capitalized if (1) the statement following is a complete sentence or (2) it introduces a formal resolution or question.

Example: This year's conference attendance was low: We did not advertise widely enough.

If a subordinate element follows the colon, however, use a lower-case letter following the colon.

Example: There is only one way to stay within our present budget: to reduce expenditures for research and development.

comma

The comma is used more often than any other mark of **punctuation** because it has such a wide variety of uses: it can link, enclose, separate, and show omissions. Effective use of the comma depends upon your understanding of how **ideas** fit together. Used with care, the comma can add **clarity** and **emphasis** to your writing; used carelessly, it can cause confusion.

The comma can prevent **ambiguity** by separating **sentence** elements that might otherwise be misunderstood. Compare the second sentence in each of the following examples.

> *Change:*   The sale of 134 units to the Lane Company was due to Bill Hendrick's efforts; so, possibly, were the 550 units to Dayco, Inc. *If so, that is 684 sales out of 1,368 that were accounted for by our sales district.* (Ambiguous. Were 684 or 1,368 accounted for by our district?)
>
> *To:*   The sale of 134 units to the Lane Company was due to Bill Hendrick's efforts; so, possibly, were the 550 units to Dayco, Inc. *If so, that is 684 sales, out of 1,368, that were accounted for by our sales district.* (Clear. It is obvious that 684 were accounted for by our district.)

TO LINK

Coordinating conjunctions (*and, but, for, or, so, nor, yet*) require a comma immediately preceding them when they are used to connect independent **clauses** unless the clauses are very short.

> *Example:*   Human beings have always prided themselves on their unique capacity to create and manipulate symbols, but today computers are manipulating symbols.

Independent clauses that are short and have single **subjects** and single **predicates** do not require a comma preceding the coordinating conjunction.

> *Example:*   The cable snapped and the power failed.

TO ENCLOSE

Commas are used to enclose nonrestrictive clauses and parenthetical elements.

> *Examples:*   Our new Detroit factory, *which began operations last month,* should add 25 percent to total output. (nonrestrictive clause)
> We can, *of course,* expect their lawyer to call us. (parenthetical element)

(For other means of punctuating parenthetical elements, see **dash** and **parentheses.**)

Yes and *no* are set off by commas in such uses as the following.

> *Examples:*   I agree with you, *yes.*
> *No,* I do not think we can finish as soon as we would like.

A **direct address** should be enclosed in commas.

> *Example:*   You will note, *Mark,* that the surface of the brake shoe complies with the specifications.

Phrases in apposition (which identify another expression) are enclosed in commas.

>   *Example:*   Our company, *the Blaylok Precision Company,* is doing well this year.

Commas enclose nonrestrictive **participial phrases**.

>   *Example:*   The lathe operator, *working quickly and efficiently,* finished early.

TO SEPARATE

Commas are used to separate introductory elements from the rest of the sentence, to separate items in a series, to separate subordinate clauses from main clauses, and to separate certain elements for clarity or emphasis.

To Separate Introductory Elements. It is generally a good rule of thumb to put a comma after an introductory clause or phrase unless it is very short. This helps indicate where the main part of the sentence begins.

>   *Example:*   *Since many rare fossils seem never to occur free from their matrix,* it is wise to scan every slab with a hand lens.

When long modifying phrases precede the main clause, they should always be followed by a comma.

>   *Example:*   *During the first series of field-performance tests last year at our Colorado proving ground,* the new motor failed to meet our expectations.

When an introductory phrase is short and closely related to the main clause, the comma may be omitted.

>   *Example:*   *In two seconds* a 20° temperature is created in the test tube.

A comma should always follow an introductory **absolute phrase.**

>   *Example:*   *The tests completed,* I began to organize the data for the final report.

Absolute phrases include participial phrases that modify the whole sentence.

>   *Example:*   *The stock market having moved up ten points in an hour,* we decided to invest in Data Corporation.

A **prepositional phrase,** if long, should be followed by a comma.

>   *Example:*   *In spite of much talk about the preeminent importance of the individual,* we seem always to expect the individual to sacrifice

personal interests to those of the smooth operation of the administrative machinery.

Certain types of introductory words must be followed by a comma. One such is a **noun** used in direct address.

> *Example:*   *Bill,* here is the statement you asked me to audit.

An introductory **interjection** (such as *oh, well, why, indeed, yes,* and *no*) must be followed by a comma.

> *Examples:*   *Yes,* I will make sure your request is approved.
> *Indeed,* I will be glad to send you further information.

An introductory **adverb** like *moreover* or *furthermore* must be followed by a comma.

> *Example:*   *Moreover,* our balance of payments will be better because of this policy.

Introductory adverbs and adverb phrases are set off with a comma because they serve the dual function of modifying the idea that follows and connecting it to the idea in the previous sentence. (See also **transition.**)

> *Example:*   We can expect a better balance of payments in the coming year. *In addition,* we should look for a better world market as a result. *However,* we should expect some shortages due to the overall economic climate.

When adverbs closely modify the **verb** or the entire sentence, however, they should not be followed by a comma.

> *Example:*   *Perhaps* we can still solve the environmental problem. *Certainly* we should try.

To Separate Items in a Series. Commas should be used to separate words in a series.

> *Example:*   Basically, plants control the wind by *obstruction, guidance, deflection, and filtration.*

Phrases and clauses in coordinate series, like words, are punctuated with commas.

> *Example:*   It is well known that plants absorb noxious gases, act as receptors of dust and dirt particles, and cleanse the air of other impurities.

When **adjectives** modifying the same noun can be reversed and make sense, or when they can be separated by *and* or *or,* they should be separated by commas.

Example: Wells may be classified as *dug, bored, driven, drilled, and jetted.*

When an adjective modifies a noun phrase, no comma is required.

Example: He was wearing his *old cotton tennis hat.* (*old* modifies the noun phrase *cotton tennis hat; cotton* modifies the noun phrase *tennis hat.*)

Never separate a final adjective from its noun.

Change: He is a conscientious, honest, reliable, worker.
  To: He is a conscientious, honest, reliable worker.

Although the comma before the last word in a series is sometimes omitted, it is generally clearer to include it. The confusion that may result from omitting the comma is illustrated in the following sentence.

Example: Random House, Allyn and Bacon, Doubleday and Dell are publishing companies.

Is "Doubleday and Dell" one company or two? "Random House, Allyn and Bacon, Doubleday, and Dell" removes the doubt.

Commas are conventionally used to separate distinct items. Use commas between the elements of an address written on the same line.

Example: Walter James, 4119 Mill Road, Dayton, Ohio 45401

Use a comma to separate the elements of a date written on the same line. However, when the day is omitted, the comma is unnecessary.

Examples: July 2, 1949
  July 1949

Use commas to separate the elements of Arabic **numbers.**

Example: 1,528,200

Use a comma after the salutation of an informal letter.

Example: Dear John,

Use commas to separate the elements of geographical names.

Example: Toronto, Ontario, Canada

Use a comma to separate names that are reversed.

Example: Smith, Alvin

Use commas to separate certain elements of **footnote** and **bibliography** entries.

> *Examples:*   Bibliography—Adelstein, Michael E. *Contemporary Business Writing.* New York: Random House, 1971.
> Footnote—[1]Michael E. Adelstein, *Contemporary Business Writing* (New York: Random House, 1971), p. 38.

To Separate Subordinate Clauses. Use a comma between the main clause and a subordinate clause when the subordinate clause comes first.

> *Example:*   By artificially stimulating the electrochemical action of the brain, scientists have learned more about the brain in the past two decades than ever before.

Use a comma following an independent clause that is only loosely related to the **dependent clause** that follows it.

> *Example:*   The plan should be finished by July, even though I lost time because of illness.

In all cases, use a comma following a long introductory dependent clause.

> *Example:*   While the angry crowd outside the embassy waited, the ambassador drank cocktails.

Be careful not to place a comma between a subject and verb, or between a verb and its **object.**

> *Change:*   The cold conditions at the test site in the Arctic, made accurate readings difficult.
> *To:*   The cold conditions at the test site in the Arctic made accurate readings difficult.

To Separate Elements for Clarity or Emphasis. **Conjunctive adverbs** (*however, nevertheless, consequently, for example, on the other hand*) joining independent clauses are preceded by a **semicolon** and followed by a comma.

> *Examples:*   Your idea is good; *however,* your format is poor.
> He has held the project together; *moreover,* he has helped everyone's morale.

Such adverbs function as both **modifiers** and **connectives.**

Commas are often used before coordinating conjunctions like *but, for,* and *yet*—even though the conjunctions are not between independent clauses—because they separate contrasting ideas.

> *Example:*   I generally agreed with him, but not completely.

Use a comma to separate two contrasting thoughts or ideas.

Examples: The project was finished on time, but not within the cost limits.
The specifications call for 100-ohm resistors, not 1000-ohm resistors.
The project was finished on time, wasn't it?
It was Bill, not Matt, who suggested that the names be changed.

Use a comma to separate a direct quotation from its introduction.

Example: Morton and Lucia White said, "Men live in cities but dream of the countryside."

Do not use a comma, however, when giving an indirect quotation.

Example: Morton and Lucia White said that men dream of the countryside even though they live in cities.

Sometimes commas are used simply to make something clear that might otherwise be confusing.

Change: The year after that Xerox and 3M outproduced all the competition.
To: The year after that, Xerox and 3M outproduced all the competition.

To clarify phrases in a series, you may need to use commas in concert with semicolons.

Example: Among those present were John Howard, president of the Howard Paper Company; Thomas Martin, president of Copco Corp.; and Larry Stanley, president of Stanley Papers.

If you find you need a comma to separate the consecutive use of the same word to prevent misreading, rewrite the sentence.

Change: The assets we had, had surprised us.
To: We were surprised at the assets we had when the company was founded.

Commas are sometimes used to separate elements in a sentence that, to provide emphasis, are not in their normal order.

Examples: The engineers worked quickly to correct the problem. (normal sequence)
Quickly, the engineers worked to correct the problem. (out of normal sequence)
I believe our policy will stand the test of time. (normal sequence)
Our policy, I believe, will stand the test of time. (out of normal sequence)

TO SHOW OMISSIONS

A comma sometimes replaces a verb in certain elliptical constructions.

> *Example:* Some were punctual; *others, late.* (replaces *were*)

CONVENTIONAL USE WITH OTHER PUNCTUATION

A comma always goes inside quotation marks.

> *Example:* Although he called his presentation "adequate," the audience thought it was superb.

When an introductory phrase or clause ends with a parenthesis, the comma separating the introductory phrase or clause from the rest of the sentence always appears outside the parenthesis.

> *Change:* Although we left late (at 7:30 p.m.,) we arrived in time for the keynote address.
> *To:* Although we left late (at 7:30 p.m.), we arrived in time for the keynote address.

Except with **abbreviations,** a comma should not be used with a **period, question mark, exclamation mark,** or dash.

> *Change:* "I have finished the project.," he said.
> *To:* "I have finished the project," he said. (omit the period)

> *Change:* "Have you finished the project?," I asked.
> *To:* "Have you finished the project?" I asked. (omit the comma)

COMMA FAULTS

Do not attempt to join two independent clauses with only a comma; this is called a "comma splice" or "comma fault."

> *Example:* It was five hundred miles to the facility, we made arrangements to fly.

Such a comma fault could be corrected in several ways.

1. Substitute a semicolon, or a semicolon and a conjunctive adverb.

> *Change:* It was five hundred miles to the facility, we made arrangements to fly.
> *To:* It was five hundred miles to the facility; we made arrangements to fly.
> *Or:* It was five hundred miles to the facility; *therefore,* we made arrangements to fly.

2. Add a conjunction following the comma.

> *Example:* It was five hundred miles to the facility, *so* we made arrangements to fly.

3. Create two sentences. (Be aware, however, that putting a period between two closely related and brief statements may result in two weak sentences.)

   Example: It was five hundred miles to the facility. We made arrangements to fly.

4. Subordinate one clause to the other.

   Example: *Because* it was five hundred miles to the facility, we made arrangements to fly.

When a conjunctive adverb connects two independent clauses, the conjunctive adverb *must* be preceded by a semicolon and followed by a comma.

   Change: It was five hundred miles to the facility, therefore, we made arrangements to fly.
   To: It was five hundred miles to the facility; therefore, we made arrangements to fly.

SUPERFLUOUS COMMAS

A number of common writing errors involve placing commas where they do not belong. These errors often occur because writers assume that a pause in a sentence should be indicated by a comma. It is true that commas usually signal pauses, but it is not true that pauses *necessarily* call for commas.

Be careful not to place a comma between a subject and **verb**, or between a verb and its **object**.

   Change: The cold conditions at the test site in the Arctic, made accurate readings difficult.
   To: The cold conditions at the test site in the Arctic made accurate readings difficult.

   Change: He has often said, that one company's failure is another's opportunity.
   To: He has often said that one company's failure is another's opportunity.

Do not use a comma between the elements of a compound subject or a compound predicate consisting of only two elements:

   Change: The director of the engineering department, and the supervisor of the quality-control section were both opposed to the new schedules.
   To: The director of the engineering department and the supervisor of the quality-control section were both opposed to the new schedules.

Change: The director of the engineering department listed five major objections, and asked that the new schedule be reconsidered.

To: The director of the engineering department listed five major objections and asked that the new schedule be reconsidered.

An especially common error is the placing of a comma after a coordinating conjunction such as *and* or *but* (especially *but*).

Change: The chairman formally adjourned the meeting, but, the members of the committee continued to argue.

To: The chairman formally adjourned the meeting, but the members of the committee continued to argue.

Change: I argued against the proposal. And, I gave good reasons for my position.

To: I argued against the proposal. And I gave good reasons for my position.

Do not place a comma before the first item or after the last item of a series.

Change: We are considering a number of new products, such as, calculators, typewriters, and cameras.

To: We are considering a number of new products, such as calculators, typewriters, and cameras.

Change: It was a fast, simple, inexpensive, process.
To: It was a fast, simple, inexpensive process.

committee

Committee is a **collective noun** that takes a singular **verb**.

Example: The *committee is* to meet at 3:30 p.m.

If you wish to emphasize the individuals on the committee, use *the members of the committee* with the plural verb form.

Example: The *members of the committee were* unanimous about the decision.

common noun

A common noun names general classes or categories of persons, places, things, concepts, actions, or qualities. Common nouns can be **abstract** (*justice*), **concrete** (*jail*), or **collective** (*jury*).

Common Noun	Proper Noun
boy	Jim Jones
city	Chicago
company	General Electric
day	Tuesday
document	Declaration of Independence

Common nouns are not capitalized unless they begin a **sentence**. (For information about the **case**, **number**, and function of common nouns, see **nouns**.)

comparative degree

Most **adjectives** and **adverbs** can be compared. Their common forms of comparison are as follows:

Examples: The new copier is *fast*. (positive)
The new copier is *faster* than the old one. (comparative)
The new copier is the *fastest* I have ever used. (superlative)

Most one-syllable words use the comparative ending *-er* and the superlative ending *-est*.

Examples: Ours was the *faster* of the two cars tested.
Ours was the *fastest* car on the track.

Most words with more than one syllable form the comparative degree by using the word *more* and the superlative degree by using the word *most*.

Examples: She is *more* talented than the rest of the writers on the staff.
She is the *most* talented writer on the staff.

Some words may use either means of expressing degree.

Examples: He was the *most angry*.
He was the *angriest*.

A few words have irregular forms of comparison.

Examples: much, more, most
good, better, best

Absolute words (such as *round, perfect, unique*) are not logically subject to comparison. However, language is not always strictly logical, and these words are sometimes used comparatively. Be careful in using such comparisons in business and technical writing, where exactness is often critical.

Example: Phase-locked loop (PLL) circuits make FM tuner performance *more exact* by decreasing tuner distortion.

The superlative form is sometimes also used in expressions that do not really express comparison (*best* wishes, *deepest* sympathy, *highest* praise, and *most* sincerely).

compare/contrast

When you *compare* things, you point out both similarities and differences. When you *contrast* things you point out only the differences.

Examples: He *compared* all the features of the two brands before buying. Their styles of selling *contrasted* sharply.

When *compare* is used to establish a general similarity, it is followed by *to*.

Example: *Compared to* the computer, the abacus is a primitive device.

When *compare* is used to indicate a close examination of similarities or differences, it is followed by *with* in formal usage.

Example: We *compared* the features of the new capacitor very carefully *with* those of the old one.

Contrast is normally followed by *with*.

Example: The new policy *contrasts* sharply *with* the earlier one in requiring that sealed bids be submitted.

When the noun form of *contrast* is used, one speaks of the *contrast between* two things or of one thing being *in contrast to* the other.

Examples: The new policy is in sharp *contrast to* the earlier one. There is a sharp *contrast between* the old and new policies.

comparison

When making a *comparison* make certain that both or all the elements being compared are clearly evident to your reader.

Change: The third-generation computer is *better*.
To: The third-generation computer is *better than the second-generation computer*.

The things being compared must be of the same kind.

> *Change:*   The *imitation alligator hide* is almost as tough as *a real alligator.*
> *To:*   The *imitation alligator hide* is almost as tough as *real alligator hide.*

Be sure to point out the parallels or differences between the things being compared. Don't assume your reader will know what you mean.

> *Change:*   Washington is farther from Boston *than Philadelphia.*
> *To:*   Washington is farther from Boston *than it is from* Philadelphia.
> *Or:*   Washington is farther from Boston *than Philadelphia is.*

A double comparison in the same sentence requires that the first be completed before the second is stated.

> *Change:*   The discovery of electricity was *one of the great if not the greatest* scientific discoveries in history.
> *To:*   The discovery of electricity was *one of the great* scientific discoveries in history, *if not the greatest.*

Do not attempt to compare things that are not comparable.

> *Change:*   Farmers say that storage space is reduced by 40 percent compared with baled hay. (*Storage space* is not comparable to *baled hay.*)
> *To:*   Farmers say that baled hay requires 40 percent less storage space than loose hay requires.

comparison as a method of development

Comparison, as a **method of development,** points out the similarities and differences between or among the elements of your subject. Comparison can be an especially effective method of development because it can be used to explain a difficult or unfamiliar subject by relating it to a simpler or more familiar one. If you were explaining the British currency system, for example, you could use this method of development by comparing the British system with the American or Canadian system. (See also **analogy.**)

complement

A *complement* is a word, **phrase**, or **clause** used in the **predicate** of a **sentence** to complete the meaning of the sentence.

Examples: Pilots fly *airplanes.* (word)
To live is *to risk death.* (phrase)
John knew *that he would be late.* (clause)

Four kinds of complements are generally recognized: **direct object** (which completes the sense of a **transitive verb**); **indirect object** (which completes the meaning of a transitive verb and the verb's direct object); **objective complement** (which completes the meaning of a verb's object); and **subjective complement** (which completes the meaning of the subject).

A direct object is a **noun** or noun equivalent that receives the action of a transitive verb; it answers the question *what* or *whom* after the verb.

Examples: John built *a business.* (noun)
I like *to work.* (verbal)
I like *it.* (pronoun)
I like *what I saw.* (noun clause)

An indirect object is a noun or noun equivalent that occurs with a direct object after certain kinds of transitive verbs such as *give, wish, cause,* and *tell.* It answers the question *to whom* or *for whom* (or *to what* or *for what*).

Examples: Give *John* a wrench. ("wrench" is the direct object)
We should buy *the Milwaukee office* a computer. ("computer" is the direct object)

An objective complement completes the meaning of a sentence by revealing something about the object of its transitive verb. An objective complement may be either a noun or an **adjective**.

Examples: They call him *a genius.* (noun)
We painted the building *white.* (adjective)

A subjective complement, which follows a **linking verb** rather than a transitive verb, describes the **subject**. A subjective complement may be either a noun or an adjective.

Examples: His brother is *an accountant.*
His brother is younger. (adjective)

complement/compliment

Complement means "anything that completes a whole." It may be used as either a **noun** or a **verb**.

Examples: A *complement* of four men would bring our staff up to its normal strength. (noun)
The two programs *complement* one another perfectly. (verb)

Compliment means "praise." It too may be used as either a noun or a verb.

Examples: The manager *complimented* the staff on its efficient job. (verb)
The manager's *compliment* boosted morale in the department. (noun)

complex sentence

The complex sentence provides a means of subordinating one thought to another because it contains one independent **clause** and at least one **dependent clause** that expresses a subordinate idea.

Example: We lost some of our efficiency (independent clause) when we moved (dependent clause).

Normally, the independent clause carries a main point, and the dependent clause carries a related subordinate point. A dependent clause may occur before, after, or within the independent clause. The dependent clause can serve within the **sentence** as its **subject**, as an **object**, or as a **modifier**.

Examples: *What he proposed* is irrelevant. (subject)
We know *where it is supposed to be*. (object)
The computer, *which can make more calculations in one hour than thousands of scientists could make in a lifetime,* is perhaps one of the greatest challenges people have ever had to face. (modifier)

Complex sentences offer more variety than **simple sentences**. And frequently the meaning of a **compound sentence** can be made more exact by subordinating one of the two independent clauses to the other to create a complex sentence (thereby establishing the relationship of the two parts more clearly). (See also **subordination**.)

Examples: We moved *and* we lost some of our efficiency. (compound sentence with **coordinating conjunction**)
When we moved, we lost some of our efficiency. (complex sentence with **subordinating conjunction**)

Learn to handle the complex sentence well; it can be a useful tool with which to express your thoughts clearly and exactly. However, be on guard against placing the main idea of a complex sentence in a dependent clause; this is one of the most common errors made with the complex sentence. For example, do not write the first sentence below if what you mean is expressed by the second sentence.

> *Example:* Production was not as great as we expected, although we met our quota. (The main idea expressed here is that production fell short of expectations.)
> Although production was not as great as we expected, we met our quota. (The main idea expressed here is that the production quota was met.)

compose/comprise

Comprise means "to include." The whole *comprises* the parts.

> *Example:* The library (the whole) *comprises* fifty thousand books (the parts).

Compose means "to create" or "to make up the whole." The parts *compose* the whole.

> *Examples:* Fifty thousand books (the parts) *compose* the library (the whole).
> The library is *composed* of fifty thousand books.

compound sentence

A compound sentence combines two or more related independent **clauses** that are of equal importance.

> *Example:* Drilling is the only way to collect samples of the layers of sediment below the ocean floor, *but* it is by no means the only way to gather information about these strata.
>
> —Bruce C. Heezen and Ian D. Macgregor, "The Evolution of the Pacific," *Scientific American* (November 1973), p. 103.

The independent clauses of a compound **sentence** may be joined by a **comma** and a **coordinating conjunction**, by a **semicolon**, or by a **conjunctive adverb** preceded by a semicolon and followed by a comma.

> *Examples:* People deplore criminal violence, *but* they have an insatiable appetite for it on television and in films. (coordinating conjunction)
> People deplore criminal violence; *however*, they have an insatiable appetite for it on television and in films. (conjunctive adverb)

It is a curious fact that there is little similarity between the chemical composition of sea water and river water; the various elements are present in entirely different proportions. (semi-colon)

A compound sentence is balanced when its clauses are of similar length and construction.

Examples: The plan was sound, and the staff was eager to begin.
Fingerprints were used for personal identification in 200 B.C., but they were not used for criminal identification until about A.D. 1880.

Balanced clauses can add interest and variety to your writing, but be careful not to overuse them because they quickly develop a monot-onous sing-song quality. (See also **parallel structure** and **balance**.)

compound-complex sentence

A compound-complex sentence consists of two or more independent clauses and at least one **dependent clause**.

Example: At the same time *that it cools and lubricates the bit and brings the cuttings to the surface,* the "drilling mud" deposits a sheath of mud cake on the wall of the hole to prevent cave-ins; it re-duces the friction *which is created by the drill string's rubbing against the wall of the hole;* and, *since the weight of the mud column bears against the wall of the hole,* it helps to contain formation pressures and prevent a blowout.

Here, the three parallel independent clauses are joined in a series linked by the semicolons and the **coordinating conjunction** *and;* each independent clause contains a dependent clause (in italics above). The first two dependent clauses are **adjective clauses** modi-fying *time* and *friction,* and the third is an **adverb clause** that modifies its independent clause as a whole.

The compound-complex sentence offers a vehicle for a more elab-orate grouping of ideas than other sentence types permit. It is not really recommended for inexperienced writers because it is difficult to handle skillfully and often leads them into sentences that become so complicated that they lose all logic and coherence. The more technically complex the subject, the more difficult the compound-complex sentence is to control effectively.

compound words

A compound word is made from two or more words that are either hyphenated or written as one word. (If you are not certain whether a compound word should be hyphenated, check a **dictionary**.)

Examples: nevertheless, mother-in-law, courthouse, run-of-the-mill, low-level, high-energy

Be careful to distinguish between compound words and words that frequently appear together but do not constitute compound words, such as *high school* and *post office*. Also be careful to distinguish between compound words and word pairs that mean different things, such as *greenhouse* and *green house*.

Plurals of compound words are usually formed by adding an *s* to the last letter.

Examples: bedrooms, masterminds, overcoats, cupfuls

When the first word of the compound is more important to its meaning than the last, however, the first word takes the *s* (when in doubt, check your dictionary).

Examples: editors-in-chief, fathers-in-law

Possessives are formed by adding *'s* to the end of the compound word.

Examples: the *vice-president's* speech, his *brother-in-law's* car, the *pipeline's* diameter, the *antibody's* action

concept/conception

A *concept* is a thought, or an idea. A *conception* is the sum of a person's ideas, or concepts, on a subject.

Examples: His final *conception* of the whole process evolved from many smaller *concepts*.
From the *concept* of combustion evolved the *conception* of the internal combustion engine.

conciseness/wordiness

Good writing is concise. Make all words, **sentences**, and **paragraphs** count by eliminating unnecessary words and phrases. Wordiness results from needless repetition of the same idea in different words and in different sentences within your writing.

Change: The modern student *of today* is more sophisticated than his father. (The phrase *of today* repeats the thought already expressed by the adjective *modern*.)

To: The modern student is more sophisticated than his father.

Change: The walls were sky-blue *in color*. (The phrase *in color* is redundant.)

To: The walls were sky-blue.

Good writers go through their writing removing every word, phrase, clause, or sentence they can omit. In doing so, they are striving to be as concise as **clarity** permits—but note that conciseness is not a **synonym** for brevity. Brevity may or may not be desirable in a given passage (depending upon the writer's **objective**), but it is always good to be concise. The writer must distinguish between language that is used for effect and mere wordiness that stems from lack of care or judgment. The following **anecdote** was related by Benjamin Franklin to Thomas Jefferson as members of the Continental Congress undertook to trim excess words and phrases from the Declaration of Independence.

> The wise old Pennsylvanian told Jefferson, in an aside, about a hatter who was opening a shop and wanted a signboard for it. What the new proprietor had in mind was a message reading, "John Thompson, Hatter, makes and sells hats for ready money," but one of his friends suggested that the word "hatter" was superfluous. Another told him that no buyer would care who made the hats, so the word "makes" was omitted. Someone else advised him to leave out "ready money," since nobody expected to buy on credit, and yet another man said that since Thompson did not propose to give the hats away the word "sells" should go. When the sign was finally erected, Franklin smiled, all that remained was the name "John Thompson" and the picture of a hat.
>
> —Richard M. Ketchum, *The Winter Soldiers* (New York: Doubleday, 1973), p. 19.

A concise sentence is not guaranteed to be effective, but a wordy sentence always loses some of its readability and **coherence** because of the extra load it must carry. Wordiness is understandable in a first draft, but it should never survive **revision**. "I would have written a shorter letter if I'd had more time" is a truism.

CAUSES OF WORDINESS

Modifiers that repeat an idea already implicit or present in the word being modified contribute to wordiness.

Examples:	*round* circles	*tall* skyscrapers
	basic essentials	descended *down*
	hot boiling water	circle *around*
	advance planning	square *in shape*
	small *in size*	as a rule . . . *usually*
	in my opinion . . . *I think*	worthy *of merit*
	balance *of equilibrium*	the reason *is because*
	realization of a dream *come true*	this country *of ours*
	visible *to the eye*	cooperate *together*
	isolated *by himself*	
	It was an *absolutely* perfect day.	

The **gobbledygook** addict is fond of such words and phrases as *factor, case, basis, elements, field, phenomenon, in terms of, in the nature of, with reference to.* Key words that seem to invite redundancy are *situation, angle, line, factor, aspect, element, consideration, considering.* Although all these words have legitimate uses, business and technical people seem to have a particular weakness for their overuse and inexact use, under the mistaken impression that they add formality to writing.

Coordinating synonyms that merely repeat one another contribute to wordiness.

Example: We must decide *finally* and *for good* on this year's budget.

Wordiness can be caused by unnecessary or redundant phrases and clauses.

Example: Our military planes, *which are manufactured in this country,* are superior to Russian planes. (unnecessary clause)

The use of **expletives, relative pronouns**, and **relative adjectives**, although they have legitimate purposes, often results in wordiness.

Change: *There are* (expletive) many supervisors in the area *who* (relative pronoun) are planning to attend the workshop *which* (relative adjective) is scheduled for Friday.

  To: Many supervisors in the area plan to attend the workshop scheduled for Friday.

Circumlocution (a long, indirect, roundabout way of expressing things) is a leading cause of wordiness.

Change: We urge you to submit any suggestions you may have on the subject, and you may be certain that your suggestions will be given our most careful attention.

To: Please give us your suggestions. We will consider them carefully.

HOW TO ACHIEVE CONCISENESS

Conciseness can be achieved by effective use of **subordination**. This is, in fact, the best means of tightening wordy writing.

Change: The law clerk's report was carefully illustrated and it covered five pages.

To: The law clerk's five-page report was carefully illustrated.

Conciseness can be achieved by using simple words and phrases.

Change: It is the policy of the company to provide the proper equipment to enable each employee to conduct the telephonic communication necessary to discharge his responsibilities; such should not be utilized for personal communications.

To: Your telephone is provided for company business; do not use it for personal calls.

Conciseness can be achieved by eliminating undesirable **repetition**.

Change: This tuning, which is offered to all our customers at no further cost to them whatsoever, is available with each piano purchased from this company.

To: Free piano tuning is offered with each purchase.

Conciseness can be achieved by making sentences positive. (See also **positive writing**.)

Change: If the error does not involve data transmission, the special function is not used.

To: The special function is used only when the error involves data transmission.

Conciseness can sometimes be achieved by changing a sentence from the passive to the active **voice**, or by changing a sentence from the indicative to the imperative **mood**. The following example does both.

Change: Card codes are normally used when it is known that the cards are to be processed by a computer, and control punches are normally used when it is known that the cards are designed to be processed at a tab installation.

> *To:*   Use card codes when you know the cards are to be processed by a computer, and use control punches when you know they are to be processed at a tab installation.

Eliminate wordy introductory phrases or pretentious words and phrases of any kind.

> *Change:*   *In connection with* your recent accident, we must *discontinue* your insurance *due to the fact that* this is your third claim within the past year. *Inasmuch* as you were insured with us *at the time of the accident, we are prepared* to honor your claim *along the lines* of your policy.
>
> *To:*   Concerning your recent accident, we are canceling your insurance because you have filed three claims in the past year. Since you were insured with us at the time of the accident, however, we will honor your claim.

Overuse of **intensifiers** (such as *very, more, most, best, quite*) contributes to wordiness; conciseness can be achieved by eliminating them. The same is true of excessive use of **adjectives** and **adverbs**.

conclusion

A good conclusion should be concise, it should reinforce your main idea, and it should tie your writing together and end it emphatically; in short, your conclusion should make your writing sound finished. A number of methods are available to help you conclude your writing effectively.

1. *Summarize your main points.* If your project is lengthy, this type of conclusion is appropriate.
2. *Offer a value judgment.* This normally takes the form of an evaluation.

> *Example:*   In my opinion, we lead our competitors in the three most important areas of industrial education: organization, training of instructors, and quality of instruction.

3. *Recommend a course of action* (or offer a challenge).
4. *Restate the main idea of your writing.*
5. *Speculate on the implications of your ideas.* Point out the potential effect of the ideas you have presented.

> *Example:*   Integrating the present three production departments under a single manager would automatically result in the use of standard procedures and allow employees to acquire broader experience. It would therefore provide a more consistent level of quality in the publications produced.

6. *Return to your opening,* to establish a sense of unity.

Be careful not to conclude with a cliché or a platitude, such as: "While profits have increased with the introduction of this new product, *the proof is in the pudding.*" Also be careful not to introduce a new idea in your conclusion.

concrete noun

Concrete nouns, as opposed to **abstract nouns**, identify those things that can be perceived by the five senses (such as *wrench, book, house, scissors, gold, water, electricity*). The difference between abstract and concrete nouns is the difference between *durability* (abstract noun) and a *stone* (concrete noun).

There are two kinds of concrete nouns: **count nouns** and **mass nouns.** Count nouns identify things that can be counted (one *wrench,* two *books,* three *dogs,* four *houses,* five *pairs of scissors*); mass nouns identify concrete materials that cannot be counted (*coffee, air, cement, corn, steel, gold, electricity*). For information about the **case, number**, and function of concrete nouns, see **nouns**. (See also **abstract words/concrete words**.)

conjunctions

A conjunction connects words, **phrases**, or **clauses**. A conjunction can also indicate the relationship between the two elements it connects (*and* joins together, *or* selects and separates).

TYPES OF CONJUNCTIONS

A **coordinating conjunction** is a word that joins two sentence elements that have identical functions. The coordinating conjunctions are *and, but, or, for, nor, yet,* and *so.*

> *Examples:* Bill *and* John work at the Los Angeles office. (joining two **proper nouns**)
> To hear *and* to obey are two different things. (joining two phrases)
> He would like to include the test results, *but* that would make the report too long. (joining two clauses)

Correlative conjunctions are coordinating conjunctions that are used in pairs. The correlative conjunctions are *either . . . or, neither . . . nor, not only . . . but also, both . . . and,* and *whether . . . or.*

Example: Bill will arrive *either* on Wednesday *or* on Thursday.

A **subordinating conjunction** connects sentence elements of different weights, normally independent clauses and **dependent clauses**. The most frequently used are *so, although, after, because, if, where, than, since, as, unless, before, that, though, when,* and *whereas*.

Example: He left the office *after* he had finished writing the report.

A **conjunctive adverb** is an **adverb** that has the force of a conjunction because it is used to join two independent clauses. The most common conjunctive adverbs are *however, moreover, therefore, further, then, consequently, besides, accordingly, also, too*.

Example: The engine performed well in the laboratory; *however,* it failed under road conditions.

PUNCTUATING CONJUNCTIONS

Two independent clauses separated by a coordinating conjunction should have a **comma** immediately preceding the coordinating conjunction if the clauses are relatively long.

Example: The Alpha project was his third assignment, *and* it was the project that made his reputation as a project leader.

If two independent clauses that are joined by a coordinating conjunction have commas within them, a **semicolon** may precede the conjunction.

Example: Even though the schedule is tight, we must meet our deadline; *and* all the staff, including programmers, will have to work overtime this week.

Two main clauses that are joined by a conjunctive adverb require a semicolon before and a comma after the conjunctive adverb. The conjunctive adverb both connects and modifies. As a **modifier**, it is part of one of the two clauses that it connects. The use of the semicolon makes it a part of the clause it modifies.

Example: The building was not finished on the scheduled date; *nevertheless,* Rogers moved in and began to conduct the business of the department from the unfinished offices.

CONJUNCTIONS IN TITLES

Conjunctions in the titles of books, articles, plays, movies, and so on should not be capitalized unless they are the first or last word in the title.

Example: The book *Technical and Professional Writing* was edited by Herman Estrin.

(See also **capital letters.**)

conjunctive adverb

A *conjunctive adverb* is an **adverb** because it modifies the **clause** that it introduces; it operates as a **conjunction** because it joins two independent clauses. The most common conjunctive adverbs are *however, moreover, therefore, further, then, consequently, besides, accordingly, also,* and *too.*

Example: The engine performed well in the laboratory; *however,* it failed under road conditions.

The two independent clauses that are joined by a conjunctive adverb require a **semicolon** before and a **comma** after the conjunctive adverb. The conjunctive adverb both connects and modifies. As a **modifier**, it is part of one of the two clauses that it connects, and the use of the semicolon makes it a part of the clause that it modifies.

Example: The new project is almost completed and is already over cost estimates; *however,* we must emphasize the importance of adequate drainage.

connected with/in connection with

Connected with and *in connection with* are wordy **phrases** that can usually be replaced by *in* or *with.*

Change: He is *connected with* the First National Bank.
  To: He is with the First National Bank.
  Or: He is employed by the First National Bank.
Change: The fringe benefits *in connection with* (or *connected with*) the job are quite good.
  To: The fringe benefits with the job are quite good.

connectives

The word *connective* is a general term for any word or **phrase** that is used to tie the parts of a **sentence** together or to indicate **subordination** or coordination between the parts of a sentence. Connectives include **conjunctions, prepositions,** and **conjunctive adverbs.**

TYPES OF CONNECTIVES

A **coordinating conjunction** joins two sentence elements that have identical functions and equal importance within the sentence. The most common coordinating conjunctions are *and, but, or, for, nor, yet,* and *so.*

Correlative conjunctions are coordinating conjunctions that are used in pairs to connect parallel constructions. The most common correlative conjunctions are *either . . . or, neither . . . nor, not only . . . but also, both . . . and,* and *whether . . . or.*

A **subordinating conjunction** connects sentence elements of different importance, often independent **clauses** and **dependent clauses**. The most common subordinating conjunctions are *so, although, after, because, if, where, than, since, as, unless, before, that, though, when,* and *whereas.*

A preposition is a connective that is used to show the relationship of a **noun** or noun equivalent, the **object** of the preposition, to some other part of the sentence. The most common prepositions are *after, about, because, before, beside, but, for, since, until, across, among, against, into, at, by, between, with, in, on, to, during, under, over, through, throughout,* and *without.* (See **prepositional phrase.**)

A conjunctive adverb is an **adverb** that has the force of a conjunction because it is used to join two independent clauses. The most common conjunctive adverbs are *however, moreover, therefore, further, then, consequently, besides, also, accordingly,* and *too.*

PUNCTUATING CONNECTIVES

Two independent clauses separated by a coordinating conjunction should have a **comma** immediately preceding the coordinating conjunction if the clauses are relatively long.

> *Example:*   I am glad I accepted the job at IBM, *and* I hope to advance rapidly there.

If two independent clauses that are joined by a coordinating conjunction have commas within them, a **semicolon** may precede the conjunction.

> *Example:*   Even though the schedule is tight, we must meet our deadline; *and* all the staff, including programmers, will have to work overtime this week.

Two main clauses that are joined by a conjunctive adverb require a semicolon before and a comma after the conjunctive adverb. The conjunctive adverb both connects and modifies. As a **modifier**, it is part of one of the two clauses that it connects. Use of the semicolon makes it a part of the clause it modifies.

> *Example:* The new office building was not finished on the scheduled date; *nevertheless,* the department moved in and began to conduct business from the unfinished offices.

Subordinating conjunctions, prepositions, and correlative conjunctions do not normally require **punctuation**.

> *Examples:* The tests were postponed *because* the equipment had not arrived. (subordinating conjunction)
> He did not receive the contract because the competition was too much *for* him. (preposition)
> It seemed that every piece tested was *either* too soft *or* too brittle. (correlative conjunction)

connotation/denotation

The *connotation* of a word is its suggested meaning beyond its primary **dictionary** definition. Words are often enriched by emotional overtones or given special meanings by regional or ethnic uses. The same word may have different connotations, depending upon the circumstances in which it is used. Would the word *bastard,* for example, mean the same thing at a neighborhood bar and in a courtroom? Likewise, the same object can be referred to by a variety of different terms that represent a wide range of connotations.

> *Example:* cur, mongrel, mutt, pooch, dog, canine, German shepherd

Be aware of the connotations of the words you use so you can anticipate your reader's reaction to them. It is wise to avoid words with ambiguous connotations. If you state that an item is *cheap,* for example, your **reader** might infer that the item is not only "inexpensive" but also "shoddy," or of poor workmanship. To help determine a word's connotation, consult your dictionary.

The *denotation* of a word is its literal or primary dictionary meaning, stripped of all emotional overtones.

> *Examples:* A bitch is the female of the dog, wolf, or fox.
> Communism is a socioeconomic system that aims at a classless society.

In most writing, it is important to choose words with denotative meanings that are as free as possible from misleading overtones.

Otherwise, the context surrounding a word must carry the burden
of clarifying the word's meaning. When you considered the word
bastard, you judged its meaning by the circumstances (courtroom,
neighborhood bar) or the context in which the word was used. Context affects both the denotation and connotation of a word. A word
may have several denotative meanings, and the context must then
make clear which one is intended.

> *Examples:* The hockey player executed a good *check.*
> The banker verified the *check.*
> The chess champion was in *check* three times, but eventually
> won the match.
> The driver was told to *check* the oil.

The connotation of a word depends entirely upon context. The
same words, therefore, may be considered derogatory or obscene in
one context but quite innocent in another.

> *Example:* The novel concerned a bastard's attempt to cope with his illegit-
> imacy.

consensus of opinion

Since *consensus* normally means "harmony of opinion," the **phrase**
consensus of opinion is redundant. The word *consensus* can only be
used of a group, never one or two people.

> *Change:* The *consensus of opinion* of the members was that the commit-
> tee should change its name.
> *To:* The *consensus* of the members was that the committee
> should change its name.

contact

The use of *contact* as a **verb** to mean "consult, confer, telephone,
speak to, or look up" should be avoided. As a verb, *contact* is too
vague; it also carries a negative **connotation** for some people who
associate the word with aggression. Unless you need to be vague,
substitute a term that means exactly what is intended.

> *Change:* I will *contact* him when I am in Boston.
> *To:* I will telephone him when I am in Boston.

continual/continuous

Continual means "happening over and over" or "frequently repeated."

Example: Writing well requires *continual* practice.

Continuous means "occurring without interruption" or "unbroken."

Example: He has been writing *continuously* for an hour.

contractions

A contraction is a shortened spelling of a word or **phrase** with an **apostrophe** substituting for the missing letters.

Term	Contraction
cannot	can't
will not	won't
have not	haven't
it is	it's

Contractions are often used in speech but should be used discriminatingly in **reports**, formal letters, and most business and technical writing. (See also **formal writing style** and **informal writing style**.)

coordinating conjunction

A coordinating conjunction is a word that joins two **sentence** elements that have identical functions. The coordinating conjunctions include *and, but, or, for, nor, yet,* and *so.*

Example: The first impact of the cutback was on the purchasing department, *but* it is now making itself felt in our department as well.

Coordinating conjunctions can join words, **phrases**, or **clauses** of equal rank.

Examples: Only crabs *and* sponges managed to escape the red tide. (words)
Our twin objectives are to increase sales *and* to lower production costs. (phrases)
The average city dweller in the United States now has 0.17 parts per million of lead in his blood, *and* the amount is increasing yearly. (clauses)

Under normal circumstances, use coordinating conjunctions only to connect **parallel structures**. Otherwise, the result is likely to be faulty coordination.

copyright

Copyright is the right of exclusive ownership by an author or an artist of the benefits resulting from the publication of his work. This right, which is protected for twenty-eight years in the United States, may be renewed by the creator or his estate for an additional twenty-eight years. After the second period, the work becomes "public domain" and may be published or reproduced by anyone without compensation to the author or his estate. For a number of years, however, Congress has extended the copyright coverage on a year-to-year basis; therefore, you cannot be certain that a copyrighted work is in the public domain simply because it is more than fifty-six years old. If you are in doubt about a copyrighted work, check it by writing to the Copyright Office, Library of Congress, Washington, D.C. 20559. There is a search fee for this service.

Copyright rules are extremely complicated. As a general rule, however, a small amount of material from a copyrighted source may be used for illustrative purposes without permission, but the copyright laws set no legal limit. As a rule of thumb, material totaling not more than two hundred words from one source may be used freely.

Published work must bear a notice of copyright. Immediately after publication, two copies of the work (along with an application for registration and a registration fee) must be submitted to the Copyright Office of the Library of Congress.

If you use copyrighted source material in your research, be aware of the following restrictions.

1. A copyrighted work cannot be legally reproduced by any method without the copyright holder's permission.

2. An unpublished work that an author submits to a publisher or to friends is covered by a common-law copyright arrangement. Such works need not bear an official copyright notice but should include a notice that the contents are not for circulation or publication.

3. Works of art that are incorporated into manufactured products can be copyrighted if they are considered purely as works of art.

correlative conjunction

Correlative conjunctions are **coordinating conjunctions** that are used in pairs. The correlative conjunctions are *either . . . or, neither*

... nor, not only ... but also, both ... and, and *whether ... or.*

> *Examples:* The shipment will arrive *either* on Wednesday *or* on Thursday.
> The shipment contains the parts *not only* for the seven ma-
> chines scheduled this month *but also* for those scheduled next
> month.

To add not only symmetry but logic to your writing, follow correlative conjunctions with parallel **sentence** elements (such as *on Wednesday* and *on Thursday* in the previous example).

A problem can develop with correlative conjunctions joining a
singular **noun** to a plural noun. The problem is with the **verb**. If you
use this construction, make the verb agree with the nearest noun.

> *Example:* Neither the treasurer nor his *associates deny* his guilt. ("Neither
> the treasurer nor his associates denies his guilt" would be
> grammatically incorrect.)

A common solution is to change the construction of the sentence.

> *Example:* His guilt is denied by neither the treasurer nor his associates.

correspondence

Business letters and **memorandums** were once extremely formal;
today, however, business correspondence is more informal and conversational. (See also **business writing style**.) Some letters, such as
contracts in letter form, are still very formal and impersonal; however, most now adopt a more personal **point of view**.

Regardless of the **tone** of a letter, the primary requirement is that
its meaning must be conveyed in a direct and clear manner. Good
letter writers strive to write in a style that is so clear that their
message cannot be misunderstood. **Clarity** should be your primary
goal in business correspondence. Unfortunately, clarity is often missing in letters and memos; consequently, inestimable hours are
wasted daily in American business and industry. It is all too common, for example, for a technical specialist or business executive to
make a proposal, have it misinterpreted, then restate it in different
terms, only to have the second version misinterpreted as well.

There are no shortcuts to achieving clarity in letters and memos.
However, clear and effective writing *can* be achieved through proper
application of the writing process—**preparation, research, organization, writing the draft**, and **revision** (see also the Checklist of the

Writing Process). Although these steps may be greatly reduced in scale and performed quickly for small letters and memos (**outlining**, for example, may be simply a matter of jotting down the main points of your intended communication and then arranging them in a logical sequence), they cannot be bypassed if you wish to write effective letters. By following the steps of the writing process, you can be assured of a good end product, and you can save your employer the expense of misunderstandings.

TYPES OF LETTERS

There are almost as many "types" of letters as there are reasons for writing them. When you apply for a job, for example, you often write a letter of application (see **application, letter of**). If you get the job, you may need to write a letter of acceptance (see **acceptance, letter of**). On the job, you may write a letter providing technical information, or you may write a letter requesting information (see **technical information, letter of** and **inquiry, letter of**). Because they are so common, this book discusses each of these types in its own entry. For other types of letters, you should rely on the Checklist of the Writing Process—concentrating on analysis of your **reader** and **objective**.

PHYSICAL APPEARANCE

Since your reader is aware of the physical appearance of your letter before anything else, any letter you sign should be neat and well organized. A good **format** will indicate to the reader that your message is likely to be well organized and clear. Neatness is more important than the particular typing style you select..

TYPING STYLES

Since there are many different typing styles for letters, you should check first to see whether your employer (or instructor) prefers a particular style (most companies provide printed forms for memos). If so, use it; if not, you may use one of the following typical forms. You may also wish to check a secretarial handbook for specific suggestions about other mechanical details. A good one is the *Reference Manual for Stenographers and Typists*, 4th ed., by Ruth E. Gavin and William A. Sabin (New York: McGraw-Hill Book Company, 1970).

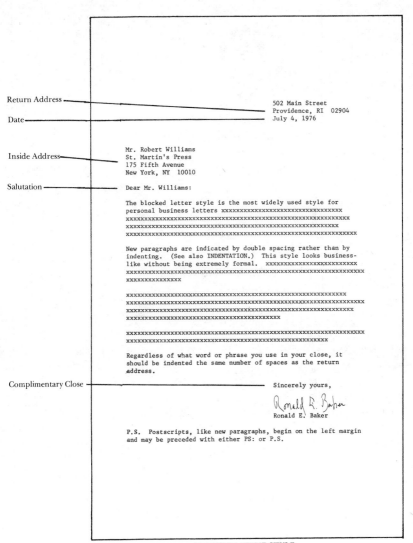

Return Address

Date

Inside Address

Salutation

Complimentary Close

502 Main Street
Providence, RI 02904
July 4, 1976

Mr. Robert Williams
St. Martin's Press
175 Fifth Avenue
New York, NY 10010

Dear Mr. Williams:

The blocked letter style is the most widely used style for
personal business letters xxxxxxxxxxxxxxxxxxxxxxxxxxxxxxx
xxxxxxxxxxxxxxxxxxxxxxxxxxxxxxxxxxxxxxxxxxxxxxxxxxxxxxxxxx
xxxxxxxxxxxxxxxxxxxxxxxxxxxxxxxxxxxxxxxxxxxxxxxxxxxxxxxxx
xxxxxxxxxxxxxxxxxxxxxxxxxxxxxxxxxxxxxxxxxxxxxxxxxxxxxxxxxxxx

New paragraphs are indicated by double spacing rather than by
indenting. (See also INDENTATION.) This style looks businesslike without being extremely formal. xxxxxxxxxxxxxxxxxxxxxxxxx
xxxxxxxxxxxxxxxxxxxxxxxxxxxxxxxxxxxxxxxxxxxxxxxxxxxxxxxxxxxxxxx
xxxxxxxxxxxxxxx

xxxxxxxxxxxxxxxxxxxxxxxxxxxxxxxxxxxxxxxxxxxxxxxxxxxxxxxxxxxxx
xxxxxxxxxxxxxxxxxxxxxxxxxxxxxxxxxxxxxxxxxxxxxxxxxxxxxxxxxxxxxxxx
xxxxxxxxxxxxxxxxxxxxxxxxxxxxxxxxxxxxxxxxxxxxxxxxxxxxxxxxxxxxxx
xxxxxxxxxxxxxxxxxxxxxxxxxxxxxxxxxxxxxxxxx

xxxxxxxxxxxxxxxxxxxxxxxxxxxxxxxxxxxxxxxxxxxxxxxxxxxxxxxxxxxxxxxx
xxxxxxxxxxxxxxxxxxxxxxxxxxxxxxxxxxxxxxxxxxxxxxxxxxxxxxxx

Regardless of what word or phrase you use in your close, it
should be indented the same number of spaces as the return
address.

                                        Sincerely yours,

                                        Ronald E. Baker
                                        Ronald E. Baker

P.S. Postscripts, like new paragraphs, begin on the left margin
and may be preceded with either PS: or P.S.

BLOCKED LETTER STYLE
(Without company letterhead)

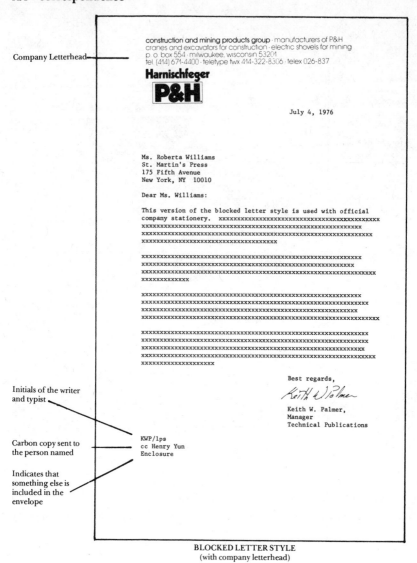

Company Letterhead

construction and mining products group · manufacturers of P&H
cranes and excavators for construction · electric shovels for mining
p. o. box 554 · milwaukee, wisconsin 53201
tel. (414) 671-4400 · teletype twx 414-322-8306 · telex 026-837

Harnischfeger

P&H

July 4, 1976

Ms. Roberta Williams
St. Martin's Press
175 Fifth Avenue
New York, NY 10010

Dear Ms. Williams:

This version of the blocked letter style is used with official
company stationery. xxxxxxxxxxxxxxxxxxxxxxxxxxxxxxxxxxxxxxxxxxxxxx
xxxxxxxxxxxxxxxxxxxxxxxxxxxxxxxxxxxxxxxxxxxxxxxxxxxxxxxxxxxxxx
xxxxxxxxxxxxxxxxxxxxxxxxxxxxxxxxxxxxxxxxxxxxxxxxxxxxxxxxxxxxxxxxx
xxxxxxxxxxxxxxxxxxxxxxxxxxxxxxxxxxxxxx

xxxxxxxxxxxxxxxxxxxxxxxxxxxxxxxxxxxxxxxxxxxxxxxxxxxxxxxxxxxxxxx
xxxxxxxxxxxxxxxxxxxxxxxxxxxxxxxxxxxxxxxxxxxxxxxxxxxxxxxxxxxx
xxxxxxxxxxxxxxxxxxxxxxxxxxxxxxxxxxxxxxxxxxxxxxxxxxxxxxxxxxxxxxxxxx
xxxxxxxxxxxxxx

xxxxxxxxxxxxxxxxxxxxxxxxxxxxxxxxxxxxxxxxxxxxxxxxxxxxxxxxxxxxxxx
xxxxxxxxxxxxxxxxxxxxxxxxxxxxxxxxxxxxxxxxxxxxxxxxxxxxxxxxxxxxxxxxxx
xxxxxxxxxxxxxxxxxxxxxxxxxxxxxxxxxxxxxxxxxxxxxxxxxxxxxxxxxxx
xxxxxxxxxxxxxxxxxxxxxxxxxxxxxxxxxxxxxxxxxxxxxxxxxxxxxxxxxxxxxxxxxxxx

xxxxxxxxxxxxxxxxxxxxxxxxxxxxxxxxxxxxxxxxxxxxxxxxxxxxxxxxxxxxxxxxxx
xxxxxxxxxxxxxxxxxxxxxxxxxxxxxxxxxxxxxxxxxxxxxxxxxxxxxxxxxxxxxx
xxxxxxxxxxxxxxxxxxxxxxxxxxxxxxxxxxxxxxxxxxxxxxxxxxxxxxxxxxxxx
xxxxxxxxxxxxxxxxxxxxxxxxxxxxxxxxxxxxxxxxxxxxxxxxxxxxxxxxxxxxxxxx
xxxxxxxxxxxxxxxxxxxxxx

Best regards,

Keith W. Palmer,
Manager
Technical Publications

Initials of the writer
and typist

KWP/lps
cc Henry Yun
Enclosure

Carbon copy sent to
the person named

Indicates that
something else is
included in the
envelope

BLOCKED LETTER STYLE
(with company letterhead)

count noun

Count nouns, as opposed to **mass nouns**, identify persons, places, or
things that can be separated into individual units and counted.

construction and mining products group · manufacturers of P&H
cranes and excavators for construction · electric shovels for mining
p. o. box 554 · milwaukee, wisconsin 53201
tel. (414) 671-4400 · teletype twx 414-322-8306 · telex 026-837

Harnischfeger

P&H

July 4, 1976

Mrs. Roberta Williams
St. Martin's Press
175 Fifth Avenue
New York, NY 10010

Dear Mrs. Williams

The full-blocked (or extreme block) style is the fastest style to
type because each line begins at the left margin. Sometimes a
subject line is placed between the salutation and the first line
of writing. Full-blocked style usually omits the colon after the
salutation.

The full-blocked style is used only on company stationery. xxxxx
xxxxxxxxxxxxxxxxxxxxxxxxxxxxxxxxxxxxxxxxxxxxxxxxxxxxxxxxxxxxxxxxxx
xxxxxxxxxxxxxxxxxxxxxxxxxxxxxxxxxxxxxxxxxxxxxxxxxxxxxxxxxxxxxxxxxx
xxxxxxxxxxxxxxxxxxxxxxxxxxxxxxxxxxxxxxxxxxxxxxxxxxxxxxxxxxxxxxxx
xxxxxxxxxxxxxxxxxx

xxxxxxxxxxxxxxxxxxxxxxxxxxxxxxxxxxxxxxxxxxxxxxxxxxxxxxxxxxxxxxxx
xxxxxxxxxxxxxxxxxxxxxxxxxxxxxxxxxxxxxxxxxxxxxxxxxxxxxxxxxxxxxx
xxxxxxxxxxxxxxxxxxxxxxxxxxxxxxxxxxxxxxxxxxxxxxxxxxxxxxxxxxxxxxxxx
xxxxxxxxxxxxxxxxxxxxxxxxxxxxxxxxxxxxxxxxxx

xxxxxxxxxxxxxxxxxxxxxxxxxxxxxxxxxxxxxxxxxxxxxxxxxxxxxxxxxxxxxxxx
xxxxxxxxxxxxxxxxxxxxxxxxxxxxxxxxxxxxxxxxxxxxxxxxxxxxxxxxxxxxxxxxxx
xxxxxxxxxxxxxxxxxxxxxxxxxxxxxxxxxxxxxxxxxxxxxxxxxxxxxxxx

Cordially,

Keith W. Palmer

Keith W. Palmer,
Manager
Technical Publications

KWP/lps
cc Henry F. Yun
   Ronald E. Baker
   File

Indicates one copy to
the permanent file

FULL-BLOCKED LETTER STYLE

Example: There were four *calculators* in the office.

For information about the **case, number**, and function of count
nouns, see **nouns**. (See also **fewer/less**.)

credible/creditable

Something is *credible* if it is believable.

Example: The statistics in this report are *credible*.

Something is *creditable* if it is worthy of praise or credit.

Example: The chief engineer did a *creditable* job.

criterion/criteria/criterions

Criterion means "an established standard for judging or testing." *Criteria* and *criterions* are both acceptable plural forms of *criterion*, but *criteria* is generally preferred.

> *Example:*   In evaluating this job, we must use three *criteria*. The most important *criterion* is quality of workmanship.

critique

A *critique* (**noun**) is a written or oral evaluation of something. The word is occasionally encountered as a **verb** meaning "to criticize," but many people dislike this usage.

> *Change:*   Please *critique* his job description as soon as possible.
> *To:*   Please prepare a *critique* of his job description as soon as possible.
> *Or:*   Please *criticize* his job description as soon as possible.

D

dangling modifiers

Verbal phrases (**gerund, participial, infinitive**) which do not clearly and logically refer to the proper **noun** or **pronoun** are called *dangling modifiers*.

DANGLING GERUND PHRASE

A dangling gerund phrase can be corrected by adding a noun or a pronoun for it to modify.

> *Change:*   After finishing the research, the job was easy.
> *To:*   After finishing the research, *we* found the job to be easy.

Another way to correct a dangling gerund phrase is to make the phrase a **clause**.

> *Change:*   After finishing the research, the job was easy.
> *To:*   After we finished the research, the job was easy.
> *Or:*   The job was easy after we finished the research.

DANGLING PARTICIPIAL PHRASE

A dangling **participial phrase** (a participial phrase that has no noun or pronoun for the phrase to modify) can be corrected by providing a subject that stands near the phrase.

> *Change:*   Keeping busy, the afternoon passed swiftly.
> *To:*   Keeping busy, *I* felt that the afternoon passed swiftly.

A dangling participial phrase may also be corrected by making the phrase a clause.

> *Change:*   Keeping busy, the afternoon passed swiftly.
> *To:*   Because I kept busy, the afternoon passed swiftly.
> *Change:*   Entering the gate, the administration building is visible.
> *To:*   As you enter the gate, the administration building is visible.

DANGLING INFINITIVE PHRASE

Correct a dangling infinitive phrase by supplying the missing noun or pronoun that provides the subject of the **infinitive phrase**.

> *Change:*   To improve typing skills, practice is needed.
> *To:*   To improve typing skills, *you* must practice.
> *Change:*   To evaluate the feasibility of the project, the centralized plan will be compared with the present system of dispersing facility sites.
> *To:*   To evaluate the feasibility of the project, the *committee* will compare the centralized plan with the present system of dispersing facility sites.

DANGLING SUBORDINATE CLAUSE

Occasionally a subject and verb are omitted from a **dependent clause**, forming what is known as an *elliptical clause*. If the omitted subject of the elliptical clause is not the same as the subject of the main clause, the construction dangles. Simply adding the subject and verb to the elliptical clause solves the problem.

> *Change:*   When ten years old, his father started the company.
> *To:*   When *Bill Krebs was* ten years old, his father started the company.
> *Or:*   Bill was ten years old when his father started the company.

(See also **misplaced modifiers**.)

dash

The *dash* is a versatile, yet limited, mark of **punctuation**. It is versatile because it can perform all the duties of punctuation (to link, to separate, to enclose, and to show omission). It is limited because it is an especially emphatic mark that is easily overused. Use the dash cautiously, therefore, to indicate more informality or **emphasis** (a dash gives an impression of abruptness) than would be achieved by the conventional punctuation marks. In some situations, a dash is required; in others, a dash is a forceful substitute for other marks.

A dash can indicate a sharp turn in thought.

Example: That was the end of the project—unless the company provided additional funds.

A dash can indicate an emphatic pause.

Examples: Consider the potential danger of a household item that contains mercury—a very toxic substance.
The job will be done—after we are under contract.

Sometimes, to emphasize contrast, a dash is also used with *but.*

Example: We may have produced work more quickly—but the result was not as good.

A dash can be used before a final summarizing statement or before **repetition** that has the effect of an afterthought.

Example: It was hot near the ovens—steaming hot.

Such a thought may also complete the meaning.

Example: We try to speak as we write—or so we believe.

A dash can be used to set off an explanatory or appositive series.

Example: Three of the applicants—John Evans, Mary Stevens, and Thomas Brown—seem well qualified for the job.

Dashes set off parenthetical elements more sharply and emphatically than do **commas**. Unlike dashes, **parentheses** tend to reduce the importance of what they enclose. Compare the following sentences.

Examples: Only one person—the president—can authorize such activity.
Only one person, the president, can authorize such activity.
Only one person (the president) can authorize such activity.

Use dashes for clarity when commas appear within a parenthetical element; this avoids the confusion of too many commas.

Example: Retinal images are patterns in the eye—made up of light and dark shapes, in addition to areas of color—but we do not see patterns; we see objects.

A dash can be used to set off a title or author's name from a **quotation.**

> *Example:* "Winning is not everything, it's the only thing"—Vince Lombardi. (Notice that the dash goes outside the quotation and the final mark of punctuation in the quotation is omitted.)

A dash can be used to show the omission of words or letters.

> *Example:* Mr. A— told me to be careful.

The first word after a dash is never capitalized unless it is a proper name.

When typing, use two consecutive **hyphens** (--) to indicate a dash.

data

The debate over whether *data* is a plural noun or a collective singular rages on. In most writing, *data* is considered a collective singular. In strictly formal scientific and scholarly writing, however, *data* is generally used as a plural, with *datum* as the singular form.

> *Examples:* The *data are* voluminous in support of a link between smoking and lung cancer. (formal)
> The *data is* now ready to be evaluated. (less formal)

Base your decision upon whether your **reader** should consider the data as a single collection or as a group of individual facts. Whatever you decide, be sure that your pronouns and verbs agree in number with the selected usage.

> *Examples:* The *data are* voluminous. *They indicate* a link between smoking and lung cancer.
> The *data is* now ready for evaluation. *It is* in the mail.

dates

In business and industry, dates have traditionally been indicated by the month, day, and year, with a **comma** separating the figures.

> *Example:* October 26, 1975.

Increasingly, however, business and industry are adopting the military day-month-year system that does not require commas.

> *Example:* 26 October 1975

The strictly numerical form for dates (10/26/75) should be used sparingly, and never on business letters or formal documents, since it is less immediately clear. When this form is used, the order in American usage is always month/day/year. For example, 5/7/76 is May 7, 1976.

CENTURIES

Confusion often occurs because the spelled-out names of centuries do not correspond to the numbers of the years.

> *Examples:* The twentieth century is the 1900s (1900–1999).
> The nineteenth century is the 1800s (1800–1899).
> The fifth century is the 400s (400–499).

(See also **A.D.** and **numbers**.)

decided/decisive

When something is *decided* it is "clear-cut," "without doubt," "unmistakable." When something is *decisive* it is "conclusive" or "has the power to settle a dispute."

> *Example:* The executive committee's *decisive* action gave our firm a *decided* advantage over the competition.

decreasing order of importance as a method of development

Decreasing order of importance is a **method of development** in which the writer's major points are arranged in descending order of importance. It begins with the most important fact or point, then goes to the next most important, and so on, ending with the least important. It is an especially appropriate method of development for a **report** addressed to a busy decision-maker, who may be able to reach a decision after considering only the most important points, or for a report addressed to various readers, some of whom may be interested only in the major points and others in all of the points.

The advantages of this method of development are that (1) it gets the reader's attention immediately by presenting the most important point first, (2) it makes a strong initial impression, and (3) it ensures that the hurried reader will not miss the most important point.

de facto/de jure

De facto means that something "exists" or is "a fact" and therefore must be accepted for practical purposes. *De jure* means that something "legally" or "rightfully" should or does exist.

> *Example:* The law states that no signs should be erected along Highway 127. Store owners have disregarded this law, and, therefore, many signs exist along Highway 127. The presence of the signs along Highway 127 is *de facto* but not *de jure*—it is "a fact" but it is not "lawful."

defective/deficient

If something is *defective* it is faulty.

> *Example:* The wiring was *defective*.

If something is *deficient* it lacks a necessary ingredient.

> *Example:* The compound was found to be *deficient* in calcium.

defining terms

The first rule of good writing is to help the **reader**. To do this, keep your reader's level of technical knowledge in mind and define any term that might not be understood.

A term is defined by placing it in a category and showing how it differs from other things in that category.

> *Examples:* An *airplane* (term) is a *machine* (category) that *flies* (difference). A *lease* (term) is a *contract* (category) that *conveys real estate for a term of years at a specified rent* (difference).

Avoid circular explanations that merely restate the term (such as "A rectifier tube rectifies.") and therefore fail to clarify the concept under discussion.

Definitions should normally be positive; focus on what the thing being defined is rather than what it is not. For example, "The kangaroo is not an American animal" could just as easily be stated "The *kangaroo* (term) is an *Australian animal* (category) with a *pouch*" (difference).

Avoid *is when, is how,* and *is where* definitions, as in "A collision is when two cars run into each other." This is not really a definition at all, since it has neither category nor difference.

Change: A contract is when people agree to something.
    To: A contract is a binding agreement between two or more persons or parties.

If a report contains a great many terms that must be defined, consider including a **glossary** of terms and definitions at the end. (See also **definition as a form of writing**.)

definite/definitive

Definite and *definitive* both apply to what is "precisely defined," but *definitive* more often refers to what is complete and authoritative.

Example: When the committee took a *definite* stand, the president made it the *definitive* company policy.

definition as a form of writing

Definition is the purpose of much business and technical writing because businesses and technologies are continually creating new terms and using familiar terms and concepts in new ways, and these terms and concepts must be defined for the **reader**. Whether you provide a brief or extended definition will depend primarily on your reader's present knowledge of the material. Sometimes one or more **paragraphs** should be devoted to defining a concept; other times you may need only a sentence definition in the body of the material or in a **glossary** at the end. But if a term is crucial to your discussion, don't take any chances—define it the first time you use it.

A variety of techniques may be employed in definition, but all definitions place a term in a category and show how it differs from other things in the category.

Example: A *lease* (term) is a *contract* (category) that *conveys real estate for a term of years at a specified rent* (difference).

(See also **defining terms**.)

A brief definition like the one in this example often needs to be extended by the use of a paragraph, or even several, to clarify the "difference." Whether you write a sentence definition or an extended sentence definition, make sure that the "categories" and "differences" are expressed in terms the reader can understand—if not, you defeat the purpose of definition. Sometimes, however, you may not need to provide a complete definition; you can clarify the meaning of a term simply by giving a **synonym** familiar to the reader.

Example: A *consignment* (term) is a *shipment* (synonym).

Occasionally, it is helpful to clarify a term by explaining its origin, which you can find in a good **dictionary**.

Example: "Diastrophism" comes from the Greek word *diastrophe* meaning "distortion," and it is applied to the distortion of the earth's crust that created oceans and mountains.

Sometimes it is helpful to point out what something *is not* in order to clarify what it *is*.

Example: A hydraulic crane is *not* like a lattice boom friction crane in one very important way. In most cases, the safe lifting capacity of a lattice boom crane is based on *the weight needed to tip the machine*. Therefore, operators of friction machines sometimes depend on signs that the machine might tip to warn them of impending danger.
   This is a very dangerous thing to do with a hydraulic crane. . . .

   —*Safe Operating Practices*, Harnischfeger Corporation, p. 26.

Extended definition may be accomplished by first defining an item, then following with concrete examples of the thing being defined. In fact, almost any **method of development** can extend a definition. For example, you might clarify a definition by dividing the subject into its component parts; that is, by using **analysis as a method of development**. Or you may use **comparison as a method of development** to point out similarities between the thing being defined and something familiar to the reader. **Cause and effect** might also be used to expand a definition; magnetism, for example, might be further identified by a discussion of its effects, or a disease by a discussion of its causes. Whatever method of development you use to expand a definition, be sure to provide both a category and a difference (or differences)—without these elements, there can be no complete definition.

In the following example from a crane operator's manual, *model W-180* is the term and *crane* is the category. Differences are specified by *self-propelled, rubber-tired, rough-terrain,* and *full-hydraulic.* The remaining explanation extends these elements.

Example: The model W-180 is a self-propelled, rubber-tired, rough-terrain, full-hydraulic crane, with the operator's cab mounted on the revolving frame. The operator's cab contains all the controls necessary to operate the crane and to drive the machine from job site to job site.

Power from the engine is transmitted to a power shift transmission through a torque converter which multiplies the engine torque to meet varying load requirements. The power shift transmission is a forward and reverse transmission that provides four speeds in either direction. From the transmission the power is transmitted to the front and rear axles by propeller shafts. The transmission is also equipped with a transfer case that allows the machine to be driven by only two wheels or all four wheels.

Hydraulic pumps mounted on the transmission and engine supply hydraulic fluid, under pressure, to all hydraulically powered machine functions. In addition to the hydraulic pumps, an engine driven air compressor supplies air pressure for actuating the vehicle brakes, shifting the transmission, controlling the engine throttle, and applying the swing brake.

—*Operator's Manual (Model W-180)*, Harnischfeger Corporation.

demonstrative adjective

The demonstrative adjectives are *this, these, that,* and *those.* They are adjectives that "point to" the thing they modify, specifying its position in space or time. *This* and *these* specify closer position; *that* and *those* specify more remote position.

> *Examples:*   *This* proposal is the one we accepted.
> *That* proposal would have been impracticable.
> *These* problems remain to be solved.
> *Those* problems are not insurmountable.

Notice that *this* and *that* are used with singular **nouns** and that *these* and *those* are used with plural nouns. Demonstrative adjectives often cause problems when they modify the nouns *kind, type,* and *sort.* Demonstrative adjectives used with these nouns should agree with them in **number**.

> *Examples:*   this kind   these kinds
> that type   those types
> this sort   these sorts

Confusion often develops when the **preposition** *of* is added ("this kind *of*," "these kinds *of*") and the object of the preposition is not made to conform in number to the demonstrative adjective and its noun.

> *Change:*   *This kind* of hydraulic *cranes* is best.
> *To:*   *This kind* of hydraulic *crane* is best.

Change: *These kinds* of hydraulic *crane* are best.
To: *These kinds* of hydraulic *cranes* are best.

The error can be avoided by remembering to make the demonstrative adjective, the noun, and the **object** of the preposition—all three —agree in number. This not only makes the sentence correct but more precise.

Using demonstrative adjectives with words like *kind*, *type*, and *sort* is often a form of laziness that can easily lead to vagueness. It is better to be more specific.

For recommendations on the placement and usage of demonstrative adjectives, see **adjectives**.

demonstrative pronoun

Demonstrative pronouns are actually the same words as **demonstrative adjectives** but they differ in usage (a demonstrative adjective modifies a **noun**, a demonstrative pronoun substitutes for a noun). The antecedent of a demonstrative pronoun must be the last noun of the preceding sentence—not the idea of the sentence—or it must be clearly identified within the same sentence.

Examples: *This* is the *specification* as we wrote it.
These are the *statistics* we needed to begin the project.
That was a *proposal* for drilling a water well.
Those were *salesmen*.

Notice that, as with demonstrative adjectives, *this* and *that* are used for singular nouns and *these* and *those* for plural nouns.

dependent clause

A dependent (or subordinate) clause is a group of words that has a **subject** and a **verb** but nonetheless depends upon a main **clause** to complete its meaning. A dependent clause can act as a unit and function in a **sentence** as a **noun**, an **adjective**, or an **adverb**.

As nouns, dependent clauses may function in the sentence as subjects, **objects**, or **complements**.

Examples: *That human beings can learn to control their glands and internal organs by direct or indirect means* is now an established fact. (subject)
The trouble is *that we cannot finish the project by May.* (subjective complement)

I learned *that drugs ordered by brand name can cost several times as much as drugs ordered by generic name.* (direct object)

As adjectives, dependent clauses can modify nouns or pronouns. Dependent clauses are often introduced by **relative pronouns** and **relative adjectives** *(who, which, that).*

Example: The man *who called earlier* is here. (modifying "man")

As adverbs, dependent clauses may express relationships of time, cause, result, or degree.

Examples: You are making an investment *when you buy a house.* (time)
A title search was necessary *because the bank would not issue a loan without one.* (cause)
The cost of financing a home will be higher *if discount points are charged.* (result)
Monthly mortgage payments should not be much more *than a man earns in one week.* (degree)

Dependent clauses are useful in making the relationship between thoughts more precise and succinct than if the ideas were presented in a series of **simple sentences** or **compound sentences**.

Change: The sewage plant is located between Millville and Darrtown. Both villages use it. (two thoughts of approximately equal importance)
To: The sewage plant, *which is located between Millville and Darrtown,* is used by both villages. (one thought subordinated to the other)
Change: Title insurance is a policy issued by a title insurance company *and* it protects against any title defects, such as outside claimants. (two thoughts of approximately equal importance)
To: Title insurance, *which* protects against any title defects, such as outside claimants, is a policy issued by a title insurance company. (one thought subordinated to the other)

Subordinate clauses are especially effective, therefore, for expressing thoughts that describe or explain another statement, or for stating where, when, how, or why an event occurred when such facts are not immediately apparent from the context. Too much subordination, or a string of dependent clauses, however, may be worse than none at all.

Change: Since interest rates on conventional loans tend to follow general conditions in the money market, *if* money is plentiful for lending and the demand for loans is low, interest rates will be forced down, *whereas* if money is scarce and the demand for loans is high, interest rates will be forced up.

To: Interest rates on conventional loans tend to follow general
          conditions in the money market: if money is plentiful for lend-
          ing and the demand for loans is low, interest rates will be
          forced down; if money is scarce and the demand for loans is
          high, interest rates will be forced up.

Change: He had selected teachers *who* taught classes *that* had a slant *that*
          was specifically directed toward students *who* intended to go
          into business.

To: He had selected teachers *who* taught classes *that* were specifi-
          cally directed to business students.

description

Description is one of the most widely used types of business and
technical writing. The most important element of description is detail; in fact, description cannot really be achieved without the effective use of detail. In business and technical writing, description must
be objective, thorough, and precise. "The smoothest engine I have
ever heard or seen" does not describe the engine; it simply offers an
opinion about it. Good description presents details with **concrete
words**. Whenever possible avoid **abstract** or **vague words**.

Example: As the oil well is being drilled, the hole is kept full of drilling
           "mud"; the weight of the drilling mud prevents the well from
           blowing in as a gusher, and it keeps fluids from the various
           zones from entering the hole.

           Once the well has been drilled to the required depth, the
           control and protection provided by the drilling mud must be
           replaced with something more permanent, and the hole must
           be further prepared for production. This process, described
           briefly and simply, involves installing large diameter pipe,
           called casing, in the hole and then pumping cement down
           through the casing and up into the space between the casing
           and the wall of the hole (called the annulus). The process of
           placing cement around the casing throughout the depth of the
           producing formation is the primary cementing operation.

           By plugging the annulus with cement, the primary cement-
           ing operation restores the isolation that existed between the
           various fluid-bearing zones before the hole was drilled and
           prevents fluid from the different zones from contaminating
           the crude oil in the producing formation.

           —*The Baker World,* Baker Oil Tools, Inc.

When describing a mechanical device it is often helpful to give a
general description of the whole device in the **introduction** or **opening** before describing the parts in detail; such an introductory de-

scription often includes the device's function. The description which follows may then include specific details about physical characteristics of each part of the device, the location of each part in relation to the whole, and how the parts work together.

Example:

General de-
scription of the
whole device

An internal combustion engine is one in which the fuel is burned directly inside the machine which converts the heat energy into work. Practically all motor cars use this kind of engine, the fuel being petrol (gasoline). The engine consists of several cylinders in which pistons are fitted. The top of each cylinder is covered over with a head which contains a hollowed-out . . . combustion chamber. A rod connects each piston with a . . . crankshaft. The burning of fuel and air in the combustion chamber produces heat energy which causes expansion of the gases formed by the process of combustion. The gases push the pistons down the cylinder and thus cause the crankshaft to rotate. A flywheel on the end of the crankshaft keeps the latter rotating smoothly between the power impulses from each cylinder; it also transmits the power developed by the engine to the clutch.

Detailed de-
scription of the
principles of
the engine's
operation

The easiest way to understand how an engine works is to keep in mind only one cylinder. For the engine to run and do work, certain things must take place over and over again in a regular order. The fuel must be sucked in, it must be compressed and burned; the resulting gases expand, and thus do work, and after expansion they must be removed. These steps make up what is known as a cycle; in most motor car engines it takes four strokes of the piston to make up one cycle. During this time the crankshaft will have made two complete revolutions. This type of engine is said to operate on a four-stroke cycle. The four strokes of the piston are named according to what they accomplish. The first is the suction, the second the compression, the third the power, and the fourth the exhaust stroke.

Summation of
how the parts
work together
to perform the
engine's func-
tion

At the start of the suction stroke, the piston is at the top of the cylinder. It moves downward and the inlet valve opens. This sucks in the charge of gases from the carburetor. The compression stroke starts when the inlet valve closes and the piston is moving upward. The mixture is ignited while under pressure by a high-tension electric spark, which is produced across the points of the sparking plug. . . . The power stroke begins with a downward thrust of the piston. The burning of the gases gives off heat, which causes expansion. Pressure is thus exerted on the piston, forcing it downward as far as it will go. This completes the power stroke. The last movement of the piston is the exhaust stroke. The exhaust valve opens toward the end of the power stroke and most of the burned gases rush out. The piston moves upward, pushing the remaining gases out of the cylinder. The four-stroke cycle is now complete.

—*Reprinted by permission,* © *Encyclopaedia Britannica,* 14th edition (1956).

An aspect of description sometimes called "rendering" is the act of showing or demonstrating, as opposed to telling, primarily through the advantageous use of images and details. Rendering makes writing more vivid and interesting by providing the reader with more details and a sense of immediacy. This technique is especially useful to business and technical people because it can help clarify and make more concrete the complex, abstract, and sometimes subtle subjects with which they must deal. For example, the following sentence is typical of much business and technical writing.

Example: Computers can scan and read punched cards.

The complex thought contained in this sentence can be rendered clearly by the skillful use of images and details from everyday life.

Example: When information appears in print, as on this page, people like you and me are able to read and understand it. However, if information is to be processed by a machine, like a computer, then other ways must be found to put these same letters and words into the machine. Computers, of course, do not have eyes like humans—but they do have electrical sensing equipment that in certain ways does almost the same thing.

   For example, most of us have walked into supermarkets through doors that open by themselves. These doors are controlled by electrical sensing equipment known as photoelectric cells, which act like eyes. Each door is controlled by two photoelectric cells that shine a beam of light to each other. As you walk through the door, the light beam is broken causing the photoelectric cells or "eyes" to sense that someone is beginning to enter. The electric eye reacts in a split second by sending a burst of electrical energy to the door's mechanical hinge, and this automatically swings the door open.

   The photoelectric sensing idea can also be used to detect the presence of a hole in a card or piece of paper.

   Thus, if holes are punched in paper to represent certain letters of the alphabet or words, it is possible for a machine to electrically sense or read this information.

—Joseph Becker, *The First Book of Information Science* (Washington, D.C.: The U.S. Atomic Energy Commission, 1973), p. 20.

In choosing details for a description of a mechanism, keep clearly in mind the purpose for which your **reader** will use what you have written. Does the reader need to understand the construction of the mechanism, or does he or she only need to know how to operate it? Will the reader need to build it? The answers to questions such as these will help you select the appropriate details to include in your description.

despite/in spite of

Despite and *in spite of* (both meaning "notwithstanding") should not be blended into *despite of.*

> *Change:* *Despite of* our best efforts, the plan failed.
> *To:* *In spite of* (or *despite*) our best efforts, the plan failed.

Although there is no literal difference between *despite* and *in spite of, despite* suggests an effort to avoid blame.

> *Examples:* *Despite* our best efforts, the plan failed. (We are not to blame for the failure.)
> *In spite of* our best efforts, the plan failed. (We did everything possible, but failure overcame us.)

diacritical marks

Diacritical marks are **symbols** added to letters to indicate their specific sounds. They include the phonetic symbols used by **dictionaries** as well as the marks used with foreign words. Some dictionaries place a quick reference list of common marks and sounds at the bottom of each page. Following is a list of common diacritical marks with their equivalent sound values. (See also **foreign words in English**.)

Name	*Symbol*	*Example*	*Meaning*
macron	–	cāke	A "long" sound that signifies the standard pronunciation of the letter.
breve	ˇ	brăcket	A "short" sound, in contrast to the standard pronunciation of the letter.
dieresis	¨	coöperate	Indicates that the second of two consecutive vowels is to be pronounced separately.

Name	Symbol	Example	Meaning
acute	´	résumé	Indicates a primary vocal stress on the indicated letter.
grave	`	crèche	Indicates a deep sound articulated toward the back of the mouth.
circumflex	^	crêpe	Indicates a very soft sound.
tilde	~	cañon	A Spanish diacritical mark identifying the palatal nasal "ny" sound.
cedilla	¸	garçon	A mark placed beneath the letter "c" in French, Portuguese, and Spanish to indicate an "s" sound.

diagnosis/prognosis

Because they sound somewhat alike, these words are often confused with each other. *Diagnosis* means "an analysis of the nature of something" or "the conclusions reached by such analysis."

> *Example:* The chairman of the board *diagnosed* the problem as the allocation of too few dollars for research.

Prognosis means "a forecast or prediction."

> *Example:* He offered his *prognosis* that the problem would be solved next year.

diction

The term *diction* is often misunderstood because it means both "the choice of words used in writing and speech" *and* "the degree of distinctness or enunciation of speech." In discussions of writing, *diction* applies to choice of words. (See also **word choice**.)

dictionary

A dictionary lists, in alphabetical order, a selection of the words in a language. It defines them, gives their **spelling** and pronunciation, and tells their function as a **part of speech**. In addition, it provides information on a word's origin and historical development. Often it provides a list of **synonyms** for a word and, where pertinent, an **illustration** to help clarify the meaning of a word.

The explanation of a word's meaning makes up the bulk of a dictionary entry. A dictionary gives primarily denotative rather than connotative meanings. It also labels the field of knowledge to which a specific meaning applies (grid, *electricity;* merger, *law*). The order in which a word's meanings are given varies. Some dictionaries give the most widely accepted current meaning first; others list the meanings in historical order, with the oldest meaning first and the current meaning last. If a word has two or more fundamental meanings, they are listed in separate **paragraphs**, with secondary meanings numbered consecutively within each paragraph. A dictionary's preface normally indicates whether current or historical meanings are listed first in an entry.

A dictionary entry also includes a word's spelling. It lists any variant spellings (align/aline, catalog/catalogue) and indicates which is most commonly used. Entries show if and where a word ought to be hyphenated—information especially helpful for compound words —and how the word can be abbreviated.

A word's pronunciation, indicated by phonetic symbols, is also given. The symbols are explained in a key in the front pages of the dictionary, and an abbreviated symbol key is often found at the bottom of each page as well. (See also **diacritical marks**.)

Information about the origin and history of a word (its etymology) is also given, usually in **brackets** at the end of the entry. This information can help clarify a word's current meaning.

Entries also include information about a word's part of speech, and its inflected forms (how it forms plurals, or how it changes form to express comparative and superlative degree). Many entries include a list of synonyms in a separate paragraph following the main paragraph. Some dictionaries label words according to **usage** levels to indicate whether a word is considered **standard English, nonstandard English**, slang, and so on. Many dictionaries supplement a word's definition by providing illustrations in the form of **maps, photographs, tables, graphs**, and the like.

TYPES OF DICTIONARIES

The following unabridged dictionaries (250,000 entries or more) attempt to be exhaustive.

1. *The Oxford English Dictionary* (Oxford, England: The Clarendon Press, 1933) is the standard historical dictionary of the English language. It follows the chronological developments of over 240,000 words, from about the year 1000 to the early part of this century, providing numerous examples of uses and sources. *A Supplement to the Oxford English Dictionary,* Vol. 1, A–G (New York: Oxford University Press, 1972), containing 17,000 entries, is now available. Volumes 2 and 3 are still being compiled.
2. *Webster's Third New International Dictionary of the English Language* (Springfield, Mass.: G. & C. Merriam Company, 1961) contains over 450,000 entries. Since word meanings are listed in historical order, the current meaning is given last. This dictionary does not list personal and geographical names, nor does it include usage information.
3. *The Random House Dictionary of the English Language* (New York: Random House, 1966) contains 260,000 entries and is encyclopedic in its use of examples. It gives a word's most widely used current meaning first and includes personal and geographical names.

Unabridged dictionaries provide complete and authoritative linguistic information, but they are impractical for desk use because of their size and expense.

Desk dictionaries are often abridged versions of larger dictionaries. There is no single "best" dictionary, but there are several guidelines for selecting a good desk dictionary. Choose a recent edition. The older the dictionary, the less likely it is to have the up-to-date information you need. Select a dictionary with upward of 125,000 entries. Pocket dictionaries are convenient for checking spelling, but for detailed information the larger range of a desk dictionary is necessary. The following are considered good desk dictionaries.

1. *The Random House Dictionary of the English Language,* College Edition. New York: Random House, 1968.
2. *The American Heritage Dictionary of the English Language.* New York: American Heritage Publishing Co., Inc., 1969.
3. *Funk and Wagnalls New Standard Dictionary of the English Language.* New York: Funk and Wagnalls, 1963.
4. *Webster's New World Dictionary of the American Language.* Cleveland: World Publishing Co., 1972.

5. *Webster's New Collegiate Dictionary*. Rev. ed. Springfield, Mass.: G. & C. Merriam Company, 1973.

differ from/differ with

Differ from is used to suggest that two things are not alike.

> *Example:* The vice-president's background *differs from* the general manager's background.

Differ with is used to indicate disagreement between persons.

> *Example:* Our attorney *differed with* theirs over the selection of the last jury member.

different from/different than

In formal writing, the **preposition** *from* is used with *different*.

> *Example:* The fourth-generation computer is *different from* the third-generation computer.

Different than is acceptable when it is followed by a **clause**.

> *Example:* The job cost was *different than* we had estimated it.

direct address

Direct address refers to a **sentence** or **phrase** in which the person being spoken or written to is explicitly named.

> *Example:* *John,* call me as soon as you arrive at the airport.

The words in a direct address are set off by **commas**.

direct object

A direct object is a **noun** (or noun equivalent) that names a person or thing that receives the action of a **transitive verb**. A direct object normally answers the question *what* or *whom*.

> *Examples:* John built a *business*. (noun)
> I like *jogging*. (gerund)
> I like *to jog*. (infinitive)
> I like *it*. (pronoun)
> I like *what I saw*. (noun clause)

(See also **indirect object, object,** and **complement**.)

discreet/discrete

Discreet means "having or showing prudent or careful behavior."

Example: Since the matter was personal, he asked Bob to be *discreet* about it at the office.

Discrete means something is "separate, distinct, or individual."

Example: The publications department was a *discrete* unit of the marketing division.

disinterested/uninterested

Disinterested means "impartial, objective, unbiased."

Example: Like good judges, scientists should be passionately interested in the problems they tackle but completely *disinterested* when they seek to solve these problems.

Uninterested means simply "not interested."

Example: Despite Jim's enthusiasm, his manager remained *uninterested* in the project.

documentation

The word *documentation* in the academic world refers to the giving of formal credit to sources used or quoted in a research paper or report; that is, the form used in a **bibliography** or a **footnote**. In the business and industrial world, *documentation* may refer also to information that is recorded, or "documented," on paper. The **technical manuals** provided to customers by manufacturers are examples of such documentation. Even **flowcharts** and engineering **drawings** are considered documentation.

double negative

A double negative is the use of an additional negative word to reinforce an expression that is already negative. It is an attempt to emphasize the negative, but the result is simply **awkwardness**.

Change: I *haven't* got *none*.
To: I have *none*.
Or: I *don't have* any.
Or: I *haven't* any.

Barely, hardly, and *scarcely* cause problems because writers sometimes do not recognize that these words are already negative.

> *Change:* I *don't hardly* ever have time to read these days.
> *To:* I *hardly* ever have time to read these days.

Not unfriendly, not without, and similar constructions do not qualify as double negatives because in such constructions two negatives are meant to suggest the gray area of meaning between negative and positive. Be careful, however, how you use these constructions; they are often confusing to the **reader** and should be used only if they serve a purpose.

> *Examples:* He is *not unfriendly.* (meaning that he is neither hostile nor friendly)
> It is *not without* regret that I offer my resignation. (implying mixed feelings rather than only regret)

The **correlative conjunctions** *neither* and *nor* may appear together in a clause without creating a double negative, so long as the writer does not attempt to use the word *not* in the same clause.

> *Change:* It was *not,* as a matter of fact, *neither* his duty *nor* his desire to fire the man.
> *To:* It was *neither,* as a matter of fact, his duty *nor* his desire to fire the man.
> *Or:* It was *not,* as a matter of fact, *either* his duty *or* his desire to fire the man.

Negative forms are full of traps that often entice inexperienced writers into errors of logic, as illustrated in the following example.

> *Example:* There is *nothing* in the book which has *not* already been published in some form, but some of it is, I believe, very little known.

In this sentence, "some of it," logically, can only refer to "*nothing* in the book which has *not* already been published." The sentence can be corrected in one of two ways. The **pronoun** *it* can be replaced by a specific **noun**.

> *Example:* There is nothing in the book which has not already been published in some form, but some of the *information* is, I believe, very little known.

Or the idea can be stated positively.

> *Example:* Everything in the book has been published in some form, but some of it is, I believe, very little known.

(See also **positive writing**.)

drawings

A drawing is useful when you wish to focus on details or relationships that a photograph cannot capture. A drawing can emphasize the significant piece of a mechanism, or its function, and omit what is not significant. However, if the precise details of the actual appearance of an object are necessary to your report or document, a photograph is essential.

There are various types of drawings, each with unique advantages. The type of drawing used for an **illustration** should be determined by the specific purpose it is intended to serve. If your **reader** needs an impression of an object's general appearance or an overview of a series of steps or directions, a conventional drawing of the type illustrated by Figure 1 will suffice.

Figure 1. Hand Signals for Crane Operation
Source: Harnischfeger Corporation

Where it is necessary to show the internal parts of a piece of equipment in such a way that their relationship to the overall equipment is clear, a cutaway drawing is necessary.

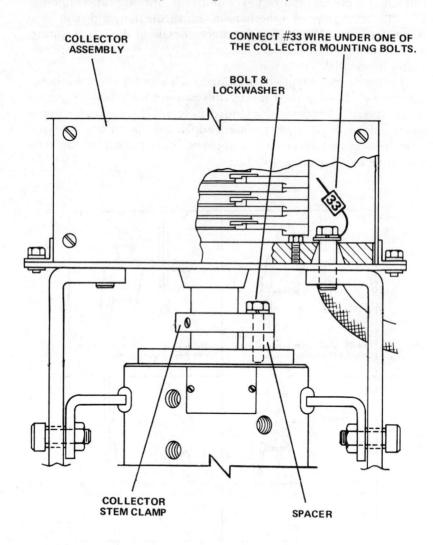

Figure 2. Detail View—Collector
Source: Harnischfeger Corporation

To show the proper sequence in which parts fit together, or when it is essential to show the details of each individual part, use an exploded-view drawing.

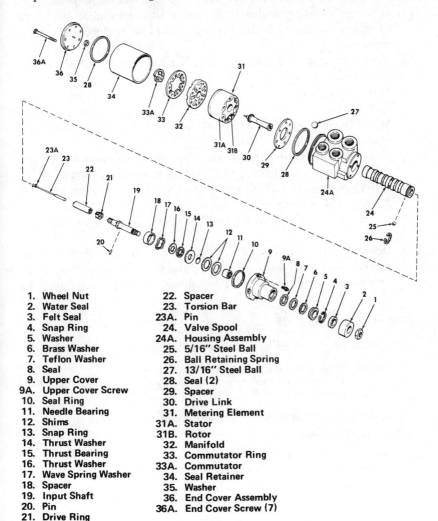

1. Wheel Nut
2. Water Seal
3. Felt Seal
4. Snap Ring
5. Washer
6. Brass Washer
7. Teflon Washer
8. Seal
9. Upper Cover
9A. Upper Cover Screw
10. Seal Ring
11. Needle Bearing
12. Shims
13. Snap Ring
14. Thrust Washer
15. Thrust Bearing
16. Thrust Washer
17. Wave Spring Washer
18. Spacer
19. Input Shaft
20. Pin
21. Drive Ring
22. Spacer
23. Torsion Bar
23A. Pin
24. Valve Spool
24A. Housing Assembly
25. 5/16" Steel Ball
26. Ball Retaining Spring
27. 13/16" Steel Ball
28. Seal (2)
29. Spacer
30. Drive Link
31. Metering Element
31A. Stator
31B. Rotor
32. Manifold
33. Commutator Ring
33A. Commutator
34. Seal Retainer
35. Washer
36. End Cover Assembly
36A. End Cover Screw (7)

Figure 3. Power Steering Valve
Source: Harnischfeger Corporation

TIPS FOR CREATING AND USING DRAWINGS

Many organizations have their own format specifications. In the absence of such specifications, the following tips will be helpful.

1. Give the drawing a clear title and a figure number (if figure numbers are used), both of which should be centered below the drawing.
2. Place the source or courtesy line, if necessary, in the lower left corner.
3. Show the equipment from the point of view of the person who will use it.
4. When illustrating a subsystem, show its relationship to the larger system of which it is a part.
5. Draw the different parts of an object in proportion to one another, unless you indicate that certain parts are enlarged.
6. Where a sequence of drawings is used to illustrate a process, arrange them from left to right.
7. Label parts in the drawing so that text references to them are clear.
8. Depending on the complexity of what is shown, labels may be placed on the parts themselves, or the parts may be given letter or number symbols, with an accompanying key. (See figure 3.)

due to/because of

Due to (meaning "caused by") is acceptable following a **linking verb**.

Examples: His short temper was *due to* work strain.
His short temper, which was *due to* strain, made him inefficient.

Due to is not acceptable, however, when it is used with a nonlinking **verb** to replace *because of*.

Change: He went home *due to* fatigue.
To: He went home *because of* fatigue.

E

each

When *each* is used as a **subject**, it takes a singular **verb** or **pronoun**.

> *Examples:* Each of the reports *is* to be submitted ten weeks after *it* is
> assigned.
> *Each* worked as fast as *his* ability would permit.

When *each* occurs after a plural subject with which it is in apposition, it takes a plural verb or pronoun. (See also **agreement**.)

> *Example:* The reports *each have* white embossed titles on *their* covers.

each and every

Although the **phrase** *each and every* is commonly used in speech in an attempt to emphasize a point, the phrase is redundant and should be eliminated from your writing. Replace it with either *each* or *every*.

> *Change:* I want *each and every* part accounted for.
> *To:* I want *each* part accounted for.
> *Or:* I want *every* part accounted for.

each other/one another

When referring to two persons or objects, use *each other*.

> *Example:* The two architects corresponded with *each other* during the
> project.

When referring to more than two, use *one another*.

> *Example:* The four firms bid against *one another* for the building contract.

economic/economical

Economic means "of or pertaining to the production, development, and management of material wealth." *Economical* simply means "not wasteful or extravagant."

> *Examples:* The strike at General Motors had an *economic* impact on the
> country.

Since gasoline will be in short supply, it has been suggested that drivers be as *economical* as possible with its use from now on.

e.g.

The **abbreviation** *e.g.* stands for the Latin *exempli gratia,* meaning "for example." Since a perfectly good English expression exists for the same use *(for example)*, there is no need to use a Latin expression or an abbreviation for a Latin expression. In addition, many people confuse *e.g.* with *i.e.*, never being certain which means what. The abbreviation *e.g.* does not save enough space to pay for having one person misunderstand your meaning—avoid *e.g.* in your writing. Use the English **phrase** *for example.*

Change: Some terms of the contract (*e.g.,* duration, job classification, and early retirement) were settled in the first two bargaining sessions.

To: Some terms of the contract (*for example,* duration, job classification, and early retirement) were settled in the first two bargaining sessions.

Or: Some terms of the contract (*such as* duration, job classification, and early retirement) were settled in the first two bargaining sessions.

elegant variation

The attempt to avoid repeating a word in a **paragraph** by substituting other words (often pretentious **synonyms**) is called elegant variation. Avoid this amateurish practice—repeat a word if it says what you mean, or use a suitable pronoun. (See also **affectation** and **long variants**.)

Change: The *use* of modules in the assembly process has increased production. *Modular utilization* has also cut costs.

To: The *use* of modules in the assembly process has increased production. The *use* of modules has also cut costs.

Or: The use of modules in the assembly process has increased production. *It* has also cut costs.

ellipses

When you omit words in quoted material, use a series of three spaced periods—called ellipsis dots—to indicate the omission. However, such an omission should not detract from or alter the essential meaning of the **sentence**.

Example: Technical material distributed for promotional use is sometimes charged for, particularly in high-volume distribution to educational institutions, although prices for these publications are not uniformly based on the cost of developing them. (without omission)

Technical material distributed for promotional use is sometimes charged for ... although prices for these publications are not uniformly based on the cost of developing them. (with omission)

When the omitted portion comes at the beginning of the sentence, it is permissible to begin the quotation with a lower-case letter to indicate the omission rather than using ellipsis dots.

Example: "When the programmer has determined a system of runs, he must create a system flowchart to provide a picture of the data flow through the system." (without omission)

The letter states, "he must create a system flowchart to provide a picture of the data flow through the system." (with omission)

When the omission comes after the end of a sentence and you continue the quotation following the omission, use four periods to indicate both the final period to end the sentence and the omission.

Example: In all publications departments except ours, publications funds—once they are initially allocated by higher management—are controlled by publications personnel. Our company is the only one to have nonpublications people control funding within a budgeted period. In addition, all publications departments control printing funds as well. (without omission)

In all publications departments except ours, publications funds—once they are initially allocated by higher management—are controlled by publications personnel. . . . In addition, all publications departments control printing funds as well. (with omission)

Use a full line of periods across the page to indicate the omission of one or more **paragraphs**.

Example: A computer system operates with two types of programs: the software programs supplied by the manufacturer and the programs created by the user. The manufacturer's software consists of a number of programs that enable the system to perform complicated manipulations of data from the relatively simple instructions specified in the user's program.

Programmers must take a systematic approach to solving any data processing problem. They must first clearly define the problem, and then they must define a system of runs that will solve the problem. For example, a given problem may require a validation and sort run to handle account numbers or employee numbers, a computation and update run to manipulate the data for the output reports, and a print run to produce the output reports.

When a system of runs has been determined, the programmer must create a system flowchart to provide a picture of the data flow through the system. (without omission)

A computer system operates with two types of programs: the software programs supplied by the manufacturer and the programs created by the user. The manufacturer's software consists of a number of programs that enable the system to perform complicated manipulations of data from the relatively simple instructions specified in the user's program.

. . . .

When a system of runs has been determined, the programmer must create a system flowchart to provide a picture of the data flow through the system. (with omission)

Do not use ellipsis dots for any purpose other than to indicate omission. Advertising copywriters, particularly those not skilled at achieving the effect they strive for with words, often use ellipsis dots to substitute for all marks of **punctuation**—and sometimes even use them where no punctuation is needed. This practice achieves no positive effect, and it is a poor one to emulate.

eminent/imminent/immanent

If someone or something is *eminent,* it is outstanding or distinguished.

Example: He is an *eminent* scientist.

If something is *imminent,* it is about to happen.

Example: He paced nervously, knowing that the committee's decision was *imminent.*

Immanent, meaning "inherent" or "indwelling," is used chiefly by theologians and philosophers to refer to the theory that a Deity pervades and sustains all material existence.

Example: The theologian suggested that God is *immanent* in all life forms.

emphasis

Emphasis is the principle by which ideas in writing are stressed according to their importance. The first step in achieving emphasis is to write simply and concisely. If a **sentence** expresses the writer's meaning simply and directly, it has the proper emphasis. But there are also mechanical means of achieving emphasis: by position within a sentence, **paragraph**, or **report**; by the use of **repetition**; by selection of sentence type; by varying the length of sentences; by the use of climactic order within a sentence; by **punctuation** (use of the **dash**); by the use of **intensifiers**; by the use of mechanical devices, such as **italics** and **capital letters**; and by direct statement (using such terms as *most important* and *foremost*).

Emphasis can be achieved by position because the first and last words of a sentence stand out in the **reader's** mind.

Change: Because they reflect geological history, moon craters are important to understanding the earth's history.
To: Moon craters are important to understanding the earth's history because they reflect geological history.
Or: Because moon craters reflect geological history, they are important to understanding the earth's history.

Notice that the revised versions of the sentence emphasize moon craters simply because the term is in the front part of the sentence. Similarly, the first and last sentences in a paragraph and the first and last paragraphs in a report or paper tend to be the most emphatic to the reader.

Example: Energy does far more than simply make our daily lives more comfortable and convenient. Suppose you wanted to stop— and reverse—the economic progress of this nation. What would be the surest and quickest way to do it? Find a way to cut off the nation's oil resources! Industrial plants would shut down, public utilities would stand idle, all forms of transportation would halt. The country would be paralyzed, and our economy would plummet into the abyss of national economic ruin. *Our economy, in short, is energy-based.*

—*The Baker World*, Baker Oil Tools, Inc.

Emphasis can be achieved by the repetition of key words and **phrases**.

Example: Similarly, atoms *come and go* in a molecule, but the molecule *remains;* molecules *come and go* in a cell, but the cell *remains;* cells *come and go* in a body, but the body *remains;* persons *come and go* in an organization, but the organization *remains.*

—Kenneth Boulding, *Beyond Economics* (Ann Arbor: University of Michigan Press, 1968), p. 131.

Different emphasis can be achieved by the selection of a **compound sentence, complex sentence**, or **simple sentence**.

Examples: The report turned in by the police detective was carefully illustrated, and it covered five pages of single-spaced copy. (This compound sentence carries no special emphasis because it contains two coordinate independent clauses.)

The police detective's report, which was carefully illustrated, covered five pages of single-spaced copy. (This complex sentence emphasizes the size of the report.)

The carefully illustrated report turned in by the police detective covered five pages of single-spaced copy. (This simple sentence emphasizes that the report was carefully illustrated.)

Emphasis can be achieved by making a sentence distinctly different in length from the preceding one.

Example: I believe that man is about to learn that the most practical life is the moral life and that the moral life is the only road to survival. He is beginning to learn that he will either share part of his material wealth or lose all of it; that he will respect and learn to live with other political ideologies if he wants civilization to go on. This is the kind of argument that man's actual experience equips him to understand and accept. *This is the low road to morality. There is no other.*

—Saul Alinsky, *Rules for Radicals* (New York: Random House, 1971), p. 25.

Emphasis can be achieved by a climactic order of ideas or facts within a sentence.

Example: Over subsequent weeks the industrial relations department worked diligently, management showed tact and patience, and the employees finally accepted the new policy.

Emphasis can be achieved by setting an item apart with a dash.

Example: Here is where all the trouble begins—in the American confidence that technology is ultimately the medicine for all ills.

Emphasis can be achieved by the use of intensifiers (*most, very, really*), but this technique is so easily abused that it should be used only with caution.

Example: The final proposal is *much* more persuasive than the first.

Emphasis can be achieved by such mechanical devices as underlining, italics, and capital letters. But this technique is also easily abused and should be used with caution.

Example: The foundations of his doctrine were embodied in . . . the *Communist Manifesto.* In a letter written in 1852 he carefully states what he regarded as original in it: "What I did that was new was to prove (1) that the existence of classes is only bound up with particular, historic phases in the development of production; (2) that the class struggle necessarily leads to the dictatorship of the proletariat); (3) that this dictatorship itself only constitutes the transition to the abolition of all classes and to a classless society." On these foundations the new movement was to be built.

—Isaiah Berlin, *Karl Marx* (New York: Time, Inc., 1963), p. 170.

The word *do* (or *does*) may be used for emphasis, but this is also easily overdone, so proceed with caution. Compare the following examples.

Examples: You believe weekly staff meetings are essential, don't you?
You *do* believe weekly staff meetings are essential, don't you?

(See also **subordination**.)

English, varieties of

There are two broad varieties of written English: standard and nonstandard. These varieties are determined through usage by those who write in the English language. As the language of the majority of educated writers, **standard English** is used to carry on the daily business of the nation. It is the language of business, industry, government, education, and the professions. Standard English is characterized by exacting standards of **punctuation** and capitalization, by accurate **spelling**, by exact **diction**, by an expressive vocabulary, and by knowledgeable **usage** choices. **Nonstandard English**, on the other hand, is the language of those not familiar with the standards of written English. This form of English rarely appears in printed material except when it is used for special effect by fiction writers. Because its users are unfamiliar with the conventions of standard English, nonstandard English is characterized by inexact or inconsistent punctuation, capitalization, spelling, diction, and usage choices. Both standard and nonstandard English find their way into everyday speech and writing in the forms of the following subcategories.

COLLOQUIAL

Colloquial English is spoken standard English or writing that attempts to re-create the flavor of this kind of speech by using words and expressions common to casual conversation. Colloquial English is appropriate to some kinds of writing (personal letters, notes, etc.) but not to most business and technical writing.

VERNACULAR

Vernacular English is the spoken form of the language, as opposed to its written form. It is the form used by the majority of those who speak the language. It differs from written English in being less cultivated and in adhering to fewer standards. To write "in the vernacular" is to imitate this kind of language. Ordinarily, such writing is confined to fiction. Vernacular can also refer to the manner of expression common to a trade or profession (one might speak of "the legal vernacular"), although **jargon** more clearly expresses this meaning.

DIALECT

Dialectal English is a social or regional variety of the language that is comprehensible to people of that social group or region but that may be incomprehensible to outsiders. Dialect, which is usually nonstandard English, involves distinct **word choices**, grammatical forms, and pronunciations. Business and technical writing, because it aims at a broad audience, should be free of dialect.

LOCALISM

A localism is a word or **phrase** that is unique to a geographical region. For example, the words *poke, sack,* and *bag* all denote "a paper container," each term being peculiar to a different region of the United States. Such words should normally be avoided in writing because knowledge of their meanings is too narrowly restricted.

SLANG

Slang refers to a manner of expressing common ideas in new, often humorous or exaggerated, ways. Slang often finds new use for familiar words ("That's a *bad* car"—meaning that the car is stylish and desirable) or coins new words ("He's a *kook*"—meaning that he is offbeat, unconventional). By their nature, slang expressions come and go very quickly. The fact that a fair number of words in the present standard English vocabulary were once considered slang indicates that when a slang word fills a legitimate need it is accepted into the language. *Skyscraper, bus,* and *date* (as in "*to go on a date*"), for example, were once considered slang expressions. Although slang may have a valid place in some writing, particularly in fiction, be careful not to let it creep into your serious formal writing.

BARBARISM

A barbarism is any obvious misuse of standard words, grammatical forms, or expressions. Examples include *ain't, irregardless, done got, drownded.*

enormity/enormousness

Enormity means "outrageousness" or "wickedness."

> *Example:* The jury was shocked by the *enormity* of his crime.

Enormousness means "greatness in size."

> *Example:* The group was amazed by the *enormousness* of the New York facility.

epithet

An epithet is a short descriptive **phrase** in apposition to someone's name. (See also **appositive**.)

> *Examples:* Alexander *the Great,* Ivan *the Terrible*

Epithet is also used to mean "a contemptuous word or phrase used to describe someone."

> *Example:* His memos always contain a few salty *epithets* to describe his colleagues.

equal/unique/perfect

Logically, *equal* (meaning "having the same quantity or value as another"), *unique* (meaning "one of a kind"), and *perfect* (meaning "a state of highest excellence") are absolute words and therefore should not be compared. However, colloquial usage of *more* and *most* as modifiers of *equal, unique,* and *perfect* is so common that an absolute prohibition against such use is impossible.

> *Example:*   Yours is a *more unique* (or *perfect*) coin than mine.

Some writers try to overcome the problem by using *more nearly equal* (*unique, perfect*). Where **clarity** and preciseness are critical, the use of **comparative degrees** with *equal, unique,* and *perfect* can be misleading. The best rule of thumb is to avoid using the comparative degrees with absolute terms. (See also **absolute words**.)

> *Change:*   Ours is a more *equal* percentage split than theirs.
> *To:*   Our percentage split is 51–49; theirs is 54–46.

-ese

The **suffix** -*ese* is used to designate types of **jargon** or certain languages or literary styles (official*ese,* journal*ese,* Chin*ese,* Pentagon*ese*).

essay questions, answering

One of the most practical applications for a systematic approach to writing is answering essay questions. The following is a procedure that has been used successfully by good students for years.

1. Read the question carefully, looking for key terms that help you determine precisely whether you are to define, describe, contrast, or trace the subject.
2. On a separate piece of paper, list the major points as you formulate your answer.
3. If time permits, develop a brief main idea statement. Quite often, the main idea statement will take the form of a restatement of the question.
4. Determine the **method of development** best suited to your subject.
5. Number the major points of your answer in the sequence best adapted to your method of development. This constitutes your **outline**.
6. Write a rough draft on your scratch sheet.
7. Correct any obvious errors in the rough draft and copy the draft onto your examination paper, continuing to revise as you do so.

Be careful to pace yourself so that you allow enough time for each question. If you must sacrifice one step of the process because time is short, omit the rough draft and write your final draft directly from your outline. The outline, however, is essential.

This method, which should take only a few minutes at most, will save you a great deal of writing time. Since it will provide a logical structure for your response, the instructor can evaluate your work more effectively—a factor that usually works to the student's advantage.

etc.

Etc. is an **abbreviation** for the Latin *et cetera,* meaning "and others"; therefore, *etc.* should not be used with *and.*

> *Change:* He brought pencils, pads, erasers, a slide rule, *and etc.*
> *To:* He brought pencils, pads, erasers, a slide rule, *etc.*

Do not use *etc.* at the end of a list or series introduced by the **phrases** *such as* or *for example* because these phrases already indicate that there are other things of the same category that are not named.

> *Change:* He brought surveying items *such as* a tripod, sleeping bags, tents, *etc.*
> *To:* He brought a tripod, sleeping bags, tents, *etc.*

In careful writing, *etc.* should be used only when there is logical progression (1, 2, 3, etc.) and when at least two items are named. It is often better to avoid *etc.* altogether, however, because there may be confusion as to the identity of the "class" of items listed.

> *Example:* He brought a tripod, sleeping bags, tents, and other surveying items.

It is always best to be as specific as possible.

euphemism

A euphemism is a word that is an inoffensive substitute for one that could be distasteful, offensive, or too blunt.

> *Examples:* *remains* for corpse
> *passed away* for died
> *marketing representative* for salesman
> *previously owned* or *pre-owned* for used

Used judiciously, a euphemism might help you avoid embarrassing or offending someone. Overused, however, euphemisms can hide the facts of a situation (such as *explosive device* for *nuclear bomb*). As a rule, call things by their right names. (See also **word choice**.)

everybody/everyone

Both *everybody* and *everyone* are considered singular and so take singular **verbs** and **pronouns**.

> *Examples:* *Everybody is* happy with the new contract.
> *Everyone* here *eats* at 11:30 a.m.
> *Everybody* at the meeting made *his* proposals separately.
> *Everyone* went *his* separate way after the meeting.

An exception to this is when use of singular verbs and pronouns would be offensive by implying sexual bias; in such a situation, it is better to use plural verbs and pronouns or to use the expression "his or her" than to offend.

> *Change:* *Everyone* went *his* separate way after the meeting.
> *To:* *They* all went *their* separate ways after the meeting.
> *Or:* Everyone went *his or her* separate way after the meeting.

Although normally written as one word, *everyone* is written as two words when each individual in a group should be emphasized.

> *Examples:* *Everyone* here comes and goes as he pleases.
> *Every one* of the team members contributed to this discovery.

(See also **indefinite pronouns**.)

ex post facto

The expression *ex post facto,* which is Latin for "after the fact," refers to something that operates retroactively. The term is normally used to refer to laws and is best avoided in other contexts.

> *Change:* The contract will be in effect *ex post facto* of the negotiations.
> *To:* The contract will be in effect after the negotiations.

exclamation mark

The purpose of the exclamation mark (!) is to indicate the expression of strong feeling. It can signal surprise, fear, indignation, or excitement. It should not be used for trivial emotions or mild surprise. It cannot make an argument more convincing, lend force to a weak statement, or call attention to an intended irony—no matter how many are stacked like fence posts at the end of a **sentence**.

USES

The most common use of an exclamation mark is after a word (**interjection**), **phrase, clause**, or sentence to indicate surprise.

Interjections are words that express strong emotion.

Examples: Ouch! Wow! Oh! Stop! Hurry!

An exclamation mark can also be used after a whole sentence, or even an element within a sentence.

Examples: The subject of this meeting—please note it well!—is our budget deficit.

In 1869, 11,000,000 passenger pigeons were shipped from Michigan in forty days, says the naturalist W. J. Shoonmaker, from *one town!*

—Robert Rienow and Leona Train Rienow, *Moment in the Sun* (New York: Ballantine Books, 1967), p. 99.

An exclamation mark can be used after a title that is an exclamatory word, phrase, or sentence.

Examples: "Our System Must Change!" is an article by Richard Moody. *The Cancer With No Cure!* is a book by Wilbur Moody.

When used with **quotation marks**, the exclamation mark goes outside unless what is quoted is an exclamation.

Example: The boss yelled, "Get in here!" Then Ben, according to Ray, "jumped like a kangaroo"!

explaining a process

Many types of business and technical writing explain a process. The explanation involves putting in the appropriate order the steps that a specific mechanism or system uses to accomplish something. The process explained could range from the legal steps necessary to form a corporation to the steps necessary to develop a roll of film. At the least, it is necessary to divide the process into distinct steps and present them in their normal order. The following guidelines will help with this type of writing.

Your opening paragraph should set the stage for the process being explained. It can do this by giving the reason the process is being performed (for example, incorporating will save tax dollars), by presenting a brief overview of the process (to give your **reader** a framework for the details that will be presented), or by explaining the function of the process (it may be part of a larger process). If the process involves the operation of a mechanism, a general **description** of the mechanism may be necessary in the opening paragraph.

The main portion of your writing should first include the details of any preparations that must be made before the process can be performed. (To develop a roll of film, for example, certain chemicals and equipment must first be made ready.) Then you must explain the steps of the process in their appropriate sequential order. Keep in mind that your reader may be completely unfamiliar with the process being described, so you must provide effective **transition** between steps to make your explanation clear. Of course, the amount and depth of detail you provide will depend on the intended use of your material. Obviously, a process that the reader must actively perform in accordance with your explanation requires more specific details than one of which the reader needs only an overview. In any case, you must thoroughly understand the process yourself. **Illustrations** carefully chosen to show the reader what to expect are invaluable.

A **conclusion** is sometimes used to point out how the process being explained is related to other processes of a larger work.

The following example explains the primary cementing operation, which is part of the process of completing an oil well.

The Primary Cementing Operation

INTRODUCTION

As the oil well is being drilled, the hole is kept full of drilling "mud"; the weight of the drilling mud prevents the well from

Reason for the process

blowing in as a gusher, and it keeps fluids from the various zones from entering the hole.

Once the well has been drilled to the required depth, the control and protection provided by the drilling mud must be replaced with something more permanent, and the hole must be further prepared for production. This process, described briefly and simply, involves installing large diameter pipe, called casing, in the hole and then pumping cement down

Overview of the process

through the casing and up into the space between the casing and the wall of the hole (called the annulus). The process of placing cement around the casing throughout the depth of the producing formation is the primary cementing operation.

By plugging the annulus with cement, the primary cementing operation restores the isolation that existed between the various fluid-bearing zones before the hole was drilled and prevents fluid from the different zones from contaminating the crude oil in the producing formation.

Function of the process

SPECIAL EQUIPMENT

Certain pieces of equipment that will be required for the primary cementing operation are installed on the casing before it is run into the well. Devices called shoes and collars, for example, are installed before the casing is run. The shoe is threaded onto the bottom end of the casing and the collar between the first and second or second and third lengths of casing. At least one of these devices must contain a back-pressure valve to prevent the cement slurry (cement and water) from flowing back into the end of the casing once it has been pumped out. If the device contains a back-pressure valve, it is called a float shoe or a float collar. If it merely has a vertical opening through it, it is called a guide shoe or a baffle collar.

Preparations that must be made before the process is performed

In deep wells, the casing must be filled with fluid as it is run in to prevent it from collapsing under the pressure of the well fluid at the greater depths. This problem is solved by installing a fill-up shoe or collar, which permits well fluid to enter the casing string but controls the rate of fill in order to prevent overfilling the casing.

Centralizers (bowed-spring devices for centering the casing in the hole) are installed at predetermined points on the casing string to ensure a uniform cementing job around the entire circumference of the casing. Wall scratchers (wire-finger devices that fold up when run into the hole and then dig into the face of the formation when the casing is lifted) are also installed to assure a good bond between the cement and the surface of the formation by removing the mudcake from the wall of the hole in the area to be cemented.

THE PRIMARY CEMENTING OPERATION

After the equipment is installed, the casing is run into the well. Great care must be taken in running the casing because if it is run too fast a "piston" effect can be created, causing pressure surges. Pressure surges can damage or seal off the producing formation or create fissures that could (1) establish a path of communication between zones that could never be repaired or even (2) result in the loss of mud control and a subsequent blowout.

Sequential steps of the process

After the casing is landed, fluid circulation is established down through the casing and up the annulus to assure free passage of the cement when the actual cementing operation begins. As soon as circulation is established, the casing is rotated or reciprocated (depending upon the type of wall scratchers used) to activate the wall scratchers and remove mudcake from the wall of the hole in the area to be cemented. Circulation is continued until the well is properly conditioned for the cementing operation.

The cement is then pumped down through the casing and up into the annulus. When the column of cement in the annulus has reached a predetermined height, the pumps are shut down and the back-check valve in the float or fill-up shoe prevents the cement slurry from re-entering the casing. When the cement cures (approximately twelve hours), the primary cementing job is completed.

A successful primary cementing job will result in a casing string permanently bonded to the formation and surrounded and protected by a cement sheath that is completely impervious to fluid migration. An unsuccessful cementing job, on the other hand, will probably have to be patched throughout the producing life of the well.

Conclusion   The primary cementing operation is only one part of the overall construction of an oil well. All the separate operations —drilling, primary cementing, completion, stimulation, production, remedial—have but one common goal: to attain the maximum recovery of oil at the lowest possible cost.

—*The Baker World*, Baker Oil Tools, Inc.

expletives

An expletive is a word that fills the position of another word, **phrase**, or **clause**. *It* and *there* are the usual expletives.

> *Example:* *It* is certain that he will go.

In this example, the expletive *it* occupies the position of **subject** in place of the real subject, *that he will go*. Although expletives are sometimes necessary to avoid **awkwardness**, most **sentences** can be better stated without them.

> *Change:* *There are* several reasons why I did it.
> *To:* I did it for several reasons.
> *Change:* *There were* many orders lost for unexplained reasons.
> *To:* Many orders were lost for unexplained reasons.
> *Or:* We lost many orders for unexplained reasons.

In addition to its usage as a grammatical term, the word *expletive* means an exclamation or oath, especially one that is profane.

explicit/implicit

An explicit statement is one expressed directly, with precision and **clarity**. An implicit meaning may be found within a statement even though it is not directly expressed.

> *Examples:*   His directions to the new plant were *explicit* and we found it with no trouble.
> Although he did not mention the nation's financial condition, the danger of an economic recession was *implicit* in the President's speech.

exposition

Exposition, or expository writing, informs the **reader** by presenting facts and ideas in direct and concise language that is usually not adorned with colorful or figurative words and **phrases**. Expository writing attempts to explain to the reader what its subject is, how it works, how it relates to something else, and so on. Exposition is aimed at the reader's understanding, rather than at his imagination or emotions; it is a sharing of the writer's knowledge with the reader. The most important function of exposition is to provide accurate and complete information to the reader and analyze it for him.

> *Example:*   A major component of an electronic data processing system is the software—the programs supplied by the manufacturer to direct the computer's internal operation. The software supplied with the NCR Century 50 System is an extensive package that includes the operating system, utility routines, applied programs, and the NEAT/3 Compiler. These programs have been designed to perform specific functions but, at the same time, to interact with one another to increase processing efficiency and to avoid duplication.
> To conserve valuable memory space, a large portion of the software package remains on disc; only the most frequently used portion resides in internal memory all of the time. The disc-resident software is organized into small modules that are called into memory as needed to perform specific functions.
> The memory-resident portion of the operating system maintains strict control of processing. It consists of routines, subroutines, lists, and tables that are used to perform common program functions, such as processing input and output operations, calling other software routines from disc as needed, and processing errors.
> The disc-resident portion of the operating system contains

routines that are used less frequently in system operation, such as the peripheral-related software routines that are used for correcting errors encountered on the various units, and the log and display routines that record unusual operating conditions in the system log. The disc-resident portion of the operating system also contains Monitor, the software program that supervises the loading of utility routines and the user's programs.

—*NCR Century Elementary Systems Manual,* NCR Corporation.

Because it is the most effective **form of discourse** for explaining difficult subjects, exposition is widely used in business and technical writing. To write exposition, you must have a thorough knowledge of your subject. As with all writing, how much of that knowledge you pass on to your reader should depend upon the reader's needs and the objective of your report.

F

fact

Expressions containing the word *fact* ("due to the *fact* that," "except for the *fact* that," "as a matter of *fact*," or "because of the *fact* that") are often wordy substitutes for more accurate terms.

> *Change:* *Due to the fact* that the sales force has a high turnover rate, sales have declined.
> *To:* Because the sales force has a high turnover rate, sales have declined.

The word *fact* is, of course, valid when facts are what is meant.

> *Example:* Our research has brought out numerous *facts* to support your proposal.

Do not use the word *fact,* however, to refer to matters of judgment or opinion.

> *Change:* It is a *fact* that sales are poor in the Midwest because of poor market research.
> *To:* In my opinion, sales are poor in the Midwest because of poor market research.

Or: Statistics suggest that sales are poor in the Midwest because of poor market research.

Or: We infer from our statistics that sales are poor in the Midwest because of poor market research.

famous/notorious/infamous

Famous means simply "well known," but *notorious* and *infamous* mean "widely known and unfavorably regarded."

Example: Abraham Lincoln was *famous*, but John Wilkes Booth was *infamous* (or *notorious*).

female

Female is usually restricted to scientific, legal, or medical contexts (a *female* patient or suspect). Keep in mind that this term sounds cold and impersonal. The terms *girl, woman,* and *lady* are acceptable substitutes in other contexts; however, be aware that these substitute words have connotations involving age, dignity, and social position.

few/a few

In certain contexts, *few* carries more negative overtones than the **phrase** *a few* does.

Examples: They have *a few* scruples. (positive)
They have *few* scruples. (negative)
There are *a few* things good about your report. (positive)
There are *few* things good about your report. (negative)

fewer/less

Fewer refers to items that can be counted (**count nouns**).

Examples: A good diet can mean *fewer* colds.
Fewer members took the offer than we expected.

Less refers to mass quantities or amounts (**mass nouns**).

Examples: *Less* vitamin C in your diet may mean more, not *fewer,* colds.
The crop yield decreased this year because we had *less* rain than necessary for an optimum yield.

figuratively/literally

Figuratively, meaning something "not actual because it is expressed as a **figure of speech**," is sometimes confused with *literally,* meaning something that is "in accordance with strict reality." Do not use *literally* when you mean *figuratively.*

> *Examples:*   In the winner's circle the jockey was, *figuratively* speaking, ten feet tall.
> When he said, "Let's run it up the flag pole," he did not mean it *literally.*

Avoid the use of *literally* to reinforce the importance of something.

> *Change:*   She was *literally* the best of the group.
> *To:*   She was the best of the group.

figures of speech

A figure of speech is an imaginative **comparison,** either stated or implied, between two things that are basically unlike but have at least one thing in common. If a device is cone-shaped with an opening at the top, for example, you might say that it looks like a volcano.

Business and technical people may find themselves using figures of speech to clarify the unfamiliar by relating a new and difficult concept to one with which the **reader** is familiar. In this respect, figures of speech help establish a common ground of understanding between the specialist and the nonspecialist. Business and technical people may also use figures of speech to help translate the abstract into the concrete; in the process of doing so, figures of speech also make writing more colorful and graphic.

Although figures of speech are not used extensively in technical or business writing, a particularly apt figure of speech may be just the right tool when you must explain or describe a complex concept. A figure of speech must be appropriate, however, to achieve the desired effect.

> *Change:*   Without the fuel of tax incentives, our economic engine would operate less efficiently. (It would not operate at all without fuel.)
> *To:*   Without the fuel of tax incentives, our economic engine would sputter and die. (This is not only apt, but it states a rather dry fact in a colorful manner—always a desirable objective.)

A figure of speech must also be consistent to be effective.

Change: We must get our research program back *on the track,* and we are counting on you to *carry the ball.* (inconsistent)

To: We must get our research program back on the track, and we are counting on you to do it. (inconsistency removed)

A figure of speech should not, however, attract more attention to itself than to the point the writer is making.

Example: The whine of the engine sounded like ten thousand cats having their tails pulled by ten thousand mischievous children.

Trite figures of speech, which are called **clichés**, defeat the purpose of a figure of speech—to be fresh, original, and vivid. A surprise that comes "like a bolt out of the blue" is not much of a surprise. It is better to use no figure of speech than to use a trite one.

TYPES OF FIGURES OF SPEECH

Analogy is a comparison between two objects or concepts that shows ways in which they are similar. It is very useful in business and technical writing, especially when you are writing to an educated but nontechnical audience. In effect, analogies say "A is to B as C is to D."

Example: Pollution (A) is to the environment (B) as cancer (C) is to the body (D).

The resemblance between these concepts is partial but close enough to provide a striking way of illuminating the relationship the writer wishes to establish.

Antithesis is a statement in which two contrasting ideas are set off against each other in a balanced syntactical structure.

Examples: Man proposes, but God disposes.
Art is long, but life is short.

Hyperbole is gross exaggeration used to achieve an effect or **emphasis**.

Examples: He murdered me on the tennis court.
The hail was like boulders.

Litotes is understatement, for emphasis or effect, achieved by denying the opposite of the point you are making.

Examples: Einstein was no dummy.
Twenty dollars is not a small price for a book.
August 6, 1945, was not a normal day for the citizens of Hiroshima.

Metaphor is a figure of speech that points out similarities between two things by treating them as being the same thing. Metaphor states that the thing being described *is* the thing to which it is being compared.

Example: He is the sales department's utility infielder.

Metonymy is a figure of speech that uses one aspect of a thing to represent it, such as *the red, white, and blue* for the American flag, *the blue* for the sky, and *wheels* for an automobile. This device is common in everyday speech because it gives our expressions a colorful twist.

Example: *The hard hat* area of the labor force was especially hurt by unemployment.

Simile is a direct comparison of two essentially unlike things, linking them with the word *like* or *as*.

Example: His feelings about his business rival are so bitter that in recent conversations with his staff he has returned to the subject compulsively, *like a man scratching an itch.*

Personification is a figure of speech that attributes human characteristics to nonhuman things or abstract ideas. One characteristically speaks of the *birth* of a planet and the *stubbornness* of an engine that will not start.

Example: Early tribes of human beings attributed scientific discoveries to gods. To them, fire was not a *child of man's brain* but a gift from Prometheus.

fine

Fine, when used in expressions such as "I feel *fine*" or "a *fine* surf," is colloquial. The colloquial use of *fine*, like that of **nice**, is too vague for serious writing. In writing, the word *fine* should retain the sense of "refined," "delicate," or "pure."

Examples: A *fine* film of oil covered the surface of the water.
A *fine* distinction was maintained between the two possible meanings of the disputed passage.
Fine crystal is currently made in Austria.

finite verb

A finite **verb** is the main verb of a **clause** or **sentence**. The nonfinite forms are the **verbals** (**infinitive**, **gerund**, and **participle**). Unlike verbals, finite verbs show **number, tense**, and **person**.

NUMBER

> *Examples:*   The punch press *stamps* thirty pieces a minute. (singular)
> The punch presses *stamp* twenty-five pieces a minute. (plural)

TENSE

> *Examples:*   The plane *will lift* from the runway with the thrust of the engine. (future)
> The plane *lifted* from the runway with the thrust of the engine. (past)
> The plane *lifts* from the runway with the thrust of the engine. (present)

PERSON

> *Examples:*   *I give* to charity through a payroll deduction program. (first person)
> *He gives* to charity through the same program. (third person)

first/firstly

Firstly is an unnecessary attempt to add the *-ly* form to an **adverb**. *First* is an adverb in its own right, and a much less stiff sounding one than *firstly*.

> *Change:*   Firstly, we should ask for an estimate.
> *To:*   First, we should ask for an estimate.

flammable/inflammable/nonflammable

Both *flammable* and *inflammable* mean "capable of being set on fire."

> *Example:*   The cargo of gasoline is *flammable* (or *inflammable*).

Since the *in-* **prefix** usually causes the word following to take its opposite meaning (*incapable, incompetent*), *flammable* is preferable to *inflammable* because it avoids possible misunderstanding. *Nonflammable* is the opposite—meaning "not capable of being set on fire."

> *Example:*   The asbestos suit was *nonflammable*.

flowchart

A flowchart is a diagram of a process that involves stages, with the sequence of stages shown from beginning to end. The process being illustrated can range from the steps involved in assembling a bicycle to the stages by which electromagnetic waves are intercepted and modified in a radio receiver (as shown below).

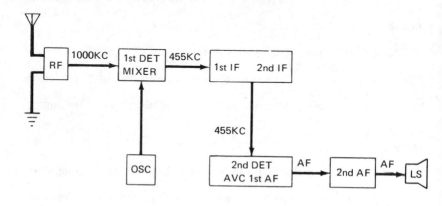

Figure 1. Flowchart of Standard Radio Receiver Showing Stages of the Process

When creating a flowchart, consider the following points.
1. Title the flowchart clearly.
2. Assign a figure number if your **report** contains several **illustrations**.
3. Use arrows to show the direction of flow.
4. Label each step in the process, or identify it with a conventional **symbol**. Steps may also be represented pictorially or in captioned blocks.
5. Include a key if the flowchart contains any symbols your **reader** may not understand.
6. Leave adequate white space on the page. Do not huddle your steps and directional arrows too close together.
7. As with all illustrations, place the flowchart as close as possible to that portion of the text which refers to it.

footnotes

Footnotes are used to indicate the source of your facts or ideas and to tell the **reader** where to find additional information about your **topic**. Footnotes can also present explanatory comments to support your ideas. Since footnotes are used to identify direct **quotations** or paraphrased material taken from other sources, they help you avoid **plagiarism** as well. In deciding what kind of information should or should not be acknowledged in a footnote, distinguish between those ideas in a field that are considered common knowledge and those that are not.

Footnote form used to present references in scientific-technical writing differs from the form used in other fields. To save space, footnotes in scientific writing are often integrated with the **bibliography** or reference section at the end of an article or chapter. Instead of being arranged alphabetically, the entries in the bibliographic or reference section are arranged in numerical sequence (1, 2, 3, etc.), according to the order in which they first appear in the text. Thus, in the text, the number one in parentheses (1) after a quotation or reference to a book or article refers the reader to the reference information in the first bibliographic entry. Number five in parentheses (5) refers the reader to the fifth entry in the bibliography, and so on. When a second number appears in the parentheses, separated from the first by a colon (3: 27), it refers to the page number of the report or book from which the information was taken.

The conventions for footnotes vary so widely in the sciences that any detailed effort to explain them all would be impossible. Although the following examples are common in scientific writing, consult publications in your field for specific format details.

BOOK

1. von Neumann, J. The computer and the brain. Yale University Press, New Haven, Conn. 1958.

ARTICLE

2. Enders, J.F. Bovine amniotic fluid as tissue culture medium in cultivation of poliomyelitis and other viruses. Proc. Soc. Exper. Biol. and Med., 1953, *82*: 100–105.

For nonscience research papers, footnotes are normally located either at the bottom of the appropriate page or at the end of a chapter or article. In either place, they are numbered consecutively, and the numbers that identify them are raised slightly above the line of print in which they occur. Within the text, the footnote number (also raised) should follow the quotation it identifies, whether the quotation is a part of or set off from the text. The number should appear at the end of the sentence when possible. When typing footnotes, single space multiple-line footnotes, and double space between them.

For the first full footnote reference to a book, the following information should be included, in the order presented: (1) author's full name; (2) complete title; (3) editor or compiler; (4) title of the series in which the book appears, if it is part of a series, and its volume or number in the series; (5) edition, if it is other than the first; (6) number of volumes for a multivolume book; (7) publication information, including city, publisher, and year; (8) volume number of that specific book, if any; and (9) page number (or numbers).

For the first full reference to a journal article, the following information should be included, in the order presented: (1) author or corporate author's name, (2) title of the article, (3) name of the journal, (4) volume and number of the journal, (5) date of the volume or issue, and (6) page number (or numbers).

BOOK, ONE AUTHOR

[1]Theodore M. Bernstein, *Watch Your Language* (Manhasset, N.Y.: Channel Press, 1958), p. 51.

BOOK, TWO OR THREE AUTHORS

[2]J.D. Hammond and Arthur L. Williams, *Essentials of Life Insurance* (New York: Scott, Foresman and Company, 1968), p. 27.
[3]Glenn Leggett, David C. Mead, and William Charvat, *Prentice-Hall Handbook for Writers,* 5th ed. (Englewood Cliffs, N.J.: Prentice-Hall, Inc., 1970), p. 203.

For more than three authors, give the first author's name followed by *et al.* (an abbreviation of the Latin *et alii,* "and others"). Then proceed with the title and other pertinent information.

BOOK EDITION, IF NOT THE FIRST

[4]Wesley E. Woodson and Donald W. Conover, *Human Engineering Guide for Equipment Designers,* 2nd ed. (Berkeley, Calif.: University of California Press, 1964), pp. 2–97.

MULTIVOLUME BOOK

[5]John Bartholemew, ed., *Times Atlas of the World,* 5 vols. (London: Times Publishing Co., Ltd., 1955–1959), 3: 27.

The volume from which the material cited was taken is noted at the end of the entry, along with the appropriate page number.

BOOK IN A SERIES

[6]E.L. Cooper, ed., *Invertebrate Immunology,* Contemporary Topics in Immunology, vol. 4 (New York: Plenum Publishing Corporation, 1974), p. 33.

EDITOR OF A COLLECTION

[7]Herman A. Estrin, ed., *Technical and Professional Writing* (New York: Harcourt, Brace & World, Inc., 1963), p. 123.

CORPORATE AUTHOR

[8]Commission on Vocational Education, *Job Selection in the 1980's* (Washington, D.C.: American Vocational Institute, 1973), p. 12.

JOURNAL ARTICLE

[9]Norman Haughness, "Clarity—The Technical Writer's Tightrope," *STC Journal* 18 (1971), 14.

SYMPOSIUM OR CONFERENCE PAPER

[10]Merril Eisenbud, "Standards of Radiation Protection and Their Implications for the Public's Health," in *Nuclear Power and the Public,* ed. Harry Foreman, M.D. (Garden City, N.Y.: Doubleday & Company, Inc., 1972), p. 107.

MAGAZINE ARTICLE

[11]"Going Private," *Newsweek,* June 3, 1975, p. 56.

ENCYCLOPEDIA ARTICLE

[12]*Encyclopaedia Britannica,* 14th ed., "Electricity."

Because the material is arranged alphabetically, page and volume numbers are unnecessary.

REPORT

[13]Parker Evans, *The Erosion of Buried Cables* (Dayton, Ohio: Ohio Bell Telephone Company, 1970), p. 27.

PAMPHLET OR BOOKLET

[14]U.S. Bureau of the Census, *We, The First Americans* (Washington, D.C.: Government Printing Office, 1973), p. 3.

THESIS OR DISSERTATION

[15]John D. Lander, "Computer Surveillance of Medicaid Claims in Tennessee (Master's Thesis, Vanderbilt University, 1973), p. 12.

PERSONAL CORRESPONDENCE

[16]Dr. Robert T. Brady, June 4, 1975, personal correspondence.

INTERVIEW

[17]Interview with Virgil Denlinger, Assistant Chief of Police, Milwaukee, Wisconsin, March 27, 1975.

SUBSEQUENT REFERENCES

In subsequent references to the same book or article, list only the author's last name and the relevant page number (or numbers).

[18]Evans, p. 32.

Where you cite more than one work by the same author, subsequent references should give (1) the author's last name, (2) a shortened title (for example, *Job Selection* for footnote example number eight above), and (3) the page number (or numbers). For coauthors, give the last name of each, or give the editor's name where that is appropriate.

To cite a single book or article in the immediately preceding footnote, use *Ibid.* (an abbreviation of the Latin *ibidem,* "the same") and the page number (*Ibid.*, p. 14.). If the page number is the same, *Ibid.* can stand alone.

[19]Hammond and Williams, p. 30.
[20]*Ibid.*

The author's name is omitted from a footnote when his full name is given in the text near the reference to, or quotation from, his work.

Footnote forms differ in varying degrees from one field of study to another and even within the same field at times. Be alert to the forms used in the organization or publication for which your material is being written. In the absence of specific guidelines, use the forms presented here, remembering to include enough accurate information so that a reader wishing to do so could find your source. Also, once you have adopted a form, be consistent.

forceful/forcible

Although *forceful* and *forcible* are both **adjectives** meaning "characterized by or full of force," *forceful* is usually limited to persuasive ability and *forcible* to physical force.

> *Examples:* The thief made a *forcible* entry into my apartment.
> John made a *forceful* presentation of his idea at the committee meeting.

foreign words in English

The English language has a long history of borrowing words from other languages. Most of these borrowings occurred so long ago that we seldom recognize the borrowed terms (also called "loan words") as being of foreign origin. (To check the origin of a word, consult the etymology portion of its **dictionary** entry.)

> *Examples:* whiskey (Gaelic), animal (Latin), church (Greek)

GUIDELINES FOR USE OF FOREIGN WORDS IN ENGLISH

Any use of foreign expressions should serve a real need. The overuse of foreign words in an attempt to impress your **reader** or to be elegant is **affectation**. Your goal of effective communication can be accomplished only if your reader understands what you write; choose foreign expressions, therefore, only when they serve the purpose of making an idea clearer.

Words not fully assimilated into the English language are set in **italics** if printed (underlined in typed manuscript).

> *Examples: sine qua non, coup de grâce, in res, in camera*

Words that have been fully assimilated need not be italicized.

> *Examples:* cliché, etiquette, vis-à-vis, de facto, résumé

When in doubt, consult a recent dictionary.

As foreign words become current in English, their plural forms give way to English plurals.

Examples: formulae becomes *formulas; antennae* becomes *antennas.*

In addition, accent marks tend to be dropped from words (especially from French words) the longer they are used in English. If the word has not been absorbed into English, however, its accent mark is a part of its spelling and to omit it is to misspell the word; the same is true of the dieresis and the German umlaut (¨). Foreign **diacritical marks** are often written in pen because American typewriters do not have them.

foreword/preface

The terms *foreword* and *preface* are sometimes used interchangeably, but are increasingly differentiated. A foreword is usually an introductory statement about a book or **report** written by someone other than the author. A preface is a statement by the author about the purpose, background, or **scope** of the book or report. The preface of this book, as an example, is on page *v*.

formal report

The formal report is commonly used in business and industry for **reports** that are especially long or important. It is popular because it is segmented. The **abstract** or preface provides a summary for those readers who need only that; the body of the report contains the details for those readers who need them; the **table of contents** provides an **outline** for those who need only certain details; the letter of transmittal often explains why the project or study being reported was initiated, and so on. The fact that the formal report is segmented also means that it lends itself to a clean and obvious organization, which serves as an aid to the reader.

Although the **format** of formal reports varies from one organization to another, all have common elements. The following are typical parts of the formal report.

LETTER OF TRANSMITTAL

A letter of transmittal (or **memorandum** if the report is for internal use only) often accompanies a formal report (see page 183). It may be merely a personal note that would not be appropriate within the report, or it may be an explanation of how, why, or under what circumstances the report was prepared. It can be stapled to the outside of the report, placed within the report, or sent in a separate envelope.

COVER

If a formal report is not bound, the cover is often a three-ring binder with a gummed label. The cover should include (1) the name of the organization, (2) the appropriate division within the company, (3) the title of the report, (4) the date, and (5) the name of the author (or authors).

TITLE PAGE

The cover information is usually repeated on the title page, with lines sometimes added for approval signatures (see page 183).

ABSTRACT

A brief summary of the report, called an abstract, is often included so that those who wish to do so may get an overview of the project.

PREFACE

A preface is a brief statement by the author to explain the background, **objective**, and **scope** of the report (see page 184).

TABLE OF CONTENTS

A table of contents, giving the main divisions of the report with their page numbers, may also be included, especially if the report is large. The outline heads and subheads may be used to create the table of contents (see page 184).

LIST OF ILLUSTRATIONS (OR FIGURES)

A list of the **illustrations** may also be included if there are more than a few illustrations in the report. This might help someone who does not need to read the report but would like to see a key **graph** or chart.

BODY

The body of the report should be typed with a good typewriter ribbon so that it is reproducible (carbon ribbons make excellent reproducible copies). The margins of the report should provide space for comments. Page numbers may appear in the upper right or bottom center of each page.

CONCLUSIONS

Some reports provide a separate section for **conclusions**. This not only gives the conclusions **emphasis** but also provides a quick summary of the report's findings for those who do not need or do not have time to read the entire report.

RECOMMENDATIONS

A separate section for recommendations, like one for conclusions, can provide emphasis and quick reference.

GLOSSARY

A **glossary** is a list of terms with their definitions.

APPENDIX

An **appendix** provides a place in the report for statistics, **tables**, and other information that may be of interest to some readers but would not be appropriate in the body of the report.

FOOTNOTES

If your report contains **footnotes**, a separate page may be provided for them after the body of the report. It is usually clearer, however, to place footnotes at the bottom of the appropriate page within the report.

BIBLIOGRAPHY

An alphabetized **bibliography** that is "full" (containing all your sources) or "selected" (the material directly referred to in the text) may also be included.

SAMPLE REPORT

The following is a sample formal report. Because formal reports are normally very long, this one has been reduced from its original size to make its inclusion in this book practical; however, enough is retained to illustrate the construction of a formal report.

TO: L. R. Bonds, Vice-President
           Education and Publications Division

FROM: H. O. Laird, Chairman
           Publications Committee

SUBJECT: Publications Committee Report

The attached report represents at least a partial
completion of Phase Two as defined in your memo of
July 30.

We recognize that there are still many things to
do and other areas that require additional study.
Therefore, one of our recommendations is that we
continue our activity and that we work on specific
subjects with individual reports.

This report represents some very serious soul-searching
work by each member of the committee. Each member has
been very helpful and willing to do his share of the
work, and I want to take this opportunity to thank
them again for it.

We look forward to meeting with you for a full
discussion of the report and an examination of specific
points you wish to pursue.

PUBLICATIONS COMMITTEE REPORT

Presented to

Mr. L. R. Bonds

Vice-President, Education and Publications Division

November 9, 1975

Table of Contents

Preface i
Table of Contents iii
Part I: A Condensed Report of Committee Observations 1
    Publications 2
    Organization 4
    Operation 6
    Personnel 8
Part II: Conclusions and Recommendations 9
Appendix A: Observations in Detail 14
    Publications 15
    Organization 23
    Operation 41
    Personnel 56
Appendix B: Individual Reports 85
    Memorandum from the Chairman 86
    Report by Walter Browser 88
    Report by Gerald Watson 92
    Report by Gunther Brown 96
    Report by Robert Helms 99

PUBLICATIONS COMMITTEE REPORT

PREFACE

This report consists of information gathered by members
of the Publications Committee from visits during
October 1975 to publications groups in the following
companies.

Xempa	Heward	Decklock
Latigil Equipment	Leweynom	Raniva
Vacuin		

Part I of the report is a condensation of the information gathered by committee members during interviews
with publications group members.

Part II of the report contains conclusions and recommendations indicated by committee observations. The
recommendations are endorsed unanimously by the
committee.

Two appendixes present the "raw data" from which the
two main parts of the report are derived. Refinement
of the material in both appendixes by the committee as
a whole led to parts I and II of the report. Appendix
A is a detailed presentation of the answers obtained
by committee members during interviews structured by a

questionnaire prepared in advance of the visits. Appendix B contains four separate reports written individually by committee members making the visits; written in unprescribed form and prefaced by a memorandum from the committee chairman, these reports are intended to complement information obtained from the questionnaire.

PART I: A CONDENSED REPORT OF COMMITTEE OBSERVATIONS

PUBLICATIONS

Publications produced by our company are similar to those produced by the corporations surveyed. Every corporation attempts to document an entire line of hardware and software. Some corporations publish for a broader audience than we do, providing technical literature for high-distribution promotional purposes. Small corporations generally produce multipurpose publications that are used for sales promotion as well as for training and reference in post-sale support of the product.

Nearly all corporations have formal writing standards guides to attempt to maintain communications quality, although enforcement of standards by editors and managers varies from loose to strict. All but one of the corporations produce a catalog of publications; these catalogs are continually updated and are reissued on schedules varying from weekly to annually. Cross-reference and key-word indexes are incorporated in catalogs produced by our company and by Heward. Readers learn of publications primarily by automatic distribution of the publications themselves.

Forms of publications vary among corporations within only a limited range. Most corporations produce both loose-leaf and bound publications. Most larger corporations publish the bulk of material side-stitched between two lightweight covers by two heavy staples, thus providing for immediate bound use and for loose-leaf use with the staples removed.

Charges assessed for publications used by customer and corporation personnel generally include only printing and distribution costs. Xempa, however, is currently attempting to establish a program to recover all costs, and Decklock charges a prorated share of all costs to users other than machine renters and pur- chasers (educational institutions, outside technicians, etc.).

Summary. We deviate little from the norm in the publications we produce, especially with respect to the larger companies surveyed by the committee. The most significant difference between our publications and those from smaller corporations is in scope of use: smaller corporations generally pursue more vigorous promotional distribution for reading by a general audience prior to sale.

ORGANIZATION

Similarities between the structure of our publications

organization and those of other corporations are not as great as the likeness of product indicates. Corporations of a size comparable to ours have product development spread geographically throughout the world, and they have separate publications organizations resident at each development site. There is no centralization of writing activities, either geographically or organizationally, as there is here. Only Leweynom is pursuing functional centralization by establishing a single "publishing house" to coordinate, standardize, edit, and produce publications written in several organizations and locations.

Publications organizations at most corporations surveyed appear to be the product of necessity rather than design. Clear corporate mandates are lacking, and only Leweynom approached publications as a product of the corporation that should be included in written project specifications. Typically among other corporations, publications management develops publications only as necessitated by each new product, in conference with higher management and nonpublications personnel in the local engineering or software support agency.

In all corporations except ours, publications funds--once they are initially allocated by higher management--are controlled by publications personnel; our company is the only one to have nonpublications

personnel control funding within a budgeted period.
Most publications groups have direct control of artwork
production, although only half control printing production. Groups that do control printing generally
avoid using a corporate printer in order to increase
printing speed and decrease printing costs. Ware-
housing and distribution, except at Leweynom, are not
under publications-organization control.

Responsibility for the accuracy of content in
technically oriented publications generally rests with
publications management, although advice is sought in
courtesy reviews by technical agencies. A legal
department is usually responsible for proper corporate-
image requirements (trademarks, logos, etc.). Customer
sales and reference publications in a few instances
undergo required reviews by nonpublications marketing
agencies.

The total budget for publications in smaller corporations appears proportionally higher than the budget
for publications in our company. Budget figures for
publications within corporations of size comparable to
ours, however, are unavailable.

Summary. Centralization of publications is unpar-
alleled in companies similar in size to ours, even
though the functions and responsibilities of our centralized publications organization do not appear dif-

ferent from those of geographically and organizationally fragmented publications agencies in other
corporations.

OPERATION

The writer's function seems to be fairly standard
throughout the industry: the writer has total responsi-
bility·for creating the publication through the final
draft. Editors assume responsibility at that point and
see the job through production. We differ from this
only in that our writers maintain responsibility for
the publication through production--we never release
complete responsibility to the editor.

Although publications departments throughout the
industry consistently become active at the planning
stage of the product-development cycle, the point at
which the writer becomes involved varies so much that
it would be futile to attempt to summarize it.

Input to the writer also seems to be fairly
standard at the following averages: research documentation, 45 percent; oral, 35 percent; writer's own
knowledge, 15 percent; and hands-on experience, 5
percent. All writers are expected to evaluate their
source material for logic and technical accuracy and to
contribute any significant result to the development of
the product.

All the companies visited are concerned about the

small amount of time they are able to devote to updating existing publications. All would like to do a
better job of updating but feel severely hampered by
lack of manpower. As the available manpower permits,
most attempt to update on an "as needed" basis.

Deadlines are established by the release date of a
new product for promotional literature and by the delivery date for technical manuals. Most companies
require that a basic set of literature be available by
each date.

No one has yet found an adequate means of evaluating the effectiveness of publications. Although
most companies visited use some variation of a comment
sheet, responses have been of no real value as a gauge
of the effectiveness of publications.

We trail our major competitors significantly in
automated production procedures, particularly in the
use of EDP systems in information-filing and text-edit
programs. Most competitors also use composers and
MTST's, but in greater numbers than we use them.

Summary. The significant points are (1) we lag
behind our competitors in EDP automation of production
facilities; (2) the industry is still groping for a
method of evaluating the effectiveness of publications;
(3) no one is able to spend adequate time on updating
because of inadequate manpower; and (4) only our

company asks writers to devote a portion of their time to the largely clerical effort of manuscript production.

PERSONNEL

With the single exception of our company, other computer manufacturers constitute the major source of writers. They simply lure writers away from their competitors. The next most common source is other departments, and the least common is the college campus. The composite background of the average writer in the industry seems to be about four years of college and five years of experience in computer technology. Most of our competitors, particularly the large ones, have four classifications of writers.

Only Heward, Latigil, and Decklock offer significant training to beginning writers, and only Heward and Latigil offer training in writing.

Limited experience with job shops and free-lance writers is fairly common, but generally negative. It has been more successful in the sales publications area than in the technical end of the business.

Summary. The significant factors here are (1) we do not compete for writers in the labor market, and (2) we put a great deal more effort into training new writers than any of our competitors except Latigil.

This seems to indicate that we may be training writers
for our competitors.

PART II: CONCLUSIONS AND RECOMMENDATIONS
Surveys of corporations comparable in size to ours
demonstrate repeatedly that separated publications
organizations in the same company provide only a fragmented approach to publications. At other large corporations, as here, publications do not measure up to
full potential as a vehicle for economically and effectively carrying information to company and customer
personnel.

At the present time, all large-company publications operations are being carried out within an
organizational structure that restrains development of
publications into a vehicle measuring up to its potential. Publications provided by different agencies
to service personnel and site representatives, for
example, sometimes involve duplication in research and
writing effort, and in addition they may cause communication difficulties between the two groups of readers.

A single publications program created by a single
knowledgeable and competent publications authority can
exercise the needed control over dissemination of
information and develop a degree of effectiveness and
professionalism unattainable by our competitors under

their current organizational structures. Single-point control would give us a competitive advantage.

The publications efforts of our competitors are fragmented for one reason: their publications efforts are decentralized. We have a potential advantage by being, for the most part, physically centralized. This gives us the opportunity to unify our publications effort--functionally as well as physically--to benefit every area of the company.

The committee, therefore, recommends that the Education and Publications Division proceed to the next logical step in organizing our publications activities: complete unification of all publications work under a single manager. Reporting to the Manager of Publications should be (1) a Manager of Support Publications, (2) a Manager of Service Publications, (3) a Manager of Educational and Promotional Publications, (4) a Manager of Production and Distribution, and (5) a Manager of Quality Assurance. The structure of the resulting unified organization is shown in the following organizational chart.

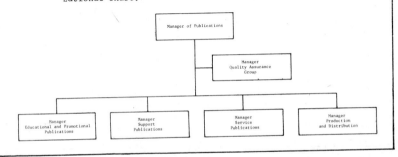

The position of Manager of Publications should be filled by a person who has extensive knowledge of and experience in publications, competent writing knowledge and experience, competent technical knowledge and experience, good knowledge of the philosophy and goals of the company, and good administrative knowledge and experience.

Second-line publications managers should be technically competent, capable of evaluating writing, good administrators, and respected by their subordinates. The Manager of Production and Distribution must have sufficient publications background to be able to coordinate activities in copy preparation, printing, and distribution.

The Publications Department should contain a Quality Assurance Group of publications professionals who operate throughout the department to ensure a uniform and consistently high quality of publications. Every member of the group should have a professional publications background, and every member should also have demonstrated competence in a technical field other than publications.

The committee unanimously endorses implementation of this recommendation because of the importance of the benefits to both corporation and customer.

formal writing style

Formal writing style is difficult to define because there is no clear dividing line between formal and **informal writing style**—elements of both appear in almost all writing. Formal writing style can perhaps best be defined by pointing to certain material that is clearly formal, such as scholarly and scientific articles in professional journals, lectures read at meetings of professional societies, and legal documents. Although **technical writing style** and **business writing style** are not as formal as they once were, technical writing (especially in such **formats** as **specifications**) tends to be somewhat more formal than business writing.

Any particular sample of writing is judged to be formal or informal depending on a number of distinctive qualities. One of the primary distinctions of formal style is that it is normally written rather than spoken. Material written in formal style is usually the work of a specialist in a particular field writing to other specialists. As a result, the vocabulary is specialized. The writer's **tone** is impersonal and objective because the subject matter looms larger in the writing than the author's personality (see **point of view**). Unlike informal writing style, formal writing style does not use **contractions**, slang, or dialect (see **English, varieties of**). **Sentences** are often elaborate because complex ideas are generally being examined.

Formal writing need not be dull and lifeless, however. By using such techniques as the active **voice**, variety in sentences, and **subordination**, formal writing can be made lively if the subject matter is inherently interesting to the **reader**.

> *Example:* Although a knowledge of the morphological and chemical constitution of cells is necessary to the proper understanding of living things, in the final analysis it is the activities of their cells that distinguish organisms from all other objects in the world. Many of these activities differ greatly among the various types of living things, but some of the basic sorts are shared by all, at least in their essentials. It is these fundamental actions with which we are concerned here. They fall into two major groups —those that are characteristic of the cell in the *steady state,* that is, in the normally functioning cell not engaged in reproducing itself, and those that occur during the process of *cellular reproduction.*
>
> —Lawrence S. Dillon, *The Principles of Life Sciences* (New York: Macmillan, 1964), p. 32.

Whether you should use a formal style in a particular instance depends on your reader and your **objective**. When writers attempt to force a formal style where it should not be used, they are likely to fall into **affectation, awkwardness**, and **gobbledygook**.

format

Format is a word used to describe the physical arrangement and general appearance of a finished writing project. A good general appearance is important to any writing project because it puts your **readers** in a favorable frame of mind toward your work and lets them know that you have put much planning and thought into it. An unpleasing appearance, on the other hand, is likely to put your readers in a negative frame of mind toward your work.

The type of writing project normally determines the format the writer uses. Such writing projects as **formal reports, memorandums, questionnaires, progress reports, proposals, technical manuals, correspondence, trip reports, résumés, instructions**, and **laboratory reports** have fairly standard formats. Some may, for example, include a **foreword** or preface, a **glossary**, a **table of contents**, an **index**, or a **bibliography**. Some may use such devices as **heads**, leaders (see **period**), **headers** and footers, **illustrations, indentation**, or **footnotes**, and others may not. Format is important because any way you can make your finished product more pleasing and accessible to your reader will help you achieve your ultimate **objective**— the clear communication of information.

former/latter

Former and *latter* should refer to only two items in a **sentence** or **paragraph**.

> *Example:* The president and his trusted aide emerged from the conference, the *former* looking nervous and the *latter* looking downright glum.

Because these terms make the **reader** look back to previous material to identify the reference, they impede reading and are best avoided.

> *Change:* We spent a great deal of time on the Jones account and very little on the Evans account, the *former* being highly profitable and the *latter* only marginally so.
>
> *To:* We spent a great deal of time on the Jones account, which was highly profitable, and very little time on the Evans account, which produced only marginal profits.

forms of discourse

There are four forms of discourse: exposition, description, persuasion, and narration. **Exposition** is the straightforward presentation of facts and ideas with the **objective** of informing the **reader**; **description** is an attempt to re-create an object or situation with words so that the reader can visualize it mentally; **persuasion** attempts to convince the reader that the writer's point of view is the correct or desirable one; and **narration** is the presentation of a series of events in chronological order. These types of writing rarely exist in pure form; rather, they usually appear in combination.

formula/formulae

The plural form of *formula* is either *formulae* (a Latin derivative) or *formulas. Formulas* is more common, however, since it is the more natural English plural. (See also **foreign words in English**.)

> *Example:* You may present the underlying theory in your introduction, but save proofs or *formulas* for the body of your report.

fortuitous/fortunate

When an event is *fortuitous,* it happens by chance or accident and without plan. Such an event may be lucky, unlucky, or neutral.

> *Example:* My encounter with the general manager in Denver was entirely *fortuitous;* I had no idea he was there.

When an event is *fortunate,* it happens by good fortune or happens favorably.

> *Example:* Our *chance* meeting had a *fortunate* outcome.

functional shift

Many words shift easily from one **part of speech** to another, depending on how they are used. When they do, the process is called functional shift, or shift in function.

> *Examples:* It takes ten minutes to *walk* from the sales office to the accounting department. (verb)
> The long *walk* from the sales office to the accounting department reduces efficiency. (noun)
> Let us *run* the new data through the computer. (verb)

May I see the last computer *run?* (noun)
I talk to the Chicago office on the *telephone* every day. (noun)
Sometimes I have to call from a *telephone* booth. (adjective)
He will *telephone* the home office from London.(verb)
After we discuss the project, we will begin work on it. (conjunction)
After lengthy discussions, we began work. (preposition)
The partners worked well together forever *after*. (adverb)

G

gender

In English grammar, gender is a term for the way words are formed to designate sex. The English language provides for recognition of three genders: masculine, feminine, and neuter (to designate those objects that have no definable sex characteristics). The gender of most words can be identified only by the choice of the appropriate **pronoun** (*he, she, it*). Only these pronouns and a select few **nouns** (*actor/actress*) reflect gender.

Gender is important to writers because they must be sure that nouns and pronouns within a grammatical construction agree in gender. A pronoun, for example, must agree with its noun antecedent in gender. We must refer to a woman as *she* or *her*, not as *it;* to a man as *he* or *him*, not as *it;* to a barn as *it*, not *he* or *she*.

An antecedent that includes both sexes, such as *everyone* and *student*, has by long-standing convention taken a masculine pronoun. When this **usage** might be offensive by implying sexual bias, however, it is better to use plural nouns and pronouns.

Examples: Every *employee* should be aware of *his* group insurance benefits.
All *employees* should be aware of *their* group insurance benefits.

It is better (though not always possible) to avoid the awkward and pedantic "his or her," "he or she" type of construction.

general-to-specific method of development

The general-to-specific **method of development** begins with a general statement, then provides facts that substantiate the statement. For example, the beginning statement, "It is evident that we need to locate additional suppliers of integrated circuits," might then be supported by the following facts: (1) the current supplier is reducing his production; (2) we are expanding into the overseas market; and (3) domestic demand for our calculators continues to increase.

gerund

A gerund is a nonfinite **verb** ending in -*ing* and used as a **noun**.

Example: *Typing* is a useful skill to acquire.

A gerund may be used as the **subject** of a verb, the **direct object** of a verb, the object of a **preposition**, a **subjective complement**, or an **appositive**.

Examples: *Estimating* is an important managerial skill. (subject of a verb)
I find *estimating* difficult. (direct object of a verb)
We were unprepared for their *coming*. (object of a preposition)
Seeing is *believing*. (subjective complement)
My primary departmental function, *programming*, occupies about two-thirds of my time on the job. (appositive)

Only the possessive form of a noun or **pronoun** should precede a gerund.

Examples: *John's* working has not affected his grades.
His working has not affected his grades.

Do not confuse a gerund with a present **participle**, which has the same form, but functions as an **adjective**.

Examples: The job involves a great deal of *writing*. (gerund, used as a noun)
You must improve your *writing* skills. (participle, used as an adjective)

glossary

A glossary is a selected list of terms defined and explained for a particular field of knowledge. An alphabetical glossary, such as is often found at the end of a textbook, can be helpful for quick reference.

If you are writing a report that will go to people who are not familiar with many of your technical terms, you may want to include a glossary. (The inclusion of a glossary does not relieve you of the responsibility of defining in the text any terms you are certain your **reader** will not know.) If you include a glossary, keep the entries concise and be sure they are so clear that any reader can understand the definitions.

> *Example:* *Bearish:* Characterized by falling stock market prices.
> *Bullish:* Characterized by rising stock market prices.
> *Certificate of Deposit:* A certificate from a bank stating that the named person has a specified sum on deposit.
> *Debenture:* A certificate or voucher acknowledging a debt.

gobbledygook

Gobbledygook is writing that suffers from an overdose of traits guaranteed to make it stuffy, pretentious, and wordy. These traits include the overuse of big and mostly **abstract words**, inappropriate **jargon**, stale expressions, **euphemisms**, and deadwood. Gobbledygook is writing that attempts to sound official (officialese), legal (legalese), or scientific; it tries to make a "natural elevation of the geosphere's outer crust" out of a molehill. Consider the following statement from an auto repair release form.

> *Example:* I hereby authorize the above repair work to be done along with the necessary material, and hereby grant you and/or your employees permission to operate the car or truck herein described on streets, highways, or elsewhere for the purpose of testing and/or inspection. An express mechanic's lien is hereby acknowledged on above car or truck to secure the amount of repairs thereto.

Translated into straightforward English, the statement gains in **clarity** what it loses in pomposity without losing its legal meaning.

> *Example:* You have my permission to do the repair work listed on this work order and to use the necessary material. You or your employees may drive my car or truck to test its performance. I understand that you will keep my car or truck until I have paid for all repairs.

Gobbledygook (also called bombast and pedantic writing) is packed with unusual words when more common ones would be clearer; it is heavy with foreign words when their English equivalents would be more appropriate; and it generally stresses trivial matters in the hope that the **reader** will be impressed with the writer's mental agility. George Orwell parodies such writing in an essay titled "Politics and the English Language." The following excerpt is typical.

> *Example:*   Objective consideration of contemporary phenomena compels the conclusion that success or failure in competitive activities exhibits no tendency to be commensurate with innate capacity, but that a considerable element of the unpredictable must invariably be taken into account.

The following revision of Orwell's passage demonstrates the clarity of direct writing.

> *Example:*   Success or failure today depends as much on chance as on your capabilities.

(See also **affectation, conciseness/wordiness,** and **word choice.**)

good/well

The confusion about the use of *good* and *well* can be cleared up by remembering that *good* is an **adjective** and *well* is an **adverb**.

> *Examples:*   John presented a *good* plan.
> The plan was presented quite *well.*

However, *well* can also be used as an adjective to describe someone's health.

> *Examples:*   He is not a *well* man.
> John is looking *well.*

got/gotten

Got is the past tense of *get.* Both *got* and *gotten* can be used as past **participles** of *get. Gotten* does stress a progressive movement, however, which is not emphasized in *got.*

> *Example:*   I *got* the new sales report, and I am pleased to see that sales have *gotten* better during the first half of the year. The semiannual report, which shows that fact, has been distributed. I know it has because Bill and I have *got* our copies already.

government proposal

A **proposal** is a company's offer to provide goods or services to a potential buyer within a certain amount of time and at a specified cost. Government proposals are usually prepared as a result of either an Invitation for Bids or a Request for Proposals that has been issued by a government agency.

INVITATION FOR BIDS

An Invitation for Bids (IFB) is inflexible; the rules are rigid and the terms are not open to negotiation. Any proposal prepared in response to an Invitation for Bids must adhere strictly to its terms.

The Invitation for Bids clearly defines the quantity and type of an item that a government agency intends to purchase. It is prepared at the request of the agency that will use the item, such as the Department of Defense. An advertisement indicating that the government intends to purchase the item is published in an official government publication, such as the *Commerce Business Daily* (available from the Superintendent of Documents, Washington, D.C. 20402). This publication is required reading for government-sales oriented organizations. The goods or services to be procured are defined in the IFB by references to performance standards called **specifications**. If, for instance, the item to be purchased is a truck, the important characteristics of that truck (height, weight, speed, carrying capacity, and so on) will be listed in the machine specification. More than one specification may apply to a single purchase, that is, one specification for the item, another for the manuals, another for welding procedures, and so forth. Bidders must be prepared to prove that their product will meet all requirements of all specifications.

A specification is restrictive, binding the bidder to production of an item that meets the exact requirements of the specification. For example, if a truck is the specified item, a company may not bid to furnish a cargo helicopter, even though the helicopter might do the job more efficiently than the truck. An Invitation for Bids requires the bidder to furnish a specific product that meets the specification parameters, and nothing else will be accepted or considered. An alternate suggestion will render the bid "nonresponsive," and it will be rejected.

Bearing in mind that the product will be tested, measured, and evaluated to see that it does, in fact, meet the requirements of the specification, price is the main criterion that enters into the selection of the vendor. However, an organization with superior engineering skills can often supply a product that meets the specification at a price well below that of a less sophisticated competitor. When a high degree of technological competence, unusual facilities, or other valid requirements make it necessary, the procuring agency may require the bidder to possess certain minimum qualifications in order to be considered; a paper clip manufacturer employing ten people, for instance, could not qualify to bid on a procurement of military aircraft.

REQUEST FOR PROPOSALS

In contrast to the Invitation for Bids, the Request for Proposals is flexible. It is open to negotiation, and it does not necessarily specify exactly what goods or services are required. Often, a Request for Proposals will define a problem and allow those who respond to it to suggest possible solutions. As an example, if a procuring agency wanted to develop a way to make foot soldiers more mobile (capable of covering difficult terrain at high speed), a Request for Proposal would normally be the means used to find the best method and select the most qualified vendor. In some instances, Requests for Proposals are presented in two or more stages, the first being development of a concept, the second being a "prototype" machine or device, and the third being the manufacture of the device selected. The procedure for preparing a proposal in response to a Request for Proposals is as follows.

The procuring agency defines the problem and publishes it as a Request for Proposals in one or more business journals. Companies interested in government business scan the appropriate publications daily. Upon finding a project of interest, the sales department of such a company obtains all available information from the procuring agency. It then presents the data to management for a decision on whether the company is interested in the project. If the decision is positive, the corporate technical staff is assigned the task of developing a "concept" to accomplish the task posed by the Request for Proposals. The technical staff normally considers several alternatives, selecting one that combines feasibility and price. The staff's concept is presented to management for a decision on whether the company wishes to present a proposal to the requesting government agency.

Assuming that the decision is to proceed, preparation of a proposal is the next step. At a minimum, the proposal should provide a clear-cut statement of the problem and the proposed solution. It should include data to show that the company is financially and technologically sound (this may require a **résumé** of the qualifications of the people in charge and an **organizational chart** to show the chain of command). A discussion of the company's manufacturing capabilities and any other advantages it may have is also advisable. However, in dealing with government agencies, bear in mind that unnecessarily elaborate and costly proposals may be construed as a lack of cost-consciousness.

In many instances, the final cost to the government is determined by negotiation after the best overall concept has been selected. However, if your concept is one that provides a simple and inexpensive solution to the problem, cost is an advantage that you should point out. If your concept is expensive, explain the benefits of advanced engineering, speed, increased capacity, and so forth.

Further information about the government procurement process can be obtained from the *Armed Service Procurement Regulations* (available from the U.S. Government Printing Office, Washington, D.C. 20402).

The following sample proposal was prepared in response to a Request for Proposals.

Example: Advantages of the Proposed 5,000 H.P. Design

> The Navy Department has indicated to Burdlorn Manufacturing Company a need for main diesel propulsion engines to be used in conjunction with gas turbines on a program with the code name of CODAG. We have been advised that the power requirement for this engine is 5,000 horsepower, plus 10 percent overload. This engine must be contained within a space 24 feet long, 11 feet high, and 7 feet wide and must not exceed 60,000 pounds in weight. In addition, at a 5,000 horsepower operating level, it is not expected that the engine will require replacement or renewal of wearing parts or other major components more frequently than every 5,000 hours. The proposed design changes will result in a very light weight engine (12 pounds/BHP) but one with durability characteristics that will not be equaled by any engine throughout the world in this compact high-horsepower output.
>
> 5,000 HORSEPOWER ENGINE
>
> Burdlorn Manufacturing Company has completed shop tests on NOBS 72393, addenda 12 and 13. During these tests, the

Navy engine serial GR-1047-0836 was operated at loads up to 4,950 brake horsepower (just 1 percent short of the 5,000 horsepower goal). As a result of these tests, we are satisfied that the 16-cylinder, 11″ bore, 12″ stroke V-engine, with a rating of 5,000 horsepower at 1,000 rpm, is well within practical limits. On the basis of an intensive review of the service history of the four (4) engines installed· on the LST-1176 and all of the research and development work conducted at the Burdlorn factory, coupled with a substantial amount of analytical design work, Burdlorn Manufacturing Company recommends that certain redesigns be effected, based on the above information.

As a result of the recent tests at loads up to 4,950 horsepower that have been run in our factory, Burdlorn Manufacturing Company has successfully dealt with the thermodynamic problems of air/fuel requirements, air flow, heat transfer, and other related problems. In proposing design criteria, which are conservative to insure the desired reliability, we have applied sufficient analysis to the individual components to make specific recommendations.

In order to summarize findings that we feel the Navy needs to evaluate our proposal, we will outline in numerical sequence the improvements and advantages based on our total experience with the 11″ bore, 12″ stroke, 16-cylinder V-engine.

1. Frame. Burdlorn Manufacturing Company recommends that the present 17 inches center distance from one cylinder to the adjacent cylinder be increased by 3 inches to provide 20 inches center distance from cylinder to cylinder in a given bank. The additional 3 inches per cylinder will mean an overall increase in engine length of 24 inches. This will mean an engine length of approximately 22 feet with the engine-driven· auxiliary equipment. This will be well within the 24 foot maximum covered by the Navy specifications. The additional 3 inches will provide the following advantages.
    a. The principal load carrying member in the frame, which is the athwartship plate, will be increased in thickness from 1/2 inch to 3/4 inch.
    b. Additional clearance is provided for welding and machining, particularly on the intermediate deck.
    c. Additional length is provided for the main and crankpin journals. This will increase the bearing areas for the main and crankpin bearings and thus gain the advantage of reduced bearing loads.

    The results of our experimental stress analysis have indicated a substantial bending movement in the top deck of the present design. Accordingly, Burdlorn Manufacturing

Company proposes to increase the thickness of the top deck. The present design uses forgings. We are proposing to use controlled quality steel castings of substantially heavier construction to reduce the stress levels.

Burdlorn Manufacturing Company has done a substantial amount of stress analysis on a similar frame on our Model FS-13-1/2″ × 16-1/2″ V-engine. On the basis of this experience, we recommend a minor redesign of the main bearing saddles to create a more even stress distribution in transmitting the load through the athwartship plates to the main bearing saddles. These main bearing saddles would be made from steel castings such as our present 13-1/2″ × 16-1/2″ engines currently use.

To provide for reduction in stress levels in the sidesheets of the engine, we propose increasing the plate thickness from 1/2 inch to 5/8 inch. In addition, we have found through extensive testing of the Navy engine and our 13-1/2″ × 16-1/2″ V-engine and also by exhaustive photoelastic stress analysis techniques that the present "hourglass" design results in a stress concentration factor at the "waist" of the frame. Accordingly, we propose a modification in this shape that will reduce the stress concentration factor due to this shape effect (see Figure 1).

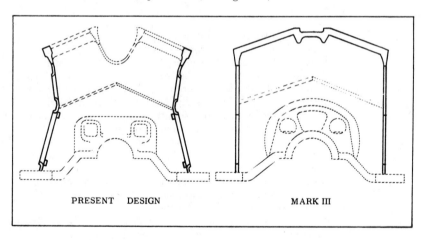

PRESENT   DESIGN   MARK III

Figure 1.   Frame Profiles

One problem experienced repeatedly on the LST-1176 was associated with the bosses for the handhole covers. Stress analysis work has shown a high stress concentration factor around these bosses because of unfused weld roots and also the increased localized stiffness caused by these bosses. Accordingly, we have designed handhole covers held in place by clamping action, which does not impose additional stress in the sidesheet due to the torquing down of the bolts against the bosses. We therefore gain the advantage by this direct means of eliminating a superimposed stress of 5,000 psi (see Figure 2).

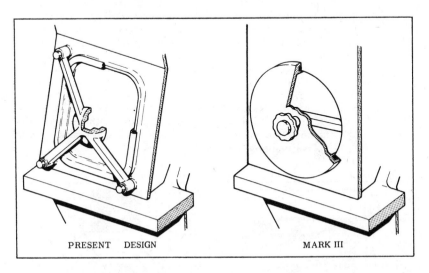

PRESENT DESIGN   MARK III

Figure 2.   Side Cover Details

An additional problem experienced on earlier frames was cracking in the air manifold. The present design provides for the air header to be welded in as an integral stress member of the frame. A number of problems are associated with this type of design, some of which are stress concentration factors in the welding together of the top deck, the air header, and the athwartship plate. A second problem associated with this type of construction is the thermogradient experienced because the air manifold temperature is regulated to approximately 100° F., whereas other heat sinks at higher temperature levels create thermal stresses in the frame that are difficult to manage. Accordingly, Burdlorn proposes a separate and independent air header that will be bolted to the frame in such a manner as not to contribute to the overall stresses or stress concentration factors of the frame weldment.

2. Valves. During the 1,000 rpm test of the engine under Navy contract NOBS 72393, a wear rate of approximately .050 inch per 1,000 hours was experienced on the inlet

valves. The wear rate on the exhaust valves was approximately .010 inch per 1,000 hours. A total wear of .100 inch would be considered acceptable for this size of valve and insert. Accordingly, it will be appreciated that a wear life of more than 5,000 hours could be expected on the exhaust valve, but a much shorter life was experienced on the inlet valve. A careful analysis of all available information has revealed only two differences between the intake valve and the exhaust valve that would contribute to this difference in wear rates. These two differences are as follows:

a. The exhaust cam is driven through a hollow shaft that is 4 inches O.D. by 2-1/2 inches I.D. The inlet cam is driven by a solid shaft that runs within the hollow exhaust camshaft and is 2-1/2 inches in diameter. It will be recognized that the relative stiffness of these two shafts in torsion is in the ratio of 5-1/2:1 as revealed by our calculations (see Figure 3).

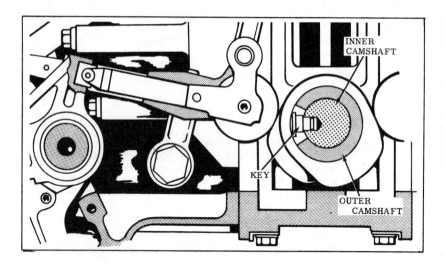

Figure 3. Present Inner and Outer Drive Shafts for Inlet and Exhaust Cams

b. The lift profiles of the intake and exhaust cams are identical; however, there is a greater dwell on the exhaust cam than there is on the inlet cam. The inlet cam has 15 degrees dwell, whereas the exhaust cam has 50 degrees dwell. The longer dwell on the exhaust cam, which cannot be incorporated in the inlet cam due to timing requirements, provides additional time in which the vibratory amplitudes in the valve train dampen or attenuate to a greater extent than the 15 degrees dwell provides on the inlet cam (see Figure 4). . . .

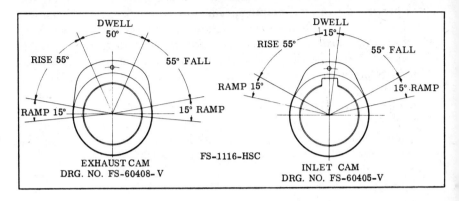

Figure 4. Comparison of Inlet and Exhaust Cam Profiles

The rest of the proposal continued to explain the design of the engine's cylinder heads, bearings, crankshaft, pistons, cylinder liners, connecting rod, and reversing mechanism.

grammar

Grammar is the systematic description of the way words work together to form a coherent language; in this sense, it is an explanation of the structure of a language. However, grammar is popularly taken to mean the sets of "rules" that govern how a language ought to be spoken and written; in this sense, it refers to the **usage** conventions of a language.

These two meanings of grammar—how the language functions and how it ought to function—are easily confused. To clarify the distinction, consider the expression "ain't." Unless used purposely for its colloquial flavor, *ain't* is unacceptable to careful speakers and writers because a convention of usage prohibits its use. Yet taken strictly as a **part of speech**, the term functions perfectly well as a **verb**; whether it appears in a declarative **sentence** ("I ain't going.") or an interrogative sentence ("Ain't I going?"), it conforms to the normal pattern for all verbs in the English language. Although we may not approve of its *use* in a sentence, we cannot argue that it is *ungrammatical*.

To achieve **clarity**, writers need a knowledge of both grammar (as a description of the way words work together) and the conventions of usage. Knowing the conventions of usage helps writers select the appropriate over the inappropriate word or expression. A knowledge of grammar helps them diagnose and correct problems arising from how words and **phrases** function in relation to one another. For example, knowing that certain words and phrases function to modify other words and phrases gives the writer a basis for correcting those **modifiers** that are not doing their job. Understanding **dangling modifiers** helps the writer avoid or correct a construction that obscures the intended meaning. In short, an understanding of grammar and its special terminology is valuable for writers chiefly because it enables them to communicate clearly and precisely.

graphs

A graph presents numerical data in visual form. This method has several advantages over presenting data in **tables** or within the text. Trends, movements, distributions, and cycles are more readily apparent in graphs than they are in tables. By providing a means for ready comparisons, a graph often shows a significance in the data not otherwise immediately apparent. Be aware, however, that although graphs present statistics in a more interesting and comprehensible form than tables do, they are less accurate. For this reason, they are often accompanied by tables giving the exact figures. There are many different kinds of graphs, most notably line graphs, bar graphs, pie graphs, and picture graphs.

LINE GRAPHS

The line graph, which is the most widely used of all graphs, shows the relationship between two sets of numbers by means of points plotted in relation to two axes drawn at right angles. The points, once plotted, are connected to one another to form a continuous line. In this way, what was merely a set of dots having abstract mathematical significance becomes graphic, and the relationship between the two sets of figures can easily be seen.

The line graph's vertical axis usually represents amounts, and its horizontal axis usually represents increments of time, as shown in Figure 1.

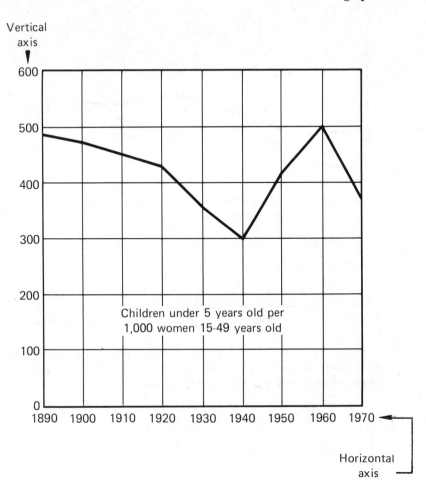

Figure 1. Fertility Ratio: 1890–1970

Source: Bureau of the Census

Line graphs with more than one line are common because they allow for comparisons between two sets of statistics for the same period of time. In creating such graphs, be certain to identify each line with a label or a legend, as shown in Figure 2. The difference between the two lines can be emphasized by shading the space between them.

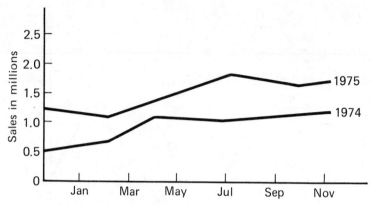

Figure 2.   Truck Sales, 1974 and 1975

Tips on Preparing Line Graphs

1. Give the graph a title that describes the data clearly and concisely, and display the title prominently.
2. Assign a figure number if your **report** includes several **illustrations**.
3. Indicate the zero point of the graph (the point where the two axes meet). If the range of data shown makes it inconvenient to begin at zero, insert a break in the scale as in Figure 3.

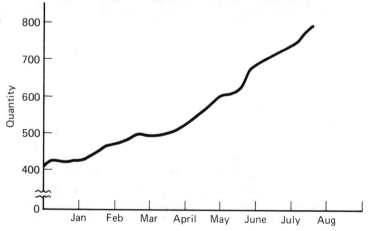

Figure 3.   Illustrating Zero Point

4. Graduate the vertical axis in equal portions from the least amount at the bottom to the greatest amount at the top. Ordinarily, the caption for this scale is placed at the upper left.
5. Graduate the horizontal axis in equal units from left to right. If a caption is necessary, center it directly beneath the scale.
6. Graduate the vertical and horizontal scales so that they give an accurate visual impression of the data, since the angle at which the curved line rises and falls is determined by the scales of the two axes. The curve can be kept free of distortion if the scales maintain a constant ratio with each other. See Figures 4 and 5.

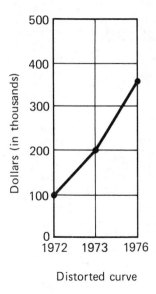

Distorted curve

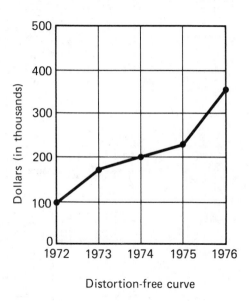

Distortion-free curve

Figure 4. Sales Growth   *Figure 5. Sales Growth*

7. Hold grid lines to a minimum so that curved lines stand out. Since precise values are usually shown in a table of data accompanying a graph, detailed grid lines are unnecessary. Note the increasing clarity of the three graphs in Figures 6, 7, and 8.

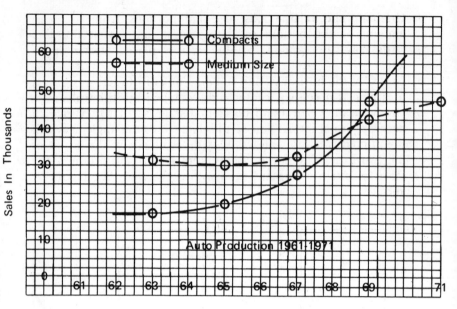

Figure 6.

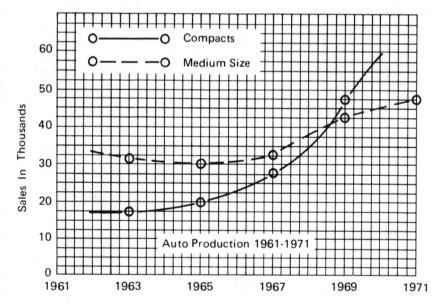

Figure 7.

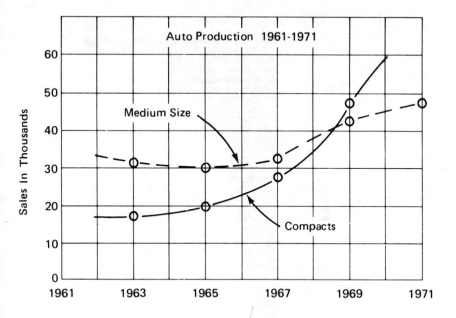

Figure 8.

8. Include a key (which lists and explains **symbols**) when necessary, as in Figure 7. At times a label will do just as well, as in Figure 8.
9. If the information comes from another source, include a source line just under the graph at the lower left.
10. Place explanatory footnotes below the graph, to the lower left.
11. Place all lettering horizontally if possible.

BAR GRAPHS

Bar graphs consist of horizontal or vertical bars of equal width but scaled in length to represent some quantity. They are commonly used to show (1) quantities of the same item at different times, (2) quantities of different items for the same time period, or (3) quantities of the different parts of an item that make up the whole.

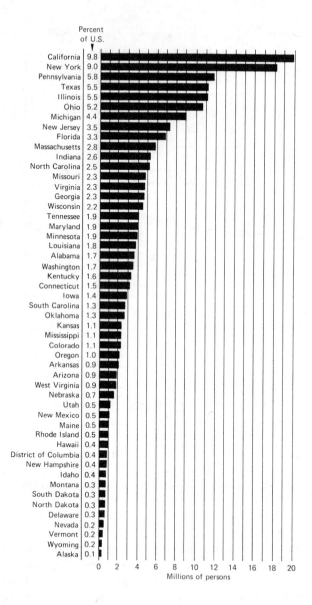

Percent
of U.S.

California	9.8
New York	9.0
Pennsylvania	5.8
Texas	5.5
Illinois	5.5
Ohio	5.2
Michigan	4.4
New Jersey	3.5
Florida	3.3
Massachusetts	2.8
Indiana	2.6
North Carolina	2.5
Missouri	2.3
Virginia	2.3
Georgia	2.3
Wisconsin	2.2
Tennessee	1.9
Maryland	1.9
Minnesota	1.9
Louisiana	1.8
Alabama	1.7
Washington	1.7
Kentucky	1.6
Connecticut	1.5
Iowa	1.4
South Carolina	1.3
Oklahoma	1.3
Kansas	1.1
Mississippi	1.1
Colorado	1.1
Oregon	1.0
Arkansas	0.9
Arizona	0.9
West Virginia	0.9
Nebraska	0.7
Utah	0.5
New Mexico	0.5
Maine	0.5
Rhode Island	0.5
Hawaii	0.4
District of Columbia	0.4
New Hampshire	0.4
Idaho	0.4
Montana	0.3
South Dakota	0.3
North Dakota	0.3
Delaware	0.3
Nevada	0.2
Vermont	0.2
Wyoming	0.2
Alaska	0.1

0   2   4   6   8   10 12 14 16 18 20
Millions of persons

Figure 9. States Ranked by Total Population: 1970

Source: Bureau of the Census

Figure 9 is an example of a bar graph showing varying quantities of the same item at the same time. Here each bar, which represents a different quantity of the same item, begins at the left scale. The left scale also provides additional information in the form of the percentage of the whole population each bar (and therefore each state) represents.

Some bar graphs show the quantities of different items for the same period of time. See Figure 10. (A bar graph with vertical bars is also called a column graph.)

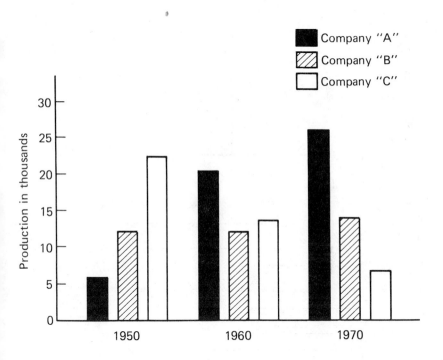

Figure 10. Auto Parts Production

Bar graphs can also show the different portions of an item that make up the whole. Here the bar is equivalent to 100 percent. It is then divided according to the appropriate proportions of the item sampled. This type of graph can be constructed vertically or horizontally and can indicate more than one whole where comparisons are necessary. See Figures 11 and 12 on page 218.

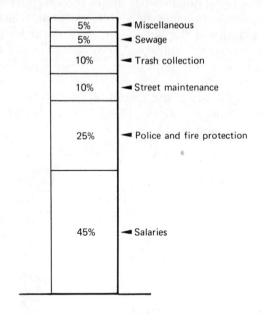

Figure 11. Your Municipal Tax Dollar

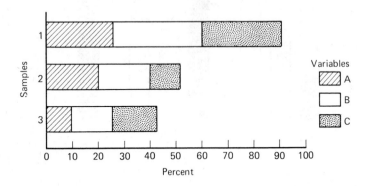

Figure 12. Example of 100 Percent Bar Graph
Showing Proportions of Three
Variables in Three Samples

If the bar is not labeled, the different portions must be marked clearly by shading or crosshatching. Include a key that identifies the various subdivisions.

PIE GRAPHS

A pie graph presents data as wedge-shaped sections of a circle. The circle equals 100 percent, or the whole, of some quantity (a tax dollar, a bus fare, the hours of a working day), with the wedges representing the various ways in which the whole is divided. In Figure 13, for example, the circle stands for a city tax dollar, and it is divided into units equivalent to the percentage of the tax dollar spent on various city services.

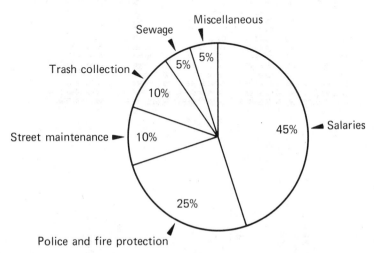

Figure 13. Your Municipal Tax Dollar

Pie graphs provide a quicker, more striking way of presenting the same information that can be presented in a table; in fact, a table often accompanies a pie graph with a more detailed breakdown of the same information.

When you construct a pie graph, keep the following things in mind.

1. The complete 360° circle is equivalent to 100 percent; therefore, each percentage point is equivalent to 3.6°.
2. To make the relative percentages as clear as possible, begin at the 12 o'clock position and sequence the wedges clockwise, from largest to smallest.
3. If you shade the wedges, do so clockwise and from light to dark.
4. Keep all labels horizontal and, most important, give the percentage value of each wedge.

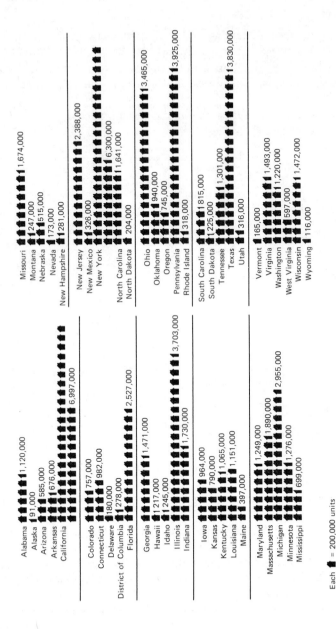

Figure 14. Number of Housing Units, by States: 1970
Source: Bureau of the Census

5. Finally, check to see that all wedges, as well as the percentage values given for them, add up to 100 percent.

Although pie graphs have strong visual impact, they also have drawbacks. If more than five or six items are presented, the graph looks cluttered. Also, since they usually present percentages of something, they must often be accompanied by a table listing precise statistics. Further, unless percentages are shown on the sections, the **reader** cannot compare the values of the sections as accurately as with a bar graph.

PICTURE GRAPHS

Picture graphs are modified bar graphs that use picture symbols of the item presented. Each symbol corresponds to a specified quantity of the item. See Figure 14. Note that precise figures are included since the graph can present only approximate figures.

Tips on Preparing Picture Graphs

1. Make the symbol self-explanatory.
2. Have each symbol represent a single unit.
3. Show larger quantities by increasing the number of symbols rather than by creating a larger symbol (it is difficult to judge relative sizes accurately).

H

half

Half a, half an, and *a half* are all correct idiomatic uses of the word *half.*

Examples: Call the client in *half an* hour.
The sales meeting lasted *a half* hour.
Your call to London will be completed in *half a* minute.

A half a (or *a half an*) is colloquial, however, and should be avoided in writing.

Change: I will finish the sales report in *a half an* hour.
To: I will finish the sales report in *half an* hour.

he/she

Since there is no singular **personal pronoun** in English that refers to both sexes, the word *he* has traditionally been used when the sex of the antecedent is unknown.

> *Example:*   Whoever is appointed (a man or woman) will find *his* task difficult.

When use of a masculine **pronoun** might be offensive, however, it is better to use a plural pronoun (or avoid use of a pronoun altogether) than to offend.

> *Example:*   *Whoever* is appointed will find *the* task difficult.
> *Change:*   An *employee* should take advantage of *his* group insurance benefits.
> *To:*   *Employees* should take advantage of *their* group insurance benefits.

You could also use the **phrase** *he or she*.

> *Example:*   *He or she* will find *his or her* task difficult.

Unfortunately, *he or she* and *his or her* are clumsy when used repeatedly; the best advice is to reword the **sentence** to use a plural pronoun. (See also **gender** and **Ms./Miss/Mrs.**)

header/footer

A header in a **report, technical manual**, or **specification** is identifying information carried at the top of each page. The header normally contains the **topic** (or topic and subtopic) dealt with in that section of the report, manual, or specification (specifications also include the identification numbers of sections and **paragraphs**).

A footer is identifying information carried at the bottom of each page. The footer generally contains the date of the document, the page number, and sometimes the manual name and section title.

Although the types of information included in headers and footers vary greatly from one organization to the next, the example on p. 223 is fairly typical.

heads

Heads (also called *headings*) are titles or subtitles within the body of a long piece of writing that serve as guideposts for the **reader**. They

Example:

Header

NCR CENTURY SOFTWARE SPECIFICATIONS

VOLUME 1, CHAPTER 1.0 NEAT/3 LANGUAGE

1.5.2 THE OPERATION CODE

THE OPERATION CODE, OR OPCODE, IS ENTERED IN THE CODING STATEMENT IN COL. 18-23.

ALL OPERATION CODES ARE 1- TO 6-CHARACTER MNEMONICS WHICH MUST BE ENTERED LEFT-JUSTIFIED IN THE OPERATION CODE FIELD OF THE CODING STATEMENT. THEY MAY CONTAIN ONLY ALPHABETIC OR NUMERIC CHARACTERS (WITH THE EXCEPTION OF THE RENAME, CONTINUATION, AND FLOWRITE INSTRUCTIONS) AND MUST BEGIN WITH AN ALPHABETIC CHARACTER. AN OPCODE MAY NOT CONTAIN A SPACE BUT MAY BE FOLLOWED BY ANY NUMBER OF TRAILING SPACES. THE SIX DIFFERENT TYPES OF OPCODE ARE THE PROCEDURAL INSTRUCTION, COMPILER PSEUDO-OPERATION, HEX OPCODE, RENAME STATEMENT, CONTINUATION STATEMENT, FLOWRITE STATEMENT AND SPUR CONTROL INSTRUCTION.

THE PROCEDURAL INSTRUCTIONS INCLUDE ALL THE NORMAL EXECUTABLE COMMANDS IN THE LANGUAGE. THE COMPILER PSEUDO-OPERATIONS, SUCH AS OVRLAY, ENTRY, AND USE, ARE USED TO PROVIDE INSTRUCTIONS TO THE COMPILER REGARDING PROGRAM CONSTRUCTION. BOTH OF THESE TYPES OF OPCODES ARE LISTED AND DISCUSSED IN SECT. 1.9-1.14.

HEX OPCODES ARE USED TO ENTER AN ABSOLUTE COMMAND CODE IN HEXADECIMAL. RENAME STATEMENTS ARE USED TO ASSIGN REFERENCES TO FOLLOWING SOURCE LINES AND CONTINUATION STATEMENTS ARE USED TO EXTEND OPERANDS. THESE OPCODES ARE DISCUSSED IN THE FOLLOWING SUBSECTIONS.

THE FLOWRITE PSEUDO-OPERATIONS MAY BE INCLUDED IN A NEAT/3 PROGRAM TO PROVIDE DOCUMENTATION IN A PROGRAM AND INPUT TO THE FLOWRITE SYSTEM. THESE PSEUDOS ARE DISTINGUISHED BY A LEFT PARENTHESIS IN COL. 18 AND A RIGHT PARENTHESIS IN COL. 23.

THE SOURCE PROGRAM UTILITY ROUTINE (SPUR) CONTROL INSTRUCTIONS ARE OMIT, COPYA, COPYP, COPYR, COPYU, COPYUI AND SETPL. THESE CONTROL INSTRUCTIONS INSTRUCT SPUR TO PERFORM VARIOUS OPERATIONS WITH PROGRAM SOURCE FILES, AND THEREFORE NEVER ACTUALLY APPEAR IN A SOURCE FILE BY THE TIME IT IS PRESENTED TO THE COMPILER BY SPUR. THESE CONTROL INSTRUCTIONS ARE DISCUSSED IN VOL. 4, SECT. 4.1.

April 14, 1973

1.5 CODING STATEMENTS 65

Footer

divide the material into manageable segments, call attention to the main topics, and signal changes of topic. If a **report**, **proposal**, or other document you are writing is long or complicated, you may need several levels of heads to indicate major divisions, subdivisions, and even smaller units of those. In extremely technical material one occasionally sees as many as five levels of heads, but as a general rule it is rarely necessary (and usually confusing) to use more than three. The following example is greatly shortened and is intended only to illustrate the use of the heads—in this case, three levels (beyond the title of the entire report).

Example: INTERIM REPORT OF THE COMMITTEE TO INVESTIGATE NEW FACTORY LOCATIONS

The committee initially considered thirty possible locations for the proposed new factory. Of these, twenty were eliminated almost immediately for one reason or another (unfavorable tax structure, remoteness from rail service, inadequate labor supply, etc.). Of the remaining ten locations, the committee selected for intensive study the three that seemed most promising: Chicago, Minneapolis, and Salt Lake City. These three cities we have now visited, and our observations on each of them follow.

CHICAGO

Of the three cities, Chicago presently seems to the committee to offer the greatest advantages, although we wish to examine these more carefully before making a final recommendation.

Location

Though not at the geographical center of the United States, Chicago is centrally located in an area that contains more than three-quarters of the U.S. population. It is within easy reach of our corporate headquarters in New York. And it is close to several of our most important suppliers of components and raw materials—those, for example, in Columbus, Detroit, and St. Louis.

Transportation

Rail Transportation. Chicago is served by the following major railroads. . . .

Sea Transportation. Except during the winter months when the Great Lakes are frozen, Chicago is an international seaport. . . .

Air Transportation. Chicago has two major airports (O'Hare and Midway) and is contemplating building a third. Both domestic and international air cargo service is available. . . .

> *Transportation by Truck.* Virtually all of the major U.S. carriers have terminals in Chicago. . . .

As you can infer from this example, the heads you use grow naturally from the divisions and subdivisions of your **outline**. If more of the preceding example were given, the heads would look like this:

> CHICAGO (first level)
> Location (second level)
> Transportation (second level)
>   *Rail Transportation.* (third level)
>   *Sea Transportation.*
>   *Air Transportation.*
>   *Transportation by Truck.*
> Labor Supply (second level)
>   *Engineering Personnel.* (third level)
>   *Manufacturing Personnel.*
>   *Outside and Consulting Services.*
> Tax Structure (second level)
> Living Conditions (second level)
>   *Housing.* (third level)
>   *Education.*
>   *Recreation.*
>   *Climate.*
> MINNEAPOLIS (first level)
> Location (second level)
> Transportation
> (and so forth)

There is no one "correct" **format** for heads. Sometimes a company settles on a standard format, which everyone within the company is then expected to follow. Or a customer for whom a report or proposal is being prepared may specify a particular format. In the absence of such guidelines, the system used in the example should serve you well. Note the following formal characteristics:

1. The first-level head is in all **capital letters**, typed flush to the left margin on a line by itself, and separated by a line space from the material it introduces.
2. The second-level head is in capital and **lower-case letters**, also typed flush to the left margin on a line by itself, and also separated by a line space from the material it introduces.
3. The third-level head is in capital and lower-case letters, but it is "run in" right on the same line with the first sentence of the material it introduces. Therefore, it is followed by a period to

set it apart from what follows, and it is underlined or italicized so that it will stand out clearly on the page.

The most important things to keep in mind about heads are the following:

1. They should signal a shift to a new topic (or, if they are lower-level heads, a new "subtopic" within the larger topic).

2. Within the larger unit they subdivide, all heads at any one level should be consistent in their relationship to the topic of the larger unit. For instance, notice in the extended list of heads on page 225 that the first-level heads ("CHICAGO" and "MINNE-APOLIS") both bear the same relationship to the larger topic of the report (possible factory locations). When the discussion narrows to Chicago, all of the second-level heads within that unit bear the same relationship to the first-level head ("CHICAGO"): they refer to Chicago's location, its transportation, its labor supply, its tax structure, and its living conditions. And the third-level heads conform to the same principle within their units.

3. The fact that one unit at a particular level is subdivided by lower-level heads does not mean that *every* unit at that particular level must also include lower-level heads. In the example, notice that under the first-level head "CHICAGO" some of the second-level units (for instance, "Transportation") are further subdivided by third-level heads and some (for instance, "Location") are not.

4. However, within any single unit, if there is one lower-level head there must be at least two (you cannot logically divide something into just one part). For instance, if the report in the example were *only* about Chicago, it would make no sense to have a first-level head "CHICAGO." Instead, "Chicago" would be made a part of the title of the report—"Interim Report on the Investigation of Chicago as a Possible Factory Location"—and the present second-level heads ("Location," "Transportation," "Labor Supply," etc.) would be made first-level heads.

5. All heads at any one level within the same next-larger unit should be parallel with one another in structure (see **parallel structure**). For instance, note in the example that all of the heads are nouns or noun phrases.

6. Too many heads, or too many levels of heads, can be as bad as too few. A highway map that showed only New York and San Francisco would not be very helpful, even to the traveler driving

from New York to San Francisco. But a map that tried to show every street and every building in every town along the way would not be much better. Keep in mind the needs of your reader.

healthful/healthy

If something is *healthful* it "gives health."

> *Example:*   Yogurt is *healthful.*

If something is *healthy* it "has good health."

> *Example:*   We provide *healthful* lunches in the cafeteria because we want our employees to be *healthy.*

helping verb

A helping verb (also called an auxiliary verb) is a **verb** that is added to a main verb to help it indicate **mood, tense**, and **voice**. In doing so, it also forms a **verb phrase**.

> *Examples:*   I *am* going.
> I *will* go.
> I *should have* gone.
> I *should have been* gone.
> The order *was given.*

All helping verbs (*be, have, do, shall, will, may, can, must, ought*) can function alone as main verbs, but they usually function as helping verbs in verb phrases. Notice that the principal helping verbs are the various forms of the main verbs *be, have,* and *do.* The verbs *shall, will, may, can,* and *must* are often called the modal auxiliaries.

herein/herewith

The words *herein* and *herewith* are typical of a bombastic type of business **jargon** that should be avoided.

> *Change:*   I have *herewith* enclosed a copy of the contract.
> *To:*   I have enclosed a copy of the contract.

historic/historical

An event is *historic* if it is of special significance.

Example: The opening of the new wing was a *historic* occasion for the hospital fund-raising staff.

Historical refers to any event that has occurred in the past; therefore, an event that is *historical* may be interesting to a historian without necessarily being *historic*.

Example: The construction of the hospital was simply a *historical* event in the life of the city.

Use the indefinite **article** *a* rather than *an* with *historic* and *historical* because the words begin with a consonant sound rather than with a vowel sound (such as *an hour*).

house organ article

A house organ is a company publication or an employee publication that is produced by the employer. Its primary purpose is to keep employees informed about the company and its operations and policies. Many different types of house organs are found in business and industry—from the gossip sheet that carries little more than bowling scores and who got married or had a baby to the more sophisticated instruments of company policy that increase the employee's understanding of the company, its purpose, and the business in which it is engaged. If your company publishes a house organ of the latter type, you may be asked to contribute an article on a subject that you are especially qualified to write about. The editor may offer some general advice but can give you little more help until you submit a draft.

Before beginning to write, consider the traditional *who, what, where, when,* and *why* of journalism (who did it? what was done? where was it done? when was it done? and why was it done?)—and then add *how,* since the *how* of your subject may be of as much interest to your fellow employees as any of the five *w*'s. Notice in the sample article at the end of this entry how much **emphasis** is placed on explaining *how* value engineering is achieved.

Before going any further, determine whether there is an official company policy or position on your subject. If so, adhere to it as you prepare your article. If there is no company policy on your subject, determine as nearly as you can what management's attitude is toward your subject.

Gather several fairly recent issues of your company house organ and study the **style** and **tone** of the writing and the approach the company has taken to various kinds of subjects in past issues. Try to emulate these as you work on your own article. Ask yourself the following questions: What is the significance of your subject to the company? What is its significance to employees? The answers to these questions should help you establish the style, tone, and approach for your article. These answers should also heavily influence the **conclusion** you write for your article.

Research for a house organ article frequently consists of **interviewing**. Interview everyone concerned with your subject. Get all available information and all points of view. (Be sure to give maximum credit to the maximum number of people.)

Writing a house organ article requires a little more imagination than writing **reports**. With a house organ, you do not have a captive audience; therefore, you must use your imagination to provide four necessary ingredients to ensure a successful article: (1) an intriguing **title** to catch **readers'** attention (a **rhetorical question** is often effective); (2) eye-catching **photographs** or **illustrations** that entice them to read your lead paragraph to see what the subject is really about; (3) a lead, or first **paragraph**, that is designed to encourage further reading into your article (this paragraph generally makes the **transition** from the **title** to the down-to-earth treatment of the subject); and (4) a well-developed presentation of your subject to hold the reader's interest all the way to the conclusion.

Your conclusion should emphasize the significance of your subject to your company and its employees. Because of its strategic location to achieve emphasis, your conclusion should include the thoughts that you want your reader to retain about your subject.

In preparing your house organ article you will find it helpful to refer to the Checklist of the Writing Process and to follow the steps listed there.

Example: ## The Shrimp Has Learned to Whistle

Former Russian Premier Khrushchev was always fond of quoting a Russian proverb that went something like this: "The shrimp will learn to whistle before such an event will come to pass." The occasion never arose while he was still in public life, but if someone had told him that American manufacturers would one day sell transistor radios for less than the Japanese could sell them, he would almost certainly have quoted his favorite proverb.

Everyone is familiar with the fact that Japanese manufacturers captured the transistor radio market from our own manufacturers because of Japan's abundant supply of cheap labor. Today, however, American radio manufacturers are regaining that market so rapidly that the perplexed Japanese have sent representatives to this country to find out how we are doing it. They have learned that the answer can be summed up in two words: Value Engineering.

Value Engineering strives to increase the efficiency with which allocated resources are used either to reduce costs while maintaining quality or to increase quality while maintaining costs. Sound like pie in the sky? Tell that to the Japanese transistor radio manufacturers!

How does Value Engineering achieve such dramatic results? By asking questions. Each product and each part of each product are analyzed in painstaking detail and subjected to a series of searching, penetrating questions: What is it? What does it do? Is it necessary? What alternate methods might do the job? What do the alternate methods cost? Which is the least expensive alternate? Will it meet the requirements? What is needed to implement it? Nothing is sacred—nothing escapes this relentless analysis.

Value Engineering is a logical, organized method of achieving a high value product that provides exactly the required performance at the lowest possible cost. It is a fundamental approach that takes nothing for granted and attacks everything about a product—including the existence of the product itself—subject only to the restriction that the performance required of the product must not be altered.

The application of Value Engineering to American industry has emerged in the last few years in response to the need for more cost consciousness in the design, development, and production of industrial products. Its contribution is sorely needed if the United States is to maintain its high wage structure and still remain competitive with the rest of the world. And in our industry, we have all the competition we can handle right here at home. Because of such intense competition, the potential contribution of Value Engineering to the valve manufacturing industry is possibly even greater than to American industry in general.

The first step in the Value Engineering procedure is a clear definition of the function of a product or part. The Value Engineer then gathers all information pertaining to the product and its technology, with particular emphasis on a complete cost breakdown. He then develops alternate methods of achieving the required function. He costs the alternatives in detail and selects the least expensive technically feasible method. This method is then subjected to testing and verification to ensure that it achieves the required performance. The final step is to summarize the results of the study, submit them to management, and implement the change if approved.

Value Engineering techniques are not restricted to the engineering and manufacturing functions—they can be applied to any operation, to any job. We could all perform our duties more efficiently if we applied the simple basic principles of Value Engineering to them daily.

The potential contribution of Value Engineering to our company can hardly be overestimated. By reducing costs, thereby placing us in a better competitive position, Value Engineering can make a tremendous contribution to our security as a leader in our industry. By improving our competitive position, Value Engineering can also help to assure our continued growth as a company. And continued company growth increases our own individual job security as employees, as well as our potential for individual growth in our own jobs.

hyperbole

Hyperbole is exaggeration to achieve an effect or **emphasis**. It is a device used to emphasize or intensify a point by going beyond the literal facts. It distorts to heighten effect.

Examples: They *murdered* us at the negotiating session.
The hail was like *boulders*.

Used cautiously, hyperbole can magnify an idea without distorting it; therefore, it plays a large role in advertising.

Example: A box of Clenso detergent can clean a *mountain of clothes*.

Everyday speech abounds in hyperbole.

Examples: I'm *starved*. (meaning "hungry")
I'm *dead*. (meaning "tired")

Use hyperbole sparingly. (See also **figures of speech**.)

hyphen

Although the hyphen functions primarily as a **spelling** device, it also functions to link and to separate words; in addition, it occasionally replaces the **preposition** *to* (0–100 for 0 *to* 100). The most common use of the hyphen, however, is to join **compound words.**

Examples: able-bodied, self-contained, carry-all, brother-in-law

Some terms are optionally one word, two words, or hyphenated words.

Example: loanword/loan word/loan-word

A hyphen is used to form compound **numbers** and fractions when they are written out.

Examples: twenty-one, one forty-second

When in doubt about whether to hyphenate a word, check your **dictionary**.

HYPHENS USED WITH MODIFIERS

Two-word and three-word unit **modifiers** that express a single thought are frequently hyphenated when they precede a **noun** (an *out-of-date* car, a *clear-cut* decision). If each of the words could modify the noun without the aid of the other modifying word or words, however, do not use a hyphen (a *new digital* computer—no hyphen). Also, if the first word is an **adverb** ending in -*ly,* do not use a hyphen (*hardly* used, *badly* needed).

A modifying **phrase** is not hyphenated when it follows the noun it modifies.

Example: Our office equipment is *out of date.*

A hyphen is always used as part of a letter or number modifier.

Examples: 5-cent, 9-inch, H-bomb, T-square

In a series of unit modifiers that all have the same term following the hyphen, the term following the hyphen need not be repeated throughout the series; for greater smoothness and brevity, use the term only at the end of the series.

Change: The third-floor, fourth-floor, and fifth-floor rooms have been painted.
To: The third-, fourth-, and fifth-floor rooms have been painted.

HYPHENS USED WITH PREFIXES AND SUFFIXES

A hyphen is used with a **prefix** when the root word is a **proper noun**.

Examples: pre-Sputnik, anti-Stalinist, post-Newtonian

A hyphen may (but not must) be used when the prefix ends and the root word begins with the same vowel. When the repeated vowel is *i,* a hyphen is almost always used.

Examples: re-elect, re-enter, anti-inflationary

A hyphen is used when *ex-* means "former."

Examples: ex-partners, ex-wife

A hyphen may be used to emphasize a prefix.

Example: He was *anti-everything.*

The **suffix** *-elect* is hyphenated.

Examples: president-elect, commissioner-elect

OTHER USES OF THE HYPHEN

To avoid confusion, some words and modifiers should always be hyphenated. *Re-cover* does not mean the same thing as *recover,* for example; the same is true of *re-sent* and *resent, re-form* and *reform, re-sign* and *resign.*

Hyphens should be used between letters showing how a word is spelled.

Example: In his letter he spelled "believed" b-e-l-e-i-v-e-d.

Hyphens identify prefixes, suffixes, or written syllables.

Example: *Re-, -ism,* and *ex-* are word parts that cause spelling problems.

A hyphen can stand for *to* or *through* between letters and numbers.

Examples: pp. 44–46
the Detroit-Toledo Expressway
A–L and M–Z

Finally, hyphens are used to divide words at the end of a line. Words are divided on the basis of their syllables, which can be determined with a dictionary. Do not divide a word, however, if only one or two letters remain. A good rule of thumb on dividing a word is to determine whether each section is pronounceable. If a word is spelled with a hyphen, divide it only at the hyphen break unless to divide the word there would confuse the **reader** because the hyphen is essential to the word's meaning. It is generally better, however, to avoid dividing words unless this would leave a large gap at the end of a line. (See also **syllabication.**)

I

idea

The word *idea* means "the mental representation of an object of thought." Do not use it as a substitute for "impression" or "intention."

Change: We started out with the *idea* of returning early.
To: We started out with the *intention* of leaving early.
Change: She left me with the *idea* that he was in favor of the proposal.
To: She left me with the *impression* that he was in favor of the proposal.

idiom

Idiom refers to a group of words that has a special meaning apart from its literal meaning. Someone who "runs for office" in the United States, for example, need not be a track star. The same person would "stand for office" in England. In both nations, the individual is seeking public office; only the idioms of the two countries differ. This difference indicates why idioms give foreign writers and speakers trouble.

Example: The judge *threw the book* at the convicted arsonist.

The foreigner must memorize such expressions; they cannot logically be understood. The native writer has little trouble understanding idioms and need not attempt to avoid them in writing, provided the **reader** is equally at home with them. Idioms are often helpful shortcuts, in fact, that can make writing more vigorous and natural.

Example: The company's legal advisers debated whether to *stand fast* or to *press forward* with the lawsuit.

If there is any chance that your writing might be translated into another language or read in other English-speaking countries, eliminate obvious idiomatic expressions that might puzzle readers. For example, the owner's manual for the 1972 Volvo automobile was obviously translated into English with British drivers in mind. Where the American expression would be "filling up," there are references to "topping up" various fluids; where Americans would expect "windshield wipers," they find "windscreen wipers"; and the rearview mirror has an "antidazzle knob" instead of an "antiglare adjustment" for night driving. Such idiomatic expressions can be an annoying hindrance to clear understanding.

i.e.

The **abbreviation** *i.e.* stands for the Latin *id est,* meaning "that is." Since *that is* is a perfectly good English expression, there is no need to use a Latin expression or its abbreviation. In addition, many people confuse *i.e.* with **e.g.,** never being certain which means what. This abbreviation does not save enough space to pay for having one person misunderstand your meaning; avoid *i.e.* in your writing.

Change: We were a fairly heterogeneous group; *i.e.,* there were managers, directors, foremen, and vice-presidents at the meeting.
To: We were a fairly heterogeneous group; *that is,* there were managers, directors, foremen, and vice-presidents at the meeting.

If you insist on using *i.e.,* punctuate it as follows. If *i.e.* connects two independent **clauses,** precede it with a **semicolon** and follow it with a **comma,** as in the above example. If *i.e.* connects a **noun** with **appositives,** precede it with a comma.

Example: We were a fairly heterogeneous group, *i.e.* managers, directors, foremen, and vice-presidents.

illegal/illicit

If something is *illicit,* it is prohibited by law or custom. *Illicit* behavior may or may not be *illegal,* but it does violate custom or moral codes and therefore usually connotes clandestine or immoral behavior.

Examples: A scandal was caused by their *illicit* behavior, and the district attorney is investigating to determine whether *illegal* acts were committed.
Explicit sexual material may be *illicit* without being *illegal.*

illustrations

The objective of using an illustration is to help your **reader** absorb the facts and ideas you are presenting. When used well, an illustration can convey an idea that words alone could never really make clear.

Example:

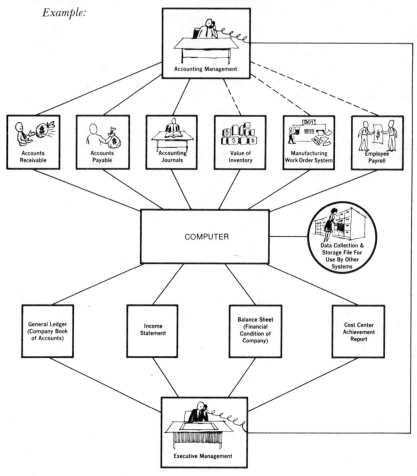

The primary objective of the accounting information system is to remove the existing time lags in data reporting. Virtually every accounting function—billing, accounts receivable, accounts payable, tax liabilities, financial statements, and so forth—will be computerized and will contain built-in auditing and checking procedures.

Illustrations should never be used as ornaments, however; they should always be functional working parts of your writing. Be careful not to over-illustrate; use an illustration only when it makes a direct contribution to your reader's understanding of your subject. When creating illustrations, consider your **objective** and your reader. You would use a different illustration of an x-ray machine, for example, for a high-school science class than you would for a group of medical doctors. Many of the attributes of good writing—simplicity, **clarity, conciseness**, directness—are equally important in creating and using illustrations.

The most common types of illustrations are photographs, **graphs**, **tables**, **drawings**, **flowcharts**, **organizational charts**, **schematic diagrams**, and **maps**. Your material will normally suggest one of these types when an illustration is needed.

TIPS FOR CREATING AND USING ILLUSTRATIONS

Each type of illustration has its unique strengths and weaknesses, and these are discussed in the specific text entry for each type. The guidelines presented here apply to most visual material you use to supplement the information in your text. Following these tips should help you create and present your visual material to good effect.

1. Keep the information as brief and simple as possible.
2. Try to present only one type of information in each illustration.
3. Label or caption each illustration clearly.
4. Include a key that identifies all **symbols**, when necessary.
5. Specify the proportions used or include a scale of relative distances, when appropriate.
6. Make the lettering horizontal for easy reading whenever possible.
7. Keep terminology consistent. Do not refer to something as a "proportion" in the text and as a "percentage" in the illustration.

8. Allow enough white space around and within the illustration for easy viewing.

9. Position the illustration as close as possible to the text that refers to it; however, an illustration should never appear ahead of the first text reference to it.

10. Be certain that the significance of each illustration is clear from the text.

11. If figure numbers or table numbers are used, as they should be if several illustrations or tables are used, number the illustrations or tables consecutively.

12. If more than six illustrations or tables appear in a **report**, list them, together with figure and page numbers, under a separate heading ("List of Figures" or "List of Tables") following the **table of contents**.

Presented with clarity and consistency, illustrations can help your reader focus on key portions of your report. Be aware, though, that even the best illustration only supplements the text. Your writing must carry the major burden of providing the context for the illustration and pointing out its significance.

imply/infer

If you *imply* something, you hint or suggest it.

   Example: His memo *implied* that the project would be delayed.

If you *infer* something, you reach a conclusion ·on the basis of evidence.

   Example: The general manager *inferred* from the memo that the project would be delayed.

In other words, the writer *implies* and the reader *infers*.

in/into

In means "inside of"; *into* implies movement from the outside to the inside.

   Example: He went back *into* the building to get the new sales brochure, which he had left *in* his office.

in order to

The **phrase** *in order to* is sometimes essential to the meaning of a **sentence**.

> *Example:* If the vertical scale of a graph line would not normally show the zero point, use a horizontal break in the graph *in order to* include the zero point.

The phrase *in order to* also helps control the **pace** of a sentence even though it is not essential to the meaning of the sentence.

> *Example:* The committee must know the estimated costs *in order to* evaluate the feasibility of the project.

Most often, however, the phrase *in order to* is just a meaningless filler phrase that is dropped into a sentence without thought.

> *Change:* *In order to* meet the deadline, we must work overtime.
> *To:* To meet the deadline, we must work overtime.

Search for these thoughtless uses of the phrase *in order to* in your writing and eliminate them.

in terms of

Although the **phrase** *in terms of* has a legitimate use, it is often used simply as a thoughtless **cliché**. When used to indicate a shift from one kind of language, or terminology, to another, it can be a useful phrase.

> *Example:* *In terms of* gross sales, the year has been relatively successful; however, *in terms of* net income, it has been discouraging.

When simply dropped into a **sentence** because it comes easily to mind, however, the phrase *in terms of* is meaningless **affectation**.

> *Change:* She was thinking *in terms of* subcontracting much of the work.
> *To:* She was thinking *about* subcontracting much of the work.
> *Or:* She was thinking *of* subcontracting much of the work.

inasmuch as/insofar as

Inasmuch as, meaning "because of the fact that," is a weak **connective** for stating causal relationships.

> *Change:* *Inasmuch as* the heavy spring rains delayed construction, the office building will not be completed on schedule.

To: *Because* the heavy spring rains delayed construction, the office building will not be completed on schedule.

Insofar as, meaning "to the extent that," should be reserved for that explicit usage rather than being used as an arbitrary replacement for *since.*

Example: *Insofar as* this report analyzes the reasons for the decline in sales, it can help us improve our sales performance next year.

Change: *Insofar as* you are here, we will review the material.
To: *Since* you are here, we will review the material.

increasing order of importance as a method of development

Increasing order of importance as a **method of development** begins with the least important point or fact, then goes to the next least important, building finally to the most important point at the end.

The primary advantage of increasing order of importance as a method of development is that your strongest point is freshest in the minds of your **readers** when they finish reading your work—in other words, you leave them with the thought you most want them to remember. The disadvantage of this method of development is the weak beginning caused by starting with your weakest point—which can risk losing your readers' interest before they get to your major points unless you provide a strong **introduction** or **opening**.

incredible/incredulous

Incredible means that some thing or some event is "unbelievable" or "nearly unbelievable."

Example: The stock market rally was *incredible* in view of the recent price of gold on the world market.

Incredulous means that a person is "skeptical" or "unbelieving" about some thing or some event.

Example: He was *incredulous* at the report of the market's rally.

indefinite adjective

Indefinite adjectives are so called because they do not designate anything specific about the **nouns** they modify.

Examples: *some* circuit boards, *any* branches, *all* aircraft engines

Notice that the **articles** *a* and *an* are included among the indefinite adjectives. (See also **a, an**.)

Example: The meeting will not start for *an* hour.

For recommendations on the placement and usage of adjectives, see **adjectives**.

indefinite pronouns

Indefinite pronouns do not specify a particular person or thing; they specify any one of a class or group of persons or things. *Any, another, anyone, anything, both, each, either, everybody, few, many, most, much, neither, none, several, some,* and *such* are indefinite pronouns. Indefinite pronouns normally require singular **verbs**.

Examples: If *either* of the vice-presidents *is* late, we will delay the meeting.
Neither of them *was* available for comment.
Each of the writers *has* his own style.

There are, of course, exceptions, as illustrated by the following examples.

Examples: *Many are* called, but *few are* chosen.
Most of them *are* aware of the problem.

A few indefinite pronouns may take either plural or singular verbs, depending on whether the nouns they stand for are plural or singular.

Examples: *Most* of the employees *are* pleased, but *some are* not.
Most of the oil *is* imported, but *some is* domestic.

(See also **pronouns**.)

indentation

Indentation means to "set in from the margin." The most common use of indentation is at the beginning of a **paragraph,** where the first line is usually indented five spaces in a typed manuscript and one inch in a longhand manuscript.

Example: It is hard to say when the stock market boom of the nineteen-twenties began. There were sound reasons why, during these years, the prices of common stocks should rise. Corporate earnings were good and growing. The prospect seemed benign. In the early twenties stock prices were low and yields favorable.

In the last six months of 1924, the prices of securities began to rise, and the increase was continued and extended through 1925. Thus at the end of May, 1924, the *New York Times* average of the prices of twenty-five industrial stocks was 106; by the end of the year it was 134.

—John Kenneth Galbraith, *The Great Crash* (Boston: Houghton Mifflin, 1961), p. 12.

Another use of indentation is in an **outline,** where each subordinate entry is indented under its major entry.

Example: II. Types of Outlines
    A. The Sentence Outline
        1. A sentence outline provides order and establishes the relationship of topics to one another to a greater degree than a topic outline.

Finally, a blocked **quotation** may be indented within a manuscript instead of being enclosed in **quotation marks**; it must, in this case, be single-spaced.

Example: The *Operators Manual* pointed out that

This is a very dangerous thing to do with a hydraulic crane. Hydraulic crane ratings are based on the strength of the material of the boom (and other components). . . .

A hydraulic crane is not like a lattice boom friction crane in one very important way. In most cases, the safe lifting capacity of the lattice boom crane is based on the weight needed to tip the machine. Therefore, operators of friction machines sometimes depend on signs that the machine might tip to warn them of impending danger.

This warning was given because many operators were accustomed to. . . .

(See also **quotations**.)

index

An index is an alphabetically arranged list of names and **topics** that is found in the back of a written work, citing the page or pages where a topic or person is discussed or (if the index is very comprehensive) mentioned.

Indexes can save the **reader** time finding information in a work because many items not found in the **table of contents** are included in the index. When researching a topic, always scan the index for pertinent entries.

Another kind of index, called a bibliographical index, lists books and articles by category or subject. The *Business Periodical Index,* for example, lists titles of articles and subjects covered in over 190 periodicals related to business. (See **reference books**.) For further information on how to use bibliographical indexes, see **library research**.

indirect object

An *indirect object* is a **noun** or noun equivalent that occurs with a **direct object** after certain kinds of **transitive verbs**, such as *give, wish, cause, tell,* and their **synonyms** or **antonyms**. It is usually a person or persons and answers the question "to whom or what?" or "for whom or what?" The indirect object always occurs before the direct object.

> *Examples:*   Wish *me* success. ("success" is the direct object)
> It caused *him* pain.
> Their attorney wrote *our firm* a follow-up letter.
> Give *the car* a push.

The meaning of an indirect object can often be expressed instead as a **prepositional phrase** with "to" or "for."

> *Examples:*   Give *John* a wrench. (Give a wrench to John.)
> Buy *him* a wrench. (Buy a wrench for him.)

The indirect object is one of the four kinds of **complements**, along with the direct object, the **objective complement**, and the **subjective complement**. (See also **object**.)

indiscreet/indiscrete

Indiscreet means "lacking in prudence or sound judgment."

> *Example:* His public discussion of the proposed merger was *indiscreet*.

Indiscrete means "not divided or divisible into parts."

> *Example:* The separate units, once combined, become *indiscrete*.

(See also **discreet/discrete**.)

individual

Avoid using *individual* as a **noun** if *person* is more appropriate.

> *Change:* Several *individuals* on the panel did not vote.
> *To:* Several *persons* on the panel did not vote.
> *Or:* Several on the panel did not vote.
> *Change:* She is an *individual* who says what she thinks.
> *To:* She is a *person* who says what she thinks.
> *Or:* She says what she thinks.

Individual is most appropriate when a single person is to be distinguished from a group.

> *Example:* The *individual* employee's obligations to the firm are detailed in the booklet that describes company policies.

infinitive

An infinitive is the uninflected form of a **verb** (*go, run, fall, talk, dress, shout*) without the restrictions imposed by **person** and **number**. Along with the **gerund** and **participle**, it is one of the nonfinite verb forms. The infinitive is generally preceded by the word *to,* which, although not an inherent part of the infinitive, is considered to be the sign of an infinitive; it also serves as a link t⟩ the rest of the **sentence**.

> *Examples:* It is time *to go* to work.
> We met in the conference room *to talk* about the new project.

An infinitive may function as a **noun**, an **adjective**, or an **adverb**.

Examples: *To expand* is not the only objective. (noun)
These are the instructions *to follow*. (adjective)
The company struggled *to survive*. (adverb)

The infinitive may reflect two **tenses**: present and (with a **helping verb**) present perfect.

Examples: to go (present tense)
to have gone (present perfect tense)

The most common mistake made with the tense of infinitives is use of the present perfect tense when the simple present tense is intended.

Change: I should not have tried *to have gone* so early.
To: I should not have tried *to go* so early.

Infinitives formed with the root form of **transitive verbs** can express both active and (with a helping verb) passive **voice**.

Examples: to hit (present tense, active voice)
to have hit (present perfect tense, active voice)
to be hit (present tense, passive voice)
to have been hit (present perfect tense, passive voice)

SPLITTING INFINITIVES

A split infinitive is one in which an adverb is placed between the sign of the infinitive, *to,* and the infinitive itself. Because they make up a grammatical unit, the infinitive and its sign are better left intact than separated by an intervening adverb. Although it may be better to split an infinitive than allow a sentence to become awkward or incoherent, only rarely is a sentence improved by splitting an infinitive.

Change: To quickly *improve* our profit margin, we must reduce our overhead costs.
To: To *improve* our profit margin quickly, we must reduce our overhead costs.

(See also **verbals**.)

infinitive phrase

An infinitive phrase consists of an **infinitive** (usually with *to*) and any **modifiers** or **complements**.

Example: The product must be able *to resist repeated hammer blows.*

Do not confuse a **prepositional phrase** beginning with *to* with an infinitive phrase. In the infinitive phrase, the *to* is followed by a **verb**; in the prepositional phrase, *to* is followed by a **noun** or **pronoun**.

Examples: We went *to the building site.* (prepositional phrase)
Our firm tries *to provide a broad variety of control* insects. (infinitive phrase)

An infinitive phrase may function as a noun, an **adjective**, or an **adverb**.

Examples: His goal is *to become sales manager.* (noun)
The need *to increase sales* should be obvious. (adjective)
We must work *to increase sales.* (adverb)

An infinitive phrase that functions as a noun may serve within the **sentence** as **subject, object**, complement, or **appositive**.

Examples: *To form her own company* was her lifelong ambition. (subject)
They want *to know when we can begin work on the project.* (direct object)
His objective is *to live well.* (**subjective complement**)
His ambition, *to form his own company,* is soon to be realized. (appositive)

The implied subject of an introductory infinitive phrase should be the same as the subject of the sentence. If it is not, the **phrase** is a **dangling modifier**.

Change: *To learn shorthand*, practice is needed.
To: *To learn shorthand,* you must practice.
Or: *To learn shorthand,* one must practice.

(The implied subject of the infinitive is *you,* or *one,* not *practice.*)

informal writing style

Informal writing style is a relaxed and colloquial way of writing **standard English**. It is the **style** found in most private letters, nonfiction books of general interest, many mass-circulation magazines, and some business **correspondence**. There is less distance between writer and **reader** because the **tone** is more personal than in **formal writing style**. **Contractions** and elliptical constructions are commonplace.

The vocabulary of an informal writing style is made up of generally familiar rather than unfamiliar words and expressions, although slang and dialect are usually avoided. Informal style approximates the cadence and structure of spoken English, while conforming to the grammatical conventions of written English.

> *Example:*   All you need is a talent for spotting the idiocies now built into the system. But you'll have to give up being an administrator who loves to run others and become a manager who carries water for his people so they can get on with the job. And you'll have to keep a suspicious eye on the phonies who cater to your uncertainties or feed your trembling ego on press releases, office perquisites, and optimistic financial reports. You'll have to give substance to such tired rituals as the office party. And you'll certainly have to recognize, once you get a hunk of your company's stock, that you aren't the last man who might enjoy the benefits of shareholding. These elegant simplicities require a sense of justice that won't be easy to hang on to.
>
> —Robert Townsend, *Up the Organization* (New York: Alfred A. Knopf, 1970), p. 11.

Most business and technical writing tends to be more formal than informal. (See also **business writing style, technical writing style**, and **English, varieties of**.)

ingenious/ingenuous

Ingenious means "marked by cleverness and originality," and *ingenuous* means "straightforward" or "characterized by innocence and simplicity."

> *Examples:*   Wilson's *ingenious* plan, which streamlined production in Department L, was the beginning of his rise within the company.
>
> I believe that the *ingenuous* co-op students bring some freshness into the company.

inquiry, letter of

One of the more common uses for business letters is to obtain information from someone. Such a letter may be as simple as a note asking the Fisher Cutbait Company for a copy of the free brochure titled *The Care and Feeding of the Piranha*, which was offered in the

August 11 issue of *Time*, or it may be as complex as asking a financial consultant to define specific requirements for floating a multi-million dollar bond issue.

Whatever the reason for the request, a typical letter of inquiry contains a clear and concise statement of the information desired: what is wanted, who wants it, why it is wanted, and how it is to be used. A letter of inquiry should contain specific questions—listed if possible—that you want answered. Finally, express your appreciation, and if possible tell the recipient how he will benefit or offer a return favor.

The objective of a letter of inquiry is to get a response, so make it as easy as possible for the recipient to respond by (1) keeping your questions to a minimum, (2) stating your questions clearly and concisely, phrasing them so they will be easy to answer, and (3) promising to keep confidential information confidential.

To save yourself and your **reader** time and trouble, plan your letter carefully; few things are more frustrating than failing to receive the answer to a question you thought you asked but did not, and your second letter might not get the prompt response your first one did. Be sure to include the address to which you wish the response sent. Those who deal with inquiries find that this vital piece of information is often forgotten. In fact, it is usually a good idea to include a stamped, self-addressed return envelope with your letter.

To sum up: state what you want, who needs it, why it is needed, and how it is to be used; ask specific questions that are easy to answer; express your appreciation. And don't forget to include your return address. See the following example. (See also **correspondence**.)

```
                                    Charles G. Patterbaugh
                                    P.O. Box 113
                                    University of Dayton
                                    Dayton, Ohio  45409

                                    March 11, 1976

      Ms. Jane Metcalf
      Engineering Services
      Miami Valley Power Co.
      P.O. Box 1444
      Miamitown, Ohio  45733

      Dear Ms. Metcalf:

      Our project team at the University of Dayton is de-
      signing an all-electric, energy-efficient, middle price
```

home. The home, which contains 2,200 square feet of
living space (17,600 cubic feet), meets all the requirements stipulated in your company's brochure titled
Insulating for Efficiency. However, we do need some
information on heating systems.

Specifically, we need the following information.
1. The proper size of heat pump to use in this climate
   for such a home;
2. The wattage of the supplemental electrical furnace
   that would be required for this climate; and
3. The estimated power consumption, and current rates,
   of these units for a year.

We will be happy to send you a copy of our preliminary
design report in consideration of your time and effort.

Very truly yours,

Charles G. Patterbaugh

Charles G. Patterbaugh

inside/inside of

In the **phrase** *inside of,* the word *of* is redundant.

Change: The switch is just *inside of* the door.
   To: The switch is just *inside* the door.

The use of *inside of* to mean "in less time than" is colloquial and
should be avoided in writing.

Change: They were finished *inside of* an hour.
   To: They were finished *in less than* an hour.

insoluble/unsolvable (or insolvable)

Although *insoluble* and *unsolvable* are sometimes interchanged when
they are used to mean "incapable of being solved," careful writers
distinguish between them.

Change: The company and the union jointly agreed that the problems
   facing the Atlanta operation were not *insoluble.*
   To: The company and the union jointly agreed that the problems
   facing the Atlanta operation were not *unsolvable.*

Insoluble means "incapable of being dissolved."

    Example: The plastic is *insoluble* even in acid.

Unsolvable means "incapable of being solved."

    Example: Until yesterday, the production problem seemed *unsolvable.*

instructions

The primary requirement in writing instructions is that they be direct and simple, a goal that is best achieved by using simple, imperative **sentences**. The imperative **mood** forces you to use the active **voice** and directs the **reader** to do something. Although instructions should be concise, do not make them telegraphic by eliminating **articles** (*a, an,* and *the*). Instructions normally use the **sequential method of development** because they are almost always to be followed in an established sequence. It is critical that steps in instructions not be presented out of sequence, since confusion could cause damage to equipment or even injury to an operator. If you need to tell the reader that two steps must be performed simultaneously, either state that fact in an introductory **paragraph** or include both steps in the same numbered item. Make certain, however, that your numbered steps are not overloaded with instructions.

    Illustrations can help clarify instructions; however, illustrations only supplement the writing, they cannot replace it.

    Example:
1. Place the socket in an upright position as shown in View A, and bring the rope around in a large, easy-to-handle loop.
2. Extend the dead end of the rope from the socket for a distance of at least one rope lay, permitting the strands to adjust around the wedge and to keep the rope in balance. Insert the wedge as shown in View B.
3. Secure the ears of the socket to a sturdy support and carefully take a strain on the live side of the rope. Pull the wedge and rope loop into position tight enough to hold the wedge in place during handling. Final wedge positioning takes place under full operating loads.
4. After pinning the socket to the hook block (or boom point), apply gradually increasing loads until the wedge is seated. Avoid applying any sudden shock loads before the wedge is in its final position. View C shows the general operating appearance of the rope socket with the wedge pulled into the socket and the end of the wedge showing.

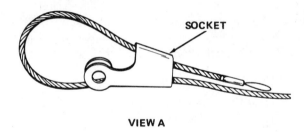

VIEW A

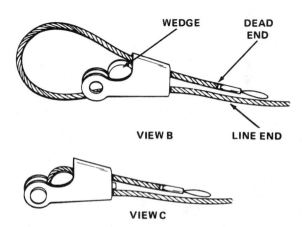

—*Operators Manual* (Model W-180), Harnischfeger Corp., pp. 2–15.

Figure 1. Installing a Rope Socket

insure/ensure/assure

Insure, ensure, and *assure* all mean "to make secure or certain." *Assure* refers to persons, and it alone has the **connotation** of setting a person's mind at rest. *Ensure* and *insure* also mean "to make secure from harm." Only *insure* is widely used in the sense of guaranteeing life or property against risk.

> *Examples:*   I *assure* you that the equipment will be available.
> We need all the data to *ensure* the success of the project.
> We should *insure* the contents of the building.

intensifiers

Intensifiers are **adverbs** that emphasize degree, such as *very, quite, rather, such,* and *too.* Although they serve a legitimate and necessary function, they can also seduce the unwary writer who is not on guard against overusing them. Too many intensifiers weaken your writing. When revising your draft, eliminate intensifiers that do not make a definite contribution to your writing.

> *Change:* It was *quite* a happy salesman who received the *very* good news that he had been offered a promotion with a *rather* substantial increase in salary.
>
> *To:* It was a happy salesman who received the good news that he had been offered a promotion with a substantial increase in salary.

The difference is not that the first example is right and the second one wrong, but that the intensifiers in the first example add nothing to the **sentence** and are therefore superfluous.

Some words (such as *unique, perfect, impossible, final, permanent, infinite,* and *complete*) do not logically permit intensification because they do not permit degrees of **comparison**. Although **usage** often ignores this logical restriction, the writer should be aware that to ignore it is, strictly speaking, to defy the basic meanings of these words. (For more detailed information, see **comparative degree**.)

> *Change:* It is *quite* impossible to implement the sales program you recommend.
>
> *To:* It is impossible to implement the sales program you recommend.

interface

Interface means "the surface providing a common boundary between two bodies or areas." The bodies or areas may be physical (the *interface* of piston and cylinder) or conceptual (the *interface* of mathematics and statistics). Do not use *interface* as a substitute for the **verbs** *cooperate, interact,* or even *work*.

> *Change:* The art department will *interface* with the public relations staff on this project.
>
> *To:* The art department will *work* with the public relations staff on this project.

interjection

An interjection is a word or **phrase** of exclamation that is used independently to express emotion or surprise or to summon attention. *Hey! Ouch! Wow!* are strong interjections. *Oh, well,* and *indeed* are mild ones. An interjection functions much as *yes* and *no*, in that it has no grammatical connection with the rest of the **sentence** in which it appears. When an interjection expresses a sudden or strong emotion, punctuate it with an **exclamation mark**.

>   *Example:*   His only reaction was a resounding, *Wow!*

Because they get their main expressive force from sound (*Wow!*), interjections are more common in speech than in writing. They are rarely appropriate to business or technical writing.

interrogative adverb

Interrogative adverbs ask questions. Typical interrogative adverbs are *where, when, why,* and *how.*

>   *Examples:*   *How* many hours did you work last week?
>   *Where* are we going when the new project is finished?
>   *Why* did it take so long to complete the job?

interrogative pronoun

Interrogative pronouns ask questions. The interrogative pronouns are *who, what,* and *which.*

>   *Examples:*   *Who* said that?
>   *What* is the trouble?
>   *Which* of these is best?

Notice that the interrogative pronouns normally do not have expressed antecedents; the antecedent is actually in the expected answer.

interviewing

The **scope** of coverage that you have established for your writing project may require more information (or more current information) than is available in written form (in the library, in corporate specifications, in trade journals, etc.). When you reach this point, consider a personal interview with an expert in your subject.

A discussion of interviewing can be divided into three parts: (1) determining the proper person to interview, (2) preparing for the interview, and (3) conducting the interview.

DETERMINING THE PROPER PERSON TO INTERVIEW

Many times your subject, or your **objective** in writing about the subject, logically points to the proper person to interview. If you were writing about the use of a freeway onramp metering device on Highway 103, for example, you would want to interview the Director of the Traffic Engineering Department; if you were writing about the design of the device, you would want to interview the manufacturer's design engineer. You may interview a professor who specializes in your subject, in addition to getting leads from him as to others you might interview. Other sources available to help you determine the appropriate person to interview are (1) the city directory in the library, (2) professional societies, (3) the yellow pages in the local telephone directory, or (4) a local firm that is involved with all or some aspects of your subject.

PREPARING FOR THE INTERVIEW

After determining the name of the person you want to interview, you must request the interview. You can do this either by telephone or by letter, although a letter may be too slow to allow you to meet your deadline.

Learn as much as possible about the person you are going to interview, and learn as much as possible about the company or agency for which he works. When you make contact with your interviewee, whether by letter or by telephone, explain (1) who you are, (2) why you are contacting him, (3) why you chose him for the interview, (4) the subject of the interview, (5) that you would like to arrange an interview at his convenience, and (6) that you will allow him to review your draft.

Prepare a list of specific questions to ask your interviewee. The natural temptation for the untrained writer is to ask general questions rather than specific ones. "What are you doing about air pollution?" for example, may be too general to elicit specific and useful information. "Residents in the east end of town complain about the black smoke that pours from your east-end plant; are you doing anything to relieve the problem?" would be a more specific question. Analyze your questions to be certain that they are specific and to the point.

CONDUCTING THE INTERVIEW

When you arrive for the interview, be prepared to guide the discussion. The following list of points should help you to do so.

1. Be pleasant, but purposeful. You are there to get information, so don't be timid about asking leading questions on the subject.
2. Use the list of questions you have prepared.
3. Let your interviewee do the talking. Don't try to impress him with your own knowledge of the subject on which he is presumably an expert.
4. Be objective. Don't offer your opinions on the subject. You are there to get information, not to debate.
5. Some answers prompt additional questions; ask them. If you do not ask these questions as they arise, you may find later that you have forgotten to ask them at all.
6. When the interviewee gets off the subject, be ready with a specific and direct question to guide him back onto the track.
7. Take only memory-jogging notes that will help you recall the conversation later. Do not ask your interviewee to slow down so you can take detailed notes. To do so would not only be an undue imposition on his time but might also disturb or destroy his train of thought.
8. If you use a tape recorder, do not let it lure you into a relaxation of discipline so that you neglect to ask critical questions.

Immediately after leaving the interview, use your memory-jogging notes to help you mentally review the interview and record your detailed notes. Do not postpone this step. Anyone, no matter how good his memory, will forget some important points if he does not do this at once.

intransitive verb

An intransitive verb is a **verb** that does not need an **object** to complete its meaning. It is able, in its own right, to make a full assertion about its **subject**. Notice in the following examples that the same verb can often be both transitive and intransitive, depending upon how it is used.

Examples: Jim *works* in an office (intransitive)
He *works* his staff very hard. (transitive)

Linking verbs are inherently intransitive since they simply connect a subject to a **modifier** or a **complement**.

Examples: The winch *is* rusted. (*Rusted* is an **adjective** modifying *winch*.)
A calculator *is* a useful tool. (*A useful tool* is a **subjective complement** renaming *calculator*.)

Some verbs, such as *lie* and *sit,* are also inherently intransitive.

> *Examples:*   The patient should *lie* on his back during treatment. (*On his back* is an **adverb** phrase modifying the verb *lie*.)
> Perhaps it would be better to *sit* and *rest.* (In this sentence, both *sit* and *rest* are intransitive verbs.)

introduction

The purpose of an introduction is to provide your **readers** with any general information they must have to understand the detailed information in the rest of your **report**. If you don't need to set the stage in this way, turn to the entry on **openings** for a variety of interesting ways to begin without writing an introduction. If you are writing a **house organ article**, an **annual report**, a **proposal**, a **police report**, a **memorandum**, or something similar, you will probably find one of the various types of openings more appropriate than an introduction. If you are preparing a **formal report**, a **laboratory report**, a **technical manual**, a **specification**, a **journal article**, a conference paper, or some similar writing project, however, you will need to present your readers with some general information before getting into the body of your report.

STATING THE SUBJECT

In stating the subject, it may be helpful to the reader to include a small amount of information on the history or theory of the subject. In addition to stating what the subject is, you may need to define it if it is one with which some of your readers may be unfamiliar. (See **definition as a form of writing**.)

STATING THE PURPOSE

The statement of purpose in your introduction should function for your article or paper much as a **topic sentence** functions in a **paragraph**. It should make your readers aware of your goal as they read your supporting statements and examples. It should also tell them why you are writing about the subject: whether your material provides a new perspective or clarifies an existing perspective.

STATING THE SCOPE

Stating the scope of your article or paper gives the reader an idea of how much or how little detail to expect. Does your article or paper present a broad survey of your topic, or does it concentrate on one facet of the topic? Keep the statement of scope brief and simple, however; lack of restraint could lead you to write an **abstract** of your article or paper instead of a simple statement of scope in your introduction.

STATING THE DEVELOPMENT OF THE SUBJECT

In a larger work it may be helpful to state how you plan to develop the subject. Is the work an analysis of the component parts of some whole? Is the material presented in chronological sequence? Or does it involve an inductive or deductive approach? Providing such information makes it easier for your readers to anticipate how the subject will be presented, and it gives them a basis for evaluating how you arrived at your conclusions or recommendations.

Example:

The steady increase in incoming orders over the past eighteen months represents a significant increase in the corporation's percentage of the market for office furniture, and the market survey conducted by a consulting firm indicates that the increase is permanent. Therefore, at its September meeting, the corporation's board of directors approved the construction of a

Subject

new manufacturing plant to increase our manufacturing capacity to accomodate the present increase in demand and the anticipated increase indicated by the market survey.

A committee was appointed by the president of the corporation to investigate various potential sites for the new manufacturing plant. The committee was to investigate all potential building sites and select several of the best alternative sites for manufacturing office furniture. These selections were to be made on the basis of such considerations as the availability of transportation, the local tax structure, the availability of labor, and the local living conditions. The purpose of this report is to submit the results of that investigation. The report offers first

Purpose
and
scope

a brief background, or summary, of the committee's complete investigation; then it presents, in complete detail, the results of the studies conducted on the three most promising building sites for the new manufacturing plant.

The committee initially considered thirty possible locations for the proposed new factory. Of these, twenty were eliminated almost immediately for one reason or another (unfavorable tax structure, inadequate labor supply, etc.). Of the remaining ten

Background

locations, the committee selected for intensive study the three that seemed the most promising: Chicago, Minneapolis, and Salt Lake City. The committee then visited these three cities, and its observations on each of them are contained in the body of this report.

Development

The report presents the significant details of each city in the following sequence: (1) the location of the city, (2) the availability of air, highway, and rail transportation, (3) the availability of labor, (4) the local tax structure, and (5) the local living conditions (housing, education, recreation, and climate).

Body
of the
report

CHICAGO

Of the three cities, Chicago presently seems to the committee to offer the greatest advantages.

Location

Although not at the geographical center of the United States, Chicago is centrally located in an area that contains more than three-fourths of the U.S. population. It is within easy reach of our corporate headquarters in New York. And it is close to several of our most important suppliers of raw materials—those, for example, in Columbus, Detroit, and St. Louis.

Transportation

Chicago is served by the following major railroads. . . .

TIPS ON WRITING INTRODUCTIONS

Not every subject needs an introduction. When your readers are already familiar with the major elements of your topic, you can save them time and hold their interest better by getting on to the details. If you do not need a full-scale introduction, turn to the entry on **openings** for a variety of interesting ways to begin without an introduction.

Introductions should be purposeful and concise. Wordy or rambling introductions usually mean that the subject has not been clearly focused. Adequate **preparation** will help solve this problem. The introduction should function like an **abstract** by giving readers a quick overview of the material, thus allowing them to decide whether they need to read the full text. A wordy introduction would defeat this purpose.

Make your **point of view** toward the subject obvious to the readers. Do not assume that readers knowledgeable about your **topic** will instinctively know your point of view toward it. Be brief, if that will suffice, but be explicit.

Finally, consider writing the introduction last. Many writers find it helpful to write the introduction last because they feel that only then do they have a full enough perspective on the writing to introduce it adequately.

inverted sentence order

An inverted **sentence** changes the normal **subject-verb-complement** sentence pattern. Inversion may occur for a variety of reasons.

1. Inverted sentence order is used in questions.

   Example: *Are* (verb) *you* (subject) going to *the office* (object of preposition)?

2. It is used in exclamations.

   Example: What *a fool* (subjective complement) *he* (subject) *is* (verb)!

3. It is also used at times simply to achieve **emphasis** and variety.

   Examples: A better *job* (direct object) *I* (subject) never *had* (verb).
   A sorry *sight* (direct object) *we* (subject) *presented* (verb).

irregardless/regardless

Irregardless is **nonstandard English** because it is a negative of *regardless* (meaning "unmindful"), which is already negative; therefore, *irregardless* is a **double negative**. Replace it with *regardless*.

   Change: *Irregardless* of the price, I will buy 100 shares of the stock.
   To: *Regardless* of the price, I will buy 100 shares of the stock.

it

The **pronoun** *it* has a number of uses. First, it can refer to a preceding **noun** that names an object or idea or to a baby or animal whose sex is unknown or unimportant to the point. *It* should have a clear antecedent.

   Examples: Darwinism made an impact on nineteenth-century American thought. *It* even influenced economics.
   The Moodys' baby is generally healthy, but *it* has a cold at the moment.

It can also serve as an **expletive**.

   Examples: *It* is necessary to sand the hull before painting.
   It is a truth universally acknowledged that there is no such thing as a free lunch.

Be on guard against overusing expletives, however.

   Change: It is seldom that we go.
   To: We seldom go.

italics

Italics (indicated by underlining on the typewriter) is a style of type used to denote emphasis and to distinguish foreign expressions, book titles, and certain other elements. *This sentence is printed in italics.* You may need to italicize words that require special **emphasis** in a **sentence**.

> *Example:*   I wish to emphasize that sales have *not* improved since we started the new procedure.

Do not overuse italics for emphasis, however.

> *Change:*   This will hurt *you* more than *me.*
> *To:*   This will hurt you more than me!

TITLES

Italicize the titles of books, periodicals, newspapers, movies, and television programs.

> *Examples:*   The book *Statistical Methods* was published in 1970.
> The *Cincinnati Enquirer* is one of the country's oldest newspapers.
> *Journal of Marketing* is published monthly for those engaged in marketing.

Abbreviations of such titles are italicized if their spelled-out forms would be italicized.

> *Example:*   The *Journal of the ABCA* is an informative publication.

Titles of chapters or articles within publications are placed in **quotation marks**, not italicized.

> *Example:*   "Does Advertising Lower Consumer Prices?" was an article in the *Journal of Marketing.*

Holy books, legislative documents, and historical events are not italicized.

> *Example:*   The Bible, Magna Carta, and the Battle of Hastings changed the history of Western civilization.

Titles of musical works are italicized, but titles of paintings and other works of art are enclosed in quotation marks.

> *Examples:*   Handel's *Messiah* (music)
> Van Gogh's "Sunflowers" (painting)
> Eliot's "The Love Song of J. Alfred Prufrock" (poem)
> Gershwin's *Concerto in F* (music)

PROPER NAMES

The names of ships, trains, and aircraft (but not the companies that own them) are italicized.

Example: They sailed to Africa on the Onassis *Clipper* but flew back on the TWA *New Yorker*.

The exceptions are craft known by model or serial designations. These are not italicized.

Examples: DC-7, Boeing 747

WORDS, LETTERS, AND FIGURES

Words, letters, and figures discussed as such are italicized.

Examples: I should replace the letter *S* and the number *6* on my old typewriter.
The word *inflammable* is often misinterpreted.

FOREIGN WORDS

Foreign words that have not been assimilated into the English language are italicized.

Examples: *sine qua non, coup de grâce, in res, in camera*

Foreign words that have been fully assimilated into the language, however, need not be italicized.

Examples: cliché, etiquette, vis-à-vis, de facto

When in doubt, consult a recent **dictionary**. (See also **foreign words in English**.)

SUBHEADS

Subheads in a report are frequently underlined (if typeset, they will be set in italics). See also **heads**.

Example: There was no publications department as such, and the writing groups were duplicated at each plant or location. Wellington, for example, had such a large number of publications groups that their publications effort can only be described as disorganized. Their duplication of effort must be enormous.

Training Writers

We are certainly leading the way in developing first-line managers (or writing supervisors) who are not only technically competent but can also train the writers under their direction and be responsible for writing quality as well.

its/it's

Its is a possessive **pronoun** and does not use an **apostrophe**.

Example: The computer has served *its* purpose well.

It's is a **contraction** for "it is."

Example: *It's* much faster than our former system.

it's me

It's me is an acceptable idiomatic expression because it is so widely used, even though (strictly speaking) it is grammatically incorrect. (See also **case**.)

J

jargon

Jargon is a highly specialized technical slang that is unique to an occupational group. If all your **readers** are members of a particular occupational group, jargon may provide a time-saving and efficient means of communicating with them. If you doubt that your entire reading audience is a part of this group, however, avoid the use of jargon.

The question that always seems to perplex business and technical people is the difference between jargon and technical terminology. Jargon is technical slang. For example, our astronauts on the moon referred to the Lunar Excursion Module as the LEM. In technical terminology, the vehicle is the Lunar Excursion Module; in the jargon of the astronauts it is the LEM. For another example, a falling stock market is called a bear market. In technical terminology, it is a falling market; in the jargon of the stock brokers, it is a bear market.

When jargon becomes so specialized that it applies only to one company or a subgroup of an occupation, it is referred to as "shop talk." Obviously, shop talk is appropriate only for those familiar with its special vocabulary and should be reserved for speech or informal **memorandums**.

When jargon becomes enmeshed in a tangle of **abstract words**, many of them pseudo-scientific or pseudo-legal, it becomes an **affec-**

tation known as **gobbledygook**. Jargon, used to this extreme, is "language more technical than the ideas it serves to express."*

Jargon and shop talk are similar in many ways to "lingo" and "cant," which are terms used to describe language that is intended to exclude outsiders from a select circle of the initiated.

job description

Job descriptions are used to refine an organization's structure and to provide information on which to base equitable salary scales. They help the management to determine whether all responsibilities within an organization are adequately covered. Well-written job descriptions provide an objective basis for evaluating employee performance and enable employees to know exactly what is expected of them.

FORMAT FOR WRITING JOB DESCRIPTIONS

Although job description formats vary from organization to organization, the following headings are typical.

Accountability. This section names, by title, the person or persons to whom the employee reports.
Scope of Responsibilities. This section provides an overview of the primary and secondary functions of the job and, if applicable, who reports to the employee.
Specific Duties. This section gives a detailed account of the specific duties of the job as concisely as possible without sacrificing meaning.
Personal Requirements. This section lists the education, training, experience, and licensing required or desired for the job.

TIPS FOR WRITING JOB DESCRIPTIONS

1. Remember, you are writing a description of a job—not of yourself.
2. Be especially aware of your **readers** (Are they managers, the board of directors, the personnel department?) and keep their needs in mind.
3. Review previous job descriptions that have been effective.

---

* Susanne K. Langer, *Mind: An Essay on Human Feeling* (Baltimore, Md.: The Johns Hopkins Press, 1967), p. 36.

The following job description is typical.

Example: Manager, Technical Publications
                              Acme Electrical Corporation

ACCOUNTABILITY

Reports directly to the Vice President, Parts and Service.

SCOPE OF RESPONSIBILITIES

The Manager of Technical Publications is expected to plan, coordinate, and supervise the design and development of technical publications and documentation required in the support of the sale, installation, and maintenance of Acme products. The manager is responsible for the administration and morale of the staff. The supervisor for instruction manuals and the supervisor for parts manuals report directly to the manager.

SPECIFIC DUTIES

Direct an organization presently composed of twenty people (including two supervisors), over 75 percent of whom are writing professionals and graphics specialists.

Screen, select, and hire qualified applicants for the department.

Prepare a formal program designed to orient writing trainees to the production of reproducible copy and graphic arts.

Evaluate the performance of members of the department and determine salary adjustments for all personnel in the department.

Plan documentation for the support of new and existing products.

Determine the need for subcontracted publications and act as a purchasing agent when they are needed.

Offer editorial advice to supervisors.

Develop and manage an annual budget for the Technical Publications Department.

Find ways to reduce costs and increase productivity.

Consult, advise, and recommend on matters pertaining to publications support of all new and existing products.

Cooperate with the Engineering, Parts, and Service Departments to provide the necessary repair and spare parts manuals upon the introduction of new equipment.

Serve as a liaison between technical specialists, the publications staff, and field engineers.

Act as Acme's technical publications voice in communicating with our customers, field engineers, and industry.

Recommend new and appropriate uses for the department within the company.

Keep up with new techniques in printing processes, typesetting, computerized text editing, art, and graphics and use them to the advantage of Acme Electrical Corporation where applicable.

PERSONAL REQUIREMENTS

B.S.E.E. (or equivalent electrical background) desired.

Minimum of three years professional writing experience with a general knowledge of graphics and production.

Minimum of two years management experience with a knowledge of the general principles of management.

Must be conversant with the needs of support people, technical people, and customers.

For additional and detailed information on the use and creation of job descriptions, see: Joseph J. Famularo, *Organization Planning Manual*, New York: American Management Association, 1971.

journal article

From time to time in your career you may wish to write a journal article. Such an article may, in fact, improve your chances for professional advancement; at the very least, publication of a journal article may get your name known among leaders in your field. In addition, a journal article can provide favorable publicity for your firm.

A journal article is an article written on a specific subject for a professional periodical. These periodicals are often the official publications of professional societies. *Technical Communication,* for example, is the official voice of the Society for Technical Communication. Other professional publications include *Electrical Engineering Review, Chemical Engineering, Journal of Marketing,* and *Business Education Forum.* There are hundreds of periodicals, of course, ranging from scientific journals that publish articles on advanced research in highly specialized areas to industrial and business periodicals that publish material of more general interest.

Although the primary effort in writing a journal article is in the **research** phase, all the other steps of the writing process—**preparation, organization, writing the draft**, and **revision**—are crucial, and you should review the entries for these steps in this handbook.

Before you begin writing, learn something about the periodical to which you will be submitting the article. Remember that, although the article is aimed at specialists in your field, your audience may also include specialists in related fields who may have little in-depth knowledge of the basics of your discipline. Read back issues of the periodical for such things as the amount and kind of detail in the articles, the length of the articles, and the **style** of the writing. Some publications may indicate the desired **format** for a manuscript that is being submitted; some may even send a style sheet (a guide to manuscript format, **footnotes**, and **bibliography**) upon request.

After you have written the article, the last (but hardly least important) item you must consider is its **title**. The title is often critical to the researcher, who may decide whether to read your article on the basis of its title. The title, therefore, must be specific—naming the main topic in as few words as possible. In addition, many editors like a title that arouses interest in the article by suggesting that it will help the reader discover something new or valuable.

The following is an example of an article for a business journal adressed mainly, but not exclusively, to marketing *specialists*.

Example:　Societal Marketing: A Businessman's Perspective*
　　　　　by Andrew Takas

In the last half a dozen years the scholarly press has published a number of papers that have argued that the concept of marketing must be expanded to include consideration of a number of societal aspects—the effects and interactions of the activities of marketers on our national life.[1] The comments of writers on the subject might be summarized thus:

1. *Satisfaction of human needs.* The key word is *human* needs—not those that are business or product oriented. An opportunity is seen for marketing techniques to be used to sell clean air, clean water, and adequate housing, for instance.

2. *Expansion to social fields.* Marketing is seen as an instrument that can be used to further all the goals of society. It is suggested that marketing techniques can be used to help achieve socially desirable goals such as population control, improved racial tolerance, and increased support of education.

3. *Consideration of societal impact.* A new imperative is presented: that business must assess not only the profitability of its actions, but also the overall effect those actions have on society.

Unfortunately, much of this thinking has taken place on a comparatively lofty plane rather than at working levels. In practice, marketers have continued to operate as if they were completely unaware of the ongoing debate.

[1] The seminal papers on the topic are probably those of William Lazer, "Marketing's Changing Social Relationships," *Journal of Marketing,* Vol. 33 (January 1969), pp. 3–9; and Philip Kotler and Sidney J. Levy, "Broadening the Concept of Marketing," *Journal of Marketing,* Vol. 33 (January 1969), pp. 10–15. A comprehensive discussion is found in the July 1971 issue of the *Journal of Marketing.*

*Reprinted from *Journal of Marketing,* Vol. 38 (October 1974), pp. 2–7, published by the American Marketing Association.

Few marketers or chief executives have ever looked at a product their companies were selling in large volume at substantial profit and said: "Let us withdraw it from the market. It doesn't harm anybody, but it doesn't do anybody any good either. It really is at best a nonessential and at worst a piece of junk. Either way it does not justify in a purely social sense the raw materials and labor that go into it."

Similarly, only a handful of sales executives may have ever looked at a proposed product and said: "We can't make any money manufacturing and selling it, but we should go ahead and do it because society needs it."

In the real world that kind of thinking cannot, and simply does not, take place. Rather, the typical planning committee conference table discussion centers around questions such as: "Will they buy it? How many units do we think we can sell? What margin will we shoot for? Will package A sell better than package B? What will be our profit target for the year? How can we take a little bit out of the cost? How can we increase our share of the industry?" No marketing practitioner can read these questions without a real sense of recognition.

The results, of course, are often desirable, but we must admit that this societally indifferent thinking process is indeed what brings goods to market and keeps them there. Otherwise there is no way to explain the existence of many products that crowd the shelves of retailers and compete for consumer dollars. Examples abound, but they all fall more or less into the "pink flamingo" category: they have a market, they neither harm nor benefit anyone dramatically, and their chief virtue is that they can be sold profitably.

In a similar way, the overriding considerations of competitive position and profitability act to resist necessary change and to delay compliance with societal needs. Why, otherwise, should it have taken four or five years first to fail to persuade and finally to legislate the auto industry into so obvious an improvement as putting all its bumpers at the same height? Another example: good ecological practice is today both popular and widely recognized as necessary, but most organizations that talk about their corporate contribution to ecology did nothing about pollution until they were literally forced to by legal or social pressures.

Why is there such a gap between advanced marketing theory and its actual practice in the marketplace? Why such a discrepancy between what wise men think ought to be done and what other wise men are actually doing? The answers apply to every level of business from policy making to operational.

Every executive makes the type of long- and medium-run decisions that could well include societal considerations. But he sees no incentive to consider them; actually, they may present him with a real disincentive. The focus of management has traditionally been, and still is, on sales and profits. As a consequence, the average sales executive spends his life struggling with sales charts, fighting for an extra percent, or looking for a new product appeal rather than considering the impact of his actions on society.

At all levels, businessmen are under continuous pressure to produce results. The lowest subordinate faces pressure from his department manager, the manager is prodded by the executive, the executive is under the eye of the chairman, and the chairman must satisfy the Board of Directors—and each one has the same clear-cut mandate. He must perform in a way that satisfies the conventional objectives: to maximize profit, to assure the survival and growth of the firm, and to maintain the individual's hold on his job. The demands and pressures of today's business simply are not consonant with theoretical musings to change the rules of the game.

The net effect of this highly pragmatic approach by marketers and their companies is to make the gap grow wider: the more they struggle with their present tasks, the more oblivious they become to the underlying problems of today, and to both the critical dilemmas and the opportunities that lie just ahead.

Given the changes of the last decades and the visible pressures of the coming ones, a marketing revolution is inevitable. Later or sooner, ultimately but surely, American marketing practice is going to be changed drastically.

The conduct of business has already been modified, of course, by considerations other than the maximization of profit. Starting from the beginning of the twentieth century, a host of legal, administrative, and ethical restrictions has severely limited the decision-making ability of the businessman. More recently, the great recognition by industry of the impact of consumerism stands out. Most marketers, incidentally, would probably reluctantly admit that they were forced into most changes, and that without strong pressure from buyers and lawmakers nothing would have happened.

But the changes we have seen thus far are trivial compared to those that surely lie ahead. Two broad reasons make this so.

First, we shall see input shortages become increasingly widespread and more severe. The last twelve months have been just the first taste of the pressures that will dramatically change us. For the first time in our lives, we are reading daily about shortages we never dreamed of only a couple of years ago. We, who had taken the availability of anything we wanted and could afford for granted, now hear that we must turn off the air conditioner, turn down the thermostat, get a smaller car, recycle our paper, and take back our empty bottles.

There is no dispute about the obvious illustration: an absolute shortage of all the petroleum we would like to consume at the price we were accustomed to paying. The problem came on us suddenly, it gives every indication that it will be permanent—and it is only the first of a number of major adjustments that we now can see lying ahead of us. In most major corporations the executive with the greatest headache in the last year probably has been the man in charge of the procurement of raw materials and, to a lesser degree, component parts.

The long-run impact on business of wide-scale shortages is fairly easy to see. In the broadest terms, planners will have to begin paying close attention to the problems of the limiting global factors. Increasingly, when *any* input *anywhere* falls short, *we* will have less. When the price of *anything* goes up *anywhere* in the world, *we* will pay more. We have already seen that when Arabian crude oil went up, we paid more for gasoline and home heating; when the Peruvian anchovies disappeared, the price of our soybeans went up; because there was a drought in the Ukraine, we paid more for bread. As population anywhere rises, we will have less of anything we want. The world has become too complex and too interdependent for us to be able to insulate ourselves.

More specifically, we shall have to adjust to a much more efficient utilization of our resources. The hey-day of the throwaway era is over. Now, for instance, we use an aluminum beer can once and throw it away. But to manufacture that aluminum can requires that two or three ounces of bauxite, probably from Jamaica, be transported some 1,500 miles to the United States. To change that bauxite to aluminum takes enough electricity to burn a hundred-watt bulb about five hours. Electricity is in increasingly short supply and higher in cost. Transportation costs are rapidly rising. The government of Jamaica has announced its determination to raise taxes and royalties on bauxite exports to eight times last year's level. How much longer will it be before the price of aluminum rises so high we can't afford to throw beer cans away? How much longer before a law is passed prohibiting the use of energy-intensive aluminum at all for beer cans?

Most broadly to the point, there will be a vastly decreased emphasis on physical products. Until now the question has been, "Will it sell?" Tomorrow the question will be, "Do we really need it?" Tomorrow's marketing manager is going to have to cope with a different kind of reality in which any product that is not absolutely necessary will find increasingly difficult justification, and probably decreased profitability.

Together with input shortages, a second factor will be operating to change the face of business: a vastly greater emphasis on meeting the goals of society rather than those of individuals, and a much more insistent demand for more public goods and services.

We can already see a well-established, broad-based, and still-growing sentiment that is demanding more and more that answers be found to the perplexing public problems of our times. The massive push of consumerism and the widely held belief of a whole new generation that there is more to life than simply owning more things are both indications of this trend. Demands for greater automobile safety, improved pollution control, safer cities, and stricter strip mining legislation all show that consumers as a group increasingly want something that business so far has not given them. New statutes to impose compliance are on the books because legislators have realized that consumers—call them voters—really want a change.

As a consequence, we can expect to see a substantial redirection of effort, skill, and funds toward public areas and away from the production of goods for private consumption. In the face of this trend it is not unreasonable to suspect that tomorrow's climate will put the brilliant, hardworking, resourceful, imaginative men who have brought marketing techniques to today's high level of effectiveness to work meeting, not individual company goals, but the broad goals of society. Tomorrow's emphasis may be to sell mass transportation instead of automobiles, literacy instead of lanolin, birth control instead of snow buggies, and schools instead of hair sprays.

If these indeed are the factors that increasingly will concern us and press on us then we are forced to recognize that traditional marketing activity is myopic. *It is simply out of tune with tomorrow's reality.*

The salad days are over even if there is still salad in the bowl. A combination of each man's concern with his own conventional problems, of reluctance to see the interrelationships of the whole picture, of fuzzy economics, expedient politics, naive faith in tomorrow, and the obvious profitability of today's course of action has kept us from facing the full impact of the realities that are swiftly descending on us.

In the long run the marketing manager as we know him is rapidly on his way to obsolescence, and conventional marketing of conventional products is dead. Dead because the need for it in its highest, most sophisticated forms has begun to cease to exist. Dead even though the marketers themselves are alive, prosperous, and well, blissfully practicing a trade that has no real future.

In the ivory towers of New York, Chicago, and Los Angeles, in the action centers of White Plains and Cincinnati, the men in the paneled offices who sit surrounded by success, comforted by the touch of expensive furniture, sustained by upward-rising sales charts, protected by echelons of assistants and secretaries, served by pocket computers and push-button telephones, gratified twice monthly by some of industry's most substantial paychecks—these men understandably cannot see and would not believe they are in an occupation that is in many ways a dead end, in others demonstrably antisocial, in concept outmoded. In terms they themselves invented, the art they are practicing is mature and has started to decline.

Now the time is at hand for the next great change. A business revolution is coming, and one of its results will be to sweep away a good part of marketing as we know it today. And, as in all other periods of change, either the leaders of the business community will take a constructive part in bringing the change about, or they will be swept away by it.

In general terms, we can already see that we face a dramatic reordering of our basic national attitudes with respect to production and consumption. The businessman who takes a realistic look down the road can see the obvious implication: the future in "product marketing" will be increasingly limited. At the same time, however, a new opportunity in selling a cluster of wholly new ideas, new concepts, and a new way of life is developing; but as do all opportunities, it comes accompanied by a real dilemma.

The basic problem is simple to state: how can the businessman's response to this new situation be made consonant with his traditional objectives?

Probably for some firms it cannot be. Some producers of frivolous products will disappear relatively quickly because their markets will evaporate and they will not be able to provide themselves with any alternative. Producers of marginally useful goods will face shrinking markets and will fight delaying actions in them. The sharpest and most resourceful will be able to stay alive longer, but there are never any victors in such a situation; there is only a continually decreasing number of survivors.

Most firms, of course, will survive, but they will do so only by making major shifts in direction and emphasis. The most successful will be those that make the greatest positive response to the new opportunities the future offers: those which look ahead constructively, interpret the future as accurately as possible, and attempt to supply the outputs and services the future demands.

But to commit corporate resources and personal futures to the uncertain, and obscure idealist, requires a rare combination of power, vision, and courage which not many corporations have. The few who do cannot throw enough weight against the national problem to make measurable headway.

Before most businessmen can act constructively, government must make one crucial change in the rules of our economic game: it must put profit into what the nation sees as its prime area of social responsibility. In no other way can we assure the maximum positive response from the business community, or even any positive response at all from substantial segments of it.

At the negative end of the spectrum another option is open: to fight. Can business be recalcitrant? Of course. It can be argued that the role of pioneer usually turns out to be a difficult and unrewarding one. The safer thing is to stay on familiar ground, to do nothing new, to preserve short-run profits, to go to court.

This may work for a while, but it is a delaying tactic rather than an answer. Sooner or later any government, seeing unmet needs and allocations of resources it considers undesirable, will move to alter the picture more to its liking. Such action takes the shape of laws and regulations that make some business activities illegal and others clearly unprofitable. Taxation can also be used: this time not as an inducement, but as a sword. In the long run the force that government can bring to bear on the businessman is irresistible, and playing legalistic tricks only delays the day of judgment. Since settlements imposed on losers tend to be much harsher than settlements arrived at voluntarily, it would seem that the astute marketer would avoid a losing battle; and the best way is to shift emphasis in time.

Because fighting the future has proven a battle certain to be lost, the most practical course often has been a compromise that approached tomorrow semi-voluntarily, holding out until the cost of further delay seemed to be rising too high and giving in only when and where it became absolutely necessary. This is the passive center of the continuum—really a nonresponse that at best delays the inevitable. But temporizing action of this sort is not a permanently rewarding answer, for defeat always waits at the end.

Common sense must argue that the positive approach is the logical one for businessmen. A businessman must, in the long run, be far better off if he takes the initiative to look for new options for his organization while he still has a reasonable opportunity to participate in writing the rules than if he waits until he is dragged kicking and screaming into forced compliance with the inevitable. Once the future arrives, opportunity disappears or is severely limited. The rules are written by others, and the individual can do no more than operate within them.

Thus far, the evaluation of future alternatives with respect to broadened marketing concepts has presented a dilemma of irreconcilables to American business, but businessmen must now reconcile them, and quickly.

Traditional marketing must take the initiative and alter its concepts and activities constructively to meet America's new needs. If it does not do so it will be increasingly regulated. Its activities will be more and more limited, and ultimately it will become of vestigial importance. Only the application of business initiative, courage, and resourcefulness will prevent the coming of new restrictions tomorrow that will make today's look like the apotheosis of *laissez faire*.

Can marketers meet the challenge? Not individually. No one company can attack the future. No one industry can effectively attempt a solution.

Can marketing meet the challenge? Yes, if all marketers move together. But government and business must first act cooperatively to develop new and acceptable rules for playing the game. Because the crucial element in securing the maximum contribution of businessmen toward the solution of the problems of tomorrow is profitability, the actions of government in providing the possibility of profit are critical in gaining the cooperation, or even the interest, of business.

Can profitability be added to societally desirable actions? Of course. A number of ways to do this already are known and others could be developed. Two of the most obvious and presently most commonly used are the underwriting of activities too risky to be acceptable within the limits of normal prudence, and favorable tax treatment that affords clear-cut opportunities for profits commensurate with the greater risks involved.

Such a combined business-government effort is necessary to generate the maximum voluntary approach by business to the problems of the future. Without the aid of government the businessman not only would be playing the familiar game of "I bet my job," but very likely also a far more dangerous one, "I bet my company." Team effort requires one major change in the thinking of both participants. For a long time they have regarded each other as adversaries; it would be helpful now for them to see each other as indispensable partners.

Perhaps that, finally, sums up the first challenge for the businessman: to find a way to lead both government and the business community into a combined, positive approach to the future.

judicial/judicious

Judicial is a term that pertains only to law courts or judges.

Example: The *judicial* branch is one of the three branches of the United States government.

Judicious is a term that pertains to anyone's careful or wise judgment.

> *Example:* The reorganization was accomplished smoothly by *judicious* management.

K

kind of/sort of

Kind of and *sort of* should be used in writing to mean only "class" or "type" of things.

> *Example:* We use a different *kind of* sales slip for cash transactions.

Do not use *kind of* and *sort of* to mean "rather," "somewhat," or "somehow."

> *Change:* It was *kind of* a bad year for the firm.
> *To:* It was a bad year for the firm.

know-how

Know-how, a colloquial term for "special competence or knowledge," should be avoided in **formal writing**. (See also **English**, **varieties of**.)

> *Change:* He has a reputation for marketing *know-how*.
> *To:* He has a reputation for marketing *skill*.

L

laboratory report

When the results of testing are to be reported, careful notes should be taken during the test. Many company laboratories have forms for reporting test results. When a form is not provided, however, bear in mind that the following kinds of information should be included in a laboratory report: (1) the reason the test was conducted, (2) the procedure used in conducting the test, (3) problems encountered during the test, (4) conclusions resulting from the test, and (5) recommendations based on the conclusions.

Be certain that test results are clearly presented. Cryptic phrases and sentence fragments are very common in laboratory reports, but they are not usually sufficient for clear communication between writer and **reader**. Use the Checklist of the Writing Process to evaluate the draft of your report, and make whatever **revision** is necessary to ensure that it is precise and coherent. Also be careful in your use of **graphs**, **tables**, and other types of **illustrations**.

Example:
Equivalent Circuits for the Capacitance-Type Humidity Sensor

ABSTRACT

Reason for conducting the test →

In the course of its development and prototype production, the capacitance-type humidity sensor has always been tested with electrical excitations quite different from those the element experiences when used with proposed transmitter and controller circuits. A study was initiated to investigate the behavior of the capacitance sensor under various excitations, including those used in the proposed circuits. The object of the study was to find an equivalent circuit for the sensor that would predict its behavior for all excitations. This report summarizes that study. Three equivalent circuits for the capacitance humidity sensor are advanced, and the existence of a fourth—the exact specification for which is beyond the range of available test equipment—is suggested. . . .

Problem encountered →

. . . .

Conclusions reached →

The conclusions drawn from the experiments are that the capacitance-type humidity sensor is a fairly complex electrical element and that its equivalent circuit is indeed a function of the nature and speed of its excitation. Specific conclusions are drawn regarding the conditions of the least and greatest variations in the components of the equivalent circuits and the possible physical origins of these variations. The report concludes with three main recommendations: (1) that we change the operating frequency of the proposed transmitter circuit to take advantage of a range of relative element invariance; (2) that we establish a production test procedure for the sensor that uses the exact excitation of the transmitter; and (3) that we build a laboratory with controlled temperature and humidity as a site for future sensor development.

Recommendations →

INTRODUCTION

Procedures used →

From the outset, the capacitance-type humidity sensor developed in the Research Division and described in Research Report 104 was, as a matter of convenience, measured and evaluated at 1000 Hz using a General Radio Type 1650-A Impedance Bridge having an internal oscillator of that frequency. However, the circuits proposed for converting the capacitance value to a more useful voltage or current level operate at considerably higher frequencies: the transmitter proposed in Research Report 104 operates at 50 to 60 KHz, and the transmitter proposed by the Electronics Division employs a modified Maxwell commutated dc bridge driven at 100 KHz. Recent tests suggest that the parameters of the sensor are different at the higher frequencies than those values measured at 1000 Hz; the tests suggest that the parameters of the equivalent circuit of the sensor are frequency-dependent.

We initiated a brief study to determine experimentally the characteristics of the capacitance-type humidity sensor over the anticipated range of application frequencies. In addition, because the Maxwell bridge transmitter subjects the sensor to a recurrent charging and discharging transient, the study included a check of sensor characteristics under transient excitation. Since the transient mode is, in a sense, a limiting frequency, this test was to provide an added check on the frequency response data. In all these efforts, we gave particular attention to determining accurately the resistances attendant with the humidity-dependent capacitance; that is, we attempted to specify how the sensor deviated from an ideal capacitor.

The object of this report is to summarize that study, to advance three equivalent circuits for the sensor, and to recommend test procedures that best characterize the sensor and an operating frequency that minimizes the frequency dependence.

THEORY OF EQUIVALENT CIRCUITS

Variable-Frequency Models

At a given frequency, any passive, two-terminal network can be shown to be equivalent to a single impedance; this impedance is variously termed the Thevenin or driving-point impedance. This impedance consists of a resistance and a reactance; depending on the frequency and the composition and configuration of the network, the reactance may be either inductive or capacitive.

When testing networks of an unknown nature, it is common practice to evaluate the unknown as an equivalent driving-point impedance. Impedance bridges are constructed on this assumption as, in general, the unknown is balanced by adjustments in a single resistance and a single reactance; the value of the unknown is then read as the values of the components of its driving-point impedance.

The complementary problem of exactly specifying a complex network known from form readings of its driving-point impedance is, at best, more difficult. If one has a network of known form, consisting of 100 resistors, capacitors, and inductors of unknown magnitude, a single reading of driving-point impedance at a known frequency is obviously insufficient to specify the values of all components. To use driving-point impedance measurements successfully, one would need 50 readings of driving-point resistance and 50 readings of driving-point reactance at 50 different frequencies to generate the needed 100 equations for the 100 unknowns. . . .

. . . .

RECOMMENDATIONS

The following recommendations are based on the results of and the conclusions drawn from this study.

The fundamental frequency of the transmitter circuit proposed by the Electronics Division for use with the capacitance-type humidity sensor should be reduced to lie in the range of 10 KHz to 50 KHz. This is the region of least R-C variation in the two-element frequency-dependent model. The transmitter, being a time-constant dependent circuit, is sensitive to both of these parameters. In general, efforts should be made to keep the frequency at the low end of this range because the transmitter is more dependent on the element's capacitance than on its resistance. However, reducing the frequency unnecessarily reduces the sensitivity of the transmitter. Accordingly, we are recommending an operating frequency of 20 KHz to 25 KHz.

Efforts should be made to devise a production test procedure for the capacitance-type humidity sensor that subjects the sensor to the type of excitation it will experience in the proposed transmitter circuit. Since there are (or may be) three important elements in the complete model of the sensor, at least three readings of each sensor should be made. Those readings might include average element current and time constant for each of two known series resistances representing limits in the source impedance of the transmitter with the span and zero adjustments set at the limits of their ranges. Time constant could be read by seeing whether the charging voltage of the sensor falls within predefined limits marked on the face of the oscilloscope. . . .

No further effort should be invested in determining an equivalent circuit for the capacitance-type humidity sensor. Even if the suggested low-level, high-speed power measurements were possible, they would probably not increase our knowledge of the sensor appreciably. To attain the next level of understanding, the sensor would have to be considered as a distributed-parameter system. Since our applications use the sensor as a lumped-parameter element, we feel that the present knowledge is adequate.

A laboratory room having closely controlled and moderately adjustable temperature and humidity should be set up as a locale for further sensor development. Present laboratory areas where humidity is uncontrolled and quite variable from day to day make routine sensor measurements difficult. All controlled work must now be done with the sensor in a controlled temperature-humidity cabinet, a definite inconvenience. With a known constant ambient, much meaningful exploratory work could be done without the need to use the controlled-conditions cabinet. . . .

lay/lie

Lay is a **transitive verb** (a **verb** that requires a **direct object** to complete its meaning) and means "to place" or "to put." Its present **tense** form is *lay*.

Example: We *lay* the foundation of the building one section at a time.

The past tense form is *laid*.

Example: We *laid* the first section of the foundation on the 27th of June.

The perfect tense form is also *laid*.

Example: Since June we *have laid* all but the last two sections of the foundation.

Lay is frequently confused with *lie*, which is an **intransitive verb** (a verb that does not require an **object** to complete its meaning) meaning "to recline" or "to remain." Its present tense form is *lie*.

Example: Injured employees *lie* down and remain still until the doctor arrives.

The past tense form (which causes the confusion) is *lay*.

Example: The injured employee *lay* still for approximately five minutes.

The perfect tense form is *lain*.

Example: The injured employee *had lain* still for approximately five minutes when the doctor arrived.

leave/let

Leave, as a **verb**, should never be used in the sense of "allow" or "permit."

Change: *Leave* me do it my way.
To: *Let* me do it my way.

Leave as a **noun**, however, can mean "permission granted."

Example: Employees are granted a *leave* of absence if they have a chronic illness.

lend/loan

Either *lend* or *loan* may be used as a **verb**, but lend is more common.

> *Examples:*   You can *loan* them the money if you wish.
> You can *lend* them the money if you wish.

Loan, unlike *lend,* can also be a **noun.**

> *Example:*   We made arrangements at the bank for a **loan.**

letters (See **correspondence.**)

libel/liable/likely

The term *libel* means "anything circulated in writing or pictures that injures someone's good reputation." When someone's reputation is injured in speech, however, the term is *slander.*

> *Examples:*   When an editorial charged our board of directors with bribing a representative, the board members sued the newspaper for *libel.*
> If the mayor supports the bribery charge in his speech tonight, we will accuse him of *slander.*

The term *liable* means "legally subject to" or "responsible for."

> *Example:*   Employers are held *liable* for their employees' decisions.

In business and technical writing, *liable* should retain its legal meaning. Where a condition of probability is intended, use *likely.*

> *Change:*   Rita is *liable* to be promoted.
> *To:*   Rita is *likely* to be promoted.

library classification system

Libraries classify and arrange books and journals by call numbers. Call numbers are normally based on the Dewey Decimal System or the Library of Congress System.

The Dewey Decimal System divides all books and journals by sets of numbers into the following ten general subject categories.

000–099   General Works
100–199   Philosophy

200–299	Religion
300–399	Social Sciences
400–499	Language
500–599	Pure Sciences
600–699	Technology (Applied Sciences)
700–799	Fine Arts
800–899	Literature
900–999	History

Each of these general categories is in turn divided into ten smaller categories. For example, the Technology classification (600–699) is broken down in the following way.

600–609	Technology
610–619	Medical Sciences
620–629	Engineering
630–639	Agriculture
640–649	Home Economics
650–659	Business and Business Methods
660–669	Chemical Technology and Industrial Chemistry
670–679	Manufacturing (metal, textile, paper, etc.)
680–689	Miscellaneous Manufactures (hardware, furniture, etc.)
690–699	Building Construction

The Library of Congress System is divided by letters into the following major subject categories.

A	General Works
B	Philosophy and Religion
C	History and Auxiliary Sciences
D	Universal History and Topography
E/F	American History
G	Geography, Anthropology, Folklore, etc.
H	Social Sciences
J	Political Science
K	Law
L	Education
M	Music
N	Fine Arts

P   Language and Literature
Q   Science
R   Medicine
S   Agriculture
T   Technology
U   Military Science
V   Naval Science
Z   Library Science and Bibliography

Business and related topics occur under the Social Sciences category (H) as follows.

HA   Statistics
HB   Economic Theory
HC   Economic History
HD   Land, Agriculture, Industry (including Labor)
HE   Transportation and Communication
HF   Commerce (including Boards of Trade, Chambers of Commerce, Tariff Policy, Business Administration, Personnel Management, and Advertising)
HG   Finance
HJ   Public Finance
HM   Sociology
HN   Social History
HQ   Social Groups
HS   Societies
HT   Communities, Classes, Races
HV   Social Pathology
HX   Socialism, Communism, Anarchism

library research

The following systematic four-step approach to library research allows you to use your research time efficiently. Although this procedure enables you to spend a relatively short amount of time in the library, it does not free you from the responsibility of being thorough in your research and of taking complete and accurate notes.

The four steps cover (1) basic sources, (2) the book and periodical stacks, (3) evaluation, and (4) check out.

BASIC SOURCES

The sources to consult first are (1) the library card file and (2) the **bibliographies** and periodical **indexes**. The card file is a file of all books contained in the library. Each book is represented in the card file by (1) an author card, (2) a subject card, and (3) a title card. If you have specific books in mind, look them up by author or title. If not, check the card file for your subject. For example, if you were researching the development of the computer, you would look behind the letter "C" in the card file, then alphabetically search for the word *computer*. Behind the computer subject and title cards you would find additional subject and title cards dealing with computers. Be thorough in searching for your topic by subject card. The examples on page 283 are title, subject, and author cards for Nigel Hawkes' *The Computer Revolution.*

The call number, which directs you to the book's location in the book stacks, is located in the upper left-hand corner on all three cards.

The library card may contain a brief summary of the book's contents. Sometimes a subject card also has the note "see also," referring you to related subject headings. Unless you are certain that you have all the information you need, it is worth your time to look up the additional references.

A book's title often indicates its contents. When it does, decide whether to look at the book on the basis of your established **objective, reader**, and **scope**. If you decide a book would not be helpful, go to the next card. If the next book appears helpful, make out a note card containing the following information: (1) call number, (2) title, (3) author (if the "author" is an organization, substitute its name), (4) date of publication, (5) publisher's name. If your writing project needs a bibliography, you can compile it from the information on these cards. (See the example on p. 284.)

Bibliographies and indexes are lists of books and articles published in broad fields, such as business or engineering. Determine which bibliography or index might deal with your subject, and then check it for appropriate titles. They are arranged alphabetically by subject, title, and author. If you find a useful one, record the pertinent bibliographic information from the entry so that it can be easily found when you begin to take notes.

TITLE CARD

AUTHOR   TITLE OF BOOK   PLACE OF PUBLICATION

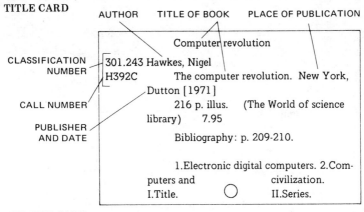

CLASSIFICATION NUMBER

CALL NUMBER

PUBLISHER AND DATE

301.243 Hawkes, Nigel
H392C   The computer revolution. New York,
         Dutton [1971]
                216 p. illus.   (The World of science
         library)   7.95
                Bibliography: p. 209-210.

                1.Electronic digital computers. 2.Computers and   civilization.
         I.Title.   ◯   II.Series.

Computer revolution

SUBJECT CARD

SUBJECT CATEGORY OF THIS BOOK

ELECTRONIC DIGITAL COMPUTERS

301.243 Hawkes, Nigel.
H392C   The computer revolution. New York,
         Dutton [1971]
                216 p. illus   (The World of science
         library)   7.95
                Bibliography: p. 209-210.

                1.Electronic digital computers. 2.Computers and   civilization.
         I.Title   ◯   II.Series

AUTHOR CARD

301.243 Hawkes, Nigel
H392C   The computer revolution. New York,
         Dutton [1971]
                216 p. illus.   (The World of science
         library)   7.95

                Bibliography: p. 209-210

                1.Electronic digital computers. 2.Computers and   civilization.
         I.Title.   ◯   II.Series.

```
   301.243                 The Computer Revolution
   H392C                   Nigel Hawkes - 1971
                           N.Y.: Dutton
```

Following is a list of periodical indexes and bibliographies that may help you get started.

> *Applied Science and Technology Index*
> *Biological and Agricultural Index*
> *Business Periodical Index*
> *Chemical Abstracts*
> *Cumulative Book Index (CBI)*
> *Education Index*
> *Engineering Index*
> *Guide to Reference Material for Science and Technology*
> *Monthly Catalog of United States Government Publications*
> *Music Index*
> *Readers' Guide to Periodical Literature*
> *Sources of Business Information*

Additional sources of information that may be helpful include handbooks, encyclopedias, manuals, and atlases. Even unbound material, such as pamphlets and leaflets, can be useful. If you need help of any kind, do not hesitate to ask a librarian. (See also **reference books**.)

BOOK AND PERIODICAL STACKS

To locate books, use the library call number from your note card. To locate periodicals, which are shelved alphabetically, use the title of the periodical.

EVALUATION

To evaluate a book, scan the **table of contents**, preface, and **foreword**, to determine the extent to which the book covers your subject. If it contains nothing of real value for your project, put it aside and write "no help" on your note card (so you will know later that you have already reviewed the book). If the entire book is full of valuable information, put it aside to take home for a thorough evaluation.

If a book has several promising passages, look them up and record summary notes on your note cards. If you lift whole sentences or passages from the original, be sure to mark them as direct **quotations** to avoid the possibility of **plagiarism**. Always include the page number with each note. Be sure to record the date of the publication on your note card.

```
301.243          The Computer Revolution
H392C            Nigel Hawkes - 1971
                     N.Y.: Dutton
                 _____

      The Babylonians credited
      with invention of abacus.


                                    p. 9
```

Next, evaluate the periodical articles you have selected. This normally must be done at the library because periodicals cannot be checked out. If an article contains more information than can be conveniently summarized on note cards, you may want to make a photographic copy to take home for fuller evaluation.

CHECK OUT

Check out the books you want to evaluate more extensively at home. Once home, you need not necessarily read the entire book; use its table of contents and index as guides, and learn to scan pages and chapters for key words and phrases pertinent to your subject. Keep your objective, reader, and scope in mind as you scan.

Be selective in your **note-taking**, and be certain to include the page number with each note. Be sure to use a separate card for each note. This phase of your research may require multiple note cards for each book. To keep them straight, enter the author's last name in the lower left corner of each card.

-like

The **suffix** *-like* is sometimes added to **nouns** to make them **adjectives**. The resulting **compound word** is hyphenated if it is unusual or might not be immediately clear.

> *Examples:*   childlike, lifelike, dictionary-like, computer-like
> Her new assistant works with *machine-like* efficiency.

like/as

In cases of confusion between *like* and *as,* remember that *like* is a **preposition** and *as* is a **conjunction**. The following rules of thumb may help clear up this confusion.

Use *like* with a **noun** or **pronoun** that is not followed by a **verb**.

> *Example:*   The new supervisor behaves *like a novice.*

Use *as* before **phrases** and **clauses** (which contain verbs).

> *Examples:*   He acted *as though he owned the company.*
> He responded *as we expected he would.*

Like may be used in elliptical constructions that omit the verb.

> *Example:*   She took to architecture *like a bird to nest building.*

If the omitted portions of the elliptical construction were restored, however, *as* would be used.

> *Example:*   She took to architecture *as a bird takes to nest building.*

(See also **connectives**.)

linking verb

A **verb** that functions primarily to link the **subject** to a **noun** or **modifier** is called a linking verb. The most common linking verb is a form of the verb *to be.*

> *Example:*   Each department *is* important to the company's overall performance.

However, many other verbs may also function as linking verbs.

Example: She *became* an investment adviser.

Other common linking verbs are *remain* and *seem.* Verbs that convey the senses (*look, feel, sound, taste, smell*) often perform only a linking function.

Example: The bookkeeper *looked* tired.

A few verbs, in different senses, may function as linking, **transitive**, or **intransitive verbs**.

Examples: He *grew* angry. (linking verb, equivalent in meaning to *became*)
He *grew* African violets in his office. (transitive verb)
The African violets *grew*. (intransitive verb)

(See also **subjective complement.**)

literature

In business and technical contexts, the word *literature* applies to a body of writing pertaining to a specific field, such as finance, insurance, or computers. We commonly speak, for example, of *medical literature* or *campaign literature.*

Example: Please send me any available *literature* on computerized translations of foreign languages.

long variants

Be on guard against inflating plain words beyond their normal value by adding extra **prefixes** or **suffixes**, a practice that creates long variants. Below is a list of some normal words and their inflated counterparts.

Normal Word	Long Variant
analysis	analyzation
certified	certificated
commercial	commercialistic
connect	interconnect
mingle	intermingle
use	utilize (see also **utilize**)
orient	orientate
visit	visitation

(See also **gobbledygook** and **word choice**.)

loose/lose

Loose is an **adjective** meaning "not fastened" or "unrestrained."

> *Example:*   He found a *loose* wire.

Lose is a **verb** meaning "to be deprived of" or "to fail to win."

> *Example:*   I hope we do not *lose* the Acme account.

lower-case and upper-case letters

The term *lower case* refers to small letters as distinguished from **capital letters** (known as *upper-case* letters). The terms were coined in the early history of printing when the printer kept the small letters in a lower "case" (or tray) below the tray where he kept capital letters.

M

malapropism

A malapropism is a word that sounds similar to one the writer intended but is, in fact, a different word.

> *Example:*   The repairman cleaned the accounting machine's *plankton*. (The part being referred to is the *platten*.)

Intentional malapropisms are sometimes used in humorous writing; unintentional malapropisms can be embarrassing to the writer. (See also **antonym** and **synonym**.)

male

Male is usually restricted to scientific, legal, or medical contexts (a *male* patient or suspect). Keep in mind that this term sounds cold and impersonal. The terms "boy," "man," and "gentleman" are acceptable substitutes in other contexts; however, be aware that these substitute words have **connotations** involving age, dignity, and social position.

maps

Maps can be used to show specific geographic features of the area represented (roads, mountains, rivers, etc.) or to show information according to geographic distribution (population, housing, manufacturing centers, etc.).

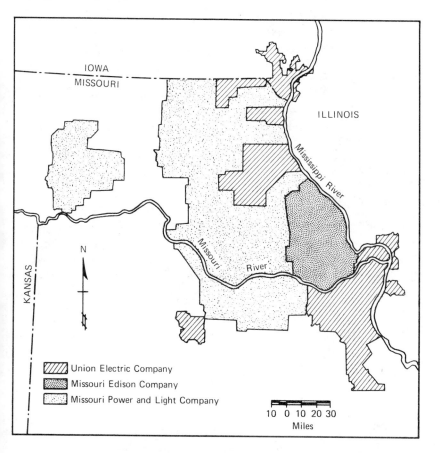

Figure 1. Location of Service Areas of Three Utilities
Source: The United States Nuclear Regulatory Commission

Bear these points in mind as you create maps for use with your text.

1. Label the map clearly.
2. Assign the map a figure number if you are using enough **illustrations** to justify use of figure numbers.
3. Make sure all boundaries within the map are clearly identified. Eliminate unnecessary boundaries.
4. Eliminate unnecessary information from your map (if population is important, do not include mountains, roads, rivers, etc.).
5. Include a scale of miles or feet to give your **reader** an indication of the map's proportions.
6. Indicate which direction is north.
7. Show the features you want emphasized by shading, dots, cross-hatching, or use of appropriate symbols when color reproduction cannot be used.
8. If you use only one color, remember that only three shades of a single color will show up satisfactorily.
9. Include a key telling what the different colors, shadings, or symbols represent.
10. Place maps as close as possible to the portion of the text that refers to them.

mass noun

Mass nouns, as opposed to **count nouns**, identify those materials that comprise a mass rather than individual units—a substance or property that cannot be separated and counted. Such words as *electricity, gold, silver, oil, water, beer, aluminum, wheat,* and *cement* are mass nouns. (For the **case** and **number** of mass nouns, see **nouns**. See also **fewer/less**.)

maybe/may be

Maybe (one word) is an **adverb** meaning "perhaps."

　　Example:　*Maybe* the legal staff can resolve this issue.

May be (two words) is a **verb phrase**.

　　Example:　It *may be* necessary to ask for an outside specialist.

media/medium

Media, the plural of *medium,* should not be used as a singular **noun** meaning "an individual means of mass communication."

Examples: The *media are* a powerful influence in presidential elections.
The most influential *medium is* television.

memorandum

The most common type of business and industrial communication is
the memorandum, almost universally referred to as a "memo." (The
plural form of *memorandum* may be either *memoranda* or *memorandums.*) Memos are commonly used for internal communications of
virtually every kind. Even though the memo may be limited in scope,
the writing process outlined in the Checklist of the Writing Process
will help you write effective memos. See the following example.
(See also **correspondence**.)

```
                                              January 3, 1976

TO:       Jason Waters, Director

FROM:     Gerald Hill, Manager

SUBJECT:  A Writing Group in Chicago

Jim Chancellor needs help with both the software speci-
fications and the software release documentation.  It
would certainly help our efficiency and productivity if
we had better specifications to work from, and it would
help the company's cause to produce better software
release documentation.

I would like to propose, therefore, that we establish a
group of writers in Chicago to help raise the quality
of specifications and software release documentation.
The implementor would write his own specification, as
he always has, but would then submit it to the manager
of this publications group for approval.  If it was not
adequate, the manager would assign it to a writer who
would work with the implementor to produce an accept-
able specification.

To staff this group, except for the manager, I strongly
suggest that we hire only newly graduated computer
science majors who can pass our writer's test.  Once
hired, they should receive adequate technical training
on our systems as well as training in writing and pub-
lications production techniques.  After receiving their
training, they should be assigned to the group in
Chicago as trainees.
```

metaphor

Metaphor is a **figure of speech** that points out similarities between two things by treating them as being the same thing. Metaphor states that the thing being described *is* the thing to which it is being compared.

> *Example:*   *The building site was a beehive,* with iron workers still at work on the tenth floor, plumbers installing fixtures on the floors just beneath them, electricians buzzing about on the middle floors, and carpenters putting the finishing touches on the first floor.

The use of metaphor can help clarify complex theories or objects, and its use in business and technical contexts is quite appropriate. For example, the life-sustaining tube connecting a space-walking astronaut to his oxygen supply in the spacecraft is called an "umbilical cord." The person who first drew this comparison knew that such a life support tube was new and unfamiliar, so to make its function immediately apparent he used a metaphor that compared it to something with which people were already familiar. A similar purpose was served when the term "window" was used to describe the abstract concept of the point at which a spacecraft reenters the earth's atmosphere. Here the strange and far-away was made near and domestic by the metaphorical use of a term familiar to everyone. Both of these expressions have gained widespread use because they helped clarify new and unfamiliar concepts.

A word of caution: beginning writers sometimes mix metaphors, which usually results in an illogical statement.

> *Example:*   Billingham's proposal backfired and now she is in hot water. (This is an incongruous statement because a backfiring automobile does not land someone in hot water.)

(See also **figures of speech**.)

methods of development

Every subject must be developed logically from a beginning to a **conclusion**. Without such direction, writing wanders aimlessly and pointlessly. An appropriate method of development is the writer's tool for keeping things under control and the reader's means of following the writer's development of a theme.

Many different methods of development are available to the writer. This book includes only those that are likely to be used by business and technical people: **sequential, chronological, order of importance, comparison, general-to-specific, specific-to-general, cause-and-effect, spatial,** and **analysis.** As the writer, you must determine the method of development that best suits your subject, your **reader,** and your **objective.**

Your subject may obviously lend itself to a particular method of development. If you were describing how to start an airplane engine, for example, you would naturally present the steps of the process in the order of their occurrence. This is the sequential method of development. If you were writing about the historical development of a corporation, you would probably describe it chronologically, from its founding to the present. This is the chronological method of development. If your subject lends itself naturally to a particular method of development, use that method—don't attempt to impose another method of development. If your subject does not lend itself naturally to a particular method of development, you must determine the best one to impose upon it—best for your subject, your reader, and your objective.

Writing projects often require the use of several methods of development, but almost always one method is primary, and the writer should have it clearly in mind while organizing the project. For example, if you were writing about the development of the Ford Motor Company and the Chrysler Corporation, you would probably use both the comparison method and the chronological method of development. Which method should be primary would depend upon whether you wished to emphasize the historical or the comparative aspects of your subject.

SEQUENTIAL METHOD OF DEVELOPMENT

The sequential, or step-by-step, method of development lends itself naturally to certain types of subjects. Probably the most common method of development, it is relatively easy to use for describing a "straight-line" series of actions that must be performed in a logical sequence. It would be the logical method of development to use, for example, when writing **instructions** for assembling a bicycle. (For further information, see **sequential method of development.**)

CHRONOLOGICAL METHOD OF DEVELOPMENT

The chronological method of development arranges events in an orderly time sequence, beginning at the start and proceeding step by step in sequential order to the end. It follows a time sequence that is intrinsic to the material, making the progression of time clear and consistent. The chronological method of development is well suited to **explaining a process** in which time relationships are important. The process of biological evolution, for example, would logically be described in chronological sequence. (For further information, see **chronological method of development**.)

ORDER OF IMPORTANCE AS A METHOD OF DEVELOPMENT

Order of importance actually includes two methods of development: decreasing order of importance, which is fairly common in business and technical writing, and increasing order of importance, which is more common in other types of writing.

When using decreasing order of importance, the writer arranges his ideas in a descending order of importance. This method of development simply begins with the most important fact or point, then goes to the next most important, and so on until it finally ends with the least important. If, for example, you were writing a **report** to a busy executive to document all the valid reasons why your pet project should be funded, you might use this method of development to impress him right at the outset with your strongest points. (For further information, see **decreasing order of importance as a method of development**.)

Increasing order of importance begins with the least important point or fact, then goes to one more important, building finally to the most important point at the end. Particularly effective for **persuasion**, this method of development is rare in business and technical writing. (For further information, see **increasing order of importance as a method of development**.)

COMPARISON AS A METHOD OF DEVELOPMENT

This method of development compares subjects by pointing out their similarities and differences. It can be especially effective in presenting new concepts because it can compare the subject being explained with another subject with which the reader is likely to be familiar. If you were explaining the British system of currency, for example, you could use this method of development by comparing the British system with the American or Canadian system. This method of development is popular with professional technical people because it is so similar to the way they instinctively evaluate technical subjects. (For further information, see **comparison as a method of development**.)

GENERAL-TO-SPECIFIC METHOD OF DEVELOPMENT

This method of development states a general premise and then provides facts that support the premise or build to a specific conclusion. For example, a management report that begins with the general statement "Companies that diversify are more successful than those that do not" would then follow with evidence to support and develop this premise. (For further information, see **general-to-specific method of development**.)

SPECIFIC-TO-GENERAL METHOD OF DEVELOPMENT

This method of development begins with a specific statement and builds to a general conclusion or premise. It is somewhat like increasing order of importance as a method of development in that it carefully builds its case and does not present its conclusion until the end. The specific-to-general method of development often uses examples and **analogies** to build to the final conclusion or premise. For example, if your subject was highway safety, you might begin with a specific highway accident and then go on to generalize about how details of the accident were common enough to many similar accidents that recommendations could be made to reduce the probability of such accidents.

CAUSE-AND-EFFECT METHOD OF DEVELOPMENT

The cause and effect method of development, by stressing the connection between a result and a preceding event, explains why something happened or why the writer predicts that something is going to happen. For example, a report on the role played by worn-out tires (cause) in highway fatalities (effect) would lend itself ideally to this method of development.

SPATIAL METHOD OF DEVELOPMENT

If you were reporting on some aspect of the operation of a national chain department store, you might start on the East Coast and develop your report geographically to the West Coast. This is the spatial method of development, which can also be used to develop a subject from bottom to top, from near to far, from inside to outside, from right to left, and so on. The spatial method should never be used unless it is natural to your subject. (For further information, see **spatial method of development**.)

ANALYSIS AS A METHOD OF DEVELOPMENT

Analysis, as a method of development, separates a whole into its component parts. It is a form of examination that seeks to distinguish and separate things, situations, experiences, or concepts—and thereby establish the identities of parts or particulars. For example, a report on the organization of a company might begin by identifying the company's major departments—manufacturing, marketing, purchasing, accounting, etc.—and then focus on one department at a time and explain its various functions. (For further information, see **analysis as a method of development**.)

minutes of meeting

Organizations and committees keep official records of their proceedings known as minutes. The secretary of such an organization is assigned to record and sometimes distribute the minutes of meetings. At each meeting, the minutes of the previous meeting are read aloud (if printed copies were not distributed) so that the group can approve or revise them. Since minutes often settle disputes and provide information (the official minutes of corporate meetings are often used as evidence in legal proceedings), they must be accurate, complete, and clear.

If you are keeping minutes and do not take shorthand, take memory-jogging notes during the meeting and then expand them with the appropriate detail immediately after the meeting. Be sure to record specific figures and names, however, during the meeting. When writing minutes, avoid subjective **adjectives** and **adverbs**, as in "Mr. Sturgess's *capable* assistant read the *extremely* comprehensive report of the subcommittee." Minutes should have a **tone** of complete objectivity and impartiality.

The minutes of meetings, according to Robert's Rules of Order, should include the following.

1. Name of the organization or committee.
2. Place and date of the meeting.
3. Kind of meeting that is being reported; that is, a regular meeting or a specially called meeting to discuss a specific subject or problem.

4. Number of members present. If the committee or board is small (ten or fewer), the names should also be given.
5. Whether the chairman and the secretary were present. If either of these officers was absent, the name of the substitute should be recorded in the minutes.
6. The statement that the minutes of the previous meeting were amended or approved or that the reading of the minutes was dispensed with.
7. A list of the reports that were read and approved. (It is not normally necessary to give a detailed account of the substance of the reports submitted.)
8. All the main motions that were made, with statements as to whether they were carried or lost. (It is not necessary to include motions that were withdrawn.)
9. Resolutions that were adopted, recorded in full. If a resolution was rejected, a simple statement to the effect that the resolution failed to pass is adequate.
10. A record of all ballots, complete with the number of ballots cast "for" and "against."

misplaced modifiers

A **modifier** is misplaced when it modifies, or appears to modify, the wrong word or phrase. It differs from a **dangling modifier** in that a dangling modifier cannot *logically* modify any word in the sentence because its intended referent is missing. The best general rule for avoiding misplaced modifiers is to place modifiers as close as possible to the words they are intended to modify.

A misplaced modifier can be a word, a **phrase**, or a **clause**.

MISPLACED WORDS

Adverbs are especially likely to be misplaced because they can appear in several positions within a sentence.

> *Examples:*   We *almost* lost all of the parts.
> We lost *almost* all of the parts.

The first sentence means that all of the parts were *almost* lost (but they were not), while the second sentence means that a majority of the parts (*almost* all) were in fact lost. Possible confusion in sentences of this type can be avoided by placing the adverb immediately before the word it is intended to modify.

MISPLACED PHRASES

To avoid confusion, place phrases near the words they modify. Note the two meanings possible when the phrase is shifted in the following sentences.

Examples: The equipment *without the accessories* sold the best. (different types of equipment were available, some with and some without accessories)
The equipment sold the best *without the accessories.* (one *type* of equipment was available, and the accessories were optional)

MISPLACED CLAUSES

To avoid confusion, clauses should be placed as close as possible to the words they modify.

Change: We sent the brochure to four local firms *that had three-color illustrations.*
To: We sent the brochure *that had three-color illustrations* to four local firms.

SQUINTING MODIFIERS

A modifier "squints" when it can be interpreted as modifying either of two sentence elements simultaneously, so that the reader is confused about which is intended.

Example: We agreed *on the next day* to make the adjustments.
Could mean: We agreed to *make the adjustments on the next day.*
Or: *On the next day we agreed* to make the adjustments.

A squinting modifier can sometimes be corrected simply by changing its position, but often it is better to recast the sentence:

Example: We agreed that *on the next day* we would make the adjustments. (if the adjustments were to be made on the next day)
Or: *On the next day* we agreed that we would make the adjustments. (if the agreement was made on the next day)

mixed construction

A mixed construction occurs when a **sentence** contains grammatical forms that are improperly combined. These constructions are improper because the grammatical forms are inconsistent with one another. The most common types of mixed constructions result from the following causes.

TENSE

    Change: The pilot *lowered* the landing gear and *is approaching* the runway. (shift from past to present tense)

        To: The pilot *lowered* the landing gear and *approached* the runway.

        Or: The pilot *has lowered* the landing gear and *is approaching* the runway.

PERSON

    Change: The *technician* should take care in choosing *your* equipment. (shift from third to second person)

        To: The *technician* should take care in choosing *his* equipment.

NUMBER

    Change: My *car,* though not as fast as the others, *operate* on regular gasoline. (singular subject with plural verb form)

        To: My *car,* though not as fast as the others, *operates* on regular gasoline.

VOICE

    Change: I *will check* your printout, and then *it will be returned* to you. (shift from active to passive voice)

        To: I *will check* your printout, and then *I will return* it to you.

(See also **parallel structure** and **agreement**.)

modifiers

Modifiers are words, **phrases**, or **clauses** that expand, limit, or make more exact the meaning of other elements in a **sentence**. Although we could create sentences without modifiers, we often need the detail and clarification they provide.

    Examples: Production decreased. (without modifiers)
              Automobile production decreased *rapidly.* (with modifiers)

Most modifiers function as **adjectives** or **adverbs**. An adjective makes the meaning of a **noun** or **pronoun** more exact by pointing out one of its qualities or by imposing boundaries upon it.

    Examples: *ten* automobiles   *this* crane
            an *educated* person   *loud* machinery

An adverb modifies an adjective, another adverb, a **verb**, or an entire clause.

Examples: Under test conditions, the brake pad showed *much* less wear than it did under actual conditions. (modifying the adjective "less")
The wear was *very* much less than under actual conditions. (modifying another adverb, "much")
The recording head hit the surface of the disc *hard.* (modifying the verb "hit")
Surprisingly, the machine failed even after all the tests that it had passed. (modifying a clause)

Adverbs become **intensifiers** when they increase the impact of adjectives (*very* fine, *too* high) or adverbs (*rather* quickly, *very* slowly). As a rule, be cautious in using intensifiers; their overuse can lead to exaggeration, and hence to inaccuracies.

DANGLING MODIFIERS

A modifying word or phrase "dangles" when it has no clear word or subject to modify. Most dangling modifiers are **verbal** phrases (**gerund, participial, infinitive**) that should modify a noun or pronoun. **Dangling modifiers** usually occur because the writer fails to provide the **subject** of a clause. (See **dangling modifiers**.)

MISPLACED MODIFIERS

A modifier is misplaced when it modifies, or appears to modify, the wrong word or phrase. It differs from a dangling modifier in that a dangling modifier cannot *logically* modify any word in the sentence since its intended referent is missing. Place modifiers as close as possible to the words they are intended to modify to avoid misplacing them. (See **misplaced modifiers**.)

mood

The grammatical term *mood* refers to the **verb** functions—and sometimes form changes—that indicate whether the verb is intended to (1) make a statement or ask a question (indicative mood), (2) give a command (imperative mood), or (3) express a hypothetical possibility (subjunctive mood).

The indicative mood refers to an action or a state that is conceived as fact.

Examples: *Was* the president there?
The president *was* there.

The imperative mood expresses a command, suggestion, request, or entreaty.

> *Example:* *Close* the sale today.
> Please *keep* this confidential.

The subjunctive mood expresses something that is contrary to fact, conditional, hypothetical, or purely imaginative; it can also express a wish, a doubt, or a possibility. The subjunctive mood may change the form of the verb, but the verb *be* is the only one in English that preserves many such distinctions.

> *Examples:* The senior partner insisted that he (I, you, we, they) *be* in charge of the project.
> If the salesman (I, you, we, they) *were* to close the sale today, we would meet our monthly quota.

Form change for the subjunctive is rare in most verbs other than *be*. Instead, we use **helping verbs** to show the subjunctive function.

> *Example:* *Had* I *known* that you were here, I would have come earlier.

The advantage of the subjunctive mood is that it enables us to express clearly whether or not we consider a condition contrary to fact. If so, we use the subjunctive; if not, we use the indicative.

> *Examples:* If I *were* president of the firm, I would change several personnel policies. (subjunctive mood)
> I *am* president of the firm, but I don't feel that I control every aspect of its policies. (indicative mood)

Be careful not to shift from one mood to another within a **sentence**; to do so makes the sentence not only ungrammatical but unbalanced as well.

> *Change:* Have the customer sign the contract (imperative); then you should collect the deposit (indicative).
> *To:* Have the customer sign the contract (imperative); then collect the deposit (imperative).

Ms./Miss/Mrs.

Ms. is a convenient form of addressing a woman regardless of her marital status, and it is now almost universally accepted. *Miss* is used to refer to an unmarried woman, and *Mrs.* is used to refer to a married woman. Some women indicate a preference for *Miss* or *Mrs.,* and such a preference should be honored. An academic or professional title *(Dr., Prof., Capt.)* should take precedence over *Ms., Miss,* or *Mrs.*

MS/MSS

MS (or ms) is the **abbreviation** for *manuscript.* The plural form is *MSS* (or mss). Do not use this abbreviation (or any abbreviation) unless you are certain that your **reader** is familiar with it.

mutual/in common

When two or more persons (or things) have something *in common,* they share it or possess it jointly.

> *Examples:* What we have *in common* is our desire to make the company profitable.
> The fore and aft guidance assemblies have a *common* power source.

Mutual may also mean shared (as in *mutual friends*), but it usually implies something given and received reciprocally, and it is used with reference only to two persons.

> *Example:* Smith mistrusts Jones, and I am afraid the mistrust is *mutual.* (Jones also mistrusts Smith.)

N

narration

Narration is the presentation of a series of events; that is, it tells a story. Narration avoids any unnecessary interruptions in movement from the beginning event to the concluding event. It uses a combination of the **sequential** and the **chronological methods of development**, presenting events as they occur both in time and in order—from start to finish sequentially and from beginning to end chronologically. Like good **description**, good narration makes effective use of details.

Example: One of the foundations engaged me to edit the manuscript of a socio-economic research report designed for the thoughtful citizen as well as for the specialist. My expectations were not high—no deathless prose, merely a sturdy, no-nonsense report of explorers into the wilderness of statistics and half-known fact. . . . Although I did not expect fine writing from a trained professional researcher, I did assume that a careful fact-finder would write carefully.

And so, anticipating no literary treat, I plunged into the forest of words of my first manuscript. My weapons were a sturdy eraser and several batteries of sharpened pencils. My armor was a thesaurus. And if I should become lost, a near-by public library was a landmark, and the Encyclopedia of the Social Sciences on its reference shelves was an ever-ready guide.

Instead of big trees, I found underbrush. Cutting through lumbering sentences was bad enough, but the real chore was removal of the burdocks of excess verbiage which clung to the manuscript. Nothing was big or large; in my author's lexicon, it was "substantial." When he meant "much," he wrote "to a substantially high degree." If some event took place in the early 1920's, he put it in "the early part of the decade of the twenties." And instead of "that depends," my author wrote, "any answer to this question must bear in mind certain peculiarities characteristic of the industry."

So it went for 30,000 words. The pile of verbal burdocks grew—sometimes twelve words from a twenty-word sentence. The shortened version of 20,000 words was perhaps no more thrilling than the original report; but it was terser and crisper. It took less time to read and it could be understood quicker. That was all I could do.

—Samuel T. Williamson, "How to Write Like a Social Scientist," *Saturday Review*, October 4, 1947.

Although most often associated with fiction, narration may just as effectively be used to follow the development of a scientific theory or a sociological trend. (See also **forms of discourse**.)

nature

Nature, used to mean "kind" or "sort," is—like those words—often vague. Avoid the word in your writing.

Change: The space program, by its very *nature,* is costly.
To: Because of the need for sophisticated equipment and highly skilled personnel, the space program is costly.
Change: The *nature* of the contract caused the problem.
To: The forfeiture clause in the contract caused the problem.

needless to say

Although the **phrase** *needless to say* often occurs in speech and writing, it is redundant because it always precedes a remark that is stated despite the inference that nothing further need be said.

> *Change:*   *Needless to say,* departmental cutbacks have meant decreased efficiency.
> *To:*   Departmental cutbacks have meant decreased efficiency.
> *Or:*   Understandably, departmental cutbacks have meant decreased efficiency.

neo-

The **prefix** *neo-* is derived from a Greek word meaning "new." It is hyphenated when used with a **proper noun** or a **noun** that begins with the vowel "o."

> *Examples:*   neo-orthodoxy, Neo-Fascism, neoplasm, neologism, neo-Darwinism

new words

New words continually find their way into the language from a variety of sources. Some come from other languages.

> *Examples:*   discotheque (French), skiing (Norwegian), whiskey (Gaelic)

Some come from technology.

> *Examples:*   software, vinyl, nylon

Some come from scientific research.

> *Examples:*   berkelium, transistor

Some come from brand or trade names.

> *Examples:*   Jello, Teflon, Kleenex

Some come from acronyms.

> *Examples:*   FORTRAN, scuba, radar

Business and technology are responsible for many new words. Some are necessary and unavoidable; however, it is best to avoid creating a new word if an existing word will do. If you do use what you believe to be a new word or expression, be sure to define it the first time you use it; otherwise, your **reader** is certain to be confused. (See also **long variants**.)

nice

Nice can be used to mean "something done with precision."

> *Example:* He made a *nice* distinction between the two plans.

Nice is overused in speech in the imprecise meaning of "pleasant" or "agreeable."

> *Change:* He is a *nice* person to work with.
> *To:* He is an *agreeable* person to work with.

Since the word is used so imprecisely in speech, use it with caution in writing. (See also **vague words**.)

no doubt but

In the **phrase** *no doubt but,* the word *but* is redundant.

> *Change:* There is *no doubt but* that he will be promoted.
> *To:* There is *no doubt* that he will be promoted.

none

None may be considered either a singular or a plural **pronoun**, depending on the context.

> *Examples:* *None* of the material *has* been ordered. (always singular with a singular noun—in this case, "material")
> *None* of the clients *has* been called yet. (singular even with reference to a plural noun ["clients"] if the intended emphasis is on the idea of *not one*)
> *None* of the clients *have* been called yet. (plural with a plural noun)

For **emphasis**, substitute *no one* or *not one* for *none* and use a singular **verb**.

> *Example:* I paid the full retail price for three of your firm's machines, *no one* of which was worth the money.

(See also **agreement**.)

nonstandard English

Nonstandard English is the written language of those who do not use the conventions or regular grammatical features of **standard**

English. Nonstandard English is therefore characterized by misspellings, unconventional **grammar** and **punctuation**, and careless **word choice**. (See also **English, varieties of**.)

nor/or

Nor always follows *neither* in **sentences** with continuing negation.

>   *Example:* They will *neither* support *nor* approve the plan.

Likewise, *or* follows *either* in sentences.

>   *Example:* The firm will accept *either* a short-term *or* a long-term loan.

Two or more singular **subjects** joined by *or* or *nor* usually take a singular **verb**. When one subject is singular and one is plural, the verb agrees with the subject nearer to it.

>   *Examples:* *Neither* the manager *nor* the secretary *was* happy with the new filing system. (singular)
>   *Neither* the manager *nor* the secretaries *were* happy with the new filing system. (plural)
>   *Neither* the secretaries *nor* the manager *was* happy with the new filing system. (singular)

(See also **correlative conjunction**.)

not

The careless placement of *not* in **sentences** can cause **ambiguity**.

>   *Change:* All executives are *not* good writers. (The implication is that *no* executive is a good writer.)
>   *To:* *Not* all executives are good writers.

notable/noticeable

Notable, meaning "worthy of notice," is sometimes confused with *noticeable,* meaning "readily observed."

>   *Examples:* His accomplishments are *notable*.
>   Our advertising campaign is having a *noticeable* effect on sales.

note-taking

The purpose of note-taking is to summarize and record the information that you extract from your research material. The great challenge in taking notes is to condense another's thoughts in your own words without distorting the original thinking. Meeting this challenge involves careful reading on your part, because to compress someone else's ideas accurately, you must first understand them.

When taking notes on abstract ideas, as opposed to factual data, be careful not to sacrifice **clarity** for brevity. You can be brief—if you are accurate—with statistics, but notes expressing concepts can lose their meaning if they are too brief. The critical test of a note is whether, after a week has passed, you will still know what the note means and from it be able to recall the significant ideas of the passage. If you are in doubt about whether or not to take a note, take it—it is much easier to discard a note you don't need than to find the source again if it is needed.

As you extract information, be guided by the **objective** of your writing and by what you know about your **readers**. (Who are they? How much do they know about your subject?)

Resist the temptation to copy your source word-for-word as you take notes. On occasion, when your source concisely sums up a great deal of information or points to a trend or development important to your subject, you are justified in quoting it verbatim and then incorporating that **quotation** into your paper. As a general rule, you will rarely need to quote anything longer than a paragraph.

If a note is copied word-for-word from your source, be certain to enclose it in **quotation marks** so you will know later that it is a direct quotation. In your finished paper, be certain to give the source of your quotation in a **footnote**; otherwise, you will be guilty of **plagiarism**.

The mechanics of note-taking are simple and if followed conscientiously can save you much unnecessary work. Consider the information contained in the following paragraph.

> Long before the existence of bacteria was suspected, techniques were in use for combatting their influence in, for instance, the decomposition of meat. Salt and heat were known to be effective and these do in fact kill bacteria or prevent them from multiplying. Salt acts by the osmotic effect of extracting water from the bacterial cell fluid. Bacteria are less easily destroyed by osmotic action than are animal cells because their cell walls are constructed in a totally different way, which makes them very much less permeable.

> —Roger James, *Understanding Medicine* (London: Penguin Books, 1970), p. 103.

The paragraph says essentially three things:

1. Before the discovery of bacteria, salt and heat were used in combatting bacteria.
2. Salt kills bacteria by extracting water from their cells by osmosis, hence its use in curing meat.
3. Bacteria are less affected by the osmotic effect of salt than are animal cells because bacterial cell walls are less permeable.

If your topic involved tracing the origin of the bacterial theory of disease, you might want to note that salt was traditionally used to kill bacteria long before people realized what caused meat to spoil, though it might not be necessary to your topic to say anything about the relative permeability of bacterial cell walls. Again, your best note-taking guides are your objective, reader, and **scope**.

As you read the following paragraph, which contains only factual data, determine which facts you should record or summarize as notes in order to be complete and accurate.

> The arithmetic of searching for oil is stark. For all his scientific methods of detection, the only way the oilman can actually know for sure that there is oil in the ground is to drill a well. The average cost of drilling an oil well is over $100,000, and drilling a single well may cost over $1,000,000! And once the well is drilled, the odds against its containing enough oil to be commercially profitable are 49 to 1. The odds against its containing any oil at all are 8 to 1! Even after a field has been discovered, one out of every four holes drilled in developing the field is a dry hole because of the uncertainty of defining the limits of the producing formation. The oilman can never know what Mark Twain once called "the calm confidence of a Christian with four aces in his hand."
>
> —*The Baker World,* Baker Oil Tools, Inc.

Now read the following list of notes and see whether they are the same as those you would have taken.

1. Many scientific methods of detection
2. Only sure way to know is to drill a well
3. Average cost of drilling a well over $100,000; actual cost can go over $1,000,000
4. Odds against profitable well: 49 to 1
5. Odds against any oil: 8 to 1
6. If existence of oil is known, 1 of 4 wells still dry because limits of field unknown

The following paragraph is less factual. As you read it, determine the opinions or ideas you would record as notes.

> Energy does far more than simply make our daily lives more comfortable and convenient. Suppose you wanted to stop—and reverse—the economic progress of this nation. What would be the surest and quickest way to do it? Find a way to cut off the nation's oil resources! Industrial plants would shut down; public utilities would stand idle; all forms of transportation would halt. The country would be paralyzed! And our economy would plummet into the abyss of national economic ruin. Our economy, in short, is energy-based.
>
> —*The Baker World,* Baker Oil Tools, Inc.

Now read the following list of notes and see whether they are approximately the same as those you would have taken.

1. Best way to stop economic progress of nation—cut off oil resources
2. Plants would close, public utilities be idled, transportation stopped
3. Economy ruined because it is based on energy

These three notes sum up all the significant ideas contained in the paragraph. A single note, such as "Our economy is energy-based," might tempt the writer because it is short and easy; however, although it sums up the ultimate significance of the paragraph, it does *not* contain all the important ideas of the paragraph. Remember that the critical test of a note is whether, after a week has passed, you will still be able to recall all the significant ideas of the passage from which it was taken.

Whether you record your notes on 3 × 5 cards or in a note pad, be sure to include the following with the first note taken from a book: author, title, publisher, place and date of publication, and page number. (On subsequent notes from the same book, you will need to include only the author and page number.) Without this bibliographic information, you cannot give proper credit when you incorporate your notes into your paper or report.

If you are rushed for time in the library, you may want to check out a book or books to review at home. If you need to take more information from periodical articles (which cannot be checked out) than can be conveniently committed to notes, you may want to make a photographic copy at the library to take home for fuller evaluation. (See also **library research**.)

nouns

A *noun* names a person, place, thing, concept, action, or quality. The two basic types of nouns are **proper nouns** and **common nouns**.

PROPER NOUNS

Proper nouns name specific persons, places, things, concepts, actions, or qualities. They are usually capitalized.

Examples: New York, Abraham Lincoln, U.S. Army, Nobel Prize, Montana, Independence Day, Amazon River, Butler County, Magna Carta, June, Colby College

COMMON NOUNS

Common nouns name general classes or categories of persons, places, things, concepts, actions, or qualities. The term "common noun" includes all types of nouns except proper nouns, although some nouns (turkey/Turkey) may be both common and proper.

Examples: human, college, knife, bolt, string, faith, copper

Abstract nouns are common nouns that refer to something which is intangible in that it cannot be discerned by the five senses.

Examples: love, loyalty, pride, valor, peace, devotion, harmony

Collective nouns are common nouns that indicate a group or collection of persons, places, things, concepts, actions, or qualities. They are plural in meaning but singular in form.

Examples: audience, jury, brigade, staff, committee

Concrete nouns are common nouns that are used to identify those things that can be discerned by the five senses.

Examples: house, carrot, ice, tar, straw, grease

A **count noun** is a type of concrete noun that identifies things that can be separated into countable units.

Examples: desks, chisels, envelopes, engines, pencils

A **mass noun** is a type of concrete noun that identifies things that comprise a mass and cannot be separated into countable units.

Examples: electricity, water, sand, wood, air, uranium

FUNCTIONS OF NOUNS

Nouns may function as subjects of **verbs**, as **complements**, as objects of verbs and **prepositions**, or as **appositives**.

> *Examples:* The *metal* bent as *pressure* was applied to it. (subjects of verbs)
> The bricklayer cemented the *blocks* efficiently. (direct object of a verb)
> The company awarded our *department* a plaque for safety. (indirect object of a verb)
> The event occurred within the *year*. (object of a preposition)
> An equestrian is a *horseman*. (subjective complement)
> We elected the sales manager chairman. (objective complement)
> George Thomas, the *treasurer*, gave his report last. (appositive)

Words usually used as nouns may also be used as **adjectives** and **adverbs**.

> *Examples:* It is *company* policy. (adjective)
> He went *home*. (adverb)

USING NOUNS

Forming the Possessive. Nouns form the possessive most often by adding *'s* to the names of living things and by adding an *of* phrase to the names of inanimate objects.

> *Examples:* The *chairman's* statement was forceful.
> The keys *of the typewriter* were sticking.

However, either form may be used.

> *Examples:* The *table's* mahogany finish was scratched.
> Two personal friends *of the chairman* were on the committee.

Plural nouns ending in "s" need only to add an apostrophe to form the possessive case.

> *Example:* The *architects'* design manual contains many illustrations.

Plural nouns that do not end in "s" require both the apostrophe and the "s."

> *Example:* The installation of the plumbing is finished except in the *men's* room.

With group words and compound nouns, add the *'s* to the last noun.

> *Examples:* The *Chairman of the Board's* report was distributed.
> My *son-in-law's* address was on the envelope.

To show individual possession with coordinate nouns, use the possessive with both.

> *Examples:* Both the *Senate's* and *House's* galleries were packed for the hearings.
> *Mary's* and *John's* presentations were the most effective.

To show joint possession with coordinate nouns, use the possessive with only the last.

> *Examples:* The *Senate and House's* joint committee worked out a compromise.
> *Mary* and *John's* presentation was the most effective.

Forming Plurals. Most nouns form the plural by adding "s."

> *Example:* *Dolphins* are capable of communication with man.

Those ending in *s, z, x, ch,* and *sh* form the plural by adding "es."

> *Examples:* How many size *sixes* did we produce last month?
> The letter was sent to all the *churches.*
> Technology should not inhibit our individuality; it should fulfill our *wishes.*

Those ending in a consonant plus *y* form the plural by changing the "y" to "ies."

> *Example:* The store advertises prompt delivery, but places a limit on the number of *deliveries* in one day.

Some nouns ending in *o* add "es" to form the plural, and others add only the "s."

> *Examples:* One tomato plant produced twelve *tomatoes.*
> We installed two *dynamos* in the plant.

Some nouns ending in *f* or *fe* add "s" to form the plural (cliff, cliffs; fife, fifes); others change the *f* or *fe* to "ves" (knife, knives).

Some nouns require an internal change to form the plural.

> *Examples:* woman/women, man/men, mouse/mice, goose/geese.

Some nouns do not change in the plural form.

> *Example:* *Fish* swam lazily in the clear brook while a few wild *deer* mingled with the *sheep* in a nearby meadow.

Most compound nouns joined by **hyphens** form the plural in the first noun (only if the main word is last is this rule reversed).

> *Example:* He provided jobs for all his *sons-in-law.*

Compound nouns written as one word add "s" to the end.

> *Example:* Use seven *spoonfuls* of freshly ground coffee to make seven cups of coffee.

If in doubt about the plural form of a word, look up the word in a good **dictionary**. Most dictionaries give the plural form if it is made in any way other than by adding "s" or "es."

noun clause

A noun clause is a subordinate **clause** that functions as a **noun**.

> *Example:* *Why the report took three months to prepare* is a mystery to me.

Noun clauses are frequently introduced by **interrogative** and **relative pronouns** and **adverbs** *(which, who, what, when, where,* and *why).* The **conjunction** *that* (not the relative pronoun) is also commonly used.

A noun clause can fit any **sentence** position that can be occupied by a noun.

> *Examples:* *That we had succeeded* pleased us. (subject)
> The treasurer admitted *that he had made a mistake.* (direct object of verb)
> Upon retirement, she's going back to *where she came from.* (object of preposition)
> Help out by doing *what you can.* (direct object of gerund)
> Give *whoever comes* a ticket. (indirect object)
> The main thing we should remember, *that we are in business to make a profit,* is the thing we seem to be forgetting. (appositive)
> He made himself *what he wanted to be.* (objective complement)

Noun clauses appear often in definitions and explanations as **subjective complements**.

> *Example:* A common theory is *that competition keeps prices low.*

nowhere near

The **phrase** *nowhere near* is colloquial and should be avoided in writing.

> *Change:* His ability is *nowhere near* Jim's.
> *To:* His ability does *not approach* Jim's.
> *Or:* His ability is *not comparable to* Jim's.
> *Or:* His ability is *far inferior* to Jim's.

number

Number is the grammatical property of **nouns**, **pronouns**, and **verbs** that signifies whether one thing (singular) or more than one (plural) is being referred to. Nouns normally form the plural by simply adding "s" or "es" to their singular forms.

> *Examples:* Many new business *ventures* have failed in the past ten *years*. *Partners* in successful *businesses* are not always personal *friends*.

But some nouns require an internal change to form the plural.

> *Examples:* Woman/women, man/men, goose/geese, mouse/mice

All pronouns except *you* change internally to form the plural.

> *Examples:* I/we, he/she, it/they

Most verbs show the singular of the third **person**, present **tense**, indicative **mood**, by adding an "s" or "es."

> *Examples:* He *stands*, she *works*, it *goes*

The verb *to be* normally changes form to indicate the plural.

> *Examples:* I *am* (He *is*) ready to begin work. (singular)
> We *are* ready to begin work. (plural)

(See also **agreement**.)

numbers

Figures are generally used to express numbers higher than one hundred because a small set of figures can be recognized more quickly than several words. Numbers smaller than one hundred are written as words.

> *Examples:* seven; thirty-nine; 248; 2,456,987

An exception is the page number of a book.

> *Example:* The diagram is on page 9.

Another exception in business and technical writing is that units of measurement are expressed in figures.

> *Examples:* 3 miles, 45 cubic feet, 9 meters, 27 cubic centimeters, 4 picas, 110 volts, 10° F.

Numbers that begin a **sentence** should always be spelled out, even if they would otherwise be written as figures.

Example: One hundred and fifty people attended the stockholders' meeting.

If spelling out such a number seems awkward, rewrite the sentence so that the number does not appear at the beginning.

Change: One hundred and fifty people attended the stockholders' meeting.
To: There were 150 people in attendance at the stockholders' meeting.
Change: Two hundred seventy-three defective products were returned last month.
To: Last month, 273 defective products were returned.

When several numbers appear in the same sentence or **paragraph**, they should be expressed alike regardless of other rules and guidelines.

Example: The company owned 150 trucks, employed 271 people, and rented 7 warehouses.

Approximate numbers are normally spelled out.

Example: More than two hundred people attended the conference.

Percentages are normally given as figures.

Example: Approximately 87 percent of the stockholders approved the merger.

In typed manuscript, page numbers are written as figures, but chapter or volume numbers may appear either way.

Examples: page 37, Chapter 2 or Chapter Two, Volume I or Volume One

The plural of a written number is formed by adding "s" or "es," or by dropping "y" and adding "ies," depending on the last letter, just as the plural of any other noun is formed. (See **nouns**.)

Examples: sixes, elevens, twenties

The plural of a figure is usually written with "s" alone.

Examples: 5s, 12s

The plural of a figure may also be written with "'s."

Examples: 5's, 12's

DATES

The year and day of the month should be written as figures. Dates are usually written in month-day-year sequence, but businesses and industrial corporations are increasingly using the military day-month-year sequence.

Example: August 24, 1975, or 24 August 1975

The **slash** form of expressing dates—8/24/75—is used in informal writing only.

TIME

Hours and minutes are expressed as figures when a.m. and p.m. follow.

Examples: 11:30 a.m., 7:30 p.m.

When not followed by a.m. or p.m., however, time should be spelled out.

Examples: four o'clock, eleven o'clock

FRACTIONS

Fractions are expressed as figures when written with whole numbers.

Examples: 27½ inches, 4¼ miles

Fractions are spelled out when they are expressed independently.

Examples: one-fourth, seven-eighths

Numbers with decimals are always written as figures.

Example: 5.21 meters

ADDRESSES

Numbered streets should be spelled out except where space is at a premium.

Example: East Tenth Street

Building numbers are normally written as figures.

Example: 4862 East Monument Street

Highways are written as figures.

Examples: U.S. 70, Ohio 271, I 94

numeral adjectives

Numeral adjectives identify quantity, degree, or place in a sequence. They always modify **count nouns**. Numeral adjectives are divided into two subclasses: cardinal and ordinal.

A cardinal adjective expresses an exact quantity.

> *Examples:* *one* pencil, *two* typewriters, *three* airplanes

An ordinal adjective expresses degree or sequence.

> *Examples:* *first* quarter, *second* edition, *third* degree, *fourth* year

In most writing, an ordinal adjective should be spelled out if it is a single word *(tenth, 312th)*. Ordinal numbers can also function as **adverbs**.

> *Example:* John arrived *first*.

(See also **first/firstly**.)

O

object

There are three kinds of *objects*: **direct object**, **indirect object**, and object of a **preposition**. All objects are **nouns** or noun equivalents (**pronoun, gerund, infinitive**, noun phrase, **noun clause**) and can be replaced by a pronoun in the objective **case**.

Direct Object. The direct object answers the question "what?" or "whom?" about a **verb** and its subject.

> *Examples:* Sheila designed a new *circuit*. (*Circuit*, the direct object, answers the question, "Sheila designed *what*?")
>
> George telephoned the *Chief Engineer*. (*Chief Engineer*, the direct object, answers the question, "George telephoned *whom*?")

A verb whose meaning is completed by a direct object is called a **transitive verb**.

Indirect Object. An indirect object answers the question "*to* whom? or *to* what?" or "*for* whom? or *for* what?" about a transitive verb, its subject, and its direct object. The indirect object always precedes the direct object.

> *Examples:*   We sent the *General Manager* a full report. ("Report" is the direct object. The indirect object, *General Manager*, answers the question, "We sent a full report *to whom*?")
>
> The General Manager gave the *report* careful consideration. ("Consideration" is the direct object. The indirect object, *report,* answers the question, "The General Manager gave careful consideration *to what*?")
>
> The Purchasing Department bought *Sheila* a new oscilloscope. ("Oscilloscope" is the direct object. The indirect object, *Sheila,* answers the question, "The Purchasing Department bought a new oscilloscope *for whom*?)

Object of a Preposition. For a discussion of objects of prepositions, see **prepositional phrase.**

objective complement

An *objective complement* is a **noun** or **adjective** that completes the meaning of a **sentence** by revealing something about the **direct object** of a **transitive verb**; it may either describe (adjective) or rename (noun) the direct object.

> *Examples:*   We painted the house *white.* (adjective)
> I like my coffee *hot.* (adjective)
> They call her *a genius.* (noun)

The objective complement is one of the four kinds of **complements** that complete the subject-verb relationship; the others are the direct object, the **indirect object**, and the **subjective complement.**

objective (purpose)

What do you want your **readers** to know or be able to do when they have read your finished writing project? When you have answered this question, you have determined the *objective* of your writing project. Too often, however, beginning writers state their objectives in broad terms that are of no practical value to them. Such an objective as "to write about the Model 6000 Accounting Machine" is too general to be of any real help. "To explain how to operate a Model 6000 Accounting Machine" is a specific objective that will help keep the writer on the right track.

The writer's objective is rarely simply "to explain" something, although on occasion it may be. You must ask yourself, "Why do I need to explain it?" In answering this question, you may find, for example, that your objective is also to persuade your reader to change his attitude toward the thing you are explaining.

A writer for a company magazine who has been assigned to write an article on the firm's new computer installation, in answer to the question *what*, could state his objective as "to explain the way the computer will increase efficiency and ultimately benefit employees." In answer to the question *why*, he might state "to ease the fear of automation that has become evident in employees."

If you answer these two questions *exactly*, and put your answers in writing as your stated objective, not only will your job be made easier but you will be considerably more confident of ultimately reaching your goal. As a test of whether you have adequately formulated your objective, try to state it in a single sentence. If you find that you cannot, continue to formulate your objective until you *can* state it in a single sentence.

Even a specific objective is of no value, however, unless you keep it in mind as you work. Guard against losing sight of your objective as you become involved with the other steps of the writing process.

observance/observation

An *observance* is the "following of a duty, custom, or law"; it is some-times confused with *observation*, meaning "the act of noticing or re-cording something."

Examples: The *observance* of Veteran's Day as a paid holiday varies from one organization to another.
The efficiency expert made careful *observations* when she vis-ited our department.

OK/okay

The expression *okay* (also spelled *OK*) is common in **informal writing** but should be avoided in more formal letters and **reports**.

Change: Mr. Sturgess gave his *okay* to the project.
To: Mr. Sturgess *approved* the project.

Change: That is *okay* with me.
To: That is *acceptable* to me.

on account of

The **phrase** *on account of*—as a substitute for *because*—should be avoided in writing.

> *Change:*   He felt that he had lost his job *on account of* the company's switch to automated equipment.
>
> *To:*   He felt that he had lost his job *because* of the company's switch to automated equipment.

on/onto/on to

On is normally a **preposition** meaning "supported by," "attached to," or "located at."

> *Example:*   Install the telephone *on* the wall.

Onto implies "movement to a position on" or "movement up and on."

> *Example:*   The union members surged *onto* the platform after their leader's defiant speech.

On is separated from *to* when *on* is used as an **adverb**.

> *Example:*   Let's go *on to* the next project.

on the grounds that (of)

The **phrase** *on the grounds that* (or *on the grounds of*) is a wordy substitute for *because*.

> *Change:*   *On the grounds of* our friendship, he felt he could ask me to substitute for him at the meeting.
>
> *To:*   *Because of* our friendship, he felt he could ask me to substitute for him at the meeting.

one

When used as an **indefinite pronoun**, *one* may help you avoid repeating a **noun**.

> *Example:*   We need a new plan, not an old *one*.

One is often redundant in **phrases** where it restates the noun, and it may take the proper **emphasis** away from the **adjective**.

> *Change:*   The computer program was not a unique *one*.
> *To:*   The computer program was not unique.

One can also be used in place of a noun or **personal pronoun** in a statement such as the following.

> *Example:* *One* cannot ignore *one's* physical condition.

In statements of this kind, to avoid the tedious repetition of *one* it is permissible to use a third-person singular personal pronoun with *one* as the antecedent.

> *Change:* *One* must do *one's* best to correct the injustices *one* sees.
> *To:* *One* must do *his* best to correct the injustices *he* sees.
> *Or:* *One* must do *her* best to correct the injustices *she* sees.

If you use *one* in this manner, be careful not to shift back and forth between *one* and *you*. However, to use one in this way at all is distinctly formal and impersonal; in any but the most formal writing you are better advised to address your reader directly and personally as *you*.

> *Change:* *One* cannot be too careful about planning for leisure time. The cost of *one's* equipment can, for example, force *one* to work more and therefore reduce *one's* leisure time.
> *To:* *You* cannot be too careful about planning for leisure time. The cost of *your* equipment can, for example, force *you* to work more and thus reduce *your* leisure time.

(See also **point of view**.)

one of those who

A **dependent clause** beginning with *who* or *that*, preceded by *one of those*, takes a plural verb.

> *Examples:* She is *one of those* executives *who are* concerned about their writing. (The subject of the dependent clause, the pronoun *who*, refers to a plural antecedent, *executives*, and is therefore plural; hence the verb, *are*, must also be plural.)
>
> This is *one of those* policies *that make* no sense when you examine them closely. (The pronoun *that*, which is the subject of the clause, refers to *policies* (plural), and so it is plural and requires a plural verb, *make*.)

Especially because people so often use singular verbs in such constructions in everyday speech and very informal writing, this rule confuses many writers. The principle behind the rule becomes clearer if *among* is substituted for *one of*. Compare the following examples with those above.

Examples: She is *among* those executives *who are* concerned about their writing. (You would not be likely to write or say, "She is among those executives who *is* concerned. . . .")

This is *among* those policies *that make* no sense when you examine them closely. (You would not be likely to write or say, "This is among those policies that *makes* no sense. . . .")

Another way to clarify the principle behind the rule is to turn the sentence around. Compare the following examples with first examples given above.

Examples: Of those executives who *are* concerned about their writing, she is one.
Of those policies that *make* no sense when you examine them closely, this is one.

When the sentences are seen turned around in this rather unnatural but perfectly logical way, you would not be likely to use *is* for *are* (in the first sentence) or *makes* for *make* (in the second sentence.) It may also be helpful to contrast these sentences with others in which the singular verb is the correct form.

Examples: She is one executive *who is* concerned about her writing. (Note that in this sentence *who* refers to a singular antecedent, *executive*. *Who* is therefore singular and takes a singular verb, *is*.)

This is one policy *that makes* no sense when it is examined closely. (*That* refers to *policy* [singular] and so requires a singular verb, *makes*.)

There is one exception to the plural-verb rule stated at the very beginning of this entry: If the phrase *one of those* is preceded by *the only* (*the only one* . . .), the verb in the following dependent clause should be singular.

Examples: She is *the only one* of those executives *who is* concerned about her writing. (The verb is singular because its subject, *who*, clearly refers to an emphatically singular antecedent, *one*. If the sentence were turned around, it would read as follows: "Of those executives, she is the only *one who is* concerned about her writing.")

This is *the only one* of those policies *that makes* no sense when you examine it closely. (If the sentence were turned around, it would read: "Of those policies, this is the only *one that makes* no sense when you examine it closely.")

Finally, it should be repeated that the plural-verb rule given at the beginning of this entry is often ignored in everyday speech and very informal writing. Indeed, in spoken English the singular form of the verb, though technically illogical, is probably far more common than the plural. However, in your professional writing, where preciseness is crucial, you are well advised to use a plural verb after *one of those who* or *one of those that.*

only

In writing, the word *only* should be placed immediately before the word or **phrase** it modifies.

> *Change:* We *only* lack financial backing; we have determination.
> *To:* We lack *only* financial backing; we have determination.

A speaker can place *only* before the **verb** and avoid **ambiguity** by stressing the word being modified; in writing, only correct placement of the word can ensure **clarity**. Incorrect placement of *only* can change the meaning of a sentence.

> *Examples:* *Only* he said that he was tired. (meaning he *alone* said)
> He *only* said that he was tired. (meaning he actually was not tired although he said he was)
> He said *only* that he was tired. (meaning he said nothing except that he was tired)
> He said that he was *only* tired. (meaning that he was nothing except tired)

openings

If your **reader** is already familiar with your subject, or if what you are writing is short, you may not need to begin your writing project with a full **introduction**. You may simply want to focus the reader's attention with a brief opening. You may also use an intriguing or interesting opening, either by itself or in conjunction with an introduction, to stimulate your reader's interest. Such types of business and technical writing as **annual reports**, **journal articles**, and **house organ articles** often *require* an interesting opening because you do not have a captive audience for such articles and **reports**.

Openings have two essential purposes: (1) to indicate the subject and (2) to catch the interest of the reader. Several types of openings achieve both purposes. If you decide that you need to use one of the following types of openings, choose one with your reader's interests, background, and education in mind. The opening should be natural, not forced; an obviously "tacked on" opening will only puzzle your reader, who will be unable to establish any meaningful connection between the opening and the body of your article or report.

STATING THE PROBLEM

One way to provide the reader with the perspective of your report is to present a brief account of the problem that led to the study or project being reported.

> *Example:* Several weeks ago a brewmaster noticed a discoloration in the grain supplied by Acme Farms, Inc. He immediately reported his discovery to his supervisor. After an intensive investigation, we found that Acme . . .

However, if the reader is familiar with the problem, or if the particular problem has been solved for a long period, a problem opening is likely to be boring to your reader.

DEFINITION

Although a definition can be useful as an opening, do not define something with which the reader is familiar or provide a definition that is obviously a contrived opening (such as "Webster defines business as . . . "). A definition should be used as an opening only if it provides insight into what follows.

> *Example:* "Conglomerate" comes from the Latin verb *conglomerare,* meaning "to roll or heap together," and it is used to refer to a corporation composed of many different companies. The remarkable growth of conglomerates over the past decade . . .

INTERESTING DETAIL

Often an interesting detail of your subject can be used to gain readers' attention and arouse their interest. This requires, of course, that you be aware of your readers' interests. The following opening, for example, might be especially interesting to members of a personnel department.

> *Example:* The small number of graduates applying for jobs at Acme Corporation is disappointing, particularly after many years of steadily increasing numbers of applicants. There are, I believe, several reasons for this development. . . .

It is often possible to find an interesting statistic to use as an opening.

Example: From asbestos sheeting to zinc castings, from a chemical analysis of the water in Lake Maracaibo (to determine its suitability
for use in steam injection units) to pistol blanks (for use in
testing power charges), the Purchasing Department attends to
the company's material needs. Approximately 15,000 requisi-
tions, each containing from one to fourteen separate items,
are processed each year by this department. Every item or
service that is bought . . .

BACKGROUND

The background or history of a certain subject may be quite interesting and may even put the subject in perspective for your reader.
Consider the following example from a house organ article describing the process of oil drilling.

Example: From the bamboo poles the Chinese used when the pyramids
were young to today's giant rigs drilling in a hundred feet of
water, there has been a lot of progress in the search for oil.
But whether four thousand years ago or today, in ancient
China or a modern city, in twenty fathoms of water or on top
of a mountain, the object of drilling is and has always been the
same—to manufacture a hole in the ground, inch by inch. The
hole may be either for a development well . . .

This type of opening is easily overdone, however; use it only if the
background information is of some value to your reader. Never use
it just as a way to get started.

QUOTATIONS

Occasionally, you can use a **quotation** to stimulate interest in your
subject. To be effective, however, the quotation must be pertinent—
not some loosely related remark selected from a book of quotations
simply because it was listed under the subject heading that fits your
writing project. Often a good quotation to use is one that predicts a
new trend or development.

Example: Richard Smith, president of P. R. Smith Corporation, recently
said, "I believe that the Photon projector will revolutionize our
industry." His statement represents a growing feeling among
corporate . . .

OBJECTIVE

In reporting on a project or activity of some kind, you may wish to
open with a statement of the project or activity's objective. Such an

opening gives the reader a basis for judging the actual results as they are presented.

Example: The primary objective of this project was to measure consumer response to our new advertising campaign. We began by establishing a sampling procedure based upon . . .

SUMMARY

You can provide a summary opening by greatly compressing the results, conclusions, or recommendations of your article or report. Do not start a summary, however, by writing "This report summarizes . . . "

Change: This report summarizes the advantages of having a new product tested by consumers before beginning mass production and distribution of the product. The major advantage is . . .

To: Having each new product consumer tested before beginning mass production and distribution has several advantages. First, it allows us to . . .

FORECAST

Sometimes you can use a forecast of a new development or trend to arouse the reader's interest.

Example: In the very near future, we may be able to call our local library and have a video tape of *Hamlet* replayed on our wall television. This project and others are now being developed at Acme Industries. . . .

SCOPE

At times you may want to present the scope of your article or report in your opening. By providing the parameters of your material—the limitations of the subject or the amount of detail to be presented—you enable your readers to determine whether they want or need to read your article or report. Be on guard against letting this kind of opening become a narrated **table of contents** or an **abstract**; if either of those is appropriate, include it—but not as an artificial opening. The scope type of opening is often useful for small writing projects where an abstract or table of contents would be inappropriate.

Example: This pamphlet provides a review of the requirements for obtaining an FAA pilot's license. It is not designed as a textbook to prepare you to take the examination itself; rather, it gives you an idea of the steps you will need to take and the costs involved.

The first requirement . . .

oral report

Business and technical people are often called upon to deliver oral reports on such things as market studies and laboratory experiments, to chair committees, to lead panel discussions, and so on. Therefore, it is important to know how to plan and deliver an oral presentation. The subject of public speaking is very large, however, and this entry is not intended to provide a comprehensive discussion of audience communication and the vocal factors influencing that communication. It is designed, rather, to provide an overall approach for preparing a presentation to an audience and tips to improve your delivery. This entry also includes specific suggestions for conducting committee meetings and panel discussions; in addition, it provides a bibliography so that you can study this important subject on your own.

TYPES OF SPEECHES

Essentially, there are three types of speeches: the *read* speech, the *impromptu* speech, and the *extemporaneous* speech.

A read (or manuscript) speech is delivered by a speaker reading directly from a carefully prepared manuscript. It is often used because a speaker wishes to be sure of every word he uses. The primary application of the read speech for business and technical people is the reading of a "paper" at a meeting of a professional society. The current trend, however, is for papers to be distributed to the audience beforehand and then summarized by the speaker. The basic weakness of a read speech is that it tends to bore the audience since it does not require the speaker to establish two-way communication with the audience.

An impromptu speech is given without advance preparation by the speaker. The impromptu speech is used primarily during a meeting in which the speaker is asked "to say a few words" about something with which he is familiar (often a project with which he is involved). The speaker must then organize his ideas either while he is speaking or in a very short time before he speaks. The only way to prepare for an impromptu speech is to anticipate that you might be asked to report to a group.

By far the most common method of oral presentation is the extemporaneous speech, which uses outlined notes prepared well ahead of the presentation. The speaker uses his outline only to remind him of what to "discuss" and in what order to present his material; he does not read from the outline. The goal of extemporaneous speech is to sound conversational and spontaneous, yet well organized. Since it is the most common and appropriate method for most of the speaking you will do, the extemporaneous method is the basis for the discussion of oral presentation in this entry. However, many of the suggestions for delivery apply to the read speech and the impromptu speech as well.

PREPARATION

In preparing a speech, you should use a process nearly identical to the **preparation** used in the writing process. Specifically, determine the needs of your audience (rather than a **reader**), determine your **objective**, and thereby establish a **scope** that will determine the amount and depth of your **research**. Then develop an effective and logical **organization** for your material.

Knowing your audience—especially their attitude about your subject—is especially important in an oral presentation. Furthermore, you must have a desire and commitment to *communicate* to your listeners; a speaker always fails when he considers his task as simply to "unload" his ideas on the audience. At times you must present ideas to an audience that is unfamiliar with your subject. Your primary job in that case is to simplify as well as explain, not to impress them with your knowledge. In fact, if you can clarify a difficult subject, that will impress your audience far more than if you smother them with technical details. Even if you are speaking at a professional meeting, aim your message at the average listener rather than at the topmost specialist in the field. In fact, the topmost specialist will be impressed with your acumen if you can bring clarity and fresh insight to your subject. Remember also that there may be visitors in the audience who are unfamiliar with the **jargon** in your field.

In making an oral presentation, you have a special need to gain and hold the attention and interest of your audience. You must not only gain their attention, but you must keep their interest as well. A good subject, a sound technical treatment, an effective organization, and a varied and forceful delivery will accomplish these goals.

Although any of the **methods of development** used for writing can be used to organize your notes into an oral report, speaking requires a slightly different treatment because your listeners remember what you say at the beginning and at the end of your presentation far better than what you say in the middle. They cannot search back to find a detail they missed or one that caught their attention. To focus their attention, therefore, you must work the most significant and most interesting aspects of your subject into your **opening** and **conclusion**.

A number of methods of development are especially useful in meeting this need. **Increasing order of importance**, for example, used with an effective opening, builds your argument so that the audience is left with the most important point as you finish. A method of development that is used primarily in speech is the *problem-solution pattern*, which first describes and analyzes the problem, then presents the criteria for evaluating possible solutions, and finally explains each solution in detail, providing the advantages and disadvantages of each one. The advantage of the problem-solution pattern is that it enables you to build audience anticipation for the possible solutions. The **cause-and-effect** method of development can also be used effectively to trace a troublesome effect (or problem) back to its first cause. Cause-and-effect holds the interest of an audience much like a detective story. The **specific-to-general** method of development can be used to present the specific reasons why a general premise is valid before presenting the premise itself. It can be useful for an audience that is skeptical of the premise and would not be receptive if they knew from the start that you were defending that premise.

CREATING THE OUTLINE

When you have determined the method of development you will use, you must create the outline from which you will deliver your presentation. Although the following example is somewhat shorter than many presentations, it shows the style and arrangement of a typical outline.

Example: Problem-Solution Method of Development

Objective: To present possible solutions to the excess aluminum inventory at the West-dale Division.

INTRODUCTION

I. Background of the Problem
   A. Since Westdale is a manufacturing plant, it uses a large amount of aluminum each year.

B. Westdale has followed a specific buying pattern.
   1. To provide a reserve supply with which to work, an extra 5,700-ton 12-day supply is on hand at all times.
   2. Story of the Allied Construction incident that shows the department's appreciation of this policy.
C. Because of an anticipated aluminum workers strike, aluminum was over-ordered, beginning in March.
D. Since the strike never started, we have a problem: what to do with the excess aluminum that will be arriving.

BODY

I. Magnitude of Oversupply
   A. Since the threatened strike was settled (in early June), we now have serious problems.
   B. Shipments will arrive for the next three months.
      1. We will have an excess of 24,000 tons by the end of September.
      2. Areas are needed to store surplus.
   C. A method of returning to normal must be found.
II. Solution must satisfy Company, Union, and Local Government.
   A. Solution One: stop ordering.
      1. This would not please the aluminum industry or the union.
         a. Aluminum-producing plants would shut down for lack of work.
         b. Workers would be laid off for months.
      2. It would not satisfy the local government.
         a. A layoff would hurt the local economy.
         b. The local government had originally asked us not to stockpile.
   B. Solution Two: cut back on orders.
      1. This solution is acceptable to the union.
         a. No plants would be entirely shut down.
         b. There would be no forced layoffs.
      2. It should suit the local government.
         a. Whole aluminum industry would not be hurt.
         b. The local economy would not be severely injured.

CONCLUSION

I. Recommendations
   A. Although the company could live with either solution, I recommend the second one.
      1. It would help long-term relations with the local government and the union.
      2. We are interested in any other suggestions.
II. Invite Questions

Many speakers find it helpful to type their outlined notes (leaving generous amounts of space between items) and put them in a loose-leaf binder so that they do not get out of order during the presentation.

The best way to rehearse your presentation is simply to "tell" it to a friend (or wife or husband) while referring to your outline notes.

VISUAL AIDS

An important decision you must make as you prepare an oral report is whether to use visual aids and, if so, what kind. Visual aids, used wisely, can help clarify and simplify your message by explaining or reinforcing your key points; however, visual aids should serve a definite purpose—they should not be used for decoration.

Much of the advice provided in the entry **illustrations** is appropriate for creating visual aids for an oral report. The size of the visual aid, however, should be determined by the size of the room in which you are making the presentation. Be sure that you are familiar with the physical arrangement and facilities of the room before you consider visual aids. Does it have a chalkboard? a projection screen? a flip chart? The answers to questions like these are obviously crucial. Once you have decided on the type of visual aid you can use, be careful not to include too much material on each visual. Avoid cluttering the visual aid; use only the most essential information. As you create the visual aid, remember that its appearance should be as professional as possible. If your company or organization has an art department, you may be able to use its facilities; if not, possibly you can enlist the help of a friend or use a professional artist.

As you are using the visual aid during your presentation, make sure to talk to the audience. Do not repeat the visual wording aloud; the wording should be a very brief summary of the ideas, and you should develop the ideas embodied in the wording. As you show the visual aid, slow your rate of speaking. Your audience has two tasks: to look at the visual aid and to listen to you. Finally, be sure to rehearse your handling of the visual aid so that your use of it during the presentation will be smooth and natural.

A device that is often quite helpful, though not strictly a visual aid, is pass-out material. If you have material to pass out, however, do not pass it out until you wish the audience to use it; if you pass it out early, you run the risk of losing the attention of your audience. If you must hand it out at the beginning, use a closed envelope with the instructions that you will tell the audience when to open it.

PRESENTATION AND DELIVERY

Opening the Presentation. Your opening is critical. You can gain the attention and respect of an audience with a good opening and lose both with a poor one.

One of the most effective openings is simply telling your audience exactly why you are making the presentation and why this subject is important to them. You may do this by telling how you became involved in the situation or how the problem or situation developed. Occasionally, you can use a **quotation** from another source that focuses attention on your subject; however, the quotation must be pertinent, not something loosely related and selected from a book of quotations simply because it was listed under a relevant subject heading. It must also be from a source that your audience respects, and you must immediately relate the significance of the quotation to your subject. Often a good quotation is one in which a new trend or development is predicted.

Although many speakers begin by telling a joke, use this technique cautiously because few people are truly funny. If you see something appropriately humorous connected to your subject or the occasion, however, humor can be an effective opening.

You may also adapt many of the methods of beginning in the entry titled **openings**.

Closing the Presentation. The best closing for an oral presentation is simply summarizing the main points or offering recommendations. You may also offer to answer any questions. If there are none, simply say "thank you." Be sure, however, that you have prepared for possible questions; it is even wise to have supplementary material on hand for questions. If you do accept questions, make sure that the rest of the group hears each question (repeat it if necessary) and that you understand the question. Finally, if someone asks a question obviously critical of something you have said, do not be defensive— deal with the question honestly and directly.

Nervousness. The only way to cope with stage fright is to accept the fact that you will be nervous, but understand that your nervousness indicates that you are anxious to please your audience. Nervousness should not, therefore, be thought of as something to be overcome; rather, you should use your nervousness to keep you alert and to provide the energy for enthusiasm. If you are interested in and enthusiastic about your subject, your listeners will respond to your message. If you are concerned about communicating *with* your audience, you will soon forget any nervousness. And if you have prepared well, your nervousness will bother you much less in the beginning. There is no substitute for knowing your subject well to instill confidence in both you and your audience. And if you become absorbed in what you are saying, you will certainly forget your initial nervousness.

Be aware of your listeners' reaction to what you are saying. An alert speaker can learn much from watching his audience. He may recognize, for example, that they are confused, bored, or possibly unable to hear. If you see these reactions, you can respond by elaborating on a confusing point, by omitting some details that are not critical and moving on to a more interesting portion of your presentation, or by increasing your volume so that all of your audience can hear you.

Vocal Factors. Many vocal factors influence voice quality. If you have particular voice problems, the best advice is to obtain professional speech instruction. The next best advice is to read authoritative material on the subject, such as the books listed at the end of this entry. Some general guidelines can be offered, however.

First, and above all else, speak loudly enough to be heard. You must project your voice so that you can give force to your message. This is especially important since natural tension will tighten the throat muscles, thereby reducing volume. Project your voice as though you were talking to the listener farthest from where you are standing. Of course, the distinctness with which you articulate each word will also help you to be heard.

As you speak, breathe as deeply as possible. Deep breathing helps you project your voice, and it relaxes the vocal cords, contributing to a deep resonant voice and eliminating a nervous "breathy" quality.

When you are speaking to an audience, speak at a slower rate than normal. This is wise because nervousness normally causes your rate of speech to speed up artificially and because an audience requires more time to absorb your message than an individual with whom you are face to face.

Finally, try to eliminate as many "vocal pauses" from your speech as possible. Vocal pauses, filler phrases, and such sounds and expressions as *ah,* and *uh,* and *you know* are so common that it may be impossible to eliminate them altogether. By consciously avoiding them in everyday speech, however, you will be able to eliminate many of them during more formal presentations.

Body Movement. Body movement during an oral presentation (contrary to what you might think) is essential. Purposeful body movement relaxes tension and prevents you from looking stiff. Appropriate movement during a presentation (not fidgety, jerky movements or foot shuffling) puts nervous energy to work. In addition, good speakers often stand on the balls of their feet (much like a boxer in a stance) so that they can move easily and maintain good posture.

Gestures should grow out of your natural movement and your own personal use of gestures. Do not try to create them or prevent them. As you gain experience, however, you can cultivate the natural gestures that you use in everyday speech. If you have nervous mannerisms, of course, you should curtail them.

Probably the most critical factor as you face an audience is eye contact. Do not stare at the wall at the back of the room or look at one person throughout your presentation. As you speak, focus on different individuals in the audience. On the other hand, do not be afraid to refer to your notes; your audience expects that you will need to refer to them periodically as you deliver your presentation.

COMMITTEE MEETINGS

One of the most common speaking occasions for business and technical people occurs when they are asked to be the chairman of a committee. If you are asked to chair a committee, there are a number of things you should do before and during the meeting to ensure a smooth discussion.

Before the meeting, learn as much as you can about the topic being discussed. Prepare an agenda well ahead of the meeting. An agenda may be flexible (if, for example, the committee is simply studying possibilities), or it may be inflexible (if the committee is implementing specific plans). Be sure to distribute the agenda well ahead of the meeting, not as the members are entering the meeting room. If the agenda is flexible, you should prepare a few questions to start the discussion and a few comments about the reason for the committee's existence or why the topic needs attention. Finally, make sure the committee is supplied with adequate physical facilities, such as a conference room, chairs, a chalkboard, and so on.

During the meeting, it is the chairman's duty to keep the committee moving in the appropriate direction; if the members insist on getting off the subject, they must be reminded that they are on a new track. If you are a committee chairman, encourage all the members to participate—don't allow a few to dominate the entire discussion. As chairman, you should build on the contributions of others—do not automatically reject someone's idea even though it may seem inappropriate. It may be useful during the meeting to have the secretary (or recorder) summarize the committee's thinking up to a certain point. Finally, remember that the members have other jobs and responsibilities, so start on time and close on time.

If you are a member of a committee, some of this advice is applicable to you. Be ready, for example, to build on the contributions of others. Furthermore, you can often help another committee member by summarizing or paraphrasing what he has said.

PANEL DISCUSSIONS

Often professional societies and organizations use panel discussions, as well as speakers, during meetings and conferences. If you are asked to lead or participate in a panel discussion, the following advice may be useful.

If you are the leader (or moderator) of a panel discussion, decide ahead of time on the format that is best for the circumstances. Will there, for example, be spontaneous questions from the audience (making the discussion a "forum")? One successful format is to have each panelist spend five to ten minutes answering a specific question, then use the rest of the time for interchange among the panelists. Questions are then accepted from the floor for a definite period of time. In any case, make sure that panel members have the questions (or areas of discussion) and the format well in advance of the meeting date so they can be fully prepared. Finally, check the physical arrangements for the discussion well in advance. (Is there, for example, adequate amplification if needed?)

During the discussion, it is the leader's duty to inform the audience of the ground rules, introduce the participants, accept and direct questions from the floor, and sum up the presentation when it is completed if that is appropriate. Obviously, the leader must be as well prepared as the panelists.

BIBLIOGRAPHY

Anderson, Virgil A. *Training the Speaking Voice.* New York: Oxford University Press, 1961.

Mambert, W. A. *Presenting Technical Ideas.* New York: John Wiley and Sons, Inc., 1968.

Micken, Ralph A. *Speaking for Results: A Guide for Business and Professional Speakers.* Boston: Houghton Mifflin Co., 1958.

Minnick, Wayne C. *The Art of Persuasion.* Boston: Houghton Mifflin Co., 1957.

Robert, Henry M. *Robert's Rules of Order.* Newly rev. ed. by Sarah Corbin Robert *et al.* Glenview, Ill.: Scott, Foresman and Co., 1970.

Wilcox, Roger P. *Oral Reporting in Business and Industry.* Englewood Cliffs, N.J.: Prentice-Hall, Inc., 1967.

organization

The purpose of organization is to shape your material into a coherent presentation of your **topic**. Without disciplined organization, the material you have gathered during your **research** would be incomprehensible to your **reader**. To provide effective organization, you must determine (1) the most effective way to develop your subject and (2) the sequence in which to present your ideas.

Direction, or **method of development**, satisfies the reader's need for a controlling shape to the development of your subject. An appropriate method of development is the writer's tool for keeping things under control and the reader's means of following the writer's development of a theme. Many different methods of development are available to the writer; this book includes those that are likely to be used by business and technical people: **sequential**, **chronological**, **increasing order of importance**, **decreasing order of importance**, **comparison**, **analysis**, **spatial**, **specific-to-general**, **general-to-specific**, and **cause-and-effect**. As the writer, you must choose the method of development that best suits your subject, your reader, and your **objective**.

Outlining provides structure to your writing by assuring that it has a beginning, a middle, and an end. It provides proportion to your writing by assuring that one step flows smoothly to the next without omitting anything important, and it enables you to emphasize your key points by placing them in the positions of greatest importance. The use of an outline makes larger and more difficult subjects easier to handle by breaking them into manageable parts. Finally, by forcing you to organize your subject and structure your thinking in the outline stage, creating a good outline releases you to concentrate exclusively on writing when you begin the rough draft.

organizational chart

An organizational chart shows how the various components of an organization are related to one another. It is useful where you want to give your **readers** an overview of an organization or where you want to show them the lines of authority within it.

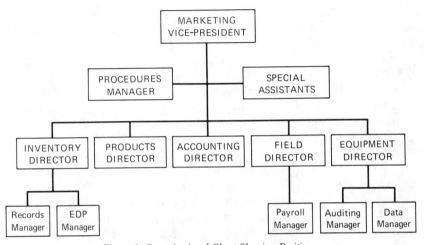

Figure 1. Organizational Chart Showing Positions

The title of each organizational component (office, section, division) is placed in a separate box. These boxes are then linked to a central authority. If your readers need the information, include the name of the person occupying the position identified in each box.

Figure 2. Organizational Box with Name of Person and Position

As with all **illustrations**, place the organizational chart as close as possible to the text that refers to it.

orient/orientate

Orientate is merely a **long variant** of *orient,* meaning "to locate in relation to something else." The shorter form should be used because it is simpler.

> *Change:* Let me *orientate* your group on our operation.
> *To:* Let me *orient* your group on our operation.

outlining

Outlining provides structure to your writing by assuring that it has a beginning (**introduction**), a middle (main body), and an end (**conclusion**). An outline gives your writing proportion so that one part flows smoothly to the next without omission of anything important. Outlining also enables you to emphasize your key points by placing them in the positions of greatest importance.

Like a road map, an outline indicates a starting point and keeps you moving logically so that you don't get lost before arriving at your conclusion. (Errors in logic are much easier to detect in an outline than in a draft.) The use of an outline makes larger and more difficult subjects easier to handle by breaking them into manageable parts; therefore, the less certain you are about your writing ability or about your subject, the fuller your outline should be. The parts of an outline are easily moved about, so you can experiment to see what arrangement of your ideas is most effective. Perhaps most important, creating a good outline frees you to concentrate on writing when you begin the rough draft (by forcing you to organize your subject and structure your thinking beforehand). Two types of outlines are generally used: (1) the topic outline and (2) the sentence outline.

The topic outline consists of short **phrases** that are listed to show the sequential order and relative importance of ideas; in this manner, a topic outline provides order and establishes the relationships of topics to one another. The topic outline alone is generally not sufficient for a large or complex writing job; however, it may be used to good advantage for structuring your main topics and subtopics in preparation for creating a sentence outline. (An outline for a small job is not as detailed as one for a larger job, but it is just as important; for example, a topic outline that lists your major and minor points can help greatly even in writing important letters.)

On a large writing project, it is wise to create a topic outline first and then use it as a basis for creating a sentence outline. In a sentence outline, the writer summarizes each idea in a single complete **sentence** that will become the **topic sentence** for a **paragraph** in the rough draft. The sentence outline begins with a main idea statement that establishes the subject, then follows with a complete sentence for each idea in the major and minor divisions of the outline. A sentence outline provides order and establishes the relationship of topics to one another to a considerably greater degree than a topic outline. A well-developed sentence outline offers a sure test of the validity of your arrangement of your material. If most of your notes can be shaped into controlling topic sentences for paragraphs in your rough draft, you can be relatively sure that your paper will be well organized before you begin its final composition. A good sentence outline, when stripped of its numbering symbols, needs only to be expanded with full details to become a rough draft.

Your outline should begin with a thesis statement, which is a statement of the main idea that you intend to develop in your report. This statement provides you with a goal that you can work toward as you create your outline. (Carried through to the final draft, the thesis statement summarizes your subject for your readers and lets them know what to expect.) A thesis statement often suggests a **method of development**.

Examples: The mission director must oversee a rigid chain of events that must occur prior to blast-off. (This thesis statement suggests a **sequential method of development**.)

Increased sales in the Chicago area appear to be a direct result of the new marketing techniques introduced there last year. (This thesis statement suggests a **cause-and-effect method of development**.)

The growth of the computer industry has closely paralleled the growth of conglomerates. (This thesis statement suggests a combination of the **chronological method of development** and **comparison as a method of development**.)

Although the following outlining technique is mechanical, it is easy to master and well suited to unraveling the complexities of large and difficult subjects.

The first step is to find the natural major divisions of your subject and write them down, then determine whether they are exactly what you need to meet the demands of your **objective**, your **reader**, and your **scope** of coverage. If they are—or when they are—arrange them in the proper order and label them with Roman numerals. For example, the major divisions for this discussion of outlining could be as follows.

Example: I. Advantages of Outlining
              II. Types of Outlining
              III. How to Outline Effectively
              IV. The Final Outline as a Basis for the Rough Draft

The second step is to establish your minor points by searching out the minor divisions within each major head. Arrange them in the proper sequence under their major heads and label them with capital letters. Keep major heads equal in importance and minor heads equal in importance; the purpose of this **parallel structure** is to keep your thinking in order. The major and minor heads for this discussion of outlining could be as follows.

Example: I. Advantages of Outlining
              II. Types of Outlining
                 A. The Topic Outline
                 B. The Sentence Outline
              III. How to Outline Effectively
                 A. Establish Major and Minor Heads
                 B. Sort Note Cards by Major and Minor Heads
                 C. Complete the Sentence Outline
              IV. The Final Outline as a Basis for the Rough Draft

Of course, you will often need more than the two levels of heads illustrated here. If your subject is complicated, you may need four or five levels to keep all of your ideas straight and in proper relationships to one another. In that event, the following numbering scheme is recommended.

Example: I. First-level head
                 A. Second-level head
                    1. Third-level head
                       a. Fourth-level head
                          (i) Fifth-level head

The third step is to mark each of your note cards with the appropriate Roman numeral and capital letter. Sort the note cards by major and minor heads (Roman numerals and capital letters). Then arrange the cards within each minor head and mark each with the appropriate sequential Arabic number. Transfer your notes to paper, converting them to complete sentences. You now have a complete rough sentence outline, and the most difficult part of the writing job is over.

The final step is to polish your rough outline. Check to ensure that the **subordination** of minor heads to major heads is logical. Remember that all major heads should be parallel and all minor heads should be parallel. Make certain that your outline follows your method of development. Check for **unity**. Does your outline stick to the subject, or does it stray into unrelated or only loosely related topics? Stay within your established scope of coverage. Resist the temptation to tell all you know unless it is all pertinent to your objective. It is much easier to correct this problem in the outline stage than in the rough draft. If some information would be of importance to only a minority of your readers, consider including that information in an **appendix**; those few readers could then pursue the subject further and the others would not be interrupted. Check your outline for completeness; scan it to see whether you need more information in any of your divisions, and plug in any information that is needed.

You now have a final, polished sentence outline. It isn't sacred, however; change it if you need to as you write the draft; the outline should be your point of departure and return. Return to it to find your place and your direction as you work.

outside of

In the **phrase** *outside of*, the word *of* is redundant.

> *Change:* Place the rack *outside of* the incubator.
> *To:* Place the rack *outside* the incubator.

In addition, do not use *outside of* to mean "aside from" or "except for."

> *Change:* *Outside of* his frequent absences, Jim has a good work record.
> *To:* *Except for* his frequent absences, Jim has a good work record.

over with

In the expression *over with,* the word *with* is redundant; moreover, the word *completed* often expresses the thought better.

> *Change:* You may use the conference room when the managers' meeting is *over with*.
> *To:* You may use the conference room when the managers' meeting is *over*.

P

pace

Pace is the speed at which the writer presents ideas to the **reader**. Your goal should be to achieve a pace that fits both your reader and your subject; at times you may need a fast pace, at other times a slow pace. The more knowledgeable the reader, the faster your pace can be—but be careful not to lose control of the pace. In the first passage of the following example, facts are piled on top of each other at a rapid pace. In the second passage, the same facts are spread out and presented in a more easily assimilated manner; in addition, a different and more desirable **emphasis** is achieved.

> *Change:* The generator is powered by a 90-horsepower engine, is designed to operate under normal conditions of temperature and humidity, produces 110 volts at 60 Hertz, is designed for use under emergency conditions, and may be phased with other units of the same type to produce additional power when needed.
>
> *To:* The generator, which is powered by a 90-horsepower engine, produces 110 volts at 60 Hertz under normal conditions of temperature and humidity. Designed especially for use under emergency conditions, this generator may be phased with other units of the same type to produce additional power when needed.

Check your draft to determine the pace at which you are presenting your facts and ideas to the reader. If you find that you are jamming your ideas too closely together, you have a problem with pacing. There are at least three solutions to such problems.

The best way to solve a pacing problem is to search out minor thoughts and subordinate them to the major points, just as, in the example, ". . . is designed for use under emergency conditions . . ." was subordinated to ". . . this generator may be phased with other units of the same type. . ."

Another solution is to consider a different type of **sentence** structure. A complex idea is normally better stated in a simple sentence structure; a series of simple thoughts is better stated in a more complex sentence structure. Notice in the example above that the first passage is one long, complicated sentence and that the same ideas are expressed in shorter sentences in the revision.

A final possible solution is to provide words and **phrases** of **transition** to alter the pace.

> *Change:* Negotiations had gone on for two days. Neither side wanted a walkout. They agreed to abide by the previous contract.
>
> *To:* *Although* negotiations had gone on for only two days, neither side wanted a walkout. *Consequently,* they decided to abide by the previous contract.

(See also **subordination**.)

paragraph

A paragraph is a group of **sentences** that support and develop a single idea; it may be thought of as an essay in miniature, for its function is to expand upon the core idea stated in its **topic sentence**. A paragraph may use a particular **method of development** to expand upon the idea stated in the topic sentence. The following paragraph uses the **general-to-specific method of development**.

> *Example:* *The arithmetic of searching for oil is stark.* For all his scientific methods of detection, the only way the oilman can actually
>
> Topic sentence ↗ know for sure that there is oil in the ground is to drill a well. The average cost of drilling an oil well is over $100,000, and drilling a single well may cost over $1,000,000! And once the well is drilled, the odds against its containing any oil at all are 8 to 1!
>
> —*The Baker World,* Baker Oil Tools, Inc.

The paragraph performs three essential functions: (1) it develops the unit of thought stated in the topic sentence; (2) it provides a logical break in the material; and (3) it creates a physical break on the page, which in turn provides visual assistance to the **reader**.

TOPIC SENTENCE

A topic sentence states the subject of a paragraph; the rest of the paragraph then supports and develops that statement with carefully related details. The topic sentence may appear anywhere in the paragraph—a fact that permits the writer to achieve **emphasis** and variety—and a topic statement may be more than one sentence if necessary.

The topic sentence is most often the first sentence of the paragraph because it states the subject that the paragraph is to develop. The topic sentence is effective in this position because the reader knows immediately what the paragraph is about.

Example: *The fundamental conception of statistics is that of an infinitely large series of measurements, or population.* Since all observable data is

Topic sentence ↗   subject to influence by uncontrollable and variable chance factors, the values recorded in a series of measurements exhibit corresponding variations. If the mean value is calculated the individual values will be seen to be more or less closely distributed around it. Since the chance factors operate equally in a positive or negative fashion, the distribution is symmetrical. The larger the number of measurements the closer will mean value approach the "true" value of the measured object. Only with an infinite number of measurements, however, will it be identical with the "true" value.

—*Documenta Geigy*, 5th ed. (Ardsley, N.Y.: Geigy Pharmaceuticals, 1956), p. 31.

On rare occasions, the topic sentence logically falls in the middle of a paragraph.

Example: It is perhaps natural that psychologists should awaken only slowly to the possibility that behavioral processes may be directly observed, or that they should only gradually put the older statistical and theoretical techniques in their proper perspective. But it is time to insist that science does not progress by carefully designed steps called "experiments," each of

Topic sentence →   which has a well-defined beginning and end. *Science is a continuous and often a disorderly and accidental process.* We shall not do the young psychologist any favor if we agree to reconstruct our practices to fit the pattern demanded by current scientific methodology. What the statistician means by the design of experiments is design which yields the kind of data to which *his* techniques are applicable. He does not mean the behavior of the scientist in his laboratory devising research for his own immediate and possibly inscrutable purposes.

—B. F. Skinner, "A Case History in Scientific Method," *The American Psychologist*, 2 (May 1956), 232.

Although the topic sentence is usually most effective early in the paragraph, a paragraph can effectively be made to lead up to the topic sentence; this is sometimes done to achieve emphasis. When a topic sentence concludes a paragraph, it can also serve as a summary or **conclusion**, based on the details that were designed to lead up to it.

Example: Energy does far more than simply make our daily lives more comfortable and convenient. Suppose you wanted to stop— and reverse—the economic progress of this nation. What would be the surest and quickest way to do it? Find a way to cut off the nation's oil resources! Industrial plants would shut down; public utilities would stand idle; all forms of transportation would halt. The country would be paralyzed, and our economy would plummet into the abyss of national economic

Topic
sentence → ruin. *Our economy, in short, is energy-based.*

—*The Baker World,* Baker Oil Tools, Inc.

Because multiple paragraphs are sometimes used to develop different aspects of an idea, not all paragraphs have topic sentences. In this situation, **transition** between paragraphs is especially important so the reader knows that the same idea is being developed through several paragraphs.

Example: *To conserve valuable memory space, a large portion of the software*

Topic Sen-
tence for all *package remains on disc; only the most frequently used portion resides*
three para- *in internal memory all of the time.* The disc-resident software is
graphs ↗ organized into small modules that are called into memory as needed to perform specific functions.

Transition → *The memory-resident portion* of the operating system maintains strict control of processing. It consists of routines, subroutines, lists, and tables that are used to perform common program functions, such as processing input/output operations, calling other software routines from disc as needed, and processing errors.

Transition → *The disc-resident portion* of the operating system contains routines that are used less frequently in system operation, such as the peripheral-related software routines that are used for correcting errors encountered on the various units, and the log and display routines that record unusual operating conditions in the system log. The disc-resident portion of the operating system also contains Monitor, the software program that supervises the loading of utility routines and the user's programs.

—*NCR Century Operating Systems Manual,* NCR Corporation

In this example, the reason for breaking the development of the idea expressed in the topic sentence into three paragraphs is to help the reader assimilate the fact that the main idea has two separate parts.

PARAGRAPH LENGTH

Paragraph length should be tailored to the reader's convenience. A series of short, undeveloped paragraphs can indicate poor **organiza-**

tion of material, in which case you should look for a larger idea to which the ideas in the short paragraphs relate and then make the larger idea the topic sentence for a single paragraph. A series of short paragraphs can also sacrifice **unity** by breaking a single idea into several pieces. A series of long paragraphs, on the other hand, can fail to provide the reader with manageable subdivisions of thought. A good rule of thumb is that a paragraph should be just long enough to deal adequately with the subject raised by its topic sentence. A new paragraph should begin whenever the subject changes significantly.

A short paragraph sometimes immediately follows a long paragraph to give emphasis to the thought contained in the short paragraph.

Example: Because it has at times displaced some jobs, automation has become an ugly word in the American vocabulary. But the all-important fact that is so often overlooked is that it invariably creates many more jobs than it eliminates. (The vast number of people employed in the great American automobile industry as compared with the number of people that had been employed in the harness- and carriage-making business is a classic example.) Almost always, the jobs that have been eliminated by automation have been menial, unskilled jobs, and those who have been displaced have been forced to increase their skills, which resulted in better and higher paying jobs for them.

In view of these facts, is automation really bad? It has made our country the most wealthy and technologically advanced nation the world has ever known!

WRITING PARAGRAPHS

The paragraph is the basic building block of any writing effort. Careful paragraphing reflects the writer's accurate thinking and logical organization. Clear and orderly paragraphs help the reader follow the writer's thoughts more easily.

Use your **outline** as a guide to paragraphing. It is easy to group ideas into appropriate paragraphs when you follow a good working outline.

Example: OUTLINE

  III. Advantages of Chicago as location for new plant
    A. Transport facilities
      1. Rail
      2. Air
      3. Truck
      4. Sea (except in winter)

B. Labor supply
   1. Engineering and scientific personnel
      a. Many similar companies in the area
      b. Several major universities
   2. Technical and manufacturing personnel
      a. Existing programs in community colleges
      b. Possible special programs designed for us

RESULTING PARAGRAPHS

Probably the greatest advantage of Chicago as a location for our new plant is its excellent transport facilities. The city is served by three major railroads. Both domestic and international air cargo service is available at O'Hare International Airport. Chicago is a major hub of the trucking industry, and most of the nation's large freight carriers have terminals there. Finally, except in the winter months when the Great Lakes are frozen, Chicago is a seaport, accessible through the St. Lawrence Seaway.

A second advantage of Chicago is that it offers an abundant labor force. An ample supply of engineering and scientific personnel is assured not only by the presence of many companies engaged in activities similar to ours but also by the presence of several major universities in the metropolitan area. Similarly, technicians and manufacturing personnel are in abundant supply. The seven colleges in the Chicago City College system, as well as half a dozen other two-year colleges in the outlying areas, produce graduates with Associate Degrees in a wide variety of technical specialties appropriate to our needs. Moreover, three of the outlying colleges have expressed an interest in establishing special courses attuned specifically to our requirements.

Consider not only the nature of the material you are developing but also the appearance of your page. An unbroken page looks forbidding.

PARAGRAPH COHERENCE AND UNITY

A good paragraph has **unity, coherence**, and adequate development. Unity is singleness of purpose, based on a topic sentence that states the core idea of the paragraph. When every sentence in the paragraph contributes to developing the core idea, the paragraph has unity. Coherence is holding to one **point of view**, one attitude, one **tense**; it is the joining of sentences into a logical pattern. Coherence is advanced by the careful choice of transitional words so that ideas are tied together as they are developed.

Example: *Any company which operates internationally today faces a host of*
Topic
sentence → *difficulties.* Inflation is worldwide. Most countries are strug-

Transition → gling with other economic problems *as well. In addition,* there
are many monetary uncertainties and growing economic na-
Transition → tionalism directed against multinational companies. *Yet* there
is ample business available in most developed countries if you
have the right products, services, and marketing organization.
To maintain the growth NCR has achieved overseas, we recently restructured our International operations into four ma-
Transition → jor trading areas. *This* will improve the services and support
which the Corporation can provide to its subsidiaries around
Transition → the world. *At the same time* it established firm management
Transition → control, insuring consistent policies around the world. *So* you
might say the problems of doing business abroad will be more
difficult this year but we are better organized to meet those
problems.

—*1974 Annual Report,* NCR Corporation

Good paragraphs often use details from the preceding paragraph,
thereby preserving and advancing the thought being developed. Appropriate **conjunctions** and the **repetition** of key words and **phrases**
can help to provide unity and coherence among, as well as within,
paragraphs.

Example: The programming language, which treats all peripheral devices as file storage units, allows your program to perform
data input or output operations depending on the specific
unit. Peripheral units from which your program can only input data are referred to as *source units;* those to which your
program can only output data are referred to as *destination
units.* Units that permit both input and output may be used as
source units, destination units, or combination *source-destination units.*

Often the nature of a peripheral device determines whether
it is a source or destination unit; at other times, however, the
use made of the unit by the program is the determining factor. By nature, a printer can only be used as a *destination unit,*
for example, and a card reader can only be used as a *source
unit.* A magnetic tape handler can be a source unit if your
program inputs data from it, or it can be a destination unit if
your program outputs data to it.

A disc unit is a good example of a *source-destination unit*
because it can furnish input data and accept output data during a single program run. However, not all programs treat
disc units as source-destination units. Many programs use one
disc unit as a *source unit* and another as a *destination unit.*

—*NEAT/3 Programming Manual,* NCR Corporation

Sometimes a paragraph is used solely for transition.

Example: . . . that marred the progress of the company.

There were two other setbacks to the company's fortunes that year which contributed to its present shaky condition: the loss of many skilled workers through the early retirement program and the intensification of the devastating rate of inflation.

The early retirement program. . .

parallel structure

Parallel sentence structure requires that **sentence** elements that are alike in function be alike in construction as well, as in the following example (in which three similar actions are stated in similar **prepositional phrases**).

Example: The stream runs *under the culvert, behind the embankment,* and *into the pond.*

Parallel structure achieves an economy of words, clarifies meaning, and pleases the **reader** aesthetically. In addition to adding a pleasing symmetry to a sentence, parallel structure expresses the equality of its ideas. This technique assists readers because they are able to anticipate the meaning of a sentence element on the basis of its parallel construction. When they recognize the similarity of word order or construction, readers know that the relationship between the new sentence element and the **subject** is the same as the relationship between the last sentence element and the subject. Because of this they can go from one idea to another more quickly and confidently.

Examples: The computer instruction contains *fetch, initiate,* and *execute* stages. (parallel words)
The computer instruction contains a *fetch stage, an initiate stage,* and *an execute stage.* (parallel phrases)
The computer instruction contains a fetch stage, it contains an initiate stage, and *it contains an execute stage.* (parallel clauses)

Parallel structure is especially important in creating your **outline**, your **table of contents**, and your **heads** because it is important for your reader to know the relative value of each item in your table of contents and each head in the body of your **report** (or other writing project).

In any type of writing, the effective use of parallel structure channels the reader's attention and helps to draw together related ideas or to line up dissimilar ideas for comparison and contrast.

> *Example:*   Her book provoked much comment: *negative from her enemies, positive from her friends.*

The power of many of Lincoln's speeches is dependent upon his use of parallel structure; in them, parallel structure harmonizes the elements within sentences and the relationships among sentences.

> *Example:*   But in a larger sense, *we cannot dedicate—we cannot consecrate—we cannot hallow*—this ground. The brave men, *living* and *dead,* who struggled here, have consecrated it far above our poor power to *add* or *detract. The world will little note nor long remember what we say here,* but *it can never forget what they did here.*
>
> —Abraham Lincoln, Address at the Dedication of the Gettysburg National Cemetery

A century later, John F. Kennedy used the same technique with striking effect.

> *Example:*   We shall *pay any price, bear any burden, meet any hardship, support any friend, oppose any foe* to assure the survival and the success of liberty.
>
> —John F. Kennedy, Inaugural Address

Although parallelism can be accomplished by the use of words, **phrases**, or **clauses**, it is most frequently accomplished by the use of **phrases**.

> *Examples:*   I was convinced of their competence *by their conduct, by their reputation,* and *by their survival in a competitive business.* (prepositional phrases)
> *Checking the engine, testing the windshield wipers,* and *gauging the tire pressure* are essential to preparing for a long trip. (gerund phrases)
> From childhood the artist had made it a habit *to observe people, to store up the impressions they made upon him,* and *to draw conclusions about mankind from them.* (infinitive phrases)

Correlative conjunctions (*either. . . or, neither. . . nor, not only. . . but also*) should always be followed by parallel structure. Both members of these pairs should be followed immediately by the same grammatical form: two words, two similar phrases, or two similar **clauses**.

Examples: Viruses carry either *DNA* or *RNA,* never both. (words)
Clearly, neither *serologic tests* nor *virus isolation studies* alone would have been adequate. (phrases)
Either *we must increase our operational efficiency* or *we must decrease our production goals.* (clauses)

To make a parallel construction clear and effective, it is often best to repeat a **preposition**, an **article**, a **pronoun**, a **subordinating conjunction**, a **helping verb**, or the mark of an **infinitive**.

Examples: The Babylonians had *a* rudimentary geometry and *a* rudimentary astronomy. (repeated article)
My father and *my* teacher agreed that I was not really trying. (repeated pronoun)
To run and be elected is better than *to* run and be defeated. (repeated mark of the infinitive)
The driver *must* be careful to check the gauge and *must* move quickly when the light comes on. (repeated helping verb)
New teams were being established *in* New York and *in* Hawaii. (repeated preposition)
The history of factories shows both *the* benefits and *the* limits of standardization. (repeated article)

FAULTY PARALLELISM

Faulty parallelism results when joined elements are intended to serve equal grammatical functions but do not have equal grammatical form. Avoid this kind of partial parallelism. Make certain that each element in a series is similar in form and structure to all others in the same series.

Change: Wilson was happy about his new assignment and getting a raise.
To: Wilson was happy about his new assignment and his pay raise.

Because faulty parallelism with correlative conjunctions (*either . . . or, neither . . . nor, not only . . . but also*) is one of the most common writing errors, the following examples are worth careful study:

Change: You may travel to the new plant either *by train* or *there is a plane.* (different grammatical forms: a prepositional phrase, *by train;* and a clause, *there is a plane*)
To: You may travel to the new plant either *by train* or *by plane.* (parallel grammatical forms: prepositional phrases)
Or: You may travel to the new plant by either *train* or *plane.* (parallel grammatical forms: nouns)
Change: We are not only *responsible to our stockholders* but also *to our customers.* (different grammatical forms: an adjective with a

modifying prepositional phrase, *responsible to our stockholders;* and a prepositional phrase, *to our customers*)

To: We are responsible not only *to our stockholders* but also *to our customers.* (parallel grammatical forms: prepositional phrases)

Or: We are not only *responsible to our stockholders* but also *responsible to our customers.* (parallel grammatical forms: adjectives with modifying prepositional phrases)

Change: We either *will pay the bill* or *we will return the shipment.* (different grammatical forms: a verb with its object, *will pay the bill,* and a clause, *we will return the shipment*)

To: Either *we will pay the bill* or *we will return the shipment.* (parallel grammatical forms: clauses)

Or: We will either *pay the bill* or *return the shipment.* (parallel grammatical forms: verbs with their objects)

Be careful not to throw your reader off balance. If you make a statement about two subjects and then follow with a further statement about one of them, complete the thought and make a balancing statement about the other subject.

Change: The Commanche Commander and the Cessna Hawk are both small aircraft; *the Commander seats four.*

To: The Commanche Commander and the Cessna Hawk are both small aircraft; *the Commander seats four* and *the Hawk seats six.*

paraphrase

When you paraphrase a written passage, you rewrite it to state the essential ideas in your own words. Because you do not quote your source word-for-word when paraphrasing, it is unnecessary to enclose the paraphrased material in **quotation marks**. However, paraphrased material should be footnoted because the ideas are taken from someone else whether the words are identical or not. Otherwise, you are guilty of **plagiarism**.

Ordinarily, the majority of the notes you take during the **research** phase of writing your **report** will paraphrase the original material (see **note-taking**).

Example: Original

By definition, the leader is a person who has followers. Thus the quality of a manager is directly related to the quality of the men who work for him, and his own results are essentially those of his workers. Tomorrow's manager will be confronted with more complex technical and commercial problems than ever before. He won't be able to do all the work himself even if he should want to; he will thereby become more dependent upon good men working for him. If he has built an organization of pipsqueaks, as management development expert Jim Hayes of Duquesne University put it, "he's nothing more than chief pipsqueak." On the other hand, if he has pulled together a team of tigers, he is the head tiger.

—George S. Odiorne, *Management by Objectives—A System of Managerial Leadership* (New York: Pitman Publishing, 1965), p. 11.

Paraphrased

In the future, managers will be confronted with more complex technical and commercial tasks than they have been in the past. Increasingly, those who manage will be dependent on those who perform these tasks. Since those performing the work will attain the results, the quality of a manager's leadership will be known by the quality of the people who work for him.

Note that the paraphrased version includes only the essential information from the original passage. Paraphrased material, consequently, will almost always be shorter than the original material. As with all summarized material, strive to put the original ideas into your words without distorting them.

parentheses

Parentheses ( ) are used to enclose words, **phrases**, or **sentences**. Parentheses can suggest intimacy, implying something that is only between the writer and the **reader**. The material within parentheses can add clarity to a statement without altering its meaning. Parentheses de-emphasize (or play down) an inserted element. Parenthetical information may not be essential to a sentence, but it may be interesting or helpful to some readers.

Example: Many American business and industrial leaders (for example, Andrew Carnegie) have risen from humble origins.

Parenthetical material applies to the word or phrase immediately preceding it.

Example: The development of IBM (International Business Machines) is a uniquely American success story.

Parentheses may be used to enclose figures or letters that indicate sequence. Enclose the figure or letter with two parentheses when it appears within a sentence, rather than using only one parenthesis.

Example: The following sections deal with (1) preparation, (2) research, (3) organization, (4) writing, and (5) revision.

Parenthetical material does not affect the **punctuation** of a sentence. If a parenthesis closes a sentence, the ending punctuation appears after the parenthesis. Also, a comma following a parenthetical word, phrase, or **clause** appears outside the closing parenthesis.

Example: Two of our regional managers, Bob Evans (Houston) and Jane Wright (Denver), do not believe the new marketing approach has had a significant impact on sales.

However, when a complete sentence within parentheses stands independently, the ending punctuation goes inside the final parenthesis.

Example: The new marketing approach appears to be a success; most of our regional managers report sales increases of 15 percent to 30 percent. (The only important exceptions are the Denver and Houston offices.) Therefore, we plan to continue . . .

In some **footnote** forms, parentheses enclose the publisher, place of publication, and date of publication.

Example: [1]Michael E. Adelstein, *Contemporary Business Writing* (New York: Random House, 1971), p. 51.

Use **brackets** to set off a parenthetical item that is already within parentheses.

Example: We should be sure to give Emanuel Foose (and his brother Emilio [1812–1882] as well) credit for his part in founding the institute.

Use parentheses with care because they are easily overused. Also be on guard against using parentheses where other marks of punctuation are more appropriate.

participial phrase

A participial phrase consists of a **participle** plus its **object** or **complement**, if any, and **modifiers**. Like the participle, a participial phrase functions as an **adjective** modifying a **noun** or **pronoun**.

Examples: The division *having the largest sales increase* wins the trophy.
Finding the problem resolved, he went to the next item on the agenda.
Having begun, we felt that we had to see the project through.

The relationship between a participial phrase and the rest of the **sentence** must be clear to the **reader**. For this reason, every sentence containing a participial phrase must have a noun or pronoun that the participial phrase modifies; if it does not, the result is a dangling participial phrase. An equally serious problem is the participial phrase that is misplaced in the sentence and so appears to modify the wrong noun or pronoun. Both of these problems are discussed below.

DANGLING PARTICIPIAL PHRASES

A dangling participial phrase occurs when the noun or pronoun the participial phrase is meant to modify is not stated but only implied in the sentence.

> *Change:*   *Being unhappy with the job,* his efficiency suffered. (His *efficiency* was not unhappy with the job; what the participial phrase really modifies—*he*—is not stated but merely implied.)
>
> *To:*   *Being unhappy with the job,* he grew less efficient. (Now what the participial phrase modifies—*he*—is explicitly stated.)

(See also **dangling modifiers** and **absolute phrase**.)

MISPLACED PARTICIPIAL PHRASES

A participial phrase is misplaced when it is too far from the noun or pronoun it is meant to modify and so appears to modify something else. This is an error that can sometimes make the writer look ridiculous indeed.

> *Change:*   *Rolling around in the bottom of the vibration test chamber,* I found the missing bearings.
>
> *To:*   I found the missing bearings *rolling around in the bottom of the vibration test chamber.*
>
> *Change:*   We saw a large warehouse *driving down the highway.*
>
> *To:*   *Driving down the highway,* we saw a large warehouse.

(See also **modifiers**.)

participle

Participles are **verb** forms that function as **adjectives**.

> *Examples:*   The *waiting* driver raced his engine.
> Here are the *revised* estimates.
> The *completed* report lay on his desk.
> *Rising* costs reduced our profit margin.

Participles belong to a larger class of verb forms called **verbals** or nonfinite verbs. (The other two types of verbals are **gerunds**, which always function as nouns, and **infinitives**, which have several functions.) Because participles are formed from verbs, they share certain characteristics of verbs even though they are adjectives: (1) they may take **objects** or **complements**; (2) they may be in the present, past, or perfect **tense**; and (3) they may be in the active or passive **voice**. But remember that a participle cannot be used as the verb of a sentence. Inexperienced writers sometimes make this mistake; the result is a *sentence fragment* (see **sentence faults**).

> *Change:* The committee chairman was responsible. His vote *being* the decisive one. (The latter is a sentence fragment, not a sentence.)
>
> *To:* The committee chairman was responsible, his vote *being* the decisive one.
>
> *Or:* The committee chairman was responsible. His vote *was* the decisive one.

TENSE

The present participle ends in "ing."

> *Example:* *Declining* sales forced us to close one branch office.

(Do not confuse present participles with gerunds, which are also verbals ending in "ing" but which always function as nouns, as in "*Running* (gerund) is his favorite occupation.")
The past participle may end in "ed," "t," "en," "n," or "d."

> *Examples:* Repair the *bent* lever.
> What are the *estimated* costs?
> Here is the *broken* calculator.
> What are the metal's *known* properties?
> The story, *told* many times before, was still interesting.

The perfect participle is formed with the present participle of the **helping verb** *have* plus the past participle of the main verb.

> *Example:* *Having gotten* (perfect participle) a large raise, the *smiling* (present participle), *contented* (past participle) employee worked harder than ever.

VOICE

Participles formed from **transitive verbs** may be in either the active or the passive **voice**. Some form of the helping verb *be* is used to form the passive voice of the perfect participle.

Examples: *Having finished* the job, we submitted our bill. (active voice)
The job *having been finished,* we submitted our bill. (passive voice)

MODIFIERS OF PARTICIPLES

Participles may be modified by **adverbs**, prepositional **phrases**, or **adverb clauses**.

Examples: *Rapidly* declining sales forced the shutdown. (adverb; the participle is *declining*)

Looking *to the future,* I felt that we should increase our research staff. (prepositional phrase; the participle is *looking*)

Having failed *because his laboratory was inadequate*, he requisitioned new equipment. (adverb clause; the participle is *having failed*)

OBJECTS AND COMPLEMENTS OF PARTICIPLES

Because participles are formed from verbs, they may take **objects** (direct and indirect) or **complements**.

Examples: *Having sold* (participle) *him* (indirect object) the new *model* (direct object), we must now provide adequate repair service.

Having been *president*, I found the adjustment difficult. (complement; the participle *having been* is formed from a **linking verb**)

Striking *the table* for emphasis, he told us exactly what he thought. (direct object; the participle *striking* is formed from a **transitive verb**)

PARTICIPLE FORMS IN VERB PHRASES

The present-tense and past-tense participle forms are combined with helping verbs to create **verb phrases**. The verb phrases function as main verbs rather than as adjectives.

Examples: I *have worked* all day.
I *am working* every day.
We *had fought* for our plan, but we *had lost*.
We *will be fighting* for our plan.
He *has planned* this trip for weeks.
He *would have been working* in any case.

parts of speech

Part of speech is a term used to describe the class of words to which a particular word belongs, according to its function in the **sentence**;

that is, each function in a sentence (naming, asserting, describing, joining, modifying, exclaiming) is performed by a word belonging to a certain part of speech.

If a word's function is to *name* something, it is a **noun** or **pronoun**. If a word's function is to make an *assertion* about something, it is a **verb**. If its function is to *describe* or *modify* something, the word is an **adjective** or an **adverb**. If its function is to *join* or *link* one element of the sentence to another, it is a **conjunction** or a **preposition**. If its function is to express an exclamation, it is an **interjection**.

party

In legal language, *party* refers to an individual.

> *Example:* The injured *party* brought suit against my client.

The term is inappropriate to general writing; when an individual is being referred to, use *person.*

> *Change:* The *party* whose file you requested is here now.
> *To:* The *person* whose file you requested is here now.

Party is, of course, appropriate when it refers to a group.

> *Example:* Arrangements were made for the members of our *party* to have lunch after the tour.

per

This common business term means "by means of," "through," or "on account of," and in these senses it is appropriate.

> *Examples:* *per* annum, *per* capita, *per* diem, *per* head

When used to mean "according to" (*per* your request, *per* your order) the expression is business **jargon** at its worst and should be avoided. Equally annoying is the phrase *as per.*

> *Change:* *Per your request,* I enclose the production report.
> *To:* *As you requested,* I enclose the production report.
> *Change:* *Per our discussion,* I will send revised instructions.
> *To:* *As we agreed,* I will send revised instructions.

per cent/percent/percentage

Percent, which is replacing the two-word *per cent,* is used when **numbers** are written out.

Example: About forty *percent* of our employees are covered by group
health insurance.

Either the word *percent* or the percent sign (%) may be used with
figures. Whichever form you choose, be consistent.

Examples: Only 25% attended the meeting.
Only 25 *percent* attended the meeting.

Percentage, which is never used with numbers, indicates a general
size.

Example: Only a small *percentage* of the managers attended the meeting.

period

A period (also called a full stop or end stop) usually indicates the
end of a declarative **sentence**. Periods also link (when used as leaders) and indicate omissions (when used as **ellipses**).

Although the primary function of periods is to end declarative
sentences, periods also end imperative sentences that are not emphatic enough for an **exclamation mark**.

Example: Send me any information you may have on the subject.

Periods may also end questions that are really polite requests and
questions to which an affirmative response is assumed.

Example: Will you please send me the specifications.

Periods end incomplete sentences when the meaning is clear from
the context. These sentences are common in advertising.

Example: Bell and Howell's new Double-Feature Cassette Projector will
change your mind about home movies. *Because if you can press
a button, now you can show movies. Instantly. Easily.*

(See also **sentences** and **sentence faults**.)

USE IN QUOTATIONS

Do not use a period after a declarative sentence that is quoted in the
context of another sentence.

Change: "There is every chance of success." she stated.
To: "There is every chance of success," she stated.

A period is conventionally placed inside **quotation marks**.

Examples: He liked to think of himself as a "tycoon."
He stated clearly, "My vote is yes."

USE WITH PARENTHESES

A sentence that ends in a closing **parenthesis** requires a period *after* the parenthesis.

Example: The institute was founded by Harry Denman (1902–1972).

If a whole sentence (beginning with an initial **capital letter**) is in parentheses, the period (or any other end mark) is placed inside the final parenthesis.

Example: The project director listed the problems facing her staff. (This was the third time she had complained to the board.)

CONVENTIONAL USES OF PERIODS

Use periods after initials in names.

Examples: W. T. Grant, J. P. Morgan

Use periods as decimal points with numbers.

Examples: 109.2, $540.26, 6.9%

Use periods to indicate **abbreviations**.

Examples: Ms., Dr., Inc.

Use periods following the numbers in numbered lists.

Example:
1.
2.
3.

PERIODS AS ELLIPSES

When you omit words in quoted material, use a series of three spaced periods—called ellipsis dots—to indicate the omission. Such an omission must not detract from or alter the essential meaning of the passage.

Example: "Technical material distributed for promotional use is sometimes charged for, particularly in high-volume distribution to educational institutions, although prices for these publications are not uniformly based on the cost of developing them." (without omission)

"Technical material distributed for promotional use is sometimes charged for . . . although prices for these publications are not uniformly based on the cost of developing them." (with omission)

When introducing a **quotation** that does not begin with the first word of a sentence (that is, when your quotation starts somewhere in the middle of a sentence of the material from which you are quoting), you do not need ellipsis dots; the **lower-case letter** with which you begin the quotation already indicates an omission.

> *Example:* "Once the client's needs have been evaluated, the sales representative must prepare a proposal designed to meet those specific needs." (without omission)
>
> His letter states that "the sales representative must prepare a proposal designed to meet those specific needs." (with omission)

If an ellipsis follows the end of a sentence, retain the period at the end of the sentence and add the three elipsis dots.

> *Examples:* "During the year, every department participated in the development of a centralized computer system. The basic plan centered on the use of the computer as a cost reduction tool. At the beginning of the year, each department received a booklet explaining the purpose of the system." (without omission)
>
> "During the year, every department participated in the development of a centralized computer system.... At the beginning of the year, each department received a booklet explaining the purpose of the system."

PERIODS AS LEADERS

When spaced periods are used in a **table** to connect one item to another, they are called leaders. The purpose of leaders is to help the reader align the data.

> *Example:*
>
> | City | Gross Sales |
> |---|---|
> | New York | $25,000 |
> | Chicago | 18,000 |
> | Detroit | 13,500 |

The most common use of leaders is in **tables of contents**.

PERIOD FAULT

The incorrect use of a period is sometimes referred to as a "period fault." When a period is inserted prematurely, the result is a sentence fragment.

> *Change:* After a long day at the office in which we finished the report. We left hurriedly for home.
>
> *To:* After a long day at the office in which we finished the report, we left hurriedly for home.

When a period is left out, the result is an incorrect "fused" (or run-on) sentence.

Change: Bill was late for ten days in a row of course Ms. Sturgess had to fire him.

To: Bill was late for ten days in a row. Of course Ms. Sturgess had to fire him.

(See also **sentence faults**.)

person

Person is the grammatical term for the form of a **personal pronoun** that indicates whether the **pronoun** represents the speaker, the person spoken to, or the person (or thing) spoken about. If the pronoun represents the speaker, the pronoun is in the first person.

Example: *I* could not find the answer in the manual.

If the pronoun represents the person or persons spoken to, the pronoun is in the second person.

Example: *You* are going to be a good supervisor.

If the pronoun represents the person or persons spoken about, the pronoun is in the third person.

Example: *They* received the news quietly.

Person	Singular	Plural
First	I, me, my	we, ours, us
Second	you, your	you, your
Third	he, him, his she, her, hers it, its	they, them, their

(See also **number** and **case**.)

Identifying pronouns by person helps the writer avoid illogical shifts from one person to another. A very common error is to shift from the third person to the second person.

Change: A *person* should spend the morning hours on work requiring mental effort, for *your* mind is freshest in the morning.

To: A *person* should spend the morning hours on work requiring mental effort, for *his* mind is freshest in the morning.

Or: *You* should spend the morning hours on work requiring mental effort, for *your* mind is freshest in the morning.

personal/personnel

Personal is an **adjective** meaning "of or pertaining to an individual person."

>   *Example:*   He left work early because of a *personal* problem.

Personnel is a **noun** meaning "a group of people engaged in a common job."

>   *Example:*   All *personnel* are required to pick up their paychecks on Thursday.

Be careful not to use *personnel* when the word you really need is *persons* or *people*.

>   *Change:*   The remaining two *personnel* will be moved next Thursday.
>   *To:*   The remaining two *persons* will be moved next Thursday.

personal pronoun

The personal pronouns are *I, me, my, mine; you, your, yours; he, him, his; she, her, hers; it, its; we, us, our, ours;* and *they, them, their, theirs*.

Don't attempt to avoid use of the personal pronoun *I* where it is natural. The use of unnatural devices to avoid using *I* is more likely to call attention to the writer than use of the pronoun *I* would.

>   *Change:*   *The writer* wishes to point out that the proposed solution has several weaknesses.
>   *To:*   *I* wish to point out that the proposed solution has several weaknesses.

The use of *we* for general reference ("*We* are living in a time of high inflation.") is acceptable. But using the editorial *we* to avoid *I* is pompous and stiff. It may also assume, presumptuously, that "we" all agree.

>   *Change:*   *We* must state unequivocally that *we* disapprove of such practices.
>   *To:*   *I* must state unequivocally that *I* disapprove of such practices.

Especially in business writing, where it can be important to distinguish commitments made by individuals from corporate commitments, bear in mind that the use of *we* can be legally construed to commit the writer's company as well as the writer personally. If you are speaking for yourself—even in your role as an employee—it is better to use *I*.

The use of *one* is also acceptable for general reference. Be aware, however, that it is impersonal and somewhat stiff and that overdoing it renders your writing awkward.

> *Change:* *One* must be careful about *one's* work habits lest *one* become sloppy.
> *To:* *People* must be careful about *their* work habits lest *they* become sloppy.

(See also **point of view**.)

persons/people

When we use *persons*, we are usually referring to individual people thought of separately.

> *Example:* At the national marketing conference, there were three very important *persons* whom I had hoped to meet.

When we say *people*, we are identifying a large or anonymous group.

> *Example:* Many *people* have never even heard of our product.

persuasion

Persuasion—an attempt to convince the **reader** that the writer's **point of view** regarding a subject is the correct or desirable one— begins with a statement of a thesis and then offers facts, statistics, and examples to support the thesis. Persuasive writing is an appeal to reason. Any opinions or generalizations offered must be supported with facts and logic. To be effective, persuasion (sometimes called argumentation) must avoid equivocation, **ambiguity**, and any trivial, irrelevant, or false claims—it must state a clear premise and reach an unmistakable **conclusion**. Although it may benefit occasionally from emotional appeal, persuasion is primarily logical, establishing the relationships among facts through the use of reason. Writers may make use of **exposition, description**, and **narration** in persuasive writing, but they subordinate them to their primary goal —to influence the reader.

> *Example:* I must ask my liberal-minded reader to join me in a restraint. Because reformers are quite human human beings, they have often given the words "reformer" and "liberal" a connotation

which amounts to saying that these types, in contrast with other Americans, are receptive to new ideas and are ready to place the good of society above any selfish interest. Undoubtedly, these virtues have been common among reformers and they have not especially characterized standpatters. The trouble is that the "liberal" and "conservative" types which many people have in mind are just so many stereotypes. Everyone is aware, for example, of labor leaders who have gone down the line for the New Deal and the Fair Deal but who are hardly open-minded or inclined to place the interest of society over their vested concern, organized labor. Conversely, some businessmen who approach apoplexy at mention of the New Deal are notably tolerant and unselfish in many ways and prove themselves strong friends of new ideas in a number of activities. The fact seems to be that the reform movement over the years has included both the flexible-minded and the guardians of the previous generation's dogmas, both people who were in the movement to give as much as they could to the community and those who were in it for what they could get out of it for themselves or their group. As a matter of fact, one of the central questions that has to be answered in any thorough study of modern America is whether at times it has not amounted to a drive to bring benefits to a minority at the expense of the majority. The author and the reader are much more likely to be satisfied with the same answers to this and related questions if neither makes the assumption that a reformer, *ipso facto,* is the noblest species of American.

—Eric F. Goldman, *Rendezvous with Destiny* (New York: Random House, 1960), p. vii.

To write persuasively, you must obey the rules of reasoning. All of your facts must be valid, you must take opposing arguments into account (not only to be honest, but to be more effective as well), and you must be careful not to overstate your case (adopting a temperate **tone** and guarding against letting yourself sound opinionated). See also **methods of development** and **forms of discourse**.

phase

Phase means "a stage of transition or development."

    Example: This is only the first *phase* of the project.

It should not be used to mean "aspect."

    Change: Have you thought about this *phase* of the subject?
        To: Have you thought about this *aspect* of the subject?

phenomenon/phenomena

Phenomenon means "any observable thing, fact, or occurrence." Its plural form is *phenomena.*

> *Examples:*   The *phenomenon* of inflation coupled with rising unemployment surprised many economists. (singular)
> Sales of cold remedies are often affected by natural *phenomena*, for example, rainfall and snow. (plural)

phrases

Below the level of the **sentence**, there are two ways to combine words into groups: by forming **clauses**, which combine **subjects** and **verbs**, and by forming phrases, which are based on **nouns**, nonfinite verb forms, or verb combinations without subjects. A phrase is the most basic meaningful group of words; it cannot make a full statement as a clause can, however, because a phrase does not contain a subject and verb combination.

> *Example:*   He encouraged his staff (clause) *by his calm confidence.* (phrase)

A phrase may function as an **adjective**, an **adverb**, a noun, or a verb.

> *Examples:*   The subjects *on the agenda* were all discussed. (adjective)
> We discussed the project *with great enthusiasm.* (adverb)
> *Working hard* is her way of life. (noun)
> The Chief Engineer *should have been notified.* (verb)

Even though phrases function as adjectives, adverbs, nouns, or verbs, they are normally named for the kind of word around which they are constructed—**preposition, participle, infinitive, gerund**, verb, or noun. (See also **absolute phrase**.)

PREPOSITIONAL PHRASE

A preposition is a word that shows the relationship of its **object** with another word; that is, it combines with its object (a noun or a **pronoun**) to form a modifying phrase; a **prepositional phrase**, then, consists of a preposition plus its object (the noun or pronoun) and its **modifiers**.

> *Example:*   *After the meeting,* the regional managers adjourned *to the executives' dining room.*

PARTICIPIAL PHRASE

A participle is any form of a verb that is used as an adjective. A **participial phrase** consists of a participle plus its object and its modifiers.

> *Example:* *Looking very pleased with himself,* the sales manager reported on the success of the policies he had introduced.

INFINITIVE PHRASE

An infinitive is the bare form of a verb (*go, run, talk*) without the restrictions imposed by **person** and **number**; an infinitive is generally preceded by the word *to* (which is usually a preposition but in this use is called the sign, or mark, of the infinitive). An **infinitive phrase** consists of the word *to* plus an infinitive and any objects or modifiers.

> *Example:* *To succeed in this field,* you must be willing *to assume responsibility.*

GERUND PHRASE

A gerund phrase, which consists of a gerund plus any objects or modifiers, always functions as a noun.

> *Examples:* *Preparing an annual report* is a difficult task. (subject of *is*)
> She liked *running the department.* (direct object of *liked*)

VERB PHRASE

A **verb phrase** consists of a main verb and its **helping verb**.

> *Example:* Company officials discovered that a computer *was emitting* more data than it *had been asked* for. After investigation, police suggested that an unauthorized program *had been run* through the computer at the coded command of another computer belonging to a different company. The police obtained a warrant to search for electronic impulses in the memory of the suspect machine. The case (involving trade secrets) and its outcome *should make* legal history.

NOUN PHRASE

A noun phrase consists of a noun and its modifiers.

> *Examples:* *Many large companies* use computers.
> Have *the two new employees* fill out *these forms.*

plagiarism

To use someone else's exact words without **quotation marks** and appropriate credit or to use the unique ideas of someone else without acknowledgment is known as plagiarism. In publishing, plagiarism is illegal; in other circumstances, plagiarism is at the least unethical. You may quote the words and ideas of another if you credit your source by **footnoting** the passage. (However, if you intend to publish or reproduce and distribute material in which you have included quotations, you will often need to obtain written permission from whoever holds the **copyright**.) You may **paraphrase** a passage without citing the source as long as the idea is not unique to one author.

point of view

Point of view is the attitude you exhibit toward your **reader** as reflected in your use of **person** (the use of **personal pronouns** such as *I, we, you,* and *they*). The writer's point of view may be impersonal.

> *Example:* It is regrettable that the material shipped on the 12th is unacceptable.

Or the writer's point of view may be personal.

> *Example:* I regret that we cannot accept your shipment of the 12th.

Although the meaning of both **sentences** is the same, the sentence with the personal point of view (using *I, we,* and *your*) reflects the fact that two *people* are involved in the communication. Years ago, business and technical people preferred the impersonal point of view because they thought it made writing sound more objective and more "businesslike." Unfortunately, however, the impersonal point of view often prevented clear and direct communication and actually caused misunderstanding at times. Today, good business and technical writing adopts a more personal point of view wherever it is appropriate.

Use of the first person (*I, we*) makes the point of view more personal since the writer speaks of himself.

> *Example:* *I* can finish the project by August 1st.

When a writer tries to avoid *I* by using *one*—when he is really talking about himself—he does not increase objectivity, but merely makes the statement impersonal.

Change: *One* can only conclude that the new advertising is not effective.
To: *I* can only conclude that the new advertising is not effective.

Never use *the writer* to replace *I* in a mistaken attempt to sound very formal or dignified.

Change: *The writer* feels that this project will be completed by the end of June.
To: *I* feel that this project will be completed by the end of June.

Do not use the personal point of view when an impersonal point of view would be more appropriate or more effective.

Change: I am inclined to think that each manager should attend the final committee meeting to hear the committee's recommendations.
To: Each manager should attend the final committee meeting to hear the committee's recommendations.

Notice in the above examples that when you write in the third person, the point of view shifts from the writer to the person or thing being discussed. If you want the subject matter to receive more **emphasis** than either you (the writer) or the reader, you should establish an impersonal point of view. This is a fairly common practice in **formal writing** because the subject matter is given greatest emphasis.

In a business letter on company stationery, be aware that use of the pronoun *we* reflects company policy, while *I* reflects personal opinion. You may decide which pronoun to use on the basis of whether the reader would most appreciate a corporate or individual concern.

Examples: *I* appreciate your suggestion regarding our need for more community activities.
We appreciate your suggestion regarding our need for more community activities.

Remember, however, that the pronoun *we* may commit your organization to what you say.

Change: *We* believe that your proposal was the best submitted.
To: *I* believe that your proposal was the best submitted.

Another way of reflecting a personal point of view is to write directly to the reader by use of the second person pronoun (*you*). This is sometimes called the "you approach," since it aims your message directly to the reader.

> *Example:*   If *you* finish *your* section of the report by the 1st, we can submit the whole report on the 5th.

When a business or technical writer tries to avoid using the pronoun *you,* the result is often awkward and sometimes even unclear.

> *Change:*   *The branch manager* should make sure that all corporate directives are carried out.
>
> *To:*   *You* should make sure that all corporate directives are carried out.
>
> *Or:*   Make sure that all corporate directives are carried out. (This is the imperative form of the sentence, in which the pronoun *you* is implied.)

Whether you adopt a personal or an impersonal point of view should depend upon your **objective** and what you know about your reader. In a business letter to an associate, you will most likely adopt a personal point of view. In a report to a large group, you will probably choose to emphasize the subject by adopting an impersonal point of view.

police report

A great many police departments have attempted, understandably, to reduce the police report to a question-and-answer form, and they have largely succeeded. No matter how good the form may be, however, it must eventually require the reporting police officer to "tell what happened." In other words, virtually every police report form has a section for the "Narrative," or "Remarks," or "Details"; it is in this section of the report that writing skill can make the difference between a mediocre report and a good one.

The basis of a good police report is, of course, the accuracy of its information. Accurate information must be gathered during the **note-taking** phase of the investigation, at times under difficult circumstances. Like notes taken for any purpose, police notes must be brief, memory-jogging, and to the point. Though brief, they must be substantial enough to trigger the necessary chain of associations later as you write the report. Do not trust your memory to help you with details you have not noted. If several incidents occur before you have time to write up any one of them, the chances of details running together in your mind are great unless your notes are complete and accurate. The shorter the elapsed time between your note-taking and completing your report, the better. Remember that it is better to include too much than too little information as you take notes. Unnecessary information can always be dropped from the final report.

A successful formula for getting complete and accurate notes involves answering a series of basic questions.

1. Who? (victim, any suspect, any witness)
2. What? (any evidence, type of crime, any property)
3. Where? (scene of the offense, location of any property, location of any evidence)
4. When? (date and time of the offense)
5. How? (manner in which the crime was committed)
6. Why? (any evident motive)

Answering these questions carefully and in full detail will give you the essential facts for your report.

Most report forms contain numerous blocks for this basic information. However, for the "Details" or "Remarks" section, you must shape the facts and impressions you have gathered into a coherent narrative. It is here, in the narrative section of the report, that you must re-create the incident for those who were not there and must therefore rely heavily on what you say, such as judges and attorneys. Even if you include all the pertinent details accurately, they will be of little benefit to the **reader** if they are disorganized.

The best way to order your facts into a clearly written narrative is to present them in the order of their occurrence; that is, the report should proceed from start to finish with a step-by-step account of the events as they occurred (see **chronological method of development**). Of course, the material should not be run together in a rambling, unbroken block of writing. Your first requirement as a writer is to help your readers—remember that they weren't there and you were. You must flesh out the bare facts and shape the material so that it communicates its meaning easily and quickly.

The beginning **paragraph** should set the scene for the investigation. It should include the pertinent facts about the time, location of events, type of crime, who responded to the call, and so on. It introduces the basic facts that will be discussed in the body of the report.

The middle, or body, of the report should reflect events as they unfolded, or in the order that can best be determined at the time. It is a good idea to number the paragraphs throughout the report, in sequence, for easy reference. Remember that your report may play a large part in the courtroom proceedings.

The end, or **conclusion**, should include information on everything pertinent to the present status of the case. What became of the persons involved? Was evidence obtained? Are there further leads to follow? Are there other persons to interview? Your conclusion should indicate whether the case has been solved and, if it has not, in what manner it is still being pursued.

Beyond the requirements of shaping complete and accurate notes into a concise, logically arranged narrative, police report writing calls for especially careful **word choice**, grammatical consistency, and accurate **punctuation**. The quickest way to find information on these categories is to look at the Checklist of the Writing Process.

Special attention must be focused on word choice in police report writing. In police work, delicate care must be used to describe what are often indelicate situations. Your training in the police vernacular will help in most situations, but using words charged with the wrong emotional overtones is a continuing problem. Be aware of a word's **connotation** before you use it. Train yourself to use neutral, unbiased, objective terms. Otherwise, you run the risk of including loaded language in your report and of laying yourself open to the charge of being biased.

> *Change:* I hauled in Billy Ray Jenkins for questioning after I spotted him loitering near the scene of the holdup. He's an obvious criminal type, with his long, greasy hair, a filthy beard, and clothes that hadn't been washed in a month. He gave me a song and dance about hitchhiking across the country. Even though he smelled like a broken wine bottle, he wouldn't let me give him the drunk test.
>
> *To:* I brought in Billy Ray Jenkins for questioning after I saw him loitering in an alley a block from the scene of the holdup. His clothes were unkempt, and his hair and beard were untrimmed. He said he was hitchhiking across the country. He smelled of alcohol but refused a drunkometer test.

The prejudice of the police officer who wrote the first example comes across clearly. The officer has, in effect, convicted the suspect in the report. In a law court, this kind of writing could only harm the prosecution's case. The second example, although not as colorful as the first, runs less risk of sounding biased and unfair.

One final concern. Be especially careful to separate fact from opinion and label each clearly. Where you or a witness offers an opinion, say so. If three witnesses agree that a break-in occurred at 2:30 a.m., you have a verified fact and can present the information as such.

But if four witnesses are pretty sure they know who assaulted them in the dark after looking at six men in a line-up, even though none actually saw his face, you are dealing with opinion and your report must say so.

positive writing

Presenting positive information as though it were negative is a trap that technical people fall into quite easily because of the complexity of the information they must write about. It is a practice that confuses the **reader**, however, and one that should be avoided.

> *Change:* If sales do *not* decline, we will *not* change our procedures.
> *To:* We will change our procedures only if sales decline.

In the first sentence, the reader must reverse two negatives to understand the exception that is being stated; the second sentence presents an exception to a rule in a straightforward manner.

On the other hand, negative facts or conclusions should be stated negatively; stating a negative fact or conclusion positively can mislead the reader.

> *Change:* New car sales for November have been maintained at 40 percent of last November's record sales volume.
> *To:* New car sales for November have dropped to 40 percent of last November's record sales volume.

possessive adjective

Because possessive adjectives (*my, your, our, his, her, its, their*) directly modify **nouns**, they function as **adjectives**, even though they are **pronoun** forms. Anything that modifies a noun functions as an adjective. This is true even of words that in most contexts function as nouns, particularly in the possessive form.

> *Example:* The *proposal's* virtues outweighed its defects.

The possessives *mine, yours, hers, ours,* and *theirs* are normally pronominal rather than adjectival. (Expressions like *mine host* are archaic.) They often function as **subjective complements**.

> *Example:* That desk is *mine.*

They can, however, serve as **subjects**.

> *Example:* My desk is in the back; *yours* is by the window.

In either case, they function as pronouns.

practicable/practical

Practicable means that something is "possible" or "feasible." *Practical* has the **connotation** of "usefulness" in addition to the meaning "capable of being used."

> *Example:* The program is *practical;* but, considering the company's recent financial problems, is it *practicable?*

Practical, not *practicable,* is used to describe a person, implying "common sense, a commitment to what works rather than to theory or abstractions."

predicate

The *predicate* is that part of a **sentence** that contains the main **verb** and any other words used to complete the thought of the sentence (the verb's **modifiers** and **complements**). The principal part of the predicate is the verb, just as a **noun** (or noun substitute) is the principal part of the **subject**.

> *Example:* Bill *piloted the airplane.* ("Piloted the airplane" is the predicate, for it tells what Bill did.)

The simple predicate is the verb (or **verb phrase**) alone; the complete predicate is the verb and its modifiers and complements.

A compound predicate consists of two or more verbs with the same subject. It is an important device for economical writing.

> *Example:* The company *tried* but *did not succeed* in that field.

predicate adjective

A *predicate adjective* is an **adjective** that follows a **linking verb** and describes the **subject**.

> *Examples:* He is *sick.*
> That flower is *artificial.*
> The milk smells *sour.*
> The proposal looks *good.*

The predicate adjective is one kind of **subjective complement;** the other is the **predicate nominative.** (See also **predicate.**)

predicate nominative

A *predicate nominative* is a **noun** construction that follows a **linking verb** and renames the **subject**.

Examples: He is my *lawyer*. (noun that renames the subject)
His excuse was *that he had been sick*. (noun clause that renames the subject *excuse*)

The predicate nominative is one kind of **subjective complement**; the other is the **predicate adjective**.

preferable

To say that one thing is "more preferable" than another is redundant. To say that one thing is *preferable* to another is sufficient.

Change: His work is *more preferable* than Bill's.
To: His work is *preferable* to Bill's.

prefix

A prefix is a letter, or letters, placed in front of a root word that changes the meaning, often causing the new word to mean the opposite of the root word.

Root Word	With Prefix
enter	*re*enter (enter again)
acceptable	*un*acceptable (not acceptable)
operate	*co*operate (operate together)
symmetrical	*a*symmetrical (not symmetrical)
honest	*dis*honest (not honest)
science	*meta*science (beyond science)

When a prefix ends with a vowel and the root word begins with the same vowel, the prefix may be separated from the root word with a **hyphen** (re-enter, co-operate, re-elect), the second vowel may be marked with a dieresis (reënter, coöperate, reëlect), or the word may be written with neither hyphen nor dieresis (reenter, cooperate, reelect). The hyphen and the dieresis are visual aids that help the **reader** recognize that the two vowels are pronounced differently. Since typewriters do not have the dieresis mark, the hyphen is the more practical way to help the reader.

Except between identical vowels, the hyphen rarely appears between a prefix and its root word. At times, however, a hyphen is necessary; for example, *reform* means "to correct" or "to improve," while *re-form* means "to change the shape of."

preparation

To write clearly and effectively does not require innate creative talent. It does require a systematic approach, however, which should logically begin with proper preparation.

Preparation consists of determining the **objective** of your writing project, its **readers**, and the **scope** within which you will cover your subject. Although these fundamentals of the writing process are often overlooked, you must come to grips with them if you hope to write well. They are the foundations upon which all the other steps of the writing process are built.

OBJECTIVE

What *exactly* do you want your readers to know or be able to do when they have finished reading what you have written? When you can answer this question—again, *exactly*—you will have determined the objective of your writing. A good test of whether you have formulated your objective adequately is to state it in a single **sentence**. This statement may also function as the thesis statement in your **outline**, although such a function should not be a requirement of your stated objective.

READERS

Know who your readers are and learn certain key facts about them, such as their educational level, technical knowledge, and needs relative to your subject. Their level of technical knowledge, for example, should determine whether you need to cover the fundamentals of your subject and which terms you must define.

SCOPE

If you know the objective of your writing project and your readers, you will know the type and amount of detail you will need to include in your writing. This is called scope, which may be defined as the depth and breadth to which you cover your subject. If you do not determine your scope of coverage you will not know how much or what kind of information to include, and therefore you are likely to invest unnecessary work during the **research** phase of your writing project. (See also the Checklist of the Writing Process.)

preposition

A preposition is a word that links a **noun** or **pronoun** (its **object**) to another **sentence** element by expressing such relationships as direction (*to, into, across, toward*), location (*at, in, on, under, over, beside, among, by, between, through*), time (*before, after, during, until, since*), or figurative location (*for, against, with*). Although only about seventy prepositions exist in the English language, they occur frequently. Together the preposition, its object, and the object's modifiers form a **prepositional phrase**, which acts as a **modifier**.

The object of a preposition, the word or phrase following the preposition, is always in the objective **case**. This situation gives rise to a problem in such constructions as "between you and *me*," a phrase that is frequently and incorrectly written as "between you and *I*."

Many words that function as prepositions also function as **adverbs**. If the word takes an object and functions as a **connective**, it is a preposition; if it has no object and functions as a modifier, it is an adverb.

Examples: The manager sat *behind* the desk *in* his office. (prepositions)
The customer lagged *behind;* then she came *in* and sat down. (adverbs)

PREPOSITION DON'TS

Do not use redundant prepositions, such as "off *of*," "in back *of*," and "inside *of*."

Change: The client arrived *at about* four o'clock.
To: The client arrived *at* four o'clock. (to be exact)
Or: The client arrived *about* four o'clock. (to be approximate)

Avoid omitting needed prepositions.

Change: He was oblivious and not distracted by the view from his office window.
To: He was oblivious *to* and not distracted *by* the view from his office window.

Avoid adding the preposition *up* to **verbs** unnecessarily.

> *Change:*　Call *up* and see if he is in his office.
> *To:*　Call and see if he is in his office.

USING A PREPOSITION AT THE END OF A SENTENCE

If a preposition falls naturally at the end of a sentence, leave it there.

> *Example:*　I don't remember which file I put it *in*.

Be aware, however, that a preposition coming at the end of a sentence can be an indication that the sentence is awkwardly constructed.

> *Change:*　The branch office is where he was *at*.
> *To:*　He was at the branch office.

COMMON USES OF PREPOSITIONS

Certain verbs (and verb forms), adverbs, and **adjectives** are used with certain prepositions. For example, we say "interested *in*," "aware *of*," "devoted *to*," "equated *with*," "abstain *from*," "adhere *to*," "conform *to*," "capable *of*," "comply *with*," "object *to*," "find fault *with*," "inconsistent *with*," "independent *of*," "infer *from*," and "interfere *with*."

USING A PREPOSITION IN A TITLE

When a preposition appears in a title, it is not capitalized if it is less than four letters.

> *Example:*　*Composition for the Business and Technical World* was reviewed recently by *Time* magazine.

A preposition of four letters or more should be capitalized when it appears in a title.

> *Example:*　The book *Managing Like Mad* should be taken seriously in spite of its frothy title.

(See also **capital letters**.)

prepositional phrase

A **preposition** is a word that shows relationship and combines with a **noun** or a **pronoun** (its **object**) to form a modifying **phrase**. A prepositional phrase, then, consists of a preposition plus its object and the object's **modifiers**.

Example: *After the meeting,* the district managers adjourned *to the executives' dining room.*

Prepositional phrases, because they normally modify nouns or **verbs**, usually function as **adjectives** or **adverbs**, although occasionally they function as nouns.

A prepositional phrase may function as an adverb of motion.

Example: Move the typewriter *onto the other desk.*

A prepositional phrase may function as an adverb of manner.

Example: Answer customers' queries *in a courteous fashion.*

A prepositional phrase may function as an adverb of place.

Example: We ate lunch *in the company cafeteria.*

A prepositional phrase may function as an adjective.

Example: The man *with the briefcase* is the new district manager.

When functioning as adjectives, prepositional phrases follow the nouns they modify.

Example: Here are the results *of our study.*

When functioning as adverbs, prepositional phrases may appear in different places.

Examples: *By five o'clock* the report will be completed.
The report will be completed *by five o'clock.*

Be careful when using prepositional phrases; separating a prepositional phrase from the noun it is modifying can cause **ambiguity**.

Change: *The man* standing by the drinking fountain *in the gray suit* is our president.
To: *The man in the gray suit* who is standing by the drinking fountain is our president.

principal/principle

Principal, meaning "an amount of money on which interest is earned or paid" or "a chief official in a school or court proceeding," is sometimes confused with *principle,* meaning "a basic truth or belief."

Examples: The bank will pay 6½% per month on the *principal.*
She is a person of unwavering *principles.*
He sent a letter of introduction to the *principal* of the high school.

Principal is also an adjective, meaning "main" or "primary."

    Example: My *principal* objection is that it will be too expensive.

progress report

The progress report, which may be issued periodically, is often used by business management to adjust manpower assignments, schedules, and budget allocations. A progress report is sometimes required as part of a sales contract. Since it describes the progress of a continuing project, a progress report should contain a "transitional" **introduction** relating the present situation to previous conditions, and it should conclude with an assessment of what has been done and an estimate of future prospects. Depending upon contractual or other requirements, a progress report may be in the form of a **report**, a letter, or a **memorandum**.

    Example: Progress Report on Rewiring the Sports Arena

Background →

    This is a progress report, as agreed to in our contract, on the rewiring program at the Sports Arena. Although costs of certain equipment are higher than our original bid indicated, we expect to complete the project without going over cost because the speed with which the project is being completed will save labor costs.

WORK COMPLETED

What has been done →

    As of August 15, we have finished the installation of the circuit breaker panels and meters, of level I service outlets, and of all sub-floor rewiring. Lighting fixture replacement, level II service outlets, and the upgrading of stage lighting equipment are in the preliminary stages (meaning that the wiring has been completed but installation of the fixtures has not yet begun).

COSTS

    Equipment used up to this point has cost $10,800, and labor costs have been $31,500 (including some subcontracted plumbing). My estimate for the rest of the equipment, based on discussions with your lighting consultant, is $11,500; labor costs should not be in excess of $25,000.

WORK SCHEDULE

What is yet to be done →

    I have scheduled the upgrading of stage lighting equipment for from August 16 to October 5, the completion of level II service outlets from October 6 to November 12, and the lighting fixture replacement from November 15 to December 17.

CONCLUSION

Conclusion →   Although my original estimate on equipment ($20,000) has been exceeded by $2,300, my original labor estimate ($60,000) has been reduced by $3,500 so that I will easily stay within the limits of my original bid. In addition, I see no difficulty in having the arena finished for the December 23 Christmas program.

pronouns

A pronoun is a word that is used as a substitute for a **noun** (the noun for which a pronoun substitutes is called its antecedent). Using pronouns in place of nouns relieves the monotony of repeating the same noun over and over. Pronouns fall into several different categories: personal, demonstrative, relative, interrogative, indefinite, reflexive, intensive, and reciprocal.

PERSONAL PRONOUNS

The **personal pronouns** refer to the person or persons speaking (*I, me, my, mine; we, us, our, ours*); the person or persons spoken to (*you, your, yours*); or the person or thing spoken of (*he, him, his; she, her, hers; it, its; they, them, their, theirs*). (See also **person**.)

Examples: *I* wish *you* had told *me* that *she* was coming with *us*.
If *their* figures are correct, *ours* must be in error.

DEMONSTRATIVE PRONOUNS

The **demonstrative pronouns** (*this, these; that, those*) indicate or point out the thing being referred to.

Examples: *This* is my desk.
These are my co-workers.
That will be a difficult job.
Those are incorrect figures.

RELATIVE PRONOUNS

The **relative pronouns** are *who* (or *whom*), *which,* and *that*. A relative pronoun performs a dual function: (1) it takes the place of a noun; and (2) it connects, and establishes the relationship between, a **dependent clause** and its main **clause**.

Example: The personnel manager told the applicants *who* would be hired.

INTERROGATIVE PRONOUNS

Interrogative pronouns (*who* or *whom, what,* and *which*) ask questions. They differ from relative pronouns in two ways: They are used only to ask questions and they may introduce independent interrogative **sentences**, while relative pronouns connect or show relationship and introduce only dependent clauses.

INDEFINITE PRONOUNS

Indefinite pronouns specify a class or group of persons or things rather than a particular person or thing. *All, any, another, anyone, anything, both, each, either, everybody, few, many, most, much, neither, nobody, none, several, some,* and *such* are indefinite pronouns.

> *Example:*   Not *everyone* liked the new procedures; *some* even refused to follow them.

REFLEXIVE PRONOUNS

A **reflexive pronoun**, which always ends with the **suffix** *-self* or *-selves,* indicates that the **subject** of the sentence acts upon itself.

> *Example:*   The secretary accidentally cut *herself* with the letter opener.

The reflexive and intensive pronouns are *myself, yourself, himself, herself, itself, oneself, ourselves, yourselves,* and *themselves.*

INTENSIVE PRONOUNS

The intensive pronouns are identical in form with the reflexive pronouns (see just above) but they perform a different function: to give **emphasis** to their antecedents.

> *Example:*   I *myself* asked the same question.

RECIPROCAL PRONOUNS

The **reciprocal pronouns** (*one another* and *each other*) indicate the relationship of one item to another. Use *each other* when referring to two persons or things and *one another* when referring to more than two.

> *Examples:*   They work well with *each other.*
> The crew members work well with *one another.*

GRAMMATICAL PROPERTIES OF PRONOUNS

Case. Pronouns have forms to show the subjective, objective, or possessive **case**.

	Subj.	Obj.	Poss.	Subj.	Obj.	Poss.
	SINGULAR			*PLURAL*		
1st Person	I	me	my, mine	we	us	our, ours
2nd Person	you	you	your, yours	you	you	your, yours
3rd Person				they	them	their, theirs
Masculine	he	him	his			
Feminine	she	her	her, hers			
Neuter	it	it	its			

A pronoun that is used as the subject of a clause or sentence is in the subjective case (*I, we, he, she, it, you, they, who*). The subjective case is also used when the pronoun follows a **linking verb**.

Examples: *He* is my boss.
My boss is *he*.

A pronoun that is used as the **object** of a **verb** or **preposition** is in the objective case (*me, us, him, her, it, you, them, whom*).

Examples: Between *you* and *me*, his facts are questionable. (object of preposition)
Mr. Davis hired Tom and *me* (not *I*). (object of verb)

A pronoun that is used to express ownership is in the possessive case (*my, mine, our, ours, his, her, hers, its, your, yours, their, theirs, whose*).

Example: He took *his* notes with him on the business trip.

Only the possessive form of a pronoun should ever be used with a **gerund**.

Example: The boss objected to *my* arriving late every morning.

Several indefinite pronouns (*any, each, few, most, none*, and *some*) form the possessive only in "of" phrases (*of any, of some*). Others, however, use the **apostrophe** (*anyone's*).

Change: *Each's* opinion was solicited.
To: The opinion *of each* was solicited.

A pronoun **appositive** takes the case of its antecedent.

Examples: Two systems analysts, Joe and *I*, were selected to represent the company. (*Joe and I* is in apposition to the subject, *systems analysts*, and must therefore be in the subjective case.)

The systems analysts selected two members of our department —Joe and *me*. (*Joe and me* is in apposition to *two members*, which is the object of the verb *selected*, and therefore must be in the objective case.)

How to Determine the Case of a Pronoun. To determine the case of a pronoun, try it with a **transitive verb**, such as *resembled.* If the pronoun can precede the verb, it is in the subjective case; if it must follow the verb, it is in the objective case.

Examples: *She* resembled her father (subjective case).
Her father resembled *her* (objective case).

If compound pronouns cause problems in determining case, try using them singly.

Examples: In his letter, John mentioned you and *me.*
In his letter, John mentioned *you.*
In his letter, John mentioned *me.*

They and *we* must discuss the terms of the merger.
They must discuss the terms of the merger.
We must discuss the terms of the merger.

When a pronoun modifies a noun, try it without the noun to determine its case.

Examples: (*We/Us*) pilots fly our own planes.
We fly our own planes. (You would not write "*Us* fly our own planes.")

He addressed his remarks directly to (*we/us*) technicians.
He addressed his remarks directly to *us.* (You would not write "He addressed his remarks directly to *we.*")

To determine the case of a pronoun that follows *as* or *than,* try mentally adding the words that are normally omitted.

Examples: The director does not have as much formal education as *he* [does]. (You would not write "*him* does.")
His friend was taller than *he* [was tall]. (You would not write "*him* was.")

Number. **Number** is a frequent problem only with a few indefinite pronouns (*each, either, neither;* and those ending with *-body* or *-one,* such as *anybody, anyone, everybody, everyone, nobody, no one, somebody, someone*), which are normally singular and so require singular verbs and are referred to by singular pronouns.

Example: As *each arrives* for the meeting and takes *his* seat, please hand *him* a copy of the confidential report. *Everyone is* to return *his* copy before *he* leaves. *No one* should be offended by these precautions when the importance of secrecy has been explained to *him.* I think *everybody* on the committee *understands* that *neither* of our major competitors *is* aware of the new process we have developed.

Person. Third **person** personal pronouns usually have antecedents.

> *Example:* John presented the report to the board of directors. *He* (John) first read *it* (the report) to *them* (the board of directors) and then asked for questions.

First and second person personal pronouns do not normally require antecedents.

> *Examples:* *I* like my job.
> *You* were there at the time.
> *We* all worked hard on the project.

PRONOUN REFERENCE

Avoid vague and uncertain references between a pronoun and its antecedents; this is the most common problem encountered with pronouns, especially *it* and *they.*

> *Change:* Studs and thick treads make snow tires effective; *they* are implanted with an air gun.
> *To:* Studs and thick treads make snow tires effective; *the studs* are implanted with an air gun.

> *Change:* We made the sale and delivered the product; *it* was a big one.
> *To:* We made the sale, which was a big one, and delivered the product.

The noun to which a pronoun refers must be unmistakably clear. Three basic problems are encountered in regard to pronoun references. One is an ambiguous reference, or one that can be interpreted in more than one way.

> *Change:* Jim worked with Tom on the report, but *he* wrote most of it. (Who wrote most of it, Jim or Tom?)
> *To:* Jim worked with Tom on the report, but *Tom* wrote most of it.

A general (or broad) reference, or one that has no real antecedent, is another basic problem.

> *Change:* He deals with social problems in his work; *this* helps him in his personal life.
> *To:* The fact that he deals with social problems in his work helps him in his personal life.

A hidden reference, or one that has only an implied antecedent, is the third basic problem.

> *Change:* In spite of the fact that our calculator division had researched the market thoroughly, we didn't sell *many.*

To: In spite of the fact that our calculator division had researched the market thoroughly, we didn't sell many calculators.

Or: In spite of the fact that we had thoroughly researched the market for calculators, we didn't sell *many*.

For the sake of **coherence**, pronouns should be placed as close as possible to their antecedents. The danger of creating an ambiguous reference increases with distance. Don't force your **reader** to go back too far to find out what a pronoun stands for.

Change: The *house* in the meadow at the base of the mountain range was resplendent in *its* coat of new paint.

To: The house, resplendent in *its* coat of new paint, was nestled in a meadow at the base of the mountain range.

Do not repeat an antecedent in **parentheses** following the pronoun. If you feel that you must identify the pronoun's antecedent in this way, you need to rewrite the sentence.

Change: The senior partner first met Bob Evans when he (Evans) was still a trainee.

To: Bob Evans was still a trainee when the senior partner first met him.

When making reference to a noun that includes both sexes (student, teacher, clerk, everyone), the pronouns *he* and *his* are traditionally used.

Example: Each employee is to have *his* annual X-ray taken by Friday.

However, some people feel that this conventional use of the masculine personal pronoun implies sexual bias. If there is danger of offending, it is often best to avoid the problem by substituting an **article** or changing the statement from singular to plural. (See also **he/she**.)

Examples: Each employee is to have *the* annual X-ray taken by Friday.
All employees are to have *their* annual X-rays taken by Friday.

proofreaders' marks

Publishers have established **symbols**, called proofreaders' marks, which writers and editors use to communicate with printers in the production of publications. A familiarity with these symbols makes it easy for you to edit your writing. They provide a convenient way for you to make improvements in your text without cumbersome rewriting or retyping.

Mark In Margin	Instruction	Mark On The Manuscript	Corrected Type
ℰ	Delete	the ~~lawyer's~~ bible	the bible
lawyers	Insert	The‸bible	the lawyer's bible
(stet)	Let stand	the ~~lawyer's~~ bible	the lawyer's bible
(cap)	Make Capital	the bible	the Bible
(lc)	Make lower case	the Law	the law
(ital)	Make italics	the lawyer's bible	the *lawyer's* bible
(tr)	Transpose	the⁀bible⁀lawyer's	the lawyer's bible
⌒	Close space	the Bi ble	the Bible
(sp)	spell out	②bibles	two bibles
#	Insert space	The|Bible	The Bible
¶	Start paragraph	The Bible ...	The Bible...
		¶ The lawyer's....	The lawyer's....
(run in)	No paragraph	...common proofreader's marks.⌐ Below is a	...common proofreader's marks. Below is a ....
(sc)	Set in small capitals	The bible	The BIBLE
(rom)	Set in roman type	The⟨bible⟩	The bible
(bf)	Set in boldface	The bible	The **bible**
(lf)	Set in lightface	The⟨bible⟩	The bible
⊙	Insert period	The lawyers have their own bible‸	The lawyers have their own bible.
∧	Insert comma	However‸ we cannot hope...	However, we cannot hope...
=/⌒/=⌒	Insert hyphens	half‸and‸half	half-and-half
⊙	Insert colon	We need the following‸	We need the following:
∧;	Insert semicolon	Use the law‸don't abuse the law.	Use the law; don't abuse the law.
ᵛ	Insert apostrophe	Johnˇs law book	John's law book
ᵛ/ˇ/	Insert quotation marks	The ˇlaw ˇis law.	The "law" is law.
(/)/	Insert parentheses	John's‸law‸book	John's (law) book
[/] /	Insert brackets	John ‸1920-1962‸went....	John [1920-1962] went....
1/N	Insert en dash	1920‸1962	1920-1962
1/M	Insert em dash	Out goal‸victory	Our goal—victory
ᵛ	Insert superior type	3ᵛ= 9	$3^2 = 9$
∧	Insert inferior type	H‸SO₄	$H_2 SO_4$
ᵛ	Insert asterisk	The lawᵛ	The law*
†	Insert dagger	The law‸	The law†
‡	Insert double dagger	The bible‸	The bible‡
§	Insert section symbol	‸Research	§Research

propaganda

Propaganda is the use of **persuasion** to gain advocates for an idea, a cause, a person, or an institution. This may be achieved by the skillful use of facts and figures, or it may be achieved by associating the subject with something that is generally admired. Although the word *propaganda* has acquired a negative **connotation** from its use in wartime, it is not necessarily negative. In business and industry, for example, public relations and advertising efforts are based on the principles of propaganda—to place an institution, a cause, an idea, or a product in a favorable light.

proper noun

A proper noun names a specific person, place, thing, concept, action, or quality. Therefore, proper nouns are always capitalized.

Proper Noun	Common Noun
Jim Jones	person
Chicago	city
General Electric	company
Tuesday	day
Declaration of Independence	document

For the **case** and **number** of proper nouns, see **nouns**.

proposal

A proposal is a company's offer to provide goods or services to a potential buyer within a certain amount of time and at a specified cost. The purpose of a proposal is to present a product or service in the best possible light and to offer reasons why it should be selected over competitive products or services. The very survival of some companies depends upon their ability to produce effective proposals.

Proposals fall into two broad categories, depending on the potential buyers. Commercial **sales proposals**, which are used in business and industrial sales, are as diverse as the minds of the people who prepare them; no special rules apply except that the product must not be misrepresented. **Government proposals**, which must be used in sales to government agencies, are usually prepared as a result of either an "Invitation for Bids" or a "Request for Proposals"; stringent rules are applied to the preparation of government proposals. Each type of proposal is explained in detail in its own entry.

prose

The word *prose* means speech or writing that is not in verse. The **adjective** *prosaic,* therefore, means "not poetic," suggesting matter-of-factness and straightforwardness; however, *prosaic* may also imply dullness of style or lack of imagination.

proved/proven

Both *proved* and *proven* are acceptable as the past **participle** of *prove,* although *proved* is currently in wider use.

    Examples: They had *proved* more obstinate than expected.
                  They had *proven* more obstinate than expected.

Proven is the more commonly used as an **adjective**.

    Example: She was hired because of her *proven* competence as a manager.

pseudo/quasi

As a **prefix**, *pseudo,* meaning "false or counterfeit," is joined to a word without a **hyphen** unless the word begins with a **capital letter**.

    Examples: *Pseudo*science (false science), *pseudo*-Americanism (pretended Americanism)

Pseudo is sometimes confused with *quasi,* meaning "somewhat" or "partial." Unlike *semi, quasi* does not mean half. *Quasi* is usually hyphenated in combinations.

    Example: *quasi*-scientific literature

(See also **bi-/semi-**.)

punctuation

Punctuation is a system of **symbols** that help the **reader** understand the structural relationship within (and the intention of) a **sentence**. Marks of punctuation may link, separate, enclose, indicate omissions, terminate, and classify sentences. Most of the thirteen punctuation marks can perform more than one function. The use of punctuation is determined by grammatical conventions and the writer's intention —in fact, punctuation often substitutes for the writer's facial expressions. Misuse of punctuation can cause your reader to misunderstand your meaning. The following are the thirteen marks of punctuation.

apostrophe	'
brackets	[ ]
colon	:
comma	,
dash	—
exclamation mark	!
slash	/
hyphen	-
parentheses	( )
period	. (including ellipses and leaders)
question mark	?
quotation marks	" " (includes ditto marks)
semicolon	;

Detailed information on each mark of punctuation is given in its own entry.

Q

question mark

The question mark (?) has the following distinct uses.

1. Use a question mark to end a **sentence** that is a direct question.

Example: Where did you put the specification?

2. Use a question mark to end any statement with an interrogative meaning (a statement that is declarative in form but asks a question).

Example: The report is finished?

3. Use a question mark to end an interrogative **clause** within a declarative sentence.

Example: It was not until July (or was it August?) that we submitted the report.

4. Use a question mark in a title that is really an interrogative clause or sentence.

Example: *Should Engineers Be Writers?* is the title of her book.

5. When used with **quotations**, the question mark may indicate whether the writer who is doing the quoting or the person being quoted is asking the question. When the writer doing the quoting asks the question, the question mark is outside the **quotation marks**.

Example: Did she say, "I don't think the project should continue"?

If, on the other hand, the quotation itself is a question, the question mark goes inside the quotation marks.

Example: She asked, "When will we go?"

If the writer doing the quoting and the person being quoted both ask questions, use a single question mark inside the quotation marks.

Example: Did she ask, "Will you go in my place?"

6. Question marks may follow a series of separate items within an interrogative sentence.

Example: Do you remember the date of the contract? its terms? whether you signed it?

7. A question mark should never be used at the end of an indirect question.

Change: He asked me whether sales had increased this year?
To: He asked me whether sales had increased this year.

8. When a directive or command is phrased as a question, a question mark is usually not used. However, a request (to a customer or a superior, for instance) would almost always require a question mark.

Examples: Will you please make sure that the books are balanced by January.
Will you please let me know if there is any way in which our Customer Service Department can assist you?

questionnaire

A questionnaire is actually an **interview** on paper. It is used when those to be interviewed are too numerous for personal interviews or when they are scattered geographically.

The questionnaire has several advantages over a personal interview.

1. The persons responding have more time to consider their answers, which may therefore be more thoughtful.
2. The questionnaire reduces the possibility that the interviewer might directly influence an answer.
3. Recipients are more accessible by mail than they are for a personal interview.
4. The questionnaire eliminates the problem of geographic limitations.
5. The cost of the questionnaire is low compared with the cost of numerous personal interviews.

The questionnaire also has disadvantages.

1. The interviewer cannot follow up on the answer to a question; that is, an unanticipated answer to one question might logically lead to another question in a personal interview.
2. Those recipients who have strong feelings about the subject are more likely to reply than those who do not, thereby possibly slanting the results.
3. The process of mailing questionnaires and waiting for replies takes considerably longer than personal interviews.

An important point to remember in creating a questionnaire is to keep it brief. Remember that the longer the questionnaire is, the less likely the recipient will be to complete and return it.

Try to ask questions that can be answered easily with a simple "yes" or "no," or with a check mark beside the appropriate answer. Avoid asking the recipient to compose written answers to your specific questions; this reduces your chances of receiving a reply, and makes it difficult to evaluate with validity those that you do receive.

Make certain that your questions are not ambiguous and that multiple-choice questions are not too limited in the responses provided. The limited choice given for the following question illustrates this point.

> *Example:* Certain steps have been taken by government to remedy our economic difficulties. How would you describe your outlook now regarding the future of the economy?
> (a) _____ Good   (b) _____ Bad

Once recognized, this problem can easily be corrected, as in the following revision.

Example: Certain steps have been taken by government to remedy our economic difficulties. How would you describe your outlook now regarding the future of the economy?

(a) _____ Very Optimistic   (b) _____ Optimistic
(c) _____ Pessimistic   (d) _____ Very Pessimistic
(e) _____ Neutral   (f) _____ Undecided

When formulating your questions, remember that you must eventually tabulate the answers. Therefore, design your questions to provide answers that can be tabulated accurately.

There are certain advantages to putting your questions in a logical sequence. If you group your questions by subject matter, you are more likely to get your respondents' best thinking and to avoid discouraging them, especially if the questionnaire is somewhat long.

Finally, your questionnaire should give recipients the opportunity to include further comments if they choose to do so, as a courtesy to them and as a clarification of their general attitude toward the subject.

If such information will be of value in interpreting the results of the questionnaire, include questions about the recipient's age, education, occupation, and so on. Also include your name, address, telephone number, the purpose of the questionnaire, and the date by which an answer is needed.

If you mail your questionnaire, be sure to include a cover letter explaining who you are, the purpose of the questionnaire, what the questionnaire will be used for, and the date by which you must receive a reply. Above all, be sure to include a stamped, self-addressed envelope. Mail the questionnaire either first-class or air mail. (Third-class or fourth-class might imply that you don't consider the questionnaire important, in addition to being too slow to be practical.)

Example:
QUESTIONNAIRE

William Patrick
3415 Idlewilde Blvd.
Slippery Rock, Pa. 60752
Phone: 523-2313

For a report on air pollution for a Clark Institute course, English 202

1. How many miles do you drive in a year? Check one.
   _____ 5,000   _____ 7,500   _____ 10,000   _____ 12,500   _____ 15,000

2. How many times each year do you have your car tuned?
   Circle: 1   2   3   4   None

3. Do you find less smoke coming from your exhaust after your car is tuned?
Check one.
_____ Yes _____ No _____ No difference

4. Have you talked with your mechanic about the problem of air pollution as it relates to a well-tuned car? Check one.
_____ Yes _____ No

5. If the answer to question 4 was "Yes," was his attitude:
_____ Cooperative _____ Uninterested _____ Evasive _____ Irritated
Comments: _____
_____
_____

Please return by April 10.

quid pro quo

Quid pro quo, which is Latin for "one thing for another," can suggest "mutual cooperation" or "tit for tat" in a relationship between two groups or individuals. The term may be appropriate to business and legal contexts if you are sure your **reader** understands its meaning.

>   *Example:*   It would be unwise to grant their request without insisting on some *quid pro quo.*

quotation marks

Quotation marks (" ") are used to enclose direct repetition of spoken or written words. They should not be used as a means of **emphasis** under normal circumstances. There are a variety of guidelines for using quotation marks.

1. Enclose in quotation marks anything that is quoted word for word (direct quotation) from speech.

>   *Example:*   She said clearly, "I want the progress report by three o'clock."

2. Do not enclose indirect **quotations**—usually introduced by *that* —in quotation marks. Indirect quotations are **paraphrases** of a speaker's words or ideas.

>   *Example:*   She said that she wanted the progress report by three o'clock.

3. Handle quotations from written material the same way: place direct quotations within quotation marks, but not indirect quotations.

Examples: The report stated, "The potential in Florida for our franchise is as great as in California."

The report indicated that the potential for our franchise is as great in Florida as in California.

4. Quotations longer than five typed lines are normally indented (*all* the lines) five spaces from the left margin, single-spaced, and *not* enclosed in quotation marks.

5. Unless it is indented as described in guideline 4, a quotation of more than one paragraph is given a quotation mark at the beginning of each new paragraph, but at the end of only the last paragraph.

6. Use single quotation marks (on a typewriter use the **apostrophe** key) to enclose a quotation that appears within a quotation.

Example: John said, "Jane told me that she was going to 'hang tough' until the deadline is past."

7. Slang, colloquial expressions, and attempts at humor, although infrequent in business and technical writing in any case, seldom rate being set off by quotation marks.

Change: Our first six months in the new office amounted to little more than a "shakedown cruise" for what lay ahead.

To: Our first six months in the new office amounted to little more than a shakedown cruise for what lay ahead.

8. Use quotation marks to set off special words or technical terms only to point out that the term is used in context for a unique or special purpose (used, that is, in the sense of *the so-called*).

Examples: The "plumbers," a White House undercover organization, was set up to stop "leaks."

The conversion of glucose to ethyl alcohol and carbon dioxide is an example of "glycolysis" (which, in Greek, means, loosely, "the breaking up of sugar") and, to emphasize the fact that it takes place "without air," it is often called "anaerobic glycolysis," "anaerobic" meaning "without air" in Greek.

—Isaac Asimov, *Life and Energy* (New York: Avon Books, 1972), p. 276.

9. Use quotation marks to enclose titles of short stories, articles, essays, radio and television programs, short musical works, paintings, and other art works.

Example: Did you see the article "No-Fault Insurance and Your Motorcycle" in last Sunday's *Journal*?

Titles of books and periodicals are underlined (to be typeset in **italics**).

> *Example:* Articles in the *Business Education Forum* and *Scientific American* quoted the same passage.

Some titles, by convention, are neither set off by quotation marks nor underlined, although they are capitalized.

> *Examples:* the Bible, the Constitution, Lincoln's Gettysburg Address, the Montgomery-Ward Catalog, the Denver Telephone Directory

10. **Commas** and **periods** always go inside closing quotation marks.

> *Example:* The "plumbers," a White House undercover organization, was set up to stop "leaks."

11. **Semicolons** and **colons** always go outside closing quotation marks.

> *Examples:* He said, "I will pay the full amount"; this was a real surprise to us.
> The following are her favorite "sports": eating and sleeping.

12. All other **punctuation** follows the logic of the context: if the punctuation is a part of the material quoted, it goes inside the quotation marks; if the punctuation is not part of the material quoted, it goes outside the quotation marks.

13. Quotation marks may be used as ditto marks, instead of repeating a line of words or numbers directly beneath an identical set.

> *Example:* A is at a point equally distant from L and M.
> B " " " " " " " S and T.
> C " " " " " " " R and Q.

In **formal writing**, this use is confined to **tables** and lists.

quotations

When you have borrowed words, facts, or ideas of any kind from someone else's work, acknowledge your debt by giving your source credit in a **footnote**. Otherwise, you are guilty of **plagiarism**. Also be sure that you have represented the original material honestly and accurately.

DIRECT QUOTATIONS

Direct word-for-word quotations are enclosed in **quotation marks**. They are usually, although not always, separated from the rest of the **sentence** in which they occur either by a **comma** or a **colon**.

Examples: The noted economist says, "If monopolies could be made to behave as if they were perfectly competitive, we would be able to enjoy the benefits both of large-scale efficiency and of the perfectly working price mechanism." (with comma)

The noted economist points out that there are three options available "when technical conditions make a monopoly the natural outcome of competitive market forces: private monopoly, public monopoly, or public regulation." (without comma)

INDIRECT QUOTATIONS

Indirect quotations, which are essentially paraphrases and are usually introduced by *that,* are not set off from the rest of the sentence by a punctuation mark.

Examples: He said in a recent interview, "Regulation cannot supply the dynamic stimulus that in other industries is supplied by competition." (direct quotation)

In a recent interview he said that regulation does not stimulate the industry as well as competition does. (indirect quotation)

Where a quotation is divided, the material which interrupts the quotation is set off, before and after, by commas, and quotation marks are used around each part of the quotation.

Example: "Regulation," he said in a recent interview, "cannot supply the dynamic stimulus that in other industries is supplied by competition."

At the end of a quoted passage, commas and **periods** go inside the quotation marks, and colons and **semicolons** go outside the quotation marks.

DELETIONS OR OMISSIONS

Deletions or omissions from quoted material are indicated by three **ellipsis** dots within a sentence and four ellipsis dots at the end of a sentence, the first of the four dots being the period that ends the sentence.

Example: "If monopolies could be made to behave . . . we would be able to enjoy the benefits of . . . large-scale efficiency. . . ."

When a quoted passage begins in the middle of a sentence rather than at the beginning, however, ellipsis dots are not necessary; the fact that the first letter of the quoted material is not capitalized tells the **reader** that the quotation begins in mid-sentence.

Change: He goes on to conclude that " . . . coordination may lessen competition within a region."

> *To:*   He goes on to conclude that "coordination may lessen competition within a region."

Such quotations should be worked into one of your sentences rather than left standing alone. Where quoted material is worked into a sentence, be sure that it is related logically, grammatically, and syntactically to the rest of the sentence.

INSERTING MATERIAL INTO QUOTATIONS

When it is necessary to insert a clarifying comment within quoted material, use **brackets**.

> *Example:*   "The industry is organized as a relatively large, integrated system serving an extensive [geographic] area, with smaller systems existing as islands within the larger system's sphere of influence."

When quoted material contains an obvious error, or might in some other way be questioned, the expression *sic,* enclosed in brackets, follows the questionable material to indicate that the writer has quoted the material exactly as it appeared in the original. (See also **sic**.)

> *Example:*   In *Basic Astronomy,* Professor Jones notes that the "earth does not revolve around the son [sic] at a constant rate."

INCORPORATING QUOTATIONS

Depending on the length, there are two mechanical methods of incorporating quotations into your text. Quotations of five lines or less are incorporated into your text and enclosed in quotation marks. (Many writers use this method regardless of length. When this method is used with multiple **paragraphs**, quotation marks appear at the beginning of each new paragraph, but at the end of only the last paragraph.) Material longer than five lines is now usually inset; that is, it is set off from the body of the text by being indented five spaces from the left margin and by triple spacing above and below the quotation. The quoted passage is single-spaced and not enclosed in quotation marks.

OVERQUOTING

Do not rely too heavily on the use of quotations in the final version of your **report** or paper. If you do, your work will appear merely derivative. The temptation to overquote during the **note-taking** phase of your **research** can be avoided if you concentrate on summarizing what you read. Quote word-for-word only where your source concisely sums up a great deal of information or points to a trend or development important to your subject. As a rule of thumb, avoid quoting anything over one paragraph.

R

raise/rise

Raise, used as a **transitive verb**, principally means "to lift something."

Example: If we cannot lower costs, we must *raise* our prices.

Rise, an **intransitive verb**, means "to go upward by one's (or its) own power."

Example: If the President signs the bill, the stock market will *rise.*

rarely ever

In the **phrase** *rarely ever,* the word *ever* is redundant and should be deleted.

Change: I *rarely ever* leave the office before 5:15.
I *rarely* leave the office before 5:15.

re

Re (and its variant form *in re*) is business and legal **jargon** meaning "in reference to" or "in the case of." *Re* is sometimes used in **memorandums**.

Example: To: Elaine Barr
From: Edgar Roden
Re: Revised Office Procedures

Re, however, is now giving way to *subject.*

Example: To: Elaine Barr
From: Edgar Roden
Subject: Revised Office Procedures

reader

If you are writing, you must expect to have a reader, or audience. If you have a reader, you must show him a certain amount of consideration by knowing who he is (his educational level, his technical knowledge, and his needs relative to your subject). Your reader's level of technical knowledge should determine whether you need to cover the fundamentals of your subject and which terms you must define (see also **defining terms**). What you know about your reader (in addition to what you know about your **objective** and your **scope**) will partially determine whether you use a **formal** or an **informal writing style**; it will determine the **tone** of your writing and the **point of view** you adopt.

The first rule of effective writing is to help the reader; you must accept this commitment if you wish to communicate your knowledge to your reader. Do not assume that the reader understands your subject. Keep his convenience in mind at all times; remember that he cannot benefit from your facial expressions, voice inflections, and gestures. Your primary job, therefore, is to help your reader by anticipating his reactions to your words.

When writing for a small audience, you will probably know all of its members; select one person from this group and write to that person. Above all, whether your audience is large or small, never try to write without writing *to* someone.

When you write for a large audience, create a composite profile of a reader and write to him. To do this, you must determine such things as the average educational level of your audience, its average level of technical knowledge, its collective attitude toward your subject, and so on.

Your commitment to helping your reader is most important; if you do not accept this commitment, you are not likely to get your message across.

reason is because

The **phrase** *reason is because* is a colloquial expression to be avoided in writing. *Because,* which in this phrase only repeats the notion of cause, should be replaced by *that.*

> *Change:* Sales have increased more than 20 percent. The *reason is because* our sales force has been more aggressive this year.

> *To:* Sales have increased more than 20 percent. The *reason is that* our sales force has been more aggressive this year.
>
> *Or:* Sales have increased more than 20 percent this year *because* our sales force has been more aggressive.

reciprocal pronoun

The reciprocal pronouns, *one another* and *each other,* indicate the relationship between two or more persons or things. When referring to two persons or things, use *each other.*

> *Example:* The two partners often disagreed with *each other.*

When referring to more than two persons or things, use *one another.*

> *Example:* The three vice-presidents talked to *one another* for an hour.

reference books

The following list provides basic sources for **library research** and general reference, although it is not intended to be exhaustive.

ABSTRACT JOURNALS

Chemical Abstracts. 1907—. (Arranged by subject and issued semi-monthly)

Dissertation Abstracts. Ann Arbor, Michigan: University Microfilms, 1952—. (Issued monthly; since 1966, Part B has been devoted to works in science and engineering)

Engineering Index. 1906—. (Arranged by subject and issued monthly)

A Guide to World Abstracting and Indexing Services in Science and Technology. Washington, D.C.: National Federation of Science Abstracting Services, 1963. (Indexed by subject and country)

International Aerospace Abstracts. 1961—. (Arranged by subject and issued semimonthly)

Journal of Economic Abstracts. Cambridge, Mass.: Harvard University Press, 1963—. (Subject index in each quarterly issue)

Metals Abstracts. Metals Park, Ohio: American Society of Metals, 1968 —. (Issued monthly)

Science Abstracts. 1898—. (Sections arranged by subject, with author and conference indexes, and issued semimonthly)

> *Section A – Physics Abstracts.* 1898—.
>
> *Section B – Electrical and Electronic Abstracts.* 1898—.
>
> *Section C – Computer and Control Abstracts.* 1966—.

ATLASES

National Geographic Atlas of the World. 4th ed. Washington, D.C.: National Geographic Society, 1975.

Rand McNally Commercial Atlas and Marketing Guide. 101st ed. Chicago: Rand McNally, 1970. (Updated annually)

Times Atlas of the World: Comprehensive Edition. London: London Times, 1975.

BIBLIOGRAPHIES

Besterman, Theodore. *A World Bibliography of Bibliographies.* 4th ed. 5 vols. Lausanne: Rowan, 1963.

Bibliographic Index: A Cumulative Bibliography of Bibliographies. New York: H. W. Wilson Co., 1937—. (Updated annually)

Philler, Theresa Ammennito, et al., eds. *An Annotated Bibliography on Technical Writing, Editing, Graphics, and Publishing 1950–1965.* Washington, D.C., and Pittsburgh: The Society of Technical Writers and Publishers, Inc., and the Carnegie Library of Pittsburgh, 1966.

Vertical File Index of Pamphlets. New York: H. W. Wilson Co., 1935—. (Subject and title index of selected pamphlets that is updated annually)

BIOGRAPHY

Biographical Index. New York: H. W. Wilson Co., 1946–1973. (A cumulative index to biographical material in books and magazines, arranged alphabetically and indexed by profession and occupation)

Jaques Cattell Press, ed. *American Men and Women of Science.* New York: R. R. Bowker Co., 1973.

Current Biography Yearbooks. New York: H. W. Wilson Co., 1940—. (Various editions for special fields)

Who's Who in America. Chicago: A. N. Marquis Co., 1899—. (A standard biographical reference work that is updated every two years)

BOOK GUIDES

Books in Print. New York: R. R. Bowker Co. (Lists author, title, publication data, edition, price, and is issued annually)

Cumulative Book Index. New York: H. W. Wilson Co., 1928—. (Lists all books published in English, with author, title, and subject listings arranged alphabetically and is issued annually with updated monthly supplements)

New Technical Books. New York: New York Public Library, 1915—. (Annotated selections, arranged by subject and updated bimonthly)

Proceedings in Print. Mattapan, Mass.: Special Libraries Association, 1964—. (Availability of conference proceedings announced, with citation, subject, agency, and price, and updated bimonthly)

BOOK REVIEWS

Book Review Digest. New York: H. W. Wilson Co., 1905—. (Authors listed alphabetically, with subject and title indexes. Issued monthly and accumulated annually)

Technical Book Review Index. New York: Special Libraries Association, 1935—. (Guide to reviews in scientific, technical, and trade journals, and is issued monthly except during July and August)

COMMERCIAL GUIDES

Encyclopedia of Associations. 9th ed. 3 vols. Detroit: Gale Research Co., 1975. (A supplement, *New Associations and Projects,* is published quarterly)

MacRae's Blue Book. 5 vols. New York: MacRae's Blue Book Co., 1975. (A buying directory for industrial material and equipment that is updated annually)

Thomas Register of American Manufacturers. 11 vols. New York: Thomas Publishing Co., 1905—. (Updated monthly)

DICTIONARIES

For desk dictionaries and unabridged dictionaries, see **dictionary**.

DISSERTATIONS

Dissertation Abstracts. Ann Arbor, Michigan: University Microfilms, 1952—. (Issued monthly; since 1966, Part B has been devoted to works in science and engineering)

ENCYCLOPEDIAS

Encyclopaedia Britannica. Chicago: Encyclopaedia Britannica Educational Corporation, 1974.

Encyclopedia Americana. New York: Grolier, Inc., 1975.

Gray, Peter, ed. *Encyclopedia of Biological Sciences.* 2nd ed. New York: Van Nostrand Reinhold Co., 1970.

McGraw-Hill Encyclopedia of Science and Technology. 3rd ed. New York: McGraw-Hill Book Company, 1971.

Newman, James R., ed. *Harper Encyclopedia of Science.* Rev. ed. New York: Harper & Row, 1967.

Sills, Donald L., ed. *International Encyclopedia of the Social Sciences.* New York: Macmillan, 1968.

FACTBOOKS AND ALMANACS

The Budget in Brief. Washington, D.C.: U.S. Bureau of the Budget, Government Printing Office. (A condensed version of the annual federal budget)

Demographic Yearbook. New York: United Nations Statistical Office, United Nations, 1949—. (An annual publication of information on all facets of world population)

Economic Almanac. New York: National Industrial Conference Board, 1940—. (Updated every two years and contains information on prices, resources, transportation involved in manufacturing)

Facts on File. New York: Person's Index, Inc., 1941—. (A weekly digest of world news, updated annually)

Statistical Abstract of the United States. Washington, D.C.: U.S. Bureau of the Census, Government Printing Office, 1879—. (An annual publication that summarizes data on industrial, political, social, and economic organizations in the United States)

GOVERNMENT PUBLICATIONS

Government Reports Announcements. Springfield, Va.: National Technical Information Service, 1946—. (A weekly listing of federally sponsored research reports arranged by subject)

Government Reports Index. Springfield, Va.: National Technical Information Service, 1965—. (A semimonthly index of reports arranged by subject, author, and report number)

Monthly Catalog of U.S. Government Publications. Washington, D.C.: Government Printing Office, 1895—. (Lists nonclassified publications of all federal agencies by subject, author, and catchword—also gives ordering instructions)

Monthly Checklist of State Publications. Washington, D.C.: Government Printing Office, 1940—. (State government publications arranged by state with an annual subject and title index)

Schmeckebier, Laurence F., and Roy B. Eastin. *Government Publications and Their Use.* Rev. ed. Washington, D.C.: Brookings Institution 1969. (A guide for locating government publications—types of publications also discussed)

GRAPHICS

Arkin, Herbert, and Raymond R. Colton. *Statistical Methods.* 5th ed. New York: Barnes & Noble Books, 1970. (See Chapter xx)

Levens, A. S. *Graphics: Analysis and Conceptual Design.* New York: John Wiley and Sons, Inc., 1968.

Nelms, Haenning. *Thinking with a Pencil.* New York: Barnes & Noble Books, 1964.

LANGUAGE USAGE

Bernstein, Theodore M. *The Careful Writer: A Guide to English Usage.* New York: Atheneum Press, 1965.

Copperud, Roy H. *American Usage: The Consensus.* New York: Van Nostrand Reinhold Co., 1970. (Compares a number of usage authorities—arranged alphabetically by entries)

Nicholson, Margaret. *A Dictionary of American English Usage.* New York: The New American Library, 1958. (Based on Fowler's *Modern English Usage*)

LOGIC

Beardsley, Monroe C. *Thinking Straight.* 3rd ed. Englewood Cliffs, N.J.: Prentice-Hall, Inc., 1966.

Brennan, Joseph G. *A Handbook of Logic.* 2nd ed. New York: Harper & Row, 1961.

Copi, Irving M. *Introduction to Logic.* 4th ed. New York: Macmillan, 1972.

PARLIAMENTARY PROCEDURE

Robert, Henry M. et al. *Robert's Rules of Order.* Newly rev. ed. by Sarah Corbin Robert, et al. Glenview, Ill.: Scott, Foresman and Company, 1970.

PERIODICAL INDEXES

Applied Science and Technology Index. New York: H. W. Wilson Co., 1958—. (Alphabetical subject list of over 50,000 periodicals issued monthly)

Business Periodicals Index. New York: H. W. Wilson Co., 1958—. (Arranged by subject and title and issued monthly)

International Bibliography of Economics. Chicago: Aldine-Atherton, Inc., 1960—. (Indexed by subject and author and issued monthly)

New York Times Index. New York: New York Times, 1913—. (Monthly index and summary of material from *The New York Times* —alphabetized by subject, personal, and organizational names)

Readers' Guide to Periodical Literature. New York: H. W. Wilson Co., 1900—. (Monthly index of general U.S. periodicals arranged alphabetically by subject)

Ulrich's International Periodicals Directory: A Classified Guide to Current Periodicals, Foreign and Domestic. 16th ed. New York: R. R. Bowker Co., 1975. (Alphabetical subject list of over 50,000 periodicals)

SECRETARIAL HANDBOOKS

Doris, Lillian, and Bessemay Miller. *The Complete Secretary's Handbook.* 3rd ed. Englewood Cliffs, N.J.: Prentice-Hall, Inc., 1970.

Gavin, Ruth, and William Sabin. *Reference Manual for Stenographers and Typists.* 4th ed. New York: McGraw-Hill Book Co., 1970.

SEMANTICS

Hayakawa, S. I. *Language in Thought and Action.* 3rd ed. New York: Harcourt Brace Jovanovich, Inc., 1972.

SPEECH AND GROUP DISCUSSION

Capp, Glen R. *Basic Oral Communication.* Englewood Cliffs, N.J.: Prentice-Hall, Inc., 1971.

Harnack, R. Victor, and Thorrel B. Fest. *Group Discussion*. New York: Appleton-Century-Crofts, 1964.

Maier, Norman. *Problem-Solving Discussions and Conferences*. New York: McGraw-Hill Book Co., 1963.

Rogge, Robert. *Advanced Public Speaking*. New York: Holt, Rinehart and Winston, Inc., 1966.

Wilcox, Roger P. *Oral Reporting in Business and Industry*. Englewood Cliffs, N.J.: Prentice-Hall, Inc., 1967.

(See also **oral report**.)

STYLE MANUALS

CBE Style Manual. 3rd ed. Washington, D.C.: American Institute of Biological Sciences, 1972. (Formerly called *Style Manual for Biological Journals*)

Government Printing Office Style Guide. Washington, D.C.: Government Printing Office.

A Manual of Style. 12th ed. Chicago: The University of Chicago Press, 1969. (Comprehensive guide to preparing manuscripts, copy editing, proofreading, format, and related topics)

Style Book and Editorial Manual. 5th ed. Chicago: Scientific Publications Division, American Medical Association, 1971.

Style Manual for Guidance in the Preparation of Papers. 2nd ed. New York: American Institute of Physics, 1967.

SUBJECT GUIDES

Corman, Edwin, ed. *Sources of Business Information*. 2nd ed. Berkeley, Calif.: University of California Press, 1964.

Jenkins, Frances B. *Science Reference Sources*. 5th ed. Cambridge, Mass.: MIT Press, 1969.

Malinovsky, Harold R., and D. Gray. *Science and Engineering Literature: A Guide to Current Reference Sources*. 2nd ed. Littleton, Colorado: Libraries Unlimited, no date set.

SYNONYMS

Dutch, Robert A., ed. *The Original Roget's Thesaurus of English Words and Phrases*. New ed. St. Martin's Press, Inc., 1965.

Roget, Peter M. *Roget's Inernational Thesaurus*. 3rd ed. New York: Thomas Y. Crowell Co., 1962.

reflexive pronoun

A reflexive pronoun, which always ends with the **suffix** *-self* or *selves*, indicates that the **subject** of the sentence acts upon itself.

Example: The secretary cut *himself* with the letter opener.

The reflexive form of the **pronoun** may also be used as an intensive to give **emphasis** to its antecedent.

Example: I collected the data *myself*.

The reflexive and intensive pronouns are *myself, yourself, himself, herself, itself, oneself, ourselves, yourselves, themselves.*

Never use a reflexive pronoun as a subject or as a substitute for a subject.

Change: Joe and *myself* worked all day on it.
To: Joe and *I* worked all day on it.

A common mistake is substituting a reflexive pronoun for *me* in a compound element.

Change: He gave it to my assistant and *myself*.
To: He gave it to my assistant and *me*.

relative adjective

Like **relative pronouns**, the relative adjectives *(whose, which,* and *what)* are pronoun forms that link **dependent clauses** to main **clauses**. The difference is that relative pronouns perform this linking function while taking the place of **nouns** but relative adjectives perform this linking function while *modifying* (describing) nouns. Some examples of the use of relative adjectives follow.

Examples: The president commended the managers *whose* divisions were the most profitable. (*whose* modifies "divisions")

He also told us *which* divisions needed to show the greatest improvement. (*which* modifies "divisions")

Finally, he told us *what* steps we should take to improve our profits. (*what* modifies "steps")

relative pronoun

Relative **pronouns** (the most common are *who, whom, which, what,* and *that*) perform a dual function: they substitute for a **noun** while linking the **dependent clause** in which they appear to a main **clause**. (Relative pronouns differ in use from **relative adjectives**, which are pronouns in form and have a similar linking function, but which *modify* [describe] nouns.) Some examples of the use of relative pronouns follow.

> *Examples:* The specifications were sent to the Engineering Manager, *who* immediately approved them. (*who* substitutes for "Engineering Manager")
>
> The project was assigned to Ed Cone, *whom* everyone respects for his skill as a designer. (*whom* substitutes for "Ed Cone")
>
> The customer's main objection, *which* can probably be overcome, is to the high cost of installation. (*which* substitutes for "objection")
>
> The memo from Martha Goldstein *that* you received yesterday sets forth the most important points. (*that* substitutes for "memo")
>
> We invited the committee to come and see *what* was being done about the poor lighting. (*what,* though it stands for no specific noun, substitutes for a noun as the subject of the dependent clause "*what* was being done . . . ," which it also links to the main clause)

The relative pronoun *who (whom)* normally refers to a person, *which* normally refers to a thing, and *that* can refer to either.

Relative pronouns can often be omitted.

> *Example:* I received the handcrafted ornament (that) I ordered.

repetition

EFFECTIVE USE

The deliberate use of repetition to build a sustained effect or emphasize a feeling or idea can be quite powerful.

> *Example:* Similarly, atoms *come and go* in a molecule, but the molecule *remains*; molecules *come and go* in a cell, but the cell *remains*; cells *come and go* in a body, but the body *remains*; persons *come and go* in an organization, but the organization *remains.*
>
> —Kenneth Boulding, *Beyond Economics* (Ann Arbor: University of Michigan Press, 1968), p. 131.

Repeating key words from a previous **sentence** or **paragraph** can also be used effectively to achieve **transition**.

Example: For many years, *oil* has been a major industrial energy source. However, *oil* supplies are limited, and other sources of energy must be developed.

INEFFECTIVE USE

Purposeless repetition, however, makes a sentence awkward and hides its key ideas.

Change: He *said that* the customer *said that* the order was canceled.
To: He *said that* the customer canceled the order.

The harm caused to your writing by careless repetition is not limited to words and **phrases**; the needless repetition of ideas can be equally damaging.

Change: In this modern world of ours today, the well-informed, knowledgeable executive will be well ahead of the competition.
To: To succeed, the contemporary executive must be well informed.

(See also **conciseness/wordiness**.)

reports

Much of the writing business and technical people do consists of reports of one kind or another. Whether the project at hand is a formal report, an informal memo, a progress report, a trip report, or a report on the results of a series of tests, application of the sequential steps presented in the Checklist of the Writing Process will serve you well. To write a successful report, you must first get clearly in mind your **readers**, your **objective**, and the **scope** of your coverage.

The **formal report** is normally used only for very large and important reports; consequently, it is quite elaborate, with a cover, a title page, a **table of contents**, and even **appendixes**.

The **progress report**, which is written periodically to report the current status of a project, is often used by management to adjust manpower assignments, schedules, and budget allocations.

The **trip report** is used to record the purpose of a business trip and its achievements. It provides needed information to management in addition to justifying the cost of the trip.

The **laboratory report** includes the reasons for a test, equipment and procedures used, problems encountered, and conclusions and recommendations resulting from the test. The most important aspects of this type of report are completeness and accuracy.

The **annual report** describes a company's financial condition and usually highlights its present strengths and suggests the directions its operations will take in the coming year.

Although **police reports** are typed on printed forms, the reporting police officer must nonetheless "tell what happened," which means that writing skill can make the difference between a mediocre report and a good one.

Business and technical people are often called upon to deliver **oral reports** on such things as market research and laboratory experiments, to chair committees, to lead panel discussions, and so on. Since being required to speak publicly in such circumstances is common, it is important to know how to plan and deliver an oral presentation.

The **memorandum** is generally used for reports within an organization. Its **tone** is often informal, and it is usually relatively brief (although it may be either narrow or broad in scope). (See also **format**.)

research

As part of the writing process, research follows **preparation** (determining the **reader, objective**, and **scope**). Research for a writing project may consist of using published material (see **library research**), experimental data (see **laboratory report**), or information from interviews and your own experience (see **interviewing** and **questionnaire**). The best research will be wasted, however, if the steps of the writing process are not carefully followed. (See the Checklist of the Writing Process.)

Certain journals—such as *Geographical Abstracts, Aeronautical Engineering Index, Journal of Economic Abstracts, Chemical Abstracts,* and *Index Medicus*—are devoted exclusively to **abstracts** of articles in professional journals and government and industrial reports; these journals save researchers time by allowing them to scan large portions of the literature in a specialized field quickly. (See also **reference books**.)

respective/respectively

Respective, an **adjective**, means "pertaining to two or more things regarded individually."

Example: The committee members prepared their *respective* reports.

Respectively is the **adverb** form of *respective,* meaning "singly, in the order designated."

Example: The first, second, and third prizes in the sales contest were awarded to Maria Juarez, Gloria Hinds, and Margot Luce, respectively.

Respective and *respectively* are often unnecessary because the meaning of individuality is already clear.

Change: The committee members prepared their *respective* reports.
To: Each committee member prepared his report.

restrictive and nonrestrictive elements

Modifying **phrases** and **clauses** may be either restrictive or nonrestrictive. A nonrestrictive phrase or clause provides additional information about what it modifies, but it does not limit, or restrict, the meaning of what it modifies. Therefore, the nonrestrictive phrase or clause could actually be removed from its **sentence** without changing the essential meaning of the sentence. It is, in effect, a parenthetical element, and so it is set off by commas to show its loose relationship with the rest of the sentence.

Examples: This instrument, *called a backscatter gauge,* fires beta particles at an object and counts the particles that bounce back. (nonrestrictive phrase)
The annual report, *which was distributed yesterday,* shows that sales increased 20 percent last year. (nonrestrictive clause)

A restrictive phrase or clause limits, or restricts, the meaning of what it modifies. If it were removed from its sentence, the essential meaning of the sentence would be changed. Because a restrictive phrase or clause is so essential to the meaning of the sentence, it is never set off by commas.

Examples: All employees *wishing to donate blood* may take Thursday afternoon off. (restrictive phrase)
Companies *that adopt the plan* nearly always show profit increases. (restrictive clause)

It is extremely important for writers to distinguish carefully between nonrestrictive and restrictive elements. The same sentence can take on two entirely different meanings depending on whether a modifying element is set off by commas (because nonrestrictive) or not set off (because restrictive). The results of a slip by the writer can be not only misleading but downright embarrassing.

Change: I think you will be impressed by our systems engineers who are thoroughly experienced in projects like yours. (The logical implication is that "you may not be so impressed by our other, less experienced, systems engineers.")

To: I think you will be impressed by our systems engineers, who are thoroughly experienced in projects like yours.

résumé

The résumé is, in effect, a catalog of what you have to offer prospective employers. As such, it is the basis for their decision to invite you for a personal interview. It tells them who you are, what you know, what you can do, what you have done, and what your job objectives are. It will serve as the focus for the interview because prospective employers can base specific questions on the information contained in it. It will also help them evaluate your interview after your departure by serving as an organized reminder of what you covered orally during the interview. The résumé, then, is an important document that deserves careful planning and execution.

Three steps are involved in preparing and using a résumé effectively. The first is to analyze yourself and your background; the second is to organize and prepare the résumé; the third is to identify those to whom you will submit the résumé.

The starting point in preparing a résumé is a thorough analysis of three categories: (1) your experience, (2) your education and training, and (3) your personal traits. List the major points for each category before actually beginning to organize and write your résumé.

EXPERIENCE

List all your employment—full-time, part-time, vacation jobs, and freelance work—and analyze each job on the basis of the following list of questions.

1. What was the job title?
2. What did you do (in reasonable detail)?
3. What experience did you gain that you can apply to another job?
4. Why were you hired for the job?

5. What special skills did you develop on that job?
6. Why did you leave it?
7. When did you start and when did you leave the job?
8. Would your former employer give you a reference?
9. What special traits were required of you on the job (initiative, leadership, ability to work with details, ability to work with people, imagination, ability to organize, etc.)?

EDUCATION

For the applicant with little work experience, such as a recent graduate, the education category is of primary importance. For the applicant with extensive work experience, education is still quite important even though it is now secondary to work experience. List the following information about your education.

1. Colleges attended, and the appropriate dates.
2. Degrees, and the dates they were awarded.
3. Major and minor subjects.
4. Courses taken or skills acquired that might be especially pertinent to the job now being applied for.
5. Cumulative grade averages and any academic honors.
6. Extracurricular activities.
7. Scholarships and awards.
8. Special training courses (academic or industrial).

PERSONAL CHARACTERISTICS

Listing your personal characteristics will help you find your personal strong points. Be as objective as possible in listing your personal characteristics. Weigh your strengths and weaknesses honestly, and determine which factors are pertinent to the job you are seeking. Some of the points that should be considered are in the following list.

1. Age and marital status.
2. Height, weight, health, and physical limitations.
3. Appearance and grooming.
4. Communication skills and speech characteristics.
5. Social attitudes (aggressive, cooperative, cheerful, tactful, moody, courteous, etc.).
6. Career objectives and plans for the future.

ORGANIZING AND WRITING THE RÉSUMÉ

After listing all items in the three separate categories, you must analyze them in terms of the job you are seeking, evaluating all the items, rejecting some of them, and finally selecting those that you will include in your résumé. Base your decisions on the following questions.

1. Precisely, what job are you seeking?
2. Who are the prospective employers?
3. What information is most pertinent to that job and those employers?
4. What details should be included, and in what order?
5. How should you present your qualifications most effectively to get an interview?

After selecting the appropriate items to be included in your résumé, consider the following requirements before beginning to write the draft of your résumé.

1. Your résumé should contain your immediate and long-range job objectives.
2. It should list the firms you have been employed by, your functions in those firms, and your specific skills.
3. It should include your professional training.
4. It should contain pertinent personal information.
5. It should be brief, preferably no more than one page. (Save details for the interview.)
6. It should always begin with your name, address, and telephone number.

The most common way to organize a résumé is by jobs held, starting with the most recent and going back to the first one. In using this organization, be sure to account for all time. Be sure also to show promotions earned (by job title) within each job, the extent of your responsibilities, and the results achieved in each job.

The second most common way to organize a résumé is by function, starting with the function most closely related to the job being applied for, followed by the next most relevant, and so on. Describe each function, using specific illustrations from your experience. This type of functional organization is used most often in advertising, public relations, contract engineering, and other occupations in which assignments change frequently.

In the actual writing of the résumé, use a terse narrative **style**. Use active **verbs**, and try to keep your use of the **personal pronoun** *I* to a minimum (but do not necessarily attempt to avoid it altogether—you are, after all, the subject of your résumé). Remember as you write the draft that your **objective** is to show the **reader** that you can contribute positively and substantially to his or her organization.

Once you have completed the draft, check the accuracy of your information and the flow of your **sentences.**

The following three sample résumés are all for the same person. The first one is a student's first résumé, and the remaining two show work experience later in her career (one is organized by job, the other by function).

```
                        R É S U M É

Carol Ann Walker                        April 12, 1970

273 East Sixth Street
Bloomington, Indiana 47401

Phone: (812) 477-3636

Job Objective: Associate copywriter, with the ultimate
               goal of working into advertising or
               public relations management.

    EDUCATION

        1970   Will graduate in June from Indiana University
               with a Bachelor of Science degree
               Major: Journalism  Minor: Mass Communications
               Grade Avg.: 3.63 (Dean's List for six
                           semesters)
               Honors: Senior Honor Society, 1969
               Activities: Business Manager of college news-
                           paper (1969), Associate Editor of
                           college newspaper (1970), pres-
                           ident of sorority (1970).

    WORK EXPERIENCE

        Summer, 1969   Elwood, Dowd, and Harvey, Indianap-
                       olis, Indiana.  Worked as editorial
                       assistant (intern), proofreading copy
                       and preparing preliminary layouts for
                       ads.  Also helped copywriters with
                       research.  Wrote copy for two indus-
                       trial ads that were used in trade
                       publications.

        Summer, 1968   Dayton Newspapers, Inc., Dayton,
                       Ohio.  Editorial staff assistant
                       (intern).  Provided research assis-
                       tance to writers for the editorial
                       page.  Prepared background material
                       for analysis of major news events.

        Summer, 1967   Oak Park Swim Club, Dayton, Ohio.
                       Life guard and instructor for pre-
                       school-age swimming classes.

        Previously earned spending money by babysitting and
```

housecleaning; had a paper route for two years
(1961-63).

PERSONAL DATA

    Age, 22; height, 5'4"; weight, 115 lbs.; health,
excellent; unmarried; hobbies are skiing, tennis,
sketching, and photography.

REFERENCES

Dr. Walter Duncan
Professor, School of Journalism
Indiana University
Bloomington, Indiana 45401
(812) 477-8283

Mr. E. P. Dowd
President, Elwood, Dowd, and Harvey
Suite 412
Midstates Building
Indianapolis, Indiana 46206
(317) 533-4422

Mr. Peter Crowley
4927 Far Oaks Lane
Dayton, Ohio 45420
(513) 299-3952

R É S U M É

Carol Ann Walker   June 14, 1976

1436 W. Schantz Avenue
Dayton, Ohio 45429

Phone: (513) 224-0773

Job Objective: Manager of Consumer Relations or Public
                  Relations for a consumer products
                  company.

WORK EXPERIENCE

    January 1973 - Present

        Kerfheimer Associates, Dayton, Ohio

        <u>Public Relations Group Leader</u> (October 1974 to
present). Creative director and project leader
for staff of five public relations specialists.
Originated public relations projects for fourteen
client companies. Most projects designed to
respond to particular problems involving such
things as consumer resistance to automated
checkout systems installed in a small supermarket
chain, press relations for an industrial firm

involved in a labor dispute, and speech writing
for the executives of a utility company to
educate the public to the need for a price
increase. (Was named Kerfheimer Creator of the
Year for 1975 for the supermarket project.)

Public Relations Specialist (September 1973 to
October 1974). (Job created as the result of a
special project.) Responsible for creating a
public relations program to renew customer
interest in a former shopping center that had
been converted (at great expense) to an enclosed
mall consisting of boutiques and specialty shops.
Created press releases and promotional materials
(printed and novelty pieces), developed slide
programs for consumer groups, and wrote television and radio spots. Had a feature article
published in the local papers, including a two-
page article in the Sunday feature magazine.

Copywriter (January 1973 to September 1973).
Created copy and preliminary layouts for advertising campaigns for clients that included home
builders, a milk producers' association, fashion
retailers, and new car dealers. (Was named Kerfheimer Creator of the Month for May 1973 and September 1973.)

June 1970 - December 1972

Elwood, Dowd, and Harvey, Indianapolis, Indiana

Associate Copywriter (September 1971 to December
1972). Worked with copywriters and account executives in preparing advertising campaigns for
clients. Assisted account executives and others
in preparing proposals to clients. Worked on
accounts where additional help was needed, not
only in writing copy but in the art department as
well. (This job was a kind of apprenticeship.)

Editorial Assistant (June 1970 to September
1971). Worked as assistant to copywriters,
account executives, and administrative executives
to perform jobs as needed: I proofread copy, did
marketing research, worked in clipping service,
wrote copy, keylined art, and created art work
for campaigns. I worked in some role in every
creative department in the firm. (Worked as
intern editorial assistant during the summer of
1969.)

Summer 1968

Dayton Newspapers, Inc., Dayton, Ohio

Editorial Staff Assistant (intern). Provided
research assistance to writers for the editorial
page. Prepared background papers for analysis of
major news events.

Part-Time Work Experience

    Worked as life guard and swimming instructor
during the summer of 1967. Earned spending money
in high school by babysitting and doing house-
work. Had a paper route for two years (1962-63).
Was business manager (1969) and associate editor
(1970) of college newspaper.

EDUCATION

    1975   Graduated Wright State University
            Degree: M.B.A. - in Management

    1970   Graduated Indiana University
            Degree: B.Sc. - in Journalism
                   (Magna cum laude)

PERSONAL DATA

    Age, 27; height, 5'4"; weight, 120 lbs.; health,
excellent; unmarried; hobbies are skiing, tennis,
photography, and sketching.

(References and a portfolio of projects will be furnished on request.)

R É S U M É

Carol Ann Walker   June 14, 1976

1436 W. Schantz Avenue
Dayton, Ohio 45429

Phone: (513) 224-0773

Job Objective: Manager of Consumer Relations or Public
                   Relations for a consumer products
                   company.

SUMMARY OF EXPERIENCE

Public Relations
Prepared public and consumer relations programs for
fourteen companies. Served as both creative director and administrative head of group of five
specialists. Wrote speeches for executives, designed campaigns in all media to overcome poor
public image and create interest in a new development. Work for eight of the fourteen companies
was done originally as a one-time, problem-oriented
project. Four of these companies were converted to
full-time clients as a result of the success of the
original projects. Clients included a supermarket
chain, industrial companies, home and apartment
builders, and a milk producers' association. (Named
Kerfheimer Creator of the Month for one project,
Creator of the Year for another campaign.)

Publicity
Created campaigns to "spread the word" about new
projects in the community; largest campaign was to
increase interest in a refurbished small shopping
center located in a deteriorating neighborhood. The
shopping center was converted to a mall, featuring
specialty shops and boutiques--fashion, food, arts
and crafts, and galleries--with no major department
stores. The mall, based on a "world bazaar" theme,
has been an outstanding commercial success.

Press Relations
Placed news releases in local and regional newspapers, feature articles in local magazine. Also
sent news and feature releases weekly to local newspapers and radio and television stations. Secured
effective participants and had them placed on local
business news and television programs, including
"Dayton Today," a program featuring local people and
places of interest. My time working for a newspaper, although limited, exposed me to the media
point of view.

Client Relations
Work as project leader and as creative director has
exposed me to the selling aspects of business--
selling campaigns, selling ideas, and selling services. Sold long-term arrangements to four clients
within a year (billings of $220,000 per year) as a
direct result of effective campaigns.

Management
Developed budgets for press and advertising campaigns, administered projects with a staff of five
people. Coordinated activities of publications
staff with art, photographic, research, and media
departments. Projects administered showed a gross
profit of 12 percent (average) over an eighteen-
month period in which billings were $920,000.

Meetings
Organized and developed programs for consumer
meetings. Created audio-visual materials to present
controlled, effective presentations. Worked with
hotel convention center and student union management
in planning the logistics for these meetings: facilities, meals, room arrangements for attendees, hos-
pitality programs, and audio-visual equipment.
Press rooms were established when appropriate.
Coordinated registration activities and created publicity for these meetings.

Community Activities
Served as publicity chairman for Girl Scout Camping
campaign and for Country Memorial Hospital fund
raising campaign. Created campaigns that exceeded
objectives, directing a staff of hard-working vol-
unteers for each campaign.

```
EDUCATION

    1975    Graduated Wright State University
            Degree: M.B.A. - in Management

    1970    Graduated Indiana University
            Degree: B.Sc. - in Journalism
                    (Magna cum laude)

PERSONAL DATA

    Age, 27; height, 5'4"; weight, 120 lbs.; health,
    excellent; unmarried; hobbies are skiing, tennis,
    photography, and sketching.

    (References and a portfolio of projects will be fur-
    nished on request.)
```

RESOURCES

Once you have written the résumé, you have made only part of the preparations necessary for the campaign to find the job you seek. The next step is to make a list of the resources that you might be able to use in planning your campaign. The following list contains possible resources that you might want to consider.

1. Companies that may have the kind of job you are looking for. (Check their **annual reports** and promotional literature.)
2. Personal friends, college instructors, and business associates.
3. College placement offices, public and private employment agencies.
4. Professional organizations.
5. Trade directories and magazines (*Thomas' Register of American Manufacturers, Dun and Bradstreet Reference Book,* government booklets for federal jobs, *College Placement Annual, Moody's Investor Services, Poor's Register of Directors and Executives, College Placement Directory, Standard and Poor's Corporation Services*).
6. Local and out-of-town newspapers.

(See also **application, letter of.**)

revision

The more natural a work of writing seems to the **reader**, the more effort the writer has probably put into revision. Anyone who has ever had to say of his own writing, "Now I wonder what I meant by that," can testify to the importance of revision. The time you invest in revision will make the difference between clear writing and unclear writing.

If you have followed the appropriate steps of the writing process, you have a very rough draft that could hardly be considered finished writing. Revision, possibly the most important single part of the writing process, is the obvious next step.

Allow as many days as possible to go by without looking at the draft before beginning to revise it. Without a cooling period, you are too close to the draft to be objective in evaluating it. Only when enough time has elapsed so that you can say, "How did I ever write that?" or "I wonder why I said that so awkwardly?" are you ready to start revising your rough draft.

A different frame of mind is required for revising than for **writing the draft**. Read and evaluate the draft, which should have been written at a boil, with cool deliberation and objectivity—from the point of view of a reader or critic. Be anxious to find and correct faults, and be honest. In revising, consider your reader first.

Do not try to do all your revision at once. Read through your rough draft several times, each time searching for and correcting a different set of problems.

Check your draft for completeness. Your writing should give readers exactly what they need, but it should not burden them with unnecessary information or get sidetracked into insignificant or only loosely related subjects. Check your draft against your **outline** to make certain that you did, in fact, follow your plan. If not, now is the time to insert any missing points into your draft. This may mean inserting a line here and there; it may mean writing a **paragraph** or passage on a separate sheet and attaching it to the appropriate page; or it may mean major additions to your rough draft, depending upon how carefully you followed your outline.

Take time to examine the facts in your draft for accuracy. Keep in mind that no matter how careful and painstaking you may have been in conducting your **research**, compiling your notes, and creating your outline, you could easily have made errors when transferring your thoughts from the outline to the rough draft. Checking the facts in your draft for accuracy is quickly and easily accomplished (especially if you took complete notes) yet can be critically important if it catches but a single error. Be certain that contradictory facts have not crept into your draft.

Be consistent with names. Make sure, for example, that you have not called the same item a "routine" on one page and a "program" on another.

Your **introduction**, if you use one, should give your purpose and provide a frame in which your reader can place the detailed information that follows in the body of your draft. Check your introduction to see that it does, in fact, provide the reader with such assistance. If you do not use an introduction, check your **opening** to see that it is useful and interesting to the reader.

To determine whether you have good **transition**, look for **unity** as a key factor. If a paragraph has unity, all its **sentences** and ideas are closely tied together and contribute directly to the main idea expressed in the **topic sentence** of the paragraph. Where transition is missing, provide it; where transition is weak, strengthen it. Also look for unity in the entire report, and provide any transition that is needed between paragraphs or sections.

Check your draft for **pace**. If you find that you are jamming your ideas too closely together, space them out and slow down the pace.

Check your use of **jargon**. If you have any doubt that your entire reading audience will understand any jargon you may have used, eliminate it from your draft.

Check your draft for **conciseness**. Tighten your writing so that it says exactly what you mean by pruning unnecessary words, **phrases**, sentences, and even paragraphs.

Replace **clichés** with fresh **figures of speech** or with direct statements.

Watch for words that could carry an undesired **connotation**. Also delete or replace vague or pretentious words, coined words, and unnecessary **intensifiers**. (See also **word choice**.)

Check your draft for **awkwardness**, determine the reason for any you may find, and correct the problem.

Finally, check your draft for possible grammatical errors. Any such errors should be caught in your check for awkwardness, but a final review may save you embarrassment.

See also the Checklist of the Writing Process.

rhetoric

Rhetoric, in its most basic sense, means the study of the theory and practice of both written and oral composition. Traditionally, college composition textbooks are referred to as "rhetorics."

Rhetoric has also been used to mean inflated or inappropriately elegant writing. Consider the following opening to a letter.

> *Example:* In regards to your most welcome inquiry of recent date, I
> want to take this opportunity to make what might be called an
> interim report.

No doubt the writer intends this **sentence** to sound polite; instead, it sounds pretentious. Avoid "rhetoric" of this type.

rhetorical question

A rhetorical question is a question that a writer asks the **reader**—a question to which a specific answer is not necessarily needed or expected. The question is often intended to make the reader think about the subject from a different perspective; the writer then answers the question in the article or essay.

> *Examples:* Is methanol the answer to the energy shortage?
> Does advertising lower consumer prices?

The answer to a rhetorical question may not be a "yes" or "no"; in the above examples, it might involve a detailed explanation of the pros and cons of the value of methanol as a source of energy or of the effect of advertising on consumer prices.

The rhetorical question can be an effective **opening**, and it is often used for a **title**. By its nature, however, it is somewhat informal, and it should therefore be used judiciously in professional writing. For example, a rhetorical question would not be an appropriate opening for a **report** or **memorandum** addressed to a busy superior in your company. When you do use a rhetorical question, be sure that it is not trivial, obvious, or forced. More than any other writing device, the rhetorical question requires that you know your reader.

S

sales proposal

Whether they sell products or services, business firms often prepare sales proposals. The purposes of a sales proposal are to describe what the seller proposes to furnish to the customer and to demonstrate that the customer's prospective purchase would be a wise investment.

HOW TO PREPARE A SALES PROPOSAL

Before a sales proposal can be prepared, you must conduct a study of the prospective customer's requirements (the relative importance of this study varies with the complexity of your product). Until you have made such a study, you cannot know either *whether* you can help the prospective customer or *how* you can help him. Once you have determined that you can and the ways in which you can, however, you are ready to prepare the proposal.

The sales proposal contains (1) a cover letter, (2) a summary of the proposal's conclusions (the ways the particular product being proposed solves the customer's particular problem), (3) a sales brochure or other description of your product that provides detailed information, (4) **illustrations** (charts, **graphs**, etc.) that demonstrate the benefits the customer will realize by using your product (cost savings, increased production, greater efficiency, etc.), (5) an explanation of the reasons why your company is well qualified to meet the customer's needs, and (6) a cost analysis that specifies in detail all the costs of the transaction you are proposing. If the transaction includes training and post-sale support or maintenance, you must provide an explanation of the training and support you are proposing.

If the proposal is long and relatively complex, include a **table of contents** at the front of it.

COVER LETTER

The cover letter accompanying the proposal should (1) express appreciation for the opportunity to make your proposal and for any assistance that has been given you in the study of the customer's requirements, (2) summarize in a single paragraph the proposal's recommendations, and (3) offer a soft sales pitch for your company and its products. See the example on page 426.

SUMMARY

The purpose of the summary is to provide the customer with an overview of your proposal and recommendations that he can use after your departure in deliberating and reaching his final decision. The summary should be brief enough that the customer will read it, yet complete enough that he will not overlook any of the significant points.

Example: Summary

The OBR Acro system is a combination of specially designed application software and an online order entry configuration

March 15, 1976

Mr. Robert X. Bostick
Bostick Hardware Supply Co.
4042 S. Plain Street
Plainsboro, Kansas 45023

Dear Mr. Bostick:

Express your
appreciation for the
opportunity to make
the proposal →

We appreciate your cooperation and assistance
in obtaining the details concerning the
various operations within Bostick Hardware
Supply Company. Information gathered during
our survey of your operations on September 26
has been analyzed by our team of specialists.

As a result of this study we are recommending
the installation of the OBR Acro at Bostick
Hardware Supply Company. The reasons for recommending OBR Acro are two. First, the installation of the Acro system will enable you
to automate your order entry, inventory
control, and accounts receivable systems.
This automation will provide a more efficient

Summarize the
proposal's
recommendations →

system that permits more effective use of
warehouse space, personnel, and assets.
Second, specific facts that were obtained
during our survey were input to our Return-on-
Investment analysis program, and it was discovered that your current return on investment
is 3.84%. We feel that this can be appreciably increased by using the OBR Acro system
as a management tool. Our recommendation
offers Bostick Hardware Supply Company the
highest degree of efficiency and economy by
employing the most modern data processing
system available today.

We would like to thank you for the opportunity
to make these recommendations. We are con-

Make a soft sales pitch
→

fident that you, your staff, and OBR will
share a mutual pride and sense of achievement
from the successful installation of the OBR
Acro system.

Sincerely yours,

William R. Jackson

William R. Jackson
Sales Manager

Enclosures

of hardware. This new system has been designed to handle your present applications more effectively while allowing for expansion and upward compatibility as your needs change in the future. The Acro software package consists of three application programs—Order Entry, Inventory Control, and Accounts Receivable. All related data-entry and data-inquiry functions can be performed through the CRT terminal with the option of entering data into the system through the card reader. This online processing system enables you to produce picking tickets, packing slips, and invoices while providing a wealth of management and control information within its many reports. In addition, Accounts Payable, Payroll, and General Ledger Applied Systems can be processed in subsequent processing runs.

Our recommendation consists of the Acro system with two CRT terminals (one located in the accounting office and one at the order desk). Operator lead-through techniques incorporated in the CRT units simplify their operation and tend to reduce the task of training order entry clerks. Use of CRT units will significantly reduce the amount of information that must be keyed into the system to process an order. Item descriptions, prices, and other types of information are retrieved from computer memory and need not be entered. CRT units permit you to offer better service to your customers by permitting your personnel to make online inquiries while talking to customers in-house or on the telephone.

Order processing is an area where a savings in manpower can be achieved while simplifying the overall task. We are recommending that a one-digit suffix be added to your present aisle numbers to aid pickers filling orders. A digit 1 refers to aisles to the left of your main aisle, and a digit 2 refers to aisles to the right of the main aisle. Sorting ordered items into the same sequence as your bin locations and printing a pick list in this sequence while using the additional one-digit code to further indicate where an item is located can result in considerable savings in the cost of processing orders.

Open-item invoicing and a full range of accounts receivable reporting, including an age analysis of delinquent accounts, are all part of the Acro system. Information necessary for an efficient collection program and information upon which decisions concerning whether marginal customers should be dropped are both vital parts of this system.

Inventory management and control can be greatly improved through the use of Acro. Automatic exception reports listing items that are out of stock or below established minimums, suggested order quantities to aid purchasing decisions, and access to the value and status of any or all items of inventory are some of the major tools available to manage your inventory.

Flash reporting is another valuable tool of the Acro system. Management is provided with up-to-the-minute information on demand. Flash reports include sales dollar volume from incoming orders, number of orders received, orders shipped, orders billed, amount invoiced and cash received from cash sales and accounts receivable receipts.

The data we gathered during our study of your operation indicate that your present return on investment is 3.84%. To provide a reasonable goal to work toward, we have made the following assumptions: (1) a 5% increase in sales, (2) a 14% decrease in inventory, and (3) a 14% decrease in accounts receivable. We have plotted the growth pattern of Bostick Hardware and determined that the pattern of growth over the past five years is approximately 15% per year. The Acro system is designed for upward compatibility within the OBR 9100 series and also larger OBR computer systems. We at OBR would like to join with Bostick Hardware in an even faster and more profitable growth in the future.

ILLUSTRATIONS

Any visual aid that you use in your sales presentation should be made a part of your proposal and left with the customer so that its impact will have a continuing effect. Oversized charts and graphs used in the sales presentation should be reduced, however, before being included in the physical proposal.

WHY YOUR COMPANY

You must convince the prospective customer that your company can meet his requirements better than its competitors can. Keep this part of your proposal brief—possibly even using a list of single-sentence items—but effective.

Example: Why OBR?

Every prospective customer is vitally concerned with the support that the manufacturer will provide for his installation. OBR is one of the oldest and largest manufacturers of business systems. In every OBR office, world wide, there are specialists in the various computer applications. Knowledge gained from successful EDP installations of all types and sizes combined with continuous training in modern system concepts and procedures have permitted OBR analysts to excel in business systems knowledge. Consequently, OBR has the experience and the manpower to provide the support required for a

computer installation. Our local OBR district office in Plainsboro is staffed with competent and knowledgeable vocational
teams who are prepared to assist with the installation of your
system.

Before your system is installed, OBR specialists are available to
(1) assist you in designing your system, (2) assist you with the
planning of your computer site, (3) assist you in planning,
coordinating, and implementing your installation, (4) provide
you with a complete library of hardware and software reference manuals, (5) aid in establishing training schedules for
your EDP staff, (6) provide programmer and operator training, (7) assist you in converting your existing programs and
files, (8) assist you in compiling and debugging your programs, and (9) assist you in developing your operating procedures.

After your computer is installed, our local specialists are available to continue this high level of support. The professional
field engineers at our Plainsboro district office are available to
maintain and assure maximum efficiency of your equipment
through preventive and remedial maintenance.

COST ANALYSIS

This section of your proposal may have little or even no writing. Its
purpose is to present the dollar figure that your proposal, if accepted, will cost the prospective customer. See the following example.

Example: Cost Analysis
OBR Acro System

Equipment Cost
OBR Sato 9100 Basic System
705–10 Processor
305–06 Disc Controller
506–13 Disc Unit
305–07 Common Trunk
934–70 Line Printer
654–03 CRT Unit
243–40 Adapter
138–60 Card Reader
Acro Applied System
Acro Accounts Payable Applied System
Acro Payroll Applied System
Acro General Ledger Applied System

	$xx,xxx.xx
Tax	x,xxx.xx
Freight	x,xxx.xx
Total Investment	$xx,xxx.xx

TRAINING AND SUPPORT

State the amount and kind of training and support offered by your proposal, as in the following example.

Example: Customer Education Program

> OBR offers a comprehensive program of customer eduation. Your personnel will be trained by a professional staff of instructors in programming and operating the OBR Acro system.
>
> Educational courses are available to each OBR user upon receipt of a purchase or rental contract. These courses are designed to cover the normal training necessary for the successful use of an OBR system. You may select qualified employees for programmer training. OBR will administer a programming aptitude test to these persons and, if approved, schedule them in the required training school.
>
> A member of top management is invited to attend an Executive EDP Seminar. In addition, you may select three managers to attend the Middle Management EDP Seminar.

Customer Support

> The following customer support will be provided to you at no charge: (1) one complete library of OBR Acro software and hardware reference manuals, (2) a ten-hour operations course, and thirty hours on-site operator training up to thirty days after certification of your system, (3) sixteen hours of test and compile computer time, (4) software distribution, and (5) program error detection/correction of any OBR applied software requiring OBR field engineering assistance.

same

When used as a **pronoun**, *same* is awkward and outmoded.

Change: Your order has been received, and we will respond to *same* (or *the same*) next week.
To: Your order has been received, and we will respond to *it* next week.
Or: We received your order, and we will comply with *it* next week.

schematic diagram

The schematic diagram, which is used primarily in electronics and chemistry and in electrical and mechanical engineering, attempts to show the operation of its subject with lines and **symbols** rather than

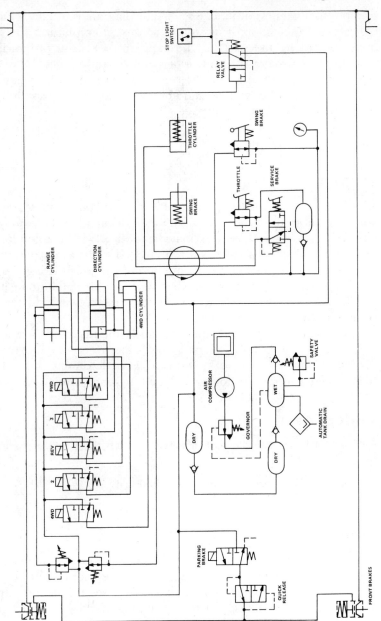

Figure 1. Air System Schematic for a Self-Propelled Hydraulic Crane
(Courtesy: Harnischfeger Corp.)

by a physical likeness of it. The schematic diagram is usually a highly abstract representation of its subject because it emphasizes the relationships among the parts at the expense of precise proportions. Because a schematic diagram is a symbolic representation of the subject, as opposed to a realistic representation of it, the schematic relies heavily on the symbols and **abbreviations** that are common to the subject. See Figure 1 on page 431.

For guidelines on how to use illustrations and incorporate them into your text, see **illustrations**.

scope

If you know your **reader** and the **objective** of your writing project, you will know the type and amount of detail to include in your writing. This is *scope,* which may be defined as the depth and breadth to which you cover your subject. If you do not determine your scope of coverage in the planning stage of your writing project, you will not know how much of what kind of information to include; as a result, you are likely to invest unnecessary work during the **research** phase of your project.

Your scope should be designed to satisfy the needs of your objective and your reader. By keeping your objective and your reader's profile in mind as you work, you can easily determine those items that should and should not be included in your writing.

seldom ever

Seldom ever is a redundant **phrase** from which the word *ever* should be eliminated.

>   *Change:* He *seldom ever* comes in on time.
>   *To:* He *seldom* comes in on time.

semicolon

The semicolon links independent **clauses** or other **sentence** elements of equal weight and grammatical rank, especially **phrases** in a series that have commas within them. The semicolon indicates a greater pause between clauses than a comma would, but not so great a pause as a period would.

When the independent clauses of a **compound sentence** are not joined by a comma and a **conjunction**, they are linked by a semicolon.

Example: No one applied for the position; the job was too difficult.

Make sure, however, that such clauses balance or contrast with each other. The relationship between the two statements should be so clear that further explanation is not necessary.

Example: The new marketing approach was very successful; every division reported increased sales.

Do not use a semicolon between a **dependent clause** and its main clause. Remember that elements joined by semicolons must be of equal grammatical rank or weight.

Change: No one applied for the position; even though it was heavily advertised.

To: No one applied for the position, even though it was heavily advertised.

USE A SEMICOLON WITH STRONG CONNECTIVES

In complicated sentences, a semicolon may be used before transitional words or **phrases** *(that is, for example, namely)* that introduce examples or further explanation.

Example: The study group was aware of his position on the issue; that is, that federal funds should not be used for the housing project.

A semicolon should also be used before **conjunctive adverbs** (such as *therefore, moreover, consequently, furthermore, indeed, in fact, however*) that connect independent clauses.

Example: I won't finish today; moreover, I doubt that I will finish this week.

The semicolon in this example shows that *moreover* belongs to the second clause.

USE A SEMICOLON FOR CLARITY IN LONG AND COMPLICATED SENTENCES

Use a semicolon between two main clauses connected by a **coordinating conjunction** *(and, but, for, or, nor, yet)* if the clauses are long and contain other **punctuation**.

Example: In most cases these individuals are corporate executives, bankers, Wall Street lawyers; but they do not, as the economic determinists seem to believe, simply push the button of their economic power to affect fields remote from economics.

—Robert Lubar, "The Prime Movers," *Fortune* (February 1960), p. 98.

A semicolon may also be used if items in a series contain commas within them.

Example: Among those present were John Howard, president of the Omega Paper Company; Carol Martin, president of Alpha Corporation; and Larry Stanley, president of Stanley Papers.

The semicolon always appears outside closing **quotation marks**.

Example: The attorney said, "You must be accurate"; the client said, "I will."

sentences

A sentence is traditionally defined as a sequence of words that contains a **subject** and a **predicate** and conveys a complete thought. A sentence normally has at least two words: a subject (something or someone) and a predicate (an assertion about the subject).

Example: Sales (subject) declined (assertion about the subject).

Modifiers—in the form of words, **phrases**, and **clauses**—can be added to the basic sentence.

Example: *Computer* sales declined *during the month of August.*

In most sentences, the subject consists of a **noun phrase** rather than a single word, and the predicate consists of a **verb** or **verb phrase** with appropriate modifiers, **objects**, or **complements**.

Example: A good personnel department (subject) screens job applicants carefully. (predicate)

TYPES OF SENTENCES

Sentences may be classified according to *structure* (simple, compound, complex, compound-complex); *intention* (declarative, interrogative, imperative, exclamatory); and *stylistic use* (loose, periodic, minor).

By Structure. A **simple sentence** consists of one independent clause. At its most basic, the simple sentence contains only a subject and a predicate.

Examples: Profits (subject) rose (predicate).
 The strike (subject) finally ended (predicate).

Either the subject or the predicate, or both, may be compounded without changing the structure of the simple sentence. A simple sentence need not necessarily be short. Although modifiers may extend the length of the simple sentence, they do not alter its basic structure as a simple sentence.

Examples: *Tom, Janet,* and *Harry* worked on the sales brochure. (compound subject)
 Tom *designed the layout and supplied the photographs.* (compound predicate)

A **compound sentence** consists of two or more independent clauses connected either by a comma and a **coordinating conjunction** or by a **semicolon**.

Example: We expect sales to increase next year, but we cannot guarantee that they will.

The **complex sentence** provides a means of subordinating one thought to another. A complex sentence contains one independent clause and at least one **dependent clause** that expresses a subordinate idea.

Example: When you have finished the report (dependent clause), bring it to my office (independent clause).

A **compound-complex sentence** consists of two or more independent clauses plus at least one dependent clause.

Example: Productivity is central to controlling inflation (independent clause), for when productivity rises (dependent clause), employers can raise wages without raising prices (independent clause).

By Intention.   By intention, a sentence may be declarative, interrogative, imperative, or exclamatory.

A declarative sentence conveys information or makes a factual statement.

Example: James Evans is president of Acme Corporation.

An interrogative sentence asks a direct question.

Example: Who is Acme's vice-president?

An imperative sentence issues a command.

Example: Get the contract.

An exclamatory sentence is an emphatic expression of feeling, fact, or opinion. It is a declarative sentence that is stated with great feeling.

Example: We got the contract!

By Stylistic Use.   A *loose* sentence is one that makes its major point at the beginning and then adds subordinate phrases and clauses that develop the major point. It is the pattern in which we express ourselves most naturally and easily. A loose sentence could be ended at one or more points before it actually ends.

> *Example:*   One of the foundations engaged me (.) to edit the manuscripts of a socioeconomic research report (.) designed for the thoughtful citizen (.) as well as for the specialist.
>
> —Samuel T. Williamson

Compound sentences are generally classed as loose, since the sentence could end after the first independent clause.

> *Example:*   The union agreed to accept an arbitrated settlement, but management refused.

Complex sentences are loose if their subordinate clauses follow their main clause.

> *Example:*   The health care delivery system today is largely a private endeavor (.) despite the fact that about 40¢ of each supporting dollar comes from the public purse.

A *periodic* sentence delays its main idea until the end by presenting subordinate ideas or modifiers first, thus holding the **reader's** interest until the end. If skillfully handled, a periodic sentence lends force, or **emphasis**, to the main point by arousing the reader's anticipation and then presenting the main point as a climax.

> *Example:*   During the last decade or so, the attitude of the American citizen toward automation has undergone a profound change.

Do not use periodic sentences too frequently, however, for overuse results in a **style** that is irritating to the reader.

A *minor* sentence is not a complete sentence. It makes sense, in its context, because the missing element is clearly implied by the preceding sentence.

> *Example:*   In view of these facts, is automation really useful? *Or economical?* There is no question that it has made our country the

most wealthy and technologically advanced nation the world has ever known.

In short, minor sentences are elliptical expressions that are equivalent to complete sentences because the missing words are clearly understood without being stated.

Examples: Why not?
How much?
Ten dollars.
At last!
This way, please.
So much for that idea.

Minor sentences are common in advertising copy and fictional dialogue; they are not normally appropriate to business or technical writing.

Example: You can use the one-minute long-distance rate any time after eleven at night all the way until eight in the morning. *Any night of the week.*

(See also **sentence construction**, **sentence variety**, and **sentence faults**.)

sentence construction

A **sentence** is the most basic and versatile tool available to the writer. Consider the many different ways the same idea can be expressed to achieve different **emphasis**.

Examples: Every person in the department, from manager to typists, must work overtime this week to insure that we meet the deadline.
To insure that we meet the deadline, every person in the department, from manager to typists, must work overtime this week.
From manager to typists, every person in the department must work overtime this week to insure that we meet the deadline.
To insure that we meet the deadline, every person in the department must work overtime this week, from manager to typists.
This week, every person in the department, from manager to typists, must work overtime to insure that we meet the deadline.

When shifting word order for emphasis, however, be aware that word order can make a great difference in the meaning of a sentence.

> *Examples:* He was *only* the accountant.
> He was the *only* accountant.

Except for **expletives**, all words or word groups in a sentence function as a **subject**, a **verb**, a **complement**, a **modifier**, a **connective**, an **appositive**, or an **absolute**. Subjects, verbs, and complements are the main elements of the sentence. Everything else is subordinate to them in one way or another. A sentence that progresses quickly from subject to verb to complement is clear and easy to understand. The problem is to write sentences that contain more information, and in more complicated form, with the same **clarity** and directness.

The basic sentence patterns in English are the following.

> *Examples:* Sales declined. (subject–verb)
> Advertising increased sales. (subject–verb–direct object)
> John showed Dr. Barnes the printout. (subject–verb–indirect object–direct object)
> Advertising made the sales drive a success. (subject–verb–direct object–objective complement)
> The advertising was effective. (subject–linking verb–subjective complement)

Most sentences follow the subject–verb–object pattern. In "The company dismissed Joe," we know the subject and the object by their positions relative to the verb. The knowledge that the usual sentence order is subject–verb–object helps **readers** interpret what they read. The fact that readers tend to expect this order explains why the writer's departures from it can be effective if used sparingly for emphasis and variety, but annoying if overdone.

An inverted sentence places the elements in other than normal order.

> *Examples:* A better job I never had. (direct object–subject–verb)
> More optimistic I have never been. (subjective complement–subject–linking verb)

Inverted sentence order may be used in questions and exclamations; it may also be used to achieve emphasis.

> *Examples:* Have you a pencil? (verb–subject–complement)
> How heavy your book feels! (complement–subject–verb)
> A sorry sight we presented! (complement–subject–verb)

In sentences introduced by expletives *(there, it),* the subject comes after its verb because the expletive occupies the subject's normal location before the verb.

> *Examples:* *There* (expletive) *are* (verb) certain *principles* (subject) of drafting that must not be ignored. (Compare: "Certain principles of drafting there are [that is, "exist"] that must not be ignored.")
>
> *It* (expletive) *is* (verb) difficult (complement) *to work* (subject) in a noisy office. (Compare: "To work in a noisy office is difficult.")

CONSTRUCTING SENTENCES FOR CLARITY

It is better to use uncomplicated sentences to state complex ideas. If readers must cope with a complicated sentence in addition to a complex idea, they are likely to become confused.

> *Change:* When you are purchasing parts, remember that, although an increase in the cost of aluminum forces all the vendors to increase their prices, some vendors will have a supply of aluminum purchased at the old price, and they may be willing to sell parts to you at the old price in order to get your business.
>
> *To:* Although an increase in the cost of aluminum forces all vendors to increase their prices, some vendors will have a supply of aluminum purchased at the old price. When you are purchasing aluminum parts, remember that these vendors may be willing to sell the parts to you at the old price in order to get your business.

Just as simpler sentences make complex ideas more digestible, a complex sentence construction makes a series of simple ideas more palatable.

> *Change:* The computer is a calculating device. It was once known as a mechanical brain. It has revolutionized industry.
>
> *To:* The computer, a calculating device once known as a mechanical brain, has revolutionized industry.

Do not string together in a series a number of thoughts which should be written as separate sentences or some of which should be subordinated to others. Sentences carelessly tacked together this way are monotonous and hard to read because all ideas seem to be of equal importance.

> *Change:* We started the program three years ago, there were only three members on the staff, and each member was responsible for a separate state, but it was not an efficient operation.

  To: When we started the program three years ago, there were only three members on the staff, each having responsibility for a separate state; however, that arrangement was not efficient.

It is often easy to improve sentences by eliminating trailing constructions and ineffective **repetition.**

 Change: We worked on the report on Friday, but we couldn't finish it because some information we needed was not available.
  To: Lack of necessary information prevented our completing the report on Friday.

CONSTRUCTING SENTENCES FOR PARALLELISM

Express coordinate ideas in similar form. By the very construction of the sentence, the reader grasps the similarity of its components.

 Example: Similarly, atoms come and go in a molecule, but the molecule remains; molecules come and go in a cell, but the cell remains; cells come and go in a body, but the body remains; persons come and go in an organization, but the organization remains.

   —Kenneth Boulding, *Beyond Economics* (Ann Arbor: University of Michigan Press, 1968), p. 131.

(See also **parallel structure.**)

CONSTRUCTING SENTENCES TO ACHIEVE EMPHASIS

Subordinate your minor ideas to emphasize your more important ideas (see also **subordination**).

 Change: We had all arrived, and we began the meeting early.
  To: Since we had all arrived, we began the meeting early.

The most emphatic positions within a sentence are at the beginning and the end. Do not waste them by tacking on **phrases** and clauses almost as an afterthought or by burying the main point in the middle of a sentence between less important points. For example, consider the following original and revised versions of a statement written for a company's annual report to its stockholders.

 Change: Sales declined by three percent in 1975, but nevertheless the Company had the most profitable year in its history, thanks to cost savings that resulted from design improvements in several of our major products; and we expect 1976 to be even better, since further design improvements are being made.

  To: Cost savings from design improvements in several major products not only offset a three-percent sales decline but made

1975 the most profitable year in the Company's history. Further design improvements now in progress promise to make 1976 even more profitable.

Reversing the normal word order is also used to achieve emphasis.

Examples: I will never agree to that.
That I will never agree to.
Never will I agree to that.

BEGINNING A SENTENCE WITH A COORDINATING CONJUNCTION

There is no "rule" against beginning a sentence with a **coordinating conjunction**; in fact, coordinating conjunctions can be strong transitional words and at times provide emphasis.

Example: I realize the project was more difficult than expected and that you have also encountered personnel problems. *But* we must meet our deadline.

Starting sentences with conjunctions is acceptable in even the most formal English. But, like any other writing device, this one should be used sparingly lest it become ineffective and even annoying. (See also **sentences**, **sentence variety**, and **sentence faults**).

sentence faults

The most common sentence faults are faulty subordination, run-on sentences, and sentence fragments.

FAULTY SUBORDINATION

Faulty subordination occurs (1) when a grammatically subordinate element, such as a **dependent clause**, actually contains the main idea of the sentence or (2) when a subordinate element is so long or excessively detailed that it dominates or obscures the main idea. Avoiding the first problem (main idea expressed in a subordinate element) depends on the writer's knowing which idea is *meant* to be the main idea. Note that both of the following sentences appear logical; which one really is logical depends on which of two ideas the writer means to emphasize.

Example: Although the new filing system saves money, many of the staff are unhappy with it.
The new filing system saves money, although many of the staff are unhappy with it.

In this example, if the writer's main point is that *the new filing system saves money,* the second sentence is correct. If the main point is that *many of the staff are unhappy,* then the first sentence is correct. It is easier than you may think to slip and put your main idea into a grammatically subordinate element (especially since people commonly do so in conversation, when they can raise their voices and make gestures to stress the main point).

The other major problem with subordination is the loading of so much detail into a subordinate element that it "crushes" the main point by its sheer size and weight.

> *Change:* If the parties to the agreement do not fully understand what is required of them under the terms of the new contract that was drawn up at the annual meeting of the district managers this past month, they should call or write the Vice-President of Finance.
>
> *To:* If the parties to the agreement do not fully understand what is required of them under the terms of the recent new contract, they should call or write the Vice-President of Finance.

RUN-ON SENTENCE

A run-on **sentence**, sometimes called a fused sentence, is two or more sentences without **punctuation** to separate them. The term is also sometimes applied to a pair of independent clauses separated by only a **comma**, although this variation is usually called a comma fault or comma splice. Run-on sentences can be corrected by (1) making two sentences, (2) joining the two clauses with a **semicolon** (if they are closely related), (3) joining the two clauses with a comma and a **coordinating conjunction**, or (4) subordinating one clause to the other.

> *Change:* The new manager instituted several new procedures some were impractical. (run-on sentence)
>
> *To:* The new manager instituted several new procedures. Some were impractical. (period)
>
> *Or:* The new manager instituted several new procedures; some were impractical. (semicolon)
>
> *Or:* The new manager instituted several new procedures, but some were impractical. (comma plus coordinating conjunction)
>
> *Or:* The new manager instituted several new procedures, some of which were impractical. (one clause subordinated to the other)

SENTENCE FRAGMENTS

A sentence that is missing an essential part (**subject**, **verb**, or **object**) is called a sentence fragment.

Examples: He quit his job. (sentence)
And quit his job. (fragment)

But having a subject and a predicate does not automatically make a clause a sentence. The clause must also make an independent statement. "I work" is a sentence; "If I work" is a fragment because the **subordinating conjunction** *if* makes the statement a **dependent clause**.

Sentence fragments are often introduced by **relative pronouns** *(who, which, that)* or subordinating conjunctions (such as *although, because, if, when,* and *while*). This knowledge can tip you off that what follows is a dependent clause and must be combined with a main clause.

Change: The new manager instituted several new procedures. *Many of which are impractical.* (The last is an adjective clause modifying *procedures* and linked to it by the relative pronoun *which.*)
To: The new manager instituted several new procedures, many of which are impractical.

A sentence must contain a **finite verb**; **verbals** will not do the job. The following examples are sentence fragments because their verbals *(providing, to work, waiting)* cannot perform the function of a finite verb.

Examples: *Providing* all employees with hospitalization insurance.
To work a forty-hour week.
The customer *waiting* to see you.

Fragments usually reflect incomplete and sometimes confused thinking. The most common type of fragment is the careless addition of an afterthought.

Change: These are my co-workers. *A fine group of people.*
To: These are my co-workers, a fine group of people.

The following examples are common types of sentence fragments.

Change: Some of our customers prefer to pay at the time of purchase. *While others find installment payments preferable.* (adverbial clause)
To: Some of our customers prefer to pay at the time of purchase, while others find installment payments preferable.
Change: The board approved the project. *After much discussion.* (prepositional phrase)
To: The board approved the project after much discussion.
Change: We reorganized the department. *Distributing the work load more evenly.* (participial phrase)

To:	We reorganized the department, distributing the work load more evenly.
Change:	The staff decided to take a break. *It being mid-afternoon.* (absolute phrase)
To:	The staff decided to take a break, it being mid-afternoon.
Change:	We consider your proposal excellent. *One of the best this year.* (appositive phrase)
To:	We consider your proposal excellent, one of the best this year.
Change:	The executive committee met yesterday for only one purpose. *To consider the proposed merger with Acme Corporation.* (infinitive phrase in apposition with *purpose*)
To:	The executive committee met yesterday for only one purpose: to consider the proposed merger with Acme Corporation.

A fragment usually should be part of the preceding sentence. Explanatory **phrases** beginning with *such as, for example,* and similar terms always belong with the preceding sentence.

A hopelessly snarled fragment simply has to be rewritten. This rewriting is most effectively done by pulling the main points out of the fragment, listing them in the proper sequence, and then rewriting the sentence.

Change:	Financing the new project and allocating funds to it during the coming year by means of a transfer of a portion of the research and development budget, but several new products must not be developed if we do.
Main Points:	1. There is a new project. 2. A way to finance it must be found. 3. Research and development money can be used to finance it. 4. If research and development money is used, the development of some new products must be curtailed.
To:	The new project can be financed during the coming year by transferring funds from the research and development budget; however, doing so would require that the development of several new products be stopped.

MISCELLANEOUS SENTENCE FAULTS

The assertion made by a sentence's predicate about its subject must be logical. "Mr. Wilson's *job* is a salesman" is not logical, but "*Mr. Wilson* is a salesman" is. "Jim's *height* is six feet tall" is not logical, but "*Jim* is six feet tall" is.

Do not omit a required verb.

Change:	The floor is swept and the lights out.
To:	The floor is swept and the lights *are* out.

Change:	I never have and probably never will write the annual report.
To:	I never have *written* and probably never will write the annual report.

Do not omit a subject.

Change:	He regarded price-fixing as wrong, but until abolished by law, he engaged in it as did everyone else.
To:	He regarded price-fixing as wrong, but until *it was* abolished by law, he engaged in it as did everyone else.

Avoid **compound sentences** containing clauses that have little or no logical relationship to each other.

Change:	My department is responsible for all company publications, and the staff includes twenty writers, three artists, and three typists.
To:	My department is responsible for all company publications. The staff includes twenty writers, three artists, and three typists.

(See also **sentences**, **sentence construction**, and **sentence variety**.)

sentence variety

Sentences may be long or short; they may be loose or periodic; they may be **simple**, **compound**, **complex**, or **compound-complex**; they may be declarative, interrogative, exclamatory, or imperative—they may even be elliptical. There is never a legitimate excuse for letting your sentences become tiresomely alike. However, sentence variety is best achieved during **revision**: do not let it concern you when you are **writing the draft**.

SENTENCE LENGTH

Varying sentence length makes writing more interesting to the **reader** because a long series of sentences of the same length is monotonous. For example, avoid stringing together a number of short independent **clauses**. Either connect them with subordinating **connectives**, thereby making some dependent, or make some clauses into separate sentences.

Change:	The company was founded ten years ago, *and* it now employs fifty people, *and* it has branch offices in two other states.
To:	The company, *which* was founded ten years ago, now employs fifty people and has branch offices in two other states.

Or: The company was founded ten years ago. It now employs fifty people and has branch offices in two other states.

Short sentences can often be effectively combined by converting **verbs** to **adjectives**.

Change: Three files *have been misplaced*. Please find those files.
To: Please find the three *misplaced* files.

Although too many short sentences make your writing sound choppy and immature, a short sentence can be effective at the end of a passage of long ones.

Example: I believe that man is about to learn that the most practical life is the moral life and that the moral life is the only road to survival. He is beginning to learn that he will either share part of his material wealth or lose all of it; that he will respect and learn to live with other political ideologies if he wants civilization to go on. This is the kind of argument that man's actual experience equips him to understand and accept. *This is the low road to morality. There is no other.*

—Saul Alinsky, *Rules for Radicals* (New York: Random House, 1971), p. 25.

In general terms, short sentences are good for emphatic, memorable statements. Long sentences are good for detailed explanations and support. There is nothing inherently wrong with a long sentence, or even with a complicated one, as long as its meaning is clear and direct. Sentence length becomes an element of **style** when varied for **emphasis** or contrast; a conspicuously short or long sentence can be used to good effect.

WORD ORDER

When a series of sentences all begin in exactly the same way, the result is likely to be monotonous. You can make your sentences more interesting by occasionally starting with a modifying word, **phrase**, or clause. This could be a single adjective, **adverb, participle**, or **infinitive**; it could be a **prepositional phrase**, a **participial phrase**, or an **infinitive phrase**; or it could be a subordinate clause.

Examples: *Exhausted,* the project director slumped into a chair. (adjective)
Recently, sales have been good. (adverb)
Smiling, he extended his hand to the irate customer. (participle)
To advance, one must work hard. (infinitive)
Work having already begun, there was little we could do. (absolute construction)

In the morning, we will finish the report. (prepositional phrase)
Reading the report, she found several errors. (participial phrase)
To reach the top job, she presented constructive alternatives when current policies failed to produce the desired results. (infinitive phrase)
Because we now know the result of the survey, we may proceed with certainty. (adverb clause)

But overdoing this technique can be monotonous; use it with moderation.

Inverted sentence order can be an effective way to achieve variety.

Examples: Then occurred the event that gained us the contract.
Never have sales been so good.

Too many inverted sentences, however, can lead to the kind of criticism that was aimed at *Time* magazine's writing style many years ago: "Backwards ran the sentences until reeled the mind." Use inverted sentence order sparingly.

Be careful in your sentences to avoid the unnecessary separation of **subject** and **verb**, **preposition** and **object**, and the parts of a **verb phrase**.

Change: The marketing manager worked closely with, despite personality differences, the advertising chief. (preposition and object separated)
To: Despite personality differences, the marketing manager worked closely with the advertising chief.

This is not to say, however, that subject and verb should never be separated by a modifying phrase or clause.

Example: John Stoddard, who founded the firm in 1943, is still an active partner.

Vary the position of **modifiers** in your sentences to achieve variety as well as precision. The following examples illustrate four different ways the same sentence could be written by varying the position of its modifiers.

Examples: Carefully, with the printed side forward, place the deck of punched cards in the hopper of the card reader.
With the printed side forward, carefully place the deck of punched cards in the hopper of the card reader.
With the printed side forward, place the deck of punched cards carefully in the hopper of the card reader.
With the printed side forward, place the deck of punched cards in the hopper of the card reader carefully.

LOOSE/PERIODIC/INSERTION SENTENCES

A loose sentence makes its major point at the beginning and then adds subordinate phrases and clauses that develop or modify the point. A periodic sentence delays its main idea until the end by presenting modifiers or subordinate ideas first, thus holding the reader's interest until the end.

Examples: The attitude of the American citizen toward automation has undergone a profound change during the last decade or so. (loose)

During the last decade or so, the attitude of the American citizen toward automation has undergone a profound change. (periodic)

Experiment in your own writing, especially during **revision**, with shifts from loose sentences to periodic sentences.

Avoid the sing-song monotony of a long series of loose sentences, particularly a series containing coordinate clauses joined by **conjunctions**. Subordinating some thoughts to others makes your sentences more interesting.

Change: The auditorium was filled to capacity, *and* the chairman of the board came onto the stage. The meeting started at eight o'clock, *and* the president made his report of the company's operations during the past year. The audience of stockholders was obviously unhappy, *but* the members of the board of directors were all re-elected.

To: By eight o'clock, *when* the chairman of the board came onto the stage and the meeting began, the auditorium was filled to capacity. *Although* the audience of stockholders was obviously unhappy with the president's report of the company's operations during the past year, the members of the board of directors were all re-elected.

You may also, for variety, alter the normal sentence order with an inserted phrase or clause.

Example: Our sales projection, drawn up six months ago, appears quite accurate.

The technique of inserting such a phrase or clause is good for **emphasis**, for providing detail, for breaking monotony, and for regulating **pace**.

(See also **sentences**, **sentence construction**, and **sentence faults**.)

sequential method of development

The sequential, or step-by-step, method of development is especially effective for **explaining a process** or describing a mechanism in operation (see **description**). It would also be the logical method for writing **instructions**.

The main advantage of the sequential method of development is that it is easy to follow because the steps correspond to the elements of the process or operation being described.

The disadvantages of the sequential method are that it can become monotonous and that it does not lend itself very well to achieving **emphasis**.

Practically all **methods of development** have elements of sequence within them. The **chronological method of development**, for example, is also sequential: to describe a trip chronologically, from beginning to end, is also to describe it sequentially.

service

When used as a **verb**, *service* means "to keep up or maintain," as well as "to repair."

> *Example:*   Our company will *service* your equipment.

When you mean the providing of a more general benefit, use *serves*.

> *Example:*   Our company *serves* (not *services*) the northwest area of the state.

set/sit

Sit (past tense: *sat*) is an **intransitive verb**; it does not, therefore, require an **object**.

> *Examples:*   I *sit* by a window in the office.
> We *sat* around the conference table.

Set (past tense: *set*) is usually a **transitive verb**, meaning "to put or place," "to establish," or "to harden (something)."

> *Examples:*   Please *set* the trophy on the shelf.
> The jeweler *set* the stone beautifully.
> Can we *set* a date for the tests?
> The high temperature *sets* the epoxy quickly.

Set, however, is occasionally intransitive.

> *Examples:* The sun *sets* a little earlier each day.
> The glue *sets* in 45 minutes.

shall/will

It was at one time fairly common to use *shall* for first-person constructions and *will* for second- and third-person constructions.

> *Examples:* I *shall* go.
> You *will* go.
> He *will* go.

This is an unnecessary distinction, however, because no one could be confused by "I will go" to express an action in the near future. *Shall* is often used in all **persons**, nonetheless, to emphasize determination that something will occur.

> *Examples:* I *shall* go.
> We *shall* go.
> They *shall* go.

sic

Sic, which is Latin for "thus," is used in **quotations** to indicate that the writer has quoted the material exactly as it appeared in the original source. It is most often used when the original material contains an obvious error or might in some other way be questioned. *Sic* is placed within **brackets**.

> *Example:* In *Basic Astronomy,* Professor Jones notes that the "earth does not revolve around the son [sic] at a constant rate."

simile

Simile is a direct comparison of two essentially unlike things, making the comparison with the word *like* or *as.* Similes state that A is *like* B.

> *Example:* His feelings about his business rival are so bitter that in recent conversations with his staff he has returned to the subject compulsively, *like a person scratching an itch.*

Like **metaphors**, similes can help illuminate difficult or obscure ideas.

Example: The odds against having your plant or business destroyed by fire are at least as great *as the odds against hitting the jackpot on a Las Vegas slot machine.* Because of the long odds, top management may consider sophisticated fire protection and alarm systems more costly than the risk merits and refuse to approve the expenditure. The plant fire protection chief is free to recommend whatever system he likes, but unless the system is required by fire codes or ordered by the insurance company, chances are it will never win top management's approval.

And yet, plants are destroyed by fire, *just as gamblers sometimes hit the jackpot on a one-armed bandit.* Losing big if fire strikes the plant, or winning big on a slot machine both depend on the chance alignment of three events or factors. . . .

—Jay R. Asher and Daniel T. Williams, Jr., "How Not to Lose the Fire Protection Gamble," *Occupational Hazards* (September 1974), p. 130.

simple sentence

A simple sentence has one **clause**. At its most basic, the simple sentence contains only a **subject** and a **predicate**.

Examples: Profits rose.
The strike ended.

Both the subject and the predicate may be compounded without changing the basic structure of the simple sentence.

Examples: *Tom, Janet, and Harry* worked on the sales brochure. (compound subject)
Tom *designed the layout and supplied the photographs.* (compound predicate)

Although **modifiers** may lengthen a simple sentence, they do not alter its basic structure.

Example: The *recently introduced* procedure works *very well.*

Inverting subject and predicate does not alter the basic structure of the simple sentence.

Example: A better job I never had.

A simple sentence may contain **noun phrases** and **prepositional phrases** in either the subject or the predicate.

Examples: The man *in the blue suit* is my boss. (prepositional phrase in the subject)
I rewrote the report *in one day.* (prepositional phrase in the predicate)

A simple sentence may include modifying **phrases** in addition to the independent clause. This fact causes most of the confusion about simple sentences.

> *Example:* Hard at work in my office, I did not realize how late it was. (This is a simple sentence because the introductory phrase is an adjective phrase and not a **dependent clause**.)

It is better to use simple sentences to state complex ideas. If readers must cope with a complicated **sentence** in addition to a complex idea, they are likely to become confused.

> *Change:* Throughout the year our company, like other companies, was confronted with a combination of management challenges—such as more intense competition in several markets, increased operating costs, and start-up costs for a number of new products—which put heavy pressure on earnings.
>
> *To:* Throughout the year our company, like other companies, was confronted with a combination of management challenges. Typical of these challenges are the intense competition in several markets, increased operating costs, and start-up costs for a number of new products. These challenges put heavy pressures on earnings.

Although simple sentences make complex ideas more digestible, a series of simple ideas should often be written in a more complex sentence.

> *Change:* The computer is a calculating device. It was once known as a mechanical brain. It has revolutionized industry.
>
> *To:* The computer, a calculating device once known as a mechanical brain, has revolutionized industry.

-size/-sized

As **modifiers**, the **suffixes** *-size* and *-sized* are more common to advertising copy than to general writing.

> *Examples:* a *king-sized* bed, an *economy-sized* carton

However, they are usually redundant unless they are part of the name of a product and should generally not be used.

> *Change:* It was a *small-size* desk.
> *To:* It was a *small* desk.

slash

Although not always considered a mark of **punctuation**, the slash performs punctuating duties by separating and showing omission. The slash is called a variety of names: slant line, virgule, bar, shilling sign.

USES

The slash is often used to separate parts of addresses in continuous writing.

Example: The return address on the envelope was Ms. Rose Howard/62 W. Pacific Court/Dalton/Ontario/Canada.

The slash often indicates omitted words and letters.

Examples: miles/hour for "miles per hour"; c/o for "in care of"; w/o for "without"

The slash separates the numerator from the denominator of a fraction.

Examples: 2/3 (2 of 3 parts); 3/4 (3 of 4 parts); 27/32 (27 of 32 parts)

The slash is sometimes used to indicate **brackets** on a typewriter that has no bracket key.

Example: Dr. Smith wrote that the earth "does not revolve around the son /sic/ at a constant rate." (See also **sic**.)

In informal writing, the slash is also used to separate day from month and month from year in **dates**.

Example: 12/29/74

so/such

So is often vague and should be avoided if another word would be more exact.

Change: She writes faster, *so* she finished before I did.
To: *Because* she writes faster, she finished before I did.

Another problem with *so* occurs with the **phrase** *so that*, which should never be replaced with *so* or *such that*.

Change: The report should be written *so* it can be copied.
To: The report should be written *so that* it can be copied.

> *Change:* The report should be written *such that* it can be copied.
> *To:* The report should be written *so that* it can be copied.

Such, an **adjective** meaning "of this or that kind," should not be used as a **pronoun**.

> *Change:* Our company does not need computers and we do not anticipate using *such*.
> *To:* Our company does not need computers and we do not anticipate using *any*.

some

When *some* functions as an **indefinite pronoun** for plural **count nouns**, or as an **indefinite adjective** modifying plural count nouns, use a plural **verb**.

> *Examples:* *Some* people *are* kinder than others.
> *Some* of us *are* prepared to leave.

Some is singular, however, when used with **mass nouns**.

> *Examples:* *Some* sand *has* trickled through the crack.
> *Some* oil *was* spilled on the highway.
> *Some* stationery *is* missing from the supply cabinet.
> Most of the water evaporates during the experiment, but *some* remains.

some/somewhat

Some, an **adjective** or **pronoun** meaning "an undetermined quantity" or "certain unspecified persons," should not replace the **adverb** *somewhat,* which means "to some extent."

> *Change:* *His writing has improved some.*
> *To:* His writing has improved *somewhat*.
> *Or:* His writing is *somewhat* improved.

some time/sometime/sometimes

Some time (two words) refers to a duration of time.

> *Example:* We waited for *some time* before calling the customer.

Sometime (one word) refers to an unknown or unspecified time.

> *Example:* We will visit with you *sometime*.

Sometimes refers to "occasional occurrences at unspecified times."

Example: He *sometimes* visits the branch offices.

spatial method of development

If you were reporting on a national chain department store, you might start with operations on the East Coast and develop your subject geographically to the West Coast. This is the spatial method of development, which can also be used to develop a subject from bottom to top, from near to far, from inside to outside, from right to left, and so on. Much **description** uses this **method of development.**

specie/species

Specie means "coined money" or "in coin."

Example: Paper currency was virtually worthless, and creditors began to demand payment in *specie*.

Species means a category of animals, plants, or things having some of the same characteristics or qualities. *Species* is the correct spelling for both singular and plural.

Example: The wolf is a member of the canine *species*.
Many animal *species* are represented in the Arctic.

specific-to-general method of development

This **method of development** begins with a specific statement and builds to a general conclusion. It is somewhat like **increasing order of importance as a method of development** in that it carefully builds its case, often with examples and **analogies** in addition to facts or statistics, and does not actually make its point until the end. For example, if your subject were highway safety, you might begin with a specific highway accident and then go on to generalize about how details of the accident were common enough to many similar accidents that recommendations could be made to reduce the probability of such accidents.

specifications

By definition, a specification is "a detailed and exact statement of particulars; especially a statement prescribing materials, dimensions, and workmanship for something to be built, installed, or manufactured." The most significant words in this definition are "detailed" and "exact." Although there are two broad categories of specifications—government specifications and industrial specifications—both require the writer of the specification to achieve a high degree of accuracy and exact technical detail. A specification must be written so clearly that no one could misinterpret any statement contained in it; therefore, do not imply or suggest—state explicitly what is needed. **Ambiguity** in a specification not only can waste money, it can result in a lawsuit. Because of the stringent requirements for completeness and exactness of detail in writing specifications, careful **research** and **preparation** are especially important before you begin to write, as is careful **revision** after you have completed the draft of your specification.

GOVERNMENT SPECIFICATIONS

Government agencies are required by law to contract for equipment strictly according to definitions provided in formal specifications. Government specifications are contractual documents that protect both the procuring government agency and the contractor.

A government specification is a precise definition of exactly what the contractor is to provide for the money he is paid. In addition to a technical description of the device to be purchased, the specification normally includes an estimated cost, an estimated delivery date, and the standards for the design, manufacture, workmanship, testing, training of government personnel, governing codes, inspection, and delivery of the item to be purchased. Government specifications are often used to prescribe the content and deadline for a **government proposal** submitted by a vendor or a company that wishes to bid on a project.

Government specifications are engineering and contractual documents with rules, **formats**, and peculiarities often known only to people trained in this specialty. What follows is a general description of the contents of a government specification. Detailed information on military and nonmilitary government specifications can be found in the following publications.

Military: *Specifications, Types and Forms.* Mil–S–83490. October 1968.
                   Standardization Policies, Procedures and Instructions. DOD–4120.3–M. January 1972.

Both are available from the Naval Publications and Forms Center, 5801 Tabor Avenue, Philadelphia, Pennsylvania 19120.

Nonmilitary: Federal Standardization Handbook. FPM12–29. July 1965. (Currently being revised.)

This handbook is available from the Government Printing Office, Washington, D.C. 20401.

Government specifications contain details on (1) the scope of the project, (2) the documents that the contractor is required to furnish with the purchased device, (3) the required product characteristics and functional performance of the purchased device, (4) the required tests, test equipment, and test procedures, (5) the required preparations for delivery, (6) notes, and (7) an **appendix**.

The "characteristics and performance" section of the specification (item three in the previous paragraph) must precisely define every product characteristic not covered by the engineering drawings, and it must precisely define every functional performance requirement the device must meet when it is operational. The "test" section of the specification (item four in the previous paragraph) must specify how the device is to be tested to verify that it meets all requirements. The test section includes the precise tests that are to be performed, the procedure to be used in conducting the tests, and the test equipment to be used (but in more general terms to avoid excluding equipment that is acceptable).

The following example is the beginning of a very long government specification for a computer installation.

Example:

Specification for JC/80 Computerized Building Automation System

1700.   PREFACE

1700.00.01   The building automation system as herein specified shall be provided in its entirety by the building automation contractor. The building automation contractor shall base his bid on the system as specified. Alternate techniques, modifications, or changes to any aspect of these specifications shall be submitted as a voluntary alternate.

Identification of this specification
Identification of a major section within this specification
Identification of a minor section within this major section
Identification of a paragraph within this minor section

1700.01.   VOLUNTARY ALTERNATES

1700.01.01   Voluntary alternates shall be fully documented and submitted to the consulting engineer ten working days prior to bid date for permission to bid the voluntary alternate. Permission to bid a voluntary alternate in no way implies that the alternate will be acceptable. Each voluntary alternate will be itemized as an add or deduct to base bid.

1700.01.02　　No voluntary alternate shall be considered from any bidder who has failed to submit a base quotation in full compliance with the building automation system specified herein.

1701.　## General Requirements

1701.01.　GENERAL

1701.01.01　The "computerized building automation system" herein specified shall be fully integrated and installed as a complete package by the building automation contractor. The system shall include all computer software and hardware, sensors, transmission equipment, required wiring, piping, preassembled control consoles, local panels, and labor supervision. Adjustment and calibration shall be provided as a prerequisite in the service contract specified hereafter.

1701.01.02　All input/output for central processing unit operation shall be ASCII (American Standard Code for Information Interchange) coded with standard EIA (Electronic Industries Association) interface hardware. Future incorporation of marketplace equipment prohibits any deviations from the standard ASCII-coded input/output or the standard EIA interface hardware.

1701.01.03　The building automation system operator shall have the capability to make several on-line adjustments to various system parameters and response to his requests shall occur immediately. The system shall be a combination of hardware and software to permit simultaneous data processing, output printing, and operator communications.

1701.02.　CONTRACTOR

1701.02.01　The building automation contractor shall have a local office within a 75-mile radius of the job site, staffed with factory-trained engineers fully capable of providing instructions and routine emergency maintenance service on all system components.

1701.03.　EXPERIENCE RECORD

1701.03.01　The building automation contractor shall have a 5-year successful history of the design and installation of fully computerized building systems similar in performance to that specified herein and shall be prepared to evidence this history as condition of acceptance and approval prior to bidding.

1701.04.　INSTALLATION

1701.04.01　The installation shall include computer programming, drawings, supervision, adjusting, validating, and checkout necessary for an operational system.

1701.04.02	The building automation contractor shall provide all other wiring necessary for system operation, including tie-ins from building automation system relays into motor starting circuits.
1701.04.03	All wiring performed by the building automation contractor shall be installed in accordance with all applicable local and national electrical codes.
1701.04.04	It shall be the responsibility of the building automation contractor to make a complete job survey prior to bid date to ascertain job conditions.
1702.	WORK PROGRESS
1702.00.01	To assure on-time completion of the project, the building automation contractor shall use a computerized quantitative weekly reporting system. Each week a progress report will be submitted to the owner's representative. The report shall be of actual construction progress, within plus or minus 1% accuracy, and shall be submitted within one week after work has been performed at the job site. Subjective reports and estimates of project completion are not acceptable.
1702.00.02	All weekly reports shall relate to manpower analysis of the project, giving dates the work is planned for completion and the number of calendar days actual job progress varies from the original plan.
1703.	CONTRACT COMPLETION, GUARANTEE, AND SERVICE
1703.00.01	All components, parts, and assemblies shall be guaranteed against defects in workmanship and materials for a period of one year after acceptance. In addition, the building automation contractor shall provide operator instruction and, if desired by the owner, system maintenance training as described hereinafter for the primary system as well as the subsystems.
1703.00.02	The following procedures shall govern the guarantee period. Within thirty days after the owner is receiving beneficial use of the building automation system, the contractor shall initiate the guarantee period by formally transmitting to the owner a 12-month service and maintenance contract marked "Paid in full." The contract shall become effective upon being dated with countersignature by the owner or his authorized representative. This service contract shall be a formal service agreement of the contractor, signed by an authorized employee, and shall include the monthly cost of the services to be provided.
1703.01.	SERVICE CONTRACT
1703.01.01	The service contract shall include the following minimum provisions:

01. Provide regularly scheduled preventive maintenance and service of at least one man-day per month by factory-trained service representatives of the building automation contractor.

02. Replace all defective parts and components as required.
03. Make available, upon request, emergency maintenance service.
04. Unless canceled by the owner 45 days prior to termination of the service agreement, the building automation contractor shall agree to continue the service on a monthly basis for an additional one-year period at the maintenance contract rates set forth in the agreement. . . .

INDUSTRIAL SPECIFICATIONS

The industrial specification is used in areas like computer software where there are no engineering drawings or other means of documentation. It is a permanent document, the purpose of which is twofold: (1) to document the item being implemented so that it can be maintained if the person who designed it is promoted, transferred, or leaves the company and (2) to provide detailed technical information on the item being implemented to all those in the company who need it (this includes other engineers and technicians, technical writers, technical instructors, and possibly salespeople and purchasing agents).

The industrial specification describes (1) a planned project (an A-spec), (2) a newly completed project (a B-spec), or (3) an old project (an F-spec). The A-spec describes how a planned project is going to be implemented, the B-spec describes how the newly completed project was implemented, and the F-spec describes the project as it finally exists after it has been operational long enough for all the problems to have been discovered and corrected. All three types of industrial specifications include a detailed technical description of all aspects of the item being described, including what was done, how it was done, what is required to use the item, how it is used, what its function is, who would use it, and so on. In addition, the A-spec often includes the estimated time to complete the project (in man-hours or man-months in addition to calendar months) and estimated costs.

The industrial specification differs from the **technical manual** that is given to the customer for the same project in that the specification contains minutely detailed information that the customer has no need for.

The following example is a specification for a computer utility routine that reads a deck of punched cards and prints in English the contents of each card. The name of the routine is CDPRNT. GAC is the name of another utility routine, and NEAT/3 is the name of a computer programming language.

Example:

2.8.8 CARD TO PRINTER

The purpose of this routine is to enable the user quickly and easily to verify and list a Hollerith Code punched card deck.

2.8.8.1 *Scope*

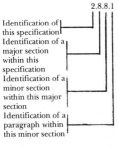

Identification of this specification
Identification of a major section within this specification
Identification of a minor section within this major section
Identification of a paragraph within this minor section

The CDPRNT routine will be of valuable use to any site that uses cards either as Monitor Control String records, NEAT/3 source lines, and/or data records. It also can be used in conjunction with other utility routines. For example, a deck of cards that has just been punched may be printed for easy visual validation. As another example, if (during an GAC run, using a card deck as the source file) an error or errors occur on the reading and translating of the cards, a simple run of the deck through the CDPRNT routine will list the cards and also verify the punch configurations against the set being used. If any of the punches are in error, the columns containing the errors are printed behind the card image in the listing.

2.8.8.2 *User Options*

The user is provided with a few simple but useful options. These are as follows:

1. *SET TYPE*— the user may choose either the extended A-set, H-set, or Site Code for translation of his cards.
2. *SLEW*— the user may slew either 1 or 2 lines between each card image on the printer.
3. *FILENAME*—an optional filename of ten characters may be entered, which will be printed at the top of each page.
4. *SPREAD*— the spread function, also optional, will differentiate between NEAT/3 Source Card types (C,D,F, etc.) and list them in a format similar to the compiler. If no entry is made on the parameter for the spread option, the cards will be printed in a straight 80-character format.

2.8.8.3 *Parameter Card*

The parameter card is designed as follows:

PAGE	LINE	REFERENCE	OPERATION	OPERANDS
1 2 3	4 5 6	7 8 9 10 11 12 13 14 15 16 17	18 19 20 21 22 23	24 25 26 27 28 29 30 31 32 33 34 35 36 37 38 39 40 41 42 43 44
		C S P E C $ U T I L	C D P R N T	S U D , , S , , S , , F I L E N A M E D O , , S ,
		C		E L P
		C		T E R
		C		W E
		C		A
		C		D
		C		

The explanation of the parameter is:

Column: 7–C indicates a control card.

8–16–SPEC$UTIL, identifies a utility routine.

18–21–CDPRNT, routine name.

24–26–SUD, symbolic unit designator of the card reader to be used as source.

28–SET, card set to be used.

H = Extended H-set

A = Extended A-set

S = SITECODE of Alternate Systems Disc

30–SLEW, signals printer number of lines to slew.

1 = Single space

2 = Double space

32–41–FILENAME, optional entry, allows the user to give a name to card file being printed. Ten-character name and version number.

43–SPREAD, an *S* entered in this column will cause the cards to be printed in NEAT/3 compiler type format. No entry in this column gives 80-character format.

S = SPREAD

□ = 80-character image

The parameter card is entered in the normal utility fashion.

There should be only one parameter card for each run.

2.8.8.4   *Card Verification*

As the card file is being read and translated, the CDPRNT routine detects any characters that cannot be translated and note the column of the card that is in error. The column or columns in error are then printed out immediately following the card image. The routine checks up to 10 errors in any single card. Upon reaching the 10th, the routine moves a message "BAD CARD" under the CHECK COLUMN heading on the print page. If such a message appears, it should inform the user that this particular card needs to be completely re-created as it has at least 10 errors in it.

2.8.8.5   *Translation Using Site Code*

By using the Site Code, the CDPRNT routine will be able to handle a nonstandard card code. The routine will expect the user to have the pack with the nonstandard code (which he has built by using SITECD routine) on the Alternate Systems Disc unit. CDPRNT will access the Site Code from the Alternate Systems Disc. The reason for specifying the alternate disc is that the program may be loaded in the standard A-set from the current systems disc, while the card file can still be translated in any code desired by the user.

spelling

The best advice for accurate spelling is to keep a good **dictionary** handy and look up the spelling of any word of which you are uncertain. Some words are spelled differently for different meanings, however, so read the definition of the word to be certain that you have found the right one. Any of the following dictionaries should serve you well for spelling.

The American Heritage Dictionary of the English Language, edited by William Morris. New York: The American Heritage Publishing Co., 1973.

Twenty-Thousand Words Spelled and Divided for Quick Reference, compiled by Lewis A. Leslie. New York: The McGraw-Hill Book Co., 1972.

Webster's New Collegiate Dictionary. Rev. ed. Springfield, Mass.: G. & C. Merriam Co., 1975.

Webster's New World Dictionary of the American Language. Second College Edition. New York and Cleveland: The World Publishing Co., 1974.

spin-off

In business usage, *spin-off* usually refers to the common stock received by stockholders of the parent corporation from the creation of a new corporation; however, it also refers to the new corporation. In technical usage, *spin-off* refers to benefits that come about in one area (for example, housing materials) as the result of achievements in another area (for example, space technology research). Do not use the term unless you are certain that all your **readers** understand it.

Example: The Teflon coating on cookware is a *spin-off* from the space program.

standard English

Standard English, unlike **nonstandard English**, is distinguished by its adherence to the conventional grammatical features of the language, by correctly spelled and carefully chosen words, and by punctuation that adheres to conventions established by the editorial policies of newspapers, magazines, publishing houses, dictionaries, usage handbooks, teachers, and others concerned with how our language is used. Because of mass education, travel, and the various media, standard English is the most common variety we encounter. Indeed, its chief advantage is that because it is commonly shared it promotes efficient understanding—a fact that explains its appropriateness to business and technical writing. It is, in fact, the language of business, industry, government, education, and the professions. (See also **English, varieties of.**)

strata

Strata is the plural form of *stratum,* meaning a "layer of material."

Examples: The land's *strata are* exposed by erosion.
Each *stratum is* clearly visible in the cliff.

style

A dictionary definition of *style* is "the way in which something is said or done, as distinguished from its substance." Arthur Schopenhauer, the German philosopher, called style "the physiognomy of the mind." A writer's style is determined by the way he thinks and by the way he transfers his thoughts to paper—uses words, **sentences**, images, **figures of speech**, **description**, **methods of development**, and so on.

A writer's style is the way his language functions in particular situations. For example, a letter to a friend would be relaxed, even chatty in **tone**, while a job application letter would be more restrained and deliberate. Obviously, the style appropriate to the one letter would not be appropriate to the other. In both letters, the audience and subject determine the manner or style the writer adopts.

Standard English can be divided into two broad categories of style —formal and informal—according to how it functions in certain situations. Understanding the distinction between a **formal writing style** and an **informal writing style** helps us to use the appropriate style in the appropriate place. We must recognize, however, that no clear-cut line divides the two categories and that some writing may call for a combination of the two styles.

When we consciously attempt to create a "style," we usually defeat our purpose. One writer may attempt to impress his **reader** with a flashy writing style, which is called **affectation**. Another may attempt to impress his reader with his scientific objectivity and produce a style that is dull and lifeless. Business and technical writing need be neither affected nor dull. It can be simple, clear, direct, and interesting—the key is to master the basic writing skills and to keep your reader in mind always. What will be both informative and interesting to your reader? When this question is uppermost in your mind, as you carefully apply the steps of the writing process, you will achieve an interesting and informative writing style. (See the Checklist of the Writing Process.)

The following passage from an article on oil drilling rescues a topic that could easily have turned into a mechanical, step-by-step exercise in tedium by the adroit use of **pace**, **emphasis**, and **parallel structure**.

Example: From the bamboo poles the Chinese used when the pyramids were young to the giant rigs drilling in a hundred feet of water today, there has been a lot of progress in the search for oil. But whether four thousand years ago or today, in ancient China or a modern city, in twenty fathoms of water or on top of a mountain, the object of drilling is and has always been the same—to manufacture a hole in the ground, inch by inch.

The hole may be either for a development well in a known field or for an exploratory (wildcat) well based on geophysical surface indications that conditions are right for the existence of oil. Except in a known field, the only way to know for certain whether oil actually exists beneath the surface of the earth is to drill a wildcat well; when the existence of oil has been verified, development wells are drilled to outline definitely the structure of the reservoir. . . .

The following guidelines will help you produce a brisk, interesting style. Concentrate on them as you revise your rough draft.

1. Use the active **voice**—not exclusively, but as much as possible without becoming awkward or illogical.
2. Use parallel structure whenever a sentence presents two or more thoughts that are equal in importance.
3. Avoid the monotony of a sing-song style by varying your sentence types and the length of your sentences.
4. Avoid stating positive thoughts in negative terms (write *40 percent responded* instead of *60 percent failed to respond*).
5. Concentrate on achieving the proper balance between emphasis and **subordination**.

Beyond an individual's personal style, there are various kinds of writing that have distinct stylistic traits, such as **technical writing style** and **business writing style**.

subject of sentence

The subject of a sentence (or clause) is a word or group of words about which the **sentence** or **clause** makes a statement. It indicates the topic of the sentence, telling what the **predicate** is about. It may appear anywhere in a sentence, but most often appears at the beginning.

Examples: *To increase sales* is our goal.
The wiring is defective.
We often work late.
That he will be fired is now doubtful.

The simple subject is a **substantive**; the complete subject is the simple subject and its **modifiers**.

Example: The procedures that you instituted have increased efficiency. (The simple subject is *procedures;* the complete subject is *the procedures that you instituted*.)

Grammatically, a subject must agree with its **verb** in **number**.

Example: The *departments have* much in common.
This *department has* several advantages.

The subject is the actor in active **voice** sentences.

Example: *Steve wrote* the report.

A compound subject has two or more elements as the subject of one verb.

Example: *The president* and *the treasurer agreed* to withhold the information.

Alternative subjects are joined by *or* and *nor*.

Example: Either *cash* or *a check* is acceptable.

Be careful not to shift subjects in a sentence; doing so may confuse your **reader**.

Change: *Radio amateurs* stay on duty during emergencies, and *sending messages* to and from disaster areas is their particular job.

To: *Radio amateurs,* who stay on duty during emergencies, are responsible for sending messages to and from disaster areas.

Or: *Radio amateurs* stay on duty during emergencies, sending messages to and from disaster areas.

subjective complement

A subjective complement is a **noun** or **adjective** in the **predicate** of a **sentence**; it completes the meaning of a **linking verb** by describing or renaming the subject of the **verb**.

Examples: The project director seems *confident.* (adjective describing the subject, *project director*)
Acme Corp. is *our major competitor.* (noun phrase renaming the subject, *Acme Corp.*)
His excuse was *that he had been sick.* (noun clause renaming the subject, *excuse*)
She is a *lawyer.* (noun renaming the subject, *she*)

The subjective complement is also known as a **predicate nominative** (noun) or a **predicate adjective** (adjective).

subordinating conjunction

Subordinating conjunctions connect **sentence** elements of varying importance, normally independent **clauses** and **dependent clauses**; they usually introduce the dependent clause. The most frequently used subordinating conjunctions are *so, although, after, because, if, where, than, since, as, unless, before, though, when,* and *whereas.* They are distinguished from **coordinating conjunctions**, which connect elements of equal importance.

Examples: He finished his report *and* he left the office. (coordinating conjunction)
She left the office *after* she finished her report. (subordinating conjunction)

When you introduce a clause with a subordinating conjunction, you make it a dependent clause.

Example: *Because we were late,* the client was angry.

The word *because* is a subordinating conjunction. Do not use the coordinating conjunction *and* as a substitute for it.

Change: We were late, *and* the client was angry.
To: The client was angry *because* we were late.

Be aware that words may serve multiple functions. *When, where, how,* and *why* serve both as **interrogative adverbs** and as subordinating conjunctions.

Examples: *When* will we go? (interrogative adverb)
We will go *when* he arrives. (subordinating conjunction)

Since, until, before, and *after* are used not only as subordinating conjunctions but also as **prepositions**.

Examples: *Since* we had all arrived, we decided to begin the meeting early. (subordinating conjunction)
I have worked on this project *since* last November. (preposition)

subordination

Subordination is a technique used by writers to show in the structure of a **sentence**, the appropriate relationship between ideas of unequal importance by subordinating the less important ideas to the more important ideas. The skillful use of subordination is a mark of mature writing.

Change: Beta Corp. now employs 500 people. It was founded just three years ago.
To: Beta Corp., which now employs 500 people, was founded just three years ago.
Or: Beta Corp., which was founded just three years ago, now employs 500 people.

Effective subordination can be used to achieve **sentence variety**, **conciseness**, and **emphasis**. For example, the sentence "The city manager's report was carefully illustrated, and it covered five typed pages" could be rewritten, using subordination, in any of the following ways.

Examples: The city manager's report, *which covered five typed pages,* was carefully illustrated. (adjectival clause)
The city manager's report, *covering five typed pages,* was carefully illustrated. (participial phrase)
The carefully illustrated report of the city manager covered five typed pages. (participial phrase)
The *five-page* report of the city manager was carefully illustrated. (single modifier)
The city manager's report, *five typed pages,* was carefully illustrated. (appositive phrase)

We sometimes use a **coordinating conjunction** to concede that an opposite or balancing fact is true; however, a subordinating **connective** can often make the point more smoothly.

Change: Their bank has a lower interest rate on loans, *but* ours provides a fuller range of essential services.
To: *Although* their bank has a lower interest rate on loans, ours provides a fuller range of essential services.

The relationship between a conditional statement and a statement of consequences is clearer if the condition is expressed as a subordinate **clause**.

Change: The bill was incorrect, and the customer was angry.
To: The customer was angry because the bill was incorrect.

Subordinating connectives (such as *because, if, while, when, though*) and **relative pronouns** *(who, whom, which, that)* achieve subordination effectively when the main clause states a major point and the **dependent clause** establishes a relationship of time, place, or logic with the main clause.

Example: Jane got the job *because* she was the most qualified applicant.

Relative pronouns *(who, whom, which, that)* can be used effectively to combine related ideas that would be stated less smoothly as independent clauses or sentences.

Change: Roger Smith is president of Interstate Insurance. He spoke at the national insurance forum last month.
To: Roger Smith, *who* is president of Interstate Insurance, spoke at the national insurance forum last month.

Avoid overlapping subordinate constructions, with each depending upon the last. Often the relationship between a relative pronoun and its antecedent will not be clear in such a construction.

Change: Shock, *which* often accompanies severe injuries, severe infections, hemorrhages, burns, heat exhaustion, heart attacks, food or chemical poisoning, and some strokes, is a failure of the circulation, *which* is marked by a fall in blood pressure *that* initially affects the skin (*which* explains pallor) and later the vital organs of kidneys and brain; there is a marked fall in blood pressure.

To: Shock often accompanies severe injuries, severe infections, hemorrhages, burns, heat exhaustion, heart attacks, food or chemical poisoning, and some strokes. It is a failure of the circulation, initially to the skin (this explains pallor) and later to the vital organs of kidneys and brain; there is a marked fall in blood pressure.

substantive

A substantive is a word, or a group of words, that functions in its **sentence** as a **noun**. It may be a noun, a **pronoun**, or a **verbal** (**gerund** or **infinitive**), or it may be a **phrase** or even a **clause** that is used as a noun.

Examples: The *report* is due today. (noun)
We must finish the project on schedule. (pronoun)
Several college graduates applied for the job. (noun phrase)
Drilling is expensive. (gerund)
To succeed will require hard work. (infinitive)
What I think is unimportant. (noun clause)

suffix

A suffix is a letter or letters added to the end of a word to change its meaning in some way. Suffixes can change the **part of speech** of a word.

Examples: The marketing survey was *useful* (adjective).
Its *usefulness* (noun) should be obvious to all.
The report was issued at just the right *time* (noun).
The report was very *timely* (adjective).

sweeping generalization

When the scope of an opinion is unlimited, the opinion is called a sweeping generalization. Such statements, though at times tempting to make, should be qualified during **revision**. Consider the following:

Examples: Anyone who succeeds in business today is dishonest.
Engineers are poor writers.

These statements ignore any possibility that someone may have succeeded in business without being dishonest or that there might be an engineer who writes superbly. Moreover, one person's definition of "success" or "dishonesty" or "poor writing" may be different from another's. No matter how certain you are of the general applicability of an opinion, use such all-inclusive terms as *anyone, everyone, no one, all,* and *in all cases* with caution. Otherwise, your opinions are likely to be judged irresponsible.

syllabication

When a word is too long to fit on a line, the proper place to divide it is often a troublesome question. The most general rule is to divide words between syllables. The following guidelines may be useful.

1. One-syllable words should not be divided.
2. Words with less than six letters should not normally be divided.
3. Fewer than three letters should not be left at the end of a line or carried over to begin a new line.
4. Words with **suffixes** or **prefixes** should be divided at, rather than within, the suffix or prefix.

   Change: su-permarket
   To: super-market

5. A hyphenated word should not be divided at the **hyphen** if the hyphen is essential to the meaning of the word. For example, *re-form* (to change the shape of something) and *reform* (to improve something) have different meanings. Thus it could be confusing to divide *re-form* at the hyphen.
6. **Abbreviations** and **contractions** should never be divided.
7. Proper names and company titles should not be divided.
8. The last word of a paragraph should not be divided.
9. The last word on a page should not be divided.

Secretarial handbooks with spellings and word divisions and **dictionaries** that indicate syllable breaks provide authoritative help. A handy guide is *20,000 Words for Stenographers, Students, Authors & Proofreaders,* compiled by Louis A. Leslie (New York: The McGraw-Hill Book Co., 1965).

symbols

From highway signs to mathematical equations, people communicate in written symbols. When a symbol seems appropriate in your writing, either be certain that your **reader** understands its meaning or place an explanation in **parentheses** following the symbol the first time it appears. However, never use a symbol when it would be clearer to write the meaning out instead. Following is a list of symbols and their appropriate uses.

Symbol	Meaning and Use
£	pound (basic United Kingdom unit of currency)
$	dollar (basic United States unit of currency)
O	oxygen (For a listing of all symbols for chemical elements, see a Periodic Table of Elements in a **dictionary** or handbook.)
+	plus
−	minus
±	plus or minus
∓	minus or plus
×	multiplied by
÷	divided by
=	equal to
≠ or ≠	not equal to
≈ or ≑	approximately (or nearly equal to)
≡	identical with
≢	not identical with
>	greater than
≯	not greater than
<	less than
≮	not less than
:	is to (or ratio)
≐	approaches (but does not reach equality with)
‖	parallel
⊥	perpendicular
√	square root
∛	cube root
∞	infinity
π	*pi*
∴	therefore (in mathematical equations)
∵	because (in mathematical equations)

( )	parentheses (See also **punctuation**.)
[ ]	brackets (See also **punctuation**.)
{ }	braces (used to group two or more lines of writing, to group figures in **tables** and to enclose figures in mathematical equations)
°F or °C	degree (Fahrenheit or Centigrade)
'	minute *or* foot
"	second *or* inch
#	number
*	asterisk (used to indicate a footnote when there are very few. When there are many footnotes, use numbers.)
&	ampersand
♂	male
♀	female
©	copyright
%	percent
%	in care of
a/o	account of
@	at (used in tables, but never in writing)
´	acute (French accent mark)
`	grave (French accent mark)
^	circumflex (French accent mark)
~	tilde (Spanish diacritical mark identifying the palatal nasal *ny*—*cañon*)
−	macron (marks a long phonetic sound, as in *cāke*)
ˇ	breve (marks a short phonetic sound, as in *brăcket*)
¨	dieresis or umlaut (mark placed over the second of two consecutive vowels indicating that the second is to be pronounced—*coöperate*)
‚	cedilla (mark placed beneath the letter "c" in French, Portuguese, and Spanish to indicate the letter is pronounced as "s"—*garçon*)
^	caret (a proofreader's mark used to indicate inserted material)
lb.	pound (measurement)
FR	franc (basic French unit of currency)
Mex $	peso (basic Mexican unit of currency)
$	peso (Philippine peso)
R	ruble (basic monetary unit of the U.S.S.R.)
¥	yen (basic Japanese unit of currency)

(See also **abbreviations**, **diacritical marks**, **proofreader's marks**, and **punctuation**.)

synonym

A synonym is a word that means nearly the same thing as another word.

Examples: purchase, acquire, buy; seller, vendor, supplier

The dictionary definitions of synonyms are usually identical; the **connotations** of such words, however, may differ. (A *seller* may be the same thing as a *supplier* but the term *supplier* does not suggest a commercial transaction as strongly as *seller*.)

Do not try to impress your **reader** by finding fancy or obscure synonyms in a **thesaurus**; the result is likely to be **affectation**. (See also **connotation/denotation** and **antonym**.)

syntax

Syntax refers to the way words, **phrases**, and **clauses** are put together to form an orderly and logical **sentence**. Because English sentences depend heavily on word order for meaning, the position a word occupies can change the meaning of the sentence.

Examples: He was *only* the messenger.
He was the *only* messenger.

T

table of contents

A table of contents is a list of chapters or sections in a book or **report**. It lists them in their order of appearance and cites their page numbers. Appearing at the front of a work, a table of contents permits the researcher to preview what is in the work and assess the work's value to him. It also aids the **reader** who may want to read only certain sections.

The length of your report should determine whether it needs a table of contents. If it does, use the major **heads** and subheads of your **outline** as a starting point.

Example: Table of Contents

Foreword i
Table of Contents iii
Part I: A Condensed Report of Observations 1
    Publications 2
    Organization 4
    Operation 6
    Personnel 8
Part II: Conclusions and Recommendations 9
Appendix A: Observations in Detail 14
    Publications 15
    Organization 23
    Operation 41
    Personnel 56
Appendix B: Individual Reports 85
    Memorandum from the Chairman 86
    Report by Walter Browser 88
    Report by Gerald Watson 92
    Report by Gunther Brown 96
    Report by Robert Helms 99

For punctuating a table of contents, see "leaders" in the entry **period**. (See also **library research**.)

tables

A table is useful for showing large numbers of specific, related statistics in a brief space. A table can present data in a more concise form than the text can, and a table is more accurate than graphic presentations because it provides numerous facts that a **graph** cannot convey. A table makes comparisons between figures easy because of the arrangement of the figures into rows and columns, although overall trends about the information are more easily seen in charts and graphs.

GUIDELINES FOR CREATING TABLES

Table Number. If you are using several tables, assign each a specific number; center the number and title above the table. The numbers are usually Arabic, and they should be assigned sequentially to

Table Number →
Title →
Boxhead →

Rule

Table 1.
RESULTS OF OPERATIONS

Column Captions

Income	1974	1973
	(000 omitted)	
Revenue from sales, services and equipment rentals	$1,979,003	$1,816,281
Costs and expenses		
Cost of sales, services and equipment rentals.....	1,116,783	1,046,097
Selling, general and administrative	579,881	551,844
Research and development	74,200	52,371
Interest	55,543	48,207
Other income, net......................	(20,027)	(24,156)
	1,806,380	1,674,363
Income before income taxes	172,623	141,918
Taxes on income	80,900	62,467
Income before minority interests.................	91,723	79,451
Minority interests in net earnings of subsidiaries....	4,558	7,490
Net income for the year	$ 87,165	$ 71,961
Primary earnings per share.................	$ 3.67	$ 3.10
Fully diluted earnings per share...............	$ 3.53	$ 3.00
EARNINGS RETAINED FOR USE IN THE BUSINESS	1974	1973
Balance January 1	$ 310,785	$ 250,224
Net income for the year	87,165	71,961
Cash dividends:		
Common—$.72 per share ($.48 in 1973).........	(16,759)	(10,923)
Preferred—$1.25 per share	(458)	(477)
Balance December 31	$ 380,733	$ 310,785

Source Line →

SOURCE: NCR Annual Report

Stub   Body

Table Number →
Title →
Boxhead →
Stub

Table 2.
Rule
Designations and Symbols of Multiples and Submultiples

Symbol	Designation	Factor	← Column Captions
T	...... Tera-	.... 10^{12}	 1,000,000,000,000
G	...... Giga-	.... 10^{9}	 1,000,000,000
M	...... Mega-	.... 10^{6}	 1,000,000
k or K	...... Kilo-	.... 10^{3}	 1,000
h	...... Hecto-	.... 10^{2}	 100
dk[1] da[2]	...... Deca-	.... 10^{1}	 10
d	...... Deci-	.... 10^{-1}	.... 0.1
c	...... Centi-	.... 10^{-2}	.... 0.01
m	...... Milli-	.... 10^{-3}	.... 0.001
μ	...... Micro-	.... 10^{-6}	.... 0.000001
n	...... Nano-	.... 10^{-9}	.... 0.000000001
p	...... Pico-	.... 10^{-12}	.... 0.000000000001

Footnotes →
[1] England and USA
[2] Continent countries

Source Line →
SOURCE: Documenta Geigy: Scientific Tables, Fifth ed.

Body

the tables throughout the text. Tables should be referred to in the text by table number rather than by direction ("Table 4" rather than "the above table"). If there are more than six tables in your **report** or paper, give them a separate heading ("List of Tables") and list them and their page numbers, together with any figure numbers, on a separate page immediately after the **Table of Contents**.

Title. The title, which is placed just above the table, should describe concisely what the table represents.

Boxhead. The boxhead carries the column headings. These should be kept concise but descriptive. Units of measurement, where necessary, should be specified either as part of the heading or enclosed in **parentheses** beneath the heading. Avoid vertical lettering where possible.

Stub. The left-hand vertical column of a table is the stub. It lists the items about which information is given in the body of the table.

Body. The body comprises the data below the boxhead and to the right of the stub. Within the body, columns should be arranged so that the terms to be compared appear in adjacent rows and columns. Leaders are often used between figures to aid the eye in following data from column to column (see Table 2). Where no information exists for a specific item, substitute a row of dots or a dash to acknowledge the gap.

Rules. These are the lines that separate the table into its various parts. Horizontal lines are placed below the title, below the body of the table, and between the column headings and the body of the table. They should not be closed at the sides. The columns within the table may be separated by vertical lines if they aid clarity.

Footnotes. **Footnotes** are used for explanations of individual items in the table. Symbols (*, #) or lower-case letters, rather than numbers, are ordinarily used to key table footnotes because numbers might be mistaken for the data in a numerical table. (Numbers are used in Table 3 of this entry because the symbols in the stub are letters.)

Source Line. The source line, which identifies where the data were obtained, appears below any footnotes (when a source line is appropriate).

Continuing Tables. When a table must be divided so that it can be continued on another page, repeat the boxhead and give the table number at the head of each new page with a "continued" label ("Table 3, continued").

technical information, letter of

The letter of technical information is an extremely common type of writing in business and industry. This type of letter is, in effect, a small technical report. It may take the form of a **memorandum** for use within your firm, or it may be a letter or a **report** to another firm.

Since this letter or memo is an abbreviated report, follow the appropriate steps of the writing process as you compose it. It is most helpful to your **reader** if you restate the problem in the letter or memo. Above all, be as clear and to the point as possible.

Consider the following letter. It addresses an updating problem peculiar to a specific computer. The writer spells out the problem by way of introduction, gives the background of the problem, and then goes on to suggest two possible solutions to it.

April 2, 1976

Parkside Office Machines Co.
123 Oceanview Drive
Seattle, Washington 98002

Ms. Judith Sparks
Technical Coordinator
Components Division
Parkside Office Machines Co.
Pines, New Jersey 04113

Dear Judy:

We've discovered a problem with our current block size restriction for the Decade 2000 computer. Many of our internal and customer publications on utility routines state that the Decade 2000 computer is normally restricted to a maximum block length of 4023 characters, but that this restriction can be lifted by setting Flag 20. This is misleading, and I am beginning to wonder if we should take a different approach. As I understand it, the problem is a hardware restriction in that the processor was wired to accommodate a maximum block length of 4023 characters. This created a problem for FRAN users because a FRAN track could accept a block of 4623 characters. The solution was to make a wiring change to make use of the first bit in the second "TA" character of control words, thereby doubling the maximum block length to 8046. This change was made about two years ago, but existing systems were not modified. Consequently, if a user who has one of the old systems sets Flag 20, the restriction is not going to be lifted as we say it will.

A couple of solutions quickly come to mind. We could

```
instruct the user to set the Flag only if his system
can accommodate an 8046-character block (if we assume
that he has this information).  We could give him the
change number of the update to the processor and in-
struct him to use Flag 20 only if his processor has
that number or greater.  I propose that we use the
second solution because the user is more likely to know
his change number than whether he can accommodate an
8046-character block.

Since the customer is directly involved, the solution
to the problem should probably be approved by your de-
partment.  Please let me know as quickly as possible
whether you approve of this solution because some of
our customer manuals are presently being revised.

                    Sincerely yours,


                    Gerald Stein
```

technical manual

Technical manuals are provided to customers and the manufacturer's technical personnel to enable the technical specialists and
customers to use and maintain the manufacturer's product. Technical manuals are normally written by professional technical writers,
although in smaller companies engineers and technicians may be
asked to write a technical manual.

The customers are normally businesses or industrial concerns.
The equipment is normally complicated mechanical, electrical, hydraulic, or pneumatic devices. The manuals may include operating
instructions, assembly and disassembly instructions, troubleshooting
guides, theory of operation, parts lists, engineering drawings, and so
on. They may be either bound or loose-leaf, although they are more
often loose-leaf to provide for easy updating.

In writing a technical manual, adhere to the Checklist of the Writing Process. **Preparation** and **organization** are especially important
because of the complexity of the project; give particular care to
outlining and review the entries on **instructions, explaining a process,** and **technical writing style.**

technical writing style

Technical writing is standard **exposition** that is usually done by a
specialist for another specialist; therefore, the **tone** is objective, with

the author's voice taking a back seat to the subject matter. Because the focus is on an object or a process, the language is utilitarian, emphasizing exactness rather than elegance. Thus the writing is usually not adorned with figurative language, except where a **figure of speech** would genuinely promote understanding. Technical writing requires an effective **introduction** or **opening**, good **organization, sentence variety**, the use of **heads**, and **illustrations**.

Effective technical writing avoids overuse of the passive **voice**. Its vocabulary is appropriately technical, although the general word is preferable to the technical word when the material allows the general word. (A jargony shorthand is a poor substitute for clear and direct writing; do not use a big or technical word merely because you know it—make certain that it belongs. See also **affectation**.)

Technical writing is direct and to the point; a theoretical treatment of the subject matter is usually avoided, as the following excerpt from a manual prepared by a computer manufacturer illustrates.

> *Example:*   The executive software controls all program-related functions, such as handling input and output operations, interpreting and executing macro instructions, providing format and translation capabilities, and handling error conditions. To conserve valuable memory space, only the pertinent software overlays are memory-resident during program execution; all other software overlays reside on disc and are called into memory only when needed.
>
> The software overlays that reside in memory during program execution are collectively called the executive software. Program-related software overlays (such as arithmetic and logic routines, the program overlay caller, the GET and PUT routines, the format and translation routines, etc.) are included in the user's object program by the compiler and are, therefore, called into memory with the program. Other executive routines and certain hardware control information are read into dedicated memory locations (called the Resident Executive Area) by Monitor at the start of the day and between programs; this group of routines and the control information comprise the Resident Executive. When necessary, the Resident Executive's Special I/O routine calls disc-resident software overlays into the Primary Software Overlay Area (PSOA), which is a 512-byte area of memory located beyond the user's program area.
>
> —*NCR Century Operating System Manual*, NCR Corporation

The **format** in this type of writing is usually clear-cut. The chief advantage of a well-defined format is that it gives the writer a mechanical way of organizing his material while helping the **reader** keep track of where the writer is going. In writing that is concerned with descriptions, processes, and sequences, a well-defined format grows out of the subject matter itself. (See also **style** and **formal writing style**.)

tenant/tenet

A *tenant* is one who holds or temporarily occupies a property owned by another person.

>   *Example:* The *tenants* of the office building were upset by the increased rent.

A *tenet* is an opinion or belief held by a person or an organization.

>   *Example:* The idea that competition will produce adequate goods and services for a society is a central *tenet* of capitalism.

tense

Tense is the grammatical term for **verb** forms that indicate time distinctions. There are six basic tenses in English: past, past perfect, present, present perfect, future, and future perfect. Each of these has a corresponding progressive form.

Basic	Progressive
I began (past)	I was beginning (past)
I had begun (past perfect)	I had been beginning (past perfect)
I begin (present)	I am beginning (present)
I have begun (present perfect)	I have been beginning (present perfect)
I will begin (future)	I will be beginning (future)
I will have begun (future perfect)	I will have been beginning (future perfect)

An advantage of the perfect tenses is that they allow you to express a prior action or condition that continues in a present, past, or future time.

>   *Examples:* I *have begun* to write the annual report, and I will work on it for the rest of the month. (*present perfect*)
>   I *had begun* to read the manual when the lights went out. (*past perfect*)
>   I *will have begun* this project by the time funds are allocated. (*future perfect*)

Note from the table that the progressive forms are created by combining the **helping verb** *be*, in the appropriate tenses, with the present **participle** (*-ing*) form of the main verb.

PAST TENSE

The simple past tense indicates that an action took place in its entirety in the past. The past tense is usually formed by adding *-d* or *-ed* to the root form of the verb.

Example: We *closed* the office early yesterday.

PAST PERFECT TENSE

The past perfect tense indicates that one past event preceded another. It is formed by combining the helping verb *had* with the past participle form of the main verb.

Example: He *had finished* by the time I arrived.

PRESENT TENSE

The simple present tense represents action occurring in the present, without any indication of time duration.

Example: I *see* the client.

A general truth is always expressed in the present tense.

Example: He learned that the saying "time *heals* all wounds" is true.

The present tense can be used to present actions or conditions that have no time restrictions.

Example: A neat desk *increases* efficiency.

The present tense can be used to indicate habitual action.

Example: I *pass* the paint shop on the way to my department every day.

The present tense can be used as the "historical present" to make things that occurred in the past more vivid.

Example: He *asks* for more information on production statistics and *receives* a detailed report on every product manufactured by the company. Then he *asks*, "Is each department manned at full strength?" In his office, surrounded by his staff, he *goes* over the figures and *plans* for the coming year.

PRESENT PERFECT TENSE

The present perfect tense describes something from the recent past that has a bearing on the present—a period of time before the present but after the simple past. The present perfect tense is formed by combining a form of the helping verb *have* with the past participle form of the main verb.

> *Examples:* He *has retired,* but he visits the office frequently.
> We *have finished* the draft and are ready to begin revising it.

FUTURE TENSE

The simple future tense indicates a time that will occur after the present. It uses the helping verb *will* (or *shall*) plus the main verb.

> *Example:* I *will finish* the job tomorrow.

FUTURE PERFECT TENSE

The future perfect tense indicates action that will have been completed at a future time. It is formed by linking the helping verbs *will have* to the past participle form of the main verb.

> *Example:* As of tomorrow, I *will have worked* here two years.

TENSE AGREEMENT OF VERBS

The verb of a subordinate **clause** should usually agree in tense with the verb of the main clause. (See also **agreement**.)

> *Examples:* When Ms. Jones *dictates* a letter, she *wants* it typed immediately.
> When Ms. Jones *dictated* a letter, she *wanted* it typed immediately.

Shift in Tense. Be consistent. The only legitimate shift in tense records a real change in time. When you choose a tense in telling a story or discussing an idea, stay with that tense. Illogical shifts in tense will confuse your **reader**.

> *Change:* Before Tom *called* the irate client, he *made* sure he *understands* the problem.
> *To:* Before Tom *called* the irate client, he *made* sure he *understood* the problem.

that . . . that

Avoid unnecessary repetition of *that.*

> *Change:* I think *that* when this project is finished *that* you should write the results.
> *To:* I think *that* you should write the results when the project is finished.

Or:	Write the results when the project is finished.
Change:	You will note *that* as you assume greater responsibility and as your years of service with the company increase, *that* your benefits increase accordingly.
To:	You will note *that* as you assume greater responsibility and as your years of service with the company increase, your benefits increase accordingly.
Or:	You will note *that* your benefits increase as you assume greater responsibility and as your years of service with the company increase.

(See also **conciseness/wordiness**.)

that/which/who

Who refers to persons, and *that* and *which* refer to animals and things.

Examples:	John Brown, *who* is retiring tomorrow, has worked for the company twenty years.
	Please return the files *that* you borrowed.
	Our Atlanta store, *which* opened last year, is very profitable.

In informal usage, *that* may refer to persons as well as to things.

Example:	The (man, book) *that* I saw was old.

That is often overused (see **that . . . that**). However, do not eliminate it if to do so would cause **ambiguity** or problems with **pace**.

Change:	We ask you sign the contract and return it to us by the 15th.
To:	We ask *that* you sign the contract and return it to us by the 15th.

Which, rather than *that,* should be used with nonrestrictive **clauses** (clauses that do not change the meaning of the basic sentence).

Example:	After John left the restaurant, *which* is one of the best in New York, he came directly to my office.

(See also **who/whom** and **relative pronoun**.)

there/their/they're

There, their, and *they're* are often confused because they sound alike. *There* is an **expletive** or an **adverb**.

Examples: *There* were more than 1,500 people at the conference. (expletive)
More than 1,500 people were *there*. (adverb

Their is the possessive form of *they*.

Example: Our employees are expected to keep *their* desks neat.

They're is a **contraction** of *they are*.

Example: If *they're* right, we should change the design.

thesaurus

A thesaurus is a book of words with their **synonyms** and **antonyms**, arranged by categories. A thesaurus gives you an idea of the scope and flexibility of the English language. Thoughtfully used, it can help you with **word choice** during the **revision** phase of the writing process. However, this variety of words may tempt you to choose inappropriate or obscure synonyms just because they are available; use a thesaurus to clarify, not to prettify, your language. Never use a word unless you are sure of its meanings; **connotations** of the word that might be unknown to you could mislead your **reader**. (See also **affectation** and **defining terms**.)

thus/thusly

Thus is an **adverb** meaning "in this manner" or "therefore." The *-ly* in *thusly* is superfluous and should be avoided.

Change: The committee's work is done. *Thusly* we should have the report by the twenty-fifth.
To: The committee's work is done. *Thus* we should have the report by the twenty-fifth.

'til/till/until

'Til is a nonstandard spelling of *till* and *until*, meaning "up to the time of." Use *till* or *until*.

Change: We worked *'til* eight o'clock.
To: We worked *till* eight o'clock.
Or: We worked *until* eight o'clock.

title

Since the title of your writing project is the first thing your **reader** sees, it should perform several functions: (1) it should indicate the specific **topic**, (2) it should suggest the project's **scope** and **objective**, (3) it should attract the reader's interest, and (4) it should possibly even reflect the **tone** of the writing.

> *Example:* "The Improvement of Technical Publications at the Mecca Corporation"

Do not create titles that are too vague, such as "Technical Publications," or titles that are too broad, such as "A Survey of Technical Publications." Titles are often important to researchers because they may have only a title on which to decide whether to read a particular article.

to/too/two

To, too, and *two* are confused only because they sound alike. *To* is a **preposition** or the mark of an **infinitive**.

> *Examples:* Send the report *to* the district manager. (preposition)
> I wish *to* go. (mark of the infinitive)

Too is an **adverb** meaning "excessively" or "also."

> *Examples:* The price was *too* high. (meaning "excessively")
> I, *too,* thought it was high. (meaning "also")

Two is a **numeral adjective**.

> *Example:* Only *two* buildings have been built this fiscal year.

tone

The word *tone,* with regard to writing, means much the same thing as it does when we speak of someone's "tone of voice." Tone involves many things, but it always reflects a combination of your attitude toward your subject and your attitude toward your **reader**. Are you bored with the subject? Unless you are very careful, boredom is likely to come through in the tone of your writing. Are you angry with the reader? Do you consider the reader stupid? These attitudes, too, are likely to come through; and therefore the tone of your writing may easily defeat your **objective**. Obviously, your choice of a formal writing style or an **informal writing style** directly affects the tone of your writing. So does your **word choice**. Your **title**, your **introduction** or **opening**, even your selected **method of development**—all of these contribute to determining tone. For instance, a title such as "Some Observations on the Diminishing Oil Reserves in Wyoming" clearly sets a tone quite different from "What Happens When We've Pumped Wyoming Dry?"

The important thing is to make sure that your tone is the best one to achieve your objective. To ensure that it is, keep your reader always in mind.

topic

In the business world, the topic of a writing project is usually determined by need. In a college writing course, on the other hand, you may have to select your own topic. If you do, keep the following points in mind.

1. Select a topic that interests you.
2. Select a topic that you can **research** adequately with the facilities available to you.
3. Limit your topic so that its **scope** is small enough to handle within the time you are given. A topic like "Air Pollution," for example, would be too broad.
4. Keep the topic broad enough so that you will have enough to write about. "Carbon Monoxide Emissions in the 1971 Chevrolet" would probably be too small. A realistic topic might be "Our Local Power Company's Effort to Reduce Toxic Emissions."
5. Select a topic for which you can make adequate **preparation** to ensure a good final **report**.

topic sentence

A topic sentence states the controlling idea of a **paragraph**; the rest of the paragraph supports and develops that statement with carefully related details. The topic sentence may appear anywhere in the paragraph—a fact that permits the writer variety in **style**—and a topic statement may also be more than one sentence if necessary.

The topic sentence is often the first sentence because it states the subject.

> *Example:*   *The arithmetic of searching for oil is stark.* For all his scientific
> methods of detection, the only way the oilman can actually
> know for sure that there is oil in the ground is to drill a well.
> The average cost of drilling an oil well is over $100,000, and
> drilling a single well may cost over $1,000,000! And once the
> well is drilled, the odds against its containing any oil at all are
> 8 to 1! Even after a field has been discovered, one out of every
> four holes drilled in developing the field is a dry hole because
> of the uncertainty of defining the limits of the producing
> formation. The oilman can never know what Mark Twain
> once called "the calm confidence of a Christian with four aces
> in his hand."
>
> —*The Baker World*, Baker Oil Tools, Inc.

On rare occasions, the topic sentence logically falls in the middle
of a paragraph.

> *Example:*   It is perhaps natural that psychologists should awaken only
> slowly to the possibility that behavioral processes may be di-
> rectly observed, or that they should only gradually put the
> older statistical and theoretical techniques in their proper per-
> spective. But it is time to insist that science does not progress
> by carefully designed steps called "experiments," each of
> which has a well-defined beginning and end. *Science is a contin-*
> *uous and often a disorderly and accidental process.* We shall not do
> the young psychologist any favor if we agree to reconstruct
> our practices to fit the pattern demanded by current scientific
> methodology. What the statistician means by the design of
> experiments is design which yields the kind of data to which
> *his* techniques are applicable. He does not mean the behavior
> of the scientist in his laboratory devising research for his own
> immediate and possibly inscrutable purposes.
>
> —B. F. Skinner, "A Case History in Scientific Method," *The American Psychologist*, II, No. 5
> (May 1956), 232.

Although the topic sentence is usually most effective early in the
paragraph, a paragraph can effectively be made to lead up to the
topic sentence; this is sometimes done to achieve **emphasis**. When a
topic sentence concludes a paragraph, it can also serve as a summary
or **conclusion**, based on the details that were designed to lead up
to it.

> *Example:*   Energy does far more than simply make our daily lives more
> comfortable and convenient. Suppose you wanted to stop—
> and reverse—the economic progress of this nation. What
> would be the surest and quickest way to do it? Find a way to
> cut off the nation's oil resources! Industrial plants would shut
> down; public utilities would stand idle; all forms of transporta-

tion would halt. The economy would plummet into the abyss of national economic ruin. *Our economy, in short, is energy-based.*

—*The Baker World,* Baker Oil Tools, Inc.

Occasionally, the controlling idea of a paragraph—what would normally be its topic sentence—is not explicitly stated but only implied. Nevertheless, if the paragraph has **unity**, a sentence stating the controlling idea *could* be written and all the sentences in the paragraph would be found to be related directly to it. However, people writing in business and industry are well advised to make their topic sentences *explicit.*

tortuous/torturous

Tortuous means "marked by twisting and winding."

Example: The highway through the mountain was *tortuous.*

Torturous means "causing pain, as to punish."

Example: The prisoner's experience was *torturous.*

toward/towards

Both *toward* and *towards* are acceptable variant spellings of the **preposition** meaning "in the direction of"; *toward* is more common in the United States, and *towards* is more common in Great Britain.

Example: We walked *toward* (or *towards*) the vice-president's office.

transition

Transition is the means of achieving a smooth flow of ideas from **sentence** to sentence and from **paragraph** to paragraph. Transition is a two-way indicator of what has been said and what will be said; it may be accomplished by a word, a **phrase**, or even a paragraph. Without the guideposts of transition, **readers** can lose their way.

Certain words and phrases are inherently transitional. Consider the following terms and their functions.

Examples: hence, therefore, consequently, as a result (All express *result.*)
for example, as an illustration, for instance, specifically (All express *example.*)
similarly, likewise, on the other hand (All express *comparison.*)
moreover, furthermore, also, too, besides (All express *addition.*)

490 transition

that is, in other words, in short, to conclude, in summary, so, thus, accordingly, but, however, conversely, indeed, in fact, no doubt (Other common words and phrases that are inherently transitional.)

Within a paragraph, such transitional expressions make for clarity and smoothness in the movement from idea to idea. Conversely, the lack of transitional devices can make the going bumpy for the reader. Consider first the following passage, which lacks adequate transition.

Example: People had always hoped to fly, but until 1903 it was only a dream. It was thought by some that human beings were not meant to fly. The Wright brothers launched the world's first heavier-than-air flying machine. The airplane has become a part of our everyday life.

Now read the same passage with words and phrases of transition added (in italics), and notice how much more smoothly the thoughts flow.

Example: People had always hoped to fly, but until 1903 it was only a dream. *Before,* it was thought by some that human beings were not meant to fly. *In 1903* the Wright brothers launched the world's first heavier-than-air flying machine. *Now* the airplane has become a part of our everyday life.

And finally, read the same passage with stronger transition provided.

Example: People had always hoped to fly, but until 1903 it was only a dream. *Before that time,* it was thought by some that human beings were not meant to fly. *However,* in 1903 the Wright brothers launched the world's first heavier-than-air flying machine. *Since then* the airplane has become a part of our everyday life.

If your **organization** and **outline** are good, your transitional needs will be less difficult to satisfy (although they must nonetheless *be* satisfied). Just as the outline is a road map for the writer, transition is a road map for the reader.

TRANSITION BETWEEN SENTENCES

In addition to using transitional words and phrases such as those shown above, the writer may achieve effective transition between sentences by repeating key words or ideas from preceding sentences, by using **pronouns** that refer (clearly) to antecedents in previous sentences, and by using **parallel structure**—that is, by repeating the pattern of a phrase or **clause**. Consider the following short paragraph, in which all these means are employed. (A few examples are indicated by italics; however, to mark them all would be confusing.)

> *Example:* Representative of many American university towns is Millville. Once a *sleepy farming community,* today *it* is the home of a large and *bustling academic community.* The *university* has, in fact, become *Millville*'s major industry, generating most of *the town*'s income—and, of course, many of *its* problems, too.

Another device for achieving transition is enumeration:

> *Example:* The recommendation rests upon *three conditions. First,* the department staff must be expanded to a sufficient size to handle the increased work load. *Second,* sufficient time must be provided for the training of the new members of the staff. *Third,* a sufficient number of qualified applicants must be available within the allotted time.

TRANSITION BETWEEN PARAGRAPHS

All the means discussed above for achieving transition between sentences—and especially the device of repetition of key words or ideas—may also be effective for transition between paragraphs. For paragraphs, however, longer transitional elements are often required. One technique is to use an opening sentence that summarizes the preceding paragraph and then moves ahead to the business of the new paragraph.

> *Example:* Mike Stanley's car battery was dead, and he arrived at the office twenty minutes late. His boss, George Brown, signaled for him to come into his office. Brown leaned back in his swivel chair, crossed his hands over his vest, and looked thoughtful. "You know, today people don't seem to take responsibility as seriously as they used to. Tardiness seems almost to be a way of life these days." Mike suppressed a groan and set his mind to receive a lecture. "What people don't seem to realize any more is that when one person is late, everyone suffers," George went on, warming to his subject. "The morale of the department suffers, the company loses money, the individual suffers when he gets a bad performance rating and doesn't get raises and promotions. . . ." Thirty minutes later, when Mike returned to his desk, Hank, at the next desk, asked him with a grin, "What did old George say?" Mike cast Hank a baleful glance and responded, "He told me to get here on time."
>
> *What Mike did for Hank was to extract the significant information*

from George's thirty-minute lecture and reduce it to a single sentence, thereby illustrating the fundamental purpose of taking notes: to summarize and record. . . .

Ask a question at the end of one paragraph and answer it at the beginning of the next.

Example: Automation has become an ugly word in the American vocabulary because it has at times displaced some jobs. But the all-important fact that is so often overlooked is that it invariably creates many more jobs than it eliminates. (The vast number of people employed in the great American automobile industry as compared with the number of people that had been employed in the harness-and-carriage-making business is a classic example.) Almost always, the jobs that have been eliminated by automation have been menial, unskilled jobs, and those who have been displaced have been forced to increase their skills, which resulted in better and higher-paying jobs for them. *In view of these facts, is automation really bad?*

    There is no question that it has made our country the most wealthy and technologically advanced nation the world has ever known. . . .

A purely transitional paragraph may be inserted to aid readability.

Example: . . . that marred the progress of the company.

    There were two other setbacks to the company's fortunes that year which also marked the turning of the tide: the loss of many skilled workers through the Early Retirement Program and the intensification of the devastating rate of inflation.

    The Early Retirement Program . . .

CHECKING FOR TRANSITION DURING REVISION

Check for **unity** and **coherence** to determine whether transition is effective. If a paragraph has unity and coherence, the sentences and ideas are tied together and contribute directly to the subject of the paragraph. Look for places where transition is missing and provide it. Look for places where it is weak and strengthen it.

transitive verb

A transitive verb is one that requires **direct object**, with or without an **indirect object**, to complete its meaning.

    The direct object is normally a **noun** or a **pronoun** that names the thing being acted upon by the **verb**. A direct object answers the question "What?" or "Whom?"

Examples: Ms. Jones wrote the *memorandum* (*Wrote* is a transitive verb.)
Ms. Jones hired John. (*Hired* is a transitive verb.)

An indirect object answers the question "*To* whom or what?" or "*For* whom or what?" That is, it normally names the person or thing that receives the direct object.

Examples: John gave *Ms. Jones* the printout. (*Ms. Jones,* the indirect object, tells "to whom"; *gave* is the transitive verb and *printout* is the direct object.)

Ms. Jones gave *the printout* careful study. (*The printout,* the indirect object, tells "to what"; *gave* is the transitive verb and *study* is the direct object.)

(See also **complement**.)

transmittal, letter of

The cover letter, or letter of transmittal, accompanying a **formal report**, **sales proposal**, or similar document may be a formal letter, or it may be an informal **memorandum**. It should include (1) the subject of the report, (2) the authorization for the report, (3) an offer to answer any questions the recipient may have, and (4) an acknowledgment of any assistance received in the preparation of the report. It may also include additional information, depending on the specific case. (See also **correspondence**.) The following is a typical letter of transmittal.

```
                                    Evans & Associates
                                    520 Niagara Street
                                    Lexington, Ky. 17302
                                    May 5, 1976

                   Boston Transit Authority
                   31 Atalmac Avenue
                   Boston, Mass. 02210

                   Gentlemen:

Authorization →    As you requested on February 2, 1975, we are
                   submitting an evaluation of your safety mea-
Subject →          sures for your intercity rail system.

                   We believe that the report is thorough and
```

<table>
<tr><td>Offer to answer
questions →</td><td>self-explanatory; however, if you would like
further clarification, we will be happy to
meet with you to answer any questions that may
arise.</td></tr>
<tr><td>Acknowledgment of
assistance →</td><td>We would like also to take this opportunity to
express our appreciation to Mr. L. K. Sullivan
of your committee for his assistance during
our stay in Boston.</td></tr>
</table>

> Sincerely,
>
> *Catherine Brown*
>
> Catherine Brown
> Director of Research
>
> Enclosure: Safety Report

trip report

The trip report is one of the more common types of reports that must be prepared by business and technical people. The trip report should state (1) the purpose of the trip, (2) the project necessitating the trip, (3) the person or persons contacted during the course of the trip, (4) the date of the trip, and (5) the conclusions reached as a result of the trip. See the following example.

                                                    February 6, 1976

TO: J. L. Watson

FROM: T. R. Santow

SUBJECT: Trip to Milwaukee the Week of January
           17, 1976.

The purpose of this trip was to gather information on
(1) operating the new disc in a single-spindle environment, (2) system scheduling, (3) data base, (4)
indexed sequential, (5) the small inquiry system, (6)
random filing system, and (7) the roll-in/roll-out
software.

Disc

I talked with Kevin Hutch, Janet Martin, and Gerald
MacDougal about the need for a separate card control
string to bring the new disc up in a single-spindle
mode. I also discussed the possibility of altering the
software so that it will search for a program on the

current system disc and then on the library disc in the
single-spindle mode, and the possibility of identifying
a library disc on the PAL printout.

I observed the disc in operation when Ralph Stevens ran
some test routines. It appeared to run faster than the
same routines run on the old disc. It soon became apparent, as I watched the tests being run, that the
speed of the actuator and the rotational speed of the
disc make the operating environment considerably different from what anyone had anticipated. Timing tests
will have to be run on the relationship between file
positions and throughput before we can write our file
placement document.

System Scheduling

I talked to Bill Wilson about S7 System Scheduling. At
the conclusion of our discussion, he agreed to send
someone to Dayton to work with us when all the necessary information is available. I also talked to Bill
about the interim publications/pilot site relationship;
he felt that we should have our interim publications,
as well as the writer, at the key pilot sites so that
documentation can be tested as well as the software and
the hardware.

Data Base

I discussed Data Base with Wayne Sewell and Ellen
Golden to get a feel for the current status of the
project, as well as for its progress, to determine when
we might expect to become involved; however, the
project does not seem to be far enough along yet for us
to be concerned.

Indexed Sequential

I discussed Indexed Sequential with Margaret Miller;
she had the information I needed, but informed me that
Indexed Sequential will not be her responsibility in
the future. On the basis of that, I tried to determine
new assignments of responsibility in Milwaukee. Things
are shifting so fast that it is difficult to keep up.

Small Inquiry System and Random Filing System

I discussed the Small Inquiry System with Wally Bevins.
He feels that the software is firm and that we should
begin work on it at our earliest opportunity. I also
discussed the Random Filing System with him; we must
add the new disc to this publication and do some additional updating.

Roll-In/Roll-Out Software

I talked to Janet Martin about Roll-In/Roll-Out specifications and found that they are as complete as we can
expect them to be. She feels that the specifications
are firm and that we should begin work on this project
soon.

trite language

Trite language is made up of words, **phrases**, or ideas that have been used so often that they are stale. Trite language necessarily contains many **clichés**.

> *Change:* *It may interest you to know* that all the folks in the branch office are *hale and hearty*. I should finish my project *quick as a wink,* and we should *clean up* on it.
>
> *To:* Everyone here at the branch office is well. I should finish my project within a week, and I'm sure it will prove profitable for us.

Trite language shows that the writer is thoughtless in his **word choice** or that he is not thinking carefully about his **topic**; he is relying instead on what others have thought and said before him. (See also **affectation**.)

try and

The **phrase** *try and* is colloquial for *try to*. Unless you are writing a casual personal letter, it is better to use *try to*.

> *Change:* Please *try and* finish the report on time.
> *To:* Please *try to* finish the report on time.

U

unity

Unity is singleness of purpose and treatment, the cohesive element that holds a piece of writing together; it means that everything in an article or paper is essentially about one thing or idea.

To achieve unity, the writer must select one **topic** and then treat it with singleness of purpose—without digressing into unrelated paths. The prime contributors to unity are a good **outline** and effective **transition**. Transition dovetails **sentences** and **paragraphs** together like the joints of a well-made drawer. Notice, for example, how neatly the sentences in the following paragraph are made to fit together by the italicized words and **phrases** of transition.

> *Example:* Any company which operates internationally today faces a host of difficulties. Inflation is worldwide. Most countries are struggling with other economic problems *as well. In addition,* there are many monetary uncertainties and growing economic nationalism directed against multinational companies. *Yet* there is ample business available in most developed countries if you have the right products, services, and marketing organization. To maintain the growth NCR has achieved overseas, we recently restructured our international operations into four major trading areas. *This* will improve the services and support which the corporation can provide to its subsidiaries around the world. *At the same time,* it establishes firm management control, ensuring consistent policies around the world. *So* you might say the problems of doing business abroad will be more difficult this year, but we are better organized to meet those problems.
>
> —*1974 Annual Report,* NCR Corporation

The logical sequence provided by a good outline is essential to achieving unity. An outline enables the writer to lay out the most direct route from **introduction** to **conclusion** without digressing into side issues that are not related, or that are only loosely related, to the subject. Without establishing and following such a direct route, the writer's work is not likely to be unified.

up

Adding the word *up* to **verbs** often creates a redundant **phrase**.

> *Change:* We have opened *up* ten new markets this year.
> *To:* We have opened ten new markets this year.

usage

Usage is a term used to describe the choices we make among the various words and constructions available in our language. The line between **standard English** and **nonstandard English**, or between formal and informal English, is determined by these choices. Your guideline in any situation involving such choices should be appropriateness: is the word or expression you use appropriate to your **reader** and subject? When it is, you are practicing good usage.

This book has been designed to help you sort out the appropriate from the inappropriate: just look up the item in question in the index. A good **dictionary** is also an invaluable aid in your selection of the right word.

utilize

Utilize should not be used as a **long variant** of *use,* which is the general word for "to employ for some purpose."

> *Change:*   You can *utilize* the fourth elevator to reach the 50th floor.
> *To:*   You can *use* the fourth elevator to reach the 50th floor.

Utilize should be reserved for the sense of "to turn to practical purposes; to make useful."

> *Example:*   We can *utilize* the computer in making our sales predictions.

V

vague words

A vague word is one that is imprecise in the context in which it is used. Some words encompass such a broad range of meanings that there is no focus for their definition. Words such as *real, nice, important, good, bad, thing,* and *fine* are often called "omnibus words" because they can mean everything to everybody. In speech we sometimes use words that are less than precise, but our vocal inflections and the context of our conversation make their meanings clear. Since writing cannot rely upon vocal inflections, avoid the use of vague words. Be concrete and specific. (See also **abstract words/ concrete words**.)

> *Change:*   It was a *meaningful* meeting, and we got *a lot* done.
> *To:*   The meeting resolved three questions: pay scales, fringe benefits, and work loads.

verb

A *verb* is a word, or a group of words, that describes an action (The antelope *bolted* at the sight of the hunters), states the way in which something or someone is affected by an action (He *was saddened* by the death of his friend), or affirms a state of existence (He *is* a wealthy man now).

TYPES OF VERBS

Verbs may be described as being either **transitive verbs** or **intransitive verbs**.

Transitive Verbs. A transitive verb is a verb that requires a **direct object** to complete its meaning.

> *Examples:*   They *laid* the foundation on October 24. ("foundation" is the direct object of the transitive verb *laid*)
> George Anderson *wrote* the treasurer a letter. ("treasurer" is the indirect object and "letter" is the direct object of the transitive verb *wrote*)

Intransitive Verb. An intransitive verb is a verb that does not require an object to complete its meaning. It is able to make a full assertion about the **subject** without assistance (although it may have modifiers).

> *Examples:*   The water *boiled.*
> The water *boiled* rapidly.
> The engine *ran.*
> The engine *ran* smoothly and quietly.

Linking Verb—Although intransitive verbs do not have an **object**, certain intransitive verbs may take a **complement**. These verbs are called **linking verbs** because they link the complement to the subject. When the complement is a **noun** (or **pronoun**), it *refers* to the same person or thing as the noun (or pronoun) that is the subject.

Examples: The conference table *is* an antique.
Mary *should be* the director.

When the complement is an **adjective**, it *modifies* the subject.

Examples: The study *was* thorough.
The report *seems* complete.

Such intransitive verbs as *be, become, seem,* and *appear* are almost always linking verbs. A number of others, such as *look, sound, taste, smell,* and *feel,* may function either as linking verbs or as simple intransitive verbs.

Examples: Their antennae *feel* delicately. (simple intransitive verb meaning that they have a delicate touch)
Their antennae *feel* delicate. (linking verb meaning that they seem fragile to the touch)

FORMS OF VERBS

By form, verbs may be described as being either finite or nonfinite.

Finite Verbs. A **finite verb** is the main verb of a **clause** or **sentence**. It makes an assertion about its subject and it can serve as the only verb in its clause or sentence. Finite verbs may be either transitive or intransitive (including linking) verbs. They are subject to changes in form to reflect person (I *see*, he *sees*), tense (I *go*, I *went*), and number (he *writes*, they *write*).

Example: The telephone *rang* and the secretary *answered* it.

Helping Verbs—A **helping verb** (sometimes called *auxiliary verb*) is a verb that is used in a **verb phrase** to help indicate **mood**, **tense**, and **voice**.

Examples: The work *had* (helping verb) begun.
I *am* going.
I *was* going.
I *will* go.
I *should have* gone.
I *must* go.

The most commonly used helping verbs are the various forms of *have (has, had), be (is, are, was,* etc.), *do (did, does),* and *can, may, might, must, shall, will, would, should,* and *could.* Phrases that function as helping verbs are often made up of combinations with the sign of the infinitive, *to:* for example, *am going to* and *is about to* (compare *will*), *has to* (compare *must*), and *ought to* (compare *should*).

The helping verb always precedes the main verb, although other words may intervene.

> *Example:* Machines *will* (helping verb) never completely *replace* (main verb) people.

Nonfinite Verbs. Nonfinite verbs are the **verbals (gerunds, infinitives**, and **participles**) which, although they are derived from verbs, actually function as nouns, adjectives, or **adverbs**.

When the *-ing* form of a verb is used as a noun, it is called a gerund.

> *Example:* Seeing is believing.

An infinitive, which is the root form of a verb (usually preceded by the word "to"), can be used as a noun, an adverb, or an adjective.

> *Examples:* He hates *to complain.* (noun, direct object of the verb *hates*)
> The valve closes *to stop* the flow. (adverb, modifies the verb *closes*)
> This is the proposal *to select.* (adjective, modifies the noun *proposal*)

A participle is a verb form used as an adjective.

> *Examples:* His *closing* statement was very *convincing.*
> The *rejected* proposal was ours.

PROPERTIES OF VERBS

Person is the grammatical term for the form of a **personal pronoun** that indicates whether the pronoun refers to the speaker, the person spoken to, or the person (or thing) spoken about. Verbs change their forms to agree in person with their subjects.

> *Examples:* I *see* (first person) a yellow tint, but he *sees* (third person) a yellow-green hue.
> I *am* (first person) convinced, and you *are* (second person) convinced; but unfortunately he *is* (third person) not convinced.

Voice refers to the two forms of a verb that indicate whether the subject of the verb acts or receives the action. If the subject of the verb acts, the verb is in the active voice; if it receives the action, the verb is in the passive voice.

Examples: The aerosol bomb *propels* the liquid as a mist. (active)
The liquid *is propelled* as a mist by the aerosol bomb. (passive)

In your writing, the active voice provides force and momentum, while the passive voice lacks these qualities. The reason is not difficult to find. In the active voice, the verb plays the key role in identifying what the subject is doing. The passive voice, on the other hand, consists of a form of the verb *to be* and a past **participle** of another verb. In the passive voice, the **emphasis** is on what is being done to the subject.

Examples: Things are seen by the normal human eye in three dimensions: length, width, and depth. (*Things* takes precedence over the eye's function.)
The normal human eye sees things in three dimensions: length, width, and depth. (Here the eye's function—which is what the sentence is about—receives the emphasis.)

Number refers to the two forms of a verb that indicate whether the subject of a verb is singular or plural.

Examples: The machine *was* in good operating condition. (singular)
The machines *were* in good operating condition. (plural)

Tense refers to verb forms that indicate time distinctions. There are six tenses: present, past, future, present perfect, past perfect, and future perfect. All verb tenses are derived from the three principal parts of the verb: the *infinitive* (without the word "to," which normally precedes it); the *past* form; and the *past participle*. Following are the six tenses of *write* (infinitive), whose other two principal parts are *wrote* (past form) and *written* (past participle).

Examples: I *write* (present tense, based on infinitive)
I *wrote* (past tense, based on past form)
I *will write* (future tense, based on infinitive)
I *have written* (present perfect tense, based on past participle)
I *had written* (past perfect tense, based on past participle)
I *will have written* (future perfect tense, based on past participle)

Note that *write* is an irregular verb; that is, its past and past participle forms are produced by internal changes: *write, wrote, written.* Regular verbs, on the other hand, form the past and past participle by the addition of the suffix *-ed, -d,* or *-t: talk, talked; believe, believed; spend,* *spent.* The tenses of regular verbs, like those of irregular verbs, are derived from the three principal parts.

> *Examples:* I *believe* (present tense, based on infinitive)
> I *believed* (past tense, based on past form)
> I *will believe* (future tense, based on infinitive)
> I *have believed* (present perfect tense, based on past participle)
> I *had believed* (past perfect tense, based on past participle)
> I *will have believed* (future perfect tense, based on past participle)

Each of the six tenses also has a progressive form. The progressive form is created by adding the appropriate tense of *be* to the present participle (the *-ing*) form of the verb.

> *Examples:* I *am writing.* (present progressive)
> I *was writing.* (past progressive)
> I *will be writing.* (future progressive)
> I *have been writing.* (present perfect progressive)
> I *had been writing.* (past perfect progressive)
> I *will have been writing.* (future perfect progressive)

CONJUGATION OF VERBS

The conjugation of a verb arranges all forms of the verb so that the differences caused by the changing of the tense, number, person, and voice are readily apparent. Following is a conjugation of the verb "drive."

Tense	Number	Person	Active Voice	Passive Voice
Present	Singular	1st	I drive	I am driven
		2nd	You drive	You are driven
		3rd	He drives	He is driven
	Plural	1st	We drive	We are driven
		2nd	You drive	You are driven
		3rd	They drive	They are driven
Progressive Present	Singular	1st	I am driving	I am being driven
		2nd	You are driving	You are being driven
		3rd	He is driving	He is being driven
	Plural	1st	We are driving	We are being driven
		2nd	You are driving	You are being driven
		3rd	They are driving	They are being driven

Tense	Number	Person	Active Voice	Passive Voice
Past	Singular	1st	I drove	I was driven
		2nd	You drove	You were driven
		3rd	He drove	He was driven
	Plural	1st	We drove	We were driven
		2nd	You drove	You were driven
		3rd	They drove	They were driven
Progressive Past	Singular	1st	I was driving	I was being driven
		2nd	You were driving	You were being driven
		3rd	He was driving	He was being driven
	Plural	1st	We were driving	We were being driven
		2nd	You were driving	You were being driven
		3rd	They were driving	They were being driven
Future	Singular	1st	I will drive	I will be driven
		2nd	You will drive	You will be driven
		3rd	He will drive	He will be driven
	Plural	1st	We will drive	We will be driven
		2nd	You will drive	You will be driven
		3rd	They will drive	They will be driven
Progressive Future	Singular	1st	I will be driving	I will have been driven
		2nd	You will be driving	You will have been driven
		3rd	He will be driving	He will have been driven
	Plural	1st	We will be driving	We will have been driven
		2nd	You will be driving	You will have been driven
		3rd	They will be driving	They will have been driven
Present Perfect	Singular	1st	I have driven	I have been driven
		2nd	You have driven	You have been driven
		3rd	He has driven	He has been driven
	Plural	1st	We have driven	We have been driven
		2nd	You have driven	You have been driven
		3rd	They have driven	They have been driven
Past Perfect	Singular	1st	I had driven	I had been driven
		2nd	You had driven	You had been driven
		3rd	He had driven	He had been driven
	Plural	1st	We had driven	We had been driven
		2nd	You had driven	You had been driven
		3rd	They had driven	They had been driven

Tense	Number	Person	Active Voice	Passive Voice
Future Perfect	Singular	1st	I will have driven	I will have been driven
		2nd	You will have driven	You will have been driven
		3rd	He will have driven	He will have been driven
	Plural	1st	We will have driven	We will have been driven
		2nd	You will have driven	You will have been driven
		3rd	They will have driven	They will have been driven

verb phrase

A *verb phrase* is a group of words that functions as a single **verb**. It consists of a main verb preceded by one or more **helping verbs**.

> *Example:* He *is* (helping verb) *working* (main verb) hard this summer.

The main verb is always the last verb in a verb phrase.

> *Examples:* You *will file* your tax on time if you begin early.
> You *will have filed* your tax when the deadline arrives if you begin early.
> You *are* not *filing* your income tax too early if you begin now.

Questions often begin with a verb phrase.

> *Example:* *Will* he *audit* their account soon?

Words can appear between the helping verb and the main verb of a verb phrase.

> *Example:* He *is* always *working*.

The **adverb** "not" may be appended to a helping verb in a verb phrase.

> *Examples:* He *cannot work* today.
> He *did not work* today.

verbals

Verbals, which are derived from **verbs**, function as **nouns, adjectives**, and **adverbs**. There are three types of verbals: gerunds, infinitives, and participles.

When the *-ing* form of a verb is used as a noun, it is called a **gerund**.

> *Example:* *Seeing* is *believing*.

An **infinitive** is the root form of a verb, usually preceded by "to" (*to* analyze, *to* build). Infinitives can be used as nouns, adjectives, or adverbs.

Examples: He liked *to jog*. (noun)
That is the main problem *to be solved*. (adjective)
The valve acts *to control* the flow of liquid. (adverb)

When a verb is used as an adjective, it is called a **participle**; present participles commonly end in *-ing*, past participles in *-ed*, *-en, -d,* or *-t*.

Examples: A *burning* candle consumes stale tobacco smoke.
The *published* report contains up-to-date information.

very

The temptation to overuse **intensifiers** like *very* is great. Evaluate your use of them carefully. Where they are appropriate, it is usually profitable to go on to clarify their meaning.

Example: Bicycle manufacturers had a *very* good year: sales across the country were up 43 percent over the previous year.

In many sentences the word can simply be deleted.

Change: The board was *very* angry about the newspaper report.
To: The board was angry about the newspaper report.

via

Via is Latin for "by way of."

Example: The equipment is being shipped to Los Angeles *via* Chicago.

The term should be used only in routing instructions and should not be used outside such contexts.

Change: His project was funded *via* the recently enacted legislation.
To: His project was funded *through* (or *as the result of*) the recently enacted legislation.

vogue words

Vogue words are words that suddenly become popular and, because of an intense period of overuse, lose their freshness and preciseness.

They may become popular through their association with science, technology, or even sports. We include them in our vocabulary because they seem to give force and vitality to our language. Ordinarily, this language sounds pretentious in our day-to-day writing.

Examples: super, interface, definitely, input, mode, variable, ballgame, parameter, communication, feedback, environment (plus many words ending in -*wise*)

Obviously, some of these terms are appropriate in the right context. It is when they are used outside that context that imprecision becomes a problem. This book discusses some vogue terms individually; use the index to find the word in question. For those not included, check a current **dictionary**.

voice

The grammatical term *voice* refers to whether the **subject** of a **sentence** or **clause** acts or receives the action. The sentence is in the active voice if the subject acts, in the passive voice if the subject is acted upon.

Examples: David Cohen *wrote* the advertising copy. (active)
The advertising copy *was written* by David Cohen. (passive)

In your writing, the active voice provides force and momentum, while the passive voice lacks these qualities. The reason is not difficult to find. In the active voice, the verb plays the key role in identifying what the subject is doing. The passive voice, on the other hand, consists of a form of the verb *to be* and a past **participle** of the main verb. In the passive voice, the **emphasis** is on what is being done to the subject.

Examples: The report *was written* by Joe Albright in only two hours. (passive voice) (*Report* takes precedence over the writing.)

Joe Albright *wrote* the report in only two hours. (active voice) (Here the writer and writing receive the emphasis.)

Things *are seen* by the normal human eye in three dimensions: length, width, and depth. (passive voice) (*Things* takes precedence over the eye's function.)

The normal human eye *sees* things in three dimensions: length, width, and depth. (active voice) (Here the eye's function—which is what the sentence is about—receives the emphasis.)

Sentences in the passive voice may state the actor, but they place the actor in a secondary position as the object of a **preposition** (*"by* the normal human eye").

The passive voice has its uses, however; when the doer of the action is not known or not pertinent, the passive voice should be used.

Example: The firm *was established* in 1929.

When the doer of the action is less important than the receiver of the action, the passive voice should be used.

Example: Bill Bryant *was presented* the award by President Colby.

As a rule, use the active voice unless you have good reason not to. Also, be careful about shifting voice in a sentence.

Change: The pocket edition *costs* so little that it *can be afforded* by anyone who wants it.

   To: The pocket edition *costs* so little that anyone who wants it *can afford* it.

wait for/wait on

Wait on should be restricted in writing to the activities of waitresses and waiters—otherwise, use *wait for.*

Example: Be sure to *wait for* (not *on*) Ms. Sturgess to finish reading the report before asking her to make a decision.

when and if

When and if (or *if and when*) is a colloquial expression that should not be used in writing.

Change: *When and if* your new position is approved, I will see that you receive adequate staff help.

   To: *If* your new position is approved, I will see that you receive adequate staff help.

   Or: *When* your new position is approved, I will see that you receive adequate staff help.

where . . . at

In **phrases** using the *where . . . at* construction, *at* is unnecessary and should be omitted.

> *Change:* *Where* is his office *at?*
> *To:* *Where* is his office?

where/that

Do not substitute *where* for *that* to anticipate an idea or fact to follow.

> *Change:* I read in the *Wall Street Journal where* the dental industry is expected to expand over the next decade.
> *To:* I read in the *Wall Street Journal that* the dental industry is expected to expand over the next decade.

while

While, meaning "during an interval of time," is sometimes substituted for **connectives** like *and, but, although,* and *whereas.* Because it has its own meaning in addition to this use as a connective, *while* often causes **ambiguity**.

> *Change:* John Evans is sales manager, *while* Joan Thomas is in charge of research.
> *To:* John Evans is sales manager, *and* Joan Thomas is in charge of research.

When used for *although* or *whereas, while* can lead to absurdity.

> *Change:* *While* the office manager was angry with his assistant, he didn't fire him.
> *To:* *Although* the office manager was angry with his assistant, he didn't fire him.

Restrict *while* to its meaning of "during the time that."

> *Example:* I'll have time to catch up on my reading *while* I am on vacation.

who/whom

Writers often have difficulty with the choice of *who* or *whom. Who* is the subjective **case** form, *whom* is the objective case form, and *whose* is the possessive case form. When in doubt about which form to use, try substituting a **personal pronoun** to see which one fits. If "he" or "they" fits, use *who*.

> *Example:* *Who* is the congressman from the 45th district?
> *He* is the congressman from the 45th district.

If "him" or "them" fits, use *whom*.

> *Example:* It depended upon *them*.
> It depended upon *whom?*
> It was they upon *whom* it depended.

It is becoming common to use *who* for the objective case when it begins a sentence, although some still object to such an "ungrammatical" construction. The best advice is to know your **reader**.

The choice between *who* and *whom* is especially complex in sentences with interjected **clauses**.

> *Change:* These are the men *whom* you thought were the architects.
> *To:* These are the men *who* you thought were the architects.

The interjected clause "you thought" tends to attract the form *whom*, a form that appears logical as the object of the verb "thought." In fact, *who* is the correct form, since it is the subject of the verb "were." Note that the interjected clause "you thought" can be omitted without disturbing the construction of the clause.

> *Example:* These are the men *who* were the architects.

whose/of which

Whose should normally be used with persons; *of which* should normally be used with inanimate objects.

> *Examples:* The man *whose* car had been towed away was angry.
> The mantle clock, the parts *of which* work perfectly, is over one hundred years old.

If these uses cause a sentence to sound awkward, however, *whose* may be used with inanimate objects.

> *Example:* There are added fields, for example, *whose* totals should never be zero.

-wise

Although the **suffix** *-wise* often seems to provide a tempting short-cut, it leads more often to inept than to economical expression. It is better to rephrase the **sentence**.

Change:	Our department rates high efficiency-*wise*.
To:	Our department has a high efficiency rating.

The -*wise* suffix is appropriate, however, to **instructions** that indicate certain space or directional requirements.

Examples:	Fold the paper *lengthwise*.
	Turn the adjustment screw half a turn *clockwise*.

word choice

As Mark Twain once said, "The difference between the right word and almost the right word is the difference between 'lightning' and 'lightning bug.'" The most important goal in choosing the right word in business and technical writing is the preciseness implied by Twain's comment. **Vague words** and **abstract words** defeat preciseness because they do not convey the writer's meaning directly and clearly. Vague words are imprecise because they can mean many different things.

Change:	It was a *meaningful* meeting. (But in what way was it meaningful?)
To:	The meeting helped both sides understand each other's position. (This version contains a specific reference to what happened to make the meeting "meaningful.")

Although abstract words may at times be appropriate to your **topic**, their unnecessary use creates dry and lifeless writing.

> Abstract: work, fast, food
> Concrete: sawing, 110 m.p.h., steak

Being aware of the **connotation** and denotation of words will help you anticipate the **reader's** reaction to the words you choose. Connotation is the suggested or implied meaning of a word beyond its dictionary definition. Denotation is the literal, or primary, dictionary meaning of a word.

Understanding **antonyms** and **synonyms** will increase your ability to choose the proper word. Antonyms are words with nearly the opposite meaning (*fresh/stale*), and synonyms are words with nearly the same meaning (*notorious/infamous*).

Malapropisms and **trite language** are likely to irritate your readers, either by confusing them or by boring them. Malapropisms are words that sound like the intended word but have different, sometimes even humorous meanings.

Example: The repairman cleaned the typewriter's *plankton*. (The correct word is *platen*.)

Trite language consists of stale and worn phrases, frequently **clichés**.

Change: We will finish the project *quick as a flash*.
To: We will finish the project *quickly*.

Avoid the use of **jargon** unless you are certain that all of your readers understand the terms you use from this specialized vocabulary. Avoid choosing words with the objective of impressing your reader, which is called **affectation**; also avoid the use of **long variants**, which are elongated forms of words clearly used only to impress *(utilize for use, telephonic communication for telephone call, analyzation for analysis)*. Using a **euphemism** (an inoffensive substitute for a word that is distasteful or offensive) may help you avoid embarrassment, but overuse of euphemisms becomes affectation. Using more words than necessary *(in the neighborhood of for about, for the reason that for because, in the event that for if)* is certain to interfere with **clarity**.

Understanding the use of **clipped forms of words**, **compound words**, **blend words**, and **foreign words in English** will help you find the appropriate word for a specific use. Clipped forms of words are created by dropping the beginning or ending of a word *(phone for telephone, ad for advertisement)*. Compound words are made from two or more words that are either hyphenated or written as one word *(mother-in-law, nevertheless)*. Blend words are created by using two words to produce a third word *(smoke + fog = smog)*.

A key to choosing the correct and precise word is to keep current in your reading and to be aware of new words in your profession and in the language. Be aware also, in your quest for the right word, that there is no substitute for a good **dictionary**.

writing the draft

If you have established your **objective**, **reader**, and **scope**, and if you have completed adequate **research** and created a good **outline**, you will find writing the rough draft fairly easy. Writing a rough draft is simply the process of transcribing and expanding the notes from your outline into **paragraphs** without worrying about refinements of language or such mechanical aspects of writing as **transition**. Refinement will come with **revision**.

It is usually best to write the rough draft quickly, concentrating entirely upon converting your outline to **sentences** and paragraphs. To achieve directness of communication, write as though you were explaining your subject to someone across the desk from you. Don't worry about a good **opening**. Just start. There is no need in the rough draft to be concerned about an **introduction** or about transition unless they come easily—concentrate on *ideas*. Don't attempt to polish or revise. Writing and revising are different activities. Keep writing quickly to achieve **unity** and proportion.

Try not to let grammatical rules get in your way; they are of little value in writing the rough draft. Learning all the grammatical rules in the world will not help you write a better rough draft, yet some people are so concerned about the proper use of **grammar** even at this early stage that it diverts energy and attention from the draft.

Don't affect a fancy writing **style**. Your function as a writer is to communicate certain information to your readers, not to impress them with your fancy footwork. Write in plain, direct, concise language. Write the draft in the style that is comfortable and natural for you.

Remember that the first rule of good writing is to help the reader. As you write the rough draft, keep your reader's level of technical knowledge in mind. This will not only help you write directly to your reader, it will also tell you which terms you must define.

When you are trying to write quickly and come to something difficult to explain, try to relate the new concept to something with which the reader is already familiar. Although **figures of speech** are not used extensively in business and technical writing, they can be very useful in explaining a complex process or piece of equipment. In the rough draft, a figure of speech might be just the tool you need to keep moving when you encounter a complex concept that must be explained or described.

Be consistent in the way you address your readers (see **point of view**). Don't switch needlessly from one form of address to another. For example, if you write *"You* will notice that . . . " one time, don't write *"One* should note that . . . " the next time. This is simply a matter of keeping your readers in mind and being considerate of them. It will not be a problem if you establish the habit of writing as if you were explaining your subject to someone across the desk from you (but in a **formal writing style** and using **standard English**, keeping in mind that your readers cannot see your gestures and facial expressions).

Most of your outline notes should become the **topic sentences** for **paragraphs** in your draft. As an example of this, notice how items III.A. and III.B. in the topic outline below become the topic sentences of the two paragraphs that follow. (And notice, too, how the subordinate items in the outline become sentences within the two paragraphs.)

Example: OUTLINE

    III. Advantages of Chicago as location for new plant
        A. *Outstanding Transport Facilities*
           1. Rail
           2. Air
           3. Truck
           4. Sea (except in winter)
        B. *Ample Labor Supply*
           1. Engineering and scientific personnel
              a. Many similar companies in the area
              b. Several major universities
           2. Technical and manufacturing personnel
              a. Existing programs in community colleges
              b. Possible special programs designed for us

RESULTING PARAGRAPHS

Probably the greatest advantage of Chicago as a location for our new plant is its excellent transport facilities. The city is served by three major railroads. Both domestic and international air cargo service is available at O'Hare International Airport. Chicago is a major hub of the trucking industry, and most of the nation's large freight carriers have terminals there. Finally, except in the winter months when the Great Lakes are frozen, Chicago is a seaport, accessible through the St. Lawrence Seaway.

A second advantage of Chicago is that it offers an abundant labor force. An ample supply of engineering and scientific personnel is assured not only by the presence of many companies engaged in activities similar to ours but also by the presence of several major universities in the metropolitan area. Similarly, technicians and manufacturing personnel are in abundant supply. The seven colleges in the Chicago City College system, as well as half a dozen other two year colleges in the outlying areas, produce graduates with Associate Degrees in a wide variety of technical specialties appropriate to our needs. Moreover, three of the outlying colleges have expressed an interest in establishing special courses attuned specifically to our requirements.

Don't let writing an introduction stop you from getting started. In fact, many good writers prefer to write the introduction last. If writing the introduction bothers you, choose the section of your outline that interests you most and start there (this is possible only if you have a good outline).

Whatever is most comfortable for you is what you should do to get started: typing, longhand—just get started! Waiting for inspiration to come along and give you a lift is simply an excuse for avoiding work. If you have made adequate **preparation**—which is the best guarantee of good writing—you are ready to begin. The actual writing should be the easiest part of the job. (See also the Checklist of the Writing Process.)

X

Xmas

"X" is similar to the Greek symbol (chi) for Christ. The expression *Xmas* is used exclusively in advertising; however, even in advertising *Xmas* is better avoided since, to some people, the term detracts from the religious significance of the holiday and is therefore offensive.

Z

zeugma

A zeugma is a construction in which an adjective or verb is forced to apply to two words even though it is grammatically or logically correct only for one of them. Poets, and occasionally public speakers, use zeugma deliberately for rhythmic effect; but it is imprecise and should therefore be avoided in business or technical writing.

> *Change:* The walls of the office *are* green, the rug blue.
> *To:* The walls of the office *are* green; the rug *is* blue.

In this case *are* (a plural **verb**) is used for both subjects, *walls* (a plural **noun**) and *rug* (a singular noun), which is grammatically and logically incorrect.

Bibliography

Adelstein, Michael E. *Contemporary Business Writing*. New York: Random House, 1971.

Anderson, Virgil A. *Training the Speaking Voice*. New York: Oxford University Press, 1961.

Barr, Doris W. *Effective English for the Career Student*. Belmont, Calif.: Wadsworth Publishing Co., 1971.

Berenson, Conrad, and Raymond Colton. *Research and Report Writing for Business and Economics*. New York: Random House, 1971.

Bernstein, Theodore M. *The Careful Writer: A Guide to English Usage*. New York: Atheneum, 1967.

————. *Watch Your Language*. Manhasset, New York: Channel Press, 1968.

Bonner, William H. *Better Business Writing*. Homewood, Illinois: Richard D. Irwin, Inc., 1974.

Brennard, Maynard J. *Compact Handbook of College Composition*. Boston: D. C. Heath and Co., 1972.

Brusaw, Charles T., and Gerald J. Alred. *Practical Writing: Composition for the Business and Technical World*. Boston: Allyn and Bacon, 1973.

Canavan, J. P. *Effective English: A Guide for Writing*. Encino, Calif.: Dickenson, 1970.

Crowell, Thomas Lee, Jr. *Index to Modern English*. New York: McGraw-Hill Book Co., 1964.

Cunningham, Donald H. *A Reading Approach to Professional Police Writing*. Springfield, Illinois: Charles C Thomas, Publisher, 1972.

Elsbree, Langdon, and Frederick Bracher. *Heath's College Handbook of Composition*. 8th ed. Boston: D. C. Heath and Co., 1972.

————. *Heath's Brief Handbook of Usage*. 8th ed. Boston: D. C. Heath and Co., 1972.

Fowler, H. W. *Modern English Usage*. New York: Oxford University Press, 1950.

Gammage, Allen Z. *Basic Police Report Writing.* Springfield, Illinois: Charles C Thomas, Publisher, 1961.

Glidden, H. K. *Reports, Technical Writing, and Specifications.* New York: McGraw-Hill Book Co., 1964.

Gorrell, Robert M., and Charlton Laird. *Modern English Handbook.* 5th ed. Englewood Cliffs, New Jersey: Prentice-Hall, Inc., 1972.

Gowan, James A. *English Review Manual.* New York: McGraw-Hill Book Co., 1970.

Guth, Hans P. *Concise English Handbook.* 3rd ed. Belmont, Calif.: Wadsworth Publishing Co., 1970.

Hand, Harry E., ed. *Effective Speaking for the Technical Man: Practical Views and Comments.* New York: Van Nostrand Reinhold Company, 1960.

Hicks, Tyler G. *Writing for Engineering and Science.* New York: McGraw-Hill Book Co., 1961.

Hodges, John C., and Mary E. Whitten. *Harbrace College Handbook.* 7th ed. New York: Harcourt Brace Jovanovich, Inc., 1970.

Houp, Kenneth W., and Thomas E. Pearsall. *Reporting Technical Information.* 2nd ed. Beverly Hills, Calif.: Glencoe Press, 1973.

Irmscher, William F. *The Holt Guide to English: A Contemporary Handbook of Rhetoric, Language, and Literature.* New York: Holt, Rinehart and Winston, Inc., 1972.

King, Lester S., M.D., and Charles G. Roland, M.D. *Scientific Writing.* Chicago: American Medical Association, 1968.

Kitzhaber, Albert R., and Donald W. Lee. *Handbook for Basic Composition.* Englewood Cliffs, New Jersey: Prentice-Hall, Inc., 1961.

Lazarus, Arnold, Andrew MacLeish, and H. Wendell Smith. *Modern English: A Glossary of Literature and Language.* New York: Grosset & Dunlop, Inc., 1972.

Leggett, Glenn, David C. Mead, and William Charvat. *Prentice-Hall Handbook for Writers.* 5th ed. Englewood Cliffs, New Jersey: Prentice-Hall, Inc., 1970.

Lemmon, Lee T. *A Glossary for the Study of English.* New York: Oxford University Press, 1971.

Mambert, W. A. *Presenting Technical Ideas.* New York: John Wiley & Sons, Inc., 1968.

A Manual of Style. 12th ed., rev. Chicago: The University of Chicago Press, 1969.

Marckwardt, Albert H., and Frederick G. Cassidy. *Scribner Handbook of English.* 4th ed. New York: Charles Scribner's Sons, 1967.

McPeek, James A. S., and Austin Wright. *Handbook of English.* New York: The Ronald Press Company, 1956.

Micken, Ralph A. *Speaking for Results: A Guide for Business and Professional Speakers.* Boston: Houghton Mifflin Company, 1958.

Mills, Gordon H., and John A. Walter. *Technical Writing.* 3rd ed. New York: Holt, Rinehart and Winston, Inc., 1970.

Minnick, Wayne C. *The Art of Persuasion.* Boston: Houghton Mifflin Company, 1957.

Monroe, Alan H., and Douglas Erlinger. *Principles and Types of Speech.* 6th ed. Chicago: Scott, Foresman and Co., 1967.

Moore, Robert H. *Handbook of Effective Writing.* 2nd ed. New York: Holt, Rinehart and Winston, Inc., 1971.

Nicholson, Margaret. *Dictionary of American-English Usage.* New York: Oxford University Press, 1967.

Nist, John. *Speaking Into Writing.* New York: St. Martin's Press, 1969.

Patterson, Frank M., and Patrick D. Smith. *A Manual of Police Report Writing.* Springfield, Illinois: Charles C Thomas, Publisher, 1972.

Pauley, Steven E. *Technical Report Writing Today.* Boston: Houghton Mifflin Company, 1973.

Perrin, Porter G. *Writer's Guide and Index to English.* 4th ed. revised by Karl W. Dykema and Wilma R. Ebbitt. Chicago: Scott, Foresman and Co., 1965.

————, and George H. Smith. *The Perrin-Smith Handbook of Current English.* 2nd ed. Chicago: Scott, Foresman and Co., 1962.

Pickett, Nell Ann, and Ann A. Laster. *Writing and Reading in Technical English.* San Francisco: Canfield Press, 1970.

————. *Handbook for Student Writing.* San Francisco: Canfield Press, 1972.

Robert, Henry M. *Robert's Rules of Order.* Chicago: Scott, Foresman and Co., 1951.

Robertson, Duncan. *Errors in Composition.* Rev. ed. Toronto: The Macmillan Co. of Canada, Ltd., 1968.

Rathbone, Robert H., and James B. Stone. *A Writer's Guide for Engineers and Scientists.* Englewood Cliffs, New Jersey: Prentice-Hall, Inc., 1962.

Roland, Charles G., M.D. *Good Scientific Writing: An Anthology.* Chicago: American Medical Association, 1971.

Rorabacher, Louise E. *A Concise Guide to Composition.* 2nd ed. New York: Harper & Row, Publishers, 1963.

Shaw, Harry, and Richard H. Dodge. *The Shorter Handbook of College Composition.* New York: Harper & Row, Publishers, 1965.

Shermann, Theodore A. *Modern Technical Writing.* 2nd ed. Englewood Cliffs, New Jersey: Prentice-Hall, Inc., 1966.

Sigband, Norman B. *Effective Report Writing for Business, Industry, and Government.* New York: Harper & Row, Publishers, 1960.

Stevens, Martin, and Charles H. Kegel. *A Glossary for College English.* New York: McGraw-Hill Book Co., 1966.

Strunk, William, Jr., and E. B. White. *The Elements of Style.* Toronto: The Macmillan Co. of Canada, Ltd., 1959.

Sypherd, W. O., Alvin M. Fountain, and V. E. Gibbens. *Manual of Technical Writing.* Chicago: Scott, Foresman and Co., 1957.

Tichy, H. J. *Effective Writing for Engineers, Managers, Scientists.* New York: John Wiley & Sons, Inc., 1966.

Ulman, Joseph N., Jr., and Jay R. Gould. *Technical Reporting.* Rev. ed. New York: Holt, Rinehart and Winston, Inc., 1959.

Watkins, Floyd C., William B. Dillingham, and Edwin T. Martin. *Practical English Handbook.* 3rd ed. Boston: Houghton Mifflin Company, 1971.

Weaver, Richard M. *A Rhetoric and Handbook.* Revised with assistance of Richard S. Beal. New York: Holt, Rinehart and Winston, Inc., 1967.

Weismann, Herman M. *Basic Technical Writing.* 2nd ed. Columbus, Ohio: Charles E. Merrill Publishing Co., 1968.

Wilcox, Roger P. *Oral Reporting in Business and Industry.* Englewood Cliffs, New Jersey: Prentice-Hall, Inc., 1967.

Wilson, Harris W., and Louis G. Locke. *The University Handbook.* New York: Holt, Rinehart and Winston, Inc., 1960.

Winterowd, W. Ross. *Structure, Language and Style: A Rhetoric Handbook.* Dubuque, Iowa: Wm. C. Brown Co., Publishers, 1969.

Woolley, Edwin C., Franklin W. Scott, and Frederick Bracher. *College Handbook of Composition.* 6th ed. Boston: D. C. Heath and Co., 1968.

Index

A

A, An, 1
  Article, 49–50
  Prefix, 375–376
A Few
  Few/A Few, 169
A Half
  Half, 221.
A Historical
  Article, 49
A La, 1–2
  Foreign Words in English,
    178–179
A Lot/Alot, 2
A While,
  Awhile/A While, 53
Abbreviations, 2–9
  Capital Letters, 73
  Clipped Forms of Words, 86–87
  Symbols, 472–474
Above, 9
Absolute Phrase, 9–10
  Comma, 93
Absolute Words, 10
Absolutely, 10
Abstract, 10–12
  Formal Report, 181
Abstract Journals
  Reference Books, 401–402
Abstract Noun, 12
  Agreement, 29
  Concrete Noun, 113
  Nouns, 310
Abstract Words/Concrete Words,
    12–13
  Word Choice, 511
Academic Degrees
  Abbreviations, 6–7
Accent Marks
  Diacritical Marks, 140–141
  Foreign Words in English, 180

Accept/Except, 13
Acceptance, Letter of, 14
  Correspondence, 121–125
Account of
  Symbols, 473
Accumulative/Cumulative, 15
Accuracy of Information
  Library Research, 281–286
  Revision, 422
  Sweeping Generalization,
    470–471
Accusative Case
  Case, 76
Acknowledgment
  Bibliography, 60–64
  Footnotes, 175–179
Acronym
  Abbreviations (Plural of
    Acronyms), 3–4
  Apostrophe, 45
  New Words, 304
Activate/Actuate, 15
Active Voice
  Voice, 507–508
Actually, 15
  Intensifiers, 251–252
Actuate
  Activate/Actuate, 15
Acute
  Diacritical Marks, 141
A.D., 15
  Abbreviations, 9
Ad
  Clipped Form of Words, 86–87
Ad Hoc, 16
  Foreign Words in English,
    179–180
Adapt/Adept/Adopt, 16
Address, Direct
  Direct Address, 144
Addresses
  Abbreviations, 7–8

Comma, 95
Numbers, 316
Slash, 453
Adept
  Adapt/Adept/Adopt, 16
Adherence/Adhesion, 16
Adjectives, 16–19
  Article, 49–50
  Comma, 94–95
  Comparative Degree, 101–102
  Demonstrative Adjective, 134–135
  Indefinite Adjective, 241
  Intensifiers, 251–252
  Modifiers, 299–300
  Objective Complement, 318
  Parts of Speech, 358
  Relative Adjective, 408
  Subjective Complement, 467
Adjective Clause, 19
  Clauses, 83–85
Adjective Phrase
  Phrases, 366
Adopt
  Adapt/Adept/Adopt, 16
Adverbs, 20–22
  Conjunctive Adverb, 115
  Interrogative Adverb, 253
  Modifiers, 299–300
  Parts of Speech, 358
Adverb Clause, 23
  Clauses, 83–85
Adverb Connective
  Conjunctive Adverb, 115
  Connectives, 115–117
  Semicolon, 433
Adverb Phrase
  Phrases, 366
Adverbial Conjunction
  Conjunctive Adverb, 115
Advice/Advise, 24
Affect/Effect, 24
Affectation, 24–26
  Elegant Variation, 152
  Euphemism, 161–162
  Gobbledygook, 200–201

Hyperbole, 231
Jargon, 262–263
Long Variants, 287–288
Vogue Words, 506–507
Affinity, 26
Affirmative Writing
  Positive Writing, 373
Afflict/Inflict, 26
Aforesaid, 26
  Above, 9
  Ex Post Facto, 162
After the Fact
  Ex Post Facto, 162
Afterthought, Introduced by Dash
  Dash, 127
Agree To/Agree With, 27
Agreement, 27–32
  Gender, 198–199
  Nor/Or, 306
  Number, 314
  Person, 362
  Tense, 483
Aids, Visual in Oral Presentation
  Oral Report, 331–332
Ain't
  Grammar, 209–210
Albeit, 32
Align
  Proofreaders' Marks, 387
All
  Agreement, 28
All Around/All-Around/
    All-Round, 32
All Ready
  Already/All Ready, 35
All Right/Alright/All-Right, 33
All-Round
  All Around/All-Around/
    All-Round, 32
All the Farther, 33
All Together/Altogether, 33
Allude/Elude, 33
Allude/Refer, 33–34
Allusion, 34

Allusion/Illusion, 34
Almanac
    Reference Books, 404
Almost/Most, 34–35
Along the Line of, 35
Alot
    A Lot/Alot, 2
Alphabetic List of Definitions
    Dictionary, 141–144
    Glossary, 199–200
Already/All Ready, 35
Alright
    All Right/Alright/All-Right, 33
Also, 35
Altogether
    All Together/Altogether, 33
a.m.
    Abbreviations, 3
Ambiguity, 35–36
Ambiguous Pronoun Reference
    Agreement, 30
    Pronouns, 385–386
Among
    Between/Among, 59
Amount
    Numbers, 314–316
Amount/Number, 36–37
Ampersand
    Symbols, 473
Amplified Definition
    Definition as a Form of Writing,
        132–134
An
    A, An, 1
    Article, 49–50
An Historical
    Article, 49
Analogy, 37
    Comparison as a Method of
        Development, 103
    Figures of Speech, 171
Analysis as a Method of
    Development, 37–38
    Methods of Development,
        292–293

And
    Conjunctions, 113–115
    Connectives, 115–117
    Coordinating Conjunction, 119
And, Beginning a Sentence with
    Sentence Construction, 441
And Etc.
    Etc., 161
And/Or, 38
And So Forth
    Etc., 161
Anecdote, 38
Anglicized Words
    Foreign Words in English,
        179–180
Animate Object, Using Possessive
        Case
    Case, 77
Annotated Bibliography
    Bibliography, 60
Annual Report, 39–43
    Openings, 323
Ante-/Anti-, 43–44
    Prefix, 375–376
Antecedent
    Agreement, 27, 30
    Pronouns, 385–386
Anticipation, Mark of
    Colon, 89–91
Anticipatory Subject
    Expletives, 166
Anticlimax
    Increasing Order of Importance
        as a Method of Development,
        240
Antonym, 44
    Synonym, 474
    Thesaurus, 485
    Word Choice, 511
Apostrophe, 44–45
    Contractions, 119
    Proofreaders' Marks, 387
    Punctuation, 390
Apparatus, Description of
    Description, 137–140

Appearance of Manuscript
  Format, 196
Appendix/Appendices, 46
  Formal Report, 182
Application, Letter of, 46–48
  Correspondence, 121–125
Appositive Phrase
  Colon, 90
  Comma, 93
Appositives, 48–49
  Capital Letters, 73
  Case, 78
  Comma, 93
  Dash, 128
Approaches
  Symbols, 472
Argument
  Persuasion, 364–365
  Propaganda, 388
Arrangement of Ideas
  Methods of Development,
    292–296
  Organization, 336–337
  Outlining, 338–341
Arrangement of Paper
  Formal Report, 180–194
  Format, 196
Arrangement of Words
  Sentences, 434–437
  Syntax, 474
Article, 49–50
  A, An, 1
  Adjectives, 16–19
  Capital Letters, 73
  House Organ Article, 228–231
  Journal Article, 265–273
As, 50
  Because, 59
  Case, 76
  Connectives, 116
  Like/As, 286
  Simile, 450–451
As . . . As/So . . . As, 50–51
As Much As/More Than, 51

As Regards/With Regard To/In
    Regard To/Regarding, 51
As Such, 51
As To Whether (when, where), 52
As Well As, 52
Associations
  Capital Letters, 72
Associations, Encyclopedia of
    Reference Books, 403
Associative Words
  Connotation/Denotation, 117–118
Assure
  Insure/Ensure/Assure, 251
Asterisk
  Proofreaders' Marks, 387
  Symbols, 473
At About/At Around, 52
Atlases
  Reference Books, 402
Attitude
  Business Writing Style, 66–68
  Point of View, 368–370
  Tone, 486–487
Attribute/Contribute, 52–53
Attribution of Ideas to Sources
  Footnotes, 175–179
Attributive Adjective
  Adjectives, 17–18
Audience
  Oral Report, 327–336
  Reader, 400
Augment/Supplement, 52
Author Card
  Library Research, 281–283
Author, Crediting
  Bibliography, 60–64
  Footnotes, 175–179
Author's Rights
  Copyright, 120
  Plagiarism, 368
Auxiliary Verb
  Helping Verb, 227
Ave.
  Abbreviations, 7–8

Average/Mean/Median, 53
Awhile/A While, 53
Awkwardness, 53–56
   Agreement, 27–32
   Dangling Modifiers, 126–127
   Expletives, 166
   Intensifiers, 251–252
   Mixed Constructions, 298–299
   Pace, 342–343
   Punctuation, 390
   Revision, 423
   Sentence Faults, 441–445
   Subordination, 469–470
   Tense, 483
   Voice, 508

B

B.A.
   Abbreviations, 6
Back of/In Back of, 57
Background Opening
   Openings, 323–326
Bad/Badly, 57
Balance, 57
   Compound Sentence, 106–107
   Parallel Structure, 349–352
   Sentence Construction, 437–441
Balance/Remainder, 57–58
Bar
   Slash, 453
Bar Graph
   Graphs, 215–218
Barbarism
   English, Varieties of, 159
B.C.
   Abbreviations, 9
   A.D., 15
Be Sure And/Be Sure To, 58
Because, 58–59
Because (in mathematical equations)
   Symbols, 472
Beginning a Sentence for Variety
   Sentence Variety, 446–447

Beginning a Sentence with a
   Conjunction
   Sentence Construction, 441
Beginning a Sentence with Numbers
   Numbers, 315
Beginning-to-End
   Chronological Method of
   Development, 81
Beginning Your Report
   Abstract, 10–12
   Introduction, 256–258
   Openings, 323–326
Being As/Being That, 59
Beside/Besides, 59
Between/Among, 59
Between You and Me, 60
Bi-/Semi-, 60
   Prefix, 375–376
Biannual/Biennial, 60
Bible
   Capital Letters, 74
   Italics, 260
Bibliographical Index
   Index, 243
Bibliography, 60–64
   Abbreviations, 7
   Documentation, 145
   Formal Report, 182
   Reference Books, 402
Bibliography for Oral Presentations
   Oral Report, 335–336
Bids
   Government Proposal, 202–209
Big Words
   Affectation, 24–26
   Gobbledygook, 200–201
   Long Variants, 287–288
   Word Choice, 512
Biographical Dictionaries and
   Encyclopedias
   Reference Books, 402–403
Biography
   Reference Books, 402–403
Blend Words, 64

New Words, 304
Word Choice, 511–512
Blvd.
Abbreviations, 7–8
Body
Tables, 476–477
Body of Report
Formal Report, 180–194
Boiling Down Ideas
Paraphrase, 352–353
Bold Face
Proofreaders' Marks, 387
Bombast
Affectation, 24–26
Gobbledygook, 200–201
Book
Capital Letters, 73
Foreword/Preface, 180
Index, 243
Table of Contents, 474–475
Book Guides, Indexes, and Reviews
Reference Books, 403
Books and Articles, List of
Bibliography, 60–64
Reference Books, 401–407
Books, Italics for Titles
Italics, 260
Borrowed Material
Bibliography, 60–64
Copyright, 120
Footnotes, 175–179
Plagiarism, 368
Borrowed Words
Foreign Words in English,
179–180
Both . . . And, 64–65
Correlative Conjunction, 120–121
Parallel Structure, 349–352
Boxhead
Tables, 476–477
Braces
Symbols, 473
Brackets, 65
Parentheses, 353–354

Proofreaders' Marks, 387
Punctuation, 389–390
Symbols, 473
Breadth of Coverage
Scope, 432
Breve
Diacritical Marks, 140–141
Symbols, 473
Brevity
Conciseness/Wordiness, 108–112
Brief, 65–66
Abstract, 10–12
Broken Type
Proofreaders' Marks, 387
Bromide
Cliché, 85–86
B.S.
Abbreviations, 6
Bullet
Heads, 222–227
Bunch, 66
Business Information Sources
Reference Books, 401–407
Business Letter Writing
Correspondence, 121–125
Reference Books, 403, 407
Business Memo
Correspondence, 121–125
Memorandum, 291
Business Writing, Types of
Acceptance, Letter of, 14
Annual Report, 39–43
Application, Letter of, 46–48
Description, 137–140
Formal Report, 180–184
Government Proposal, 202–209
House Organ Article, 228–231
Inquiry, Letter of, 247–249
Instructions, 250–251
Job Description, 263–265
Journal Article, 265–273
Memorandum, 291
Progress Report, 380–381
Proposal, 388–389

Résumé, 413–421
  Sales Proposal, 424–430
  Transmittal, Letter of, 493–494
Business Writing Style, 66–68
  Style, 464–466
Businessese
  Affectation, 24–26
  Business Writing Style, 66–68
But
  Coordinating Conjunction, 119
Buzz Words
  Affectation, 24–26
  Vogue Words, 506–507

C

ca. (circa)
  Abbreviations, 7
Call Letters
  Library Classification System,
    279–281
Call Numbers
  Library Classification System,
    279–281
Call Out
  Graphs, 210–221
Can/May, 69
Cancel Out, 69
Cannot/Can Not, 69
Cannot Help But, 69
  Double Negative, 145–146
Cant
  Jargon, 262–263
Canvas/Canvass, 69
Capital/Capitol, 70
Capital Letter, Indicating
  Proofreaders' Marks, 387
Capital Letters, 70–74
Carbon Copy Notation
  Correspondence, 123–125
Card File (or Catalog)
  Library Research, 281–283
Cardinal Number
  Numeral Adjectives, 317

Caret
  Symbols, 473
Case (grammatical) 74–79
  Pronouns, 382–385
Case (usage), 79
Causal Relationship
  Because, 58–59
Cause-and-Effect Method of
    Development, 79–80
  Methods of Development,
    292–293, 295
Cedilla
  Diacritical Marks, 141
  Symbols, 473
Censor/Censure, 80
Center Around, 80
Century
  A.D., 15
  Dates, 129–130
cf. (compare)
  Abbreviations, 7
Ch. (chapter)
  Abbreviations, 7
Chairing a Committee
  Oral Report, 334–335
Chairman/Chairwoman/
    Chairperson, 80–81
  Gender, 198–199
  He/She, 222
Character, 81
Charts
  Illustrations, 236–238
Checklist of the Writing Process, xx
Choppy Writing
  Awkwardness, 54
  Pace, 342–343
  Sentence Variety, 446
  Subordination, 469
  Transition, 489–491
Chronological Abbreviations
  Abbreviations, 9
Chronological Method of
    Development, 81
  Methods of Development, 292–294

Circa (ca)
  Abbreviations, 7
Circle Chart (pie graph)
  Graphs, 219–221
Circumlocution
  Affectation, 24–26
  Conciseness/Wordiness, 110–111
  Gobbledygook, 200–201
Cite/Site/Sight, 81
Clarity, 81–83
  Ambiguity, 35–36
  Awkwardness, 53–56
  Coherence, 87–88
  Conciseness/Wordiness, 108–111
  Dash, 127
  Defining Terms, 131–132
  Emphasis, 155–157
  Figures of Speech, 170–171
  Idiom, 234–235
  Pace, 342–343
  Parallel Structure, 349–352
  Positive Writing, 373
  Sentence Construction, 439–440
  Subordination, 468--470
  Transition, 489–492
  Unity, 496–497
  Word Choice, 511–512
Classification
  Analysis as a Method of
    Development, 37–38
Classification System, Library
  Library Classification System,
    279–281
Clauses, 83–85
  Adjective Clause, 19
  Adverb Clause, 23
  Dependent Clause, 135–137
  Noun Clause, 313
Clearness
  Clarity, 81–83
Clench/Clinch, 85
Cliché, 85–86
  Figures of Speech (worn), 171
  Revision, 423
  Trite Language, 496

Climactic Order of Importance
  Emphasis, 156
  Increasing Order of Importance,
    240
  Methods of Development,
    292–294
Clinch
  Clench/Clinch, 85
Clipped Form of Words, 86–87
  Word Choice, 512
Close of Letter
  Correspondence, 123–125
Close of Paper
  Conclusion, 112–113
Close-Space Marks
  Proofreader's Marks, 387
Closing an Oral Presentation
  Oral Report, 332–333
Co.
  Abbreviations, 5
Coherence, 87–88
  Clarity, 81–83
  Conciseness/Wordiness, 108–111
  Emphasis, 155–157
  Methods of Development,
    292–296
  Outlining, 338–341
  Pace, 342–343
  Revision, 421–423
  Subordination, 468–470
  Transition, 489–492
  Unity, 496–497
Cohesive Writing
  Coherence, 87–88
Coined Words
  Blend Words, 64
  New Words, 304
  Word Choice, 512
Col. (column)
  Abbreviations, 7
Collective Noun, 89
  Agreement, 29
  Nouns, 310
Colloquial English
  English, Varieties of, 157–159

Standard English, 464
Colon, 89–91
  Proofreaders' Marks, 387
  Punctuation, 390
Column Captions
  Tables, 476–477
Column Graph
  Graphs, 217
Combinations of Words
  Compound Words, 108
Combined Words
  Blend Words, 64
Comma, 91–100
  Proofreaders' Marks, 387
  Punctuation, 390
Comma Fault
  Comma, 98–100
  Sentence Faults, 442
Comma Splice
  Comma, 98–99
  Semicolon, 433–434
  Sentence Faults, 442,
Comma with Parentheses
  Comma, 98
  Parentheses, 354.
Command, Giving
  Instructions, 250–251
  Mood, 300–301
Commercial Guides
  Reference Books, 403
Commercial Proposal
  Proposal, 388–389
  Sales Proposal, 424–430
Committee, 100
Committee Meetings
  Oral Report, 327–336
Committee Minutes
  Minutes of Meeting, 296–297
Common
  Mutual/In Common, 302
Common Noun, 100–101
  Nouns, 310
Commonly Confused Terms
  Usage, 497–498

Communication, Oral
  Oral Report, 327–336
Companies, Names of
  Abbreviations, 4–5
  Capital Letters, 72
Company Financial Report
  Annual Report, 39–43
Company News
  House Organ Article, 228–231
Comparative Degree, 101–102
  Adjectives, 17
  Adverbs, 21
  Modifiers, 299–300
Compare/Contrast, 102
Comparing Similar Ideas
  Analogy, 37
  Metaphor, 292
  Simile, 450–451
Comparison, 102–103
  Absolute Words, 10
  Adjectives, 16–19
  Adverbs, 20–22
  Analogy, 37
  Figures of Speech, 170–172
  Methods of Development,
    294–295
Comparison as a Method of
    Development, 103
  Analogy, 37
  Methods of Development,
    294–295
Comparison, Double
  Comparison, 102–103
Complement, 103–104
  Linking Verb, 286–287
  Objective Complement, 318
  Subjective Complement, 467
  Verbs, 499
Complement/Compliment, 104–105
Completeness
  Checklist of the Writing Process,
    xx
  Revision, 421–423
Complex Sentence, 105–106
  Sentences, 435

Compliment
  Complement/Compliment,
    104–105
Complimentary Close
  Capital Letters, 71
  Correspondence, 123–125
Compose/Comprise, 106
Composing the Report
  Checklist of the Writing
    Process, xx
  Writing the Draft, 512–515
Compound Antecedent
  Agreement, 32
Compound-Complex Sentence, 107
  Sentences, 435
Compound Constructions
  Case, 77
Compound Fractions
  Hyphen, 232
Compound Noun
  Case, 77
  Compound Words, 108
  Nouns (forming plurals), 312–313
Compound Numbers
  Hyphen, 232
Compound Predicate
  Predicate, 374
Compound Pronoun
  Case, 78
Compound Sentence, 106–107
  Sentences, 435
Compound Subject
  Agreement, 30
  Subject of Sentence, 466–467
Compound Words, 108
  Word Choice, 512
Comprise
  Compose/Comprise, 106
Concept-Conception, 108
Concepts
  Capital Letters 72
Conciseness/Wordiness, 108–111
  Affectation, 24–26
  Gobbledygook, 200–201
  Revision, 421–423

Concluding a Sentence
  Exclamation Mark, 162–163
  Period, 359
  Punctuation, 390
  Question Mark, 390–391
Conclusion, 112–113
  Abstract, 10–12
  Formal Report, 182
Concrete Noun, 113
  Abstract Words/Concrete Words,
    12–13
  Nouns, 310
  Word Choice, 511
Concrete Words
  Abstract Words/Concrete Words,
    12–13
  Word Choice, 511
Concrete Writing
  Connotation/Denotation, 117–118
  Description (rendering), 137–140
  Word Choice, 511
Condensed Report
  Abstract, 10–12
  Brief, 65–66
Conditional Mood
  Mood, 301
Conducting a Committee Meeting or
    Panel Discussion
  Oral Report, 334–335
Conducting an Interview
  Interviewing 253–255
Conference Proceedings Guide
  Reference Books, 406–407
Conference Speaking
  Oral Report, 335
Confused Meaning
  Ambiguity, 35–36
Conjugation of Verbs
  Verbs, 503–505
Conjunctions, 113–115
  Capital Letters (Conjunctions in
    Titles), 73
  Connectives, 115–117
  Coordinating Conjunction, 119
  Correlative Conjunction, 120–121

Parts of Speech, 358
Sentence Construction (Beginning
  a Sentence with a Conjunction),
  441
Conjunctive Adverb, 115
  Comma, 96
  Compound Sentence, 106
  Connectives, 115–117
  Semicolon, 443
Connected With/In Connection
  With, 115
Connectives, 115–117
  Because, 58–59
  Conjunctions, 113–115
  Conjunctive Adverb, 115
  Coordinating Conjunction, 119
  Correlative Conjunction, 120–121
  Preposition, 337–378
  Semicolon, 433
  Subordinating Conjunction,
    467–468
Connotation/Denotation, 117–118
  Revision, 423
  Word Choice, 511
Consensus of Opinion, 118
Consistency, Grammatical
  Mixed Construction, 298–299
Construction
  Sentence Construction, 437–441
Contact, 118
Contents, Table of
  Table of Contents, 474–475
Context
  Connotation/Denotation, 117–118
  Note-Taking, 306–309
Continual/Continuous, 118–119
Continuity
  Coherence, 87–88
  Unity, 496–497
Contract Report
  Formal Report, 180–182
Contractions, 119
  Apostrophe, 44–45
  Clipped Form of Words, 86–87
Contrary to Fact

Mood, 300–301
Contrast
  Compare/Contrast, 102
  Comparison as a Method of
    Development, 103
Contrasting Coordinates
  Comma, 96–97
Contribute
  Attribute/Contribute, 52–53
Conversation
  Quotation Marks, 394
Conversational English
  English, Varieties of, 157–159
  Standard English, 464
Convincing Your Reader
  Persuasion, 364–365
  Propaganda 388
Coordinating Conjunction, 119
  Comma, 92
  Compound Sentence, 106–107
Coordination
  Balance, 57
  Coordinating Conjunction, 119
  Parallel Structure, 349–352
Copy Marking
  Proofreaders' Marks, 387
Copying
  Copyright, 120
  Footnotes, 175–179
  Plagiarism, 368
  Quotations, 396–399
Copyright, 120
  Plagiarism, 368
Corp.
  Abbreviations, 4–5
Corrections
  Proofreaders' Marks, 387
  Revision, 421–423
Correlative Conjunction, 120–121
  Connectives, 115–117
  Parallel Structure, 350–351
Correspondence, 121–125
  Acceptance, Letter of, 14
  Application, Letter, 46–48
  Inquiry, Letter of 247–249

Point of View, 368–370
Reference Books, 406
Technical Information, Letter of, 478–479
Tone, 486–487
Transmittal, Letter of, 493–494
Count Noun, 124–125
Agreement, 28
Amount/Number, 36–37
Mass Noun, 290
Nouns, 310
Courtesy Line
Drawings, 150
Cover
Formal Report, 181
Cover Letter
Formal Report, 180–181
Transmittal, Letter of, 493–494
Credible/Creditable, 125
Credit, Giving
Bibliography, 60–64
Copyright, 120
Documentation, 145
Footnotes, 175–179
Note-Taking, 306–311
Plagiarism, 368
Quotations, 396–397
Criterion/Criteria/Criterions, 126
Critique, 126
Cube Root
Symbols, 472
Cumulative
Accumulative/Cumulative, 15
Currency Signs
Symbols, 472–473
Curved Brackets
Parentheses, 353–354
Customer Manual
Technical Manual, 479
Cutaway Drawing
Drawings, 148

D

Dagger (Inserting)
Proofreaders' Marks, 386–387

Dangling Modifiers, 126–127
Absolute Phrase, 9–10
Infinitive Phrase, 244
Misplaced Modifiers, 297–298
Participial Phrase, 355
Prepositional Phrase, 379
Dash, 127–129
Emphasis, 156
Punctuation, 390
Data, 129
Collective Noun, 89
Data Sheet
Résumé, 413–421
Dates, 129–130
Apostrophe, 45
Comma, 95
Numbers 316
Slash, 453
Days
Capital Letters, 72
Dates, 129–130
Deadwood
Conciseness/Wordiness, 108–111
Decided/Decisive, 130
Declarative Mood
Mood, 300–301
Declarative Sentence
Sentences, 435
Decreasing Order of Importance as a Method of Development, 130
Deduction
General-To-Specific Method of Development, 199
De Facto/De Jure, 131
Defective/Deficient, 131
Defining Terms, 131–132
Connotation/Denotation, 117–118
Definition as a Form of Writing, 132–134
Dictionary, 141–143
Reader, 400
Definite/Definitive, 132
Definite Article
A, An, 1
Article, 49–50

Definition
  Defining Terms, 131–132
  Dictionary, 141–143
Definition as a Form of Writing,
  132–134
Definition Openings
  Openings, 324
Definitions, List of
  Dictionary, 141–143
  Glossary, 199–200
Degree (Temperature/Mathematics)
  Symbols, 473
Degree of Comparison
  Comparative Degree, 101–102
Degrees, Academic
  Abbreviations, 6–7
Deity
  Capital Letters, 74
  Xmas, 515
De Jure
  De Facto/De Jure, 131
Delete Mark
  Proofreader's Marks, 386–387
Delivery of Speech
  Oral Report, 327–334
Demonstrative Adjective, 134–135
  Adjectives, 16
Demonstrative Pronoun, 135
  Pronouns, 381
Denotation
  Connotation/Denotation, 117–118
  Defining Terms, 131–132
  Dictionary, 141–142
Dependent Clause, 135–137
  Clauses, 84
  Comma, 96
  Complex Sentence, 105–106
  Compound-Complex Sentence,
    107
  Subordination, 468–470
Depicting
  Description, 137–140
Depth of Coverage
  Scope, 432
Derivation of Words

Dictionary, 141–143
Description, 137–140
  Forms of Discourse, 197
Description of a Job
  Job Description, 263–265
Description of a Mechanism
  Description, 137–140
Description of a Mechanism in
    Operation
  Explaining a Process, 163–166
Description of a Process
  Explaining a Process, 163–166
Descriptive Adjective
  Adjectives, 16
Descriptive Clause
  Adjective Clause, 19
Descriptive Grammar
  Grammar, 209–210
Descriptive Word
  Modifiers, 299–300
Descriptive Writing
  Description, 137–140
Desk Dictionaries
  Dictionary, 141–143
Despite /In Spite Of, 140
Detail Drawing
  Drawings, 147–150
Developing Ideas
  Methods of Development,
    292–296
  Organization, 336–337
  Paragraph, 343–349
  Sentence Construction, 439–441
Device, Description of
  Description, 137–140
  Explaining a Process, 163–166
Dewey Decimal System
  Library Classification System,
    279–280
Diacritical Marks, 140–141
  Symbols, 473
Diagnosis/Prognosis, 141
Diagram
  Flowchart, 174
  Schematic Diagrams, 430–430

Dialect
  English, Varieties of, 158
Dialogue
  Quotation Marks, 394–395
Diction, 141
  Word Choice, 511–512
Dictionaries, Biographical
  Reference Books, 402–403
Dictionary, 141–144
  Abbreviations, 2–9
  Connotation/Denotation, 117–118
  Defining Terms, 131–132
  Foreign Words in English,
    179–180
  Spelling, 463
Dictionary Meaning
  Connotation/Denotation, 117–118
Dieresis
  Diacritical Marks, 140–141
  Symbols, 473
Differ From/Differ With, 144
Different From/Different Than, 144
Differences and Similarities
  Comparison as a Method of
    Development, 103
Differentia
  Defining Terms, 131–132
Digest of Report
  Abstract, 10–12
Dignified Writing
  Affectation, 24–26
Digression
  Anecdote, 38
Direct Address, 144
  Comma, 92
Direct and Indirect Word Meanings
  Connotation/Denotation, 117–118
Direct Object, 144
  Indirect Object, 243
  Object, 317–318
  Transitive Verb, 492–493
Direct Quotation
  Comma, 97
  Copyright, 120

Footnotes, 175–179
  Plagiarism, 368
  Quotations, 396–397
Directions
  Instructions, 250–251
Directions, Geographical
  Capital Letters, 71
Discourse, Forms of, 197
  Description, 137–140
  Exposition, 167–168
  Narration, 302–303
  Persuasion, 364–365
Discreet/Discrete, 145
Discussion Guides
  Reference Books, 406
Discussions, Panel
  Oral Report, 335
Dishonesty
  Plagiarism, 368
Disinterested/Uninterested, 145
Dissertation Abstracts
  Reference Books, 404
Ditto Marks
  Quotation Marks, 394–396
Divided by
  Symbols, 472
Dividing a Word
  Dictionary, 142
  Hyphen, 232
  Syllabication, 471
Dividing Months
  Bi-/Semi-, 60
Dividing Years
  Biannual/Biennial, 60
Division
  Analysis as a Method of
    Development, 37–38
Documentation, 145
  Abbreviations, 7
  Bibliography, 60–64
  Copyright, 120
  Footnotes, 175–179
  Literature, 287
  Note-Taking, 306–309

Plagiarism, 368
Documents, Government
  Reference Books, 404–405
Dollar Sign
  Symbols, 472
Dots, Spaced
  Ellipses, 152–154
  Period, 360–361
Double Comparison
  Comparison, 102–103
Double Dagger, Indicating
  Proofreaders' Marks, 386-387
Double Negative, 145–146
Double Possessive
  Case, 77
Dr.
  Abbreviations, 68
Draft
  Writing the Draft, 512–515
Drawings, 147–150
  Illustrations, 236–238
Due To/Because of, 150

E

Each, 151
  Agreement, 29
Each and Every, 151
Each Other/One Another, 151
  Reciprocal Pronoun, 401
Earth
  Capital Letters, 72
Economic/Economical, 151–152
Econòmic Groups
  Capital Letters, 71
Economical Writing
  Conciseness/Wordiness, 108–111
-ed
  Participle, 355–356
  Tense, 482, 483
Editing Guides
  Proofreaders' Marks, 386–387
  Reference Books, 407
Effect

Affect/Effect, 24
Cause-and-Effect Method of
  Development, 79–80
e.g., 152
  Abbreviations, 7
Either . . . Or
  Correlative Conjunction, 120–121
  Parallel Structure, 350–351
Elegant Variation, 152
  Affectation, 24–26
Elimination
  Definition as a Form of Writing,
    132–134
Ellipses, 152–154
Elliptical Construction
  Clauses, 84–85
  Comma, 98
  Dangling Modifiers, 127
  Sentences (Minor Sentence),
    436–437
  Zeugma, 515
Elude
  Allude/Elude, 33
Em Dash
  Proofreaders' Marks, 387
Eminent/Imminent/Immanent,
  154–155
Emotional Overtones
  Connotation/Denotation, 117–118
Emphasis, 155–157
  Coherence, 87–88
  Comma, 93
  Dash, 127–129
  Sentence Construction, 437–439
Employment
  Acceptance, Letter of, 14
  Application, Letter of, 46–48
  Résumé, 413–421
-en
  Participle, 356
En Dash
  Proofreaders' Marks, 386–387
Enclosure Notation
  Correspondence, 123–125

Encyclopedias
  Footnotes, 177
  Reference Books, 404
Ending a Sentence
  Ellipses, 152–154
  Exclamation Mark, 162–163
  Period, 359–360
  Punctuation, 389–390
  Question Mark, 390–391
Ending Your Report
English, Varieties of, 157–159
  Nonstandard English, 305–306
  Standard English, 464
Enormity/Enormousness, 159
Ensure
  Insure/Ensure/Assure, 251
Epithet, 159
  Appositives, 48–49
  Capital Letters, 73
Equal/Unique/Perfect, 159–160
  Absolute Words, 10
Equal To
  Symbols, 472
-er
  Adjectives, 17
  Adverbs, 21
  Comparative Degree, 101–102
-ese, 160
  Jargon, 262–263
  New Words, 304
  Suffix, 470
Esq. (Esquire)
  Abbreviations, 6
Essay Questions, Answering,
    160–161
-est
  Adjectives, 17
  Adverbs, 21
  Comparative Degree, 101–102
  Intensifiers, 251–252
et al.
  Abbreviations, 7
etc., 161
Etymology

  Dictionary, 141–143
Euphemism, 161–162
  Affectation, 24–26
  Connotation/Denotation, 117–118
  Word Choice, 512
Events
  Capital Letters, 72
Everybody/Everyone, 162
  Agreement, 31
Everyone
  Agreement, 31
  Everybody/Everyone, 162
Ex Post Facto, 162
Exact Writing
  Abstract Words/Concrete Words,
    12–13
  Connotation/Denotation, 117–118
  Description (Rendering), 137–140
  Word Choice, 511–512
Exaggeration
  Hyperbole, 231
Except
  Accept/Except, 13
Excess Words
  Conciseness/Wordiness, 108–111
  Revision, 423
Exclamation
  Interjection, 252–253
Exclamation Mark, 162–163
  Punctuation, 389–390
Exclamatory Sentence
  Interjection, 252–253
  Sentences, 435–436
Experiment, Results of
  Laboratory Report, 274–278
Explaining a Process, 163–166
Expletives, 166
Explicit/Implicit, 167
Exploded-View Drawing
  Drawings, 149
Exposition, 167–168
  Forms of Discourse, 197
Extemporaneous Speech
  Oral Report, 327–328

Extended Definition
   Definition as a Form of Writing,
      132–134
Extent of Coverage
   Scope, 432

F

f./ff. (following)
   Abbreviations, 7
Fact, 168–169
Fact Books
   Reference Books, 404
Fact Sheet
   Résumé, 413–421
Factual Writing
   Exposition, 167–168
False Coordination
   Balance, 57
   Subordination, 468–470
False Elegance
   Affectation, 24–26
Family Relationships
   Capital Letters, 73
Famous/Notorious/Infamous, 169
Fancy Words
   Affectation, 24–26
   Elegant Variation, 152
   Long Variants, 287–288
   Word Choice, 512
Fancy Writing
   Affectation, 24–26
   Gobbledygook, 200–201
   Jargon, 262–263
Fashionable Words
   Vogue Words, 506
Fault
   Comma, 98–99
Faulty Parallelism
   Parallel Structure, 351–352
   Subordination, 468–470
Faulty Pronoun Reference
   Pronouns, 385–386
Faulty Subordination

Sentence Faults, 441–442
Federal Government Publications
   Reference Books, 404–405
Feel Bad/Feel Badly
   Bad/Badly, 57
Female, 169
Feminine
   Agreement, 31
   Gender, 198–199
   He/She, 222
   Ms./Miss/Mrs., 301–302
Few/A Few, 169
Fewer/Less, 169
Figurative Language
   Figures of Speech, 170–172
Figuratively/Literally, 170
Figure Numbers
   Drawings, 150
   Flowcharts, 174
   Graphs, 212
   Illustrations, 238
   Maps, 290
Figures
   Numbers, 314–316
Figures, List of
   Formal Report, 181
   Illustrations, 236–238
Figures of Speech, 170–172
   Analogy, 37
   Cliché, 85–86
   Hyperbole, 231
   Metaphor, 292
   Simile, 450–451
Films
   Capital Letters, 73
   Italics, 260
Final Draft
   Revision, 421–423
Financial Report
   Annual Report, 39–43
Finding Information
   Interviewing, 253–255
   Library Research, 281–286
   Questionnaire, 391–394

Research, 411
Fine, 172
Fine Writing
  Affectation, 24–26
Finite Verb, 173
  Verb, 500
First/Firstly, 173
First Name Spelled Out
  Abbreviations, 5
First Person
  Person, 362
  Point of View, 368–370
Flammable/Inflammable/
    Nonflammable, 173
Flow Chart, 174
  Illustrations, 236–238
Flow of Writing
  Clarity, 81–83
  Coherence, 87–88
  Conciseness/Wordiness, 108–111
  Pace, 242–243
  Transition, 489–492
  Unity, 496–497
Flowery Writing
  Affectation, 24–26
  Gobbledygook, 200–201
fm
  Abbreviations, 5
Font (type)
  Proofreaders' Marks, 386–387
Footer
  Header/Footer, 222
Footnotes, 175–179
  Abbreviations, 7
  Formal Report, 182
  Graphs, 215
  Tables, 476–477
For
  Because, 58–59
For Example
  e.g., 152
  Transition, 489–490
Forecast Opening
  Openings, 326

Forceful/Forcible, 179
Foreign Punctuation
  Diacritical Marks, 140–141
  Foreign Words in English,
    179–180
Foreign Words in English, 179–180
  A La, 1–2
  Ad Hoc, 16
  Ex Post Facto, 162
  Italics, 261
  Quid Pro Quo, 394
  Word Choice, 512
Foreword
  Foreword/Preface, 180
  Formal Report, 181
Foreword/Preface, 180
Form Changes in Words
    (Inflectional Changes)
  Adverbs, 21
  Nouns, 311–313
Formal English
  Formal Writing Style, 195–196
  Style, 464–466
  Usage, 497–498
Formal Report, 180–194
Formal Writing Style, 195–196
  Style, 464–466
Format, 192
  Correspondence, 122–125
  Formal Report, 180–182
  Header/Footer, 222
  Heads, 222–227
  Indentation, 242
  Memorandum, 291
  Specifications, 455–463
Formation of Words
  Blend Words, 64
  New Words, 304
Former/Latter, 196
  Above, 9
Forms of Discourse, 197
  Description, 137–140
  Exposition, 167–168
  Narration, 302–303

Persuasion, 364–365
Formula/Formulae, 197
Fortuitous/Fortunate, 197
Fraction
 Numbers, 316
 Slash, 453
Fragment
 Awkwardness, 54
 Sentence Faults, 442–443
 Sentences (Minor Sentence),
  436–437
Franc
 Symbols, 473
French Terms
 A La, 1–2
 Foreign Words in English,
  179–180
Functional Shift, 197–198
Fused Sentence
 Period, 361–362
 Sentence Faults, 442
Fused Word
 Blend Words, 64
Future Perfect Tense
 Tense, 483
Future Tense
 Tense, 483

G

Gender, 198–199
 Agreement, 31
 He/She, 222
 Ms./Miss/Mrs., 301–302
General English
 Standard English, 464
General-to-Specific Method of
  Development, 199
 Methods of Development, 295
General Types of Writing
 Description, 137–140
 Explaining a Process, 163–166
 Exposition, 167–168
 Forms of Discourse, 197

Instructions, 250–251
 Narration, 302–303
 Persuasion, 364–365
General Words
 Abstract Words/Concrete Words,
  12–13
 Vague Words, 498–499
 Word Choice, 511–512
Generalization
 Sweeping Generalization,
  470–471
Genitive Case (Possessive)
 Apostrophe, 44–45
 Case, 76–78
 Its/It's, 261–262
 Possessive Adjective, 373–374
Geographical Directions
 Capital Letters, 7–8
Geographical Locations
 Abbreviations, 2–9
 Capital Letters, 7–8
German Accent Marks
 Diacritical Marks, 140–141
Gerund, 199
 Substantive, 470
 Verbals, 505–506
Gerund Phrase
 Dangling Modifiers, 126
 Gerund, 199
 Phrases, 367
Getting Ready
 Preparation, 376–377
Giving Instructions
 Instructions, 250–251
Gloss Over
 Euphemism, 161–162
Glossary, 199–200
Goal of Writer
 Objective (Purpose), 318–319
Gobbledygook, 200–201
 Affectation, 24–26
 Blend Words, 64
 Conciseness/Wordiness, 108–111
 Long Variants, 287–288

God
  Capital Letters, 74
Good/Well, 201
Got/Gotten, 201
Government Proposal, 202–209
  Proposal, 388
Government Publications
  Reference Books, 404–405
  Specifications, 456–460
Government Specifications
  Specifications, 456–460
Grammar, 209–210
  Parts of Speech, 357–358
Grammatical Agreement
  Agreement, 27–32
Grammatical Properties of Verbs
  Verb, 501–503
Graphic Illustrations
  Graphs, 210–221
  Illustrations, 236–238
  Reference Books, 405
Graphs, 210–221
  Illustrations, 236–238
Grave
  Diacritical Marks, 140–141
  Symbols, 473
Greater-Than Symbol
  Symbols, 472
Grid Lines
  Graphs, 210–221
Group Discussion Guides
  Reference Books, 406–407
Group Nouns
  Collective Noun, 89
Group, Speaking Before
  Oral Report, 332–334
Grouping of Words
  Clauses, 83–85
  Phrases, 366–367
  Sentences, 434–437
Guide to Reference Books
  Reference Books, 401–407

H

Habitual or Customary Actions
  Tense, 482
Hackneyed Expressions
  Clichés, 85–86
  Trite Language, 496
Half, 221
Handbooks
  Reference Books, 401–407
Hasty Generalization
  Sweeping Generalization,
    470–471
Have
  Infinitive, 245–246
  Tense, 482–483
He
  Case, 74–75
  Gender, 198–199
  Person, 362
  Personal Pronoun, 363–364
He/She, 222
  Case, 74–75
  Gender, 198–199
Header/Footer, 222
  Format, 196
Heads (Titles and Subtitles),
    222–227
  Format, 196
  Outlining, 340
Healthful/Healthy, 227
Helping Verb, 227
  Verb, 500–501
Herein/Herewith, 227
Historic/Historical, 227–228
  Article, 49–50
Historical Events
  Capital Letters, 72
Historical Present
  Tense, 482
History of Words
  Dictionary, 141–142
Holidays
  Capital Letters, 72

Honorable (as title)
   Abbreviations, 6
Horizontal Axis
   Graphs, 210–221
Hours
   Numbers, 316
House Organ Article, 228–231
   Openings, 323
How to Begin Your Report
   Introduction, 256–258
   Openings, 323–326
How to End Your Report
   Conclusion, 112–113
However
   Conjunctive Adverb, 115
Hyperbole, 231
   Affectation, 24–26
   Figures of Speech, 171
Hyphen, 231–233
   Dash, 127–129
   Prefix, 375–376
   Proofreaders' Marks, 386–387
   Punctuation, 389–390
   Syllabication, 471

I

I
   Case, 74–76
   Person, 362
   Personal Pronoun, 363–364
Ibid.
   Abbreviations, 7
Idea, 234
Ideas, Developing
   Methods of Development,
     292–296
   Organization, 336–337
   Outlining, 338–341
Identical-With Symbol
   Symbols, 472
Idiom, 234–235
   Ambiguity, 36
   English, Varieties of, 157–159

Idiomatic Uses of Prepositions
   Prepositions, 378
Idiomatic Uses of Words
   Idiom, 234–235
i.e., 235
   Abbreviations, 7
If and When
   When and If, 508
Illegal/Illicit, 235
Illogical Constructions
   Sentence Faults, 441–445
Illogical Shift
   Mixed Construction, 298–299
Illusion
   Allusion/Illusion, 34
Illustrations, 236–238
   Drawings, 147–150
   Flowcharts, 174
   Graphs, 210–221
   Maps, 289–290
   Organizational Charts, 337
   Schematic Diagrams, 430–431
   Tables, 475–477
Illustrations, List of
   Formal Report, 181
   Illustrations, 236–238
Imaginative Comparison
   Figures of Speech, 170–172
Immanent
   Eminent/Imminent/Immanent,
     154–155
Imperative Mood
   Mood, 300–301
   Sentences, 436
Implicit
   Explicit/Implicit, 167
Implied Meaning
   Connotation/Denotation, 117–118
Implied Subject
   Sentences, 437
Imply/Infer, 238
Importance, Relative
   Subordination, 468–470
Imprecise Words

Ambiguity, 35–36
  Vague Words, 498–499
Impromptu Speech
  Oral Report, 327
In/Into, 238
In-/Un-
  Prefix, 375,376
In Back Of
  Back Of/In Back Of, 57
In Care Of
  Symbols, 473
In Case Of
  Case (Usage), 79
In Common
  Mutual/In Common, 302
In Connection With
  Connected With/In Connection
    With, 115
In Order To, 239
In Re
  Re, 399
In Regards To
  As Regards/With Regard To/In
    Regard To/Regarding, 51
In Spite Of
  Despite/In Spite Of, 140
In Terms Of, 239
Inanimate Object, Possessive
    Form of
  Case, 77
Inasmuch As/Insofar As, 239–240
Inc.
  Abbreviations, 4–5
Incident
  Anecdote, 38
Incomparable Words
  Absolute Words, 10
Incomplete Comparison
  Ambiguity, 35–36
  Comparison, 102–103
Incomplete Sentence
  Sentence Faults, 442–444
Inconsistency, Grammatical
  Mixed Constructions, 298–299

Increasing Order of Importance as a
    Method of Development, 240
  Methods of Development, 294
Incredible/Incredulous, 240
Indefinite Adjective, 241
  Adjectives, 16–19
Indefinite Article
  A, An, 1
  Article, 49–50
  Indefinite Adjective, 241
Indefinite Pronouns, 241
  Case, 74–79
  Pronouns, 382
Indeed
  Interjection, 252–253
Indentation, 242
  Paragraph, 343
  Quotations, 398
Independent Clause
  Balance, 57
  Clauses, 84
  Comma, 92
  Complex Sentence, 105–106
  Compound Sentence, 106–107
  Compound-Complex Sentence,
    107
  Conjunctions, 114
  Dependent Clause, 135–137
  Semicolon, 482–433
  Simple Sentence, 451–452
Independent Grammatical Unit
  Absolute Phrase, 9–10
Independent Phrase
  Absolute Phrase, 9–10
Index, 243
  Bibliography, 60–64
  Reference Books, 406
Indicative Mood
  Mood, 300–301
  Sentences, 434–435
Indirect and Direct Word Meanings
  Connotation/Denotation, 117–118
Indirect Object, 243
  Complement, 103–104

Direct Object, 144
Object, 317–318
Predicate, 374
Transitive Verb, 492–493
Indirect Quotation
Comma, 97
Indirect Reference
Allusion, 34
Indiscreet/Indiscrete, 244
Individual, 244
Induction
Specific-to-General Method of
Development, 455
Industrial Specification
Specifications, 455–456
Infamous
Famous/Infamous/Notorious, 169
Infer
Imply/Infer, 238
Inferior Type
Proofreaders' Marks, 386–387
Infinitive, 244–245
Substantive, 470
Verb, 501
Verbals, 505–506
Infinitive Phrase, 245–246
Dangling Modifiers, 127
Infinity
Symbols, 472
Inflammable
Flammable/Inflammable/
Nonflammable, 173
Inflated Words
Long Variants, 287–288
Inflectional Changes in Words
Adverbs, 21–22
Nouns, 311–312
Inflict
Afflict/Inflict, 26
Informal English
Informal Writing Style, 246–247
Style, 464–466
Usage, 497–498
Informal Report

Memorandum, 291
Informal Writing Style, 246–247
Style, 464–466
Information, Locating
Library Research, 281–286
Reference Books, 401–407
Research, 411
Information, Requesting
Inquiry, Letter of, 247–249
Questionnaire, 391–394
Technical Information, Letter of,
478–479
-ing Ending
Gerund, 199
Participle, 355–357
Ingenious/Ingenuous, 247
Initials
Abbreviations, 29
Inoffensive Words
Euphemism, 161–162
Inquiry, Letter of, 247–249
Correspondence, 121–125
Insert Mark
Proofreaders' Marks, 386–387
Insertion Sentence
Sentence Variety, 448
Inset
Indentation, 242
Inside/Inside Of, 249
Inside Address
Correspondence, 122–125
Insofar As
Inasmuch As/Insofar As, 239–240
Insoluble/Unsolvable (or Insolvable),
249–250
Institutions
Abbreviations, 4–5
Capital Letters, 72
Instructional Manual
Technical Manual, 479
Instructions, 250–251
Insure/Ensure/Assure, 251
Intensifiers, 251–252
Adverbs, 20–22

Conciseness/Wordiness, 112
  Emphasis, 155–157
  Modifiers, 299–300
Intensive Pronoun
  Pronouns, 382
  Reflexive Pronoun, 408
Intention of Writer
  Objective (Purpose), 318–319
  Point of View, 368–370
Interesting Detail Opening
  Openings, 324–325
Interface, 252
  Vogue Words, 506–507
Interjection, 252–253
  Capital Letters, 73
  Comma, 94
  Exclamation Mark, 162–163
  Parts of Speech, 357–358
Internal Correspondence
  Memorandum, 291
Interoffice Communication
  Memorandum, 291
Interpolation Within Quotation
  Brackets, 65
Interpretations, Multiple
  Ambiguity, 35–36
Interrogation
  Interviewing, 253–255
Interrogative Adjective
  Adjectives, 16
Interrogative Adverb, 253
  Adverbs, 20
Interrogative Mood
  Mood, 300–301
Interrogative Pronoun, 253
  Pronouns, 382
Interrogative Sentence
  Question Mark, 390
  Sentences, 435
Interviewing, 253–255
  Checklist of the Writing Process,
    xx
  Questionnaire, 391–394
  Research, 411

Into
  In/Into, 238
Intransitive Verb, 255–256
  Verb, 499
Introduction, 256–258
  Foreword/Preface, 180
  Revision, 422–423
  Rhetorical Question, 424
Introductory Words and Phrases
  Comma, 93–94
  Expletives, 166
  Gerund, 199
  Infinitive Phrase, 245–246
  Introductions, 256–258
  Transition, 491
Inverted Commas
  Quotation Marks, 394–396
Inverted Sentence Order, 258–259
  Emphasis, 155
  Sentence Construction, 438–439
  Sentence Variety, 447
  Style, 464–466
Investigation
  Interviewing, 253–255
  Library Research, 281–286
  Questionnaire, 391–394
  Research, 411
Irregardless/Regardless, 259
Irregular Verb
  Verb, 508
-ism
  Suffix, 470
Is To (Ratio)
  Symbols, 472
Is When (or Where)
  Defining Terms, 131–132
It, 259
  Gender, 198–199
It Is
  Expletives, 166
It Is I
  Case, 75
Its/It's, 261–262
  Case, 75

It's Me, 262
  Case, 75
Italics, 259–261
  Emphasis, 259–260
  Foreign Words in English,
    179–180
  Proofreaders' Marks, 386–387
  Quotation Marsk, 396
Items in a Series, Punctuating
  Comma, 94–95
  Semicolon, 434

J

Jargon, 262–263
  Affectation, 24–26
  Blend Words, 64
  Revision, 423
  Word Choice, 511–512
Job Description, 263–265
Joining Words
  Conjunctions, 113–115
  Connectives, 115–117
Joint Possession
  Case, 77
Journal Article, 265–273
Journals of Abstracts
  Reference Books, 400–401
Journals
  Bibliography, 62
  Footnotes, 176–177
Jr.
  Abbreviations, 6
Judicial/Judicious, 273–274
Juxtaposition
  Ambiguity, 36

K

Kind (Singular and Plural Forms of)
  Demonstrative Adjective, 134–135
Kind Of/Sort Of, 274
Know-How, 274

L

Laboratory Report, 274–278
Language Usage Guides
  Reference Books, 405
Languages
  Capital Letters, 70–74
Latin Words
  Foreign Words in English
    179–180
Latter
  Above, 9
  Former/Latter, 196
Law
  Police Report, 370–373
Lay/Lie, 278
Lead-Ins
  Openings, 323–326
Lead Sentence
Leading a Committee
  Oral Report, 334–335
Leading a Panel Discussion
  Oral Report, 335–335
Leaders
  Format, 196
  Period, 361
Leave/Let, 278
Legal Rights of Author
  Copyright, 120
  Plagiarism, 368
Legal Terms
  Ad Hoc, 16
  Brief, 65
  De Facto/De Jure, 131
  Ex Post Facto, 162
  Quid Pro Quo, 394
Legalese
  Affectation, 24–26
  Gobbledygook, 200–201
Lend/Loan, 279
Length
  Paragraph, 345–346
  Sentence Variety, 445–446
Less

Fewer/Less, 169
Less-Than Symbol
Symbols, 472
Let
Leave/Let, 278
Let-Stand Mark
Proofreaders' Marks, 386–387
Letterhead
Correspondence, 121–125
Letter of Acceptance
Acceptance, Letter of, 14
Correspondence, 121–125
Letter of Application
Application, Letter of, 46–48
Correspondence, 121–125
Résumé, 413–421
Letter of Inquiry
Correspondence, 121–125
Inquiry, Letter of, 247–249
Letter of Technical Information
Correspondence, 121–125
Technical Information, Letter of,
478–479
Letter of Transmittal
Correspondence, 121–125
Transmittal, Letter of, 493–494
Letter Report
Correspondence, 121–125
Memorandum, 291
Letter Writing
Correspondence, 121–125
Reference Books, 406
Letters of the Alphabet
Abbreviations, 2–9
Capital Letters, 73
Italics (indicating a letter), 261
Levels of Heads
Heads, 224–227
Levels of Usage
English, Varieties of, 157–159
Lexical Meaning
Connotation/Denotation, 117–118
Dictionary, 141–142
Lexicon

Dictionary, 141–143
Libel/Liable/Likely, 279
Library Card
Library Research, 281–283
Library Classification System,
279–281
Library of Congress System
Library Classification System,
280–281
Library Research, 281–286
Lie
Lay/Lie, 278
Lightface Type
Proofreaders' Marks, 386–387
-like, 286
Suffix, 470
Like
Comparison as a Method of
Development, 103
Like/As, 286
Simile, 450–451
Like/As, 286
Likely
Libel/Liable/Likely, 279
Limiting Adjective
Adjectives, 16–17
Limiting Your Topic
Scope, 432
Line Drawing
Drawings, 147
Line Graph
Graphs, 210–215
Lingo
Jargon, 262–263
Linking Verb, 286–287
Verb, 500–501
Linking Words
Conjunctions, 113–115
Connectives, 115–117
Prepositions, 377–378
List of Books and Articles
Bibliography, 60–64
Reference Books, 401–407
List of Definitions

Dictionary, 141–144
Glossary, 199–200
List of Figures or Illustrations
Formal Report, 181
Illustrations, 236–238
List of Items, Punctuating
Comma, 94–95
List of Names
Index, 243
List of Numbers
Tables, 475–477
List of Terms
Glossary, 199–200
List of Topics
Index, 243
Table of Contents, 474–475
List of Words
Dictionary, 141–144
Glossary, 199–200
Thesaurus, 485
Listener Response
Oral Report, 327–334
Literal Meaning
Connotation/Denotation, 117–118
Dictionary, 141–144
Literally
Figuratively/Literally, 170
Literature, 287
Literature, Searching
Library Research, 281–286
Research, 411
Litote
Figures of Speech, 171–172
Loan
Lend/Loan, 279
Loan Words
Foreign Words in English,
179–180
Localism
English, Varieties of, 157–160
Locating Information
Library Research, 281–286
Logic
Reference Books, 405–406

Logical Thinking
Coherence, 87–88
Comparison, 102–103
Defining Terms, 131–132
Metaphor (mixed), 292
Methods of Development,
292–296
Mixed Construction, 298–299
Organization, 336–337
Outlining, 338–341
Sweeping Generalization,
470–471
Long Quotation
Quotations, 398
Long Variants, 287–288
Affectation, 24–26
Gobbledygook, 200–201
Word Choice, 512
Loose/Lose, 288
Loose Sentence
Sentences, 436
Sentence Variety, 448
Lose
Loose/Lose, 288
Lower-Case and Upper-Case
Letters, 288
Capital Letters, 70–74
Proofreader's Marks, 386–387
Ltd.
Abbreviations, 5
Lucid Writing
Clarity, 81–83
-ly Ending
Adverbs, 21

M

M.A.
Abbreviations, 6
Macron
Diacritical Marks, 140
Symbols, 473
Magazine
Bibliography, 62–63

Footnotes, 177
House Organ Article, 228–231
Journal Article, 265–273
Magazine, Italics for Title
  Italics, 260
Magnification
  Hyperbole, 231
Main Idea Statement
  Conclusion, 112–113
  Introduction, 256–258
  Objective (Purpose), 318–319
  Outlining, 338–341
Main Verb
  Verb Phrase, 505
Making an Indirect Reference
  Allusion, 34
Malapropism, 288
  Word Choice, 511
Male, 288–289
Male, Symbol for
  Symbols, 473
Manual
  Technical Manual, 479
Manuscript
  Abbreviations, 7
  Format, 196
  MS/MSS, 302
Manuscript Preparation
  Proofreaders' Marks, 386–387
Manuscript Speech
  Oral Report, 327–332
Map Books
  Reference Books, 402
Maps, 289–290
  Illustrations, 236–238
Mark of Anticipation
  Colon, 89–91
Mark of Possession
  Apostrophe, 44–45
Masculine
  Agreement, 31
  Gender, 198–199
  He/She, 222
Mass Noun, 290
  Agreement, 28

Amount/Number, 36–37
Count Noun, 125
Nouns, 310
May
  Can/May, 69
Maybe/May Be, 290
M.D.
  Abbreviations, 6
Me
  Case, 76, 78
Mean
  Average/Mean/Median, 53
Meaning
  Ambiguity, 35–36
  Connotation/Denotation, 117–118
  Defining Terms, 131–132
  Dictionary, 141–143
  Glossary, 199–200
Measurement
  Abbreviations, 5
  Numbers, 314–316
Mechanical Arrangement
  Format, 196
Mechanism, Description of
  Description, 137–140
Mechanism in Operation
  Explaining a Process, 163–166
Media/Medium, 290–291
Median
  Average/Mean/Median, 53
Meeting, Conducting
  Oral Report, 334–335
Meeting, Minutes of
  Minutes of Meeting, 296–297
Memorandum, 291
  Correspondence, 121–125
Messrs.
  Abbreviations, 6
Metaphor, 292
  Figures of Speech, 172
Methods of Development, 292–296
  Analysis, 37–38
  Cause-and-Effect, 79–80
  Chronological, 81
  Comparison, 103

Decreasing Order of Importance
as a Method of Development,
130
Definition as a Form of Writing,
132–134
General-to-Specific, 199
Increasing Order of Importance,
240
Sequential, 449
Spatial, 455
Specific-to-General, 455
Methods of Discourse
Description, 137–140
Exposition, 167–168
Forms of Discourse, 197
Narration, 302–303
Persuasion, 364–365
Metonymy
Figures of Speech, 172
Military Format of Dates
Dates, 129–130
Military Proposal
Government Proposal, 202–209
Military Specification
Specifications, 455
Military Titles
Abbreviations, 6
Capital Letters, 73
Minor Sentence
Sentences, 434, 436–437
Minus Symbol
Symbols, 472
Minutes
Numbers, 316
Symbols, 473
Minutes of Meeting, 296–297
Misplaced Modifiers, 297–298
Dangling Modifiers, 126–127
Modifiers, 300
Miss
Ms./Miss/Mrs., 301–302
Missing Words
Ellipses, 152–154
Missing Subject
Dangling Modifiers, 126–127

Misused Word
Malapropism, 288
Mixed Construction, 298–299
Mixed Metaphor
Metaphor, 292
Mixed Words
Blend Words, 64
Malapropism, 288
Modal Auxiliary Verb
Helping Verb, 227
Mode
Vogue Words, 506–507
Moderator of Panel Discussion
Oral Report, 335
Modifiers, 299–300
Adjectives, 16–19
Adverbs, 20–22
Dangling Modifiers, 126–127
Misplaced Modifiers, 297–298
Money
Symbols, 472, 473
Months
Abbreviations, 9
Comma, 137
Dates, 129–130
Months, Dividing
Bi-/Semi-, 60
Mood, 300–301
Verb, 500
More
Adjectives, 17
Adverbs, 21
Comparative Degree, 101–102
Intensifiers, 251–252
More Than
As Much As/More Than, 51
Most
Adjectives, 17
Adverbs, 21
Almost/Most, 34–35
Comparative Degree, 101–107
Intensifiers, 251–252
Move (up, down, left, right)
Proofreaders' Marks, 386–387
Movies, Titles of

Capital Letters, 73
  Italics, 260
Mr.
  Abbreviations, 7
Mrs.
  Abbreviations, 7
  Ms./Miss/Mrs., 302–302
Ms./Miss/Mrs., 301–302
  Abbreviations, 7
MS/MSS, 302
  Abbreviations, 7
Much
  Intensifiers, 251–252
Multi-Author Books
  Bibliography, 62
  Footnotes, 176
Multiple Interpretations
  Ambiguity, 35–36
Multiple Words as a Unit
  Compound Words, 108
Multiplied-By Symbol
  Symbols, 472
Mutual/In Common, 302
Myself
  Reflexive Pronoun, 408

N

Name in Different Words
  Appositives, 48–49
Namely (Viz.)
  Abbreviations, 7
Names
  Capital Letters, 71
  Comma, 92, 94
  Epithet, 159
  Italics, 260–261
Names, First
  Abbreviations, 5
Names, List of
  Index, 243
Naming
  Direct Address, 144
Naming Adjective

Demonstrative Adjective, 134–135
Naming Pronoun
  Demonstrative Pronoun, 135
Narration, 302–303
  Forms of Discourse, 197
Nature, 303
Nearly Equal To
  Symbols, 472
Needless to Say, 304
Negation
  Definition as a Form of Writing,
    132–134
Negative, Double
  Double Negative, 145–146
Negative Writing
  Positive Writing, 373
Neither . . . Nor
  Correlative Conjunction, 120–121
  Nor/Or, 306
  Parallel Structure, 350–351
Neo-, 304
  Prefix, 375–376
Neologism
  New Words, 304
New Words, 304
Newspaper Indexes
  Reference Books, 406
Newspaper, Italics for Title
  Italics, 260
Newspaper Article
  House Organ Article, 228–231
Nice, 205
  Vague Words, 498–499
No./Nos.
  Abbreviations, 7
No
  Comma, 94
  Interjection, 252–253
No Doubt But, 305
  Double Negative, 145–146
Nominative Absolute
  Absolute Phrase, 9–10
Nominative Case
  Case, 74–79

Nominative, Predicate
Predicate Nominative, 375
None, 305
Nonfinite Verb
Verbals, 505–506
Nonflammable
Flammable/Inflammable/
Nonflammable, 173
Nonliteral Use
Idiom, 234–235
Nonrestrictive
Clauses, 83–85
Comma, 92
Modifiers, 299–300
Restrictive and Nonrestrictive
Elements, 412–413
Nonspecific Words
Abstract Words/Concrete Words,
12–13
Vague Words, 498–499
Word Choice, 511
Nonstandard English, 305–306
English, Varieties of, 157–159
Usage, 497–498
Nor/Or, 306
Normative Grammar
Grammar, 209–210
Not, 306
Not . . . No
Double Negative, 145–146
Not Equal To
Symbols, 472
Not Greater Than
Symbols, 472
Not Identical With
Symbols, 472
Not Less Than
Symbols, 472
Not Only . . . But Also
Correlative Conjunction, 120–121
Parallel Structure, 349–351
Notable/Noticeable, 306
Note Cards
Note-Taking, 306–309

Note-Taking, 306–309
Library Research, 284–285
Minutes of Meeting, 296–297
Paraphrase, 352–353
Plagiarism, 368
Notes for Oral Presentation
Oral Report, 327–331
Notorious
Famous/Infamous/Notorious, 169
Noun Clause, 313
Clauses, 83–85
Noun Formed from Verb
Gerund, 199
Noun Phrase
Phrases, 366–367
Noun Predicate
Predicate Nominative, 375
Noun Substitute
Pronouns, 381–386
Nouns, 310–313
Agreement, 27–32
Case, 74–79
Collective Noun, 89
Common Noun, 100–101
Count Noun, 124–125
Gerund, 199
Mass Noun, 290
Noun Clause, 313
Parts of Speech, 357–358
Proper Noun, 388
Substantive, 470
Nowhere Near, 313
Number, 314
Agreement, 27–32
Amount/Number, 36–37
Collective Noun, 89
Finite Verb, 173
Mixed Construction, 299
Pronoun, 384–385
Symbols, 473
Verb, 502, 503–505
Number, Beginning a Sentence with
Numbers, 315
Numbering

Bibliography, 64
Footnotes, 175–178
Numbers, 314–316
Comma, 95
Numerical Adjectives, 317

O

Object, 317–318
Complement, 103–104
Direct Object, 144
Indirect Object, 243
Objective Complement, 318
Predicate, 374
Prepositions, 377–378
Verb, 499
Object-Verb-Subject Sentence Order
Inverted Sentence Order,
258–259
Objective, 318–319
Objective Complement, 318
Objective (Purpose), 318–319
Point of View, 368–370
Preparation, 376–377
Objective Case
Case, 76
Complement, 103–104
Pronouns, 384
Objective Complement, 318
Adjective, 16–19
Complement, 103–104
Objective Opening
Openings, 325–326
Objective Point of View
Point of View, 368–370
Observance/Observation, 319
O'clock
Numbers, 316
Of Which
Whose/Of Which, 510
Officialese
Affectation, 24–26
Gobbledygook, 200–201

OK/okay, 319
Omitted Letters
Apostrophe, 45
Contractions, 119
Dash, 129
Slash, 453
Omitted Words
Comma, 98
Dash, 129
Ellipses, 152–154
Sentences (Minor Sentence),
436–437
Slash, 453
Omnibus Words
Vague Words, 498–499
On Account of, 320
On/Onto/On To, 320
On the Grounds That (of), 320
On To
On/Onto/On To, 320
One, 320–321
Agreement, 28, 29, 31
Point of View, 368–370
One Another
Each Other/One Another, 151
Reciprocal Pronoun, 401
One of Those Who, 321–323
Only, 323
Onto
On/Onto/On To, 320
Op. Cit.
Abbreviations, 7
Opening Statement
Introduction, 256–258
Openings, 323–326
Openings for Speeches
Oral Report, 327–336
Operation of a Mechanism
Explaining a Process, 163–166
Opposite Meaning
Antonym, 44
Option
Government Proposal, 202–204

Or
  Conjunctions, 113–115
  Nor/Or, 306
Oral Communications Guide
  Reference Books, 406–407
Oral Report, 327–336
Order of Importance
  Decreasing Order of Importance
    as a Method of Development,
    130
  Increasing Order of Importance
    as a Method of Development,
    240
  Methods of Development, 294
Order of Words
  Syntax, 474
Ordered Writing
  Checklist of the Writing Process,
    xx
  Methods of Development,
    292–296
  Organization, 336–337
  Outlining, 338–341
Ordering Ideas
  Organization, 336–337
  Outlining, 338–341
Ordinal Numbers
  Numeral Adjective, 317
Organization, 336–337
  Methods of Development,
    292–296
  Outlining, 338–341
Organizational Chart, 337
  Illustrations, 236–238
Organizations
  Abbreviations, 4–5
  Capital Letters, 72
Organizing Ideas
  Organization, 336–337
  Outlining, 338–341
Organizing the Report
  Checklist of the Writing Process,
    xx

Methods of Development,
  292–296
Organization, 336–337
Outlining, 338–341
Orient/Orientate, 338
  Long Variants, 287–288
Origin of Words
  Dictionary, 142
Out-of-Date
  Hyphen, 232–233
Outline for Oral Presentation
  Oral Report, 329–331
Outlining, 338–341
Outside of, 341
Over With, 341
Overloaded Sentence
  Pace, 342–343
Overstatement
  Emphasis, 156–157
  Hyperbole, 231
  Style, 465
Overtones
  Connotation/Denotation, 117–118
Owing To
  Due To/Because Of, 150
Ownership
  Apostrophe, 44–45
  Possessive Adjective, 373–374
  Pronouns, 382–385
Ownership of Written Material
  Copyright, 120
  Plagiarism, 368
Oxygen, Symbol for
  Symbols, 472

P

p. (page)
  Abbreviations, 7
Pace, 342–343
  Coherence, 87–88
  Revision, 421–423
Page Number
  Numbers, 314

Pamphlets
  Bibliography, 63
  Footnotes, 178
  Reference Books, 402
Panel Discussion
  Oral Report, 334
Paper
  Title, 486
  Topic, 487
Paper, Reading of
  Oral Report, 327
Paragraph, 343–349
  Emphasis, 155
  Format, 196
  Indentation, 242
  Outlining, 338–341
  Proofreaders' Marks, 386–387
  Transition, 489–489, 491–492
  Unity, 496–497
Parallel
  Symbols, 472
Parallel Structure, 349–352
  Balance, 57
  Conjunctions, 113–114
  Sentence Construction, 440
Paraphrase, 352–353
  Note-Taking, 307–309
  Plagiarism, 368
Parentheses, 353–354
  Brackets, 65
  Comma, 98
  Dash, 128
  Proofreaders' Marks, 386–387
  Punctuation, 389–390
Parentheses with Comma
  Comma, 98
  Parentheses, 354
Parenthetical Element
  Comma, 92
  Dash, 128
  Parentheses, 353–354
  Restrictive and Nonrestrictive
    Elements, 412–413
Parliamentary Procedure
  Reference Books, 406

Participial Phrase, 354–355
  Dangling Modifiers, 127
  Phrases, 367
Participle, 355–357
  Dangling Modifiers, 127
  Participial Phrase, 366–367
  Verbals, 505–506
Particular-to-General Method of
    Development
  Specific-to-General Method of
    Development, 455
Parts, Description of
  Description, 137–140
Parts List
  Technical Manual, 479
Parts of Speech, 356–357
  Adjectives, 16–19
  Adverbs, 20–22
  Conjunctions, 113–115
  Interjection, 252–253
  Nouns, 310–313
  Prepositions, 377–378
  Pronouns, 381–386
  Verbs, 499–505
Party, 358
Pass-Out Material During Oral
    Presentation
  Oral Report, 331
Passive Voice
  Voice, 507–508
Past Participle
  Participle, 356
Past Perfect Tense
  Tense, 482
Past Tense
  Tense, 482
Patterns, Sentence
  Sentence Construction, 437–441
Pedantic Writing
  Affectation, 24–26
  Gobbledygook, 200–201
People
  Capital Letters, 71
  Personal/Personnel, 363
  Persons/People, 364
Per, 358

Slash, 453
Per Cent/Percent/Percentage,
  358–359
  Numbers, 315
  Symbols, 473
Perfect
  Absolute Words, 10
  Equal/Perfect/Unique, 159–160
  Tense, 481–482
Period, 359–362
  Format (leaders), 196
  Proofreaders' Marks, 386–387
  Punctuation, 389–390
Period Fault
  Period, 361–362
Period, Spaced
  Ellipses, 152–154
  Period, 360–361
Periodic Report
  Progress Report, 380–381
Periodic Sentence
  Emphasis, 155
  Sentence Variety, 448
  Sentences, 436
Periodical Indexes and Guides
  Reference Books, 406
Periodicals
  Bibliography, 63
  Footnotes, 177
  Library Research, 283–284, 285
Permissible Fragment
  Sentences (Minor Sentence),
    436–437
Perpendicular
  Symbols, 472
Person, 362
  Agreement, 27–32
  Finite Verb, 173
  Mixed Construction, 288–289
  Number, 314
  One, 320–321
  Point of View, 368–370
  Pronouns, 383
  Verb, 501–505
Personal/Personnel, 363

Personal Data Sheet
  Résumé, 413–421
Personal Pronoun, 363–364
  Point of View, 368–370
  Pronouns, 381
Personal Title
  Abbreviations, 2–9
  Capital Letters, 70–74
Personality in Writing
  Style, 464–466
Personification
  Figures of Speech, 172
Persons
  Agreement, 27–32
  Gender, 198–199
  He/She, 222
Persons/People, 364
Perspective of Writer
  Point of View, 368–370
Persuasion, 364–365
  Forms of Discourse, 197
  Propaganda, 388
  Rhetoric, 423–424
Peso
  Symbols, 473
Phase, 365
Ph.D.
  Abbreviations, 2–9
Phenomenon/Phenomena, 366
Phone
  Clipped Form of Words, 86–87
Phonic Marking
  Diacritical Marks, 140–141
Phrases, 366–367
  Absolute Phrase, 9–10
  Infinitive Phrase, 245–246
  Participial Phrase, 354–355
  Prepositional Phrase, 378–379
  Verb Phrase, 505
Pi
  Symbols, 472
Pictorial Illustrations
  Drawings, 147–150
  Illustrations, 236–238
Picture Graph

Graphs, 221
Pie Graph
    Graphs, 219–221
Place Names
    Capital Letters, 71–72
Plagiarism, 368
    Copyright, 120
    Note-Taking, 306–307
Planets
    Capital Letters, 72
Planning Your Report
    Preparation, 376–377
Plays, Titles of
    Capital Letters, 72
    Italics, 260
Pleonasm
    Appositives, 48
    Conciseness/Wordiness, 108–111
    Repetition, 409–410
Plural
    Abbreviations (Plural of
        Acronyms), 3
    Agreement, 27–32
    Apostrophe, 45
    Compound Words, 108
    Dates, 130
    Nouns, 311–313
    Number, 314
    Numbers, 315
Plus
    Symbols, 472
p.m.
    Abbreviations, 3
Point of View, 368–370
    Description, 139–140
    Exposition, 167–168
    Narration, 302–303
    One, 320–321
    Person, 362
    Personal Pronoun, 363–364
    Persuasion, 364–365
    Reader, 400
    Tone, 486–387
Police Report, 370–373
Political Divisions

Capital Letters, 71–72
Political Title
    Abbreviations, 6
    Capital Letters, 73
Pompous Style
    Affectation, 24–26
    Gobbledygook, 200–201
Popular Words
    Vogue Words, 506–507
Portmanteau Words
    Blend Words, 64
Position Description
    Job Description, 263–265
Position of Modifiers
    Adjectives, 17–18
    Adverbs, 21–22
Positive Degree
    Adjectives, 17
    Adverbs, 21
Positive Writing, 373
    Conciseness/Wordiness, 108–111
Possession, Mark of
    Apostrophe, 44–45
    Case, 76–78
Possessive Adjective, 373–374
    Adjectives, 16–19
Possessive Case
    Agreement, 27–32
    Apostrophe, 44–45
    Case, 76–78
    Compound Words, 108
    Gerund, 199
    Nouns, 311–312
    Pronouns, 382–385
Pound
    Symbols (monetary), 472, 473
    Symbols (measurement), 473
pp. (pages)
    Abbreviations, 7
Practical/Practicable, 374
Précis
    Abstract, 10–12
    Paraphrase, 352–353
Preciseness
    Vague Words, 498–499

Word Choice, 511–512
Predicate, 374
  Complement, 103–104
Predicate Adjective, 374
  Subjective Complement, 467
Predicate Complement
  Objective Complement, 318
Predicate Nominative, 375
  Subjective Complement, 467
Predicate Noun
  Predicate Nominative, 375
Preface
  Foreword/Preface, 180
  Introduction, 256–258
Prefable, 375
Prefix, 375–376
  Hyphen, 232–233
  Suffix, 470
Preliminaries
  Preparation, 376–377
Preparation, 376–377
  Checklist of the Writing Process,
    xx
  Objective (Purpose), 318–319
  Reader, 400
  Scope, 432
Preposition, 377–378
  Capital Letters (Used in Titles), 73
  Parts of Speech, 357–358
Prepositional Phrase, 378–379
  Comma, 93
  Phrases, 366–367
Prescriptive Grammar
  Grammar, 209–210
Present Participle
  Participle, 356
Present Perfect Tense
  Tense, 482–483
Present Tense
  Participle, 356
  Tense, 482
Presentation, Oral
  Oral Report, 327–336
Pretentious Words
  Long Variants, 287–288

Pretentious Writing
  Affectation, 24–26
  Gobbledygook, 200–201
  Jargon, 262–263
Prewriting
  Checklist of the Writing Process,
    xx
  Preparation, 376–377
Principal/Principle, 379–380
Printer, Marks for
  Proofreaders' Marks, 386
Problem Opening
  Openings, 323–326
Problem-Solution Pattern for
  Speeches
  Oral Report, 329
Proceedings Guide
  Reference Books, 403
Process Description
  Explaining a Process, 163–166
Process, Explaining
  Explaining a Process, 163–166
Professional Article
  Journal Article, 265–273
Prognosis
  Diagnosis/Prognosis, 141
Progress Report, 380–381
Prolixity
  Conciseness/Wordiness, 108–111
Pronominal Adjective
  Adjectives, 17
Pronouns, 381–386
  Agreement, 30–32
  Appositive, 48–49
  Case, 74–79
  Demonstrative Pronoun, 135
  Indefinite Pronouns, 241
  Parts of Speech, 357–358
  Person, 362
  Personal Pronoun, 363–364
  Point of View, 368–370
  Reciprocal Pronoun, 401
  Reflexive Pronoun, 408
  Relative Pronoun, 408–409
  Substantive, 470

Pronoun Antecedent
  Agreement, 30–32
Pronoun Reference
  Agreement, 30–32
  Ambiguity, 36
  Pronouns, 385–386
Pronunciation
  Diacritical Marks, 140–141
  Dictionary, 141–143
Pronounciation Symbols
  Diacritical Marks, 140–141
Proofreaders' Marks, 386–387
Propaganda, 388
  Persuasion, 364–365
Proper Name
  Italics, 260–261
Proper Noun, 388
  Nouns, 310
Proportion
  Drawings, 147–150
Proposals, 388–389
  Government Proposal, 202–210
  Sales Proposal, 424–430
Prose, 389
Proved/Proven, 389
Pseudo-/Quasi-, 389
Public Documents
  Reference Books, 404–405
Public Domain
  Copyright, 120
Public Speaking
  Oral Report, 327–336
Publication Information
  Bibliography, 60–64
  Footnotes, 176
  Reference Books, 401–407
Publication of Article
  Journal Article, 265–273
Punctuating Abbreviations
  Abbreviations, 3–4
Punctuating Conjunctions
  Conjunctions, 114
Punctuating Connectives
  Connectives, 116–117
Punctuating Items in a Series

Comma, 95
Semicolon, 434
Punctuation, 389–390
  Apostrophe, 44–45
  Brackets, 65
  Colon, 89–91
  Comma, 91–100
  Dash, 127–129
  Diacritical Marks, 140–141
  Exclamation Mark, 162–163
  Hyphen, 231–233
  Parentheses, 354
  Period, 359–362
  Question Mark, 390–391
  Quotation Marks, 394–396
  Semicolon, 432–434
  Slash, 453
  Symbols, 473
Purple Passage
  Affectation, 24–26
  Gobbledygook, 200–201
Purpose of Writing
  Objective (Purpose), 318–319

Q

Qualifier
  Modifiers, 299–300
Quantitative Noun
  Nouns, 310
Quasi-
  Pseudo-/Quasi-, 389
Query Letter
  Inquiry, Letter of, 247–249
  Question Mark, 390–391
Question, Rhetorical
  Rhetorical Question, 424
Questioning as Research
  Interviewing, 253–255
  Questionnaire, 391–394
Questionnaire, 391–394
  Interviewing, 253–255
  Research, 411
Questions, Asking
  Interrogative Adverb, 253

Interrogative Pronoun, 258
Interviewing, 253–255
  Mood, 300–301
Quid Pro Quo, 394
Quotation Opening
  Openings, 325
Quotations, 396–399
  Copyright, 120
  Dash, 129
  Ellipses, 152
  Footnotes, 175–179
  Plagiarism, 368
Quotation Marks, 394–396
  Italics, 259–261
  Proofreaders' Marks, 386–387
  Punctuation, 389–390
Quoting Copyrighted Material
  Copyright, 120
  Plagiarism, 368
  Quotations, 396–397

R

Races and Nationalities
  Capital Letters, 71
Radio and Television Stations
  Abbreviations, 5
Raise/Rise, 399
Rank
  Abbreviations, 6
  Capital Letters, 72
Rarely Ever, 399
Ratio
  Symbols, 472
Re, 399
Reader, 400
  Defining Terms, 131–132
  Objective (Purpose), 318–319
  Point of View, 368–370
  Preparation, 376–377
  Scope, 432
Reading a Speech
  Oral Report, 327
Real
  Vague Words, 498–499

Reason is Because, 400–401
Reciprocal Pronoun, 401
  Pronouns, 382
Recommendations
  Formal Report, 182
Recording Information
  Note-Taking, 300–309
Recording Minutes of Meetings
  Minutes of Meetings, 296–297
Reducing Ideas
  Paraphrase, 352–353
Redundancy
  Conciseness/Wordiness, 108–111
  Repetition, 409–410
Refer
  Allude/Refer, 33–34
Reference
  Pronouns, 385–386
Reference Books, 401–407
Reference Cited
  Bibliography, 60–64
  Footnotes, 178
Referring Indirectly
  Allusion, 34
Reflexive Pronoun, 408
  Pronouns, 382
Regardless
  Irregardless/Regardless, 259
Regular Verb
  Finite Verb, 173
  Verbs, 503
Rehearsing Oral Presentation
  Oral Report, 332–334
Relationship of Words
  Grammar, 209–210
  Syntax, 474
Relationships, Family
  Capital Letters, 73
Relative Adjective, 408
  Adjectives, 16–19
Relative Adverb
  Adverbs, 20–22
Relative Importance
  Subordination, 468–470
Relative Pronoun, 408–409

Agreement, 29
Pronouns, 381
Religious Titles
Abbreviations, 6–7
Capital Letters, 73
Remainder
Balance/Remainder, 57–58
Remote Pronoun Reference
Pronouns, 385–386
Rename
Appositive, 48–49
Rendering
Description, 139
Repeated Material in Columns
Quotation Marks (Ditto Marks),
396
Tables, 475–477
Repetition, 409–410
Awkwardness, 53–56
Conciseness/Wordiness, 108–111
Emphasis, 155–157
Transition, 489–492
Rephrasing
Paraphrase, 352–353
Revision, 421–423
Reports, 410–411
Annual Report, 39–43
Formal Report, 180–194
Laboratory Report, 274–278
Memorandum, 291
Oral Report, 327–336
Police Report, 370–373
Progress Report, 380–381
Trip Report, 494–495
Reporting Test Results
Laboratory Report, 274–278
Requesting Information
Correspondence, 121–125
Inquiry, Letter of, 247–249
Questionnaire, 391–394
Research, 411
Research Material, Sources of
Interviewing, 253–255

Library Research, 281–286
Questionnaire, 391–394
Specifications, 455–463
Research Paper
Checklist of the Writing Process,
xx
Library Research, 281–286
Research, 411
Resemblance
Analogy, 37
Comparison, 102–103
Comparison as a Method of
Development, 103
Respective/Respectively, 411–412
Restrictive and Nonrestrictive
Phrases, 412–413
Adjective Clause, 19
Clauses, 84
Result
Cause-and-Effect Method of
Development, 79–80
Résumé, 413–421
Reversed Sentence Order
Inverted Sentence Order,
258–259
Reviews, Books
Reference Books, 403
Revision, 421–423
Checklist of the Writing Process,
xx
Transition, 489–492
Rewriting
Revision, 421–423
Rhetoric, 423–424
Rhetorical Question, 424
Rights of an Author
Copyright, 120
Plagiarism, 368
Rise
Raise/Rise, 399
Robert's Rules of Order
Minutes of Meeting, 296–297
Oral Report, 334–335
Reference Books, 406

Roget's Thesaurus
  Reference Books, 407
  Thesaurus, 485
Roman Type
  Proofreaders' Marks, 386–387
Root Form of the Verb
  Infinitive, 244–245
Rough Draft
  Checklist of the Writing Process,
    xx
  Revision, 421–423
  Writing the Draft, 512–515
Round
  Absolute Words, 10
Ruble
  Symbols, 473
Rule
  Tables, 476–477
Rules of Grammar
  Grammar, 209–210
Rules of Order
  Minutes of Meeting, 296–297
Run-On Sentence (fused)
  Period, 361–362
  Semicolon, 433
  Sentence Faults, 442

S

Sales Proposal, 424–430
  Proposals, 388–389
Salutation
  Capital Letters, 71
  Comma, 95
  Correspondence, 122–125
Same, 430
Same Meaning
  Synonym, 474
Same Thing in Different Words
  Appositives, 48–49
  Paraphrase, 352–353
Schematic Diagram, 430–432
  Illustrations, 236–238
Scholarly Article

Journal Article, 265–273
Science Encyclopedias
  Reference Books, 404
Scientific Names
  Capital Letters, 72
Scientific Writing Style
  Technical Writing Style, 479–481
Scope, 432
  Checklist of the Writing Process,
    xx
  Objective (Purpose), 318–319
  Preparation, 376–377
  Reader, 400
Scope Openings
  Openings, 326
Seasons
  Capital Letters, 72
Second Person
  Person, 362
Seconds
  Abbreviations, 5
  Symbols, 473
Secretarial Handbooks
  Reference Books, 406
Section Symbol
  Proofreaders' Marks, 386–387
Section Title
  Heads, 222–227
Seldom Ever, 432
-self
  Reflexive Pronoun, 408
Semantics
  Connotation/Denotation, 117–118
  Defining Terms, 131–132
  Reference Books, 405–406
Semi-
  Bi-/Semi-, 60
Semicolon, 432–434
  Conjunctive Adverb, 115
  Proofreaders' Marks, 386–387
  Punctuation, 390
Sentences, 434–437
  Balance, 57
  Complement, 103–104

Complex Sentence, 105–106
Compound-Complex Sentence, 107
Compound Sentence, 106–107
Sentence Construction, 437–441
Sentence Faults, 441–445
Sentence Variety, 445–448
Simple Sentence, 451–452
Transition, 489–490
Sentence, Beginning
Expletives, 166
Sentence Construction, 438–439
Sentence Construction, 437–439
Sentences, 434–437
Sentence, Ending
Exclamation Mark, 162–163
Period, 359–362
Punctuation, 390
Question Mark, 390–391
Sentence Faults, 441–445
Sentence Fragment
Period 361–362
Sentences, 436–437
Sentence Faults, 442–444
Sentence Length
Sentence Variety, 445–446
Sentence Opening
Expletives, 166
Sentence Construction, 438–439, 441
Sentence Outline
Outlining, 338–341
Sentence Portion Following Verb
Predicate, 374
Sentence Structure
Sentence Construction, 437–441
Sentence Variety, 445–448
Inverted Sentence Order, 258–259
Sentences, 434–437
Style, 464–466
Sentence Word Order
Inverted Sentence Order, 258–259

Separating a Word
Dictionary, 142
Hyphen, 233
Syllabication, 471
Separating Adjectives
Comma, 94–95
Sequence of Tenses
Tense, 481
Sequential Method of Development, 449
Methods of Development, 293
Series
Agreement, 28
Series of Items, Punctuating
Comma, 94
Semicolon, 434
Service, 449
Set/Sit, 449–450
Set In
Indentation, 242
Sex
Agreement, 31
Chairman/Chairwoman/Chairperson, 80–81
Gender, 198–199
He/She, 222
Ms./Miss/Mrs., 301–302
Shall/Will, 450
She
Case, 75
Gender, 198–199
He/She, 222
Shift
Functional Shift (of Part of Speech), 197–198
Mixed Construction, 298–299
Mood, 301
Person, 362
Subject of Sentence, 466–467
Tense, 483
Voice, 508
Shilling Sign
Slash, 453
Shop Talk

Jargon, 262–263
Shortened Word Forms
  Abbreviations, 2–9
  Clipped Form of Words, 86–87
  Contractions, 119
Sic, 450
Sight
  Cite/Site/Sight, 81
Signature
  Correspondence, 122–125
Signs, Mathematical
  Symbols, 472
Similar Meaning
  Synonym, 474
Similarities and Differences
  Comparison as a Method of
    Development, 103
Simile, 450–451
  Figures of Speech, 172
Simple Predicate
  Predicate, 374
Simple Sentence, 451–452
  Sentences, 434–435
Simple Verb
  Finite Verb, 173
  Verbs, 500
Since
  As, 50
  Because, 58–59
Single Quotation Mark
  Apostrophe, 44–45
  Quotation Marks, 395
Singular
  Agreement, 27–32
  Data, 129
  Number, 314
Sit
  Set/Sit, 449–450
Site
  Cite/Site/Sight, 81
-size/-sized, 452
Slang
  English, Varieties, of, 158–159
  Quotation Marks, 395

Slang, Technical
  Jargon, 262–263
Slant Line
  Slash, 453
Slash (virgule), 453
  Proofreaders' Marks, 386–387
  Punctuation, 390
Small Capital Letters
  Proofreaders' Marks, 386–387
Small Letters
  Lower-Case and Upper-Case
    Letters, 288
  Proofreaders' Marks, 386–387
So
  Intensifiers, 251–252
So . . . As
  As . . . As/So . . . As, 50–51
So Called
  Quotation Marks, 395
So/Such, 453–454
Social Groups
  Capital Letters, 71
Social Varieties of English
  English, Varieties of, 157–159
Some, 454
Some/Somewhat, 454
Some Time/Sometime/Sometimes,
  454–455
Somewhat
  Some/Somewhat, 454
Sort (Singular and Plural Forms)
  Demonstrative Adjective, 134–135
Sort Of
  Kind Of/Sort Of, 279
Sound Value for Letters
  Diacritical Marks, 140–141
  Foreign Words in English,
    179–180
Source Line
  Drawings, 147–150
  Graphs, 210–221
  Tables, 476–477
Sources, Citing
  Bibliography, 60–64

Footnotes, 175–179
Sources of Information
  Library Research, 281–286
  Reference Books, 401–407
  Research, 441
Space, Inserting
  Proofreaders' Marks, 386–387
Spaced Periods (Ellipses)
  Ellipses, 152–154
  Format, 196
  Period, 360–361
Spatial Method of Development, 455
  Methods of Development,
    295–296
Speaking
  Oral Report, 327–336
Special Events
  Capital Letters, 72
Specie/Species, 455
Specific Words
  Abstract Words/Concrete Words,
    12–13
  Concrete Noun, 113
  Word Choice, 511–512
Specific-to-General Method of
    Development, 455
  Methods of Development, 295
Specifications, 455–463
Speech
  Oral Report, 327–336
Speech and Group Discussions
  Oral Report, 327–336
  Reference Books, 406–407
Speech, Figures of
  Figures of Speech, 170–172
Speech, Parts of
  Parts of Speech, 357–358
Specs
  Specifications, 455–463
Speed of Presenting Ideas
  Pace, 342–343
Spell-Out Mark
  Proofreaders' Marks, 386–387
Spelling, 463

Dictionary, 141–142
Spelling Numbers
  Numbers, 314–316
Spin-Off, 463–464
Splice
  Comma, 98–99
Split Infinitive
  Infinitive, 245
  Verbals, 505–506
Spoken English
  English, Varieties of, 157–159
Square Root
  Symbols, 472
Sr.
  Abbreviations, 7
St.
  Abbreviations, 8
Stacks
  Library Research, 281–285
Stale Expressions
  Cliché, 85–86
  Trite Language, 496
Standard English, 464
  English, Varieties of, 157–158
  Usage, 497–498
Star-Shaped Mark of Punctuation
    (Asterisk)
  Symbols, 473
Start-to-Finish
  Sequential Method of
    Development, 449
Starting
  Introduction, 256–258
  Openings, 323–326
State Government Publications
  Reference Books, 405
Statement of Finance
  Annual Report, 39–43
States
  Abbreviations, 8
Statistics
  Reference Books, 405
  Tables, 475–477
Status Report

Progress Report, 380–381
Step-by-Step Method of
    Development
Sequential Method of
    Development, 449
Stet
    Proofreaders' Marks, 386–387
Story
    Anecdote, 38
    Narration, 302–303
Strata, 464
Street Names
    Abbreviations, 7–8
Structure of Writing
    Organization, 336–337
    Outlining, 338–341
Stub
    Tables, 475–477
Style, 464–466
    Formal Writing Style, 195–196
    Informal Writing Style, 246–247
Style Manuals
    Reference Books, 407
Subheads
    Heads, 222–227
    Italics, 261
Subject
    Substantive, 470
Subject, Anticipatory
    Expletives, 166
Subject Card
    Library Research, 281–285
Subject Guides
    Reference Books, 407
Subject, Missing
    Dangling Modifiers, 126–127
Subject of Report
    Topic, 487
Subject of Sentence, 466–467
    Agreement, 27–32
    Substantive, 470
Subject-Verb Agreement
    Agreement, 27–30
    Collective Noun, 89

Compound Words, 108
Subject-Verb-Object Pattern
    Sentence Construction, 438
Subjective Case
    Case, 75–76
    Pronouns, 382–384
Subjective Complement, 467
    Adjectives, 16–19
    Agreement, 29
    Complement, 103–104
Subjective Overtone
    Connotation/Denotation, 117–118
Subjective Point of View
    Connotation/Denotation, 117–118
    Point of View, 368–370
Subjunctive Mood
    Complement, 104
    Mood, 300–301
Submitting an Article for
    Publication
    Journal Article, 265–266
Subordinate Clause
    Clauses, 84
    Comma, 96
    Dangling Modifiers, 127
    Dependent Clause, 135–137
Subordinating Conjunction,
    467–468
    Conjunctions, 113–115
Subordination, 468–470
    Clauses, 84
    Coherence, 87–88
    Conciseness/Wordiness, 111
    Conjunctions, 114
    Dependent Clause, 135–137
    Emphasis, 155–156
    Sentence Construction, 438, 439,
        440
    Sentence Variety, 445–448
    Sentences, 436
Substandard English
    English, Varieties of, 157–159
    Nonstandard English, 305–306
Substantive, 470

Gerund, 199
Infinitive, 244–245
Nouns, 310–313
Pronouns, 381–386
Subject of Sentence, 466–467
Substituting Inoffensive for
   Offensive Words
   Euphemism, 161–162
Subtitles
   Heads, 222–227
Such
   So/Such, 453–454
Suffix, 470
   -ese, 160
   Hyphen, 232–233
   -like, 286
   -wise, 510–511
Suggestive Meaning
   Connotation/Denotation, 117–118
Summarizing
   Note-Taking, 306–309
   Paraphrase, 352–353
Summary
   Abstract, 10–12
   Brief, 65–66
Summary Opening
   Openings, 326
Superior Type
   Proofreaders' Marks, 386–387
Superfluous Details
   Revision, 421–423
   Scope, 432
Superlative
   Adjectives, 16–19
   Adverbs, 20–22
   Comparative Degree, 101–102
Supp. (supplement)
   Abbreviations, 7
Supplement
   Augment/Supplement, 53
Survey
   Questionnaire, 391–394
Sweeping Generalization, 470–471
Syllabication, 471

Dictionary, 141–142
Hyphen, 233
Syllables, Dividing
   Syllabication, 471
Syllogism
   General-to-Specific Method of
      Development, 199
Symbols, 472–474
   Abbreviations, 2–9
   Diacritical Marks, 140–141
   Proofreaders' Marks, 386–387
   Punctuation, 389–370
Symmetry
   Balance, 57
   Parallel Structure, 349–352
Synonym, 474
   Antonym, 44
   Dictionary, 141–143
   Euphemism, 161–162
   Reference Books, 407
   Thesaurus, 485
   Word Choice, 511–512
Synopsis
   Abstract, 10–12
   Brief, 65–66
Syntax, 474
System of Library Classification
   Library Classification System,
      279–281

T

Table Numbers
   Tables, 475–477
Table of Contents, 474–475
   Formal Report, 181
   Format, 196
Tables, 475–477
   Illustrations, 236–238
Tabular Illustrations
   Illustrations, 236–238
   Tables, 475–477
Taking Notes
   Note-Taking, 306–309

Tale
  Anecdote, 38
Tautology
  Conciseness/Wordiness, 108–111
  Repetition, 409–410
Technical Article
  Journal Article, 265–273
  Openings, 323
Technical Book Reviews
  Reference Books, 403
Technical Books
  Reference Books, 403
Technical English
  Technical Writing Style, 479–481
Technical Information, Letter of,
    478–479
  Correspondence, 121–125
Technical Papers
  Oral Report, 327–334
Technical Slang
  Jargon, 262–263
Technical Terminology
  Defining Terms, 131–132
  Jargon, 262–263
Technical Writing Types
  Abstract, 10–12
  Description, 137–140
  Explaining a Process, 163–166
  Formal Report, 180–194
  Government Proposal, 202–209
  Inquiry, Letter of, 247–249
  Instructions, 250–251
  Job Description, 263–265
  Journal Article, 263–273
  Laboratory Report, 274–278
  Memorandum, 291
  Progress Report, 380–381
  Proposal, 388–389
  Sales Proposal, 424–430
  Specifications, 455–463
  Technical Manual, 479
  Transmittal, Letter of, 493–494
Technical Writing Style, 479–481
Television and Radio Stations

Abbreviations, 5
Telling a Story
  Narration, 302–303
Tenant/Tenet, 481
Tenet/Tenant
  Tenant/Tenet, 481
Tense, 481–483
  Agreement, 27–32
  Finite Verb, 173
  Mixed Construction, 298–299
  Verbs, 502–505
Term Paper
  Checklist of the Writing Process,
    xx
  Title, 486
Terms Commonly Confused
  Usage, 497–498
Terms, Defining
  Defining Terms, 131–132
Terms, List of
  Glossary, 199–200
Test Results, Reporting
  Laboratory Report, 274–278
Text, Reference
  Reference Books, 401–407
Than
  Case, 76
That
  Demonstrative Adjective, 134–135
  Demonstrative Pronoun, 135
That Is
  i.e., 235
That . . . That, 483–484
That/Which/Who, 484
The
  Article, 49–50
There Are (There Is)
  Expletives, 166
  Sentence Construction, 438
Therefore
  Symbols, 472
There/Their/They're, 484–485
Thesaurus, 485
  Dictionary, 141–143

These
   Demonstrative Adjective, 134–135
   Demonstrative Pronoun, 135
Thesis Statement
   Outlining, 338–339
Third Person
   Person, 362
This
   Demonstrative Adjective, 134–135
   Demonstrative Pronoun, 135
Thus/Thusly, 485
Those
   Demonstrative Adjective, 134–135
   Demonstrative Pronoun, 135
Three-Dimensional Drawing
   Drawings, 147, 150
Tightening Up
   Conciseness/Wordiness, 108–111
   Revision, 423
'Til/Til/Until, 485
Time
   Abbreviations, 3, 9
   A.D., 15
   Capital Letters, 72
   Numbers, 316
   Tense, 481–483
Time Method of Development
   Chronological Method of
      Development, 81
Tired Expression
   Cliché, 85–86
   Trite Language, 496
Title Card
   Library Research, 282–283
Title of Books, Plays, Movies, etc.
   Articles, 50
   Capital Letters, 73
   Conjunctions, 114–115
   Dash, 129
   Italics, 260
   Prepositions, 378
Title, 486
Title of Person
   Abbreviations, 5–7
   Capital Letters, 73

Title of Section
   Heads, 222–227
Title Page
   Formal Report, 181
Titles
   Heads, 222–227
To
   Infinitive, 244–245
To/Too/Two, 486
Tone, 486–487
   Point of View, 368–370
Too
   Intensifiers, 251–252
   To/Too/Two, 486
Topic, 487
Topic Outline
   Outlining, 338–340
Topic Sentence, 487–489
   Paragraph, 343–344
Topics, List of
   Index, 243
Tortuous/Torturous, 489
Toward/Towards, 489
Trade Journal Article
   Journal Article, 265–273
Trailing Sentence Constructions
   Sentence Construction, 440
Transition, 489–492
   Clarity, 81–83
   Coherence, 87–88
   Pace, 242–243
   Paragraph, 345, 347–348
   Repetition, 409–410
   Revision, 423
   Unity, 496–497
Transitive Verb, 492–493
   Verbs, 499–505
Transmittal, Letter of, 493–494
   Correspondence, 121–125
Transpose Mark
   Proofreader's Mark, 386–387
Transpotition
   Inverted Sentence Order,
      258–259
   Sentence Construction, 438–439

Travel Report
  Trip Report, 494–495
Trip Report, 494–495
Trite Language, 496
  Cliché, 85–86
Try and, 496
Two
  To/Too/Two, 486
Two-Way Indicator
  Transition, 489–492
Type (Singular and Plural Forms)
  Agreement, 28
  Demonstrative Adjective, 134–135
Typed Manuscript
  MS/MSS, 302
Types of Business and Technical
    Writing
  Abstract, 10–12
  Acceptance, Letter of, 14
  Annual Report, 39–43
  Application, Letter of, 46–48
  Description, 137–140
  Explaining a Process, 163–166
  Formal Report, 180–194
  Government Proposal, 202–209
  House Organ Article, 228–231
  Inquiry, Letter of, 247–249
  Instructions, 250–251
  Job Description, 263–265
  Journal Article, 265–273
  Laboratory Report, 274–278
  Memorandum, 291
  Progress Report, 380–381
  Proposal, 388–389
  Résumé, 413–421
  Sales Proposal, 424–430
  Specifications, 455–463
  Technical Manual, 479
  Transmittal, Letter of, 493–494
Types of Words
  Abstract Words/Concrete Words,
    12–13
  Blend Words, 64
  Clipped Form of Words, 86–87
  Compound Words, 108

Foreign Words in English,
  179–180
New Words, 304
Word Choice, 511–512

U

Umlaut
  Diacritical Marks, 140–141
  Foreign Words in English,
    179–180
  Symbols, 473
Un-/In-
  Prefix, 375–376
Unabridged Dictionaries
  Dictionary, 142–143
Unattached Modifier
  Dangling Modifiers, 126–127
Unclearness
  Ambiguity, 35–36
  Vague Words, 499
Underlining
  Emphasis, 157
  Italics, 259–261
Unequal Importance
  Subordination, 468–470
Uninterested
  Distinterested/Uninterested, 145
Unique
  Absolute Words, 10
  Equal/Unique/Perfect, 159–160
Unity, 496
  Clarity, 81–83
  Coherence, 87–88
  Conciseness/Wordiness, 108–111
  Paragraph, 347–349
  Point of View, 368–370
Universal Truth
  Tense, 482
Unlike and Like
  Comparison as a Method of
    Development, 103
Unrelated Idea
  Unity, 496–497
Unrelated Phrase

Absolute Phrase, 9–10
Unsolvable
Insoluble/Unsolvable, 249–250
Unspecific Words
Abstract Words/Concrete Words,
12–13
Vague Words, 498–499
Word Choice, 511
Until
'Till/Till/Until, 485
Up, 497
Upper Case
Lower-Case Letters, 288
U. S. Government Publications
Reference Books, 404–405
Usage, 497–498
Usage Guides
Reference Books, 405
Utilitarian Writing
Exposition, 167–168
Instructions, 250–252
Utilize, 498
Long Variants, 287–288

V

Vague Pronoun Reerence
Agreement, 30–32
Pronouns, 385–386
Vague Words, 498–499
Abstract Words/Concrete Words,
12–13
Word Choice, 511
Vagueness
Ambiguity, 35–36
Vague Words, 498–499
Vantage
Point of View, 368–370
Variety
Sentence Variety, 445–448
Variety of Vocabulary
Synonym, 474
Thesaurus, 485
Verb Phrase, 505

Verb, 500–501
Verb Used as a Noun
Gerund, 199
Verbals, 505–506
Gerund, 199
Infinitive, 244–245
Participle, 355–357
Verbatim
Plagiarism, 368
Quotations, 396–397
Verbiage
Conciseness/Wordiness, 108–111
Verb, 499–505
Gerund, 199
Helping Verb, 227
Infinitive, 244–245
Intransitive Verb, 255–256
Linking Verb, 286–287
Mood, 300–301
Participle, 355–357
Parts of Speech, 357–358
Transitive Verb, 492–493
Verbals, 505–506
Voice, 507–508
Vernacular
English, Varieties of, 158
Vertical Axis
Graphs, 210–215
Very, 506
Intensifiers, 251–252
Via, 506
Viewpoint of Writer
Point of View, 368–370
Sweeping Generalization,
470–471
Vigorous Writing
Description (Rendering), 139
Figures of Speech, 170–172
Positive Writing, 373
Style, 464–466
Voice, 507–508
Virgule
Slash, 453
Virtual Sentence

Sentences (Minor Sentence), 436–437

Visual Aids in Oral Presentation
Oral Report, 331–332

Visual Aids in Writing
Drawings, 147–150
Flowcharts, 174
Graphs, 210–221
Maps, 289–290
Organizational Charts, 337
Schematic Diagrams, 430–431
Tables, 475–477

Vita
Résumé, 413–421

Vivid Writing
Description, 137–140
Figures of Speech, 170–172

Vocabulary
Dictionary, 141–144
Glossary, 199–200
Thesaurus, 485
Word Choice, 511–512

Vocative Expression
Direct Address, 144

Vogue Words, 506–507
Word Choice, 512

Voice, 507–508
Mixed Construction, 299
Verb, 501–502

W

Wait For/Wait On, 508

We
Person, 362
Point of View, 368–370

Weighing Ideas
Balance, 57
Parallel Structure, 349–351

Well
Good/Well, 201

When and If, 508

Where/That, 509

Where At, 509

Which
That/Which/Who, 484

While, 509

Who
That/Which/Who, 484
Who/Whom, 509–510
Case, 79
Interrogative Pronoun, 253

Whose/Of Which, 510

Will
Shall/Will, 450

-wise, 510–511
New Words, 304
Suffix, 470

Wish, Verb Form Used With
Mood, 300–301

With Regard To
As Regards/With Regard To/In Regard To/Regarding, 51

Without Subject
Dangling Modifiers, 126–127

Word Association
Connotation/Denotation, 117–118

Word Beginnings
Prefix, 375–376

Word Book
Dictionary, 141–144
Glossary, 199–200
Thesaurus, 485

Word Choice, 511–512
Abstract Words/Concrete Words, 12–13
Antonym, 44
Blend Words, 64
Clipped Form of Words, 86–87
Compound Words, 108
Connotation/Denotation, 117–118
Euphemism, 161–162
Foreign Words in English, 179–180
Jargon, 262–263
Long Variants, 282
Malapropism, 288
New Words, 304

Revision, 423
Thesaurus, 485
Vague Words, 498–499
Vogue Words, 506–507
Word Division
    Dictionary, 141–142
    Hyphen, 233
    Syllabication, 471
Word Endings
    Suffix, 470
Word-for-Word
    Plagiarism, 368
    Quotations, 396–397
Word Group
    Clauses, 83–85
    Phrases, 366–367
    Sentences, 434–437
Word List
    Dictionary, 141–144
    Glossary, 199–200
    Thesaurus, 485
Word Meaning
    Connotation/Denotation, 117–118
    Dictionary, 141–144
    Glossary, 199–200
Word Order
    Sentence Construction, 437–441
    Sentence Variety, 445–448
    Syntax, 474
Word Types
    Abstract Words/Concrete Words,
        12–13
    Blend Words, 64
    Clipped Form of Words, 86–87
    Compound Words, 108
    Foreign Words in English,
        179–180
    New Words, 304
    Vague Words, 498–499
    Vogue Words, 506–507
Wordiness
    Conciseness/Wordiness, 108–111
    Repetition, 409–410
Words, Commonly Confused

Usage, 498
Words, Defining
    Defning Terms, 131–132
    Dictionary, 141–144
    Glossary, 199–200
Works Cited
    Bibliography, 60–64
    Footnotes, 175–179
Worn Figures of Speech
    Cliché, 85–86
    Trite Language, 496
Writer's Objective
    Objective (Purpose), 318–319
Writing
    Abstract, 10–12
    Acceptance, Letter of, 14
    Annual Report, 39–43
    Application, Letter of, 46–48
    Business Writing Style, 66–68
    Checklist of the Writing Process,
        xx
    Conclusions, 112–113
    Correspondence, 121–125
    Description, 137–140
    Explaining a Process, 163–166
    Exposition, 167–168
    Formal Report, 180–194
    Formal Writing Style, 195–196
    Forms of Discourse, 197
    Government Proposal, 202–209
    House Organ Article, 228–231
    Informal Writing Style, 246–247
    Inquiry, Letter of, 247–249
    Instructions, 250–252
    Introduction, 256–258
    Journal Article, 265–273
    Laboratory Report, 274–278
    Memorandum, 291
    Minutes of Meeting, 296–297
    Narration, 302–303
    Persuasion, 364–365
    Police Report, 370–373
    Progress Report, 380–381
    Proposal, 388–389

Résumé, 413–421
Sales Proposal, 424–430
Style, 464–466
Technical Information, Letter of,
    478–479
Technical Manual, 479
Technical Writing Style, 479–481
Transmittal, Letter of, 493–494
Trip Report, 495–496
Writing the Draft, 512–515
Writing Letters
Correspondence, 121–125
Writing Process
Checklist of the Writing Process,
    xx
Writing Project
Checklist of the Writing Process,
    xx
Writing Styles
Business Writing Style, 66–68
Formal Writing Style, 195–196
Informal Writing Style, 246–247
Style, 464–466
Technical Writing Style, 479–481
Writing the Draft, 512–515
Writing Types, General
Description, 137–140
Exposition, 167–168
Forms of Discourse, 197
Narration, 302–303
Persuasion (Argumentation),
    364–365
Wrong Word
Malapropism, 288
Word Choice, 511–512

X

Xerox
Copyright, 120
Plagiarism, 368
Xmas, 515

Y

Year
Biannual/Biennial, 60
Dates, 129–130
Years
Abbreviations, 9
A.D., 15
Numbers, 316
Yes
Comma, 92
Interjection, 252–253
You
Business Writing Style, 66–68
Person, 362
Personal Pronoun, 363–364
Point of View, 368–370
Pronouns, 381–383

Z

Zero Point
Graphs, 212
Zeugma, 515
Zip Code Abbreviations,
    Abbreviations, 8